THE FOUNDATIONS
OF MYSTICISM

A four-volume series

**THE PRESENCE OF GOD:
A HISTORY OF WESTERN CHRISTIAN MYSTICISM**

THE FOUNDATIONS OF MYSTICISM

Vol. I of
The Presence of God:
A History of Western Christian Mysticism

by
Bernard McGinn

CROSSROAD □ NEW YORK

The Crossroad Publishing Company
370 Lexington Avenue, New York, NY 10017

Printed in the United States of America

Library of Congress Cataloging-in-Publication Data

McGinn, Bernard, 1937-
    The presence of God : a history of Western Christian mysticism /
by Bernard McGinn.
        p.   cm.
    Includes bibliographical references and indexes.
    Contents: v. 1.   The foundations of mysticism.
    ISBN 0-8245-1121-2 (v. 1); 0-8245-1404-1 (v. 1, pb.)
    1. Mysticism—Europe—History.   I. Title.
BV5077.E85M34   1991
248.2'2—dc20   91-23931
                                                              CIP

This volume is dedicated

to my students, past and present,

at the Divinity School of the

University of Chicago,

who have been helpful critics,

frequent instructors,

and friends.

A Note on the Cover Illustration

This mosaic illustration of two thirsty stags or deer approaching a fountain to drink is an ancient Christian symbol of the desire of the mystic to imbibe the presence of God. This particular representation is from a window aedicule in the Mausoleum of Galla Placidia in Ravenna, constructed about 425 C.E. An earlier but more fragmentary version, in a mosaic from San Giovanni in Fonte in Naples (ca. 400–410), testifies to the popularity of the theme in Christian art of the late fourth and the early fifth centuries, the period of the origins of Western Christian mysticism.

Origen appears to have been the first to give allegorical explanations for the various kinds of deer referred to in the Old Testament, identifying the "roe or young hart" of Song of Songs 2:9 (LXX) with Christ (see his *Commentary on the Song of Songs* 3.11; *Homily on the Song of Songs* 2.11–12). But Origen also saw in the varying images of harts, stags, and deer (e.g., Song 2:9; Ps 41:1; Ps 28:7–9; Job 39:1–4; Prov 5:19; etc.) symbols of the devout Christian who desires to overcome vices (deer kill serpents) and attain God (*Commentary on the Song of Songs* 3.12). Following this latter exegesis, the early Latin mystical authors all commented on the mystical meaning of the deer. The most famous treatment is in Augustine's *Homily on Psalm* 41 (see chapter 7, below, p. 239), but we find the deer as a symbol of the mystic also in Ambrose (e.g., *Exposition of Psalm* 118.11.9) and in Cassian (e.g., *Conference* 10.11).

Contents ▣

**Appendix: Theoretical Foundations.
          The Modern Study of Mysticism**

Preface 回

THE IDEA FOR A multivolume history of Christian mysticism first occurred to me in 1982. Had I known then what toils this inspiration, however worthy, would bring, I might have shown more hesitation in taking it up.

My involvement with many projects, not least with Crossroad's *Encyclopedia of World Spirituality*, contributed much to ongoing research on this history, to which I have come to give the general title *The Presence of God*, but these commitments also delayed the time when my research was mature enough to begin the actual writing of the project. In an area of this scope, further reading often tended merely to convey how much there was still to read.

Two major changes in the original plan emerged from these years of research and writing. My original intention had been to deal with the entire history of Christian mysticism, both East and West. It soon became clear to me, however, that this was far too ambitious, given both my own linguistic limitations (especially of Syriac and Russian — languages crucial for Eastern Christian mysticism), as well as the often underdeveloped state of current research. Hence, the mysticism of Eastern Christianity will be treated in these volumes only insofar as it is a direct resource for the forms of mysticism that developed in the Latin West from the fourth century on. The most crucial aspect of this Eastern influence, of course, is found in the writings of the great Greek patristic mystics who will be treated in the first part of this volume, especially Origen and Dionysius.

A second major change occurred during the actual writing of the first volume, which I was finally able to begin in the spring of 1987. My original intention to have the first volume cover Christian mysticism down through the twelfth century proved to be too sanguine. Six months of concentrated research and writing on the Cistercian mystics (time that I spent as the guest of the Institute for Advanced Studies of Hebrew University in Jerusalem) demonstrated that there was far too much material in these twelve centuries to think of encompassing it all in a single volume. Hence, although I will argue that there is a basic continuity in the developing forms of Western mysticism from the fourth through the twelfth centuries, I have decided to split the original first volume into two. This first volume, entitled *The Foundations of Mysticism,* will be primarily concerned with the presentation of the historical roots of Western mystical traditions in Judaism, in Greek religious philosophy, and in early Christianity. It will close with a treatment of the founding fathers of Western mysticism (Ambrose, Augustine, and Cassian). The second volume, *The Development of Mysticism,* will carry the story down through the twelfth century.

Over these past eight years my research into mysticism has profited from the kindness of many. Some of these contributions have directly affected this volume and its successors. I would like to single out the most important. First, a special word of thanks to the staff of Crossroad Publishing Co., especially Werner Mark Linz and Frank Oveis, who have been both generous in their support of the project and patient of its necessary delays. Second, my gratitude to those friends and colleagues I prevailed upon to read various portions of the manuscript while it was still in gestation. Their suggestions and criticisms were helpful in many ways that I have tried to single out in the chapters that follow. Of course, none of them are to be blamed for the final results, especially since I have at times stubbornly maintained views that wiser heads have doubted. I would also like to thank my wife, Patricia, for valuable assistance in various stages of the writing, and particularly the final editing of this long book. My research assistants over the past eight years have all made valuable contributions in many ways, none more than Shawn Madison Krahmer, who provided crucial assistance in the final editing stages.

The mention of these student assistants leads to a final and wider expression of gratitude. This volume is dedicated to my students at the Divinity School over the years — a dedication eminently justified for all that they have contributed to this history.

Bernard McGinn
August 28, 1990
Feast of St. Augustine

General Introduction 回

T
HE PRESENT VOLUME is the first of four dedicated to the
history and theology of Western Christian mysticism.
Though the importance of the topic should be obvious, the
perspective from which this and the succeeding volumes
are being written is not.

The impetus to undertake this task has come from many sources,
some personal and some common to the current study of religion.
The past two decades have witnessed a remarkable resurgence of
interest in the study and practice of Christian spirituality, not least in
mysticism traditionally understood as the acme of the spiritual path.
Though the challenge of secularism has marginalized religion for
many in the modern world, it has also provided the occasion for others
to discover profound depths in their religious traditions. Partly on the
basis of such rediscoveries, new forms of interreligious dialogue have
emerged, and, among these, discussions of the nature of mysticism
have been prominent. The global ecumenical situation in which we
now find ourselves has facilitated a new level of awareness and discussion of the richness of humanity's spiritual heritage. From both the
specifically Christian and the ecumenical point of view, mysticism is
a topic of central concern today.

It is true that a large body of literature has been devoted to the
study of mysticism over the past century. I have tried to review some
of the major contributions in the appendix to this volume. Nevertheless, from the theological point of view, it is remarkable how few
synoptic presentations exist and how limited and unsatisfactory many
of these are. The difficulties of the task doubtless help explain this fact,
but they cannot serve as an excuse for avoiding attempts to correct the

xi

situation. The present moment calls out for a more complete and critical knowledge of the history of Christian mysticism, as well as more adequate contemporary theological appraisals of the phenomenon. I believe that these two tasks are so interdependent that neither can be successfully undertaken apart from the other.

Since the beginning of the present century, theology has struggled with the relation between the historically contingent and changing character of Christian belief and practice and the universal and permanent truth claims implied in the Christian message. Although there is no commonly agreed upon analysis or answer to this central concern, it is fair to say that there is consensus that the problem of history cannot be solved by avoiding it. Most contemporary Christian thinkers would claim that we need more — and better — history if we are ever to get at the crucial theological issues. Whereas former eras frequently presented Christian belief and practice by means of an analysis of its essential and "unchanging" features, modern theology more often finds it fruitful to study the historical development of a doctrine or practice in order to approach its inner meaning. History may not have the last word when it comes to systematic or constructive questions concerning Christian faith, but a strong case can be made that it should always have at least the first. The great French historian of theology Marie-Dominique Chenu once said, "A perfect history of theology, if one existed, would yield a theology of history."[1] Perfection lies beyond human reach, but I think that a more adequate contemporary theology of mysticism is possible only on the basis of a more satisfactory history of Christian mysticism.

Any remotely adequate contemporary theology of mysticism must begin not from an abstract consideration of the essential characteristics of mystical experience as such (assuming that such an exercise is even possible), but rather from an attempt to draw from the decisive stages in the history of Christian mysticism a coherent interpretation that may serve as the ground for a renewed contemporary theory and practice of mysticism. *The Presence of God* will seek to address both tasks, that is, both the historical and the constructive dimensions of a theological understanding of Christian mysticism.

Historical reconstruction, when well done, is more than mere description: it is always guided and informed by explanatory perspectives that are at least implicitly constructive. The four volumes that will comprise *The Presence of God* are both a history and a historical theology of Western Christian mysticism. The first two volumes, *The Foundations of Mysticism* and *The Development of Mysticism,* present an account of the first major period — or, perhaps better, layer — of Christian mysticism, which was created in the third and fourth centuries and flourished down through the twelfth. This layer may well be called the monastic layer, since it was closely tied to the values and practices of monasticism. The third volume, *The Flowering of Mysticism*, will treat the period from the thirteenth century through the sixteenth, a time when new forms of religious life and practice produced a second rich layer which interacted with the monastic component in the later Middle Ages and the Reformation era. These centuries saw the creation of classic "schools" of mysticism, which sought to spread mystical practices to all groups in Christian society through the medium of the vernacular languages, not the learned Latin of the clergy. The fourth volume of *The Presence of God* will be entitled *The Crisis of Mysticism* and will deal with the challenges to Christian mystical ideals from within and without that became evident in the seventeenth century and that have continued to the present. The final part of this last volume will also endeavor to summarize in constructive fashion what this account of Western mysticism means for contemporary reflection on the nature of Christian mysticism.

The Nature of Mysticism: A Heuristic Sketch

According to the great mystical Doctor of the Church St. Teresa of Avila:

> I used sometimes, as I have said, to experience in an elementary form, and very fleetingly, what I shall now describe. When picturing Christ in the way I have mentioned, and sometimes even when reading, I used unexpectedly to experience a consciousness of the presence of God of such a kind that I could not possibly doubt that he was within me or that I was wholly engulfed in him. This was in no sense a vision: I believe that it is called mystical theology.[2]

This quotation from Teresa's *Vida*, or *Life*, introduces some of the major issues that govern the account of mysticism to be presented in these volumes, especially the consciousness of the divine presence. But I would like to begin from the perhaps curious fact that Teresa identifies this conscious presence with mystical theology. This goes contrary to the position of many modern students of mysticism who have wished to distinguish between mysticism and mystical theology, and between mystical experience and its theological interpretation. Evelyn Underhill, for instance, in differentiating true mystics from those philosophers (and, we may add, theologians) who reflect on mystical experience said of the latter "they are no more mystics than the milestones on the Dover Road are travellers to Calais."[3] This *bon mot* masks an important misconception that has plagued the modern study of mysticism. Although it may be possible to make

theoretical distinctions between mysticism and mystical theology, I believe
that it is dangerous to separate the two in the history of Christianity.[4]

The fact that the term "mystical theology" antedated the coining of the
term "mysticism" by over a millennium points us in the right direction for
appreciating the complex and unbreakable bonds between mysticism conceived of as a religious way of life and mystical theology. Mystical theology
has often been understood in terms of misleading models of a simple
distinction between experience and understanding that do justice neither
to the texts of the mystics nor to the complexities of the relations between
experience and understanding that modern epistemological and cognitional theories have presented to us. Mystical theology is not some form of
epiphenomenon, a shell or covering that can be peeled off to reveal the
"real" thing. The interactions between conscious acts and their symbolic
and theoretical thematizations are much more complex than that, as the
following volumes will try to show. Rather than being something added on
to mystical experience, mystical theory in most cases precedes and guides
the mystic's whole way of life.

Those who define mysticism in terms of a certain type of experience of
God often seem to forget that there can be no direct access to experience
for the historian. Experience as such is not a part of the historical record.
The only thing directly available to the historian or historical theologian is
the evidence, largely in the form of written records, left to us by the Christians of former ages. Until recent years, overconcentration on the highly
ambiguous notion of mystical experience has blocked careful analysis of the
special hermeneutics of mystical texts, which have usually been treated
without attention to genre, audience, structure, and even the simplest procedures for elucidating study of the text. Mystical masterpieces, which are
often close to poetry in the ways in which they concentrate and alter
language to achieve their ends, have all too often been treated like phone
books or airline schedules: handy sources for confirming what we already
expect.

A recognition of the interdependence of experience and interpretation
can help avoid some of the false problems evident in scholarship on mysticism. The emphasis on mystical experience has led not only to neglect of
mystical hermeneutics but also to an emphasis on first-person, autobiographical accounts of special visionary or unitive experiences of God. First-
person accounts are rare in the first millennium of Christian mysticism, for
reasons that will appear in this volume. Debates about whether authors like
the Pseudo-Dionysius were "really" mystics because they lack such accounts
are sterile. Authors whose "autobiographical" statements were found to be
based on prior literary sources (the most famous example is Augustine's

dependence on Plotinus in the Ostia vision described at the end of the ninth book of the *Confessions*) also have had their mystical credentials questioned or withdrawn. Much of this confusion and unproductive debate could be avoided by a more nuanced understanding of the textually and theologically mediated nature of all Christian mysticism.[5] Theologically speaking, the issue is not, Was this person really a mystic because he or she claims to have had the kind of experience I define as mystical? but, What is the significance of her or his writings, autobiographically mystical or not, in the history of Christian mysticism?

It is also important, as far as possible, to try to see mysticism against the broader historical development of the Christian religion. In the history of Christian mysticism one neglects the wider context only at the cost of missing important elements of the significance of the phenomenon. The paradoxical intersection of the timeless and time implied in the mystery of the Incarnation is nowhere more evident than in the ways in which "timeless" mystical consciousness of God's presence has been conditioned by changes and developments in the church and in society at large. For example, the mystical piety of the fathers and mothers of the desert cannot be understood apart from monasticism seen as an institutional response to significant shifts in the religious climate of late antiquity. Again, radically new features present in the mysticism of the thirteenth century need to be understood within the context of important social upheavals in medieval civilization and their effect upon the fabric of Christendom. Though these volumes will be primarily a history of theological ideas, a study of the ways in which the direct consciousness of God's presence has been fostered and understood in the history of Western Christianity, they will try, at least in minimal fashion, to note key elements in the historical background that affected these conceptions.

If mysticism needs to be understood contextually, and if the mystical text and its place in the tradition—not mystical experience (whatever it may be)—are the primary objects of study, we must still ask what mysticism is. The final part of the fourth volume of this series, as mentioned above, is intended to present a more complete and constructive understanding based on the history of Christian mysticism, especially in the Latin West. But in the spiral of historical understanding (to use H.-I. Marrou's phrase),[6] it is important to present here at the outset at least a preliminary and heuristic notion of what I mean by mysticism.

Rather than trying to define mysticism (any simple definition of such a complex and controversial phenomenon seems utopian), I prefer to give a sense of how I understand the term by discussing it under three headings: mysticism as a part or element of religion; mysticism as a process or way of life; and mysticism as an attempt to express a direct consciousness of the presence of God.

It was perhaps the greatest insight of Friedrich Baron von Hügel's great book, *The Mystical Element of Religion,* to emphasize that mysticism is only one part or element of a concrete religion and any particular religious personality.[7] No mystics (at least before the present century) believed in or practiced "mysticism." They believed in and practiced Christianity (or Judaism, or Islam, or Hinduism), that is, religions that contained mystical elements as parts of a wider historical whole. These elements, which involve both beliefs and practices, can be more or less important to the wider body of believers. They also can be present in varying degrees of intensity and development. When they reach a level of fully explicit formulation and paramount importance for certain adherents of the religion, I would argue that we can speak of mysticism proper, though even then mysticism is inseparable from the larger whole. Thus, in the history of early Christian mysticism presented in this volume, I will argue that there have been mystical elements present in the Christian religion from its origins but that the first great tradition of explicit mysticism came to birth when a theory of mysticism first fully laid out by Origen in the third century found institutional embodiment in the new phenomenon of monasticism in the fourth century. This combination characterizes the first stage, or layer, in the history of Christian mysticism spoken of above.

Second, it is important to remember that mysticism is always a process or a way of life. Although the essential note — or, better, goal — of mysticism may be conceived of as a particular kind of encounter between God and the human, between Infinite Spirit and the finite human spirit, everything that leads up to and prepares for this encounter, as well as all that flows from or is supposed to flow from it for the life of the individual in the belief community, is also mystical, even if in a secondary sense. Isolation of the goal from the process and the effect has led to much misunderstanding of the nature of mysticism and its role as an element of concrete religions.

This goal, essential characteristic, or defining note has most often been seen as the experience of some form of union with God, particularly a union of absorption or identity in which the individual personality is lost. If we define mysticism in this sense, there are actually so few mystics in the history of Christianity that one wonders why Christians used the qualifier "mystical" so often (from the late second century on) and eventually created the term "mysticism" (first in French, "la mystique") in the seventeenth century.[8] This suggests that at the very least, it is necessary to expand the notion of union, recognizing that there were several, perhaps even many, understandings of union with God held by Christians over the centuries.[9]

But it may also be argued that union with God is not the mos
category for understanding mysticism.

Inspired in part by the seminal work of Joseph Maréchal,[10] but especially
by my reading of the texts that have been accepted as mystical classics in
the history of Christianity, both East and West, I have come to find the term
"presence" a more central and more useful category for grasping the unifying note in the varieties of Christian mysticism. Thus we can say that the
mystical element in Christianity is that part of its belief and practices that
concerns the preparation for, the consciousness of, and the reaction to what
can be described as the immediate or direct presence of God.[11]

The ways in which this special form of encounter with God have been
understood are multiple. One thing that all Christian mystics have agreed
on is that the experience in itself defies conceptualization and verbalization,
in part or in whole. Hence, it can only be presented indirectly, partially,
by a series of verbal strategies in which language is used not so much infor-
mationally as transformationally, that is, not to convey a content but to
assist the hearer or reader to hope for or to achieve the same consciousness.
Even those mystics who have paradoxically insisted on "strong" ineffability
have tried to use all the resources of language — and often to create new
ones — to assist this transformative process. From this perspective, it comes
as no surprise that union is only one of the host of models, metaphors, or
symbols that mystics have employed in their accounts. Many have used it,
but few have restricted themselves to it. Among the other major mystical
categories are those of contemplation and the vision of God, deification, the
birth of the Word in the soul, ecstasy, even perhaps radical obedience to the
present divine will. All of these can be conceived of as different but complementary ways of presenting the consciousness of direct presence.

A full explanation of this broad and flexible understanding of mysticism
must await the final volume, but the reader is owed at least a brief comment
here on my understanding of the crucial terms "consciousness," "presence,"
and "direct" or "immediate."

Much of the modern discussion of mysticism, of which I have tried to
present some key moments in the appendix to this volume, has revolved
around the analysis of the nature and kinds of mystical experience. There
are reasons for thinking that this discussion has reached an impasse. Part
of this, at least, seems due to the imprecision and ambiguity of the term
"experience," which many investigators scarcely bother to define — as if they
were sure that everyone has the same thing in mind when the term is used.
The term mystical experience, consciously or unconsciously, also tends to
place emphasis on special altered states — visions, locutions, raptures, and
the like — which admittedly have played a large part in mysticism but which

many mystics have insisted do not constitute the essence of the encounter with God. Many of the greatest Christian mystics (think of Origen, Meister Eckhart, and John of the Cross) have been downright hostile to such experiences, emphasizing rather the new level of awareness, the special and heightened consciousness involving both loving and knowing that is given in the mystical meeting. For this reason alone we can welcome the suggestions of some recent investigators who have found the term "consciousness" a more precise and fruitful category than "experience."[12] Obviously, "consciousness" can be used just as ambiguously as "experience." In the last volume of this series I hope to say a good deal more about the way in which I find the term helpful and also about its relation to experience, which is a category that should not be totally rejected. In preferring to emphasize consciousness rather than experience at this stage, I am primarily interested in underlining the necessity for exploring forms of language that will be both more true to the historical record and potentially more accurate and flexible in investigating its significance.

The second term in need of comment is "presence." It would be easy to draw up a lengthy list of texts from the mystics (like the one from Teresa cited above) that speak of a special consciousness of the divine presence as the goal of all their hopes and efforts. But this would be to tell only half the story. Precisely because of the incommensurability between finite and Infinite Subject, Christian mystics over the centuries have never been able to convey their message solely through the positive language of presence. The paradoxical necessity of both presence and absence is one of the most important of all the verbal strategies by means of which mystical transformation has been symbolized. The relationship has been portrayed in many forms. Sometimes, among the more positive, or cataphatic, mystics, it is primarily a successive experience, as in the coming and going of the Divine Lover presented in the Song of Songs and studied by the great mystical commentators on the Song, such as Origen and Bernard of Clairvaux. At other times, among the negative or apophatic mystics, presence and absence are more paradoxically and dialectically simultaneous. If the modern consciousness of God is often of an absent God (absent though not forgotten for the religious person), many mystics seem almost to have been prophets of this in their intense realization that the "real God" becomes a possibility only when the many false gods (even the God of religion) have vanished and the frightening abyss of total nothingness is confronted. If everything we experience as real is in some way present to us, is not a "present" God just one more *thing*? This is why many mystics from Dionysius on have insisted that it is the consciousness of God as negation, which is a form of the absence of God, that is the core of the mystic's journey. The author of *The Cloud of Unknowing* speaks of this with particular power:

> Leave aside this everywhere and this everything, in exchange for this nowhere and this nothing. . . . A man's affection is remarkably changed in the spiritual experience of this nothing when it is achieved nowhere. . . . It seems to him, sometimes, in this labor, that to look upon it is to look into hell.[13]

In a more modern vein, the twentieth-century mystic Simone Weil has expressed it thus: "Contact with human creatures is given us through the sense of presence. Contact with God is given us through the sense of absence. Compared with this absence, presence becomes more absent than absence."[14]

This is not the place to analyze in greater detail exactly what is meant by the consciousness of presence, nor can the issue of the paradoxicality of presence and absence in the encounter with God be pursued now. I merely wish to point out the many dimensions of the issues as we begin to follow them in the history of Christian mysticism. I have spoken, however, of this presence of God (or present-absence as the case may be) as direct or immediate. My final heuristic comment relates to the choice of these terms.

When I speak of mysticism as involving an immediate consciousness of the presence of God I am trying to highlight a central claim that appears in almost all mystical texts.[15] Mystics continue to affirm that their mode of access to God is radically different from that found in ordinary consciousness, even from the awareness of God gained through the usual religious activities of prayer, sacraments, and other rituals. As believers, they affirm that God does become present in these activities, but not in any direct or immediate fashion. Mystical religious texts are those that witness to another form of divine presence, one that can, indeed, sometimes be attained within the context of the ordinary religious observances, but which need not be. What differentiates it from other forms of religious consciousness is its presentation as both subjectively and objectively more direct, even at times as immediate.

This experience is presented as subjectively different insofar as it is affirmed as taking place on a level of the personality deeper and more fundamental than that objectifiable through the usual conscious activities of sensing, knowing, and loving. There is also an objective difference to the extent that this mode of the divine presence is said to be given in a direct or immediate way, without the usual internal and external mediations found in other types of consciousness.

It is important to note that this immediacy describes the actual mystical encounter itself, not the preparation for it, nor its communication in speech or in writing. Human consciousness in its total activity is always mediated both by the subject's previous history and by the mediations necessarily found in all thought and speech. What the mystics are talking about is what lies "between" these necessary mediations, if I may express it in this way. The mystics may well be mistaken about this form of immediacy, but I think that it is important, at least in a preliminary way, to underline this element in their claims before subjecting them at a later time to a more intense scrutiny.

It is interesting to note that some of the major modern theories of mysticism, such as that of Jacques Maritain in his *The Degrees of Knowledge*, have sought to incorporate this immediate relationship into their accounts.[16] I have also found Bernard Lonergan's notion of the possibility of a "mediated immediacy" (though he does not directly relate this to mysticism) as a helpful way of thinking about the issue.[17] It is in this still primarily heuristic sense that I am using the term.

Obviously, these remarks about the nature of Christian mysticism will raise many questions, both because of their brevity and perhaps also because of their inherent ambiguities and shortcomings. The large task of writing the history of Western Christian mysticism, much of which still lies before me, as well as the reactions of students, readers, and critics, will, I hope, help me to refine them. They represent my current position in a spiral of understanding whose firstfruits I present in this volume.

Abbreviations

ACW   *Ancient Christian Writers. The Works of the Fathers in Translation.* Edited by Johannes Quasten, Joseph C. Plumpe, Walter J. Burghardt and Thomas Comerford Lawler. Westminster, MD, and New York: Newman Press, 1946— . The most recent reprint is Mahwah, NJ: Paulist Press.

ANF   *The Ante-Nicene Fathers. Translations of the Writings of the Fathers down to A.D. 325.* Edited by Alexander Roberts and James Donaldson. Edinburgh, 1866–72. 10 vols. The most recent reprint is Grand Rapids: Eerdmans, 1981.

CC   *Corpus Christianorum. Series Latina.* Turnhout: Brepols, 1954— .

CSEL   *Corpus scriptorum ecclesiasticorum latinorum.* Vienna: Hoelder-Pichler-Tempsky, 1866— .

CWS   *The Classics of Western Spirituality.* Edited by Richard Payne, John Farina, and Bernard McGinn. Mahwah: Paulist Press, 1978— .

DS   *Dictionnaire de spiritualité ascétique et mystique doctrine et histoire.* Edited by Marcel Viller, assisted by F. Cavallera, J. de Guibert, et al. Paris: Beauchesne, 1937— . 15 volumes to date (through Thiers, March 1990).

FC   *The Fathers of the Church. A New Translation.* Founded by Ludwig Schopp. Edited by Roy J. Deferrari, et al. Washington, DC: The Catholic University of America Press, 1947— .

GCS   *Die griechischen christlichen Schriftsteller der ersten drei Jahrhunderte.*
        Berlin: Akademie-Verlag, 1897 —   .

LC   Loeb Classical Library. Cambridge, MA: Harvard University
        Press, 1913 —   .

LXX   Septuagint version of the Hebrew Bible. See *Septuaginta, id est*
        Vetus Testamentum Graece iuxta LXX interpres. Edited by Alfred
        Rahlfs. 2 vols. Stuttgart: Deutsche Bibelgesellschaft, 1980.

NPNF   *The Nicene and Post-Nicene Fathers of the Christian Church.* Edited
        by Philip Schaff and Henry Wace. Buffalo and New York,
        1886–90. First Series: 14 volumes. Second Series: 14 volumes.
        The most recent reprint is Grand Rapids: Eerdmans, 1983.

PG   *Patrologiae cursus completus. Series graeca.* Edited by J. P. Migne.
        Paris, 1857–66. 161 volumes.

PL   *Patrologiae cursus completus. Series latina.* Edited by J. P. Migne.
        Paris, 1844–64. 221 volumes.

SC   *Sources chrétiennes.* Edited by Jean Daniélou et al. Paris: Cerf,
        1940 —   .

Vg   Vulgate version of the Christian Bible. See *Biblia Sacra iuxta*
        Vulgatam Versionem. Edited by Robert Weber et al. Stuttgart:
        Deutsche Bibelgesellschaft, 1983.

WS   *World Spirituality. An Encyclopedic History of the Religious Quest.*
        General Editor, Ewert Cousins. New York: Crossroad,
        1985 —   .

PART I

The Historical Roots of Western Mysticism

Introduction

THIS HISTORY WILL be concerned with Latin Christian mysticism beginning in the fourth century with the development of Western monasticism and the towering figure of Augustine of Hippo. But the history of Western mysticism cannot be understood without some knowledge of its roots in Judaism, in Greek religious philosophy, and above all in the history of early Christianity. The full influence of these earlier traditions is an important part of the story that follows for many reasons. Perhaps the most vital is that Christian mysticism forms a continuous tradition of a distinctively exegetical character. The activity of reading, interpreting, and praying the Bible and other classic texts has been a key ingredient in its history. Jewish and early Christian modes of reading the sacred text were important models for later Christian mystical modes of interpretation. What may be more surprising is the way in which pagan Greek exegetical traditions also paved the way.

Christian modes of preparing for the direct experience of the presence of God were tied to particular ascetical practices, sacramental rituals, and forms of prayer; but they also were based on the spiritual values, patterns of life, and paradigmatic figures revealed in the scripture and explained by the fathers. The incorporated experience and inherited language that guided the believer toward the divine encounter were fundamentally scriptural—it was through the assimilation of the word of God within the worshiping community that the mystical life was made possible. It is no surprise, then, that most of the literature that forms the evidence for this first volume is directly exegetical in nature. The early Christian mystics of East and West did not normally use their own personal experience of God as

3

the subject for their teaching, the way Teresa of Avila and others later would, but sought to penetrate the mystical depths of the Bible to find the place where the meeting between God and humanity is realized. This exegetical basis of early Christian mysticism helps explain certain characteristics of the materials presented in Part I.[1]

As mentioned in the introduction, there will be no attempt to give a general summary of either the non-Christian or Greek Christian roots of Western mysticism. Rather, the following chapters will merely try to set the stage, that is, to provide the minimum information needed to understand how Western Christianity made use of its heritage. My concentration will be on those elements in the Jewish, Greek, and early Christian background that seem indispensable for understanding what came to birth in the Latin West in the fourth and fifth centuries.

The question of the existence of mysticism, or at least of a mystical element, in the Hebrew Bible and the literature of the Second Temple period is a difficult scholarly problem, which depends not only on the definition of mysticism being used but also on complex philological and historical issues that only a student trained in the exacting skills of biblical and Jewish studies could hope to penetrate. I have neither the skills nor the intention to take up these problems in a direct way. But there can be no question that the Hebrew scriptures, in both their original Jewish form and as the Christian Old Testament, were understood, at least in part, as mystical books by many later readers. Certain great figures, such as Abraham, Jacob, and especially Moses, were treated as paradigmatic mystics whose experiences and whose life histories became the models through which others sought to achieve contact with God. Favored texts, especially the Psalms and the Song of Songs, were thought to contain in their spiritual or mystical meaning an account of the soul's journey to God.

The same is true for the New Testament. It is not necessary to prove that either Paul or the author of John's Gospel was a mystic in order to vindicate the importance of these texts for the study of Christian mysticism. What is important is the way in which Paul and John became foundational, that is, the mode of reading used and the particular incidents and texts singled out for attention. For example, Paul's account of his rapture into heaven (2 Cor 12:2–4) provided an important warrant for visionary experiences of this type in Christian history. The exegesis of passages in the Gospel of John on the union between Christ and the believer has been central to Christian mysticism almost from the beginning. In the history of Western mysticism the ways in which the books of the Bible were read is more important than the determination of what these texts may have meant in their original context. The biblical scholar needs to explore the original meaning; the historical theologian must try to find out what the passage signified to the later believing community.

In a similar vein, we do not really need to determine to what extent Plato was or was not a mystic (though like A. J. Festugière I think that he was)[2] in order to understand that Platonic *theōria* is crucial in the history of Western mysticism. Platonism and Neoplatonism are indispensable parts of our story, far more so than those aspects of Greek religion, especially the mystery cults, which would require more attention if this were a history of pagan Greek mysticism. Obviously, I will not attempt to give a full history even of Greek philosophical mysticism here, but will treat only those elements that directly or indirectly had a substantive role in the development of Western Christian mysticism. The key figures of Plato, Philo, Plotinus, and Proclus will bulk large in this story.

The history of early Christian mysticism, especially in the Greek-speaking world, is directly related to subsequent Western developments, not only through monasticism, the institutional matrix of most Western mysticism down to the twelfth century, but also through the legacy of the great church fathers of the East who were translated into Latin. The history of Eastern Christian mysticism in the first five centuries of the Christian era, that is, down to the time of the division of the Eastern and Western empire, remains to be written, despite some survey accounts,[3] as well as many detailed studies of great value. It will be enough here to try to survey those aspects of Greek Christian mystical traditions between roughly 150 and 500 C.E. that decisively shaped the heritage that the West shared with the East. Subsequent contact between East and West insofar as it impinges on the history of mysticism will be taken up when necessary in the subsequent volumes.

While the major intent of this first part of volume 1 is to set up the historical and hermeneutical basis for the history of Western Christian mysticism, these five chapters will also suggest an approach to the mysticism of the ancient world that is directly related to the general theme of these volumes. From at least the beginning of the fourth century B.C.E., the ancient Mediterranean world, especially in Israel and Greece—the two major influences on later Christian mysticism—had experienced a crisis of access to God or the gods as traditional religious structures came under question in a new and rapidly changing historical situation. The most influential answers to this changed religious world were set out in the writings of Plato (427–347 B.C.E.) and in the Jewish apocalypses (beginning at least as early as the third century B.C.E.). The apocalypses and the philosophical-religious tradition begun by Plato were major components of the background of Christian mysticism, and not just because of some historical accident. They were ways of making God accessible to a world in which the divine was no longer present in its traditional forms, and as such they made Christianity and Christian mysticism possible.

The Christian religion itself can be seen as another of the creative answers of Hellenistic antiquity to the question of where God is to be found. Jesus of Nazareth was himself an heir of the apocalyptic religious mentality, in part or in whole. After his death, his earliest followers showed considerable skill in the ways in which they adapted their belief in the divinity manifested in Jesus, now the risen and ascended Christ, to the world in which they lived. The presence of God which Jewish apocalypticists and early mystics realized in their ascents to the divine realm and which Platonists sought through a flight to the contemplation of ultimate reality, Christians insisted could be attained only through the risen Lord, the true *theophania theou.* Like their Jewish and pagan contemporaries, the adherents of the new religion believed that this participation in divine life involved an ascent to the heavenly realm; unlike them, they insisted that this ascent could only be effected in Christ and the community that formed his body. The divine presence experienced in Jesus was accessible through the community and its sacramental rituals, particularly in baptism as foundation and Eucharist as crown. It was to be consummated, if necessary, through public witness to Christ as God in the act of martyrdom.

Historical interpretation, at least on a large scale, can rarely be more than plausible suggestion. The larger the screen, the more tenuous any single line of meaning will seem to those who know the bewildering complexity of the sources and the issues. This is especially true for the following chapters. Each tries to portray a world about which volumes have been written, volumes often penned to controvert what others have said. At best I hope that they will constitute something like Plato's "likely story," a way of gaining insight about some difficult but vital issues.

The first chapter examines the Jewish matrix, that is, the roots of Christian mystical traditions in the Judaism of the Second Temple period. The main themes pursued will be the visionary contact with God found in some Jewish apocalypses and the way in which the developing Jewish sense of scripture as a canon in need of ongoing interpretation set the stage for Christian use of the Hebrew Bible. The second chapter, "The Greek Contemplative Ideal," will examine the development of pagan philosophical mysticism, especially in the history of Platonism, down to the time of Proclus (d. 485 C.E.), concentrating on those themes and figures with lasting influence on the West. A number of theologians have viewed the Greek notion of mystical contemplation as an intrusion into Christianity of at best dubious worth.[4] The position that I will argue for is akin to one that Friedrich Heiler once expressed as follows:

> It was indeed the fusion of these two currents, of Biblical Christianity and Hellenism, that created the incomparable wealth of Christian contemplative piety. It began in the age of the New Testament and continued in the following centuries. The profoundest contemplative experience of the ancient world entered into Christianity, where it was purified and completed.[5]

The third chapter, entitled "Jesus: The Presence of God on Earth," will briefly examine Christian origins as revealed in the New Testament and other early texts from about 50 to 150 c.e. Any attempt to identify the New Testament as a mystical text or even one containing mystical elements, implicit or explicit, is bound to be controversial. A very important tradition of Protestant biblical scholarship has opposed finding any mysticism in the foundational Christian documents in order to maintain the uniqueness of the Christian religion and its founder. Catholic, Anglican, and some Protestant scholars have argued for a New Testament mysticism, though on diverse grounds and with divergent understandings of the term. I do not intend to defend the case for a distinctive New Testament mysticism, but I will look at how certain New Testament texts were plausibly interpreted as guides for the mystical life, beginning as early as the late second century c.e.

The final two long chapters in this part will be more directly related to our main topic. The classic Greek tradition of mystical theology was heralded by Clement of Alexandria, but was first realized by Origen, one of the greatest geniuses in the history of Christianity. From his time down to the end of the fifth century a succession of teachers established the basic lines of the Eastern Orthodox understanding of the Christian life in which all authentic Christianity is mystical, at least potentially. A number of these fathers, especially the mysterious writer who called himself Dionysius, were translated into Latin and eagerly read in the West. Though these two chapters will concentrate on providing a synoptic view of the mystical thought of the major Greek figures known in the West, they will also look at two larger developments that affected all later Christian mysticism, wherever found.

Chapter 4, "Mystical Elements in Early Greek Christianity," will investigate the second-century debate over Gnosticism. If not a mystical religion as such, Gnosticism certainly contained important mystical elements, and yet Gnostic Christianity was rejected by the predominate, or Orthodox, tradition. This rejection set certain boundaries for later Christian mysticism that have continued to influence its history. Finally, in chapter 5, "The

Monastic Turn and Mysticism," I will take up the origins and the meaning of the new institution of monasticism that came to birth in the fourth century and was both the main institutional locus for Christian mysticism in the following centuries and a potent intellectual influence on its development.

CHAPTER 1

The Jewish Matrix

W HEN ALEXANDER THE GREAT smashed the army of the Persian king Darius in 333 B.C.E. at the battle of Issus, the ancient world entered a new era. The failure of the Greek city-state, which had precipitated the century of crisis that led to the rise of Macedon and triumph of Alexander, was now to be followed by the rapid conquest and transformation of the ancient empires and kingdoms of the Near and Middle East. The story of Alexander's severing of the Gordian knot provides an apt prophetic image for the decisive beginning of a new era.

Alexander's conquest was not only a political event of epochal significance but also the catalyst of profound cultural and religious change. Hellenism, the spread of Greek language and Greek cultural values to the new subject peoples, was bound to affect the traditional religions of the Eastern peoples that were so closely tied to their native dynasties and age-old ways of life. The phenomenon is evident throughout the ancient East — Egypt, Persia, Babylonia — but perhaps nowhere more so than among the Jews.

In 536 B.C.E. a number of Jews had returned to Palestine from exile in Babylonia. By about 515 they had succeeded in building a somewhat impoverished replacement for the great Temple destroyed in 587. The religious practices of the period of the Second Temple (515 B.C.E.–70 C.E.), especially its later phases after the irruption of Alexander, form the Jewish matrix for both Christianity and the rabbinic Judaism that was to develop in the wake of the destruction of this Second Temple. In the words of one recent historian of the period:

> The issues after Alexander are those of the meeting between two powerful cultures — Hellenism and Judaism — and the patterns and modes that

9

developed between them. The Jewish reaction to Hellenism ran the whole gamut from enthusiastic assimilation to pietistic rejection. . . . In broadest terms, this is perhaps the most crucial of the issues in the history of Judaism of that age.[1]

The process was complicated by many factors, not least because it involved not only the Jews of Palestine but also the Jewish diaspora scattered throughout the Near East, especially in Egypt. Several notable works in recent decades have attempted to lay out the dynamics of this rich cultural and religious interchange.[2]

One thing immediately evident about Judaism in the Hellenistic period proper (332–167 B.C.E.), in the succeeding Hasmonean times (167–63 B.C.E.), and under Roman rule (after 63) is the variety of the religious life, evidenced in intense debates over the nature of Judaism. Indeed, the marked sectarianism of late Second Temple period makes any determination of a normative Judaism at this time exceedingly questionable.[3] Some of the new elements produced in this intensely creative religious world laid the groundwork for the growth of mysticism both in rabbinic Judaism and in early Christianity. Foremost among these was the new relation to God and the heavenly world found in the apocalypses, the most important Jewish literary creation of the centuries before the birth of Christ.

Recent research has enriched our understanding of the apocalypses as illustrating a major shift in Jewish beliefs not only about God's role in history but also about the relations between God and the human person.[4] Since the end of the eighteenth century, scholars have investigated how the genus of revelatory literature best known through the canonical books of Daniel and the Apocalypse of John introduced a new way of understanding history and its approaching end into Western religious traditions. This theology of history—apocalyptic eschatology, as it is called today—differs from the view of history found in the ancient Hebrew prophetic tradition and also from that present in the Wisdom traditions, however much it may owe to both. Its deterministic view of God's control over history centers on the conviction that present events, usually trials or difficulties of various sorts, are to be understood as the beginning of a triple drama of the last times conceived according to a pattern of present crisis, imminent divine judgment, and subsequent reward for the just. The divine plan for universal history, hidden from the ages, was believed to have been revealed by God through angelic intermediaries to the seers of old and recorded by them in the books we call apocalypses.[5]

It is only within recent years that a more careful distinction between apocalypse as a form of literature and apocalyptic eschatology as a view of history has enabled scholars to begin to grasp the role of the apocalypses in the growth of mysticism.[6] According to one recent definition, "apocalypse is a genre of revelatory literature with a narrative framework, in which a revelation is mediated by an otherworldly being to a human recipient, describing a transcendent reality which is both temporal, insofar as it envisages eschatological salvation, and spatial insofar as it involves another, supernatural world."[7] The manner of revelation seems to have much to do with the relative weight given to the temporal or spatial poles of the message. On this basis, a distinction has been made between two basic types of apocalypses, one in which the seer is taken on a heavenly journey and the other which lacks such a journey. In the former type the message tends to concentrate on the revelation of celestial and cosmological secrets, though sometimes communal and personal eschatological elements are included; the latter tends to be more taken up with the meaning of history and its approaching end, frequently including reviews of world history, and *ex eventu,* or after-the-fact prophecy.[8]

Both the genre and the message of the apocalypses reveal important new religious attitudes found in late Second Temple Judaism, attitudes that relate to God, the cosmos, and the means by which God communicates to humanity.

For the ancient Jews, God communicated through his word, initially speaking through human agents, the judges, and the prophets. Though the process of the formation of the Hebrew Bible is quite complex, it was well advanced by the second century B.C.E., though there was not a formally closed canon till much later.[9] During the last centuries before Christ we can detect a broad movement away from the word of God as found in oral proclamation to an emphasis on the word of God fixed in the written text. To be sure, the interpretation of scripture begins in the scripture itself,[10] and there was much precedent in Jewish history for the emphasis on the text that became so evident in the last two centuries B.C.E. But, according to Michael Stone, "sacred traditions were becoming books, even sacred books, and a basic change in the nature of Judaism took place once the sacred book became clearly established."[11] Very little Jewish literature of the period 400–200 B.C.E. survives. The wealth of texts beginning about 200 gives evidence of a desire to vindicate the relevance of the sacred text qua sacred text for the present situation of the Jews through a variety of means.

The continuing centrality of the sacred text for the life of the community was mediated in part through the creation of new genres that either expanded on the biblical story, used it as a source for moral lessons, or commented on it directly. Many of these ways of appropriating the Bible, after a complex series of transformations, are to be found also in Christianity and in rabbinic Judaism of the early centuries c.e. James L. Kugel in a recent study of these early interpreters puts it well:

> the work they performed was of immense significance, not only for the career of Scripture itself but for the beliefs and attitudes of all who held that Scripture sacred. They established the basic patterns by which the Bible was to be read and understood for centuries to come (in truth, up until the present day), and, what is more, they turned interpretation into a central and fundamental religious activity.[12]

Two broad factors in the Jewish exegetical culture of the late Second Temple period were especially significant for subsequent Christian readings. First, the emerging sense of the sacred text as both authoritative and formative for the piety and practice of believers; and, second, the belief that the text contained deeper meanings and dimensions than those readily available to all readers. This latter conviction was shared by contemporary Greeks, who frequently sought more profound religious and philosophical meanings hidden in the mythic and poetic texts of their tradition.[13] Philo was not the first, but was certainly the most influential, of those Jews who sought to meld Jewish and Greek approaches to the holy books, following the "inspired men who take most of the contents of the Law to be visible symbols of things invisible, expressing the inexpressible" (*De specialibus legibus* 3.178).[14] By the second century c.e., Christian exegetes would be referring to such deeper meanings of the Old Testament as "mystical," the earliest usage of the term in Christian literature. While not every mystical sense of scripture pertains to mysticism in the explicit sense, the mystical meaning of the Bible has an indissoluble connection with the story of Christian mysticism, both in the East and in the West.

The apocalypses represent another response to the codification of the sacred text. Though replete with scriptural reminiscences, they never exegete the biblical text as such. Rather, in a remarkably audacious way, they claim an inspired authority equal to the canonical books.[15] One late apocalypse (4 Ezra 14) summarizes this claim by telling the story of how Ezra received ninety-four books from God during a forty-day period (like Moses)—the twenty-four public books of the Hebrew canon and seventy secret books in which is "the spring of understanding, the fountain of wisdom, and the river of knowledge" (4 Ezra 14:47).

The apocalypses are written texts claiming to be both inspired and ancient, claims based on the use of pseudonymity, that is, ascribing a piece to a seer or holy man of the past. Thus, an apocalypse is a new book pretending to be an old one. The Jewish apocalypses purport to be written down and hidden by the sages of ancient days—Adam, Enoch, Abraham,

Moses, Ezra, Baruch, Daniel, and the like. Pseudonymity, common in both Jewish and non-Jewish literature of the time, indicates a belief that revelation lies in the distant past and is fixed in written texts, and it also implies that those who sought to identify themselves with the heroes of Israel's past felt that they could claim an equally inspired authority for writings issued in the seer's name.[16]

Although it is difficult to identify the particular religious or social groups responsible for the writing of the apocalypses, there can be no doubt that they are in general the product of a scribal elite. These sages, or "skilled ones" (*maśkîlîm* [Dan 12:3]), learned scholars and exegetes who composed and interpreted sacred texts, were quite different from the priests, the masters of Temple-centered ritual, and were doubtless in many ways a challenge to them. Jacob Neusner sees them as one of the three ideal types of Jewish piety (along with the priest and the messiah) whose creative interaction marked the period.

> Priest, sage, soldier—all these figures stand for Israel, or part of the nation. When all would meld into one, that one would stand for some fresh and unprecedented Judaism. Jesus represented as perfect priest, rabbi, messiah, was one such protean figure. The Talmudic rabbi as Torah incarnate, priest manque, and model of the son of David, was another.[17]

To these three, however, we may add the figure of the visionary, one evident to us in all the apocalypses, but especially in those where the recipient is described as undertaking a journey to the heavenly world.

The evidence of the Dead Sea Scrolls has shown that the earliest surviving apocalypse is not the book of Daniel, as had long been thought, but the Book of Watchers found in chapters 1–36 of the compilation of five apocalyptic texts known as *1 Enoch*.[18] In chapter 14 of this third-century B.C.E. vision, Enoch, who according to Gen 5:24 walked with God and then vanished "because God took him," ascends to heaven, where the divine theophany is manifested to him. This is the first personal account of a bodily ascension in Jewish literature. The text is of such importance that it deserves quotation:

> And behold I saw the clouds: And they were calling me in a vision; and the fogs were calling me; and the course of the stars and the lightnings were rushing me and causing me to desire; and in the vision, the winds were causing me to fly and rushing me high up into heaven. . . . And I observed and saw inside it [the second heavenly house] a lofty throne—its appearance was like crystal and its wheels like the shining sun; and I heard the voice of the cherubim; and from beneath the throne were issuing streams of flaming fire. It was difficult to look at it. And the Great Glory was sitting upon it—as for his gown, which was shining more brightly than the sun, it was whiter

than any snow. None of the angels were able to come in and see the face of the Excellent and Glorious One; and no one of flesh can see him. . . . And the Lord called me with his own mouth and said to me, "Come near to me, Enoch, and to my holy Word." And he lifted me up and brought me near to the gate, but I continued to look down with my face. (*1 Enoch* 14:8, 18–21, 24–25)[19]

In order to understand the religious significance of this powerful vision we must reflect on the fact that the Jewish apocalypses were part of a wide range of revelatory literature that proliferated in the Hellenistic world at a time when traditional means of access to the will of God or the gods seem to have become problematic to many. The otherworldly-journey apocalypses in particular bear comparison with a variety of texts — Greek, Roman, and Near Eastern — which speak of forms of ascent to the heavenly world where a new and more direct encounter with the divine takes place. In a recent survey of these texts, Alan Segal has claimed, "it is possible to see the heavenly journey of the soul, its consequent promise of immortality and the corollary necessity of periodic ecstatic journeys to heaven as the dominant mythical constellation of late classical antiquity."[20] The claim to dominance aside, there can be no question of the importance of these visionary ascensions.

Despite the attention given to the literature of ascension for almost a century, many confusions and unanswered questions still remain. For one thing, we have no clear picture of exactly what to include under the traditional category of *Himmelsreise der Seele* that was popularized through the writings of Wilhelm Bousset, R. Reitzenstein, R. Bultmann, and others. Ioan Culianu points out that these older studies illegitimately lumped together at least three different kinds of literature — otherworldly revelatory journeys (i.e., apocalypses of various kinds — Jewish and other), the descent and ascent of a supermundane being, and the ascent and/or descent of the soul as such.[21] Morton Smith points out that ascents can take place in four ways: in dreams, in waking visions, by the soul leaving the body, or bodily ascents either in this life or in resurrection,[22] though the distinction between sleeping dreams and waking visions is difficult to make in many antique texts.[23] Obviously, more careful study both of literary genera and the kinds of ascension they describe is needed before any determination can be made of whether or not they may be considered mystical or proto-mystical literature. But the ascensional texts can be, and were, understood by later mystics, Jewish and Christian, as providing a warrant and an example for their own hopes and practices.

Older accounts found the origin for the heavenly journey of the soul in Persian sources, even postulating the existence of an Iranian redemption myth about the descent of the heavenly man to redeem humanity and to show the way back to heaven. This myth was supposed to have been influential in Greece from the time of Plato, and subsequently in Judaism, Christianity, and Gnosticism.[24] More recent trends in scholarship have run counter to this questionable construction, as evidenced in both Segal and Culianu.[25] The latter suggests two basic types of heavenly ascents of the soul (i.e., nonbodily journeys): the Greek type, in which the soul ascends through the seven planetary *spheres,* and the Jewish type, in which the soul ascends through seven (or sometimes three) *heavens.*[26] It was not through Persian myth but through Greek science and cosmic piety, and through Jewish apocalypticism, that the ascension motif was incorporated into Western religious traditions.

The Jewish apocalypses include dreams and symbolic visions seen while on earth (the usual way in which apocalyptic eschatology is conveyed, as in Daniel 7–12), as well as visionary journeys to heaven, where cosmological mysteries, the heavenly court, and the divine throne and its occupant are beheld. The character and significance of these heavenly visions and the role of the visionary in Jewish religion have become a topic of concern in recent scholarship, though much remains to be investigated, particularly from a comparativist point of view.[27] Enoch's ascension described above implies both a bodily journey to the celestial world (based on Gen 5:24) and a direct experience of God (though perhaps more of an auditory than a visual experience). In the *Testament of Levi* (probably second century B.C.E.) during a dream vision the patriarch is lifted up through three heavens until "the angel opened for me the gates of heaven and I saw the Holy Most High sitting on the throne" (5:1). There are a number of other descriptions of such direct experiences of God in the surviving Jewish apocalypses and related literature.[28]

The visionary ascent to heaven speaks of an important shift in conceptions of the way in which humans gain access to the divine presence, one that directly relates the Jewish apocalypses to the major theme of these volumes. To the question of where God is to be found — or even where he is to be seen — the Jews of earlier ages had a standard answer: in the Temple.[29] The divine presence that the rabbis came to call the *shekhinah* was first found in the portable "tent of assembly" (Exodus 25–30; 35–40), and later in the Jerusalem Temple in both its first and its second periods. It became the center of the religious life of the people of Israel. "That is where I will meet you and speak to you. I will meet the sons of Israel in the place consecrated by my glory (*kābôd*). . . . I will remain with the sons of Israel, and I will be their God" (Exod 29:42b–43, 45). The highest spiritual experience, the essence of a visit to the Temple, was "to see the face of

Yahweh" (Deut 16:16; cf. Ps 11:4-7).[30] In this way, the Israelite could put himself in line with his forefathers, the patriarchs of old, like Abraham who saw God on the mountain of Isaac's sacrifice (as suggested in the Hebrew text of Gen 22:14), and Jacob who met God and wrestled with him face to face at the ford of Jabbok (Gen 32:23-32). Moses, too, had seen God, though in a limited way, both in the fiery bush (Exod 3:2-6) and again on Sinai (Exodus 19, and esp. 33:11, 18-23). All these texts were to be as important to Christian mystics over the centuries as they had been to pious Jews during the time prior to the birth of Christ.

The prophets also enjoyed the favor of the vision or experience of God, and in various localities, as evidenced by Elijah's famous vision on Mount Horeb (1 Kgs 19:9-18). But in time, God's presence came to be localized in the Temple at Jerusalem, as the famous vision described in Isaiah 6 shows:

> In the year of King Uzziah's death [740 B.C.E.] I saw the Lord Yahweh seated on a high throne, his train filled the sanctuary; above him stood two seraphs, each one with six wings. . . . And they cried out to one another in this way, "Holy, holy, holy is Yahweh Sabaoth. His glory fills the whole earth." The foundations of the threshold shook with the voice of the one who cried out, and the Temple was filled with smoke. (Isa 6:1-4)

Another possibility, however, becomes evident at the time of the destruction of the First Temple and the Babylonian captivity. While an exile in Babylonia, the prophet Ezekiel received a vision, which, if it is not the most famous in the Hebrew Bible, is at least the most obscure.

> There the hand of Yahweh came upon me. I looked; a stormy wind blew from north, a great cloud with light around it, a fire from which flashes of lightning darted, and in the center a sheen like bronze at the heart of the fire. In the center I saw what seemed like four animals. (Ezek 1:4-5)

This "chariot vision" in which the divine presence appears mounted on a throned cart drawn by four mysterious creatures has been a source of inspiration for later mystics, both Jewish and Christian.[31] The prophetic attack on the Temple and its cultus (e.g., Jer 7:4) had paved the way for a new situation in which Ezekiel was able to experience the divine presence in all its majesty independently of Jerusalem, though he closes his book with an eschatological vision of the perfect Temple in the restored holy city (Ezekiel 40-48).[32] Gershom Scholem pointed out that Ezekiel's experience stands at the beginning of an important trajectory of visions of God mounted on the divine chariot that is picked up in *1 Enoch* and like-minded apocalypses and that stretches into the early centuries of the Christian era, when the "work of the chariot" (*ma'aseh merkavah*) was a central theme of rabbinic mystical literature, customarily known as Merkavah mysticism.[33]

(It is important to underline the fact that the vision in *1 Enoch* involves not only the manifestation of Yahweh outside Jerusalem, as in the case of Ezekiel, but also a crucial new element — the seer's ascent *into* heaven.)

"The heavens are the heavens of the Lord, but the earth he has given to the sons of men" (Ps 115:16). When the apocalyptic seer is given the power to ascend to heaven, he receives a gift generally denied to the prophets. (Elijah's ascension in 2 Kgs 2:2-15 in the fiery chariot forms an exception, but, like Enoch in Genesis, he does not return to bring a message back.) Penetration into the heavenly realm of God, presented in crudely descriptive or highly evocative ways, was to remain an important part of both Jewish and Christian mystical speculation. In its historical origins it underlines the fact that the vision of God to be attained in the Jerusalem Temple was no longer sufficient for all Jews in the last centuries B.C.E..

While we have no evidence that the authors of the otherworldly-journey apocalypses had made any decisive break with the Temple cultus and priesthood in the way the Qumran community had, they witness to a relativizing of the Temple as the sole place where God is to be found and therefore to possibilities of divine–human encounter outside traditional religious structures. These prepared the way for the Jewish and Christian mystics of the first centuries C.E. What the former discovered in their ascents to the heavenly palaces in which the *shekhinah* was to be found, the latter encountered through Christ, God's ultimate presence in and also beyond this world.

Because the visionary accounts found in the Jewish apocalypses are invariably pseudonymous, it has often been thought that they are purely literary creations that have no relation to meditational techniques or the actual religious experiences of their authors. The visions described in early Jewish mysticism and rabbinic texts are also not put in the first person, though they lack apocalyptic pseudonymity, that is, direct speaking in another's persona.[34] It would be a mistake, however, to separate the "literary" too sharply from the "real," especially in a Judaism in which meditation on scripture seems to have been becoming a central part of religious and even mystical praxis.[35] (We have much explicit evidence for this in later Jewish mysticism.) Although direct proof is lacking, there seem to be good arguments for claiming that the visionary accounts found in the otherworldly-journey apocalypses are based, at least in part, on the practices and experiences of individuals and groups in the Judaism of the time. Hence, a number of recent investigators are willing to call them "mystical" and grant them whatever degree of reality we wish to assign to that term.[36]

It is not only the fact that the seer ascends to heaven but also the kind of message that he receives there that shows the religious shift present in apocalyptic literature. In the words of Ithamar Gruenwald, "seen from the point of view of scripture, the type of knowledge found in the apocalypticism is unprecedented in its scope, depth, and what is more important, in its finality."[37] This pertains both to the secrets about the meaning of history shown in texts like Daniel and 4 Ezra and to the revelations concerning creation, the angelic world, astronomy, calendrical lore, and the fate of souls after death found in the otherworldly-journey apocalypses. Paradoxically, to the apocalyptic authors God seems both nearer and farther away than he was to the prophets and earlier Jewish leaders. The seer gets to ascend to the divine realm, to become part of the celestial court, and to learn secrets not revealed to other mortals;[38] but from the perspective of the community of Israel, God seems more distant, his providential control hidden and not easy to find during a time when the power of evil is growing and the faithful are either threatened or actually undergoing persecution.

The form of redemption promised in the apocalypses is different from that present in older strata of Judaism. An expansion takes place in two directions: spatially and temporally. The national and concrete historical perspectives found in early Judaism are spatially expanded in various ways until "redemption becomes cosmic," in Michael Stone's phrase.[39] Temporally, the transcendence of death through personal immortality has been seen as the central message of apocalyptic eschatology,[40] and it is well known that the notion of resurrection from the dead makes its earliest appearance in these apocalypses (e.g., Dan 12:2; *1 Enoch* 51:1–5). The same message, if delivered in a different manner, is found also in the otherworldly-journey apocalypses. Wilhelm Bousset in his study of the ascent of the soul long ago observed, "The ecstasy through which one has the power to raise oneself up through the heavens to the Highest God is nothing else than an anticipation of the heavenly journey of the soul after death."[41] Ecstatic mystical experience and personal immortality are two sides of the same coin — the former the foretaste of the latter, which serves as its completion. This is suggested by our apocalypses and confirmed in another major and related religious phenomenon of late Second Temple Judaism, the turn to new forms of wisdom literature.

"If the pursuit of wisdom had ancient roots in Israel, it is nonetheless true that it became an ever-growing force in Jewish intellectual life during the years of the direct contact with Hellenism," James Kugel reminds us.[42] The Wisdom of Ben Sira (or Ecclesiasticus, composed early in the second century B.C.E.), the *Psalms of Solomon* (first century B.C.E.), and especially the Wisdom of Solomon, dated as early as the second century B.C.E. by some, but more likely written ca. 40 C.E., are primary examples of this tendency, which has close ties with the philosophical tradition in Hellenistic Judaism evident in such figures as Aristobulus and especially Philo (who will be treated in the next chapter). Ben Sira and the Wisdom of Solomon are both part of the Septuagint (LXX), the Bible of the Jewish diaspora later adopted by the Christians. If the concern for cosmic secrets in the other-worldly apocalypses brings them close to the ambit of the developing cosmic piety of the Hellenistic tradition,[43] this proximity of interest is heightened in the wisdom literature, where, as in Greek cosmic piety, the experience of God reaches the believer through meditation on the order of the universe.[44] Elements of a more personal relationship to God, or at least to a divine power, are also discovered here.

This is most evident in the Wisdom of Solomon, where the author speaks of Wisdom, a quasi-divine power pervading the universe, with the flavor of a love relationship:

> Bright and unfading is Wisdom, easily beheld by those who love her, and found by those who seek her. She is the first to make herself known to those who desire her (6:12-13). . . . Her I loved and sought out from my youth, and longed to make her my bride, and I became a lover of her beauty. She magnifies her noble birth by enjoying intimacy with God, and the Master of All loved her (8:2-3).

This form of relation with a divine personification (person?) is close to what we will find in Philo's attitude toward the Logos, which has often been described as an expression of mystical piety.[45] The author of Wisdom does not ascend to heaven to see God in mythological fashion, but he does attain nearness to God in a more philosophical way through his inner devotion to Wisdom, as the famous *sorites* of Wis 6:17-20 indicates. Although the differences between the apocalypses and the wisdom literature are obvious, they are at least historically related in constituting the two major ways in which the Jews dealt with the effects of historical change on their religious values during the turmoil of the Hellenistic period.[46]

The Wisdom of Solomon shares a general sense of cosmic optimism that we can find in the Stoics and other philosophical schools of Hellenistic thought. Although the apocalypses certainly show an interest in the secrets of the cosmos, they are not generally as optimistic about the world or universe. Of course, the apocalyptic authors do not believe that the cosmos is a creation of an evil deity or power, but especially in the historical apocalypses we find a strong sense that the present age or aeon is under the control of the evil angelic powers and is therefore not redeemable. What has been variously called "cosmic paranoia" and the "demonization of the cosmos," which reaches its fulfillment in Gnosticism, also had roots in many aspects of Hellenistic philosophy and religion, not just in Judaism.[47] The connections between the Jewish apocalypses and the full-fledged Gnosticism of the second century C.E. are certainly real and have been detailed by a number of scholars,[48] but we should not forget Ioan Culianu's reminder, "The Gnostic 'demonization of the cosmos' presupposes a new vision of the world, which, as a whole, is neither Babylonian, nor Jewish, neither Greek, nor Iranian."[49]

The subsequent history of the religious forms initiated in the apocalypses and other texts of the late Second Temple period is not directly related to the history of Christian mysticism, especially in its Western Latin manifestations. The first great era of Jewish mysticism, known as Merkavah mysticism because of its fascination with the exegesis of the chariot vision of Ezekiel 1, and sometimes as Hekhalot, or "Palace," mysticism, because of the many texts that describe the divine palaces found during the ascent, would form a major topic for comparative study with early Christian mysticism, especially since both shared so much common background, but there is little evidence for any direct contact. By the second century of the Christian era, which appears to be when the Merkavah literature begins, Christianity and rabbinic Judaism were already bitter opponents, both claiming that they alone were the true heirs of the Jewish heritage. No period of Jewish mysticism offers more problems for study than this primal era, especially since the texts that represent our surviving evidence have so many problems of dating and transmission. Recent work, especially by Ithamar Gruenwald, has demonstrated the direct link between apocalyptic literature and the Merkavah texts.[50]

One interesting analogy between the earliest stage of Jewish mysticism and emerging Christian mysticism involves the Song of Songs, a text favored by mystics of both traditions. There is still no commonly agreed upon date for the Song. It is not referred to in the other books of the Hebrew Bible or in the New Testament.[51] Rabbinic sources indicate some dissension about its inclusion in the canon, but also note its strong defense by Rabbi Akiva (first third of second century C.E.): "No man of Israel ever disputed about the Song of Songs, that it did not defile the hands [i.e., was not a sacred book]. The whole world is not worthy of the day on which the Song of Songs was given to Israel, for all the Scriptures are holy, but the Song of Songs is the Holy of Holies."[52] The Song does not appear in the first century of Christian literature, its earliest citations coming in the mid-second-century *Odes of Solomon* and in Melito of Sardis (ca. 170 C.E.). We may speculate that the Song took on new importance for both Christians and Jews in the course of the second century C.E. as both groups sought to vindicate why this erotic poem was a part, indeed a central part, of the divine message to humanity.

Rabbi Akiva is also, interestingly enough, the hero of the most famous story of early Merkavah mysticism, the account of the four rabbis who entered *pardes* (literally, an orchard; metaphorically, paradise), which in Akiva's case is often associated with the verse from Song of Songs 1:4, "The King brought me into his chambers."[53] Building on the work of Gershom Scholem and Saul Lieberman, Joseph Dan argues that the rabbinic evidence suggests that Akiva, the great hero of early Merkavah mysticism, was also the source for a new understanding of the Song of Songs based on three elements: (1) that the book was given to Israel on Mount Sinai; (2) that it is the holiest of all the biblical books; and (3) that its author was not Solomon but "the King who owns peace," that is, God himself.[54] In other words, the book is a divine self-description, the kind that seems expanded upon in the unusual Merkavah text known as the *Shi'ur Qomah.*[55] In Dan's words, "A new concept and meaning of the Song of Songs emerged in rabbinic academies and transformed esoteric homiletics [e.g., midrashic speculation on Ezekiel 1] into mystical activity."[56]

Whether or not Dan's hypothesis is convincing to all students of early Jewish mysticism, it seems difficult to doubt that the Song of Songs did play a role in the Merkavah texts and in some rabbinic literature that may reflect a mystical milieu. The early rabbinic commentaries on the Song make it quite clear that the Bride is to be identified with the people of Israel. This corporate and historical-allegorical reading of the Song of Songs was influential on Origen, the first surviving Christian mystical commentator on the book, who knew that the rabbis placed it among the four esoteric texts reserved for advanced students.[57]

Origen was certainly influenced in his interpretation of the Song by the standard Jewish reading, though he altered it to argue that the true message concerned Christ and the church. Did he know of Jewish mystical readings, which may have interpreted the Bride as the individual soul who ascends to the Divine Lover? Although this has been asserted by some authors,[58] no solid proof has yet been brought forward. In short, Origen knew Jewish corporate or communal interpretations of the Song and used them selectively for his own purposes, but his properly mystical reading still seems to be his own creation.

The example of the Song of Songs may offer a paradigm of the relations between Jewish and Christian interpretations of the books sacred to both religions. The Jewish exegetes of the last centuries B.C.E. prepared the ground in a general way for both their rabbinic and their Christian successors, especially by making the practice of interpretive reading central and by creating many of the tools that helped refine such reading. In particular cases, it may even be possible to determine direct lines of contact on specific points, ones that may be of importance for the history of Christian mysticism; but, by and large, after the late first century c.e., Jewish exegesis and Christian exegesis form parallel (and often conflicting) traditions. The one major exception was the allegorical interpretation of Philo, which had an important influence on Christian exegesis, both in East and West, and not least in the area of mysticism. (This will be taken up in the next chapter.)

The Old Testament might be described as the common book that divides Christians and Jews. Even the names they use for it — Old Testament and Hebrew Bible (*tanakh*) — reflect their different perspectives, as do the number and order of the books contained. The first Christian Bible was not even the Hebrew text itself, but was rather the Septuagint (LXX), the interpretive Greek translation emanating from the diaspora in Egypt and containing the Apocrypha, or deuterocanonical books, such as the Wisdom of Solomon. Despite these differences, the sacred books of the Jews are part of the foundation of Christianity and of all Christian mysticism.

The religious world of late Second Temple Judaism provided a matrix for Christian mysticism in two related ways — through the mystical, or at least protomystical, ascents to the vision of God found in the apocalypses, and through the movement toward the establishment of a canon of the sacred texts of Israel and the creation of the tools and techniques to render it continuously alive for the believing community. Although my argument in this chapter has been more suggestive than demonstrative, I am convinced that to neglect the Jewish roots of Christian mysticism and to see it, as many have done, as a purely Greek phenomenon is to risk misconstruing an important part of its history.

CHAPTER **2**

The Greek
Contemplative Ideal

I N THE SECOND CHAPTER of his *Dialogue with Trypho* (ca. 150 C.E.)
the apologist Justin recounts the story of his pursuit of the love
of wisdom through the various philosophical schools culminating
in the Platonists. Through their instruction he thought that he
had already become so wise that in his words "I wished to see God
immediately because this is the goal of Plato's philosophy" (2.6).
Justin's meeting with a mysterious Christian seer convinced him that
the Platonists promised what they could not deliver and helped him
see the error of their claims that the soul can see God by its own power
because it is unbegotten and immortal, that is, naturally divine (*Dial.*
4–6).[1] But were the Platonists wrong to think that seeing God is the
goal of human life?

A later Christian story gives a more ambiguous witness to pagan
and Christian encounter. In the "Alphabetic Collection" of the *Sayings
of the Desert Fathers,* the Abba Olympios tells of the pagan priest who
slept in Olympios's cell at Scete and asked him, "Since you live like this,
do you not receive any visions (*ouden theoreite*) from your God?" When
Olympios responded that he did not, the priest contrasted the mysteries
revealed to pagan priests when they sacrifice with the lack of visions
of the Christian monks, concluding, "Truly, if you see nothing, then
it is because you have impure thoughts in your hearts, which separate
you from your God, and for this reason his mysteries are not revealed
(*apokalyptetai*) to you." The desert elders approved of this judgment
when it was reported to them on the grounds that "impure thoughts
separate God from man."[2] However we evaluate the religious confron-
tations tantalizingly revealed in these two texts—radical opposition,
correction, analogy, appropriation, or transformation—one thing is

obvious: the language involved is not only Greek, but Plato's Greek, that is, the description of the soul's return to God through purification (*askēsis*) followed by contemplative vision (*theōria*). Contemplation is only one of the historically and culturally conditioned forms in which Christian mysticism has come to birth, but it is one of the most ubiquitous and enduring.[3]

In his noted book *Contemplation et vie contemplative selon Platon,* André Jean Festugière remarked, "When the Fathers 'think' their mysticism, they platonize,"[4] a dictum that is true also for many subsequent Christian mystics. The major influence of Plato and the Platonic tradition on the history of Christian mysticism cannot be denied, though like the use of the term "contemplation," the import of this influence has also been vigorously debated. Some modern Protestant theologians, beginning with Albrecht Ritschl, have judged the history of Christian mysticism to be at root nothing more than an invasion of Christian faith by a fundamentally different and alien Hellenic religious element.[5] Even Festugière, who did not see the contemplative ideal as incompatible with Christianity, argued for a fundamental difference between the ascetical spirituality of the early Christians and the philosophical spirituality of mystical contemplation introduced in the third century C.E.[6] The purpose of this chapter is not so much to judge these views (they will be more directly critiqued in chapter 4) as to present the main lines by which the contemplative ideal of Plato and his followers influenced Western Christian mysticism. This sketch must be selective, but some issues will require more detailed treatment than others.

Plato

To begin with Plato is, of course, to start *in medias res.*[7] Historians of religion have devoted much effort to investigating to what degree earlier elements in Greek religion that influenced Plato, especially Pythagoreanism and Orphism, and early Greek philosophers, such as Parmenides and Heracleitus, may or may not be termed mystical. Ugo Bianchi, for example, finds in Greek religion two tendencies: an "Olympian," or distant, conception of divinity, and the "mystical" conception that recognizes an interference of the divine and human levels. He locates Plato in the third, or "mysteriosophical," type of Greek mystical religion.[8] But these questions need not delay us, since they are only distantly relevant to the study of those Eastern and Western Christians who were influenced, frequently only indirectly, by Plato (ca. 429–347 B.C.E.).

"In the days of my youth my experience was the same as that of many others. I thought that as soon as I should become my own master I would immediately enter into public life." These lines from the *Seventh Letter* ascribed to Plato introduce a brief but plausible account of the sage's disillusionment with Athenian politics, especially following the death of Socrates, and his lifelong dedication to philosophy in accordance with his conviction that "the classes of mankind . . . will have no cessation from evils until either the class of those who are right and true philosophers attains political suprem- acy, or else the class of those who hold power in the State becomes, by some dispensation of Heaven, really philosophic" (324 B, 326 AB).[9] Whether or not the *Seventh Letter* is really from Plato, it provides us with an insight into the historical context within which the great philosopher pursued his thought.[10] Plato lived at a time when the inner crisis of the traditional Greek *polis* and the religion intimately bound up with it had become evident, and there seems to be no reason to deny that this had a profound effect on his decision to abandon the public arena to cultivate the wisdom necessary to build a more just human society. The reform of the *polis* meant the reform not only of its citizens, but of its religion as well. If society is out of joint, it can only be because humanity's whole attitude toward the universe and its divine source was in need of repair. Plato's philosophy is powered by an unremitting desire for reform: personal, political, and religious.

This is not the place to attempt to give any summary of Plato's philos- ophy, however brief. What is needed here is only a sketch of those aspects of his thought that were influential on later Christian mysticism, especially in the West. To call Plato a mystic is a controversial issue, as we shall see, though I have no hesitation, along with Festugière and others, in doing so.

Plato views the true human subject, or soul, as a searcher always restless short of permanent possession of the Absolute Good which beatifies. Such possession is achieved through *theōria,* or contemplation, which is the fruit of an ascending purification (*katharsis, askēsis*) of both love and knowledge and which reaches its goal when *nous,* the divine element in the soul, is assimilated to its supernal source. We need to inquire more closely into each of these elements: *theōria;* its relation to love and knowledge; *nous;* and its source, the Absolute that Plato referred to as the One, the Good, and the Beautiful.

Plato's thought is characterized by a sharp distinction (although never an absolute separation) between the world of appearances and the world of Forms or Ideas, between *doxa* (opinion) and *epistēmē* (real knowledge), between temporality and unchanging immortality. Contemplation can be described as the way in which *nous,* a divine exile in the world of appear- ances, opinions, and time, unites the two realms through its intuitive contact with the presence of the Absolute.[11] Peter Manchester has characterized the religious context within which Plato wrote as follows:

> The religious experience of eternity and time that is distinctive of Mediterranean spirituality in our period is an orientation to temporal presence. . . . It is an experience of a divine Presence in the human present, a presence reflected both in the cosmos of nature and in the life of the mind. Here the characteristic religious problem is the competence of speculative mysticism to encounter divine creative power.[12]

For Plato contemplation provided new access to the divine in an age when the traditional divinities of the Greek *polis* had begun to lose their numinosity, at least among the sensitive searchers after truth pictured in Socrates and his circle.[13] Just as the Jewish visionaries of the Hellenistic world were to respond to their changing religious situation by finding new ways of access to God, especially ascensions to the heavenly realm, Plato, as Festugière has shown, stands at the head of two new traditions in Greek reflective piety—"the desire of union with the ineffable God," and "the desire of union with the God of the world, the cosmic God."[14] Both traditions were to affect Christian mysticism, though Christian suspicion of the divinization of the cosmos lessened considerably the influence of the latter tradition.[15]

No single text in Plato lays out all the dynamics of his contemplative spirituality, but a brief look at three famous passages will help illustrate the key themes. The first of these is *Symposium* 201D–212A, the speech in which Socrates recounts Diotima's instruction in "love matters" (*ta erotika*).

In this lengthy account, the seer explains that Love (*erōs*) is a medium between the beautiful and the ugly, describing his birth as the result of the union of *Porus* (Resource, the son of Cleverness or Craft) and *Penia* (Poverty or Need). As a mediating *daimōn*, or spirit, Love connects the heavenly and earthly realms. The lover's love for beautiful things is essentially a desire for the happinesss (*eudaimonia*) that comes from the permanent possession of true Beauty, which is identical with the Good (206D). Such possession cannot be perfect if it comes to an end, and therefore love involves a longing for immortality (cf. 207A, 207D, 208B, 212A).

Diotima's stress upon love's striving to gain its object may seem to imply that love is only desire for selfish possession, but she insists that the ultimate goal of love is not for mere possession, but for generous begetting—"It is of engendering and begetting upon the beautiful" (206E). Begetting according to the body is not condemned, but the begetting according to the soul which brings forth virtues is praised as more noble (208A–209E).

Diotima's teaching concludes with the famous description of the "straight path" (*orthōs*) to the "rites and revelations" of love.[16] Beginning from the love of one beautiful body, the lover must come to love all beautiful bodies. Then he must turn to the beauty of souls, which will lead him to the beauty of laws and institutions and of every kind of knowledge (*epistēmē*). Finally, "turning rather towards the main ocean of the beautiful [he] may by contemplation (*theōrōn*) of this bring forth in all their splendor many fair fruits of discourse and meditation in a plenteous crop of philosophy" (210D). To the one who has thus prepared himself and been strengthened in this passage, "suddenly (*exaiphnēs*) he will have revealed to him, as he draws to the close of his dealings in love, a wondrous vision, beautiful in its nature" (210E). This sudden appearance of the very Form of the Beautiful, "existing ever in singularity of form independent by itself" (211B), brings the lover to contemplation of Divine Beauty (*to theion kalon* [211E]) and enables him to bring forth true virtue (212A). It makes the lover both a "friend of god" and immortal.[17]

It is clear from this text that Plato's notion of love is not purely egotistical and self-serving, as Anders Nygren claimed;[18] rather, true *erōs* is love for the Good that seeks to beget the good, either the good of human offspring or of virtue.[19] But is the union with the Beautiful-Good that is attained at the height of the path a personal one? Certainly not in the sense in which later monotheistic mystics strive for union with the God of revelation, but Plato's description of the unitive vision with the Beautiful-Good is not totally impersonal either. Too easy an imposition of modern views of what constitutes the personal over against the impersonal seems to be at work in some interpretations of Plato.[20] The fact that Plato describes the Form that takes possession of the lover as a god, or at least as divine, certainly left the door open for personalized readings that may go beyond but that are not necessarily contrary to his descriptions of that indescribable supreme moment.[21] Nor is it clear that Plato's view of the goal is as purely intellectual as some have argued, that is, that the mind's gaze upon science or knowledge is only an abstract conception.[22] A full case cannot be presented here, but I would be inclined to follow the lead of Festugière, who argues that the seeing involved in Plato's contemplation is not a defining, but is based on "an immediate union . . . of a mystical order" in which both knowledge and love play complementary roles in attaining an intuitive contact with the presence of true Being.[23] While beatitude for Plato is essentially a cognitive state, because the Good that is grasped in the act of contemplation is identified with the Beautiful that is the goal of *erōs*, contemplation also produces loving joy in the soul.[24] René Arnou, in his treatment of Plato's view of contemplation, summarizes with a clarity that merits full citation:

Platonic contemplation appears as a sudden and immediate vision of true Being, or, if one ascends as far as possible on the scale of values, a union with the Supreme Good, a mysterious union which is not just the vision of an object by a subject, but the taking possession of the subject by a superior reality in such a way that the love that responds to the attraction of the Beautiful and the Good enjoys a role just as necessary as the intelligence which gazes.[25]

A second passage that will be helpful for illustrating Platonic contemplation is Socrates' second speech in *Phaedrus* 243E–257B. Here, in order to prove that the madness of love is not an evil but a gift of the gods, Socrates first gives a dialectical argument proving that the soul is the uncreated and immortal principle of motion (245C–246A). In trying to describe the form or nature of the soul, however, Socrates must resort to a myth, the famous comparison of soul, both divine and human, to a pair of winged horses and a charioteer, a description based on the well-known three parts of the soul (*nous, thymos,* and *epithymia*) found frequently in the dialogues.[26] The souls of the gods ascend the height of heaven's dome without difficulty and pass outside to be carried around to view the region where the "divine intelligence" (*dianoia theou*) and any like it "rejoices in seeing reality (*to on*) for a space of time and by gazing on truth is nourished and made happy" (247D). The human soul, however, has lost the wings that enable it to share in the divine nature (246E) and thus has fallen to earth (248CE) to be entombed in the body (250C). All human souls will eventually get their wings back after a ten-thousand-year cycle, but the philosopher has a shortcut to this goal because he can remember when his soul "rose up into real being" (*anakypsasa eis to on ontos* [249C]) and was "initiated into perfect mysteries" (ibid.; cf. 250BC).

In our fallen condition it is beauty entering in by means of sight, "the sharpest of the physical senses" (250D), that begins the philosopher's return. Plato emphasizes the shock and suddenness of the appearance of beauty in the beautiful boy. "But he who is newly initiated, who beheld many of these realities, when he sees the godlike face and form which is a good image of beauty, shudders at first, and something of its old awe comes over him . . ." (251A). Indeed, the description of love madness that follows (251A–252C) emphasizes the action of beauty on the lover through the eyes as a gift — almost as a grace.[27] The rather complex account of the kinds of godlike souls found in the beloved (252C–253C) echoes the concern of the *Symposium* for the begetting of virtues upon the beautiful loved one.

The return to the analysis of love madness in terms of the charioteer and winged-horses myth (253C–256D) makes evident that as long as the better element, or charioteer of the soul (*nous*), restrains the lower elements, or horses, from the physical consummation of love, the cultivation of virtue will lead the lovers on to the goal of true contemplation. This implies, as Martha Nussbaum has shown, that the *Phaedrus* differs from the *Symposium* not only in recognizing the role of the madness of love but also in emphasizing the role that personal erotic attachment continues to play in the soul's ascent.[28]

One final, even better known, Platonic text, the "Allegory of the Cave" from *Republic,* book 7 (514A–518B), also deserves comment. In no other text does Plato so poignantly (and pessimistically) describe the contrast between the dim and illusory nature of life in our world of shadows and the possibility of a life lived in clear view of the supernal world of Forms where the Good, the Form of Forms, reigns like a supreme sun making all things visible. One of the prisoners, chained from birth and condemned to watch mere shadows of images cast by firelight (514A–515C), can only with great difficulty learn to progress through the levels of contemplation to gaze eventually upon the sun itself (516AB). Were he to return to the other captives to try to instruct them and to release them from their prison, he would appear so strange and out of place that they would ridicule and perhaps even kill him, just as Socrates was killed (517A). Nevertheless, the whole purpose of the allegory, as later becomes clear (e.g., 519C–521B), is to insist that such a return is the philosopher's vocation. He alone can guide the *polis* of blind captives toward a more just social order, just as most later Christian mystics will insist that the contemplative love of God must yield to active love of neighbor within the body of Christ as long as we remain in this life.

Plato's explanation of the allegory underlines the message that in the soul's ascent to the "intelligible region" (*ton noēton topon* [517B]) the Idea of the Good is the highest and ultimate vision. The philosopher who has beheld these "divine contemplations" (*theiōn theoriōn* [517D]), later described as "the contemplation of essence and the brightest region of being" by means of the "eye of the soul" (518C), must always keep in mind how hard the passage of ascent and descent between the two worlds really is.[29] Though the "Allegory of the Cave" has been most often mined for its insights into Plato's metaphysics, speculation and spirituality cannot be separated in the philosopher. Ancient philosophy, as Pierre Hadot has shown, is always a spiritual exercise, a training for the best form of living.[30] The famous "Allegory of the Cave" is essentially an account of the spiritual path that begins with awakening (without the stress on the erotic element in this case) and proceeds through painful purification and gradual illumination to end in vision.[31]

Let us try to summarize the characteristics of Platonic contemplation on the basis of these three texts, supplementing them where necessary from other places in the dialogues and letters. For Plato, the path to human happiness begins with the awakening of the soul through the manifestation of beauty (generally the beauty of the young male in Plato's cultural world). Platonic spirituality has been contrasted with Christian as a kind of auto-salvation in which the philosopher raises himself to the goal solely by his own efforts. While there is surely a great distance between Christian conceptions of fallen humanity's need for grace and what we find in Plato, there are some surprising analogies that have often been missed.[32] Many scholars have noted that the *Symposium* and other texts make clear the necessity for a freely given manifestation or "sudden" (*exaiphnēs*) appearance of the transcendental goal at the end of the process, thus arguing that the summit is not achieved solely by personal effort. But even so acute an investigator as A. J. Festugière misses the importance of the external initiative (might we say "grace"?) of the "sudden" shock of beauty which begins the whole process.[33] To be sure, the gift of beauty given in the beautiful boy is not a *direct* intervention of the Absolute, but is it not at least its manifestation in our world of shadows?

The ascetic or cathartic process by which the sage both restrains his passions and cultivates virtue in his soul is another aspect of the Greek contemplative tradition beginning with Plato that greatly influenced later Christian spirituality,[34] although Plato's thoughts in this area are less developed than those of later Neopythagoreans, Stoics, and Neoplatonists. We can find in his dialogues a kind of tension between world-affirming views in which material reality and erotic relations are used as integral parts of the ascension process (e.g., *Symposium,* and especially the *Phaedrus*) and more negative views, where discipline of and flight from the body as the soul's prison give a more pessimistic, almost dualistic tone to the ascetical program.[35] Even in the more optimistic accounts, however, Plato stresses the essential importance of the transition from a material to a purely spiritual level of knowing and loving. Various appraisals of the role of Platonic and general Hellenic notions of asceticism in the history of Christian spirituality, frequently quite negative ones, have been made.[36] It is only by following the history of the development and intent of asceticism within the broader context of Christian mysticism, as intended in these volumes, that we can hope to appreciate the complexity of this issue.

The gradual purification of love and knowledge achieved through the philosopher's moral and intellectual efforts is the necessary preparation for the sudden manifestation of the ultimate reality of the Form of Forms, variously described as Beauty, the Good, and the One. Plato, like later mystics in the Eastern and Western Christian traditions, insisted that this Ultimate Reality cannot be adequately set forth in language. Nowhere is his profound affinity with much Christian mysticism more evident than in his resolute presentation of what those thinkers who refuse to admit that there can be any form of knowing higher than conceptual thought have always considered a nonsensical delusion — the paradox of continuing to try to suggest with words an ineffable First Principle said to be beyond description.[37]

Negative, or apophatic, theology will form a major part of the story of these volumes, on both the historical and the systematic level. More systematic issues must be left for the final volume, but it may be useful to introduce some necessary distinctions at this time. As Stephen Gersh reminds us, there are *subjective* negative descriptions of God or the First Principle according to which God is said to be unknowable and ineffable to our mode of perception and expression. (We can also distinguish between unknowability, which relates to the mind, and inexpressibility, which relates to the mind's ability to communicate what it knows, though most authors will assert that the latter implies the former.) There are also *objective* negative descriptions in which God or the First Principle is described apophatically without reference to our mode of conceiving.[38] (The two modes of apophaticism may imply each other — that is, God is unknowable in himself and *therefore* unknowable to us — but need not do so.) Subjective apophatic descriptions may be further divided into (a) absolute subjective apophaticism in which God is unknowable and inexpressible to all humans and in every way, and (b) various relative forms of subjective apophaticism in which God is unknowable: (i) only to some or most; (ii) not at all times (i.e., he may reveal himself); and (iii) not to all forms of knowledge. Plato's apophatic thought is not developed in as explicit a way as that of many of his followers, but we can say that it is primarily a form of relative subjective apophaticism that, like many others, combines all three subtypes.

Throughout Plato's writings there are affirmations of the transcendental and therefore unknowable nature of the goal of contemplation. What is not clear is whether or not all these descriptions refer to one and the same reality and whether this reality should be described as the "Really Real" (*to ontos on*), or whether it lies beyond all formulations based on the Greek verb "to be" (*einai*). Later Platonists who insisted that the First must be superior to everything that in any way "is" (conceiving "is" as being predicated of a "something" that exists) found much warrant for their views in Plato; but this may be reading back more coherence into the philosopher's thought than actually to be found in the texts.

Affirmations of at least relative subjective apophaticism in Plato's texts are not hard to find. *Symposium* 211A says of the Beautiful that there is no explanation or knowledge of it (*oude tis logos oude tis epistēmē*). A much-cited text from the *Timaeus* asserted that "to discover the Maker and Father of this Universe were a task indeed; and having discovered him, to declare him unto all men were a thing impossible (*kai heuronta eis pantas adynaton legein* [28C]).[39] A rather obscure passage in the *Seventh Letter,* also much quoted by later authors, has Plato say of the knowledge of the highest subjects of his teaching that "it does not at all admit of verbal expression like other studies, but, as a result of continued application to the subject itself and a communion (*synousios*), it is brought to birth in the soul on a sudden (*exaiphnēs*), as light that is kindled by a leaping spark" (341CD). At least one text in Plato expresses a more objective apophaticism. In book 6 of the *Republic,* the Idea or Form of the Good is said to be "not being but still more than being," an affirmation fraught with questions, but one that was a cornerstone for those Neoplatonists, like Plotinus, who placed the First Principle beyond all being.[40] These and other like texts,[41] for the ancients at least, provided the background for understanding the dialectical puzzles of the *Parmenides,* traditionally seen as the height of Plato's metaphysics.

The fact that the dialogue that was viewed for centuries as Plato's ultimate wisdom is now seen as a curious puzzle, a philosophical joke, or a purely logical exercise by many modern interpreters is eloquent witness to the gap that separates so much contemporary philosophy from its history.[42] Still, a number of recent readings have defended the metaphysical interpretation of the ancient Platonists that was the basis for the dialogue's role in the history of mysticism.[43]

The two parts of the *Parmenides* deal first with the difficulties involved in the relation of the Forms or Ideas to things in the world (127A–134E), and second with the application of Parmenidean dialectic to *to hen,* the Form or Idea of the One (134E–166C). The issues in the first part revolve largely around the idea of participation (*methexis*), a crucial element in Plato's metaphysics. The complex argument of the second part is based on the dialectical premise that "one must consider not only what happens if a particular hypothesis is true, but also what happens if it is not true" (136A). As applied to the supposition that the One does or does not exist, this involves considering eight hypotheses — four for the premise that the One exists,[44] and four for the premise that it does not exist.[45] The clash of the various hypotheses and the problems and possible fallacies in the argument have been the subject of learned commentary, ingenious explanation, and outright rejection for millennia. The first hypothesis has been especially important in the history of the apophatic tradition. In arguing that if the One exists, then, because it is not many and has no parts it must lack both members of contrary predicates like rest and motion, same and different, like and unlike, equal and unequal, Plato concludes by observing that since the One is totally outside time and therefore outside being (*ousia*): "Then the One has no name, nor is there any description (*logos*) or knowledge (*epistēmē*) or perception (*aisthēsis*) or opinion (*doxa*) of it. . . . And it is neither named nor described nor thought nor known, nor does any existing thing perceive it" (142A). Thus, the first hypothesis leads to the conclusion that nothing can be affirmed of the One; it surpasses all sense as well as rational knowledge, and even all being, at least being conceived as *ousia*. We can only say what it is not.[46] But if this One is the Absolute Principle, the heart of Plato's metaphysics, as the Neoplatonists and others have claimed,[47] it is identical with the Beauty that suddenly reveals itself to the lover in the *Symposium* (210E) and with the Good of the *Republic,* which is both the Form of Forms and beyond *ousia* (506D–509B). The Absolute, though beyond words and beyond being, is capable of revealing itself to the *nous* in the philosopher's soul in a form of direct intuition that Plato sometimes calls *noēsis.* In the words of E. R. Dodds, "The supreme act of cognition will thus not be strictly cognitive at all, but will consist in the momentary actualization of a potential identity between the Absolute in man and the Absolute outside man."[48] This is the height of Platonic contemplation — not merely a seeing, but an awareness of identity with the present Ultimate Principle.[49]

In describing the real lover of knowledge (*philomathēs*) in *Republic* 6, Plato had said that he "would hold on his way . . . till he came into touch with the nature of each thing in itself by that part of his soul to which it belongs to lay hold of that kind of reality . . . and through that approaching it, and consorting with reality really (*tō onti ontos*), he would beget intelligence and truth . . ." (490B). The contact between the Absolute Principle and the philosopher, therefore, is possible only because the philosopher's soul — or, to speak more precisely, the higher dimension of the soul that Plato often calls *nous* — is itself of divine origin as *Timaeus* 90BD insists.

"Like is known by like," as Greeks as far back as Empedocles had claimed.[50] Hence, the soul is both divine in origin and capable of being divinized, that is, of reviving and perhaps even radicalizing its innate divinity. An important passage in the *Thaeatetus* says "we should make all speed to take flight from this world to the other, and that means becoming like the divine so far as we can" (*homoios theō kata to dynaton* [176B]). Divinization then is the goal of Plato's philosophy: the philosopher gains immortality by being assimilated to God.[51] Certainly, Plato's notion of divinization is not that of later Christian mystics, especially because of his teaching that the soul is naturally divine and not just divinizable; but the fact that divinization is the culmination of Plato's journey did much to facilitate the adaptation and accommodation of aspects of Plato's contemplative ideal to the service of Christian mysticism.[52]

But was Plato a mystic? Scholars have disagreed, not only because they have read Plato differently but even more because they have had different understandings of what constitutes a mystic.[53] At least three major issues separate the interpreters. First, is Plato's concept of the goal of *theōria* a purely intellectual one, and, if so, does this exclude him from the camp of the mystics? Second, is Plato's view of human perfection something that the philosopher achieves by his own efforts, or does it allow for at least something like a gift or "grace" from the Source? Third, does Plato's belief in the divinity and natural immortality of the soul rule out true mysticism on his part? On all three issues we can say that Plato shows essential differences from later Christian mystics, but we can doubt if that necessarily means that he is not a mystic.

It is questionable that A. H. Armstrong and others are correct in seeing Plato's *theōria* as a purely intellectual vision that does not transcend the level of reason. A. J. Festugière's view that Plato unites both a rationalist and a mystical tendency in his thought is more convincing.[54] And even if Plato were to be convicted of holding a purely intellectual union with the Supreme Idea, why should we deny to him the kind of rational or intellectual mysticism that has been affirmed of a number of Neoaristotelian and Neoplatonic authors?[55] On the second point, Plato's philosophy is not a salvation religion with a distinct savior figure and a developed notion of the necessity of divine assistance, but the "grace" provided by the beautiful beloved does seem to have a necessary if not sufficient role at the beginning of the path toward contemplation, and, as we have seen above, there is a sense in which both the beginning and the end of the philosopher's journey to immortal happiness are a "gift." Finally, while it is true that for Plato *theōria* is the activation of the soul's natural divinity, a supreme self-realization quite different from Christian self-abnegation following the model of Christ,[56] Plato does not differ from Plotinus in this regard, and it is difficult to see why those who would affirm that the latter is a true mystic should deny the title to the former. To be sure, the question of whether or not Plato was a mystic is not vital to our argument. It is enough to know that he was read as one, and it is to some of those readings, direct and indirect, we will soon turn.

The path from Plato to Proclus is much better known today than it was even a few decades ago. Numerous bibliographies and general accounts,[57] as well as specialized studies of individuals and important themes have recently appeared. The customary divisions in the history of the Platonic tradition of the Old Academy, that is, Plato's immediate school (ca. 350–100 B.C.E.), Middle Platonism (ca. 100 B.C.E.–ca. 250 C.E.), and Neoplatonism (ca. 250 C.E. on), still have some use, but more for chronological reasons than as indicating fundamental shifts in working out the inner dynamics of Plato's thought.[58] The world of Middle Platonism, filled with important but shadowy figures whose works often survive only in fragments, has been favored in recent years with a number of useful surveys.[59] The role of other significant philosophical schools and tendencies, especially Aristotelianism, the Stoics, and the Neopythagoreans, as well as philosophically oriented religious movements like Gnosticism, Hermetism, and that reflected in the Chaldean Oracles, makes the spiritual world of the Roman *oikoumenē* of the first three centuries C.E. a very complicated one.

Many of these schools and movements had at least some relationship to early Christianity and its mysticism, but in this context it is impossible to consider them all. One important general tendency of the era was the shift toward conceiving of philosophy as an exegetical enterprise based on authoritative, even revealed, texts. From the time of the collapse of the Athenian schools in the first century B.C.E., we can trace greater emphasis on the foundational texts of the various philosophical traditions, a growing emphasis on textuality over orality.[60] This did not mean that philosophy lost its goal as a form of life, a spiritual path. Rather, the increasing role that documents like the Orphic Hymns and Chaldean Oracles played in school exegesis heightened the religious dimensions of philosophy even over what we have seen in Plato. This is evident in many figures, but especially in three central philosophers whose thought is both representative of the time and also directly relevant to Latin Christian mysticism—Philo (ca. 20 B.C.E.–ca. 50 C.E.), Plotinus (205–270 C.E.), and Proclus (410–485 C.E.).[61]

Philo

Philo was an Alexandrian Jew who was roughly a contemporary of Jesus and Paul. (Christian legend has him meeting St. Peter in Rome!). Jerome's treatise *On Famous Men* (based mostly on Eusebius) says of Philo, "Among the Greeks the popular saying was 'Either Plato philonizes or Philo platonizes,' so much were they alike in thought and expression" (*Famous Men* 11 [*PL* 23:659]). Philo, however, was more than just another platonizer; he was the first figure in Western history to wed the Greek contemplative ideal to the monotheistic faith of the Bible, a union since applauded by many, but condemned by others, both Jews and Christians, as a form of miscegenation. Philo's special place in the history of Judaism, Platonism, and even Christianity—for his most avid ancient readers were Christians[62]—resides in his attempt to use the best Greek philosophy (largely Platonic) both apologetically, that is, to prove that Judaism was the true religion, and speculatively, that is, to draw out the inner meaning of the biblical narratives and ritual practices that formed the heart of Judaism. From the perspective of contemporary Greek philosophy, he was doing with the Bible what other philosophers were already engaged upon with other "sacred" texts; from the perspective of his later Christian readers, many of his techniques and his conclusions foreshadowed how they were to seek to join biblical revelation and Greek philosophy in the service of a mystical ideal.

Philo's mystical thought anticipates classic Christian mysticism especially in its exegetical character. For the great Jewish thinker the meaning of life had been revealed in the scripture, but not all had the eyes to read it. As David Winston puts it, "If the main intent of the Philonic enterprise is a Greco-Jewish reconciliation, its main instrument is a vast and detailed allegorical interpretation of Scripture, partly through a line-by-line exegesis, known as the Allegory of the Law, and partly through a more thematic treatment designated as the Exposition of the Law."[63] The nature of Philo's allegorical exegesis has been much studied, but still remains controversial in some aspects. Philo came at the end of what was apparently a lengthy line of philosophically-minded Jews who made use of pagan techniques of allegorical interpretation in the service of effecting a rapprochement between faith and philosophy.[64] Adopting a middle position between the extreme allegorists who "frivolously neglect the letter" and the small-minded literalists, Philo urged readers of scripture "to go forward in quest of the allegorical interpretation (*tropikas apodoseis*), in the conviction that the words of the oracles are as it were shadows cast by bodies, whereas the significations therein revealed are the things that have true existence" (*De confusione linguarum* 190).[65] The major purpose of the intricate and dense forest of Philonic allegory is to show the soul its way home to God.[66]

While some scholars have denied Philo the title of mystic,[67] many of the major Philo students of the present century, from Erwin Goodenough to David Winston, have argued convincingly that the Jewish philosopher should be understood in light of a form of Middle Platonic mysticism widespread in the late Hellenistic world.[68] Philo's importance rests on the merger he effected between this form of Greek contemplative piety, with its growing emphasis on the transcendence of the divine First Principle, and his Jewish faith grounded in the Bible and in the practices and laws of his people. This reconciliation was achieved not only by seeking a deeper and more universal meaning in the scriptures, but also by transforming Platonic contemplation into a more personalistic mode.[69] Although H. A.

Wolfson's interpretation of Philo, which seems to transfer to the Jewish philosopher Plato's role in A. N. Whitehead's famous remark about Western philosophy being a series of footnotes to Plato, is doubtless exaggerated, the Jewish thinker's status as a pioneer in Western mystical thought cannot be doubted.

One reason why Philo was able to serve as a model for Christian authors was the role he gave to the Logos, or Divine Word or Reason, as an intermediary between the absolutely transcendent and unknowable God and the human soul.[70] Philo's Logos doctrine has deep roots in Hellenistic Judaism's speculation about the figure of Sophia, or Wisdom,[71] as well as in certain aspects of Middle Platonism, especially in the gradually emerging intradeical interpretation of Plato's world of Ideas (i.e., the teaching that the Ideas are to be found in the mind of God). Aristotle's criticism of Plato's theory of Ideas (e.g., *Metaphysics* 1:978b–991b) had shown how difficult it was to maintain a separate realm of Ideas as in some sense a cause of the world. One solution, first explicitly found in Philo but almost certainly something he inherited from previous Middle Platonists, was to move the Ideas into God, to identify them with the Divine Mind that causes the universe.[72]

Like the One of the first hypothesis of the *Parmenides*, Philo's God is beyond all the predicates of human language, that is, he is subjectively apophatic. "Who is capable of asserting of the Primal Cause that it is incorporeal or corporeal, or that it possesses quality or is qualityless, or, in general, who could make a firm statement concerning his essence or quality or state or movement?" (*Legum allegoriae* 3.206 [Winston, p. 141]).[73] But Philo's God, the biblical God who gives his name in Exod 3:14,[74] is not beyond being; he is "the Existent which truly exists" (*to on ho esti alētheian on* [*De mutatione nominum*] 7). Although no proper name can be given to him (ibid., 8–12), "the bare fact that he is" (*to einai monon*) can be apprehended (*Quod deterius* 89).[75]

The existence of the inconceivable God can be known through analogy because he reveals himself in two ways, first, through the intelligible universe, or elder son, that is, his Logos, and, second, and derivatively through the sensible universe as through a younger son.[76] Philo's teaching about the Logos is rich and controversial; a broad picture will have to suffice here. The Logos is "the Idea of Ideas (*idea ideōn*)" (*De migratione Abrahami* 103),[77] the first-begotten son of the Father (*De confusione linguarum* 63; *De posteritate Caini* 63), a "second God."[78]

> To his chief messenger and most venerable Logos, the Father who engendered the universe has granted the singular gift, to stand between and separate the

creature from the Creator. . . . "And I stood between the Lord and you" (Deut 5:5), neither unbegotten as God, nor begotten as you, but midway between the two extremes, serving as a pledge for both. . . . (*Quis rerum divinarum heres sit* 205 [Winston, p. 94])

The Logos, then, is both a Platonic mediating principle, the medium that joins two extremes (see *Timaeus* 31C), and more, insofar as he is a "vivid and living hypostatization of an essential aspect of deity, the face of God turned toward creation," as David Winston puts it.[79] As the manifestation of the hidden God, the Logos reveals the two essential aspects of God's relation to the world, the creative power (*poietikē dynamis*) and the ruling or conserving power (*basilikē dynamis*).[80]

The Logos is also central in the soul's return to God, both primordially and consequently. "For just as God is the Pattern of the Image [i.e., the Logos], which was just named Shadow, so does the Image become the pattern of others, as Moses makes clear at the beginning of the Law Code by saying, 'And God made man after the Image of God' (Gen 1:27); thus the Image had been modeled after God, but man after the Image . . ." (*Legum allegoriae* 3.96 [Winston, p. 101]).[81] The Logos is immanent in all things, but in a special way in the human mind. The presence of the Logos within the soul, that is, within the higher dimension or *nous* (Philo followed Plato in adhering to a tripartite understanding of the soul) (*Leg.* 3.115 [Winston, pp. 119–20]), makes possible both knowledge of the existence of God (e.g., *De migratione Abrahami* 184–86) and the return of the soul to God from its present fallen state.

In the *Phaedrus,* as we have seen, Plato constructed an elaborate myth of the fall of the soul. Philo did not need to do this, since Genesis supplied him with the story of Adam, Eve, and the serpent in the Garden of Eden. For the Jewish writer, the Genesis account was not a collection of mythical fictions (*mythou plasmata*), "but modes of making ideas visible, bidding us to resort to allegorical interpretation guided in our renderings by what lies beneath the surface" (*Op.* 157 [LC 1:125]). Philo's allegorical reading, in which the serpent stands for the pleasure that tempts the woman (woman here represents sense perception, i.e., *aisthēsis*) in order to pull the "sovereign mind" (*hegemonē nous*) of the man away from heavenly realities and down to the things of this world, was the first in a long line of interpretations of the Eden story as a timeless message about the inner conflict and fall in every soul (*Op.* 157–59 [LC 1:124–34]).[82]

If the story of the Fall signifies the disordered soul which has forgotten its true nature as image of the Logos, the hidden message of the other books of the Pentateuch, especially the histories of the patriarchs and the story of Moses, presents a typology of those souls who have regained their true

nature by following the path to mystic contemplation.[83] Like Plato, Philo
holds that ultimate bliss resides in the vision of God, or "knowledge of him
who truly is" (*epistēmē tou ontos ontos;* see *De decalogo* 87 [LC 7:46]).[84] "For the
beginning and end of happiness is to be able to see God" (*Quaestiones et Solutiones in Exodum* 2.51 [LC *Suppl.* 2.99]). Also like Plato, the Jewish philosopher describes the true contemplative in terms taken from the language
of the Greek mysteries. Thus Moses, "entering into the dark cloud, the
invisible region, abides there while being initiated into the most holy
mysteries. He becomes, however, not only an initiate, but also a hierophant
and instructor of divine rites (*hierophantēs orgiōn kai didaskalos theiōn*), which
he will impart to those clean of ear" (*De gigantibus* 54 [Winston, p. 69]).

This ascent into an invisible region in order to be initiated into mysteries
begins with a discipline of the body and an ascetical life-style that Philo
sketched in his treatise *The Contemplative Life* (*Peri biou theoretikou,* or *De vita
contemplativa*), written in praise of the Therapeutae, an Essene-like Jewish
contemplative group near Alexandria.[85] They are described as aiming "at
the vision of the Existent" (*Cont.* 11) and as having secured "God's friendship" (*theou philia* [*Cont.* 90]) through virtue.

The power that motivates the contemplative life leading to the vision of
God is a divine *erōs* (*De somniis* 2.232 [Winston, p. 165]), but Philo makes
it clear that this love is not a native gift of the soul but is rather an inspiration by which God calls us upward to himself.[86] Philo gives greater
emphasis than Plato to the role of ecstasy (*ekstasis,* literally, "standing outside" [the self]) in the upward path:

> . . . but escape also from your own self and stand outside from yourself, like
> persons possessed and corybants seized by Bacchic frenzy and carried away
> by some form of prophetic inspiration. For it is the mind that is filled with
> the Deity and no longer in itself, but is agitated and maddened by a heavenly
> passion, drawn by the truly Existent and attracted upward to it. (*Her.* 70
> [Winston, p. 169])[87]

Andrew Louth has pointed out another difference between Philo and Plato.
Since the Jewish thinker holds that the soul is only a created image of the
Logos, not a part of the Logos itself, to come to know one's inner self on
the journey up to the Existent is to gain an awareness of the "absolute
nothingness of created being" (*en pasi tou genetou . . . oudeneian*). "And the
man who has despaired of himself is beginning to know him that is" (*Som.*
1.60 [LC 5:326–29]).[88] Divinization for Philo thus implies a self-naughting
absent in much of the pagan mystical tradition, though we shall see an
analogue in Plotinus.

Philo was the first to introduce into mystical literature the famous oxymoron of "sober intoxication" (*methē nephalios*) to describe the way in which the mind is taken out of itself in the upward way. "It longs for the intelligible, and on beholding in that realm beauties beyond measure, the patterns and originals of the sensible things in the world below it is possessed by a sober intoxication, like those seized with corybantic frenzy . . ." (*Op.* 71 [Winston, p. 173]).[89] Nevertheless, it is not clear in Philo if ecstasy and sober intoxication are to be seen as stages characterizing the way to the contemplative goal or as attempts to express aspects of that goal itself.

David Winston has claimed that "man's highest union with God, according to Philo, is limited to the Deity's manifestation as Logos."[90] But some texts, at least, seem to hold out the possibility for vision of the Existent in himself, not, of course, a comprehension or understanding of his nature, but some form of contact with *that* which is. In one place he says, "It is fitting for those who have entered into comradeship with knowledge to long to see the Existent (*to on idein*), but if they are unable, to see at least his image, the truly holy Logos . . ." (*Conf.* 97 [Winston, p. 171]).[91] Other texts seem even clearer about the possibility of some form of vision, or cleaving,[92] and, in at least one case, union (*henōsis*) with God, the Existent One,[93] though, like Plato, Philo holds that this happens suddenly,[94] and that its duration is brief.[95]

Philo goes beyond Plato, however, in ascribing the supreme vision (however we are to conceive it) to the historical figures of the Bible — Enoch, Abraham, other patriarchs, and most especially to Moses. The leader of the Jewish people is described as having a "prophetic mind" which becomes "filled with God" and therefore "like the monad" so that "he is changed into the divine" (*QE* 2.29 [LC *Suppl.* 2:69–70]; cf. 2.40). Making Moses the ideal mystic, the divinized man, marks an important moment in the history of mystical traditions, for both Jews and Christians, if only because it links the generalized and often abstract subjective apophaticism of the Hellenic tradition with a personal life story that could, at least in part, be imitated — the account in Exodus of how Moses ascended to meet God in the cloud and darkness that hung upon Sinai.[96]

The mention of Moses' prophetic mind points to modern disputes about the nature of Philo's account of contemplation. H. A. Wolfson argued that the direct mode of access to God of which Philo speaks is always the result of a divine prophetic revelation that bypasses human reason, while David Winston distinguishes between ecstatic and hermeneutical prophecy, viewing Philo's notion of contact with God as an intellectual experience based on reason's intuitive function, a development of an "ontological" proof for God's existence innate in the mind.[97] The latter position, stressing the intellectual character of contemplation, seems closer to Philo's texts, but one still wonders if it does full justice to the ecstatic and apophatic elements found in Philo's frequent appeals to Bacchic frenzy and the divine darkness that Moses experienced. Did Philo himself enjoy such experiences? At times the Alexandrian speaks of the inspiration that he had enjoyed during his philosophical studies,[98] or in writing,[99] but it is questionable whether he wishes to equate this with the vision of God, the Supreme Existent.

Ancient Mystery Religions

Philo, even more than Plato, raises the question of the relation between Greek mystical philosophy and the ancient mystery religions. Erwin Goodenough saw Greek philosophy as the prime instrument in the metamorphosis of the various oriental mythologies into the mystery religions. He viewed Philo as the summation of a process by which "Judaism was at once transformed into the greatest, the only true Mystery. . . . The objective of this Judaism was salvation in the mystical sense."[100] Though Goodenough may have pushed his evidence too far in some instances (as in his arguments for secret Jewish mystery rituals), his interpretation does bring out Philo's relation to his Hellenistic milieu and the special character of his Judaism. Hans Jonas, who held that the transition from myth to mystical philosophy was in part mediated by the mystery cults, also understood Philo as playing an important role in the complex interactions between myth, mystery, and mysticism at the beginning of the common era.[101] His interpretation sought to draw the Jewish philosopher closer to the thought world of Gnosticism.[102] What was the relation between the mystery cults and traditions of late antiquity and the Greek contemplative ideal?

Despite the study devoted to them since the nineteenth century, basic puzzles remain in our knowledge of the mystery religions — or, perhaps better, mystery cults.[103] Their origins, both individually and as a general phenomenon, are still in doubt, though now there seems to be some agreement that the mysteries are fundamentally products of Greek piety, even that the "Oriental" mysteries are the result of Hellenic interpretations of Eastern myths. As to whether or not the great mysteries, like those of Eleusis, Dionysius, Orpheus, the *Magna Mater,* Isis, and Mithras, are to be seen as in some way "mystical," judgments have varied depending largely on the view of mysticism employed. Ugo Bianchi, with his broad distinction between the Olympian and the mystical strains in Greek religion, has no difficulty in granting them mystical status because they witness to the interference of the divine and human levels of reality.[104] Walter Burkert, on the other hand, understanding mysticism as "the transformation of consciousness by meditation," denies that the mysteries were mystical.[105]

Nevertheless, he admits that "in religious terms, mysteries provide an immediate encounter with the divine,"[106] an experience that might well be described as implicitly mystical. Previous investigators, such as Albrecht Dieterich and Hans Jonas, gave the mysteries a major role in the development of late antique mysticism, both pagan and Christian. In his study of the images of union between a god and a human found in the mysteries (eating, sexual congress, divine sonship, rebirth, and the heavenly journey), Dieterich claimed to have uncovered a form of thought found in all mysticism and argued that Catholic Christianity was the "universal heir of ancient mysticism."[107] Hans Jonas utilized Dieterich's materials, but gave the mysteries only an intermediary role in the transition from myth to mysticism.[108] Today it seems likely that whatever role the mysteries had in the development of Christian mysticism, it was largely one mediated through the philosophical appropriation of the myths of the mystery cults.[109]

The relation between the mysteries and Greek philosophy, according to Kurt Rudolph, is based on the philosophers' conviction that "knowledge of God was attainable only by a path resembling the one followed in the mysteries at the ritual and religious level."[110] The occasional use of the language of the mysteries in Plato eventually broadened to include full allegorical readings of the myths and rituals of the cults, a process that reached its fulfillment in Neoplatonism. Pierre Hadot has argued that even though the Neoplatonists use the adjective *mystikos* only sparingly, the notion of intuitive experimental vision of mystery as the summit of philosophical contemplation was something that the philosophers adopted from the traditional use of *mystikos* found in the Greek mysteries.[111]

The mutual interaction between philosophy and mystery in late antiquity was certainly influential on Gnosticism (an issue to be taken up in chapter 4); it is evident also in texts such as the Chaldean Oracles and the Hermetic treatises. The importance of the Chaldean Oracles for later pagan mystical philosophy was first demonstrated by Hans Lewy in his *Chaldaean Oracles and Theurgy: Mysticism, Magic, and Platonism in the Later Roman Empire.*[112] Written in the late second century, probably by Syrian magicians, the Oracles, which became a sacred scripture for many Neoplatonists,[113] are a good example of the "sacramental mysticism" of Greek mysteriosophical religion.[114] A number of key themes in these obscure texts, especially the insistence that it is only through a secret highest level of human intelligence described as the "flower of nous" (*anthos nou*) that contact with the "Father Above" is possible, were to be important in later apophatic mysticism.[115]

Even more important were the Hermetic writings, or *Hermetica,* ascribed to the Egyptian god Thoth, who was identified with the Greek Hermes. Composed under Egyptian, Jewish, and Greek influence between the first and third centuries C.E., the philosophical *Hermetica* (popular treatises on the occult sciences were also ascribed to Hermes) were widely known in late antiquity and were to exercise both direct and indirect influence, if only of a secondary nature, on the history of Christian mysticism.[116] Although the writings of the *Corpus Hermeticum* are too varied to speak of a single Hermetic doctrine, these revelatory texts display the basic concerns of Alexandrian Hellenism on two central issues: the nature of God, especially the opposition between the Cosmic God and the unknown Primary God, and the story of the soul's fall into and ascent from the earthly realm.[117] An oscillation between optimistic and pessimistic views of the universe, even more marked than in Plato, is evident. Some passages display a strong mystical character. In the tenth treatise of the standard corpus (called "The Key"), Hermes instructs his disciple about the possibility of the vision of the Good, or "the God and Father," affirming that it can be briefly and imperfectly enjoyed in this life, but that the perfect vision (*thea*) "that changes the whole person into [divine] being" (*kai holon auton eis ousian metaballei*) and "makes the soul a god" (*psychēn apotheothēnai*) must wait until death.[118]

The negative theology of the Hermetic literature has been well studied by Festugière in the fourth volume of his *La révélation d'Hermès Trismégiste*. Through the treatise known as the *Asclepius*, a third-century work surviving in a fourth-century Latin translation, Hermetic apophaticism had some direct influence on the West.[119] Indeed, a central element in all the religious literature of the second and third centuries C.E., both the properly philosophical and the mysteriosophical, was the growing stress on the transcendence and unknowability of the Highest God. Middle Platonists such as the philosopher Albinus, Neopythagoreans such as Numenius, Gnostics of various persuasions, the authors of the Chaldean Oracles and the *Hermetica*, as well as Christians such as Clement and Origen, despite their marked differences of opinion on many issues, all insisted on the radical, if not quite absolute, unknowability of God.[120] However unknowable the First remained in its own nature, second-century thinkers such as Numenius also believed that some form of contact was possible in this life. In a famous fragment from his lost treatise *On the Good* (*Peri tagathou*) Numenius compared the contemplative to "a man sitting on a watch-tower, having caught a quick glimpse of a small fishing-boat, one of those solitary skiffs, left alone by itself. . . . Just so, then, must a man withdraw far from the things of sense, and commune in solitude with the Good alone (*homilēsai tō agathō monō monon*). . . ."[121]

The many forms of mysticism, or at least of mystical philosophy, of the first centuries C.E. defy easy categorization. A. J. Festugière proposed a

typology of late Hellenistic mysticism (i.e., 100 B.C.E.–400 C.E.) that distinguished between theoretical forms stressing the sage's ability to raise himself
up to contact with the First Principle, the Father beyond all understanding,
or at least the astral God of this world, and the mysticism of salvation based
on a pessimistic view of the world and emphasizing the necessity for divine
intervention to effect the movement up to the divine goal.[122] These forms
were united in finding the vision of God the ultimate aim and goal.[123] This
rich background was absorbed and transformed into something new by
Plotinus, the purest mystic of pagan antiquity.

Plotinus

Plotinus was born in Egypt about 205. Dying in Rome in 270, he had
lived through an era of great turmoil in Roman history, though this would
be difficult to detect from his writings.[124] His treatises were edited and
published by his pupil Porphyry in the early fourth century in six books of
nine treatises called the *Enneads.* They are among the greatest masterpieces
of mystical as well as of philosophical literature.

Investigations of Plotinus's mystical thought have been many, from
pioneering studies such as those of Joseph Maréchal and René Arnou,
through the more recent work of scholars like A. H. Armstrong, Jean
Trouillard, Pierre Hadot, Werner Beierwaltes, and others.[125] From this
literature a general picture emerges that corrects many earlier misconcep-
tions, though given the difficulty of Plotinus's thought a number of issues
remain problematic.

Plotinus certainly enjoyed what moderns would call mystical experiences. His pupil Porphyry in the fascinating life he wrote of his master
testifies: "his end and goal was to be united (*henothēnai*), to approach the
God who is over all things. Four times while I was with him he attained
that goal" (*Life of Plotinus* 23).[126] Plotinus himself speaks in autobiographical tones in several passages, such as the famous opening of *Ennead* 4.8.1:

> Often have I woken up out of the body to myself and have entered into myself,
> going out from all other things; I have seen a beauty wonderfully great and
> felt assurance that then most of all I belonged to the better part; I have
> actually lived the best life and come to identity with the divine; and set firm
> in it I have come to that supreme actuality, setting myself above all else in
> the realm of Intellect. Then after that rest in the divine (*en tō theiō stasin*),
> when I have come down from Intellect to discursive reasoning, I am puzzled
> how I ever came down. (LC 4:396–97)

This passage deals with union or identity between the self or soul and the
Intellect or Nous. It has usually been taken as indicating a brief ecstatic

experience of the kind described by Porphyry, but Dominic O'Meara argues that the "often" refers not to the union itself, but to the philosopher's experience of puzzled reflection upon the habitual state of union of the higher soul with the Intellectual Principle.[127] Plotinus actually seems to want to have it both ways, because elsewhere he claims that the unitive state is both an ontological constant, though not consciously so to the lower soul (see, e.g., 4.8.8; 5.1.12; and 6.4.14), and also the conscious goal which his mysticophilosophical teaching is designed to foster. Philosophy exists to raise the lower soul or self to consciousness of its higher identity, the transcendent self which enjoys identity with pure Intellect, and through Intellect even with the unknown One. This experience must always be short and exceptional as long as the soul remains in the body.[128]

A passage from *Enn.* 5.8.11 helps to clarify this. Here he describes in a fashion that must be autobiographical a form of oscillation between (1) discursive preparation for mystical encounter, in which there is still a distinction between the one who sees and what is seen, and (2) the unity of mystical awareness, which is necessarily followed by (3) a return to a new, but refined, discursiveness.

(1) . . . one of us, being unable to see himself, when he is possessed by that god brings his contemplation to the point of vision, and presents himself to his own mind and looks at a beautified image of himself. . . .

(2) . . . but then he dismisses the image, beautiful though it is, and comes to unity with himself, and making no more separation, is one and altogether with god silently present, and is with him as much as he wants to be and can be.

(3) But if he returns again to being two, while he remains pure he stays close to the god, so as to be present to him again in that other way if he turns to him again. (LC 5:272–73)

No other ancient author has portrayed the psychology of mystical states with their complex passages between the consciousness of duality and unity with greater subtlety than Plotinus.[129]

Another noted passage from *Enn.* 6.9.9 speaks in an even more personal tone:

Anyone who has had this experience will know what I am talking about. He will know that the soul lives another life as it advances toward the One, reaches it and shares in it (*metaschousa autou*). . . . It needs nothing more. On the contrary, it must renounce everything else and rest in it alone, become it alone (*touto genesthai*), all earthiness gone, eager to be free, impatient of every fetter that binds below in order so to embrace the real object of its love with its entire being that no part of it does not touch the One.[130]

Such texts show that not only did Plotinus try to portray the experience of the passage between the unity of mystical consciousness and the duality of everyday thinking, but that he also had a dual notion of unification, one that involved union with the Nous, or Intellect, as well as a higher uniting with that which is beyond all thought and being, the unknowable One (*to hen*). The differing modes of union portrayed in Plotinus's mystical accounts form the experiential basis for the understanding of the structure of reality that he developed out of the classical philosophical tradition.[131]

Plotinus's ability to combine abstruse philosophical analysis with a tone of deep personal feeling is unique — reading him is like being invited to embark on a journey of exploration into uncharted territory in search of hidden treasure: a bracing and perhaps dangerous enterprise. His doctrine of the One, for example, certainly has its roots in the negative theology of his predecessors, but is far richer than that found in earlier authors. The constant interpenetration of metaphysics and mysticism in his thought means that a brief sketch of Plotinian metaphysics is needed before turning to a more detailed consideration of his notion of mystical contemplation and union.

Plotinus conceived of three transcendent levels of reality, or hypostases, beyond the visible universe — the One, the Intellect, and the Soul. In reality, this scheme is made more complex by his distinction of Soul into upper and lower levels: the higher Universal Soul (*psychē*); and Nature (*physis*), or that Soul as embodied in matter. To show the roots of Plotinus's hypostases in the evolution of Greek thought, with the One or Absolute Unity being a development of the Parmenidean-Platonic tradition, the Intellect (One-Many) a combination of Aristotelian and Middle Platonic elements, and the World Soul (One and Many) partly Platonic and partly Stoic in heritage, is not to reduce Plotinus to a mere compiler, nor is it to settle the question of whether or not he is a consistent thinker — an issue that does not seem to have much bothered his ever-questing mind.[132]

Plotinus's three hypostases have been interpreted in a number of ways, most often as a hierarchical structure, a map of the ontological levels of reality in which the lower stages flow from the higher ones through the necessary nontemporal process of procession or emanation (*proodos*) and return through conversion (*epistrophē*).[133] Many interpreters have also stressed an introspective reading of this hypostatic structure, seeing Plotinus's thought as a "metapsychology," that is, as a presentation of the reality of all things through the analysis of consciousness.[134] As Gerard O'Daly puts it: "'Procession' and 'conversion' (or return) are temporal metaphors for the moment in which the self's originative vision of its principle — a vision that is permanent — is made conscious to itself as pre-intellectual, in an instant of unmediated contact."[135]

Both views are correct and highlight important dimensions of the Plotinian enterprise, but they are incomplete without the invocation of a third approach, the dialectical one. On the basis of Plotinus's own critique of the notion of levels of being implied in the emanation model (e.g., 6.4–5; 6.8), as well as his attempts to express — insofar as it is open to expression — how the One both is and is not the reality of all things, and both is and is not conscious, Plotinus presents a mystical dialectic of immanence and transcendence whose purpose is to lead the soul to its ultimate liberation.[136] Freedom comes through the realization of what it means to say that "the One is all things and not a single one of them" (*Enn.* 5.2.1).

Each of these aspects of Plotinian thought gives rise to different mystical possibilities that together generate a complex of ideas that had great importance for subsequent Christian mysticism.[137] The hierarchical scheme of emanation and return is the best known. Its spiritual possibilities are well illustrated in the famous treatise on Beauty (*Enn.* 1.6). Here the controlling metaphors are those of journey, ascent, passionate striving, return to the source, and vision, as in the *Symposium* on which the text is based. This inquiry into the nature of beauty and its role in the soul's return to its source begins, as did Plato, with the beauty of bodies, which Plotinus holds does not reside in the symmetry of parts but in the participation of the higher Form (1.6.1–3). The recognition of the true nature of bodily beauty is the starting point for an ascent that proceeds to the beauty of "ways of life and kinds of knowledge" (1.6.4), then to the beauty of the soul purified by virtue so that it is "entirely belonging to the divine" (1.6.6), until finally, "passing in the ascent all that is alien to the God, one sees with one's self alone That alone (*autō monō auto monon idē*), simple, single and pure, from which all depends and to which all look and are and live and think" (1.6.7).[138] The text concludes with a passionate invocation of the necessity for purification and introversion in order to reach "the Fatherland from which we have come" (1.6.8),[139] as well as the reminder that this process is one of deification — "You must become first all godlike and all beautiful if you intend to see God and beauty" (1.6.9).[140]

Plotinus was a resolute intellectualist, but the profoundly erotic tone of *Enn.* 1.6 shows us that he did not think that knowing alone could bring the soul back to its source.[141] Even in Plato, as we have seen, *erōs* was not so much a selfish desire for personal possession and enjoyment of the beautiful as a creative desire to beget beauty on the beloved. In Plato, however, because *erōs* always involves a deficiency of some sort, it could not be ascribed to the divine world. In Plotinus, erotic love has an ambit both more cosmic and more transcendental. *Ennead* 6.8.15 says of the Good,

"He is at once lovable, and love, and love of himself" (*kai erasmion kai erōs ho autos kai hautou erōs*). Of course, the One or Good is absolutely self-sufficient (6.8.10), without any hint of desire for anything outside itself (3.8.11). But in recognizing that *erōs* is not defined by need, Plotinus made a major breakthrough in classical thought that enabled him to speak of a Supreme Reality in which seeker and sought become truly one. Although this transcendent *erōs* has no concern for what is below it (Plotinus explicitly denies that God loves the world [e.g., 5.5.12]),[142] we must remember that the erotic One remains the source for all that is and that the whole universe is essentially erotic in the sense that its being is marked by passionate striving for return to the Source (e.g., 3.5.1–2 and 4).[143] From a Christian perspective, Plotinus's inability to relate *erōs* above and below, transcendental Eros and human eros in our terms, is a limitation, though he does affirm that all love for beauty is in some way a reflection of the Good (e.g., 6.7.22 and 31), and that "the Good is gentle and kindly and gracious, and present to anyone when he wishes" (5.5.12).

The role of love in the soul's return to its source is among the most constant themes in Plotinus's thought. Drawn upward by the shock of beauty, the soul eventually becomes love itself (6.7.22). When it has attained union with Nous, it will be able to exercise both of the inherent powers of this supreme Intellectual Principle:

> Intellectual-Principle, thus, has two powers, first that of grasping intellectively its own content, the second that of an advancing and receiving whereby to know the transcendent; at first it [the soul] sees, later by that seeing it takes possession of Intellectual-Principle, becoming one only thing with that: the first seeing is that of Intellect knowing, the second that of Intellect loving; stripped of its wisdom in the intoxication of the nectar; it comes to love; by this excess it is made simplex and is happy; and to be drunken is better for it than to be too staid for these revels. (*Enn* 6.7.35)[144]

Nous erōn is what makes possible the final stage of union with the One.[145] Plotinus is not afraid to describe this *erōs* in language adopted from lower, more common, forms of love: "And if anyone does not know this experience, let him think of it in terms of our loves here below, and what it is like to attain what one is most in love with" (6.9.9). As "many lovers of the One" (6.5.10), our destiny is to continue to enjoy loving union with the One as far as possible in this life and the next (e.g., 1.6.7; 3.5.4).

The second approach to Plotinus's thought, stressing the introspective and metapsychological dimension, is also well illustrated in many texts. According to Emile Bréhier, what was new in Plotinus

> . . . was ushering into the intelligible world the individual subject itself with the concrete richness and infinity of its determinations. . . . For nothing like

things exist in true reality. There exist only subjects which contemplate and in which contemplation exists in a varying degree of concentration and purity. . . . Pure subject—the One; the subject ideally separated from its object—Intelligence; finally, the subject which scatters and disperses itself in a world of objects.[146]

More recently, Werner Beierwaltes has analyzed the Plotinian One as the nonreflective element in reflection, "the *Aufhebung* of the reflexive into the pre-reflexive which is its consummation."[147] It would demand an extensive textual presentation to follow the details of Plotinus's introspective understanding of the nature of Soul and Intellect. Here it must suffice to consider how the "metasubjective" understanding of the One is the undercurrent of all of Plotinus's mystical thought.

Plotinus's refusal to allow any predicates to be ascribed to the One in proper fashion is among the best-known aspects of his thought.[148] To use the terminology adopted above, his apophaticism is both objective and subjective, and it would appear at first absolutely so. "It is . . . truly ineffable (*arrēton*): for whatever you say about it, you will always be speaking of 'something'" (*ti*) (5.3.13). Objectively, it is frequently described as "beyond being" (*epekeina ousias,* or *tou ontos,* following *Republic* 509B),[149] and also beyond knowing—"The One, as it is beyond Intellect, so is beyond knowledge (*gnōsis*), and as it does not in any way need anything, so it does not need knowing. . . . For knowing is one thing [or "one something"—*hen ti kai to gignōskein*]; but That is one without the something" (5.3.12).[150] But Plotinus does qualify his apophaticism, not only by his admission of some form of contact with the One but also through his struggle to construct a critical dialectical language about it. His linguistic strategies are evident in many places in the *Enneads,* but nowhere more profoundly than in the second half of *Enn.* 6.8 (7–21), "On Free Will and the Will of the One."

In trying to understand in what sense will and activity can be used in relation to the One, Plotinus experiments with a new language based on ungrammatical and frequently puzzling usages and expressions qualified throughout by the particle *hoion* ("quasi," or "so to speak"), a language designed to suggest the eminent reality of the One without attempting the impossible task of circumscribing or objectifying it in any way.[151] The One can never be objectified, because it is a pure transcendent subject,[152] and hence it is through a series of appeals to the immanent activity of acting, knowing, and willing that Plotinus creates his new language. Basically, he invites the reader to try to imagine a spontaneous immanent activity not directed at an object and not proceeding from a subject, but which in some indescribable way *is* the subject itself.

The Good does not exist either by necessity or by chance (6.8.7). It is as it must be, but without any "must" — "being what it wills to be (*touto ousan ho thelei*), or rather projecting into existence what it wills, itself higher than will, will a thing beneath it" (6.8.9).[153] The Good or First is described as having an activity (*energeia*) identical with itself, but this is not the kind of activity that can be distinguished from essence (*ousia*). Rather, the form of willing that can be ascribed to the One (*hoion*) is to be found in the formula "he is as he willed himself to be," as long as this willing is not distinguished, even mentally, from essence or nature (6.8.13). Activity in the One can be described as a "quasi essence" (*hoion ousia* [9.8.13, 7–8, 26–28]). This is why Plotinus can go on to identify the One with Love, or at least Self-Love (see 6.8.15, the passage already referred to). In 6.8.16 the contortions of language are expanded in new directions, as Plotinus concedes to the One a "quasi intellect" (*hoion nous*), or a "super-intellect" (*hypernoēsis*), which does not *have* but *is* the knowing that it loves.[154] This eternal "self-directed activity" (*energeia menousa*) is the being of the One. "If then this Act never came to be but is eternal — a waking without an awakener, an eternal wakening and supra-Intellection — he is as he waked himself to be" (6.8.16).[155]

This profound exploration of the inner dynamics of the One helps explain the complex relations between the First Principle, or One, and Nous, or Intellect.[156] In 6.8.18 Plotinus says that in seeking the One we seek what is within all things just as the center of a circle is within its radii and circumference.[157] That which is "around" the center is preeminently the Nous, or Intellect, which both is and is not the One in a more radical sense than any other reality. Insofar as Nous is essence, being, and thought, it is projected outside the One (6.8.19). But this is to understand Nous as the product or term of an activity, whereas in its more proper sense Nous *is* an activity, a fact that makes it more difficult to make an easy distinction between Nous and the One that makes itself. Plotinus's language usually tries to suggest how the One is active without the self-reflexivity which is of the essence of Nous, but one controversial passage seems to move self-reflexivity back into the One and thus bring Nous and the One even closer together. *Enn.* 5.1.7 appears to say, "In turning towards itself the One sees. The seeing is Nous" (*ē hoti tē epistrophē pros hauto hēora; hē de horasis hautē nous*).[158] Thus we should beware of excluding Nous from having a role even in the highest stage of mystical union. Hadot argues that in one sense we never surpass the level of Nous, because we "reach and share" in the One (6.9.9) by *becoming* Nous in the first constitutive moment or stage of its reality — not Nous as it thinks itself and consequently all things, but Nous as it is lovingly one (*nous erōn*) with its Source before it is projected forth.[159]

What does this complex apophaticism based on the analysis of reality as a form of transcendental subjectivity mean for Plotinian mysticism? This will not become fully evident until we consider the dialectical element in Plotinian thought — a component that qualifies the emanational picture and provides a more inclusive metaphysical perspective for the metapsychological account.

In *Enn.* 6.5.12, at the end of the double treatise investigating the omnipresence of being, Plotinus asks how the All is to be found in everything. The answer is discovered in the rejection of particularity:

> Now it is because you approached the All and did not remain in a part of it, and you did not even say of yourself "I am just so much," but by rejecting the "so much" you have become all. . . . You will increase yourself then by rejecting all else, and the All will be present to you in your rejection. . . ." (LC 6:358-59)[160]

In numerous other places the philosopher asserts that "all things are one" (6.5.1), or "we are all and one" (6.5.7), or that the three hypostases exist within us waiting for us to turn our attention to them (5.1.5-7, 10-13). The critique of the metaphors of emanation (useful as they are for expressing certain truths about the relation of the One to all things) found in 6.4-5 (especially 6.4.7 and 11, and 5.3) emphasizes an understanding of the omnipresence of the One in all things that Plotinus found he could best express in dialectical language drawn from Plato's *Parmenides*.[161] This dialectical presence of the One is nowhere more powerfully presented than in *Enn.* 6.9, the famous treatise on the Good or One that is perhaps the best summary of Plotinian mysticism.

All things must share in unity in order to exist, but what is the source of unity? It is not in the Soul (6.9.1), and not even in the Being that is identical with Nous (6.9.2), because (adopting the negative pole of the dialectical view of the One) Nous-Being is all things and the One cannot be all things and remain the One. In 6.9.3 Plotinus applies the full range of Parmenidean negative dialectic to the One, arguing that contrary terms such as rest and motion cannot be properly predicated of it because these apply in proper fashion only to the realm of being. Our rising up to contemplation of the One is a form of progressive simplification which does not directly penetrate the One, "but revolving, as it were, around it, tries to express our own experience of it, now drawing nigh to it, now falling back from it as a result of the difficulties involved."[162] This mode of attainment is not through scientific or philosophical reasoning (*epistēmē, noēsis*), but through "a presence transcending knowledge" (*kata parousian epistēmēs kreittona* [6.9.4]).[163] In a passionate plea emphasizing the personal responsibility of the lover to rise up to the One, Plotinus concludes with a statement that expresses both the negative and the positive pole in the One's relation to all things:

> The One is absent from nothing and from everything. It is present only to those who are prepared for it and are able to receive it, to enter into harmony with it, to grasp and to touch it by virtue of their likeness to it, by virtue of that inner power similar to and stemming from the One when it is in that state in which it was when it originated from the One. Thus will the One be "seen" as far as it can become an object of contemplation. (*Enn. 6.9.4*, trans. O'Brien).[164]

The affirmation of mutually opposed predicates to indicate the simultaneous transcendent-immanent nature of the One grounds a brief survey of negative theology (6.9.5–6) and the famous concluding sections of the text (6.9.7–11) in which Plotinus explores the positive (#8–9) and negative (#10–11) aspects of the "constant presence-in-absence of the One."[165] In order to attain the One, the soul must strip itself of all other forms and turn to the god within in order to be able to reveal to others "transcendent communion" (*synnousian* [6.9.7]).[166] Using his familiar metaphor of the circle, Plotinus now stresses the immanence of the One in all things as the center of the entire spiritual circle of reality, or as the conductor of a chorus whose members have become distracted (6.9.8).[167] "We are not separated from the One, not distant from it, even though bodily nature has closed about us and drawn us to itself" (6.9.9). The One is the source of the divine *erōs* that burns in the soul and of which earthly unions are only a shadow— to love and be united with the One is to be divinized, "it is like a flame" (ibid.).

Finally, in 6.9.10–11, Plotinus puzzles over the duration and nature of the union attained at the height of contemplation. Vision attained in this life is always of brief duration because of the way in which the body binds us to things below, but the actual union is an identity of seer and seen in which "the man who obtains the vision becomes, as it were, another being. He ceases to be himself, retains nothing of himself."[168] Like two centers that co-incide but are still potentially separable, we sense the goal not as "other, but as one with us" (*ouk . . . heteron alla hen pros heauton*). Invoking the language of the mystery cults to describe the experience, one not so much of seeing as of being "oned," (*mē hēoramenon all' henōmenon* [6.9.11]), Plotinus ends by piling up descriptions of this *ekstasis* (#11, line 22) in which like joins like. Mystical union is both a self-transcendence and a penetration to the soul's true identity: "when it is not anything else, it is nothing but itself. Yet, when it is itself alone and not in a being, it is in That [i.e., the One]" (6.9.11, my translation). As Hadot puts it, "One can define Plotinian mystical experience as the arousing of the presence of the transcendent 'I'."[169]

The use of *ekstasis* to describe this union, though rare, is a significant element in Plotinus's mystical thought.[170] Jean Trouillard suggests that the term *enstasis* might actually be more fitting, though both words would mean the same thing for Plotinus.[171] But it is now time, having examined some representative texts, to summarize what Plotinus meant by contemplation and union with the First Principle, or the One.

A full study of the many Plotinian texts on contemplation is beyond our scope here.[172] Following the lead of Arnou, it is possible to give a brief summary of what *theōria* and its equivalents meant for Plotinus.[173] "Contemplation and vision have no limits" (*kai gar ouk exei peras hē theōria oude to theōrēma*), according to *Enn.* 3.8.5. This indicates that contemplation is the very life of the soul, both the "making" that produced it and its reductive longing to return to its Source. "All things come from contemplation and are contemplation" (3.8.7). The living contemplation of itself that characterizes Nous still implies a duality, however, and Nous's contemplation of the One is not a contemplation of the Source precisely *as one*. The One itself, of course, is beyond contemplation and desire (3.8.11), but because we possess its likeness in ourselves we can attain it by a kind of "simple intuition" (*epibolē athroa* [3.8.9]). The intuition found at the summit of contemplation is described by a broad range of metaphors throughout the Plotinian corpus — illumination, influx, fecundation, possession, etc.[174] As in Plato, it appears "suddenly" (*exaiphnēs* [e.g., 6.7.34 and 36]) in the form of a presence (*parousia*) surpassing all forms of knowledge.[175] In the supreme moment the soul loses consciousness of itself (e.g., 6.7.34), taking on the mode of "knowing" ascribed to the One in texts like 6.8.16. This experience beatifies and divinizes the soul.[176]

Considerable discussion has been devoted to this union through contemplation. The term *henōsis* is not used in the *Enneads* for union with the One, but Beierwaltes has argued that Plotinus's mysticism centers on *henōsis* conceived of as a form of *unio mystica*.[177] The texts that we have reviewed, such as 6.7.34 and 6.9.9 (where the verbal form *henōthenai* occurs), support this case. Plotinus's view of union is not pantheistic as some still claim — the One both is and *is not* all things.[178] It has been debated whether or not it should be termed monistic. The crucial issue, according to John Rist, is "can this 'otherness' which divides the soul from the level of Nous and the One be annihilated, and what would the consequences be of such an annihilation for Plotinus's system in general, or at least for the nature of his mysticism?"[179] Others have rightly questioned whether the ascription of modern understandings of terms like monism and theism makes sense when applied to a thinker as distant in time and as subtle and original in thought as Plotinus.[180]

The comparison of union to the coincidence of circles in 6.9.10, the use of the term *tautotēs* ("the self-same") to characterize the union in 6.9.8 (line 29),[181] and the frequent appearance of phrases stating that the two become one (e.g., throughout 6.9),[182] all seem to argue for a form of identity; but most recent interpreters claim that a careful study of Plotinus actually indicates that he does not teach any form of annihilation of the soul or absolute identity with the Supreme.[183] It appears more correct to characterize Plotinus's view of mystical union as a dialectical one. The One always *is* the soul transcendentally, but since the One is also always *more* than Soul, the two can never be absolutely identified, even when the soul rises from its ordinary conscious "I" to the transcendent "I" present with the Source. During this life, the philosopher's goal is to cultivate the identity pole of the dialectic, to attempt to realize the supranoetic loving union that is the soul's deepest reality; but this can never be achieved in more than transitory fashion while in the body: the centers that coincide will always separate. Will it be different after death? Plotinus obviously hopes that it will, but he maintains a discreet silence. Perhaps what exists now will always be the case.

Plotinus, the greatest of pagan mystics, has often been viewed through Christian eyes. While paying tribute to his serenity of spirit and profundity of thought, many have noted how far he is from Christian mystical ideals. There is no reason to deny or even to downplay these differences, but they did not prevent him from having a powerful effect on many Christians, both in the East and the West.[184]

Like Plato, Plotinus has an important place for a givenness by which the One suddenly manifests itself to the mystic,[185] but this unexpected appearance of the Supreme is not what Christians have generally meant by grace. As a kind of automatic reflex from above attendant on the soul's efforts to awaken its divinity, it is certainly far from Augustine's view of grace and even from the more synergistic theologies of grace found in the Greek fathers. The essential root of this distance is that Plotinus had quite a different conception of the nature of the human person from Augustine and other Christians (and even from many later Neoplatonists). As A. H. Armstrong puts it, "Plotinus . . . , on the strength of his own experience, knew perfectly well that he was two people,"[186] that is, his true self was the undescended soul living in union with Nous, the divine transcendent *I*, not the reflexively conscious lower self. Where the soul is naturally divine, rather than a created spirit, the Christian concept of grace can have no real place.

Plotinus has also been accused of advocating a kind of "auto-salvation" in which the philosopher realizes his own divinization through intense self-effort — a charge not totally accurate perhaps, given the subtlety of his views on freedom and necessity, but one that tries to express the important difference between Plotinian and Christian contemplation found in Plotinus's assertion that "to obtain the vision is solely the work of him who desires to obtain it" (6.9.4).[187] Is salvation even the right term to use in relation to Plotinus's thought? For Plotinus, the One, or perhaps better, our recognition of the One in us, is a true liberation (e.g., 6.4.14–15; 6.5.12; 6.8.12), but it is not the work of a liberator or savior. Despite the "subjective" model Plotinus used to understand the nature of reality, and the personalistic tone of his moving accounts of union (e.g., 6.7.35; 6.9.11), the One and the Intellect are not persons in the sense that Jesus Christ as Savior is, nor does Plotinian contemplation culminate, the way most Christian mysticism does, in union with a personal (or tripersonal) God. Discrete personality as we know it here below has no place in the Plotinian goal.

Plotinus closes *Ennead* 6.9 with the famous phrase about the "flight of the alone to the Alone" (*phygē monou pros monon*), a theme that underlines the essentially private and individual nature of his mysticism. It is true that there are qualifying factors to Plotinian individualism, both external and internal — for example, his life of teaching and spiritual guidance to others, and the cosmic piety reflected in his use of the metaphor of the chorus and dance of all things about the One — but the liberation that Plotinus strives for is a private and personal affair, as well as one that seems limited to a philosophical elite. No community or church, even the community of philosophers, has a constitutive role in it. Nor does this mysticophilosophical goal have anything to do with any specific historical person or event: it is eternally present and needs no historical process to bring it to realization. It would be difficult to exaggerate the distance between this and contemporary Christian notions of mystical union, as we shall see. Despite these differences, I hope that this brief exposition has suggested some of the reasons why Plotinian thought was worthy to be one of the major formative influences on Christian mysticism, in the West as well as the East.

Later Neoplatonism

The subsequent history of contemplative mysticism in the pagan Neoplatonic schools is not a short story.[188] In concluding an already long chapter, I will note only the essential aspects of the story, those that exercised real influence on the history of Western mysticism, especially some elements in the thought of Proclus which, through the medium of his disciple the Pseudo-Dionysius and other "cryptoproclean" writings such as the *Book of Causes*,[189] were important for later Western speculative mysticism.

Porphyry

Plotinus's pupil Porphyry (ca. 232–ca. 304) was known as a resolute enemy of Christians, but this did not prevent him from having a significant influence on Christian thought, especially in logic. His influence was most marked in the West, where translations of several of his works into Latin made him known both to the fathers and the medieval scholastics.[190] Two aspects of Porphyry's metaphysics that had an impact on Christian speculative mysticism deserve brief note here.

Plotinus had claimed that the First Principle, or One, must be beyond being, basing his view on the *Parmenides* and the growing apophaticism of the late antique world. But his reading of the *Parmenides* was not the only possible one, as fragments of an anonymous Greek commentary that Hadot has ascribed to Porphyry (or at least someone of his school) indicate.[191] Although these fragments (esp. nos. 1, 2, and 4) proclaim an apophaticism as radical as anything in Plotinus, in the fifth fragment, commenting on *Parmenides* 142B, the author refuses to view "being" as a secondary reality, making instead a distinction between two kinds of being—*to einai*, the infinitive form, and *ousia*, the traditional substantive.

> And so existence (*to einai*) is double: the first pre-exists being (*prouparxei tou ontos*), the second is that which is produced by the One that is beyond being (*ek tou ontos tou epekeina henos*) and which is itself existence absolutely (*tou einai ontos to apolyton*) like the Idea of Being. . . . It is like thinking pure existence (*leikon einai*).[192]

Seeing the One as the true existence (*to einai monon*) goes far beyond anything explicitly found in Plotinus (though it is perhaps hinted at in some of the more cataphatic passages in *Enn.* 6.7 and 6.8). It marks a new stage in the history of Neoplatonic metaphysics,[193] one that was influential on the Christian Neoplatonist Marius Victorinus in his anti-Arian treatises of the early 360s.[194] Though it does not appear to have had a direct influence on later Christian speculative mysticism, the crucial role of a dialectical notion of God as pure existence in mystical union is foreshadowed in the Porphyrian text.

A second metaphysical theme of import for later Christian speculative mysticism also appears to have first become explicit in Porphyry. In *Enn.* 6.8.16 (line 34) Plotinus had affirmed that the One as "Awakener without awakening" is "beyond Being and Intellect and Life" (*epekeina ousias kai nou kai zōēs*). A number of passages, building on Plato's *Sophist* 248E, use this triad of powers in a generic way to describe the activities of Nous (e.g., 5.4.2; 6.8.8 and 15). In the sixth of the fragments of the Porphyrian *Parmenides* commentary, a section describing the two states of Intellect,

Intellect in the first state is seen as identical with the ineffable One, while in the second state, the One-Intellect as cause is characterized as Being-Life-Intelligence (*hyparxis, zōē, noēsis*). Here Being signifies the One as Principle, Life as the procession of all things from it, and Intelligence as the revision or return.[195] This incipient absorption of the Neoplatonic triad describing the "One-Being" into the pure One is also found in the contemporary Neoplatonist Iamblichus,[196] and was developed in an original way by Victorinus in his anti-Arian trinitarian treatises. Though the dynamic possibilities of this new approach to a triadic expression of transcendence in immanence for Christian Trinitarian mysticism were not to become a reality prior to the dissemination of the Dionysian writings, here too Porphyry's metaphysics was a harbinger of things to come.

Proclus

The main channel of communication for these and other tendencies of late Neoplatonism to Christian thought was Proclus, the last great pagan philosopher, whose thought forms an indisputable background to the Dionysian corpus. According to John M. Rist, "where Plotinus is a mystic, Proclus seems to know only a theory of mysticism."[197] This view does not square with the picture of Proclus drawn in his pupil Marinus's life of his master, though Proclus's writings, with their dry and logical style, are rarely as gripping as the *Enneads*. Such views seem based on a confusion of the autobiographical and the mystical which I continue to find dubious.[198]

With Proclus the evolution of the ideal of contemplative piety that began with Plato reaches its culmination. For the Athenian philosopher, theology is an exegetical science,[199] a form of knowing (*epistēmē*) which is also a spiritual exercise (*gymnasia*) that consists in the proper understanding of Plato's thought, particularly in the *Parmenides*.[200] As he put it in the prayer that opens his commentary on the dialogue: "I beg all the divine classes to form in me a perfect disposition for participating in Plato's thoroughly epoptic and mystical doctrine, which he himself reveals to us in the *Parmenides*" (*In Parm.* 1.618).[201] It comes as no surprise that Proclus's major work was entitled the *Platonic Theology*.[202] It should be noted, however, that while Plato's philosophy formed the subject matter of Proclus's mystical or "epoptic" science, it did so merely because it was the best epistemic manifestation of the reality more easily accessible in oracular revelation (the Chaldean Oracles) and through the theurgic manipulation of the divine character traits or symbols found in all things. As a passage from the *Platonic Theology* puts it:

There are three true characters which fill divine beings and extend across all
the divine classes: goodness, knowledge, and beauty; and there are also three
true characters which bring together what has been filled . . . : faith, truth,
and love. Through them the world is preserved in existence and joined to the
primordial causes by an intermediary, whether it be love's madness, divine
philosophy, or theurgic power, which is better than all wisdom and all human
knowledge. . . . (1.25)[203]

Proclus's mystical philosophy thus contains a ritual element lacking in both
Plato and Plotinus.

What the Athenian found in the hypotheses of the *Parmenides* and the
other Platonic dialogues was a complex hierarchical world of levels of
reality based on Plotinus's three hypostases and evolving according to the
fundamental dynamic law of remaining in the source (*monē*), proceeding
from it (*proodos*), and returning to it (*epistrophē*). As proposition 35 of his
Elements of Theology puts it: "The effect must either remain simply, or revert
simply, or proceed simply, or combine the extreme terms, or combine the
mean term with one of the other two; or else combine all three. By exclusion, then, every effect remains in its cause, proceeds from it, and reverts
upon it."[204]

This dynamic principle is well illustrated in what Proclus has to say
about the famous triad of Being-Life-Intellect (*on-zōē-nous*) in *Elements of
Theology,* prop. 103:

All things are in all things, but in each according to its proper nature: For
in Being there is life and intellect; in Life, being and intellect; in Intellect,
being and life; but each of these exists upon one level intellectually, upon
another vitally, and on the third existentially.[205]

However, this first and highest triad that interpenetrates all things is not the
First Principle, but is the product of the utterly unknowable Unity of the
One. "Immediately beyond Being must stand a not-Being which is Unity
and superior to Being" (*kreitton tou ontos kai hen*).[206] Stephen Gersh, following
E. Corsini, has shown how Proclus and his predecessors based this deriva-
tion of transcendental plurality from Absolute Unity on an interpretation
of the *Parmenides* that understood the negations of the first hypothesis as
dealing with the One and the affirmation of the second as treating of the
procession of the One into triads.[207] The revolution that was to take place
in the Christian Neoplatonism of the Pseudo-Dionysius was when both
hypotheses were applied to the same trinitarian God as negative and positive
expressions of the single Creative Source.[208]

The same law of remaining-proceeding-returning is also illustrated in
the distinctive teaching about the divine henads that Proclus developed
from Iamblichus and other predecessors. The henads, outlined in the

Elements of Theology propositions 113–65, are participated forms of the One found throughout all reality and identified with the traditional Greek gods.[209] They serve a function both metaphysical — insofar as they mediate between the One and the many — and religious — because it is through them that Proclus incorporates a notion of "provident love" (*pronoetikos erōs*) into his vision of the universe. It is by means of their presence in us that the soul is able to return to its source.

Unlike Plotinus, Proclus never says that the Ultimate One is in any way *erōs*, but he goes further than Plotinus in giving yearning *erōs* a consistent cosmic role. Speaking of the highest level of henads in his *Commentary on the First Alcibiades,* Proclus asserts that from these three intelligible henads or gods (that is, Goodness, Wisdom, and Beauty) the triad of faith, truth, and love "proceeds thenceforward to all divine orders and radiates to all union with the intelligible."[210] Thus, universal *erōs* gives harmony to the cosmos. "From above, then, love ranges from the intelligibles to the intra-mundane making everything revert to divine beauty. . . ."[211] Love comes down from the gods themselves in order to make possible the loving return: "So gods love gods, the superior their inferiors providentially (*pronoetikos erōs*), and the inferior their superiors reflexively" (*epistreptikos erōs*).[212] *Erōs* now, even more clearly than before, is not just an expression of human need, but is a universal force binding together all levels of reality and drawing them up toward the One. Proclus seems to have been helped in achieving this synthesis by his recognition that in its origin, *erōs* is not a passive state, something caused in us by the sight of the beautiful object, but that it is primarily an activity coming down from above. "We must observe that divine love is an activity, wanton love a passivity; the one is coordinate with intellect and divine beauty, the other with bodies."[213]

Finally, Proclus's metaphysical system established an apophaticism of such daunting purity that it may be difficult to see how the soul could ever contemplate or come to mystical union with a source so remote. "Affirmations cut off reality in slices,"[214] and Proclus was ever a man for the whole. Negations may provide access to the higher realms of emanation, but even they do not allow any penetration to the Ultimate One beyond the One that in some way produces what is below it. The only form of negation that may in some way approach the Ultimate is the "negation of negation," a mysterious transcendental movement to another dimension. Although there are texts in Plotinus that implicitly affirm a negation of negation in relation to the One (e.g., 6.8.9, lines 39–41), Proclus is the first Western thinker to give the negation of negation a central role in his metaphysics. In the second book of the *Platonic Theology* (e.g., 2.10), and especially toward the conclusion of the seventh book of his *Commentary on the Parmenides* (a part that survives only in the medieval Latin translation of William of Moerbeke), we find classic texts on this important theme.[215]

Proclus distinguishes the One which participates in Being (*unum participatur ab ente*) from the unparticipated and exalted One (*le unum imparticipatum, le unum le exaltatum,* in the terminology of scholastic Latin). It is our bond with the former which makes possible the return to the latter: "For all things are connected with the One Being inasmuch as they all participate in existence (*substantia*): the One Being is the monad of beings. Through it they move mystically to the One it contains, and then through this to the One that transcends the existent" (*In Parm.* 7).[216] Proclus claims that this Supreme One lies beyond even oneness and that no attribute taken from anything else is applicable to it.[217] It is completely unknown and inexpressible, though in a supereminent way: it possesses *superexcellentia* even with regard to itself.[218] Even negations express nothing about it: "negative propositions that have been stated do not express anything about the One, but do refer to the One."[219] It alone transcends the principle of contradiction.[220]

What then are the meaning and religious significance of the act of referring to the One? Here Proclus takes what we might call a psychological or introspective turn, one not unlike what we have seen in the metapsychological interpretation of Plotinus, but more explicitly formulated. As he puts it:

> The question arises, however, how is it that we call it "one" when the thing itself is altogether unnameable? We should rather say that it is not the One that we call "one" when we use this name, but the understanding of unity which is in ourselves. . . . All [things] long for the first cause and have a natural striving towards it. And this fact shows us that the predilection for the One does not come from knowledge, since if it did, what has no share in knowledge could not seek it; but everything has a natural striving after the One, as also has the soul.[221]

So the attempt to name the One is really naming our natural desire for the One, that is, activating the One's image in us. This imprint, characterized as striving, or *erōs*, is what makes the mystic ascent possible.[222]

Proclus then, like Plato and Plotinus before him, insisted that it was because of a divine something in the soul that return was possible, though unlike Plotinus he thought that the soul was totally fallen and not still partly in the upper realm.[223] Plotinus, as we have seen, located this divine element in the Nous, though he sometimes spoke of something more Nous than Nous itself, a "supreme aspect of Nous" (6.9.3, line 27), or "inner Nous" (5.3.14, line 15). Proclus identifies it with the *anthos nou,* or "flower of Nous," a term he found in the Chaldean Oracles. In one place he also refers to the "flower of the whole soul" in a manner which seems to indicate a still higher imprint in the soul that forms the point of contact for union with the unknowable One.[224]

Proclus remains subjectively apophatic in an absolute sense, at least insofar as any form of knowledge of the imparticipable One is concerned. But he does believe that union, that is, *henōsis*, with the One is possible. The term is found often in his works, having one of its most impressive statements in book 7 of the *Parmenides* commentary:

> [The soul] mounts towards the incomprehensible supereminence of the One itself, borne in its direction by a longing for its nature, revolving round it, wanting to embrace it, seeking with supreme passion to be present to it, unifying itself as far as possible and purging all its own multiplicity so that somehow it may become perfectly one. Impotent to comprehend that incomprehensible or to know the unknown, yet according to the manner of its own procession it loves its inexpressible apprehension of participation in the One. For in order to receive something, the soul must first co-exist with that thing; but what would this mean in the case of the intangible? Thus the One transcends all discursive knowledge and intellection and all contact. And only unification (*unio, henōsis*) brings us near the One, since just because it is higher than any existence it is unknown. (*In Parm.* 7)[225]

This is "the ecstasy which frees us from all other preoccupations so that we can unite ouselves to god alone."[226] Like his Greek forebears, Proclus continues to refer to it as a contemplation, one which for him reaches its goal through the negation of negation. "For by means of a negation Parmenides has removed all negations. With silence he concludes the contemplation of the One" (*In Parm.* 7).[227]

Proclus's influence on Christian mysticism through Dionysius is evident not only in the notion of cosmic love and the quasi-theurgic elements of Dionysian sacramentalism, but especially in the dialectical view of the One as the negation of negation. The appropriation of these elements into Christian thought involved profound adjustments and transpositions that will occupy us in the chapters to come.[228] Proclus forms an interesting example of an anti-Christian writer in an explicitly Christian world who managed to exercise a profound influence on the religion he hated. Christian Procleanism was to be of singular importance both in metaphysics and in mysticism — a paradox that highlights the many ambiguities in the relations between the Greek contemplative tradition and Western Christian mysticism.

CHAPTER 3

Jesus: The Presence
of God on Earth

THE SEARCH FOR new ways to attain the presence of God that marked the *oikoumenē* of the late Hellenistic world forms an important part of the background to the history of Christian mysticism. The two preceding chapters have analyzed aspects of both the Jewish and the Greek religiophilosophical developments that were important to this story. Although the connections are not always direct, the apocalyptic ascents to the heavenly realm and the Platonic pursuit of *theōria* help explain why Christian mysticism took some of the particular forms that it did. If our stress on the theme of desire to experience the presence of God casts light on the new religious world of late Hellenism, this chapter will argue that it also provides a way to view the distinctiveness of the Jesus movement that appeared in Palestine in the third decade of the first century C.E.

The Presence of God in Jesus

Christians (as they came to be called when they spread outside Palestine into Gentile areas; see Acts 11:26) were those who affirmed that the invisible God worshiped by the Jews had become present in a final and unsurpassable way in Jesus of Nazareth, a wandering Jewish preacher briefly active around the year 30. Though Jesus had been executed by the Roman authorities (one of the few facts about his life on which there is no disagreement), his followers believed that he had manifested his divine power by rising from the dead and ascending to heaven. These events had inaugurated the new aeon of the kingdom of God, which was soon to become universal when Jesus would return to earth manifesting his divinity in a great *parousia* (literally, "presence," or "advent"). During the interim period between the resurrection and the second coming, it was only in and through belief in Jesus who had become the Christ, that is, the "Anointed One," or messiah, that saving contact with God was possible.

The essential issue for the groups of Jews and later Gentiles who came to believe that Jesus was the messiah was not so much how God was present in him (the christological question that continues to exercise and divide theologians to the present), as it was how contact with Jesus as the manifestation of the divine was to be gained and fostered in order to reach salvation. His earliest followers insisted that this could be achieved only as a member of the community he had founded and which he had left as his presence in the world—there could be no such thing as purely individual adherence to Christ as Savior. Entry into the community of believers (the *ekklēsia*) through confession of faith (*pistis*) in Jesus as Lord and a ritual of ablution or baptism that was understood as a mysterious participation in his death and resurrection was the necessary starting point. Life within the community was a wholly new mode of living, based on strict morality, mutual love and sharing of goods, and an intensive ritual life of prayer centered on a liturgical meal which Jesus had initiated before his death and in which he was believed to become present in the eating of consecrated bread and wine. All of this was designed both to manifest and to nurture the Christian's growing identity with the risen Lord. Given the animosities the new group aroused, first among Jews who did not accept Jesus as the messiah and soon with the Roman authorities who were suspicious of new religions, especially of one that would not recognize the state gods, some believers might even be called to what the community believed was the ultimate identification with Jesus, witnessing (*martyrein*) to faith in him by dying for him. Although the number of Christian martyrs was never very large, the ideal of martyrdom was a significant part of the identity of the new religion.

Jesus himself, like any pious Jew, was doubtless well instructed in the Hebrew scriptures, but he was not a scribe as were the apocalypticists studied in chapter 1. He was a preacher, the content of whose message centered on the kingdom of God (another point about him on which there appears to be a reliable consensus). Jesus the preacher of the message became Jesus the preached message and soon Jesus the written message, as elements of his preaching and the stories about him, especially the account of his sacrificial death and rising, were fixed in written form.[1] How much of these sayings and stories about Jesus may reflect his own words and actions and how much is basically the product of the faith of the early communities is an important and controversial issue in which a clear consensus has not yet emerged and most likely never will. Important as the issue is, the question, not directly relevant to our purpose, will not be taken up here.

Though the role of the written word in Christianity is always secondary to Christ conceived of as the Word (*Logos*) of God, the importance of scripture must be clearly grasped if we wish to understand the nature of Christian mysticism, because mysticism, especially down to the twelfth century, was for the most part directly exegetical in character. The cultivation of immediate consciousness of the divine presence took place within the exercise of reading, meditating, preaching, and teaching the biblical text, often within a liturgical or quasi-liturgical context.[2]

It is no surprise that sacred texts played such a large role in the new religion. The earliest Jewish-Christian communities, accustomed to the reading and interpretation of the Hebrew Bible as a central part of their ritual life, continued to read and pray the sacred texts of the Jews, though in a new way. Not only did the Jesus movement rapidly adopt the Greek version of the Hebrew Bible (the Septuagint, or LXX) as their standard text, but its members from the start began to read the book christologically, that is, essentially as a witness, prophecy, or extended preparation for the coming of Jesus. The written materials about Jesus, which during the last three decades of the first century c.e. achieved their final development in the new genre known as gospels, often portray Jesus as showing how the Hebrew sacred texts were fulfilled in him.

The principle around which the Christian Bible was created was also fundamentally christological. The Greek version of the Hebrew Bible (by ca. 200 c.e. Christians were calling this the "Old Testament") was the word of God because it had announced and prepared for the coming of the Christ. By the second half of the second century c.e. selected Christian writings which were customarily used in liturgical assemblies and which were thought to convey the authentic message of Jesus because they were deemed to have been written by the first leaders of the community (*apostoloi*) were being gathered into an authentic "canon" or list which was soon called the "New Testament."[3] These texts, as interpreted by the church, especially by its authoritative leaders (*episkopoi*, or bishops), were not only the norms for correct belief, but also a means by which Jesus Christ, who in the second century came to be more and more identified as God's preexistent Word, became present in the assembly.

In sum, early Christianity was characterized by its belief that God had become present in Jesus Christ, who since his return to heaven is made accessible through word and rite in the midst of the community of believers. These distinctive elements — ecclesiological setting, scriptural matrix, and sacramental practice — constitute the core of early Christianity and are integral to all Christian mysticism, but especially to its formative stages.

This picture may seem to imply that Christianity was essentially a mystical religion from its origins. That is not my argument. The formation of Christian mysticism in the proper sense was the result of a historical process that was not complete for several centuries. The mysticism of Latin Christianity, which is the explicit subject of these volumes, was not evident before the latter part of the fourth century. I wish to suggest, however, along with Friederich von Hügel, that from the start Christianity contained a mystical element, or at least that central themes in the new religion were capable of a mystical interpretation in the sense that they could be understood and appropriated by later believers in such a way as to lead to special modes of direct awareness of the divine presence in Jesus.[4]

Even to speak of early Christianity as containing a mystical element, of course, is controversial. While thinkers in the Orthodox tradition have little difficulty in seeing early Christianity as a mystical religion and its theology as fundamentally mystical theology, the other branches of Christianity have not been as certain. Many Catholic authors have defended the mystical character of at least parts of the New Testament and of the Christian writings of the apostolic and subapostolic periods,[5] often by distinguishing between two senses of mysticism: the implicit, general, or objective mysticism of the new life "hidden with Christ in God" (Col 3:3), and explicit, special or subjectively realized mysticism, that is, the conscious experience of God's presence in the soul.[6] Other Catholic or Anglo-Catholic writers have been more doubtful, preferring to see mysticism as a largely Greek phenomenon centering on the contemplative ideal that entered Christianity in the second century, though they view this form of piety as one compatible with the Gospel message.[7] A central tradition in modern Protestant thought, from Ritschl and Harnack, through Barth and Brunner, to Bultmann and beyond, has denied any connection between Christian origins and mysticism and has viewed the introduction of Greek mysticism into Christianity as an unfortunate infection. But other Protestant theologians, most notably Albert Schweitzer, have emphasized the importance of distinctive forms of mysticism found in the New Testament and other early Christian writings.[8]

If we understand mysticism as some form of union of identity with God through purely contemplative practice, especially one that bypasses the mediatorial role of Christ and the place of scripture and the community, it is indeed difficult to say that there is much mysticism in the first century or more of Christianity (or even after that for that matter). But if we take mysticism in the broader and more flexible sense argued for in this volume, the first century of Christian writings provides considerable evidence for the existence of a mystical element, if not of fully formed and explicit theories of mysticism. Paul and John were not mystics in the sense that we can speak of Origen or Augustine as mystics; but the writings of Paul and John, as well as of other early Christian authors, pseudonymous or not, are certainly susceptible of mystical readings, and such readings form the historical foundation of all later Christian mysticism, both East and West.

Some modern scholars have maintained that these readings were misreadings, because they do not conform to historical-critical canons of interpretation or to particular theological interpretations of the essence of Christianity. The perspective that guides my presentation, however, is that the historical-critical reading of scripture does not theologically exhaust its meaning and that the search for some original "essence of Christianity" apart from its history has been an illusory one. The mystics, who have played an important part in Christian history even if they were not there at the beginning, would insist that only a spiritual reading can reveal the full intent of scripture.[9] It was through such spiritual readings that Christian mysticism lived and grew.

In what follows I will try to indicate those elements or strands in the various documents of the first century of Christian writing (primarily but not solely those that later come to be called the New Testament) which formed Christian mysticism and which have continued to shape it over the centuries. I shall not try to argue the case for a specific New Testament mysticism, even a Pauline or Johannine mysticism, as some have done. This may be possible, but such attempts often have an anachronistic ring and have been relatively inattentive to the developmental character of Christian mysticism. If we see Christian mysticism as centered on finding God present in his holy word in the midst of the community, however, we must take at least a brief look at those sections of the scriptural word which most readily offered themselves for readings of the mystical type.

New Testament Writings

Synoptic Gospels

Between ca. 70 and ca. 90 C.E. the mass of oral and written materials that reflected the Christian community's memories about Jesus were put together in the documents we know as the Synoptic Gospels ascribed to Matthew, Mark, and Luke.[10] Though posterior to Paul's authentic letters (which date ca. 50–58 C.E.), the Synoptics enshrine important early materials along with later redactional elements. In the Synoptic Gospels, Jesus is presented not only as teacher and savior but also as model to be imitated.[11] This view of the Redeemer had a significant practical role in much later Christian mysticism. "Anyone who does not take up his cross and follow in my footsteps is not worthy of me" (Matt 10:28 and parallels). Such imitation, of course, most often was conceived of in terms of bearing with the difficulties, internal and external, encountered in living the Christian faith, though later it was also applied to modes of specialized piety based on various conceptions of the "apostolic life" lived by Jesus and the earliest communities.[12] However, the imitation of Christ also could be taken to imply what Paul was to call having "the mind of Christ" (e.g., 1 Cor 2:16), that is, being able to understand and to be conscious of "the depths of God" (1 Cor 2:10: *ta bathē tou theou*), because the special God-consciousness that Jesus displayed several times in the Synoptics, especially in the famous "John-like" text of Matthew 11:27 and Luke 10:22, has been made accessible to his followers: "No one knows the Son except the Father, just as no one knows the Father except the Son *and those to whom the Son chooses to reveal him.*" Later mystics were often to appeal to this text as a warrant for their claims to immediate and special knowledge of God.

An unusual event (possibly a misplaced Easter narrative) found in all three Synoptic Gospels was used to confirm this: the account known as the Transfiguration (see Matt 17:1-9; Mark 9:2-10; Luke 9:28-36). Here Peter, John, and James (a select group) ascend a mountain to pray with Jesus and see him glorified and talking with Moses and Elijah. All three accounts speak of a cloud that "overshadowed" (*epeskiazen*) the disciples in which they heard the voice of God saying, "This is my Son, the Beloved" ("Chosen One" in Luke).[13] Though the origin and meaning of this story have been much debated by modern scripture scholars, one can easily see how it could suggest the possibility of ecstatic contact with God through the mediation of the glorified Jesus. The Synoptic accounts of the Easter visions granted to the apostles and select special friends of Jesus, especially Mary Magdalene (Matt 28:9-10; Mark 13:9) were understood in the same way. Because the risen Lord lives on in word and sacrament, special experiences of his presence were thought to remain a constant possibility.

The Synoptic Gospels make use of a number of the concepts or themes that later Christian mysticism was to employ in order to describe the goal of the mystical path. Most prominent among these are the notions of perfection and the vision of God. Both are found in the famous Matthean text known as the Sermon on the Mount (Matt 5:1-7:29, which is related to the Sermon on the Plain in Luke 6:17-49). In the midst of the sermon, Jesus summarizes his moral teaching with the admonition, "You must therefore be perfect just as your heavenly Father is perfect" (Matt 5:48). Just what the perfection of the new life entailed was understood in various ways by later Christians, many of them involving mystical elements. Jesus began his great address with the well-known eight beatitudes praising those who possess the values and virtues central to "good news" (*euangelion*) of salvation. The fifth beatitude — "Happy the pure in heart: they shall see God" (Matt 5:8) — became one of the key texts in the history of Christian mysticism. What the Gospel writer may have intended by this seeing of God (*ton theion opsontai*) is capable of a number of interpretations, but it is difficult to fault the educated Greek Christians who from the second century on sought to understand Christ's promise of "seeing God" in terms of the Platonic traditions of contemplative *theōria* sketched in chapter 2. Even in modern times powerful theological voices have used Matt 5:8 as the scriptural basis for their understanding of Christian ethics and mystical theology.[14]

Perhaps the most unusual use of the Synoptic Gospels in the service of traditional Christian mysticism is that which is the strangest for the modern reader — and the farthest from the historical-critical mentality — the practice of spiritual interpretation. The Gospel writers had portrayed Jesus as interpreting the Jewish scriptures as being fulfilled in him (e.g., Matt 5:17–19; 26:54; Luke 4:21), and Paul had spoken of the sacred books of the Jews as containing both "types" (*typoi* [1 Cor 10:6, 11]) and "allegorizings" (*allegoroumena* [Gal 4:24]) of the Christian message. (Spiritual readings of sacred texts were characteristic of both Jewish and Greek religious hermeneutics in the Hellenistic world, as we have seen in the two preceeding chapters.) A distinctive feature of Christian exegesis, however, was its application of the techniques of such reading to its own developing canon of sacred writings. It may well have been Gnostic Christians who first began the full-fledged spiritual interpretation of Christian texts, especially those of the Gospel of John; but this challenged other Christians to adopt deeper readings of many of the events and sayings of Jesus that were compatible with the developing orthodox, or "Great Church" tradition, as we find in the case of Clement of Alexandria.[15] After ca. 200 c.e. any number of passages in the stories or sayings found in the Synoptics were accorded spiritual readings, which gave them a vital role in the development of Christian mysticism.

Two examples must suffice. The parable of the Sower (Matt 13:4–23; Mark 4:1–20; Luke 8:11–15), whether or not it reflects an original address of Jesus the preacher, shows obvious signs of a redactional reading which verges on spiritual interpretation. This process was furthered by later exegetes who saw the different levels of growth of the gospel seed as indicating stages of perfection in the Christian life, with the hundredfold crop signifying the perfect spiritual believer, often what we would call the mystic.

The Gospel of Luke tells of the visit of Jesus to the house of Martha and Mary, where he chided Martha for being busy about many things, "yet few are needed, indeed only one," and praised Mary "who has chosen the better part" (10:38–42). Mary, Martha, and their brother Lazarus are also featured in an extended account in the Gospel of John (11:1–44); and a Mary of Magdala was noted as one whom Jesus had delivered from demons (Luke 8:2), who had stood by at his crucifixion (Mark 15:40), and who had been favored with an Easter appearance (see above). This abundance of Marys, though noted by early Christian exegetes, did not prevent Mary Magdalene, through a convergence of identities, from becoming a potent paradigm for Christian mysticism. By identifying Mary Magdalene with the penitent prostitute of Luke 7:36–50, spiritual interpreters created one of the basic mystical "biographies" that helped shape later Christian spirituality. Though less important than Moses in Christian antiquity, the story of Mary Magdalene, the sinner who through the depth of her love and repentance became the special lover of Jesus, was of major import in later mysticism. Elements of Mary Magdalene's privileged position appear in Gnostic texts which give her preference over the establishment figure of Peter.[16] Origen is the earliest witness to one of the key elements in the mystical use of the Magdalene legend—the interpretation of the Lukan account of Jesus' praise of Mary's choice of the "one thing needed" as signifying the preeminence of contemplative love (Mary) over active service (Martha).[17]

Pauline Writings

Although Christian mystics have used materials from the Synoptic Gospels extensively in their writings, the Pauline and Johannine texts have been the favored New Testament resources for later mystics, just as are the Psalms and the Song of Songs from the Old Testament. The debate about Pauline mysticism has been particularly acute in the twentieth century. Prescinding from arguments over whether or not Paul, a Pharisaic Jewish convert to Christianity of ca. 40 C.E., actually was or was not a mystic by various modern definitions, the writings of this great missionary offer the most direct evidence for the intimate connection between apocalypticism and the roots of Christian mysticism.

The Jesus movement of the earliest followers of the Jewish teacher and preacher has been described as an apocalyptic sect within Judaism—a characterization which captures some, if perhaps not all, of the meaning of the new movement. However much Jesus himself may or may not have shared in the apocalyptic mentality that looked for the imminent arrival of the new aeon,[18] there can be no question that his first followers understood his resurrection and expected parousia in apocalyptic terms. This is especially evident both from Paul's authentic letters (1 Thessalonians, Galatians, 1 and 2 Corinthians, Philippians, and Romans)[19] and from his life.

Anselm Stolz was the first to point out the central role that Paul's account of his apocalyptic rapture to the third heaven (2 Cor 12:1-6) played in the history of Christian mysticism.[20] Along with the Exodus story of Moses' encounter with God atop Mount Sinai, it has served as a model narrative for mystical experience of the divine presence. Recent research has also noted that it is unique in the religious literature of the time in being the only autobiographical account of an apocalyptic ascent to the heavenly realm.[21] Paul actually seems to recount two experiences, an ascent to the third heaven, and a higher ascent to paradise:

> I know a man in Christ who fourteen years ago—whether in the body or out of the body I do not know, God knows—was caught up to the third heaven. And I know that this man—whether in the body or separate from the body I do not know, God knows—was caught up into Paradise and he heard unutterable words which are unlawful to speak. (trans. James Tabor)

Paul's remarkable firsthand account highlights the basic shifts that apocalypticism underwent in early Christianity. Jewish apocalypticism is always pseudonymous with its accounts of visionary ascents being ascribed to ancient biblical figures. In Christianity, Paul speaks of his own apocalyptic ascents, using them to ground his preaching authority, just as later the John of the Apocalypse would speak in his own name of the visions granted him. Paul answers Jewish opponents in Corinth who had boasted of their special experiences by stressing that he had been raised to paradise itself, which according to James Tabor, "seems to always symbolize God's intimate presence and access to the tree of life."[22] Unlike others raised to heaven, Paul experiences no fear. While they receive messages to be communicated to the faithful, the apostle is given a revelation of "unutterable words" (*arrēta rhēmata*), a higher gift than any of his opponents. Like Moses, who encountered God in cloud and darkness, this mystery cannot be revealed to anyone who has not had the experience: it is essentially apophatic.[23] Paul's experience here is presented in auditory terms, but in other places he speaks of seeing Jesus (e.g., 1 Cor 9:1; 15:8), presumably references to the conversion experience on the road to Damascus recounted three times in the Acts of the Apostles (9:1-9; 22:6-21 [which includes reference to another appearance of Jesus when Paul was praying in the Temple at Jerusalem]; and 26:12-18). Thus Paul, like Peter, Stephen, and other early Christian leaders, was a visionary as well as an apostle.[24]

The teaching found in the Pauline epistles also must be taken into account in surveying the apostle's influence on later Christian mysticism. Numerous works have attempted to delineate the main lines of a Pauline mysticism. The most famous of these, Albert Schweitzer's *The Mysticism of Paul the Apostle,* is one of the classics of twentieth-century study of mysticism.[25] I do not intend to argue the case for a specific Pauline mysticism here, but rather to highlight key themes in Paul's writings which Christian mystics have used as the scriptural foundations for their teaching.

In 1 Cor 13:12 in the midst of his famous Hymn to Love, Paul contrasts the imperfection of the present with the perfection of what is to come: "Now we are seeing a dim reflection in a mirror; but then we shall be seeing face to face. The knowledge that I have now is imperfect; but then I shall know as fully as I am known."[26] Although Paul speaks more often of faith (*pistis*), the necessary ground of the believer's relation to the risen Lord, both knowledge (*gnōsis*) and love (*agapē*) play crucial roles in his thought. The connection of the perfection of *agapē* with face-to-face vision and a higher *gnōsis* here in 1 Corinthians 13, even though Paul is speaking about the future heavenly state, was often subsequently interpreted as applying, at least to some degree, to this life, possibly because another famous text, 2 Cor 3:12–18, presents the contrast between clouded and full vision in terms of the veiled understanding of the Old Testament time (symbolized by Moses' veiling of his face in Exod 34:34) and Christ's removal of the veil in the time of the New Testament:

> Now this Lord is the Spirit, and where the Spirit of the Lord is, there is freedom. And we, with unveiled faces reflecting like mirrors the brightness of the Lord, all grow brighter and brighter as we are turned into the image (*eikon*) that we reflect; this is the work of the Lord who is Spirit. (2 Cor 3:17–18)

The word translated as "reflecting" (*katoptrizomenoi*) was often understood as "gazing" or "contemplating" (*speculantes* is both the Old Latin and the Vulgate translation).[27] Thus, the text could be read to mean that it is by contemplation of the glory of the risen Christ that the image of God in us (Gen 1:26) is being conformed to the Word, the Father's perfect Image (cf. Rom 8:29; 1 Cor 15:49; 2 Cor 4:4; and esp. Col 1:15–20, a deutero-Pauline text). The linking of contemplation and the perfecting of the image of God made this passage one of the most important in the history of Christian mysticism. These two central passages, when combined with Matt 5:8 and the Johannine theme of seeing God in Christ (to be treated below), provided ample warrant for the important role that "christologized" Platonic *theōria* was to play in Christian mysticism. Seeing the Christian life as the gradual restoration of a damaged image or lost likeness of God was a theme that later authors found in (or read into) a variety of biblical texts, especially those in Paul.[28]

Agapē and *gnōsis,* along with vision or contemplation (*theōria*), are among the most important terms in the history of Christian mysticism. All these words have histories so complex (and often controversial) that all that can be provided here are a few introductory remarks to set the stage for later discussions, when we will look at how different Christian writers understood them.

Agapē was not a Christian creation, but it was a rare word until the early Greek-speaking Christians adopted it as the special designation for the love which God directs toward us and which we, through his grace, can in turn address to him.[29] It occurs in the Synoptic Gospels (e.g., Luke 11:42; Matt 24:12), but it was largely through its frequent employment by Paul and John that *agapē/caritas* became so important in Christianity. The passage on *agapē* in 1 Corinthians 13 is the most famous single Pauline text on love, but there are many others.[30] There can be no doubt that the first Christians seized on *agapē* to distance their view of love from what they understood to be represented by *erōs* (a term that does not occur in the New Testament) and even *philia,* a generic term for liking, affection, and friendship, which is used there at times (*philein* appears 25 times to 141 appearances for *agapan* and 116 for *agapē*). Anders Nygren in his famous *Agape and Eros* has argued for a radical difference between the two kinds of love, claiming that those Christians beginning with Origen who defended the equivalence of *agapē* and *erōs* perverted the true meaning of Christian love. But, as we shall see in later chapters, the issue is not so simple; the opposition that seems to be implied by the New Testament's preference for *agapē* over *erōs* may apply only to what the philosophers came to call profane *erōs,* and not the heavenly or sacred version.

Gnōsis is a word whose history is, if anything, even more complex than *agapē.* The term, which in its Christian usage may be translated as "knowledge by personal acquaintance," was widely used in Greek and was given both philosophical and religious meanings. Paul himself used it freely—it is not until the later Pastoral epistles pseudonymously ascribed to him that we get warnings about false *gnōsis* (e.g., 1 Tim 6:20–21). Though the word is used to describe God's own knowledge (e.g., Rom 11:33), it is most often used for the knowledge that we have of God, especially in the letters to the Corinthians. *Gnōsis* appears as one of the gifts of the Spirit (1 Cor 12:8). We may say that in its deepest sense it signifies the personal knowledge of the hidden mysteries of God that the risen Lord progressively reveals to the faithful (e.g., 2 Cor 2:14 and 10:5; Phil 3:8). God "has shone in our minds (*kardiais*) to radiate the light of the knowledge of God's glory (*tēs gnōseōs tēs doxēs*), the glory on the face of Christ" (2 Cor 4:6). But *gnōsis* has its limits for Paul. The Hymn to *Agapē* says that it is inferior to love (1 Cor 13:8), and Paul also warns the Corinthians against the *gnōsis* that inflates self-importance unless it is accompanied by the *agapē* that provides growth (1 Cor 8:1–11). One summation of the connection between the two, which we may take as the distinctly New Testament way of dealing with the relation of love and knowledge in the spiritual life, comes in the deutero-Pauline text of Eph 3:16–19:

> Out of his infinite glory, may he give you the power through his Spirit for your hidden self to grow strong, so that Christ may live in your hearts through faith, and then, planted in love and built on love, you will with all the saints have the strength to grasp the breadth and the length, the height and the depth; until, knowing the love of Christ, which is beyond all knowledge (*gnōseōs*), you are filled with the utter fullness of God (*plērōma tou theou*).

Is Pauline *gnōsis* a mystical knowledge? Insofar as *gnōsis* is a hidden knowledge of divine realities that involves a personal relation to Christ, it certainly can be read in this way. Of course, more specific understandings of how any mystical knowing of God relates to other forms of knowledge, especially to the knowledge of Christ given in faith, are not to be found in Paul.

The close personal relation between the believer and Christ in Paul's thought is expressed through the famous formula "in Christ." Adolf Deissmann was the first to study the significance of this phrase and its cognates: it occurs 164 times in all the letters ascribed to Paul, both genuine and spurious.[31] Being "in Christ" always refers to the believer's situation in this life, the phrase "with Christ" (*syn Christō* or *kyriō*) being reserved for the life to come (e.g., 1 Thess 4:17; 2 Cor 5:8; Phil 1:23). Galatians contains some of the most striking formulations, as when Paul announces, "I have been crucified with Christ, and I live now not with my own life but with the life of Christ who lives in me" (Gal 2:19–20). "All baptized in Christ, you have all clothed yourselves in Christ, and there are no more distinctions between Jew and Greek, slave and free, male and female, but all of you are one in Christ Jesus" (Gal 3:27). The formation in Christ (Gal 4:19) that begins with preaching and baptism incorporates all believers into one body in the Lord so that they can continue to grow in their identification with him. Albert Schweitzer has stressed the apocalyptic background to this Pauline sense of oneness with Christ—the community of believers, both dead and alive, already share in the resurrection existence which will be fully realized at the parousia.[32] This solidarity with the risen Lord allows the apostle to speak not only of believers living in Christ but also of Christ living in them (e.g., Phil 1:21; Gal 2:20).

The relation between Christ and the Spirit (see 2 Cor 3:17–18 cited above) facilitates a further set of formulas concerning the Spirit and the believer. According to Romans 8, "the law of the spirit of life in Christ Jesus has set you free from the law of sin and death" (8:1) to the extent that "the Spirit of God has made his home in you" (8:9). Thus, "he who raised Jesus from the dead will give life to your own mortal bodies through his Spirit living in you" (8:11). The power of this theme is particularly evident in the well-known passages in Rom 5:5 ("the love of God has been poured into our hearts by the Holy Spirit who has been given to us") and Gal 4:6 ("The proof that you are sons is that God has sent the Spirit of his Son into our hearts: the Spirit that cries, 'Abba, Father'"). Although Paul does not make use of the language of divinization, his insistence on our shared sonship with Christ and the inhabiting of the Spirit was to be used by later mystics to support belief that the Christian life implied a form of divinization. This divinization was conceived of as a spiritual union with God in Christ. In 1 Cor 6:16–17, Paul, attacking fornication as a sin against our bodies that are now members of the body of Christ, says: "As you know, a man who goes with a prostitute is one body with her, since the two, as it is said, become one flesh [see Gen 2:24]. But anyone who is joined to the Lord is one spirit with him." This formula of becoming one spirit with the Lord, while Paul does not seem to intend it in any mystical sense,[33] was perhaps the most often-cited scriptural warrant for an understanding of mystical union that emphasizes personal intercommunion and eschews any form of identity or union of indistinction.[34]

These are some of the most important Pauline passages that were to be used over the centuries as guides for attempts to realize as fully as possible what the presence of God in Christ should mean for the believer. Paul's fame as the apostle raised up to the third heaven and to paradise (the tradition usually understood these as the same)[35] made him the archetypal mystic. Naturally, there are elements of anachronism in seeing the apostle to the Gentiles as a mystic in the later classic sense, but perhaps this is no more anachronistic than viewing him as nothing more than a preacher of the contrast between law and gospel. Paul was the most complex religious personality of his time, and his ebullient and sometimes confusing creativity gave rise to a multitude of possibilities in Christian history.

Johannine Writings

From the perspective of the history of Christian mysticism, we confront a similar situation in turning to the Johannine writings. A number of interpreters have been willing to speak of a Johannine mysticism,[36] or at least to compare elements in the Johannine teachings with forms of Hellenistic mysticism,[37] whereas other exegetes have insisted that there is nothing really mystical about the Fourth Gospel and its related texts.[38]

The Johannine corpus is later than the Pauline and more distant from its supposed apostolic source. Whereas six of the letters ascribed to Paul are viewed as authentic and early, the Gospel, three letters, and the apocalypse that gained admittance to the New Testament under the name of John (whom the Synoptics mention as one of the select inner circle of the apostles) cannot be considered as products of this disciple's pen. The Apocalypse of John obviously comes from quite a different John, probably a Jewish-Christian prophet active in Asia Minor during the nineties of the first century C.E. The Gospel and letters have considerable similarity of thought and expression, so that modern scholarship has tended to consider them as products of a Johannine school in which several writers who placed themselves in the tradition of the apostle were active.[39] These writers had knowledge of many of the Jesus materials used by the Synoptics (and perhaps even of these Gospels themselves), but it is obvious that they set out to write a very different kind of account of the life and teaching of Jesus. John's Gospel appears to have been written in several stages and was completed in the decade before 100 C.E.; the three epistles mirror problems and debates in the Johannine community in the early years of the second century C.E.[40] Tradition asserts Ephesus as the location of the community, but this cannot be historically demonstrated.

The striking difference between the Synoptics and John suggests why the Christian tradition has always looked on John's Gospel as the "spiritual Gospel," a foundational text for mystical appropriations of the Christian message.[41] The author is interested in portraying how Jesus invites his followers not just to conversion and participation in the new community and its sacramental life, but also to a deeper understanding of the meaning of that life through an enlightenment whose goal is an experience of union with God through Christ begun in this life and completed in the next.[42] John, the beloved disciple (see John 13:25), is presented as a model of the kind of believer who has attained this deeper level of Christian existence. Indeed, John deliberately upstages Peter (whom the Synoptics treat as the leader of the disciples) in several places (see, e.g., John 19:26–27; 20:3–10; 21:7).[43] Although the term *gnostikos* is not found in the New Testament, it is not an exaggeration to say that the Fourth Gospel portrays John as the perfect *gnostikos,* or "gnostic believer," about whom there was to be so much debate in the following two centuries, when the Gnostics came to see in Paul and especially in John the roots of their own understanding of

Christianity. This is not to say that Paul or John was a Gnostic (any more than we can say that they were explicit mystics); but the debate between the Gnostics and the adherents of the "Great Church," or orthodox tradition, over the correct reading of Paul and John was important in the formation of orthodox mysticism, as will be seen in the next chapter.[44]

Even more than with Paul, a reading of John's Gospel and the Johannine letters, especially 1 John, immediately displays themes capable of a mystical interpretation. The vision of God, evident in some Pauline passages noted above, is central to John's presentation of the role of Jesus as Savior. The role of special knowledge or enlightenment, and especially of *agapē*, is given prominence. Indeed, it is John, at least the John of 1 John 4:8, who says that "God is *agapē*" (*hoti ho theos agapē estin*), something that no previous author had said in explicit fashion. Finally, while Paul's understanding of existence "in Christ" could be interpreted as indicating some kind of union with the Savior, John speaks explicitly of oneness with Christ and with God. A brief look at each of these themes will highlight what later mystics found so congenial in the Johannine texts.

Invisibility and visibility—hidden presence and manifested mystery— this dialectic of seeming incompatibilities has always been the stuff of mystical attempts to experience the divine presence. The Prologue of John's Gospel, the text that has probably attracted more commentary than any other in the New Testament, gives special emphasis to this theme. In summarizing this profound meditation on the role of the Logos in his relation to God (John 1:1), in creation (1:2–5) and in redemption (1:9–14), John appeals to the language of vision: "No one has ever seen God; it is only the Son, who is nearest to the Father's heart, who has made him known" (1:18). The invisibility of God is a common theme in early Christian writings, especially in John (e.g., John 6:46; 1 John 4:12), but John insists that through the Word's taking on flesh (1:12) we gain the ability actually to see God's glory (1:14). The one who sees Christ sees or knows the Father (8:19; 12:45; 14:9). This theme of seeing God, which is a special way of knowing him, is an essential part of John's message.[45] 1 John 3:2 uses a formula that complements what we have seen in 1 Cor 13:12: "My dear children, we are already the children of God but what we are to be in the future has not yet been revealed; all we know is, that when it is revealed we shall be like him because we shall see him as he really is." The vision of God, both here and hereafter, that John speaks of has been compared with notions of seeing God found in earlier authors like Philo of Alexandria, as well as later materials such as the pagan *Hermetica,* but important differences remain.[46]

The knowledge of God of which John speaks, like the vision of him, is totally Christocentric. Throughout this Gospel, Jesus is presented as the enlightener, the one who alone brings knowledge of God to humanity (e.g., 1:9; 3:11–12; 6:44–45; 7:16–18, 26–28; 9:1–41 [the story of the man born blind]; 10:14–15; 12:46, 50; and 13:31–17:26 [the Last Supper discourses]). Though John never uses the term *gnōsis*, no New Testament author more often speaks of knowing (*gignōskein*) God or Christ. John sums up this teaching in one of the famous "I-am statements" that dot the book: "I am the Way, the Truth and the Life. No one can come to the Father except through me. If you know me, you know my Father too. From this moment you know (*gignōskete*) him and have seen him" (John 14:6–7).

Knowledge of God is knowing that God not only loves us but that he himself is love (*agapē*).[47] "God is love" (1 John 4:8), and "God loved the world so much that he gave his only Son, so that everyone who believes in him may not be lost but may have eternal life" (John 3:16). The descending love by which the Father loves the Son (John 5:20) and through him loves us is communicated to believers as the inner form of their new life. The famous Last Supper discourse (or, better, discourses [13:31–14:31; 15:1–17:26]), the high point of John's teaching, is centered on mutual love as the cement of the Christian life. At the outset of the first speech, Jesus lays down mutual love as the new commandment: "I give you a new commandment: love one another; just as I have loved you, you must also love one another" (13:34). Those who demonstrate their love for Christ by keeping this command-ment will be loved by both the Father and the Word, "and we will come to him and make our home with him" (14:23). The second discourse returns to the same theme, beginning with a lengthy passage (15:9–17) detailing the downward flow of *agapē* from the Father through Jesus to his "friends," who are again commanded to love one another. Later he insists on the circle of love by which the Father loves the disciples because they have loved the Christ who reveals him (16:26–27). He concludes with the famous prayer that asks that the very union that binds Father and Son may also unify all who love them:

> Father, may they be one in us, as you are in me and I am in you, so that the world may believe that it was you who sent me. I have given them the glory you gave to me, that they may be one as we are one. With me in them and you in me, may they be so completely one that the world will realize that it was you who sent me and that I have loved them as much as you have loved me. (17:21–23)

The emphasis on the love of God which descends from the Father through his Beloved Son to the community of believers, who demonstrate the depth of their adherence to the new life in Christ by the fervor of their mutual love, is repeated throughout the first letter (e.g., 1 John 2:3–11; 3:1, 10–24;

and esp. 4:7–5:4). Such texts were a powerful source for the teaching of later Christian mystics that true love could never be a private affair between Christ and the individual, but that the real measure of our love for Christ is our love for others.[48]

The *agapē* of which John speaks so powerfully brings about a connection with God that, as 17:21–23 shows, can be described as a sharing in the union enjoyed by the Father and the Son. Union language characterizes the Johannine texts as no other early Christian document.[49] This union, of course, is resolutely christological. Given the style of this Gospel, in which long discourses placed in Jesus' mouth explain the deeper, hidden meaning of signs, events, and rituals, the "in Christ" formula of Paul is replaced by the phrase *en emoi* ("in me"), frequently used in conjunction with the verb *menein* ("remaining, dwelling").[50] What is particularly striking about John's use is the mutuality of relations he underscores on all the levels of union. "Do you not believe," Jesus asks the disciples in the first supper discourse, "that I am in the Father and the Father is in me?" (14:10; cf. 10:38; 17:21). That the Father dwells within him means that it is the Father himself who performs the saving works (14:11): "The Father and I are one" (10:30). Mutuality of indwelling extends to the relationship of Jesus and his disciples, as the Last Supper discourse affirms (e.g., 14:20; 17:23) and illustrates in parable fashion under the image of the vine and branches (15:1–8). Through Jesus, the believer can come to enjoy mutual indwelling with the Father (14:23; 17:21; 1 John 4:15–16). The Paraclete, or Spirit of Truth, whom Jesus promises to send upon the disciples to continue his work, is also said to be "with you . . . in you" (14:17), though the reverse formula of the believer being in the Spirit is not used. In 1 John this union is described as a *koinōnia* or fellowship (1:3, 6–7), a term Paul had used to indicate the believer's fellowship with Christ (e.g., 1 Cor 1:9) and the Spirit (e.g., 2 Cor 13:13; Phil 2:1), but which is not used in the Gospel.[51]

Three final observations concerning the way in which John's works could be and were read by later Christian mystics will conclude these brief remarks. The first is the opening that John gives to a specifically trinitarian mysticism. John does not have anything like the developed trinitarian theology of later Christianity, but his use of "dwelling in" in relation to the Father, the Word, and (more ambiguously) the Spirit provided the clearest biblical ground for attempts to understand how God becomes present to the faithful in an interpersonal way in which we become partakers of the inner life of the three divine persons. Second, the Johannine texts, although they do not speak openly of divinization, give support to the Pauline notion of our sonship in and with Christ conceived as a new begetting from above (e.g., John 1:12; 3:3–7; 1 John 2:29; 3:9–10; 4:7; 5:18–19). John's claim that the Paraclete will come to dwell within the disciples (14:17) was also used to support Paul's notion that the believers' bodies are temples of the Holy Spirit (1 Cor 6:19). Later mystics buttressed their appeals to the sparse New Testament references to divinization, especially 2 Peter 1:4, which speaks of sharing in the divine nature (*theias koinōnoi physeōs*), with references to these Pauline and Johannine passages. Finally, we should note that John's Gospel, more than any other New Testament text, impels the reader to undertake a deeper appropriation of the Christian sacramental rituals, especially baptism (John 3:1–5:47) and the Eucharist (6:1–7:52). John did not deny the importance of the sacraments in achieving the new life in Christ, but like his later mystical interpreters, he did not think of sheer participation in the rites themselves as the final stage.[52]

The other parts of the New Testament, which had largely reached its final canonical form by ca. 200 C.E., also included themes and texts that later mystics were to use for their own purposes. The apocalypse ascribed to John, while subject to considerable debate over its authenticity and inclusion in the canon, provided clear evidence and authorization for ecstatic visionary experience (e.g., Apoc 1:10; 4:1–2; etc.). It remained an important resource for visionary forms of mysticism down through the ages. The final books of the New Testament (composed ca. 100–140 C.E.), the literature of emergent Catholicism as it has been called, could also be occasionally mined for mystical interests, though the major concerns of these writings reflect disciplinary and institutional issues.

Other Early Christian Writings

The first century of Christian existence left a number of other literary witnesses, including texts that at least some Christian communities considered scriptural or inspired until the New Testament canon took its final form. These writings, often called the "Apostolic Fathers," were all written in Greek, though some of them were known in translation to later Latin-speaking Christians. The *Shepherd of Hermas,* a quasi apocalypse combining visions, commandments, and parables, was translated into Latin and read by some medieval authors, but it never became a real influence. Written in several stages between ca. 100 and 140 C.E., the *Shepherd* testifies to how important apocalyptic visions continued to be in many second-century Christian circles. The *Didache,* or *Teaching of the Twelve Apostles,* at least parts of which go back to the first century C.E., was also translated into Latin, but it too was little read and offers no real ammunition for mystical interpretations. Another group of texts that were translated into Latin in the Middle Ages, though apparently not widely read, merits discussion, if only because it has often been seen as the best representative of a special form of early Christian mysticism — the seven letters of Ignatius, bishop of Antioch, who was martyred in Rome perhaps about the year 110 c.e.[53]

More than a few scholars have attempted to describe Ignatius's mysticism. Albert Schweitzer argued that Ignatius took over Paul's mysticism of being in Christ, but filled it with Hellenistic content by conceiving of it in terms of the union of flesh and spirit.[54] F. A. Schilling in 1932 also saw Ignatius as a mystic because of his "continuous 'in-Christ' experience" and his prophetic consciousness. Theo Preiss, in an important article in 1938, identified the mysticism of the imitation of Christ and of unity with God in Ignatius, claiming that the bishop transformed early Christian consistent eschatology into a eucharistic piety aimed toward immortality of the soul rather than the general resurrection.[55] More recently, Louis Bouyer and Virginia Corwin have each claimed the bishop of Antioch for the ranks of the mystics, though on different grounds.[56]

The evidence for Ignatius's mysticism to some extent overlaps with that seen in Paul (the bishop knew at least some letters of Paul and praises him in *Eph.* 12.2), and to some extent goes beyond it. Like the apostle, Ignatius often speaks of being "in Christ,"[57] and of Christ being "in us."[58] He also uses the formula "in God."[59] But with a few exceptions (e.g., *Eph.* 8.2; 15.3), Ignatius's expressions provide little opening to any reading in terms of a deeper and more personal appropriation of the shared communal identity of all believers in Christ.[60]

Much the same seems to be true of his use of the language of union. To be sure, union and uniting are the leitmotif of the bishop's thought — Christ's union with the Father (e.g., *Mag.* 7.1–2), the union of the divine and the human in the Redeemer (e.g., *Eph.* 7.2), and the unity of the church in the one Eucharist (e.g., *Phil.* 4.1) are all important notions. A number of interpreters, such as Preiss and Corwin, have read Ignatius's use of words such as union (*henōsis*), unity (*henōtes*), and concord (*homonoia*) as indicating mystical union. The "blameless unity" of the church with Christ and the Father, developed with the use of musical metaphors in *Eph.* 4.2–5.1, is, however, clearly more a communal than a personal concept, as are the unions of flesh and spirit and of faith and love prayed for in *Mag.* 1.2. The union of the Father and the Son is the source and model for the unity of the Christian community (e.g., *Mag.* 7.1–2; *Tr.* 11.2; *Smyr.* 12.2; *Phil.* 5.2; 8.1; *Pol.* 8.3); but, as William Schoedel insists, Ignatius "does not use the word [i.e., *henōsis*] to describe the communion between God and human beings."[61] Of course, one could argue that it is the objective sense of unity given by God that also predominates in the Johannine texts considered above; but John seems to allow for a more subjective appropriation in which the believer comes to a deeper personal awareness of loving oneness with the Father and the Son (e.g., John 17:21-23).

Ignatius does not speak about acquiring or gaining union with God, nor does he have any role for the vision of God, here or hereafter (the goal of the Christian life is immortality and eternal life, as in *Pol.* 2.3). What is distinctive of his teaching, however, is the notion of "attaining" (*tygchanein;* or, in the intensified form, *epitygchanein*) God or Christ, which he uses nineteen times (fifteen times of himself, three times of all Christians, and once of Polycarp).[62] The bishop sees his attaining to God principally in terms of his coming martyrdom, as his letter to the Romans makes clear (e.g., 1.2; 2.1; 5.3; 9.2): "let me be the food of wild beasts through whom it is possible to attain God" (4.1).[63] By this attaining to God he will become a true disciple (e.g., *Eph.* 1.2; *Rom.* 4.2). He also uses the term in a more general sense, as in *Smyr.* 9.2: "God is your reward, whom you will attain if you endure everything for him."[64] Attaining God is a future possibility, one that is realized at death; but (unlike union) it seems to imply a personal relation with God. If mysticism is not restricted to the language of union or identity, and if death is conceived of as the goal of the Christian life, then the language of attaining seems open to a mystical interpretation.[65] Did Ignatius intend such a meaning? One's answer to this seems to depend on the prior question of how we conceive the relation between the ideal of martyrdom (for which Ignatius's letters are the most powerful personal witness in early Christianity) and the issue of mysticism.

The notion of suffering as a form of imitation of Jesus, especially the ultimate suffering of death, took its root in New Testament texts from the Synoptics (e.g., Matt 5:10; 10:38; 16:24 and parallels), from Paul (e.g., Rom 8:17; 1 Cor 4:10-13; 2 Cor 1:5-6; Phil 1:29; 3:10), and elsewhere (e.g., Col 1:24; 1 Pet 2:21; 4:16; Apoc 22:14). The story of Stephen recounted in the Acts of the Apostles (6:8-7:60) is particularly instructive. As the "proto-martyr" in the later Christian tradition, Stephen's witness to faith in Jesus as messiah causes a transfiguration in which his face appears to his opponents as the face of an angel (6:15). "Filled with the Holy Spirit, [he] gazed into heaven and saw the glory of God, and Jesus standing at God's right hand" (7:55). Similar visionary experiences of the heavenly world, with analogies to apocalyptic visions and perhaps even to later mystical ones, are found in the martyr acts of the second century.[66]

Writing in expectation of his martyrdom, Ignatius recounts no visions, but his letters do provide material for the conception of martyrdom as the perfect imitation of Christ. This is especially evident in *Rom.* 6.1-8.1, the impassioned address in which the bishop begs the Roman community not to interfere with his coming death: "Allow me to be an imitator of the

suffering of my God. If anyone has him within himself, let him understand
what I want, and let him sympathize with me, knowing what constrains
me."[67] The intense desire for death (which in Ignatius borders almost on
a morbid fascination) at its deepest level is a desire to be with Jesus and
the Father. The peculiar tortured metaphors of *Rom.* 7.2–8.1 bring this out
in a powerful way:

> For I write you (fully) alive, longing to die. My longing (*erōs*) has been
> crucified, and there is no matter-loving fire in me. There is water living and
> speaking in me, saying from within me, "Come to the Father" [cf. John
> 7:38–39]. I take no pleasure in the food of corruption nor yet in the pleasures
> of this life. I want the bread of God, which is the flesh of Jesus Christ, of the
> seed of David; and for drink I want his blood which is incorruptible love. I
> no longer want to live in human fashion; and this will be so if you want it;
> want it, that you may also be wanted.[68]

But Ignatius can also widen the compass of imitation to include all forms
of dedication and endurance through suffering based on the example of
Jesus. This is the sense of *Eph.* 10.3: "Let us be eager to be imitators of the
Lord—who was wronged more? who was defrauded more? who was
rejected more?" For Ignatius, the whole Christian life is an imitation of
Christ (*Phil.* 7.2), but this life reaches its culmination (for those called to
it) in the perfect imitation of martyrdom.

Martyrdom, as portrayed in Ignatius's letters and the more authentic of
the martyr acts, was *the* Christian ideal of perfection in the second century.[69] Can this ideal be described as mystical? Certainly not if mysticism
is conceived of only as a particular experience of union with God achieved
at some point during this life. But if mysticism is taken more broadly as
a process of transformation effected by desire for and consciousness of the
immediate presence of God, then mysticism need not always use union
language, and a mysticism realized in dying may be no stranger in Christianity than it is in ecstatic Kabbala, such as the *Zohar*, where it is only at
death that the mystic experiences the marriage to the supernal *shekhinah*
that completes his lifelong task. Marcel Viller argued that martyrdom not
only involved the ideal of Christian perfection for its time (something that
can be conceived of in purely ethical terms) but also implied a special form
of immediate relation to Christ that is suggested by some of the martyr
acts.[70] In the *Martyrdom of Saints Perpetua and Felicitas*, for instance, when the
slave Felicitas is taunted by one of her captors because her expressions of
pain in childbearing indicate her inability to bear the torments of the
arena, she replies: "What I am suffering now, I suffer by myself. But then
another will be inside me who will suffer for me, just as I shall be suffering
for him."[71] In the third century, Origen incorporated the martyr ideal of the

presence of Christ into his mystical theology with no difficulty, as we shall see below. Of course, there was no such explicit development of what we might call the mystical side of martyrdom in the second century, but it seems difficult to deny that it is at least implied.

This acknowledgment raises once again the issue of the extent to which mysticism is an importation into Christianity from foreign soil. Even so sympathetic and eminent a scholar as A. J. Festugière argued that there were essentially two strands in Christian spirituality during the early centuries: an ascetical Christianity based on unselfish *agapē*, which expressed itself in martyrdom and reached a culmination in early monasticism; and a secondary strain, that of contemplative mysticism, which entered Christianity in the latter second century and was based on *erōs* for the vision of God as the key to personal happiness. Festugière identified the distinction between the active and the contemplative lives as a key to these complementary types.[72]

This is an attractive—but I think too simple—view of what happened. Christian piety did undergo crucial changes and developments in the second half of the second century, and many of these had to do with the importation of important religiomystical notions from the world in which the Christians lived. But the issues that gave rise to Christian mysticism in the full sense were more the outcome of internal debates about the meaning of life in Jesus, the risen Lord, than importations from without (if the inner/outer distinction has any sense). The new understandings of Christianity validated themselves by appeals to those elements in the tradition (especially in the sacred texts that by that time were well on the way to becoming what we call the Christian Bible) which expressed the possibility, perhaps even the obligation, for all believers to strive for a deeper consciousness of the presence of the Redeemer. Christian writers did not conceive of this as possible apart from life in the *ekklēsia*, nor did they think that it implied the absorption of the individual into an undifferentiated divine source. (This is why those who interpret all mysticism as absorptive union have misunderstood the mystical elements in early Christianity.) Early Christian mystics did introduce numerous elements, such as the distinction between the active and contemplative lives (and here Festugière is correct) that were certainly not in the biblical texts. But other key themes could certainly find a rooting there, and it will be an important part of the chapters that follow to trace how this was done.

Mystical Elements in Early Greek Christianity

ALONG WITH THEIR LEGACY from the first Christians, the Greek fathers were also the heirs to both the new religious forms created by the Jews of the Second Temple period and the contemplative ideals of the Greek philosophers. However complicated and sometimes indirect the channels of communication, the Christian authors of the period ca. 150–500 C.E. cannot be understood apart from this dual inheritance, but their appropriation of Jewish and Greek understandings of how humans can experience direct contact with the present God was fundamentally affected by their conviction that it was in Jesus Christ that the ultimate appearance of the saving God had been realized. As we have seen in chapter 3, the foundational Christian documents that came to be known as the New Testament proclaimed both that Jesus was God present in the world and also that he had invited his followers to share in the new life begun at the resurrection. Even the earliest documents of the New Testament suggest different understandings of what it meant to call Jesus God and diverse ways of coming to share in the divine life.

Therefore, it is not surprising that the past generation of patristic scholarship has been so concerned with uncovering the diversity of early Christianity, especially in showing how the orthodox, or Great Church tradition, which has remained foundational to the mainline Christian churches of both East and West, should not be thought of as the only and original form of Christian belief, but that it is actually the historical product of the intense debates about the meaning of Christianity that characterized the second century of our era.[1] Even after the formation of the orthodox center in Christianity, the great doctrinal disputes of the later patristic centuries and the movement of

84

Christianity out into other linguistic and cultural contexts demonstrate the continuing variety and complexity of the new religion. This variety is evident in the diverse ways of appropriating belief in Jesus as Savior found in early Christian spirituality.[2]

This initial diversity, as well as the subsequent rich development of the Christian churches, helps explain why modern interpreters have used so many different categories to organize their presentations of the spirituality and mysticism of the early church. Some have concentrated on the idea of Christian perfection; others on that of divinization or on the related themes of contemplation, gnosis (knowledge), or the vision of God. Nor have other important ideas been neglected, such as divine birth, likeness to God, enjoyment of God, perfect prayer, ecstasy, and union with God.[3] Most of these themes can be found also in the Greek contemplative tradition, but in Christianity they were utilized within the context of a community of belief centered on the confession of Jesus Christ as God and Redeemer. Hence, they always involved a relationship to him, frequently one expressed in terms of following Christ, or imitating Christ.[4]

These overlapping perspectives demonstrate one of the characteristic features of patristic thought — a density of expression which often combines various genera and themes that later generations of theologians were to divide into discrete categories. To separate out any single element in these writings, which frequently mingle exegetical, doctrinal, sacramental, and spiritual dimensions, is to risk a false simplicity and even a dangerous misconstruction. But as long as we do not claim that any single approach of and by itself can reveal all aspects of an author's thought, we can still fruitfully use the presence of God as realized in Jesus Christ as a key to open up some of the main elements of Greek patristic mysticism.

Our concern, of course, is not with Greek patristic mysticism as such, but only with those themes and figures that had a direct and decisive influence on later Latin traditions. This chapter is not a historical summary of the mysticism of the Greek fathers;[5] it is a survey of some decisive moments without which the history of later Western mysticism cannot be understood (especially the struggle against Gnosticism), and a look at several crucial figures, particularly Origen, Evagrius, and the Pseudo-Dionysius, who were read in the Latin world.

A crucial consideration, one in which the early Christian community shows its relation to the Jewish matrix briefly sketched in chapter 1, concerns the exegetical context of early Christian mysticism. Jesus, the divine Word or Logos in the flesh, brought the message of salvation, the *euangelion* or good news of redemption, in an oral form. But that message soon came to be fixed in written documents, a move that illustrates the transition from oral to written sacred communication characteristic of the whole late ancient world. The Christian communities vindicated their ownership not only of the books about Jesus and the activities of his first followers but also of the sacred books of the Jews, in an essentially christological way. Since the whole of God's revealed message was about the Redeemer, the Jewish scriptures as promise, the Christian writings as fulfillment, they claimed that only the followers of Jesus possessed the proper key for understanding them. However much Christian authors adopted the exegetical tools of the Jewish scribes and rabbis and also of the Greek litterateurs and philosophers, it was always in the service of this overarching hermeneutic. Scripture, christologically interpreted, was the ground of all Christian thought, including mysticism, especially in the first centuries.[6]

It is equally important to remember that the Christian community antedated and was the source of the Christian scriptures. The risen Lord was first present in the body of those who confessed his name in prayer, ritual, and their life together before that presence was fixed in written form in the community's sacred texts. In other words, the New Testament, as well as the Christian reading of the Old Testament (to give the two parts of the Christian Bible the names they had acquired by ca. 200 C.E.), were the *products* of Christian spirituality just as much as they were also its sources. This reciprocal relation between community and text has characterized Christianity not only in the first century of its development (roughly the time of the writing and formation of the New Testament), but throughout its history through the ongoing process of interpretation within a community setting, especially in catechesis and preaching. The language and the themes that the Greek fathers used to understand the action of the saving Word and our relation to him, though often adopted from the Greek contemplative tradition, functioned within a context rather different from that found in Greek religion and religious philosophy. The Christian context was one of a mutually reciprocal presence of a saving Mediator in both the community and the text. Despite the diversity of the early Christian communities, and notwithstanding the differences in tonality and emphasis found in the various early Christian mystics (even those who represent the emerging center, or "orthodox" view of the Great Church tradition), Christian mysticism, especially in its formative phases, was always both ecclesial, that is, realized only in and through the community, and scriptural, that is, tied to the spiritual, hidden, or "mystical" meaning of the sacred texts.[7]

In the previous chapter we investigated the extent to which writings of the first century of the existence of the new religion (ca. 50–150 C.E.) contain elements that were considered mystical in the later tradition, either

by classical Christian mystics of the late patristic and medieval periods or
by modern interpreters (as in the case of Ignatius's letters). But it is important to point out that historians have generally seen the later second
century C.E. as a more crucial period in the history of Christian mysticism.
The great debates over the meaning of *gnōsis* as a special form of higher
knowledge of God, and the writings of major figures of the "Alexandrian
school" of Christian teaching, especially Clement and Origen, give this
period special importance.

The Second Century and
the Beginnings of Christian Mysticism

The late second century C.E. was decisive for the formation of Christianity as an organized religious entity. Without in any way detracting from
the originating importance of the first century of Christianity's existence,
it was in the last two quarters of the second century that Christians
confronted difficult questions of ethos and organization and created the
responses that formed the loose communities of believers into a more
organized religious entity whose intellectual and institutional achievements
had much to do with its eventual success. It was the church of the year
200 — a church with monarchical episcopate, bonds of communion among
episcopal sees, generally similar liturgy and sacraments, official lists (i.e.,
canons) of sacred books, formulas of belief (i.e., creeds), and, above all, an
ideology of a tradition (*paradosis*) of common belief handed down from the
apostles — that was to become the religion of the empire in the fourth
century.

During the second century, those who confessed the name of Jesus as
Lord were forced to confront the difficult issues of self-definition. What
does it mean to be a Christian? Who decides who is truly a Christian? How
is the decision made?[8] The necessity for self-definition was impelled both
from within and from without, that is, both by those whom believers saw
as external foes (Jews and pagans) and by internal disputes about who was
a true Christian. Each of these quarrels had its effect on the future of Christian mysticism.

Against the Jews, Christian authors, as we have seen, claimed that they
alone were the *verus Israel,* the real heirs of Abraham, Moses, and the
prophets. The polemics over the true nature of Israel that marked late
Second Temple Judaism prepared the way for the gradual separation and
ultimate split between Judaism and Christianity that is evident especially
after the destruction of the Temple in 70 C.E.. One sign of the increasingly
polemical struggle between early Christianity and early rabbinic Judaism

in the second century is how their mystical traditions developed in such independent fashion.

The second context within which the Christians of the second century sought to define their particularity was that of their relation to the Hellenistic culture that was so central to Roman society. Though strongly influenced by Jewish thought forms, the Christians of the second century clearly rejected contemporary Judaism. Even more strongly influenced by the Hellenistic culture in which they lived (how could it be otherwise?), their reaction to this world was more complex. It is not easy to know what the mass of Christians thought about the Roman *imperium*. Many doubtless continued to view it as a world marked for apocalyptic destruction, as had the prophet John, the author of the Apocalypse (ca. 95 c.e.). But judging from the handful of authors whom chance or design has preserved for us, most Christians seem to have sought accommodation and conversion, not condemnation and aversion. While they were resolute in attacking the lax morality and polytheistic rites of the Roman world, they were also anxious to convince the Roman elite that Christianity fostered upright living, good citizenship, and philosophic truth—in other words, that Christianity was the fulfillment not only of the promises made to the Jews but also of the truths about God which the Word had sowed in all humanity and which were conspicuous in the lives and teachings of the best Greek lovers of wisdom, such as Socrates and Plato.[9] The apologetic literature of early Christianity composed roughly ca. 125–200 witnesses to a rising Christian self-confidence, which claimed that the new religion, despite its suspect origins and unusual beliefs such as the resurrection of the dead, was the summation of all the truths that the wise men of old had held in partial fashion.[10] This generally positive attitude fostered by the apologists toward the Greek philosophical tradition, especially Platonism, did much to prepare the ground for the appropriation of *theōria* and related themes into Christianity.[11]

The division between "external" and "internal" debates is, of course, somewhat artificial. Judaism contained many Hellenistic elements; many Christians were converts from Judaism or paganism; and the Christian "heresies" were themselves often the expressions of complex reactions among various religious and cultural elements. Still, it is important to stress that the most decisive elements in shaping Christian identity in the second century were the debates among those who thought of themselves as followers of Jesus and not Christian polemics against Jews and apologies directed toward the pagan world.

Three debates were critical in forming the "Great Tradition," the gradually emerging consensus about the content of belief and the structure of the community which came to be described as catholic (i.e., universal) and orthodox (i.e., rightly believing) Christianity.

For the history of Christian mysticism, the dispute over the finality of revelation, which was the essential issue in the quarrel against Montanus (a prophet from Asia Minor active ca. 160) and his followers, may have some relevance as a prototype for later struggles between pneumatic inspiration (claimed by some mystics) and institutional authorization, but there is no proof that Montanism had any direct influence on subsequent Christian mysticism. The struggle over Montanism helped the church clarify the importance of episcopal authority at the same time that it underlined the finality of the revelation given through Jesus and available in the sacred books of the community.

The activities of Marcion of Pontus, who came to Rome about 140 and who taught an uncompromising Pauline form of Christianity which totally rejected the Old Testament, were of considerable importance in vindicating the significance of the spiritual interpretation of the Old Testament and in moving the Christian communities toward the establishment of a more ample canon of approved books. The most decisive struggle of the second century, however, both for the church at large and for the history of Christian mysticism, was over *gnōsis,* the nature of the saving knowledge, or acquaintance with God, brought by Christ.

The Gnostic Threat

Almost a century ago, Dean Inge quipped that "Gnosticism was rotten before it was ripe,"[12] a comment that reflected the orthodox Christian attacks by Irenaeus, Hippolytus, Epiphanius, and others. Inge's greater contemporary, Adolph von Harnack, thought differently. In his *History of Dogma* he argued that the Gnostics were the first theologians and that Gnosticism, as a form of "acute hellenization" of Gospel Christianity, was the precipitating factor in the moderate hellenizing reaction that gave rise to the history of dogma defined as "a work of the Greek spirit on the soil of the Gospel."[13] During the twentieth century, research into the history of Gnosticism moved into the province of the history of religions, especially with the publication of the first volume of Hans Jonas's *Gnosis und spätantike Geist* in 1934.[14] The discovery in 1945 of a cache of Coptic translations of lost Gnostic documents near Nag Hammadi in Upper Egypt revolutionized contemporary knowledge and evaluation of Gnosticism.[15] Historical research and the concerns of both existentialist philosophy and Jungian psychology reinforced each other in unusual ways to fuel an outpouring of interest, both public and scholarly, in Gnosticism in general.[16] In the second half of the twentieth century, Gnostic myths seem as popular in some intellectual circles as they once were among those of the second century. Despite the vast differences between ancient Gnosticism and contemporary neo-Gnostics,[17] Inge's orthodox prejudice at times seems to have been reversed, so that the Gnostics, viewed as adherents of a liberal-minded, proto-feminist, democratic form of Christianity, become the true, though defeated, heroes and heroines of early Christianity.

The new discoveries have increased our knowledge but have not always brought firm answers to the debates over Gnosticism that have troubled scholars for the past century. We still continue to ask the same basic questions about Gnosticism (even presuming that we can talk about it as in some way *one* thing):[18] Where? When? What? That is, where was its milieu or source? When did it originate? What are its essential characteristics?[19] From our perspective, a further question must also be asked: How are we to evaluate its significance for the history of Christian mysticism?

In the absence of a general consensus regarding the answers to the first three questions, it is difficult but still necessary to try to give some kind of response to the final issue, especially because many scholars, such Hans Jonas, have given Gnosticism a central role in the transition from myth to mysticism.[20] More recent authors have not hesitated to speak of Gnostic mysticism, or at least to admit a mystical element in Gnosticism.[21]

It seems undeniable that many if not most Gnostics thought of themselves as Christians. Gnosticism may have arisen independently of Christianity, possibly in Jewish circles,[22] and there are Gnostic texts (e.g., the *Allogenes* and the *Zostrianos* from Nag Hammadi) that have no overt Christian references; but most Gnostic writings witness to belief in Jesus as Savior. It is clear that Gnosticism became important primarily in its Christian forms.[23]

The fact that the Gnostic view of the universe expresses a dualistic understanding of reality that sees the material world as a mistake of some sort ("The world came into being through trangression," as the *Gospel of Philip* puts it),[24] led some older scholars, such as R. Reitzenstein to posit an ultimately Iranian origin for Gnosticism. Others saw it as a logical development from the eschatological dualism of Jewish apocalypticism, especially after the failure of apocalyptic hopes for the new aeon.[25] Still others noted its closeness to some increasingly pessimistic cosmological speculations of Middle Platonism. But we cannot reduce Gnosticism to a search for its origins. This would be to negate the originality and power of its vision. There can be no question that the Gnostics were eclectic, picking and choosing what they found useful. Plotinus, who was as unhappy with the Gnostics as the average church father, recognized this when he complained: "Generally speaking, some of these peoples' doctrines have been taken from Plato, but others, all the new ideas they have brought in to establish a philosophy of their own, are things they have found outside the truth."[26] As Kurt Rudolph has pointed out, one of the peculiarities of the Gnostic tradition "lies in the fact that it frequently draws its material from the most varied existing traditions, attaches itself to it, and at the same time sets it in a new frame by which this material takes on a new character and a completely new significance."[27]

This practice contributes to the difficulty in finding an adequate definition for Gnosticism, especially one that would fit all the sects, groups, and texts that at one time or another have been called Gnostic. Debate continues on this issue, but it is notable that the definitions given by scholars, though expressing various nuances, have much in agreement.[28] We may say, then, that the core ideas of the various forms of Gnosticism revolve around dualism, the innate divinity of the soul (or its higher part), and salvation through gnosis.

Some recent scholars have tried to identify an original, or classic, form of Gnosticism, as Bentley Layton does for the "Sethian" Gnosticism enshrined in such texts as the *Apocryphon* (or *Secret Book*) *of John*. Many others, such as Kurt Rudolph, aver that "according to the present state of research, it is still too early to posit a common 'original' system."[29] In the midst of these disagreements among experts, we may admit to a certain confusion — one that is compounded by reading the Gnostic texts themselves.[30]

Irenaeus of Lyons, who more than any other figure formed the orthodox reaction against Gnosticism in his work *Against Heresies* (ca. 180), briefly summarizes the teaching of one Saturninus, an early Gnostic, in a way that highlights what the emerging church tradition found objectionable about Gnostic beliefs:

> And he postulates that the Savior was unengendered, incorporeal, and formless, and was shown forth as a human being only in appearance. And — he says — the God of the Jews is one of the angels. And because the parent wished to destroy all the rulers, the anointed (Christ) came for the destruction of the God of the Jews and for the salvation of those who might be persuaded by him: and these are those who have the spark of life in them. Indeed, there are — he says — two human races which were modeled by the angels, one wicked and the other good. . . . And he says that marriage and the engendering of offspring are from Satan. And most of his followers abstain from (the flesh of) living things. . . . (*Against Heresies* 1.24.1 [Layton, p. 162])

Fundamental to all Gnosticism was the rejection of the Genesis account of the creation of the material world by the highest God because of his desire to communicate his goodness. For the Gnostics, this world was the product of an inferior power, weak and evil, or sometimes the result of some kind of problem or ignorance in the spiritual realm or *plērōma* (as in the *Gospel of Truth* 17:4–20). In mythic terms, especially as set forth in the *Apocryphon of John* and related texts, the production of the material universe is part of an elaborate and deliberately confusing mythology of the production and eventual return of various levels of spiritual being to the ultimately Unknowable Source, or Highest One.[31] The orthodox picture of the evils of Gnosticism (whether or not it was actually realized in all the groups condemned as Gnostic) centered on this rejection of the Bible's account of creation, as well as the docetic view of Christ, the rejection of marriage, and false asceticism — all of which imply the dualism that has so interested those historians of religion who have sought to understand Gnosticism within a historical continuity of forms of dualistic religion.[32]

The fathers of emerging orthodoxy were especially worried about the Gnostics because it is clear that their interpretation of Christ's saving action was quite attractive, at least with some groups, in the second century. Some of the Gnostic teachers, especially the great, if shadowy, figure Valentinus (ca. 100–175), who came to Rome from Alexandria about 140 and established a group that continued to exist for several centuries, first within the Roman church itself and later as a separate form of Christianity, even claimed an "apostolic tradition" stretching back to Paul that paralleled the claims of his orthodox opponents like Irenaeus.[33] Indeed, there is considerable disagreement about how far Valentinus and the Valentinian schools that flourished in the East with leaders like Theodotus and in the West with Ptolemy and Heracleon were really dualistic and docetic at all.[34]

How much of the appeal of the Gnostics came from the mystical elements in their systems of thought and piety, and what did these contribute to early Christian mysticism? It is difficult to know for sure. Somewhat simplistically, we may approach these questions by distinguishing positive from negative dimensions of the issue.

Positively, the Gnostic texts display important affinities with many of the key themes found in the Hellenistic mysticism considered in chapter 2 — descent and ascent of the soul, negative theology, contemplation and vision of God, divinization and unification with the divine. In the Gnostic sources, however, these mystical topoi appear within a mythic pattern in which salvation is achieved through that gnosis by means of which some persons (not all) come to recognize the hidden divine nature of their fallen souls. This seems to be the key to the mystical element in Gnosticism.

It may be possible, as Bentley Layton suggests, to distinguish various types of Gnostic mysticism.[35] Texts such as *Zostrianos*, the *Allogenes* (or "Foreigner") and *The Three Tablets of Seth*, all of which portray a similar strong form of the Gnostic dualistic myth, express a mysticism based on the fall and ascent of the soul that has at least part of its ancestry in the stages of ascent to the Source described in texts such as Plato's *Symposium* 210A–212A. Thus, the sage Zostrianos recounts his ascent through the aeons to the gnosis found in attaining the First Principle and then his descent to spread the message to humanity:

> And there I saw all these (spiritual beings) as they exist, in one. And I became unified with all of them, and I blessed the Concealed Aeon, the Virgin Barbelo and the Invisible Spirit. And I became wholly perfect; received power; was inscribed in glory; was sealed; and there was wreathed with a perfect wreath. . . .
>
> And I descended to the perceptible world, and I put on my ignorant material image. . . .
>
> I awakened a multitude that were lost, saying, "O living people! O holy seed of Seth! Understand! Do not let yourselves [appear?] inattentive to me. Elevate your divine element as being god. . . ." (*Zostrianos* 129:6–130:18 [Layton, p. 139])

In the *Allogenes* the mystical journey is an interior one in which the nameless seer (the "Foreigner"), after a hundred years of deliberation, receives a vision of the aeons corresponding to the structure of the pleroma or totality of spiritual reality (50:7–59:37 [Layton, pp. 144–45]). In this text the vision of the "First One" leads to an attempt to understand and express the Inexpressible Source by means of a series of paradoxes and contradictory predications that recall the hypotheses on the One of Plato's *Parmenides* (*Allogenes* 61–67 [Layton, pp. 146–48]).[36] These texts have a clear emphasis on the vision or beholding of the First Principle: "We have beheld! We have beheld! We have beheld that which is First really existent as it really exists — as it exists!" as the Sixth Hymn in the quasi-liturgical *Three Tablets of Seth* puts it (124:18–19 [Layton, pp. 156–57]).[37] This beholding leads to a state of *gnōsis* that is described as a unification (123:30–33); and sometimes even as a divinization (*Zost.* 44:21).[38] Despite the strong Platonist element in these texts, more authentic Platonists, like Plotinus, were quick to point out the distance between Plato and Gnostic cosmological dualism.[39]

Works that represent the Gnosticism of Valentinus and his followers, especially the famous *Gospel of Truth,* a sermon on salvation by gnosis which many think actually comes from Valentinus, give a rather different picture of the Gnostic's goal. They have little emphasis on the fall and ascent of the soul, but rather present a kind of mysticism of immanence in which the major themes are containment and awakening.[40] The gospel that Jesus brings reveals the mystery of the uncontained Father, who contains all things in himself:

And as for him, they discovered him within them — the inconceivable uncontained, the Father, who is perfect, who created the entirety. Because the entirety was within him and the entirety was in need of him — since he retained within himself its completion, which he had not given unto the entirety — the Father was not grudging. . . . (*Gos. Truth* 18:31–39 [Layton, p. 254])

The homily is basically a plea to escape forgetfulness, to awake to the mystery of the existence of all in God through the gnosis that comes from the Father in the manifestation of the Son (e.g., 30:23–36). This awakening, not unlike that of Paul (Gal 5:6), is the work of faith that brings the fullness of love (*Gos. Truth* 34:28–33).[41] It leads to a form of mystical union described as a state or place of repose which the author attests that he himself has enjoyed (42:25–43:22). Hippolytus, another of the patristic opponents of the Gnostics, preserves the story of Valentinus's mystical vision of the Logos as a newborn infant, the source of all his teaching, thus corroborating Valentinus's claims to mystical experience (Hippolytus, *Refutation* 6.42.2).

The Gnostic, possibly Valentinian, Hymn of Christ found in the apocryphal *Acts of John* also seems to imply a similar mysticism of immanence or containment in which Christ is both savior and saved, the uniter and what is united, as he invites his disciple to join him in his dance and "see yourself in me who am speaking."[42] Another Valentinian text, the *Epistle to Rheginus*, speaks of a "resurrection of the spirit" which takes place in this life as the believer recognizes the nonexistence of the material world and becomes aware of the unchanging permanence of spiritual reality.[43] In the Valentinian anthology known as the *Gospel of Philip* there is considerable emphasis on the ancient theme of Greek piety (also found in the New Testament, e.g., 1 Cor 13:12; 1 John 3:2) of becoming like the spiritual reality we behold:

People cannot see anything in the real realm unless they become it. . . . If you have seen any things there, you have become those things: if you have seen the Spirit, you have become the Spirit; if you have seen the Anointed (Christ), you have become the Anointed (Christ); if you have seen the [Father, you] will become the Father. . . . There, you will see yourself; for you shall [become] what you see. (*Gos. Phil.* 38 [61:20–35; Layton, p. 337])[44]

Layton ascribes the difference between these two forms of Gnostic mysticism, which we may call fall-and-ascent mysticism and immanence-awakening mysticism, to the influence of the pre-Gnostic "Thomas school" writings on Valentinian Gnosticism.[45] These texts, such as the well-known *Gospel of Thomas* (a selection of wisdom *logia* ascribed to Jesus, including many sayings known from the Synoptic Gospels) and the Hymn of the Pearl, emphasize the recognition of the divine identity within the soul (e.g.,

Gos. Thom. 3, 18, 22, 77), and they also speak of the believer becoming Jesus (*Gos. Thom.* 108).[46] Nevertheless, the relations between the various forms of Gnostic and pre-Gnostic Christian traditions remain conjectural at best, and the mystical elements in the Thomas texts are less clear than in the properly Gnostic writings.

These characteristics of what many scholars have identified as Gnostic mysticism allow us to ask what effect such mysticism may have had on the subsequent history of Christian mystical traditions. Here the orthodox rejection of Gnosticism in the second and third centuries points clearly in a negative direction. Those elements in later Christian mysticism that appear to be similar to aspects of Gnostic mysticism can often be explained by appealing to common Jewish, Greek, and New Testament roots rather than by postulating any real contact with Gnostic sources themselves. This is not to deny Gnosticism an important role in the history of Christian mysticism, though one more negative than positive. The Gnostic debates set norms which later Christian mystics would trangress only at the peril of their relation to the wider orthodox body. Gnosticism might be termed the first great Christian mystical heresy, though historically speaking it would be inadequate to define Gnosticism purely in terms of mysticism and its "heresy" solely on these grounds.

Recent study, especially that of G. Stroumsa, has highlighted the differences between Gnostic asceticism and the major lines of early Christian asceticism which were to triumph in the birth of the monastic movement. Gnostic self-denial, fitting its dualistic origins, was more concerned about sexual purity than about general moral progress and personal integration.[47] Here the Christian fathers, even those for whom virginity was a paramount value, seem closer to the more inclusive moral programs of the contemporary Hellenistic philosophers than to the Gnostic views.[48] Gnostic mysticism also displays essential differences from the developing orthodox view of mysticism — at least as our "orthodox" sources present it. The future of Christian mysticism was shaped by the reaction to Gnosticism in a permanent way.

Justin Martyr, who died in Rome about 165, appears to have been one of the earliest orthodox opponents of Gnosticism and Gnostic mysticism.[49] For someone whose conversion from Platonism to Christianity hinged on his discovery that the Platonists were wrong about the innate divinity of the soul (Justin, *Dialogue* 2.4–6),[50] Gnostic harping on this theme (something that seems to have been a characteristic of almost all Gnostic groups) must have seemed a dangerous regression. Though Justin's view of the relation of the cosmos to God cannot be viewed as a clear expression of subsequent

Christian theories of creation from nothing, his recognition that the cosmos and the soul were both radically dependent on and yet different from God is an important moment in the history of Christian thought and of Christian mysticism: "If the world is begotten, souls are also necessarily begotten" (*Dialogue* 5.1). It is difficult to think that it was Justin alone who gave this point the weight that it seems to have enjoyed in the polemic against Gnostic mysticism. It is far easier to suppose that Gnostic insistence on the divine seed in all humans made the issue ripe for discussion and that orthodox believers came to see that Christianity necessarily implied that the soul was not naturally divine.

The speculative mysticism that was soon to flourish in orthodox Christianity, even that of Clement and Origen, who shared certain values with the Gnostics, insisted on the distinction between the divine realm and the created realm. The soul might be capable of divinization, but it was not naturally or innately divine. Orthodox and Gnostic Christians could make use of many of the same themes to describe the goal of the redemptive process—divinization, vision, perfection, unification—but these themes tended to take on different meanings in terms of how one viewed the soul's origin.

A second area in which we can detect important differences between Gnostic mysticism and the developing mysticism of orthodox Christianity concerns the relation of faith (*pistis*) and love (*agapē/erōs*) to the gnosis through which Gnostics believed that salvation was communicated.[51] This is a more complicated area, if only because gnosis plays an important role in the New Testament (see chapter 3) and the notion that Gnostics did not appreciate the roles of faith and love goes contrary to many texts. For instance, Irenaeus admitted that the Carpocratians taught that "we are saved by faith and love, all else is indifferent" (*Against Heresies* 1.20.3), and texts of the Valentinians show that they too valued the faith and love that their hero Paul had preached. Though we still lack an adequate treatment of how the different groups of Gnostics understood the roles that faith and love played, there can be no doubt that the orthodox reaction, rightly or wrongly, took the Gnostics to task for slighting the importance of faith and love in relation to the higher knowledge of gnosis.

Because gnosis was such a central term in some New Testament texts, the more speculative opponents of the Gnostics, such as Clement of Alexandria and to a lesser extent Origen, were not ready to abandon it to the enemy. They insisted on a careful understanding of how gnosis grows out of faith and love and does not contradict them—an issue that the Gnostics, even those who had something good to say about faith and love, seem to have left largely unexamined. Later forms of Christian mysticism almost invariably took great care to spell out how the knowledge given in the faith and the love commanded in the gospel are related to higher forms of direct awareness of God and the soul's relation to him (whether these are called gnosis or not). It is difficult not to see this obsession as at least in part a reaction to the challenge of the unbridled dependence on gnosis among the "heretical" mystics of the second century. Tertullian, in his *Prescription against the Heretics,* summarizes the essential orthodox complaint: "Let vain imagining yield to faith; let vaunting yield to salvation. Either they ought to stop making such a fuss, or else be quiet. To know nothing against the rule of faith is to know everything" (14 [*PL* 2:32A]).[52] This was another crucial part of the negative legacy Gnosticism left for later Christian mysticism.

Gnosis, of course, is tied to a distinctive understanding of revelation. Here too the orthodox reaction established certain boundaries for the functioning of mysticism that were to have a long history. The Gnostics claimed multiple sources of revelation: the recognized scriptures, if read in the proper way; new revelatory texts based on hidden messages of the risen Jesus to certain select souls; and also, as we have seen in the case of Valentinus, the visionary and mystical experiences of the Gnostic teachers themselves. In other words, the Gnostics, not unlike the Montanists, believed in an ongoing process of revelation often tied to visionary experience, in sharp contrast to the orthodox stress on revelation as restricted to the message given to the first apostles and delivered to the community through an established hierarchy.[53] Visionary experience, possibly of a mystical kind, was not totally excluded from the developing orthodox view of Christianity. Visions were important to a number of the Christian martyrs, as the *Martyrdom of Saint Polycarp* (5, 9) and the *Martyrdom of Saints Perpetua and Felicitas* (4, 7, 8, 10, 11–13) show.[54] Origen was willing to speak, if rarely, about the times that the Logos had visited him.[55] What distinguishes these visions from the Gnostic variety is their private character; that is, they were directed to strengthening and/or illuminating the individual believer for some task. Even when they teach or illuminate, they do so not by conveying some new and deeper message but by confirming the meaning of the tradition of the church. The function of visions in later Christianity continues to adhere to these norms. We see here a clear confirmation of Gershom Scholem's view about how mystical illuminations generally relate to established religious structures.[56]

There is still a final area in which Gnosticism may be said to have exerted a real influence on all subsequent Christian mysticism, if largely in a negative way. This concerns the content of gnosis and its relation to the text of scripture. Louis Bouyer has argued that the false or "pseudo-gnosis" of the Gnostics was a deformation of the true gnosis found in Paul and John, and that Justin, Irenaeus, Clement, and their successors were basically concerned about reemphasizing the historical dualism of early Christianity, based on apocalypticism, over against the false metaphysical dualism introduced in the second century.[57] This theory has the merit of underlining the continuity of the theme of gnosis in early Christianity, but unfortunately it also seems to be a modern version of the second-century orthodox ideology in which heresy must always be a perversion of an original truth rather than (in some cases at least) an early tradition or experimental possibility later judged inadequate for particular historical reasons. The issue debated in the second century was not so much the value of gnosis — everyone admitted that — but rather its content: What does gnosis convey, and how it is communicated? That is, how does the believer arrive at true gnosis? On these related questions, the proto-orthodox tradition came up with very different answers from those found in Gnosticism.

The Gnostic speculative thinkers, especially the Valentinians, were among the most original exegetes of the second century. Recent study has disclosed both the originality of their views and the influence that they had on subsequent interpreters, especially Origen.[58] Given the interaction between exegesis and experience that marks Christian mysticism from the beginning, this is another indication of the significance of their role. But here too the Gnostics seem more important for what their views led the orthodox to rule out than for what they contributed in a positive way. However much Origen and others learned from Heracleon and the other Gnostic exegetes, the fundamental lesson they absorbed was the incorrectness of Gnostic exegesis. This was not because the Gnostics practiced the wrong method of exegesis; they were the most accomplished proponents of the spiritual interpretation, which was to be widely employed by many later Christians, especially in Alexandria. They were rejected because their use of this method came up with the wrong meaning.

Method is usually subservient to commitment, despite what some modern theories of religion have held. Few disagreements are more severe than among those who use the same means to arrive at radically different conclusions. The Gnostics of the second century, even the Valentinians it seems, made use of spiritual exegesis of both the Old and the New Testaments in order to discover an esoteric message reserved for the few.[59] This message disclosed that the true meaning of the Christian books was actually that of the Gnostic myths, usually dualistic and always pessimistic about the material world. The Christian fathers who opposed Gnosticism, even those who were close to some aspects of it, insisted that spiritual or allegorical interpretation of the scriptures could be valid only if it did not conflict with the exoteric message of salvation enshrined in the customary preaching and teaching of the community. The Christian mysteries conveyed, by definition, a message open to all. Though the "true gnostics" (as Clement called them) might come to understand it on a deeper level than ordinary believers, spiritual exegesis did not reveal a different message, especially not one about powers and hidden mysteries at best only hinted at in the texts of the established books. In short, the most important effect that Gnosticism had on the subsequent history of Christian mysticism was to make esotericism of any sort suspect, especially an esotericism based on secret modes of scriptural interpretation. Later Christian exegetes, of course, continued to make use of the spiritual interpretation of the Bible to convey the deeper level of the text. The full implications of the message might not be immediately evident to all and believers might even require prolonged ascetical and spiritual training in order to grasp these implications. But the message by definition was open to all Christians; it was not the property of the few. As Augustine put it in the ninety-eighth of his *Homilies on John,* one of the most detailed discussions of the dangers of esotericism in the Christian tradition: "There seems to be no necessity that some secret teachings are kept silent and hidden from the faithful who are still children in the manner of matters to be spoken privately to the advanced, that is, to the more intelligent" (*Homilies on John* 98.3 [*PL* 35:1881]).[60]

Gnostic mysticism, like most Jewish mysticism, was fundamentally esoteric in nature. Christian mysticism, at least the mysticism that is usually judged orthodox, is not. In the history of Christian mysticism, Gnosticism is not only the first great divide, but like all mystical "heresies" it remains a continual divide. Many later Christian mystics will echo positions found in the Gnostic texts, though usually without any possibility of direct dependence. The difficulties that some of these mystics were to encounter in propounding their message will not be unrelated to this central shaping experience the Christian church underwent in the second century.

Major Orthodox Spokesmen

The major orthodox spokesmen of the second half of the second century—Justin, Irenaeus, Clement—were all anti-Gnostic, but to treat them only from this perspective neither does them theological justice nor reveals their role in developing the mystical theology of the Great Church tradition. Justin, who wrote at the time when the debate over the Gnostic brand of Christianity was heating up, was primarily interested in convincing Jews and Greeks of the truth of the gospel. Irenaeus used the Gnostics as an opportunity to create the first truly complete, if not systematically organized, expression of Christian faith, one that has continued to be a resource in the history of theology in a way that no other second-century writing has.[61] Clement, who shared much with the moderate Gnostics, was adamant in condemning their errors. But his real concern was not with polemics but with the presention of his own genial, if eclectic, version of Christianity to his educated contemporaries.

Justin and Irenaeus

It is difficult to call Justin and Irenaeus mystical theologians, though they do witness to the growing desire of the orthodox party not to relinquish to the enemy mystical themes such as the vision of God. Justin's famous account of his conversion at the beginning of his *Dialogue with Trypho* is the earliest extensive discussion in Christian literature of the Greek ideal of the vision of God, one that is less surprising for its knowledge of the theme than for its highly qualified judgment (*Dialogue* 3–6).[62] Justin was well acquainted with Plato and the Platonists, but his conversion marked a fundamental break with Platonism, not least on the issue of the preexistent divine nature of the soul. Under the instruction of the aged seer who socratically leads him to see the inconsistencies of the Platonic doctrines of anamnesis and metempsychosis, Justin advances to a Christian position that does not deny to the *nous* begotten by God the possibility of vision of its unbegotten Source, but insists that this is the reward for virtuous living given to a *nous* that has been adorned by the Holy Spirit, not something owed it by nature.[63] Given this critique of Platonic views of *theōria* in the *Dialogue,* it is not surprising that Justin, despite much use of Plato in his two *Apologies,* makes no other references to vision as the goal of human life, though he does use other contemporary Platonic expressions, as when he speaks of the soul's "fellowship" (*synousia*) with God (*Apology* 1.10.3).[64]

For Irenaeus, in contrast, seeing God is central. As a famous text in *Against Heresies* puts it, "The glory of God is a living man and the life of man is the vision of God" (*Against Heresies* 4.20.7).[65] Hans Urs von Balthasar has argued that Irenaeus's theology, in opposition to Gnosticism, concentrates on "seeing what is," a *videre* that "is less Plato's contemplation than simply standing before the clear message of the facts."[66] Though some have called Irenaeus a mystical theologian,[67] it is more accurate to see his theology as mystical only in the very broad sense in which the Eastern Orthodox tradition understands all right-believing theology as mystical—that is, as an expression of faith in the mysteries revealed by Christ and handed down by the church — and not mystical in the more narrow sense used here, which centers on the believer's response to the more immediate experience of the presence of God in this life.

Irenaeus's theological synthesis endeavored to clarify how the invisible God has come to be seen through the manifestation of his incarnate Son, recapitulating all history — a crucial part of the dogmatic basis for future mystical theologies of both the East and the West. His insistence on the reality of the "seeing" of the historical Jesus who shows the identity of God the Creator and God the Redeemer was both a powerful attack on Gnostic notions of seeing God and a cogent reminder to the orthodox camp that the promise that the pure of heart will see God (Matt 5:8: *opsontai*) is integral to Christian belief. This important text, popular with the Valentinians,[68] was recaptured for the orthodox party by Irenaeus and his contemporaries.[69] It was to become a central biblical proof text for both Clement and Origen.[70] Irenaeus is also the first of the theologians of the Great Church to make much of the theme of deification, though he tends to do so in contexts attacking docetic views of the Incarnation rather than in terms of analyses of the Christian's progress to perfection.[71]

Clement of Alexandria

Clement is the first Christian writer who gives us a fairly full treatment of many ideas, such as vision, divinization, and union, that were later central to orthodox mysticism. Hence, it is not without some justification that A. Levasti termed him "the founder of Christian mysticism,"[72] though I believe that the statement goes too far. Clement not only is the major proponent of "true gnosis" as fundamental to the life of the church, but he also is the first to fit gnosis within the framework of a Christian appropriation of Middle Platonic apophatic theology. The theme of the vision of God (Platonic *theōria*) provides a key to understanding how this Alexandrian author laid the groundwork for later Christian mystical theology.

For those who think of mysticism as a pagan invasion of Gospel Christianity, who believe that deification is not a biblical notion,[73] and who are sure that the vision of God promised in Matt 5:8 is not compatible with Platonic *theōria*, Clement of Alexandria (d. ca. 215) will always be a problematic figure. Born in Athens, perhaps about 150, he was a convert to Christianity who taught in Alexandria but fled the city during the persecution of the emperor Severus. Even to those who do not see him as a perverter of Christianity, Clement appears an innovator in his attempt to bring together his Christian faith and an advanced form of traditional

Greek literary and philosophical education (*paideia*). Though it goes too far in my estimation to call him either the "founder of Christian mysticism," as did Levasti, or even "the creator of Christian mystical theology," in the words of Dom John Chapman,[74] he was the first to treat in detail a number of the major themes that later became central to Christian mysticism. Indeed, he was the one who introduced both the adjective "mystical" and the adverb "mystically" into Christian literature, using them over fifty times in his works to describe everything from Christ (e.g., *Paedagogus* [*The Teacher*] 1.7.59) and his teaching (e.g., *Stromateis* [*Miscellanies*] 6.15.127) to the deeper understanding of the scripture (e.g., *Strom.* 5.6.37) and the "mystical practice or habit" of the Gnostic Christian (e.g., *Strom.* 6.9.78).[75]

Clement found the grounds for all of his major conceptions in scriptural texts, however much he expressed them in the language of Greek religious philosophy. To see him as a mere parrot of Greek philosophy does justice neither to the limits of his Hellenic ecumenism nor to the depth of his dedication to the incarnate Christ, the one teacher of all.[76] Though Clement was not a direct influence on later Latin mystical thought, his position as a significant innovator, his role in the response to Gnosticism, and the impact he had on Origen, make necessary a summary sketch of his views.

Justin, good Platonist that he had been, became convinced that the Platonists had been wrong about the natural divinity of the soul, which is probably why he tended to neglect the mystical elements of Platonism while stressing the cosmological ones, which confirmed the centrality of the Logos. Clement, on the other hand, eagerly appropriated a full range of contemporary Platonic mystical themes—divine unknowability, vision, deification—into his thought. But he did so on the basis of two clear perceptions: first, that the soul is not naturally divine; and, second, that gnosis (important as it is) is not a precondition for salvation.

In a revealing text from the *Excerpts from Theodotus,* a workbook of passages from a Valentinian author with Clement's own comments, Clement put his finger on the difference between the Platonic-Gnostic view of the soul's nature and the one he propounded on the basis of his understanding of the church's tradition:

> We admit that the elect seed is both a spark kindled by the Logos and a pupil of the eye and a grain of mustard seed and leaven which unites in faith the genera which appear to be divided. But the followers of Valentinus maintain that when the animal body was fashioned a male seed was implanted by the Logos in the elect soul while it was asleep. . . . Therefore when the Savior came, he awakened the soul and kindled the spark. . . . And after the

Resurrection, by breathing the Spirit on the apostles, he was blowing off and removing dust like ashes, but kindling and giving life to the spark.[77]

Though obscurely put (as we might expect in this unfinished work), Clement's sense of a contrast between his position and that of the Valentinians is clear—both can use the same terms about the inner reality of the soul, but they understand them in different ways. The Gnostics take them to indicate an original divinity given only to the few, one forgotten in taking on flesh and rekindled only in the resurrection. Clement understands the "seed" and like metaphors as expressing the *potentiality* for divinization present in all souls and realized when the soul "unites in faith" (*henopoiousa eis pistin*) through participation in the Christian community.[78] This position conforms to the picture richly, though often confusingly, presented in his major works, the *Paedagogus* and the *Stromateis*. It also points to the second major contribution of Clement, his refusal to make gnosis and its possessors (the "Gnostics") the norm of salvation in Jesus.

Clement's thoughts on this issue may not be fully resolved. Two positions seem to be at war in his writings. One affirms the superiority of the Gnostic over the ordinary believer and even argues, not unlike the Valentinians, for a kind of "true church" within the church. The other insists that all believers can be saved (though they may enjoy different rewards) and that all spiritual life and insight are grounded in the teaching of the ecclesial community.[79] From later perspectives, Clement's modified esotericism may seem suspect; from the viewpoint of the struggles of second-century Christianity it highlights his important break from the hard-line Gnostics.

The seventh book of the *Stromateis* summarizes (insofar as Clement ever "summarized" anything) his teaching about the perfect Gnostic's superiority over the simple believer:

> Though the simple believer may succeed in one or other of the points mentioned, yet it must be remembered that he cannot do so in all, nor with perfect science (*epistēmē*) like the Gnostic. And further, of our Gnostic's apathy (*apatheia*), if I may use the term, according to which the perfecting of the believer advances through love (*agapē*), till it arrives at the perfect man, at the measure of the stature (Eph 6:3), being made like to God (*exomoioumenē theiō*) and having become truly equal to the angels (*isangelos* [Luke 20:36])—of this apathy many other evidences from Scripture occur to me. . . . (*Strom.* 7.14.84 [3.60.2–8]).[80]

This passage includes most of Clement's favorite conceptions, described, as usual, in an unsystematic way. Some brief comments on them will reveal much about the Alexandrian's thought.[81]

Although the difference between the simple believer and the Gnostic is central to Clement, his view of the Gnostic is not that of the Gnostics themselves, even the moderate ones, like Valentinus. Belief, not gnosis, is the key to salvation (e.g., *Strom.* 4.18.114; 6.14.108–14). Though the Gnostic will receive the greater reward, what he acquires is not something new or hidden. "The life of the Gnostic is, in my view, no other than the works and words which correspond to the tradition of the Lord" (*Strom.* 7.16.104 [3:73.19–20]; cf. 2.6.31). Gnosis, then, is not something innate in a naturally divine core of the soul, but it is the gift of Christ the Redeemer (*Strom.* 5.4.19; *Paed.* 1.11.57), one that can be acquired more fully through training (e.g., *Strom.* 6.9.78).

Clement is also at pains to sketch out the relations between gnosis and faith and love, far more so than most of the heterodox Gnostics were. It is difficult, however, to systematize a clear theory. Gnosis begins in the historical faith given by Christ: "We define wisdom as certain knowledge, a sure and unbreakable gnosis of divine and human realities, comprehending the present, past and future, which the Lord taught us both through his presence and through the prophets" (*Strom.* 6.7.54 [2:459.9–12]). But the relation between gnosis and love is complex. Some texts portray a progression that gives love (*agapē*) higher status: "Knowledge (*gnōsis*) [is] added to faith and love to knowledge, and to love, the heavenly inheritance" (*Strom.* 7.10.55 [3:41.7–8]; cf. 7.10.57). In many passages, however, the relation between love and gnosis is reciprocal: charity is perfected in gnosis (e.g., *Strom.* 2.9.45; 4.7.54; 6.15.21), and gnosis reaches its fulfillment in charity (e.g., 6.9.78). The discussion in *Stromateis* 7.10.55–58 is a full, though still opaque, summary of Clement's attempts to deal with this problem. Though he does not provide a very successful resolution, Clement appears as a predecessor of later attempts by Christian mystics to deal with two complex and interrelated dyads: reason and ordinary belief on the one hand; and illuminated knowledge (Greek *gnōsis;* Latin *intellectus*) and love (*agapē, erōs*) on the other.

Gnosis, as Clement understands it, has many dimensions. It is the spiritual interpretation of scripture (e.g., *Strom.* 4.4.15; 6.15.31), as well as the knowledge that results from this hermeneutical effort. While it makes use of the philosophy of Plato, who is praised as "a friend of truth and almost inspired by God" (*Strom.* 1.8.42 [2:28.3–4]),[82] its perfection depends primarily on moral effort, the practice of the life of virtue. As P.-T. Camelot has shown, Clement's view of gnosis is an inseparable combination of both theological demonstration and mystical contemplation.[83]

The true Gnostic is the one who has attained the vision of God, *theōria theou.* Clement is the writer responsible for domesticating this term in Christianity — it occurs some eighty-four times in his writings. "The goal of life is vision," as he puts it in the first book of the *Stromateis* (1.25.166

[2:104.1–2]).[84] *Stromateis* 7.3.13 gives a representative text which helps to relate gnosis and *theōria* when it speaks of the Gnostic souls who "keep always moving to higher and yet higher regions, until they no longer greet the divine vision in or by means of mirrors (1 Cor 12:13), but with loving hearts feast forever on the uncloying, never-ending sight. . . . This is the apprehensive vision (*kataleptikē theōria*) of the pure of heart (Matt 5:8)" (*Strom.* 7.3.13 [3:10.10–16]).[85] Clement is obviously speaking here of the perfection of vision (Paul's "face-to-face" vision) which will be enjoyed in heaven, but other texts indicate that such vision will begin on earth: "it is through intelligent action, in obedience to the commands, that the Gnostic arrives at the goal of contemplation . . . till at last he receives the holy reward of his translation hence" (*Strom.* 7.13.83 [3:59.23–25]). *Theōria*, then, is the fruit or goal of gnosis (e.g., 4.22.136). It achieves that perfection which is the goal of human life, a perfection that Clement sometimes speaks of as a union or uniting with God (*Strom.* 7.10.57 [3:41.26–30]).[86] His teaching about divine union is again neither systematic nor developed, but it is clear that he does not propose any type of mystical identity or union of indistinction.[87]

The attaining of *theōria* in this life is a gradual process. Clement speaks of "mystic stages" (*tas prokopas tas mystikas*) that lead to the vision of God (7.10.57).[88] This process of perfection is characterized also in two other closely related ways: as the passage of the soul to a state of "passionlessness" (*apatheia*), and as the gift of divinization (*theopoiēsis*).

Clement's understanding of *apatheia* has been much criticized and also often misunderstood. There can be no question that the Alexandrian took over the language and also much of the meaning of *apatheia* from Stoic moral teaching.[89] But the notion that Clement's "apathetic Gnostic" is a person without feelings, utterly indifferent to the world and unconcerned about his fellow humans is a basic misunderstanding. Stoic moral theory distinguished between the feelings or urges (*oreixeis*) that were necessary as long as we are embodied and the unruly passions (*pathē*) that prevented the soul from correctly evaluating what these feelings might mean for responsible action. As Peter Brown puts it, "Passions were not what we tend to call feelings: they were, rather, complexes which hindered the true expression of feelings. . . . What Clement envisaged, in the ideal of *apatheia*, was a state of final serenity of purpose."[90] Stoic *apatheia*, though primarily introspective, was not incompatible with service to the human community, as witnessed in Clement's older contemporary, the philosopher-emperor Marcus Aurelius (121–180 c.e.). The christianization of *apatheia* heightened the sense of service by giving it a christological focus. In the important discussion of *apatheia* that is found in *Stromateis* 6.9, Christ and, after his resurrection, the apostles are taken as the paradigms for the Gnostic who cannot be dislodged from the love that he bears for God and who can therefore exercise this love toward all without being troubled by passions.[91]

Clement's notion of *apatheia* is based on a distinctive anthropology and moral theory that can make his expressions easy to misunderstand. They were his way (imperfect to be sure) of trying to express how Christ's absolute love for his Father is the moral norm for Christians. The "apathetic" Gnostic, like most later ideals of Christian mysticism, is both active and contemplative: "For the end of the gnostic on earth is in my opinion twofold, in some cases scientific contemplation (*theōria epistemonikē*), in others action" (*Strom.* 7.16.102 [3:72.7-8]). Indeed, Clement, who lived in a time of the revival of persecution, saw the Gnostic martyr as the most perfect type of the perfection of love.

This emphasis on the twofold goal of contemplation and action highlights another place where Clement introduces an important theme that later mystics were to investigate in detail. Nicholas Lobkowicz, in his history of the relations between theory and practice, echoes the doubts of many: "At first sight the message of the Gospel would seem to contain little to support the exaltation of theoretical endeavors and contemplative life found in the Ancients."[92] But Lobkowicz goes on to show both how certain Gospel texts, such as the Mary and Martha incident recounted in Luke 10, were spiritually interpreted to give support to discussions of the relation of contemplation and action, and, more importantly, how Christianity also effected an inner transformation of the original meaning of the categories.[93]

In Greek philosophy *theōria* and *praxis* (literally "watching" and "doing") originally signified two modes of activity at the basis of two forms of life, what we would call the philosophical and the political pursuits. Most Greeks, despite Plato's ideal of the philosopher-ruler, failed to see any real relationship between the two. *Theōria* in the beginning was a broad term that included elements of both scientific theorizing and contemplative gazing or vision of the divine world. Later Greek philosophers, especially among the Neoplatonists, emphasized the contemplative aspect, just as they for the most part denigrated the practical life of politics in comparison with the life of contemplative union with the First Principle. Clement and after him Origen and the other Christian fathers show a similar understanding of *theōria* as primarily a vision of God, and they also agree in according this contemplation supremacy among all human endeavors. Where they do not agree with late pagan philosophers is in their refusal to reject *praxis,* because they had come to understand it not as politics but as the practice of the love for neighbor (*agapē*) enjoined by Jesus (Matt 22:37-39; John 13:34-35), Paul (1 Cor 13:2) and John (1 John 2:9). To cite

Clement once again: "These three things our philosopher attaches to himself: first, speculation (*theōria*); second, the performance of the precepts; third, the forming of good men — these concurring form the Gnostic" (*Strom.* 2.10.46 [2:137.14–16]). Although Clement is not always clear on how the contemplative and the active dimensions of the Christian life are to be related, his insistence that neither can be dismissed is a crucial element in later Christian moral and mystical thought.

Clement was also the first Christian author to make extensive use of the notion of divinization, or becoming like God, as a description of Christian perfection. His *Discourse* (*Protrepticus*) proclaims the famous formula: "I say, the Logos of God became man so that you may learn from man how man may become God" (1:8 [1:9.9–11]).[94] Later in the same work he also introduces the Greek verb for divinizing (*theopoiein*) into Christian literature when he speaks of God divinizing the human through his teaching (*Prot.* 11.114 [1:81.1]).[95] The teaching appears throughout the *Stromateis* in countless passages, either ones using the familiar terminology of becoming "like God" (*homoiosis theou*) (e.g., *Strom.* 2.22.131 [2:185]),[96] or others employing the language of participation (e.g., *Strom.* 5.10.63 [2:369.1–2]). To cite just one central text from book 7: "he who obeys the Lord and follows the prophecy given through him, is fully perfected after the likeness of his teacher, and thus becomes a god [*theos* without the article] while still moving about in the flesh" (*Strom.* 7.16.101 [3:31.19–21]).[97]

Clement does not use the text from 2 Pet 1:4 about becoming partakers in the divine nature as a warrant for his teaching on divinization, but he does make use of two other texts popular with the fathers, Ps 81:6 (e.g., *Paed.* 1.5.26) and Luke 20:36 (e.g., *Strom.* 4.25.155; 7.14.84). These passages are useful proof texts, but the root of the Christian doctrine of divinization, developed by the Greek fathers on the basis of a Platonic background, is not to be found in just a few proof texts, but rather in the consonance the fathers saw between the believer's identification with Christ, the God-man, as taught by Paul and John, and the teaching of the best philosophers about the goal of human existence. Sharing in the divine nature, becoming *isangelos*, or equal to the angels (Luke 20:36), is not to become identical with Christ or the Hidden Father. In the fluid language of participation, it is to become "godlike," that is, to be divinized. One may well think of it as the Christian answer to the false "divinizations" of Greek culture heroes, such as Hercules, and contemporary emperors, that is, as another part of their corrective response to the world around them. Divinization, one of the central soteriological concepts of Eastern Christianity, was an important part of the background of later, full-blown theories of mysticism, as we shall see them in thinkers such as Origen and Augustine.

Clement's distinction between the divinity of the Logos and the divinization we gain through him makes special sense against the background of
his strongly apophatic view of the divine nature. Here too Clement is a
trailblazer, though again a rather disorganized one. As a part of the broad
movement of Middle Platonism toward a more radically transcendent view
of the First Principle, Clement utilized a number of the familiar Platonic
tags about the unknowability and inexpressibility of God,[98] but does not
seem to have evolved a consistent dialectical apophaticism on the basis of
Parmenidean paradoxes, as Plotinus and his followers later did. The Alexandrian author framed his apophaticism, like all his thought, within his
sense of the agreement of the best philosophers with the Johannine message
that "no one has ever seen God; it is only the Son, who is nearest to the
Father's heart, who has made him known" (John 1:18). Many of his considerations of divine unknowability are set within a context of an argument
whose purpose is to emphasize Christ as the only source we have into the
Divine Abyss.[99] The opening of the fifth book of the *Stromateis* summarizes:
"Now neither is knowledge without faith, nor faith without knowledge. Nor
is the Father without the Son, for the Son is with the Father. And the Son
is the true teacher respecting the Father" (*Strom.* 5.1.1 [2:326]).[100]

The relationship of Clement's theology to the gospel and to the history
of Christian thought in general is part of the wider question about the
legitimacy of the mystical element in Christian faith. Theologians and
historians of Christianity who are suspicious of mysticism have been quick
to point out how much Clement took from his Greek background and how
little of his theology conforms to their own definitions of the essence of
Christianity.[101] Other scholars have judged Clement more leniently, if not
always uncritically.[102] Certainly, Clement's works are both unsystematic
and to some degree one-sided. Some elements of the esotericism of his
opponents and also of the intellectualism of some of his Platonic forebears
cling to a theology that, for all it problems, still tries to present a Christian
view of the soul's relation to God.[103]

Origen: The Master of Early Christian Thought

Origen *adimantios* ("man of steel") is one of the most remarkable figures
in the history of Christianity.[104] Twenty years older than that other great
third-century Egyptian mystical thinker, Plotinus (both apparently studied
under the mysterious and influential Platonist Ammonius Saccas), he was
born into a pious Christian family of Alexandria about 185 c.e. Origen's
father, Leonides, saw to it that he was well educated in both the classical
Hellenic *paideia* and in the scriptures. When Leonides died a martyr in the

persecution of Septimius Severus in 202, the young Origen was restrained from offering himself for martyrdom only by his mother's hiding his clothes. Shortly after this he was appointed catechist for the Christian community, a position he held until his departure from Alexandria for Caesarea about 233.

The young catechist was both a model of the classical philosopher and the Christian ascetic in his devotion to study, rigorous lifestyle, and avoidance of sexual pleasure (Eusebius speaks of his voluntary emasculation). "For very many years he persisted in this philosophic way of life, putting away from him all inducements to youthful lusts, and at all times of the day disciplining himself by performing strenuous tasks, while he devoted most of the night to the study of Holy Scripture" (Eusebius, *Church History* 6.3.9). Under the patronage of a wealthy Christian, Ambrose, Origen began his extensive literary production between 215 and 220. The Christian philosopher's growing fame led to trips to Rome, to Athens, to Arabia, and to Palestine. While in Palestine he was ordained presbyter, which led to a break with Demetrius, bishop of Alexandria. This was the cause for his abandonment of Alexandria for Caesarea, where he spent the final twenty years of his life in the same intense preaching, teaching, and writing that had characterized his earlier years. Gregory Thaumaturgos, who studied with him at Caesarea, gives the following testimony to the effect of his teaching:

And thus, like some spark lighting upon our inmost soul, love was kindled and burst into flame within us — a love at once to the Holy Word, the most lovely object of all, who attracts all irresistibly towards himself by his unutterable beauty, and to this man, his friend and advocate. . . . And in my estimation there arose but one object dear and worth desire — to wit, philosophy, and that master of philosophy, that divine man. (*Panegyric* 6.83–84)[105]

The long peace that the church had enjoyed during Origen's adult life was broken by the emperor Decius in 250. Origen, who had never ceased to regard martyrdom as the true goal of the Christian, was arrested and tortured, but not put to death. He appears to have died in 253 or 254.

Perhaps only a third of Origen's vast corpus, said by some to have numbered six thousand volumes (i.e., papyrus roles), by others two thousand, survives because of the destruction of many writings after his condemnation for heresy in the sixth century.[106] What does remain, however, is sufficient to provide a good picture of this immensely creative and influential thinker. Although his treatise *On First Principles* (*De principiis* in its surviving Latin text), which is a speculative consideration of the foundations of Christian thought, is his best known work, and although he wrote other important treatises, especially *On Prayer* and *Exhortation to Martyrdom,* Origen was first and foremost an exegete, perhaps the greatest that Christianity has ever known.[107] His work on scripture falls into three basic categories: establishment of the text, preaching, and detailed commentary. First, he sought to provide Christians with a critical biblical text through his compilation of the *Hexapla,* or six-column version of the Old Testament. He also labored to explain difficulties and obscurities in the text by means of his *scholia.* Second, he preached the moral and spiritual meaning of the whole Bible to the Christian liturgical community in the hundreds of homilies he delivered both at Alexandria and later at Caesarea (some 279 survive). Finally, he wrote extensive commentaries on the full inner meaning, verse by verse, of almost all the biblical books. Many of the most important of these, such as that on Genesis, are lost. Fortunately, those that remain, especially the surviving books of his great *Commentary on John*[108] and the three remaining books of the original ten of his *Commentary on the Song of Songs,*[109] are crucial to understanding his mystical thought.

Origen is exemplary of most of the figures to be considered in the first two volumes of this history in combining the roles of exegete, theologian (both dogmatic and speculative), and mystic.[110] Furthermore, his mysticism, while not monastic in the technical sense to be considered in the following section, can be described as at least protomonastic.[111] Origen's ascetic life-style and his fostering of the ideal of virginity look forward to the "monastic turn" in early Christian spirituality; and his thought, as mediated through Evagrius Ponticus, Gregory of Nyssa, Cassian, and others, was the major force that shaped the theology that grew out of the desert experience. Through both his direct and his indirect influence, he occupies a special position in later Christian theories of mysticism.

Given the intimacy of the relation of exegesis, speculative theology, and mysticism found in Origen's thought, it is impossible to present any one of these elements without giving at least some attention to the others. Though it may be true that Origen was not a systematic theologian in the sense that Thomas Aquinas and John Calvin were (no patristic theologian was),[112] he wrote from a coherent and carefully thought out perspective, even when the positions he advanced were tentative or even experimental. His theology was formed primarily by the tradition of the teaching of the Christian community (in both his life commitment and his thought Origen was always a church teacher),[113] but as a good Alexandrian he also thought that this message was the true "philosophy," the love of wisdom that the Greeks had aimed at, but had not been able to achieve.

Ancient philosophy, especially as found in Plato, had discerned wisdom's true object in the study of the meaning of the cosmos and its mirror image, the human conceived as microcosm. Origen did not deny the importance of these correlative sources for true wisdom, but as a Christian he was convinced that fallen humanity could no longer find the truth through contemplation of the heavens or the study of humans in society. In our present condition, the truth about the self cannot be known from the first "intelligible world," but is only accessible through a new noetic object: the intelligible world of the revealed scriptures. The intimate relation between reading the scripture and reading the self (and, by extension, knowing how to read the cosmos) is brought out in a well-known passage from the treatise on hermeneutics found in the fourth book of *On First Principles:*

> One must therefore portray the meaning of the sacred writings in a threefold way upon one's own soul, so that the simple man may be edified by what we may call the flesh of scripture . . . , while the man who has made some progress may be edified by its soul, as it were; and the man who is perfect . . . may be edified by the spiritual law. . . . For just as man consists of body, soul and spirit, so in the same way does the scripture, which has been prepared by God to be given for man's salvation. (4.2.4)[114]

Note that this isomorphism is dynamic: the true relation of the three components of the human is discerned through the personal appropriation of the three levels of the scriptural message. Karen Torjesen suggests that the process can be likened to placing the believer *within* the text and inscribing its meaning on his or her soul.[115] Origen is interested not so much in determining different meanings of the text as in using the encounter with the text as the paradigm for the spiritual education (*paideia*, training) by means of which the goal of life is attained.

Several excellent studies of Origen's exegesis exist, so only those points necessary for understanding his mysticism need to be taken up here. In determining the literal sense of the biblical text, Origen was conscious of a twofold task: first, grasping the grammatical sense of the words (*pros rhēton*), the work he undertook in the *Hexapla* and *scholia;* and, second, discovering the historical reality of the passage (*kath' historian*). To deny that a passage was to be taken literally was merely to say that it could not or did not happen historically (see *De prin.* 4.2.5), not to claim that the grammatical meaning of the words did not contain a deeper message for believers. Scripture in its entirety is nothing else than the Logos teaching each believer in and through the church. The Logos eternally begotten from the Father's self-emptying, who in turn emptied himself by taking on flesh, now becomes present and active in us through the mediation of his presence in the inspired words of the scripture.[116]

Following Paul, Origen taught the necessity of advancing beyond the "letter that kills" to the level of spiritual meaning (1 Cor 10:1–11; 2 Cor

3:4–18; Gal 4:21–31) by making use of the events and persons of the Old Testament as "types" (*typoi,* 1 Cor 10:11) and "allegories" (*allēgoroumenoi,* literally, "things spoken allegorically" in Gal 4:24) of present realities. In order to find out what the Logos is teaching in any passage, it is necessary to make use of a wide variety of allegorical and typological tools (Origen and the fathers did not clearly distinguish between these two approaches, despite the claims of some modern writers).[117] These techniques are to be applied to the New Testament as well as the Old, though with the important difference that the teaching of the Logos is direct in the former and mediated through others in the latter. Allegorical and typological exegesis is part of Origen's inheritance from both the Jewish and the Hellenistic past. His real originality, as Torjesen suggests, was in being the first Christian to describe the personal appropriation of the Logos's teaching as an "anagogic" reading, one designed to lift the soul above. "The scribe of the gospel is one who knows how, after studying the narrative of the events (*historias*), to ascend to the spiritual realities (*epi ta pneumatika aptaiston anagogē*) without stumbling."[118] The goal of interpretation is to realize the Bible's teaching through our own ascension to God, a process that Origen once expressed as wishing "to gallop through the vast spaces of mystic and spiritual understanding" (*Commentary on Romans* 7.11 [*PG* 14:1132D]).[119]

Ascent of the soul back to its source in God implies a prior descent, thus introducing us to Origen's speculative thought, one deeply colored by Platonism, but a Platonism in many ways altered and transformed.[120] Origen's Platonism is resolutely Christian in distinguishing God as true being (*ousia*) from everything else, that is, all that constitutes the world of becoming; and it is essentially Platonic in finding in God's supreme goodness the ground for his connection with the created realm.[121] The Alexandrian, like all Greek Christian writers of the pre-Constantinian period, was concerned to counter the attacks of Marcion and the Gnostics on the goodness of the Creator God; but against the religious view of paganism, which saw God and the gods as all participating in an essentially good cosmos, he was equally anxious to maintain God's transcendence of the world. In his treatment of the divine nature in *On First Principles* 1.1 he makes it clear that God alone is true and substantial being; all other things exist "accidentally" by participating in him.[122] Because he does not participate in being but all beings participate in him, Origen is willing at times to use Plato's formula (*Republic* 509B) and speak of God as being beyond being itself,[123] though he does not have a highly developed apophatic theology.[124]

The transcendental manifestation of the goodness of God the Father (Origen, following Johannine usage, restricted the term *ho theos* to the

Father, using *theos* of the Son and Holy Spirit) (*Comm. on Jn.* 2.1-2 [12-18]) is to be found in the generation of the Son, who is the Logos, the only true image of God. Two things are evident in Origen's doctrine of the Logos (and by extension his less-developed teaching about the Holy Spirit): first, his insistence that the Son is truly divine and coeternal with the Father; and, second, his use of what later theology would describe as subordinationist language in trying to express the difference between the Father and the Son.[125] More important from the speculative point of view, as well as for Origen's mystical theology, is the Logos's role in the creation of the world, the extradivine manifestation of the Father's goodness. The absolute unity of the Father first becomes manifest in the Logos in whom he creates the intelligible universe, that is, the ideas or causes which are the prototypes for everything that comes to exist in the actual universe. This creation (like Meister Eckhart's virtual creation of all things in their Principle, the Word) is eternal (cf. *De prin.* 1.4.3-5). We know these divine ideas (though only partially and in a divided manner) through the various titles or names (*epinoiai*) that are given to Christ. Much of Origen's Christology consists in the analysis of the *epinoiai,* as book 1 of the *Commentary on John* shows. The Logos is both the model of creation and the intelligent agent through which the Father produces it.[126]

If God is good and all-powerful, how are we to account for division, hierarchy (implying higher and lower), and especially evil in the world? The thrust of Origen's theodicy leads him to one of the characteristic (and to later generations most questionable) aspects of his teaching—the affirmation of a prior and perfect creation whose fall made necessary the world we inhabit. In his first *Homily* on Genesis, Origen asserts ". . . that first heaven, which we said is spiritual, is our mind, which is also itself spirit, that is, our spiritual man which sees and perceives God" (*Hom. on Gen.* 1.2).[127] The original spiritual creation was composed of "intellects" (*noi*) all created equal after the pattern of the only true image, the Logos (*Hom. on Gen.* 1.12-13). This is the creation described in the first chapter of Genesis. These intellects, each guided by a *pneuma,* or participation in the Holy Spirit, were joined to spiritual bodies and lived a joyous life of contemplation of God, "a pure and perfect reception of God into itself" (*De prin.* 4.4.9).[128] Together they constituted the supreme unity of the preexistent church under the headship of the one intellect which was perfectly united in love with the Logos, that is, the intellect of the preexistent Christ.

The fundamental characteristic of these intellects, however, was the freedom given to them by God—divine goodness and the freedom of spiritual creation are the lynchpins of Origen's thought. It was this freedom that made possible the original fall from perfect contemplation:

For the Creator granted to the minds created by him the power of free and voluntary movement, in order that the good that was in them might become their own, since it was preserved by their own free will. But sloth and weariness of taking trouble to preserve the good, coupled with disregard and neglect of better things, began the process of withdrawal from the good. (*De prin.* 2.9.2 [Butterworth, p. 130])

Origen, like other Platonists both pagan and Christian, has difficulty explaining the nature of this fall (can there really be an *explanation* of evil?). Perhaps, as Patricia Cox suggests, we may best think of it as "a failure of imagination."[129] There is no denying, however, that this postulate of a prior fall was important for the consistency of Origen's theodicy. Diversity and evil in our present world do not denigrate the Creator's goodness, but measure the degree of the fall from perfect contemplation. Angels are intellects who remain within contemplative "striking distance" of the original harmony. Humans are intellects who fell farther and were provided a second, material creation as the arena,—or, better, schoolroom—to work out their destinies. Demons are fixed (perhaps) in unalterable opposition to God. The material creation (which Origen apparently found mentioned in the "tunics of skins" of Gen 3:21) was not so much a punishment as an educational opportunity. This accounts for the ambiguous role of matter in Origen's thought. Matter is not evil; it is a good gift of a good Creator. But it is a limited good whose real purpose is to teach intellects to ascend above it in the their path back to unimpeded vision of God.

The fallen intellects constitute the core of the human person, whom, as we have seen, Origen thinks of as constituted by three levels. Following the famous Pauline formula (1 Thess 5:23), Origen distinguished: (1) *pneuma,* or spirit, the created participation in the Holy Spirit, which has become inert in fallen humanity; (2) *pyschē,* or soul, which is the "cooled" state of intellect in the fallen condition, able either to be redirected above to contemplation of God through the instruction of spirit, or else dragged below by the *sensus carnalis* (see Rom 8:6) to the level of (3) *sōma,* the body, humanity's material component.[130] But the body, it must be emphasized, is not evil; rather, it is a boon given by the Creator "to challenge the potentially mighty spirit of each to stretch beyond itself," as Peter Brown notes following *On First Principles* 3.2.3.[131] Because each intellect was created "after the image," that is, as a participation in the Logos,[132] it remains capable of regaining its original state of contemplative likeness to God (see Gen 1:26) through the pedagogic activity of the Logos. Origen at one place advises his listeners: "Let us always, therefore, contemplate that Image of God so that we can be transformed to his likeness" (*Hom. on Gen.* 1.13).[133]

If the process of restoration or return can be effected only through the activity of the Logos, we can ask how the Logos actually repairs the damage done by the fall and restores all things to the Father. In this area, too, Origen's Christian Platonism is the prototype for many subsequent theologies in its understanding of how the Platonic world model of emanation and return requires a twofold activity of the second person of the Trinity. As pure Logos, he serves as model and artificer (thus combining the roles of the Ideas and the Demiurge from the *Timaeus*), and, as *Logos-sarx*, he becomes the necessary medium of return.

In good Platonic fashion, two extremes can only be joined by some medium (*Timaeus* 31C). The Logos or Word can take on a body only through the mediation of the unfallen intellect of the preexistent Christ.[134] As Origen puts it in book 2 of *On First Principles:*

> . . . that soul of which Jesus said, "No man taketh from me my soul" (John 10:18), clinging to God from the beginning of the creation and ever after in a union inseparable and indissoluble, . . . was made with him in a pre-eminent degree one spirit, just as the apostle promises to them whose duty it is to imitate Jesus, that "he who is joined to the Lord is one spirit" (1 Cor 6:17). From this soul, then acting as a medium between God and flesh (for it was not possible for the nature of God to mingle with a body apart from some medium), there is born, as we said, the God-man. . . . (*De prin.* 2.6.3 [Butterworth, p. 110])

Through Jesus' unfailing love and unbroken contemplation of God, his soul becomes the model and teacher for all other souls as they awaken the *pneuma* within themselves and begin to return to God.

If the Creator's loving goodness is the fundamental principle grounding the flow of all things out from God, both in the first and the second creations, the oft-repeated axiom, "the end is always like the beginning," forms the basis for Origen's understanding of the return of all things to the Father through Christ.[135] "We believe that the goodness of God through Christ will restore his entire creation to one end, even his enemies being conquered and subdued" (*De prin.* 1.6.1 [Butterworth, p. 52]). This insight, which Origen found expressed in Paul's words that in the end God will be "all in all" (1 Cor 15:28) is fundamental to his mysticism. It also involves serious problems, from the viewpoint of later Christian orthodoxy, concerning his view of the universal return of all spirits, perhaps even the demons, to God in the *apokatastasis.*[136]

The central metaphor Origen uses for this process of return is that of a journey upward, an ascension — the notion that may well be taken as the main motif of his mysticism.[137] This mode of presenting the life of the spirit, of course, is one common to many religious traditions, and there can be no doubt that Origen's adaptation of it was dependent on a generalized

Platonic world view; but his *theologia ascendens* (to use von Balthasar's phrase) departs from Platonism both in its Christocentrism and in its biblical foundation.[138] The whole message of scripture is the descent and ascent of the Incarnate Word to rescue the fallen intellects. Thus, the history of Israel and the other nations recounted in the Old Testament is to be read as an account of the fall and rise of souls.[139] The New Testament recounts the Word's descent and ascent more directly, though still mysteriously. All the other metaphors that Origen employs to present the message of return, especially those of warfare and of growth or education,[140] are subservient to the unifying symbol of the *pascha,* the passage above achieved by and in Christ.[141] Though it would be incorrect to ascribe the popularity of the ascent motif in Christian mysticism to Origen alone, there can be no doubt that his emphasis on itinerary had great influence on many later mystics.

The Alexandrian's presentations of the soul's journey are multiple, nuanced, and even poetic in character.[142] They are presented in the language of scripture personally appropriated through the act of exegesis. Marguerite Harl has pointed out that the Greek fathers, especially Clement, Origen, and the Cappadocians, used the adjective *mystikos* not to describe their own experience or language but rather to characterize the language of scripture and, by extension, those Christian rituals and activities in which the Word also is objectively present.[143] As Origen said in introducing the story of Rebecca: "The words which have been read are mystical; they are to be explained in allegorical mysteries" (*Hom. on Gen.* 10.1).[144] The difficult and wandering journey by which the soul returns to God begins from the clear "bread" of direct scriptural language, but can only advance through ingestion of the "wine" of scripture, its obscure and poetic speech, which intoxicates and draws upward. Here words must be understood in strange and transposed ways, more connotatively than denotatively.[145] Allegory is the continual search for God through successive recognitions of the truth (*Hom. on Num.* 17.4).[146]

Thus Origen's "theological poiesis"[147] is an exegetical process in which religious experience, especially mystical experience, is realized in the act of making the language of the Bible at its deepest and incommunicable level into the soul's language. As Harl puts it: "The Bible furnished Christian writers citations corresponding to a verbal and gestural thematizing of the encounter with God. . . . Citation makes it possible for the experience of a single person not to remain isolated: it authenticates individual experience by situating it within the collective experience of the people of God."[148] No one in Christian antiquity achieved this more fully than Origen, who, according to Harl, "knew his most vivid religious experiences within that particular Christian *place* which is the work of exegesis."[149]

Origen presents the soul's exegetical-mystical ascent according to a basic triple pattern of pedagogy which he took over from Greek philosophy but argued could be truly learned only from the Bible.[150] He found the pattern clearly illustrated in the three books ascribed to Solomon. Proverbs teaches what the Greeks call moral science, the proper manner of virtuous living which corresponds to the life of the patriarch Abraham and to what later Christians would call the purgative way. Ecclesiastes presents natural science, that is, enlightened knowledge of the natures of things and of how they are to be used as God intended (corresponding to Isaac and the illuminative way). Finally, the Song of Songs is the textbook for what Origen calls "epoptics," or "disciplina inspectiva," which "instils love and desire of celestial and divine things under the image of the Bride and the Groom, teaching how we come to fellowship with God through paths of love and charity" (*Comm. on Song* prol. [ed. 76.14–16; Lawson, p. 41]). When the soul has completed the first two courses of study, "it is ready to come to dogmatic and mystical matters and to arise to the contemplation of divinity with pure spiritual love" (ibid. [ed. 78.17–19; Lawson, p. 44]). This is the science of Jacob who became Israel (etymologically, "he who sees God"). It forms the unitive or properly mystical level — in one place Origen even calls this mode of knowing *mystika*, that is, "mystics" (*Comm. on Lam.* frg. 14 [GCS Origen 3:241.3ff.]).[151]

These three broad stages (ancestral of so much to come) do not, of course, mean that the journey is either simple or direct. In his twenty-seventh homily on Numbers Origen presents a more complicated itinerary of gain and loss, presence and absence, figured in the forty-two stages or camps of Israel's wandering through the desert from the Egypt of this world to the promised heavenly land (Numbers 33) (*Hom. on Num.* 27 [GCS Origen 7:255–80]).[152] It is not necessary to follow all the details of this reading (much of it based on etymologies of the place-names involved) to grasp the essentials of the message. "The true food of a rational nature is the Word of God" (*Hom. on Num.* 27.1), but the Word gives himself to different readers according to their capacities. Only those capable of mystical insight will catch the hint that the forty-two camps to which Israel ascends "in their power" (Num 33:1) and the forty-two generations of Christ's ancestors given in the Gospels indicate that "the person who ascends, ascends with him who descended from there to us" (*Hom. on Num.* 27.3); that is, a strict relation ties our ascent to Christ's descent. The conversion that begins with our departure from Egypt (interpreted both as moral conversion in this life and the soul's departure from the body in death) initiates a complex itinerary marked by constant warfare against demonic temptation (i.e., the pursuit of pharaoh and his army).[153] The goal is not the darkness encountered on Sinai's height (the apophatic symbol favored by Philo and later by Gregory of Nyssa and Dionysius), but the light and abundance of the promised land.[154] While Origen neither denies the ultimate unknowability of the Father nor neglects the negative scriptural symbols that portray this, his temperament (like that of Augustine and Bernard — to mention only two of his most illustrious successors) inclines him to concentrate on the positive rather than the negative aspects of the enjoyment of God's presence. The oft-repeated characterization of Origen as "mystic of light" is true, at least on this point.

The journey as portrayed by Origen includes a consideration of what later generations will call the discernment of spirits (*Hom. on Num.* 27.11), as well as more properly mystical aspects, such as in the mention of ecstasy in stage 23 ("Thara" or "Terah" of Num 33:27), which Origen interprets as a "contemplation of amazement . . . when the mind is struck with amazement by the knowledge of great and marvellous things" (see *Hom. on Num.* 27.12). This ecstasy, as we shall see below, is not a ravishing from the senses, but a sudden new insight into the divine mysteries revealed in scripture.

In developing the theme of the soul's return to God, Origen makes use of a variety of symbols and images drawn from the Bible. Crouzel has distinguished a group of symbols of grace (light, life, and food) from what he calls "nuptial themes," and doubtless different perspectives could enrich and alter these classifications.[155] Given the Alexandrian's claim that the Song of Songs is the central textbook for "epoptics," that is, the place where scripture reveals the heart of its message about the love of the descending Christ for the fallen soul, it is in the interpretation of the erotic language of the Song that the deepest inscription of the mystical message takes place.

Origen's use of erotic symbolism — such as the wound of love (Isa 49:2; Song 2:5), the kiss of the lovers (Song 1:1 and elsewhere), the embrace (Song 2:6) — introduces us to one of the most complex and controversial aspects of the history of Christian mysticism.[156] The Alexandrian stands at the head of those Christian mystics who have argued that of all the positive or cataphatic modes of speaking available to the mystic, erotic language is the most appropriate way of using speech to surpass itself.[157] This claim has been harshly judged, especially by those modern scholars who argue that the insistence of many Christian mystics on abstention from sex as a necessary condition for achieving real experience of God in this life is artificial and even dangerous.

The arguments of some modern psychologists that the introduction of considerable erotic language about God into a mystical account cannot be more than a disguise and an attempt at sublimating hidden sexual urges,[158] and the claims of some philosophers that Western philosophical and theological notions of love are erotic idealizations that remove the subject from the reality of desire by making it the basis for some form of mental glorification,[159] illustrate the fundamental differences between the way traditional Christian mystics viewed love and desire and how this force is often seen in the contemporary world. The mystics insisted that they were neither disguising nor idealizing eros, but rather transforming it by leading it back to its original form. While this issue will be taken up in more detail in the final volume of this series, what we need to do at the outset, especially in the case of Origen, is to be as clear as we can about what he thought he was and was not doing in giving erotic language this privileged position.

Simone Weil once noted that "to reproach mystics with loving God by means of the faculty of sexual love is as though one were to reproach a painter with making pictures by means of colors composed of material substances."[160] Origen, the first Christian mystic to discuss the transformation of desire, would have agreed. While Origen recognized that the erotic and the sexual were not the same (the power of desire can be directed to material objects other than those of sexual gratification) (*Comm. on Song* prol. [ed. 8; Lawson, p. 36]), as an heir to the Greek tradition of eros he gave the pursuit and enjoyment of the beloved person the status of paradigm for all the modes of eros. But Origen also agreed with Plato and the other sages that although eros is usually experienced in relation to a human lover, it is in reality a heavenly force: "the power of love is none other than that which leads the soul from earth to the lofty heights of heaven, and . . . the highest beatitude can only be attained under the stimulus of love's desire" (ibid. [ed. 63.9–11; Lawson, p. 24]). Plato taught this, as we have seen, because he conceived of eros as a demigod, a desire to attain what is perfect and to beget from this attainment. Origen, adapting Platonic eros to his Christian faith, makes a daring breakthrough—God himself must be Eros if the eros implanted in us is what returns us to him.

The debate initiated by Anders Nygren over the validity of Origen's equation of the *agapē* with which the Greek Bible identifies God (e.g., 1 John 4:8) and the *erōs* of the Greek tradition (twice used of God in the Septuagint translation!) has obscured one of the most radical shifts in the history of Platonism.[161] The Christian belief in a transcendent God who "chooses" (however we understand this) to "go out" of himself in creation implies something like the yearning desire of *erōs,* and hence Origen says "I do not think one could be blamed if one called God Passionate Love (*erōs/amor*), just as John calls him Charity" (*agapē/caritas*) (*Comm. on Song* prol. [ed. 71.22–25; Lawson, p. 35]). Therefore, "you must take whatever scripture says about charity (*caritas*) as if it had been said in reference to passionate love (*amor*), taking no notice of the difference in terms; for the same meaning is conveyed by both" (ibid. [ed. 70.32–71.1; Lawson, p. 34]). Pagan Neoplatonists, especially Plotinus and Proclus, were tentatively to follow suit in giving *erōs* a transcendental role, perhaps in emulation of the Christians, though this would be difficult to prove.[162]

Origen took the notion of God as Eros with great seriousness. Few ancient thinkers have more clearly expressed the tension between the realization of God's yearning for the world and the power of the Parmenidean notion of the absolute unchangeability of the Ultimate. "God so loved the world" (John 3:16) was not a mere metaphor for him. Many are aware that in a few texts Origen dares to assert a kind of "suffering" in God,[163] and some Origen scholars, such as Hans Urs von Balthasar, have argued that the "passion of Word" in emptying himself to take on flesh is one of Origen's most profound theological insights.[164]

If, as Origen believed, eros has its source above and has been implanted in us by God-Eros (we could call this EROS I), the motive force powering the soul's ascent must be the transformation of the eros gone awry in us (eros ii) back to its transcendental starting place. Origen's *Commentary on the Song of Songs* contains the first Christian theoretical exposition of this transformation.[165]

The transformation is governed primarily by the teleological specification of the objects of desire, that is, Origen begins by insisting that eros ii can only be transformed by turning it away from the inferior material and human objects to which it has become directed in its fallen state. Hence, any form of erotic practice, especially sexual love (even that legitimately allowed by the church) is irrelevant (or more likely harmful) for the transformative process.[166] Origen's emphasis on the privileged role of virginity as the manifestation of the soul's preexisting purity and God-directed freedom, well analyzed by Peter Brown in *The Body and Society,*[167] marks the earliest theoretical defense of the strict division between sexual practice and mystical endeavor. It has also been one of the distinctive marks of classical Christian mysticism, though we cannot ascribe the triumph of the ideal of virginity to Origen's influence alone, as we shall see in the following section.

Origen bases this disjunction on the identification of Paul's notion of the inner and the outer person (e.g., 2 Cor 4:16), that is, the flesh and the spirit, with the two creations. The inner person is the one created "in the image and likeness of God" (Gen 1:26); the outer is that "formed from the slime of the earth" (Gen 2:7). The objects to which the latter directs eros ii, be they either unworthy lower things such as money, vainglory, or sexual pleasure, or even the higher goods of human arts and learning, are all transitory and unworthy of true eros. The only true goal of eros is the spiritual good of the first creation, the manifestation of EROS I: "by that which is good we understand not anything corporeal, but only that which is found first in God and in the powers of the soul — it follows that the only laudable love is that which is directed to God and to the powers of the soul" (*Comm. on Song* prol. [ed. 72.25–73.1; Lawson, p. 36]). Thus, for one who thinks only on the level of *amor carnalis,* the Song of Songs should not even be read (Origen here cites the rabbinic prohibition against reading the Song before mature years);[168] but the one who possesses *amor caelestis,* namely, that soul who has been pierced by the dart or wound of love from the Word himself, finds in the Song the central message of the Bible (*Comm. on Song* prol. [ed. 66:29–67.16; Lawson, pp. 22–23]).[169]

But how exactly does the spiritual person learn to read the inner text behind the erotic images and longing language of the lovers in the Song of Songs? Here Origen bridges the gap between the inner and the outer person, between heavenly and carnal love, by means of the teaching about the spiritual senses of the soul (*aisthēsis pneumatikē, aisthēsis theia*) that he developed from Clement of Alexandria. This is one of his most important contributions to the history of Christian mysticism.[170]

According to the Alexandrian, "the divine scriptures make use of homonyms, that is to say, they use identical terms for describing different things . . . so that you will find the names of the members of the body transferred to those of the soul; or rather the faculties and powers of the soul are to be called its members" (*Comm. on Song* prol. [ed. 64.16–65.19; Lawson, pp. 26–27]). Therefore, any bodily description contained in the Bible (and what book of scripture contains more potent descriptions of body parts and bodily activities than the Song?) is actually a message about the inner person's relation to the Word because this person possesses "spiritual senses" analogous to the senses of taste and touch, hearing, smell, and sight by which the outer person relates to the material world.[171] Seeking the proper understanding of the erotic language of the Song is the exemplary exercise by which these higher and finer "senses" of the fallen, dormant intellect are awakened and resensitized by the spirit in order to be made capable of receiving the transcendental experience of the presence of the Word. Through these "organs of mystical knowledge,"[172] which Origen calls "a sensuality which has nothing sensual in it,"[173] "the sharpness of sensual experience is brought back to its primordial intensity," as Peter Brown puts it.[174]

On this basis, the language of the Song becomes the best way to read the inner text of the soul.[175] Origen's patient explorations of the shades of meaning implied in the differing spiritual senses (he insisted that some could be regained without others) allowed him to present a richer picture of the relations between the soul and the Word than any Christian thinker before him. His surviving exegesis of the Song, both in the three books of the commentary and the two homilies, provides numerous examples of how the spiritual senses guide the soul's mystical transformation.[176] The same teaching appears throughout his works. Consideration of a few examples will demonstrate his strategy.

Let us start with three erotic images of the senses of touch and taste present in the Song: the kiss of the mouth, the taste of the breasts, and the wound of love. The famous opening verse of the Song ("Let him kiss me with the kisses of his mouth") was to continue to engender multiple interpretations from the exegetes, not only because of the necessity for allegorical rendering of the whole book, but also because of the rather unusual expression of the verse (i.e., why "kisses of the mouth"?). Origen's interpretation, as usual, is both ecclesial and personal, moving through five levels of interpretation (not always as clearly defined as here): (1) from the grammatical citation of the text and (2) its dramatic or historical reconstruction, to (3) the deeper meanings of what it has to say about Christ's relation to the church, (4) its general message about the soul's itinerary, and (5) how we are to appropriate the message as our own.[177] It is not necessary to follow all the steps in detail. The message is that the sensation of receiving kisses is to be read as the mind's reception of the teaching of the Word, conveyed both to the church and the individual soul. "When her mind is filled with divine perception and understanding without the agency of human or angelic ministration, then she may believe that she has received the kisses of the Word of God himself" (*Comm. on Song,* book 1 [ed. 91.12-17; Lawson, p. 61]).[178]

A similar intellectualized reading is given to the images of tasting of breasts that obtrude throughout the Song. "Thy breasts are better than wine" (Song 1:2b LXX) is interpreted as referring to the *principale cordis* (Greek *hēgemonikon*), the inner ground of the heart of Christ upon which John, the beloved disciple, reposed. The treasures of wisdom and knowledge (Col 2:3) that the perfect soul drinks from Christ's breast are even better than the wine she received from the Law and the Prophets (*Comm. on Song,* book 1 [ed. 91-101; Lawson, pp. 62-70]).[179] The two later references to breasts in the surviving commentary also interpret the image in terms of teaching and knowledge. "We will love thy breasts more than wine" (Song 1:3c) is taken as spoken by the maidens, or weak souls, to the Bride, the perfect soul whose own breasts (*hēgemonikon*) are now full from her drinking of Christ's "fullness of spiritual teaching" (*Comm. on Song,* book 1 [ed. 110-111;

Lawson, pp. 87–88]). In Song 1:13 Christ is the "sachet of a myrrh-drop," an odd phrase that Origen understands to refer both to the self-emptying of the Word in becoming flesh, and to "the contents of the divine teachings and the intricacy and complication of the propositions of theology." This hangs between the breasts, which, Origen says, "as we told you before, [are] the ground of the heart in which the church holds fast Christ, or the soul holds the Word of God, fast bound and tied to her by the chains of her desire."[180] (Note that the two earlier passages involved the spiritual sense of taste; in the latter, the sense of smell is to the fore.)

The image of the wound of love, which Origen already referred to in the prologue to the commentary, is more complex. As Crouzel has shown, Origen put together two texts, Isa 49:2 LXX ("He set me as a chosen arrow") and Song 2:5 LXX ("I am wounded with *agapē*), to create a rich and original teaching about the Word as the arrow or dart of the Father (and alternately the sword of Eph 6:17), whose love strikes or wounds the soul (the surviving texts all have an individual, not an ecclesial, application).[181] The theme appears in numerous places in his writings. In the Song commentary the two major treatments have a personal and poignant tone in which the desire for the Word's teaching is expressed as a transcendental erotic obsession:

> If there is anyone anywhere who has at some time burned with this faithful love of the Word of God; if there is anyone who has at some time received the sweet wound of him who is the chosen dart, as the prophet says; if there is anyone who has been pierced with the loveworthy spear of his knowledge, so that he yearns and longs for him by day and night, can speak of naught but him, would hear of naught but him, can think of nothing else, and is disposed to no desire nor longing nor yet hope, except for him alone — if such there be, that soul then says in truth: "I have been wounded by charity." (*Comm. on Song,* book 3 [ed. 194.6–13; Lawson, p. 198])[182]

In passages such as these the spiritual sense of touch brings out a dimension of personal urgency not always found in relation to the other spiritual senses.[183]

This also seems to be suggested by the passages where Origen breaks through the calm web of his didactic tone with expressions of his own longing for the coming of the Word. In book 3 of the *Commentary,* he interprets the embrace of the right and left hands of the Groom (Song 2:6) in a strictly ecclesial way with a warning about the necessity for not taking the erotic image literally (*Comm. on Song,* book 3 [ed. 195–97; Lawson, pp. 200–203]). But in *Homily* 1.2 he applies the verse to the individual soul in a personal way: "For there is a certain spiritual embrace, and O that the Bridegroom's more perfect embrace may enfold my Bride!" (*Hom. on Song* 1.2 [ed.

31.19-22; Lawson, p. 270]).[184] Perhaps the most noted passage in the homilies, one of the few places where he speaks directly of himself, is a description, both exegetical and personal, combining the senses of spiritual seeing and touching:

> God is my witness that I have often perceived the Bridegroom drawing near me and being most intensely present with me; then suddenly he has withdrawn and I could not find him though I sought to do so. I long, therefore, for him to come again and sometimes he does so. Then, when he has appeared and I lay hold of him (*manibus comprehensus*), he slips away once more; and, when he has so slipped away, my search for him begins anew. (*Hom. on Song* 1.7 [ed. 39.17-22; Lawson, p. 280])[185]

Even though we may agree with Marguerite Harl that the Alexandrian is referring to the experience of a special presence of the Word in the act of interpretation, it is not necessary to deny that he is speaking in a voice that is at once that of the Bride in the text and his own.[186]

Although Origen uses the full range of the erotic images of the Song of Songs to describe how the spiritual senses contact the Divine Lover, spiritual "touch" and spiritual "vision" have a certain priority and seem to communicate a more intimate connection. Good Greek that he was, Origen always conceived of the goal of the soul's journey in terms of knowledge, the higher knowledge (*gnōsis*) and mystical vision (*mystikē theōria;* see *Comm. on Jn.* 13.25) of the mystery of Christ.[187] The "spiritual" (*pneumatikos*) or "perfect" (*teleios*) Christian—Origen preferred these terms to Clement's "true Gnostic"—possessed a knowledge of Christ that was both "tactile" (i.e., indicated a real encounter) and "visual" (i.e., denoted mutual possession according to the maxim "like is known by like"). Though Origen admitted two classes of believers in the church (e.g., *Hom. on Gen.* 1.7; *Comm. on Jn.* 1.7), and therefore can be said to incline to a degree of elitism, he, like Clement, was also aware of the danger of making any fundamental division in the body of believers.[188] He makes no appeal to secret tradition or knowledge. While the spiritual elite are superior to simple believers, this places on them obligations of prayer and instruction like those he himself displayed throughout his career as a catechist and homilist.

It is relatively easy to describe the content of this higher knowledge, at least in broad terms, because Origen provides us with several lists of the basic categories of spiritual truths which the Word conveys through the scriptures (notably in *De prin.* 4.2.7). Considerable disagreement exists, however, about whether this knowing is best described in "intellectual" or in "affective" terms.

Henri Crouzel, whose *Origène et la "connaissance mystique"* is the basic work on the subject, says that for Origen "knowledge is a vision or direct contact, it is a participation in its object, better still it is union, 'mingling' with its object, and love."[189] This knowledge involves a personal relation to Jesus of which Origen often spoke in moving fashion, as we have seen.[190] The intimacy of the union is suggested not only by the dominant image of the Bride and Groom, but also (in a different way) by the procreative symbol of birthing. Thus, Origen can speak of the loving soul as both Bride and Mother: "And every soul, virgin and uncorrupted, which conceives by the Holy Spirit, so as to give birth to the Will of the Father, is the Mother of Jesus" (*Comm. on Mt.* frg. 281 [GCS Origen 12.1:126.10–15]).[191] In his view of the mystic's soul as at once virgin and mother, Origen is an initiator of a potent theme in the history of Christian mysticism,[192] one that displays surprising parallels with later mystics, for example, Meister Eckhart.[193]

Thus, Origen's mystical gnosis is intellectual but also affective, a possession of the truth that satisfies both the noetic and the erotic dynamism of the soul. While we have seen that there is clearly room for a loving dimension in Plotinus's view of contemplation of the *Nous,* the heightened affectivity we find in Origen is closer to that present in many later Christian mystics, such as Augustine.[194] Although he does not use the formula popular later in the Middle Ages that "love is a form of knowing" (*amor ipse intellectus est*), there are many ways in which he agrees with it. In a text in the nineteenth book in the *Commentary on John* he understands Adam's "knowing" of Eve as an analogue for mystical gnosis, however much some might be offended by the comparison. Citing 1 Cor 6:17 ("Anyone who is joined to the Lord is one spirit with him"), he concludes: "Therefore, whoever unites with a prostitute knows (*egnōketō*) the prostitute; whoever unites with his wife, his wife, and, more than he and in a holy fashion, whoever unites with the Lord knows (*egnōketō*) the Lord" (*Comm. on Jn.* 19.4 [21–24] [SC 290:58.25–27]).[195]

The controversy about whether Origen is to be seen as primarily a Platonic intellectual mystic or an affective Christian one is wrong on at least two counts.[196] It is doubtful that any such general division makes sense, at least in the history of Christian mysticism; and it is also inadequate to describe the Platonic mystical tradition as a purely intellectual one, as I tried to demonstrate in chapter 2. Origen's mysticism centers on the transformation of eros ii, the power of yearning desire implanted in the soul by the God who is EROS I. Thus, eros ii must be led away from its pursuit of material satisfactions and be educated by the Word to pursue its true object, the inebriating wine of the truths about the divine realm.[197] This is a new type of knowing, as Harl has shown, a *pathein* not a *mathein,* that is, the experience of something received in the soul, not something learned by one's own efforts.[198] It is, to be sure, a transformation whose goal is most often described in terms of knowing. We may wish to call it a type of *amor intellectualis Dei,* but we must not forget that it remains an *amor.* Von Balthasar is certainly correct in speaking of Origen's "passionate and tender love for the Word."[199] As the prologue to the *Commentary on the Song* puts it: "after realizing the beauty of the divine Word, we can allow ourselves to be set on fire with saving love, so that the Word itself deigns to love the soul in which it has encountered longing for it" (ed. 79.19–21; Lawson, p. 46). For Origen, God was fire and flame—"Our God is a consuming fire" (Heb 12:29)—a fire that both warms and illuminates.[200] According to Henry Chadwick, "in his capacity for combining as a unity in himself intellectual passion with warm personal devotion to God in Christ and the practical virtues of a Christian, Origen is perhaps unique among the Fathers."[201]

According to Origen, the effect of the transformation of eros ii experienced in this life is set forth in the text of the Song in which the Bride asks the friends of the Groom (i.e., all the holy teachers, angelic and human), "Set charity in order in me" (Song 2:4b LXX). Learning the different degrees of charity, that is, loving the proper objects in the right way, means loving God without measure, loving our neighbors as ourselves according to their role in Christ's body, loving enemies (though not as ourselves)—in short, ordering all human affections according to the truth of the scriptures.[202] The Alexandrian is the first to make the order of charity an important element in theological speculation. Later, Augustine and especially the twelfth-century mystics will make much of it.

Another key theme of later Christian mysticism in which Origen played an important role (though Clement led the way) was the consideration of the relation of action and contemplation. If the original state of the unfallen intellects was one of perfect contemplation of the Father, the very structure of creation confirmed the superiority of the contemplative over the active life that the Greek philosophical tradition had maintained.[203] In terms of the soul's itinerary, the levels of *ethica* and *physica* (the purgative and illuminative stages) represent the necessary *praxis,* the activity that leads to *apatheia,* the state of harmonious internal balance that overcomes the unruly passions.[204] This makes it possible for the soul to live, as far as possible in this life, on the contemplative or theoretic level of *epoptica.* Origen was the first to find a Gospel basis for the superiority of contemplation over action in the account of Jesus's visit to Bethany (Luke 10:38–42), where the Savior praises Mary, representing the contemplative life, over Martha, the type of the active life.[205] He does insist, however, that both modes must work together in the soul's pedagogy.[206]

The basic structure of the mystical life as the transformation of eros is not a solitary path, a Plotinian "flight of the alone to the Alone." It is rooted in the life of the church, which serves as the moon in relation to the sun of Christ (*Hom. on Gen.* 1.5–7). In and through the Word's love for the church the Divine Lover comes to meet the individual soul — the mystical interpretation of the Song of Songs presupposes the ecclesial one or, better, is another dimension of it. The grace of Christ needed to strengthen the weakened wills of fallen souls is conveyed first to the "great sacrament" of the church,[207] and through the church's ritual and pedagogical activities to the individual believers.[208] But grace must be personally appropriated, as is especially evident in two treatises Origen wrote on the Christian life, *On Prayer* and *Exhortation to Martyrdom*.

On Prayer (*Peri euchēs*), written for his patron, Ambrose, about 233, is not the earliest Christian treatise on the subject, but it is the first extensive treatment of private prayer for the mature believer.[209] In analyzing the "what we ought," or the correct words for prayer, and the "as we ought," the dispositions of the one who prays (*Prayer* 2.2 [Greer, p. 83]), Origen is concerned to show that prayer, which involves the action of all three persons of the Trinity in us, should pervade the entire life of the Christian. "For the only way we can accept the command to 'pray constantly' (1 Thess 5:17) as referring to a real possibility is by saying that the entire life of the saint is a single great prayer. What is customarily called prayer is, then, a part of this prayer" (*Prayer* 12.2 [Greer, p. 104]). The work's penetrating theological commentary on the Lord's Prayer and its concrete directions concerning the actual manner of praying show how deeply speculation and piety were intertwined for Origen.

The *Exhortation to Martyrdom* is important for showing how Origen's view of mystical theory appropriated and reinterpreted the earliest Christian ideal of attaining God present in Christ — the supreme act of witnessing to Jesus by dying for him. Throughout his life, the studious ascetic insisted that martyrdom was the ideal for the believer,[210] but his understanding of this ideal reflects his own theological vision. While he still views martyrdom as an *imitatio Christi* in ways not unlike those found in earlier literature (e.g., *Exhortation* 12, 28, 36–37, 42), the martyr is now seen not so much oppositionally, as the one who confronts pagan demonism through his speaking out for Jesus, as "gradationally" (to use Alison Elliot's term), that is, as the one who brings to perfection the soul's desire to separate itself from the earthly body and material things (e.g., *Exhortation* 3, 12).[211] This separation process is part of the erotic transformation by which Christ the Bridegroom (*Exhortation* 10, 31) elevates the soul, who has died to this life, to the *theōria* of heavenly realities in face-to-face vision (*Exhortation* 13). Because the rational being of the soul "has a certain kinship with God," we should not fear the death that will burst the soul's bonds so that we can "enjoy with

Christ Jesus the rest proper to blessedness, contemplating him, the Word, wholly living" (*Exhortation* 47 [Greer, p. 76]).

The language of contemplation (*theōria*) dominates Origen's descriptions of the goal of the mystical itinerary, just as it had in Clement.[212] The Alexandrian teacher emphasizes that the Father, as the completely immaterial First Principle of all, cannot be seen (e.g., *De prin.* 1.1.5; 1.1.8). But the Word, as the Father's perfect Image both knows him and is known by him (Matt 11:27); hence, the Word made flesh becomes the "cleft in the rock" of Moses' vision (Exod 33:21–23)[213] in which we can come to know, that is, to "see" God with the heart, or interior sense of vision, as the beatitude "blessed are the pure of heart for they shall see God" (Matt 5:8) promises.[214] Christ is the only way by which we can gain access to this vision: he is our guide to the delights of "mystical and ineffable contemplation" (*mystikēs kai aporretou theōrias*) (*Comm. on Jn.* 13.24 [146] [SC 222:110.46]).[215] The vision begins in this life, but will only be completed in the universal restoration when the intellect "will think God and see God and hold God and God will be the mode and measure of its every movement" (*De prin.* 3.6.3).

Those foreshadowings of the ultimate vision that begin in this life through the awakening of the interior, spiritual senses are, as we have stressed, insights into the divine mysteries, deeper ways of understanding God. Though Origen sometimes spoke of them as involving *ekstasis*, or *enthysiasmos*, or *sobria ebrietas* (a description first found in Philo),[216] we must not think of these terms as implying ecstasies or trancelike states such as those found in the apocalyptic visionaries or in the Montanists. Origen, like Meister Eckhart and others, was largely indifferent to rapture and altered states in his concentration on the new knowledge of God conveyed to the soul by the Divine Lover.[217]

The Alexandrian was not averse to speaking of contemplation of God as involving or leading to the deification or divinization of the soul. "The intellect which is totally purified and is raised above the material to attend to the contemplation of God with the greatest attention is deified (*theopoiēsthai*) by what it contemplates," as an important text from the *Commentary on John* puts it (32.27 [339] [GCS Origen 4:472]). Becoming "like God," as we have seen, was central to Greek philosophical mysticism since the time of Plato (see *Thaeatetus* 176B), but in arguing with the Platonist Celsus, Origen was anxious to underline the distinctive character of Christian divinization:

> For Christians see that with Jesus human and divine nature begin to be woven together, so that by fellowship with divinity (*to pros to theioteron koinōnia*) human nature might become divine, not only in Jesus, but also in all those who believe and go on to undertake the life which Jesus taught, the life which

leads everyone who lives according to Jesus' commandments to friendship with God and fellowship with Jesus. (*Against Celsus* 3.28)

This participation in the divine nature, Origen insists, is not because the soul itself is of divine origin, as the Platonists and Gnostics held. Interpreting Exod 15:11 in light of Ps 81:6 and John 10:43 (not 2 Pet 1:4), Origen can speak of "those gods who by grace and participation in God are called gods," but he goes on to underline that "no one is found like God in either power or nature" (*Hom. on Ex.* 6.5).[218] Such a participation in God, according to Origen, can advance from the level of similarity to that of becoming one thing, the consummation in which God will be "all in all" (*De prin.* 3.6.1).

Language of union (though not the modern term "mystical union") is fairly frequent in Origen's writings. Occasionally he uses the same term (*henōsis*) to express union with God that was later employed more extensively by the pagan Neoplatonists and by Dionysius.[219] Origen did not, however, have the same thing in mind.[220] His understanding of union, based on his view of the distinction between Creator and creature, is always modeled on that of the lovers in the Song of Songs. Hence he often invokes the passage from 1 Cor 6:17 that would become the classic proof text for the loving union of hearts and minds to the exclusion of any union of identity or indistinction. Commenting on Song 2:10–13, he says: "For the Word of God would not otherwise say that she was his neighbor, did he not join himself to her and become one spirit with her" (*Comm. on Song,* book 3 [ed. 223.21–22; Lawson, pp. 239–40]).[221] A text from *Homily on Numbers* 17 conceives of the nature of such union as a never-ending ascension into God, a foreshadowing of the doctrine of *epektasis* that Gregory of Nyssa was to develop so fully (17.4 [GCS Origen 7:160–61]).

Origen scholars have debated whether the contemplation and love of the Word are merely intermediate steps in the soul's journey, that is, one that will be surpassed in a supreme final vision and union with the Father. That the issue of Logos mysticism versus God mysticism, though perhaps an artificial distinction, is raised by his works is another indication of the centrality of Origen in the subsequent history of Christian mysticism, since the finality of the Word's mediation became a question that was to be raised again and again. The major reason Origen has sometimes been accused of abandoning the role of the Logos has been the universalism of his speculative theology, in which the Son will eventually hand over all things to the Father. Although a few texts might be read as suggesting that the Word then ceases his mediational activity,[222] this is by no means the only conclusion that can be drawn from the Origenian teaching that the end must be like the beginning. The whole issue of his *apokatastasis* is one fraught with problems, both because of the experimental character of his thought and later misrepresentations of his views. A number of passages in his works indicate that he could not conceive of any state of affairs in which the Word did not remain the essential link between the Father and his creation.[223]

One final controversial area in the investigation of Origen's mysticism may be mentioned in conclusion. Given the modern creation of the category "mysticism" and its identification with autobiographical accounts of experiences of ecstatic union with God, much ink has been spilled over whether or not Origen was "really" a mystic or only a speculative theologian or mystical theorist.[224] If historical determination that someone has actually enjoyed such experiences is the only criterion for who is a mystic, then there can be no proven mystics. Origen is, of course, one of the few patristic writers who does speak at times in something like the autobiographical voice in these matters—or at least he speaks the scriptural texts of union with the Divine Lover in his own voice. But if the effect of someone's writings about how the soul is to seek the divine presence in this life becomes the test, then Origen might be called the Christian mystic *par excellence,* because, as von Balthasar has put it, "there is no thinker in the Church who is so invisibly all-present as Origen."[225]

Finally, we can also ask, as many have done, if Origen's thought is to be judged ultimately as a Platonizing of Christianity, despite his critical remarks about Plato and the Greek philosophers.[226] The answer, I believe, lies in making some necessary distinctions. First, Origen's remarkably coherent view of the universe and the soul's destiny would be inconceivable without the speculative system developed by ancient philosophy, especially by the Platonic tradition. But it is also true that he distanced himself from pagan Platonists in essential ways through his Christian beliefs. The pagans were appalled by the Christian view of the cosmos and of human destiny—Origen and Plotinus, for all they had in common, were mortal enemies. The great Alexandrian used Platonism as a vehicle to help him develop his understanding of the implications of the Christian message: his was fundamentally a Christian account.[227]

CHAPTER 5

The Monastic Turn
and Mysticism

T HE MOST DECISIVE factor in the Greek Christian background
of Western mysticism was not the struggles of the second
century, nor even Origen's impressive theology of mysticism
in the third century, but the creation and triumph of
monasticism in the fourth century. The monastic turn was the great
religious innovation of late antiquity, and monastic institutions and
values have continued to affect the history of Christianity to the
present. Fourth-century monasticism was striking as much for its
novelty as for its success.

As suggested in the general introduction to this volume, the history
of Christian mysticism displays a kind of layering effect in which
earlier expressions live on into later periods to interact with new ideas,
systems, and institutions to create ever more complex possibilities.
The volumes in this history have been designed to present what I take
to be the three great layers, or overlapping traditions, in the history
of Western Christian mysticism. The first layer, whose foundations are
being studied in this volume and whose subsequent history will
appear in the next, was inseparable from the history of monasticism.
Though its fundamental conceptions were rooted in Judaism, Hellenism, and early Christianity, ideas need institutions to have effects.
It was through the institution of monasticism that the mystical theories
found in Origen, and those of Augustine and the other early Latin
mystics, reached into the centuries to come. These spiritual systems,
whether or not they were created specifically for a monastic context,
soon became monastic.

The second major layer, beginning about 1200 with the new surge
of piety evident in the mendicant and beguine movements, fed on this

first "monastic" component but also challenged it in important ways, not only through the variety of its institutions but especially through its stress on the possibility of attaining mystical perfection in all walks of life, as Meister Eckhart (one of its major exponents) and others insisted. This new stage in the history of Western mysticism (to be studied in volume 3) saw considerable development down through the sixteenth century. A third overlapping tradition, one problematic and complex in its relation to both earlier strands, began in the seventeenth century and may be said to continue in various ways down to the present. It will treated in the fourth volume of this history.

Monasticism's decisive role in the history of the earliest layer of Western mysticism is largely due to the way in which it served as a precipitating factor for the transition from the broad ascetical and mystical tendencies of early Christianity to specific life-styles and teaching traditions suited to convey mysticism in the narrower and more technical sense. This was especially important during the centuries when societal and ecclesiastical collapse and confusion made anything except physical survival seem like a luxury. Monasticism virtually alone provided the context within which some Christians could cultivate the knowledge of scripture and the life of penance and prayer that prepared the believer for more special forms of immediate contact with God in this life. Male and female monastics came to be viewed as the ideal Christians, the religious virtuosi who combined ascetical self-mastery and the knowledge needed to attain God.

This emphasis on the special position of the monastics bore the seeds of future problems, especially in relation to the universality of the call to Christian perfection. Monastics might become the victims of their own success, considering themselves — and being considered by others — the only "real" Christians. In this way, forms of esotericism and elitism similar to those found in the Gnostic "perfect" were in danger of being reintroduced into Christianity.[1]

The presence of these dangers is evident in the precautions that the first monastics took against them. At least insofar as it was assimilated by the fourth-century church, monasticism generally stood opposed to esoteric teaching,[2] insisting, along with episcopal authority, on the universal and public accessibility of the message of salvation preached in the churches. The issue of elitism is more complex. Emphasis on the necessity of flight from the world and the need for a program of sexual denial, asceticism, and contemplative prayer as preconditions for attaining perfection would seem to make it difficult, if not impossible, for all but monastics to reach the goal. But the stories of the early desert fathers are filled with reminders that Christian perfection is measured by humility, charity, kindness, and patience, not by more specialized spiritual gifts—almost as if the desert dwellers needed to be told this again and again.[3] Later monastics may not always have remembered the message.

Early in the 330s, just a few years after the proclamation of the peace of the church by Constantine, Eusebius of Caesarea, the emperor's advisor and court theologian, already hailed the monks with extravagant praise: "Giving the monks (*monachoi*) a home was God's first and greatest provision for mankind, because they are the front rank of those advancing in Christ" (*Comm. in Ps.* 67:7 [*PG* 23:689b]).[4] This early witness by such an important church leader indicates how rapidly the new mode of life was accepted by the hierarchy and integrated into the life of the church.

Monastic Origins

The roots of monasticism lie deep in the history of Christianity. Despite the attempts of some scholars to tie monasticism to Jewish or even pagan sources, the new way of life evolved from the ascetical lifestyles found in early Christianity through adaptation to changing historical circumstances.[5] Though the monks looked back to a series of Old and New Testament models and prototypes, especially figures associated with the desert, like Moses, Elijah, and John the Baptist, the gradual evolution of recognized forms of ascetical life within village Christianity in the third century was the historical matrix out of which monasticism sprang. Recent work, especially by Peter Brown, has given us new insights into the ways in which the monks as "holy men" carved out new roles for themselves as special mediators between the divine and human realms,[6] as well as a more complete picture of the growth of the ideal of virginity that was to be realized especially in the male and female ascetics of the desert.[7] This does not mean, however, that we are any closer to fathoming the full mystery of the move out into the desert that marked the beginning of monasticism in the true sense.

The evidence for various kinds of free-form asceticism, that is, of small groups of men and women living ascetic lives in the context of village Christianity, was widespread in the third century c.e. Variously called *apotaktitai* (Greek), *remnuoth* (Coptic), *iḥîdāyā* (Syriac) and *sarabitae* (Latin), they were recognized as a particular order or group (Greek *tagma*) in the church and are referred to as *monachoi* ("solitary ones") as early as 324 in a papyrus text.[8] By the last quarter of the third century some of these ascetics had already begun the practice of *anachōrēsis,* or withdrawal from society into the desert, a separation that involved both an external geographical shift of momentous nature and a new kind of exploration of the inner geography of the soul.[9]

Though the move toward severe asceticism and a life of sexual abstention was widespread in late antiquity, being found among pagan philosophers as well as Christians,[10] the monks went far beyond the philosophers, not only in the degree of their asceticism but also in the way in which they turned their backs on society to achieve perfection through solitary struggle against the devil and encounter with God. The martyr, the ideal Christian of the first three centuries, witnessed to pagan society's demonic nature by dramatic confession of Christ in the public context of courtroom and arena; the monk, who became the martyr's successor in the new Christian empire of the fourth century,[11] went the martyr one better, breaking with human society to achieve autarkic perfection and complete control over the demons through "a long drawn out, solemn ritual of dissociation—of becoming a total stranger."[12] The prototype of this new creation was Antony, the "Father of Monks" (ca. 250–356).

Antony, the "Father of Monks"

The historical Antony presents a number of puzzling problems, especially because the sources concerning him give rather different views.[13] For his subsequent influence, however, it was the Greek life written by Athanasius about 357 and rapidly translated into Latin that was the channel through which his fame became so potent in Christian spirituality.[14] This artfully constructed account presents a spiritual itinerary of conversion, withdrawal, purgative struggle, and transformation. The personalization of the mystical path begun with Philo's presentation of Moses and the patriarchs here reaches a new stage, as Athanasius portrays his contemporary, Antony the *monachos*, as the ideal mystic initiate.

The *Life* falls into two unequal parts: the first fourteen chapters detail the mystical itinerary, and the longer second part (chaps. 15–94) presents tales of Antony's wisdom and miraculous powers. Antony, a young peasant orphan of relative affluence, experienced a conversion through hearing the gospel message of voluntary poverty (Matt 19:21). In what was by then a typical pattern, he placed himself under the tutelege of an older ascetic in the neighborhood of his village. "There were not yet many monasteries in Egypt, and no monk at all knew the great desert, but each of those wishing to give attention to his life disciplined himself in isolation, not far from his own village" (*Life* 3 [Gregg, p. 32]). Antony's life of discipline (*askēsis*) was essentially a battle with the demons within and without. A series of three increasingly difficult temptations are presented (chaps. 5–10), in which Antony conquers the forces of evil through his dependence on Christ, who appears to him and strengthens him at the conclusion of the *agōn*. Antony then took the decisive step of leaving society behind to retreat into the desert and eventually barricade himself in an abandoned fort where he continued his warfare against the Enemy for twenty years. About the year 305, his friends came to tear down the door of the fort and reveal the transformed Antony:

> Antony came forth as though from a shrine, having been led into divine mysteries and inspired by God.[15] This was the first time that he appeared from the fortress for those who came out to him. And when they beheld him, they were amazed to see that his body had maintained its former condition, neither fat from lack of exercise, nor emaciated from fasting and combat with demons. . . . The state of his soul was one of purity, for it was not constricted by grief, nor relaxed by pleasure, nor affected by either laughter or dejection. . . . He maintained utter equilibrium, like one guided by reason and steadfast in that which accords with nature. (*Life* 14 [Gregg, p. 42])

The language of mystical initiation is here given specific Christian overtones, especially through the invocation of *apatheia* and the presentation of Antony as the new Adam, the renewed human who, through Christ's power, regained all that Adam lost. Antony achieved mastery over himself, over the world, and especially over the demons whose powers were so frightening to the late antique mind.

> Through him the Lord healed many of those present who suffered from bodily ailments; others he purged of demons, and to Antony he gave grace of speech. Thus he consoled many who mourned, and others hostile to each other he reconciled in friendship, urging everyone to prefer nothing in the world above the love of Christ. . . . He persuaded many to take up the solitary life. And so, from then on, there were monasteries in the mountains and the desert was made a city by monks, who left their own people and registered themselves for citizenship in the heavens. (*Life* 14 [Gregg, pp. 42–43])

The miracle stories and long addresses of the saint contained in the second part flesh out the picture of the powers that Antony attained because of the dominance of the "intellectual part" within him (see, e.g., chaps. 20, 45, and esp. 73–74, where Antony attacks the philosophers' notion of an uncreated soul).[16] Though Antony's greatest gift was the typical desert value of the discernment of spirits, he is portrayed as a visionary in easy and familiar contact with the heavenly world and with the ability to foresee the future (e.g., chaps. 34–37, 43, 59, 65, 82).

Hagiographical Literature

The eremitical mode of life pioneered by Antony found many successors, both historical and legendary. One popular tale, best known in Jerome's version, even told of a predecessor of Antony, Paul the first hermit, whose control over animals (a frequent theme) was a sign of his power as a new Adam. Soon certain areas in the Egyptian desert, especially at Kellia and Scetis south of Alexandria, became famous as locations frequented by the desert ascetics. The primary historical source for this mode of early monasticism, one that communicated its image to later generations both in the East and the West, was the *Sayings of the Fathers* (*Apophthegmata Patrum*), collections of originally oral materials enshrining statements and exemplary stories whose origins go back well into the fourth century but whose literary formation was a long and complicated process with interesting analogies to the ways in which Jesus materials came to be collected in the Gospels.[17] Two major collections were formed by the first half of the sixth century. The "Systematic," or "Anonymous Collection," translated into Latin from a lost Greek original about 550, is composed of some twenty-two books of sayings organized under key spiritual topics (e.g., compunction, patience, discretion, prayer, charity, etc.). It was very widely read in the medieval period and beyond.[18] There is also an "Alphabetical Collection" (*Alphabeticon*), which organizes its sayings and stories (many overlapping with the other collection) according to a list of the famous men and women of the desert.[19]

The *Sayings* and the many lives, often legendary, of the desert saints cannot be called mystical literature in a direct way, but this material does witness to a style of life which, especially when fused with Origenist theology, created the monastic mystical tradition. The basic pattern of withdrawal–purgation–transformation was the structure that gave shape and purpose to the other values and practices of the first monastics. Flight from the world to the solitary and silent life of the inhospitable desert remained the foundation:

> When Abba Arsenius was still at the palace, he prayed the Lord saying: "Lord, show me the way to salvation." And a voice came to him: "Arsenius, run from men and you shall be saved." He went to become a monk, and again prayed in the same words. And he heard a voice saying: "Arsenius, be solitary: be silent: be at rest. These are the roots of a life without sin." (*Sayings* 2.1 [Chadwick, p. 40])

The desert, traditionally the home for demons and not for humans, was the place where the encounter with the spirits of evil—demons of lust, of gluttony, of anger, of desire for possessions, and the like—could be more readily encountered and mastered through the patient penance of the cell. These demonic powers, always present within the soul, became luminously real in the intense heat and introspective atmosphere of the desert. When

Abraham questioned Abba Poemon about how the demons fight against him, Poemon responded: "The demons fight against you? They do not fight against us at all as long as we are doing our own will. For our own wills become the demons, and it is these that attack us in order that we may fulfill them" (*Alph. Coll.* Poemon 67 [Ward, p. 148]).

Asceticism, while of great value, is not portrayed as an end in itself, but always as a means to the goal of transformation. To a hunter who up-braided him for talking gladly with the brethren, Abba Antony offered the example of the overstrung bow in danger of snapping. "So it is with God's work," he concluded. "If we go to excess, the brothers quickly become exhausted. It is sometimes best not to be rigid" (*Sayings* 10.2 [Chadwick, p. 106]).[20] Obedience to the abba — or spiritual father — discretion, discernment,[21] humility, patience, and charity receive the greatest stress in the purgative process. The final goal, as in the case of Antony, is best described as a transformation by which the ascetic becomes an *epigeios theos,* a "god upon earth," as Abba Macarius the Great was described.[22] In the *Sayings* and related literature this divinization is often symbolized through the language of fire, sometimes in a visionary context. A brother of Scetis, looking through the window, sees Abba Arsenius "like fire from head to feet," because "he was a brother worthy to see such sights" (*Sayings* 18 [Chadwick, p. 187]). When Abba Lot asks Abba Joseph about how to lead a more perfect life, "then the old man rose, and spread out his hands to heaven, and his fingers shone like ten candles: and he said: 'If you will, you could become a living flame'" (ibid. 12.8 [Chadwick, p. 124]).[23] Though the process of divinization is generally a long and slow one, some texts stress that the proper intention is all. Abba Allois said, "If a man wills, in one day he can come by evening to a measure of divinity" (ibid. 11.6 [Chadwick, p. 132]).

These two forms of Christian monasticism, the free-form asceticism con-nected with Christian villages and the life of the solitary eremites or anchorites of the desert, were soon joined by a third, the organized communities, that is, *koinōniai* or *coenobia,* whence we derive the term "cenobitism."

Pachomius, born about 290 in Upper Egypt, was a pagan Egyptian peasant press-ganged into the imperial army. Upon his discharge about 313 he was baptized and began to live the anchoritic life under Abba Palamon. But Pachomius's vocation was to be different from that of the desert dwellers, as a story from the "First Greek Life" relates:

Once, journeying through that desert a considerable distance, he came to a deserted village called Tabennesi. There he prayed to express his love of God.

And as he protracted his prayer à voice came to him — until that time he had not yet had a vision — and the voice said to him, "Stay here and build a monastery; for many will come to you to become monks."[24]

The "First Sahidic Life" indicates that Pachomius's first attempt to form a loose anchoritic community was not successful. It was only after five years, perhaps ca. 320, that he imposed a rule of life on his community and began to enjoy some success.[25] Pachomius thus became the earliest monastic legislator, though the regulations that survive under his name probably represent the order of the houses following his model at the end of the fourth century.[26] The flavor of Pachomius's view of monasticism with its emphasis on the harmony of the *koinōnia*, the community of brethren, is perhaps best reflected in a saying of his recorded in the "First Greek Life":

> In our generation in Egypt I see three important things that increase God's grace for the benefit of all those who have understanding: the bishop Athanasius, the athlete of Christ contending for the faith unto death; the holy Abba Antony, the perfect model of the anchoritic life; and this *koinōnia*, which is a model for all those who wish to assemble souls in God, to succour them until they be made perfect. (chap. 136 [*Pachomian Koinonia* 1:395])

By the time of the founder's death in 346, nine houses of men and two of women followed his rule. The Pachomian communities were to grow to be large and powerful, especially in Upper Egypt where they eventually constituted a string of monastic villages containing thousands of monks and nuns.

Athanasius's role in disseminating Antony's fame, as well as the praise given to him in the Pachomian *logion*, raises the important issue of the relation between the new phenomenon of monasticism and the established structure and hierarchy of the church. There can be no question that monasticism was originally a far stranger, more threatening phenomenon than it now appears through the screen of our somewhat tendentious sources. Jean Leclercq and others have rightly spoken of "le monachisme sauvage," monasticism as an a-social phenomenon that went counter to the values of the civilized world of late antiquity and was doubtless more in tension with established ecclesiastical structures than we customarily imagine.[27] What is most surprising about this non-Greek phenomenon emerging from the fringes of society was how quickly it was appropriated by the hellenized church leaders of the fourth century. (Of course, Christianity itself was not to remain unchanged in the encounter.) Although monasticism was rapidly organized and even routinized in the service of the imperial church, the marginal and critical function of monasticism has continued to mark it throughout its history. Monasticism lives in a creative tension between charism and legislation, between critique and support of both society and church.

The full story of the spread of monasticism throughout the Roman world in the fourth century cannot detain us here. Though Egypt played a definite originating role, monasticism was not just a diffusion from the land of the Nile. The ascetic tendencies present throughout Christianity, especially in Palestine and Syria, but also in Asia Minor, North Africa, and even Italy, Gaul, and Spain, quite soon produced their own distinctive forms of monasticism. We shall look at the Western examples more fully in the next section of this volume. Tensions among the different forms of monastic asceticism are evident. Through a process still not totally clear to us, by the latter part of the fourth century the two new monastic forms, that is, the anchoritic or eremitical way of life and the cenobitical life lived according to a rule, had turned against the older, loosely organized small groups of "apotaktic" monastics who were by then generally condemned as false ascetics and hypocrites. They came to be blamed, justly or unjustly, for any moral or doctrinal dangers present in the new mode of life, that is, anything that for various reasons was not assimilated into the structure of the imperial and orthodox church.

The monastic way of life proved a powerful stimulus to the creation of new types of religious literature. To the hagiographical texts and stories about the men and women of the desert — literature that can be described as at least implicitly mystical — was soon added explicitly theological writings that represent some of the classics of Christian mysticism. In the last decades of the fourth century three great mystical writers with various ties to monasticism appeared: Gregory of Nyssa; the mysterious author whose writings circulated under the name of Macarius; and Evagrius Ponticus. Although other Eastern fathers, especially Athanasius and Basil, were to be of great import in Western theology and spirituality over the centuries, the particular focus of this volume allows consideration only of these three, and even here detailed consideration will be accorded only to Evagrius.

Gregory of Nyssa

Gregory of Nyssa, the younger brother of Basil, the great Cappadocian monastic legislator and anti-Arian bishop, was born about 335 and died about 395. Research of the past decades, beginning with Jean Daniélou's *Platonisme et théologie mystique: Doctrine spirituelle de Saint Grégoire de Nysse* (1944), has vindicated for Gregory a position as one of the most penetrating and original thinkers of Greek Christianity and one of the major mystical theorists of the ancient church. Gregory was well educated, both in the classics of Greek culture (he shows easy familiarity with much of Plato and had also read Plotinus) and in the earlier Greek fathers, especially Origen (though he disagreed with the Alexandrian on several key issues). Gregory was a prolific writer, responsible for major dogmatic works such as the *Great Catechetical Oration* and the twelve books *Against Eunomius,* important exegetical tomes such as the treatise on the creation account entitled *On the Making of Man* (*De opificio hominis*), and a variety of ascetical and mystical commentaries and treatises. Among the moral/mystical works three stand out: the *Life of Moses* (*De vita Moysis*) in which the Jewish leader is taken as a model of the soul's spiritual journey to God; the fifteen homilies *On the Song of Songs,* dedicated to Olympias, the wealthy deaconess of Constantinople who was to be John Chrysostom's patroness; and the eight homilies *On the Beatitudes.*[28]

Gregory's original and subtle mystical theory has been much studied in the past half century.[29] His writings were influential on some authors, such as the pseudonymous Dionysius, who were widely read in the Latin West. The bishop's own works, unlike those of Origen, did not become available in Latin, with the exception of the *On the Making of Man,* which was twice translated, once by Dionysius Exiguus in the sixth century and again by John the Scot in the ninth. Through this channel Gregory's doctrine of creation and his anthropology had an impact on some Western thinkers, not only on John the Scot but also on some later mystical authors, such as William of St. Thierry (these influences will be taken up in the next volume). But Gregory's own mystical theology, now recognized as one of the most powerful in the history of Christianity, did not have a direct role in the West, though there are many interesting analogies in later Western mystics. For this reason I will limit myself here to a few general remarks about his significance.

In the wake of the Arian controversy, the major doctrinal dispute of the fourth century, the Greek fathers were forced to examine the doctrine of God with more care and in greater depth than had hitherto been the case. The creation of orthodox trinitarian theology marks a watershed in the history of Christian thought, one that was bound to have its effect on all aspects of subsequent Christianity, including mysticism. Gregory, the last and most subtle of the Cappadocian fathers, not only played a crucial role in the development of trinitarian theology, but also in the Christian view of the divine nature as unlimited and therefore incomprehensible.[30]

Origen, as we saw in the last chapter, had little room for apophaticism. This may well be rooted in the fact that the Alexandrian adhered to the classical Greek view, which equated limitlessness (*apeiron*) with imperfection. In several places Origen actually admitted that God, or at least God's power, is limited.[31] This seems to be the source for his conception that the intellects of the first creation had attained a "satiety" (*koros*), a fullness of contemplative possession of the divine nature from which they fell (*De prin.* 2.8.3).[32] Gregory of Nyssa decisively broke with Origen on this issue, insisting that God was boundless, unlimited, and therefore absolutely incomprehensible.[33] As he says in the *Life of Moses:*

> He [Moses] learns from what was said (Exod 33:20) that the Divine is by its very nature infinite, enclosed by no boundary. . . . Since what is encompassed is certainly less than what encompasses, it would follow that the stronger prevails. Therefore he who encloses the Divine by any boundary makes out that the Good is ruled over by its opposite. . . . It is not in the nature of what is unenclosed to be grasped. But every desire for the Good which is attracted to that ascent constantly expands as one progresses in pressing on to the Good. Never to reach satiety (*koros*) of desiring is truly to see God. (*De vita Moysis* 2.236–39)[34]

Gregory created the first systematic negative theology in Christian history, one that was to have a profound effect a century later on the mysterious Dionysius.[35] The most distinctive feature of this apophaticism for his mystical thought was the famous doctrine of *epektasis,* his teaching (often invoking Phil 3:13) that the goal of the Christian life, both here and in heaven, is the endless pursuit of the inexhaustible divine nature. This theme appears constantly in the *Life of Moses,* and it is also the way in which he interpreted the restless and unfulfilled character of the encounters with the Divine Lover recounted in the Song of Songs. In the twelfth of his *Homilies on the Song of Songs* he says:

> When she hoped, like Moses, that the king's face would appear to her (Exod 33:13–22), the one whom she desired escapes her grasp. She says, "my beloved has passed by" (Song 5:6), but he did so not to forsake her soul's desire, but to draw her to himself. . . . The bride never ceases going in nor going out, but she rests only by advancing towards that which lies before her and by always going out from what she has comprehended.[36]

Epektasis gives Gregory's reading of the Song a flavor not found in Origen—both a greater erotic tension on the level of language and a more systematic treatment of the paradoxical character of every perception of the divine presence (*aithēsis tou parousias*) as an experience of a presence that is also an absence. "She realizes that her sought-after love is known only in her impossibility to comprehend his essence, and that every sign becomes a hindrance to those who seek him" (*Hom.* 6).[37]

All the main lines of Gregory's mystical thought—his understanding of the spiritual senses, his treatment of the stages of the soul's itinerary, as well as his teaching on the perception of the divine presence, on ecstasy, on the nature and kinds of contemplation, on divinization, and on union — are affected by this profound apophaticism. Gregory's thought played a key role in the history of later Greek mysticism, but it will not be taken up in more detail here because of its lack of direct influence in the West.

Macarius the Great

The fifty *Spiritual Homilies* (*Homiliai pneumatikai*) ascribed to Macarius (d. ca. 390), did exercise considerable influence in the West, but largely after their translation and printing in the sixteenth century.[38] Despite their ascription to a name famous among Egyptian anchorites, these homilies and the corpus associated with them (consisting of a treatise known as the "Great Letter" and various letters, dialogues, and *logia*) were probably composed in a Syrian-Mesopotamian milieu sometime late in the second half of the fourth century.[39]

The most vexing question about the *Homilies* (really a series of monastic spiritual conferences) is their relation to Messalianism, a mystical (or better *the* mystical) heresy of Eastern Christianity. As with so many heresies, we are dependent on the accounts of heresy hunters, often much posterior in time, to such an extent that it is difficult to know what beliefs the real Messalians might have held and whether or not there were actually ever very many of them.[40] The historian Theodoret tells us:

> About the same time the heresy of the Messalians sprang up. Those who have rendered their name into Greek call them Euchites [i.e., "those who pray"]. Besides the above, they bear other appellations. They are sometimes called Enthusiasts, because they regard the agitating influences of a demon by whom they are possessed as the presence of the Holy Spirit. Those who have imbibed this heresy shun all manual labor as a vice; they abandon themselves to sleep, and they declare their dreams to be prophecies.[41]

(The term "Messalians" is derived from the Syriac word for prayer, as is the Greek "Euchites.")

The descriptions of Messalianism from later antiheretical writers like Timothy of Constantinople and John of Damascus depend on conciliar condemnations begun at Side (ca. 390 in Asia Minor) and expanded on at Constantinople (426) and Ephesus (431). These attacks indicate that the Messalians were monastics who stressed the role of constant prayer in overcoming sin to such an extent that they undervalued the role of baptism, the other sacraments, and the whole ecclesiastical establishment. The other troubling element in Messalianism seems to have been an emphasis on the physicality of good and evil in the ascetic life. For instance, the devil's presence could be removed through the expulsion of bodily secretions.

Likewise, the true "spirituals" (*pneumatikoi* was what the Messalians called themselves) were known for their ability to "see" the Trinity with their physical eyes.[42] Accusations about idleness echo what the new forms of monastic asceticism said about the surviving apotaktic forms of early monasticism. Messalianism appears to have become a lightning rod for the suspicions of late fourth- and early fifth-century church leaders about the dangers involved in the monastic movement.

A. Villecourt and H. Dörries demonstrated clear parallels between passages in the Macarian *Homilies* and excerpts from a Messalian work known as the *Asceticon*, condemned at Constantinople and Ephesus.[43] In addition, some manuscripts of the *Homilies* bear the name of Symeon, and a Symeon the Mesopotamian was known as a Messalian leader. Was Macarius/Symeon a Messalian, and could the *Homilies* or other parts of the Macarian corpus be identical with the *Asceticon?* Debate continues on both issues, but recent scholarship has shied away from too "Messalian" a reading of Macarius, although there is considerable willingness to admit that much of the material may go back to Symeon of Mesopotamia, now generally viewed as a "moderate" Messalian. The text certainly stresses themes that bring it close to aspects of Messalian thought, such as the necessity for continual pure prayer (e.g., *Hom.* 15.22), and the ongoing cohabitation of sin and grace in the heart of the believer (e.g., *Hom.* 17.15; 41.2); but it also opposes a number of the teachings of condemned Messalianism, such as the denigration of baptism and of good works. Consequently, the Macarian corpus has been viewed by a number of recent investigators as either a critique of the exaggerations of the "strict" Messalians,[44] or else as a witness to the original monastic piety of Asia Minor and Syria, which was subsequently altered by extremists.[45]

The Macarian *Homilies,* with their distinctive emphasis on God as fire and light, their deft probing of the continuing struggle between good and evil in the human heart, and their teaching on the role of Christ and the Holy Spirit in the progress of the life of pure prayer that leads to God, form one of the most characteristic components of Eastern Christian mysticism. Though these conferences are not devoid of intellectual substance, their view of the spiritual combat is basically practical. There are aspects of Macarian teaching, such as the discussion of the spiritual senses (e.g., *Hom.* 4.7; 28.5), which bear comparison with Origen; but the essence of the Macarian position was developed independently of Origenism, and the Macarian "conception of man as a single psychosomatic whole"[46] is different from the view of body and soul we find in Origen, Gregory, and Evagrius despite their appreciation of the complex interdependence of the two in the fallen state. Macarius's insistence on the need for attaining God "in experience (*peira*) and plenitude (*plerophoria*)," especially in the perception of the divine light (e.g., *Hom.* 1.12; 43.1), foreshadows much to come in the Eastern tradition, especially in such mystics as Symeon the New Theologian and Gregory Palamas. It may well be, as Gilles Quispel suggests, that we have in Macarius no "Seinsmystik," or mysticism of being in the manner of Origen, Gregory of Nyssa, and those influenced by Greek philosophical mysticism, but a "Gestaltsmystik," or a mysticism of the divine form, rooted in Jewish Christianity and analogous to such roughly contemporary Jewish mystical texts as the *Shi'ur Qomah.*[47] A kind of "physical" vision or contact with God is implied in a number of texts (e.g., *Hom.* 4.11).

It is interesting to note that Macarius appears to have been the first to adopt the now-classical Christian modifier *mystikos* to describe the kind of union a person can enjoy with God in this life, speaking of both a *synousia mystikē* and *koinōnia mystikē.*[48] If the Macarian homilies are really Messalian, then, as John Meyendorff notes, the entire tradition of Eastern spirituality falls under the same accusation because of the influence they had on many later authors.[49]

Evagrius Ponticus

In the case of Evagrius Ponticus, the third of the great Greek Christian mystics of the end of the fourth century, we are dealing with a direct link between the desert experience and Origenist systematics, as well as a writer who had considerable influence on Western Christian mysticism, albeit more through his disciple John Cassian than through the impact of his own writings, though some were indeed available in Latin.[50] It will be necessary, then, to spend more time with this important mystic whose writings have been said to form "the first complete system of Christian spirituality,"[51] though others would wish to reserve this accolade for Origen.

Born in Pontus about 345, Evagrius was trained by the Cappadocian fathers, being ordained lector by Basil and deacon by Gregory Nazianzenus. His brilliant career as an opponent of the Arians in Constantinople was brought to an end by his conversion to the ascetic life as a result of a personal crisis, his involvement with a married woman. He fled the capital and went first to Jerusalem, where he met Melania and Rufinus, and then on to the Egyptian desert, where he lived from about 383 until his death in 399. Influenced by, among others, two of the most famous abbas, Macarius of Alexandria and Macarius the Great, Evagrius himself became a figure of note among the ascetic heroes of the desert, as stories about him, especially in the *History of the Monks in Egypt* (*Historia monachorum in Egypto*) and in his pupil Palladius's *Lausiac History* (*Historia Lausiaca*), demonstrate.[52]

Although rather different from most of the other hermits in his education and social background, he came to be appreciated for his asceticism and modesty, as well as for wisdom.

Evagrius's role in monastic mysticism is especially tied to his place in the history of desert Origenism.[53] Some of the earliest monastic documents, such as the letters of Antony, show the presence of Origen's thought, though it is not easy to say how such speculation reached a simple Egyptian peasant. But Origen's teaching had remained a force in Alexandria through the third and fourth centuries, and hence we should not be surprised that a number of important fourth-century abbas show evidence of the great thinker's influence.[54] Athanasius himself summoned the monk Didymus the Blind (313–398) to become Alexandria's catechist. (Didymus was a convinced follower of Origen, who trained Rufinus and Jerome among others.) Late in the fourth century we have evidence of a strong Origenist movement in the desert south of Alexandria led by Abba Isidore, Evagrius, and the four "Tall Brothers."[55] There was tension between the learned Origenists and the simple monastics, who were often accused of being "Anthropomorphites" for their concrete and even materialistic views of God. But the Origenists themselves also came under fire. The patriarch Theophilus, after originally supporting the Origenists in their struggle against the Anthropomorphites, turned against them in 400 and savagely persecuted the "Tall Brothers" and others.

The first Egyptian Origenist crisis, part of a wide reaction throughout Christianity against the Alexandrian's teaching, does not seem to have seriously affected Evagrius's name—he continued to be read and translated. The great Origenist crisis of the sixth century, however, proved a different matter. Sparked by the interest of Palestinian monks in the writings of Origen, Didymus, and Evagrius, this controversy soon spilled over into imperial ecclesiastical policy. The emperor Justinian (527–565), ever eager to display his theological expertise, personally compiled a list of Origen's errors, which he sent to Mennas, the patriarch of Constantinople. A synod held in the city in 543 approved the condemnation of these ten errors, and the Second Ecumenical Council of Constantinople of 553 c.e. issued an official anathema of fifteen Origenist propositions, many of them based on Evagrius's writings.[56] The result of this was not only the accusation of heresy that has ever since been attached to the teaching of Origen, Didymus, and Evagrius, but also the destruction of many of their writings. Though some Greek texts of Evagrius remain, far more of his work survives in Syriac and in Armenian.

Evagrius's most important work is the great trilogy sometimes called the *Monachikos* that mirrors the basic structure of his view of the mystical life.

This consists of the *Praktikos,* one hundred chapters on the ascetic life, which survive in the Greek original, together with the *Gnostikos,* fifty chapters on how the "Gnostic," or true contemplative, teaches spiritual knowledge (Syriac and Armenian translations with many Greek fragments). The longest part of the trilogy is the great *Kephalaia Gnostica,* six hundred chapters of ninety axioms each surviving in two Syriac versions (S1 and S2) which give the heart of Evagrius's speculative mysticism.[57] In addition, there is the important work on prayer surviving in Greek, the *De Oratione,* or *On Prayer,* consisting of 153 chapters,[58] and a number of primarily ascetical works directed to monastics, such as the *Antirrhetikos* (a treatise on the eight principal sinful tendencies) and the *Mirror for Monks and Nuns.* Evagrius's biblical commentaries, notably his commentary on the Psalms, are just beginning to be recovered and studied;[59] and there are more than sixty letters extant, mostly in Syriac. At least two of these are of importance for understanding his mystical thought, the *Letter to Melania* (*Epistola ad Melaniam*) and the *Letter of Faith* (*Epistola fidei*), which survived under the name of Basil.[60] Rufinus and Gennadius of Marseilles translated a good deal of Evagrius into Latin, though not all the versions survive.[61]

Most of Evagrius's major works appear in the chapter, or century form, that is, as collections of often enigmatic aphorisms organized in groups of hundreds. The Pontic hermit was the first Christian author to use this genre, which, despite its similarity to some Hellenistic philosophical works, such as the *Sentences of Sextus,* seems to have been rooted in the central mode of early monastic teaching, the giving of a "word" of counsel to the neophyte monk by his abba.[62] More imitated in the East than in the West, the century genre contributes to our difficulty in understanding Evagrius's teaching: his thought is filtered through a deliberate stylistic veil in which less is more, as well as through an accidental linguistic one because of the fate of his teaching. The novel format may also have something to do with those evaluations of Evagrius which see him as an overly rigid and schematic thinker, one who set Origen's experimental and flexible speculations into a hard crystalline form. Though it would be difficult to deny all elements of this evaluation, Evagrius's chapters, when carefully studied, reveal a subtle and at times deliberately ambiguous mode of thought. His gnomic chapters are like the tips of mystical icebergs, revealing their true size and configuration only after prolonged meditation and extensive exploration beneath the surface.

Even more than with Clement and Origen, Evagrius's mysticism has seemed problematic, even not fully Christian, to some investigators. Von Balthasar, for example, concludes his insightful paper "The Metaphysics and Mystical Theology of Evagrius" with the claim that "the mystical teaching of Evagrius in its fully developed consistency stands closer to Buddhism than to Christianity."[63] The Swiss theologian judges Evagrius to be a "pure mystic," one in whom the transcendental experience of the knowing self has been fully realized, but he denies that Evagrius can be considered a Christian mystic because of the way in which he emptied the major Christian beliefs of their specific meaning.[64] Irenée Hausherr, one of the most learned students of Greek and Byzantine mystical thought, expressed similar doubts about the desert author.[65] But other interpreters, such as Karl Rahner, John Eudes Bamberger, Antoine Guillaumont, and most recently Gabriel Bunge, have given more positive evaluations.[66] Despite the controversy, all recent investigators agree on one thing: Evagrius is one of the major figures in the history of Christian mysticism.

Evagrius's theology is fundamentally Origenist, though he differed from his Alexandrian teacher in important particulars. Evagrius's basic view of reality, like Origen's, is realized in three great stages — creation, fall and second creation, and the eventual return.

The presence of movement, inequality, and evil in the world makes it necessary to postulate a prior harmonious creation of equal spiritual beings (*logikoi*, or "rationals," in Evagrius's terminology), as well as a future return of all spiritual beings to God and the eventual destruction of evil.[67] "Among creatures," as he says, "some were produced before judgment and some after judgment. With regard to the first no one has provided information, but with regard to the second he who was on Horeb [i.e., Moses] has given an account."[68] The first creation, which enjoyed absolute unity with the Trinity, fell away from its contemplative perfection through "negligence" (see *KG* 1.49; 3.22, 28). Evagrius is even less informative than was Origen about the essence of this primordial fault, one that lies deeper than the "sins" which take place in the second creation.

The negligence of the first creation brought about God's immediate judgment on the *logikoi* and the production of the second creation, which is characterized by movement, multiplicity, and matter. This creation is effected in and through Christ, the only unfallen *logikos*.[69] As the spiritual created being who is perfectly united to the Logos, the second person of the Trinity, he alone knows the essential principle (*logos*) of each thing that belongs to the second creation.[70]

The *logikoi* are assigned places or conditions (*systaseis*) in the second creation in proportion to the degree of their negligence, winding up as angels, humans, or demons. The *logikos* or *nous*, the rational identity of each spiritual being, descends or "thickens" into *psychē* or soul (see, e.g., *Praktikos* 35–39; 56–57; *KG* 2.29), which is composed of three elements: *nous* (taken in a secondary sense as the rational element in the soul), *epithymia* (desire or sensuality), and *thymos* (rejection or irascibility).[71] The angels are those beings in whom *nous* predominates;[72] *epithymia* is strongest in humans, and *thymos* controls the demons.[73] All three kinds of beings have bodies adapted to their spiritual constitutions. These God-given bodies, Evagrius argues, are both indicators of the state of the *nous* within and aids in the return process (e.g., *Praktikos* 53). Evagrius's complex anthropology (which is also an angelology and a demonology) can be described as tripartite (*nous, psychē, sōma*) or bipartite (*psychē, sōma*) depending on the perspective adopted. It is perhaps best illustrated in diagram form (see fig. 1).[74]

Figure 1

ANTHROPOLOGY OF EVAGRIUS PONTICUS

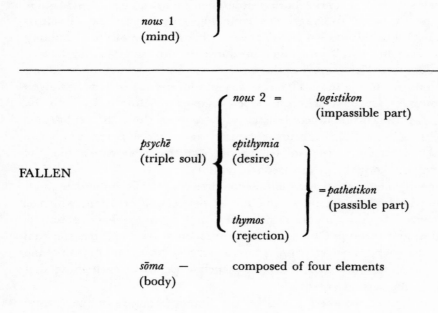

The return of the fallen rational creation to its source is accomplished in three stages. "Christianity is the dogma of Christ our Savior. It is composed of *praktikē* [i.e., of ascetic living], of the contemplation of the physical world [i.e., *physikē*], and of the contemplation of God [i.e., *theologikē*]" (*Praktikos* 1 [Bamberger, p. 15]).[75] The two contemplative stages are subdivisions of what Evagrius usually calls *gnostikē*, that is, the "gnostic" life, so here too an alternate binary pattern emerges. This twofold pattern (Evagrius's terminology is closer to Plato and Clement than to Origen) was one of the Pontic abba's major contributions to Christian spirituality, an important prototype of the later distinction between the ascetical and the mystical, or the practical and contemplative lives.[76]

The three stages (*praktikē, physikē, theologikē*) mark the levels by which *nous* is restored to its former place.[77] At the end of the *Gnostikos* Evagrius summarizes thus: "The goal of *praktikē* is to purify the intellect and to render it impassible; that of the *physikē* is to reveal the truth hidden in all beings; but to remove the intellect from all material things and to turn it toward the First Cause is a gift of *theologikē*" (*Gnostikos* 49 [ed. Guillaumont, p. 191]).[78]

In many ways Evagrius's most evident contribution, at least in the West, is to be found in the area of ascetical theory, the knowledge of *praktikē*.[79] Relying on the traditions of introspection of the desert fathers, as well as his own probing mind, the Pontic master fashioned tools of permanent value for later Christian spirituality, especially in his teaching on the eight principal *logismoi*, the direct ancestors of the well-known "Seven Deadly Sins."[80] The *logismoi* are conceived of as evil or passionate thoughts or tendencies present in the soul through the pull of *epithymia* and *thymos*, and the deceptions of *nous* 2 (see fig. 1). They make true contemplation impossible and are the means the demons use to keep *psychē* from becoming *nous* 1, its true self.[81] The exterior asceticism of deprivation of sleep, food, and sex is a necessary but not sufficient condition for undertaking the real struggle, the ascesis of controlling the fallen gravity of gluttony (*gastrimargia*), impurity (*porneia*), avarice (*philargyria*), depression (*lypē*), anger (*orgē*), impatient discouragement or dissatisfaction (*akēdia*), vainglory (*xenodoxia*), and pride (*hyperphania*).[82] Evagrius's subtle and sensible exposition of the nature of the *logismoi* and the way to recognize and combat them makes him one of the masters of what came to be called the "discernment of spirits."[83]

As in Origen, the process of return can take place only through the taking on of flesh by the preexistent Christ. "Christ is the only one who has the Unity within him and he has received the judgment of the *logikoi*" (*KG* 3.2 [ed. Guillaumont, p. 99]). He traces his wisdom in the corporal nature of the *logikoi* the way a pedagogue traces letters for a child (*KG* 3.57). His descent makes possible our ascent and eventual divinization. As a passage from the *Letter to Melania* puts it:

And as in this world there were not two beings, God and man, but one, God for himself and man for us; thus in his world too, there are not two beings, God and man, but one God who for himself is God and God who is man because God has become man. As the one has become man for the other, thus also the other becomes God for the one. (12 [Parmentier, p. 19])[84]

Despite the difficulties that his thought later encountered for its Origenist insistence on the preexistence of Christ, in his day Evagrius was resolutely orthodox, as rigorously opposed to Apollinaris's denial of a human soul in Christ (e.g., *KG* 6.79) as he was to Arian subordination of the Word to the Father.

Evagrius's teaching on the ascent of *nous* through the power of the incarnate Christ centers on three closely related, at times interchangeable, terms. Two are familiar to us already, *theōria* and *gnōsis*, the other is less central to former mystical theorists, but essential for Evagrius: *proseuchē*, that is, prayer. No author of the Greek patristic tradition used these terms more frequently, and few have spoken of them with equal sophistication.[85] *Theōria* is most often used for characterizing how the *nous* comes to understand created reality. *Gnōsis* taken as "the knowledge of something" is used in the same way. But *gnōsis* understood as "essential gnosis" (*gnōsis ousiados*) describes the goal of the entire process: not knowledge *of* something, but the knowledge that *is* the Holy Trinity (e.g., *KG* 2.3, 47; 3.6; 4.42, 77, 87, 90; 5.55–56, 62, 88; 6.10, 14, 34). However, the terms at times appear interchangeable.[86] Prayer is also used both for all the activities by which *nous* ascends and for the unitive knowing that is the goal.[87]

The interdependence of the three terms is well brought out by what Evagrius has to say about their relation to *nous*. That *theōria* and *gnōsis* constitute the essential life of *nous* is clear, but much the same can also be said for prayer as "the activity which is appropriate to the dignity of *nous*" (*Prayer* 84 [Bamberger, p. 69]).[88] While some levels of prayer can be considered preludes to the highest *gnōsis* (*Prayer* 86), prayer in the truest sense is coextensive with essential *gnosis* of the Trinity, as we learn from the famous axiom: "If you are a theologian you truly pray. If you truly pray you are a theologian" (*Prayer* 60 [Bamberger, p. 65]). What the abba calls "pure prayer" (e.g., *Prayer* 30, 67, 70, 72, 97) or "true prayer" (e.g., *Prayer* 53, 55, 60, 75, 80, 113, 153) is the gradual stripping away of all images and forms in order to attain formless and conceptless direct contact with the unnumbered and formless Trinity.[89] "Prayer is the continual intercourse of the spirit with God. What state of soul then is required that the spirit might thus strain after its Master without wavering, living constantly with him without intermediary?" (*Prayer* 3 [Bamberger, p. 56]).

Many commentators have noted that Evagrius's equation of pure prayer with *gnōsis/theōria* of the Trinity is one of the most distinctive contributions of his thought, especially within the context of the monastic life.[90] Bamberger points out that traditional forms of monasticism, both the Basilian version of the Christian East and the later Benedictine version of the West, actually have nothing to say about contemplative prayer in their founding documents. Evagrius is one of the first who made contemplative prayer the essence of the monastic life and thus linked the forces of monasticism and mysticism in a powerful way.[91] The affirmation that such prayer attains unmediated contact with God shows that while the desert abba did not use the notion of divine presence as an explicit category of his mystical theory, this central thread of Christian mysticism is implied in his writings.

In several places Evagrius distinguishes the various changes or transformations that mark the stages of movement from *praktikē* through *gnostikē* to the goal of union.[92] We cannot take any real steps on the path of *theōria* until the soul has been purified through the asceticism of the *bios praktikos*. In the *Letter to Anatolius* that prefaces the *Praktikos*, Evagrius summarizes his program through the words he puts in the mouths of the desert hermits as they confer the monastic habit on neophytes:

> The fear of God strengthens faith, my son, and continence in turn strengthens this fear. Patience and hope make this latter virtue solid beyond all shaking and they also give birth to *apatheia*. Now this *apatheia* has a child called *agapē* who keeps the door to deep knowledge of the created universe. Finally, to this knowledge succeed theology and supreme beatitude. (*Prak.* pref. [Bamberger, p. 14])[93]

Evagrius's teaching on *apatheia* is spelled out in considerable detail. He distinguishes between an imperfect *apatheia* gained while the struggle with the demons continues and the perfect *apatheia* attained when they are overcome.[94] (The necessity for the continuing operation of *apatheia*, either perfect or imperfect, for any kind of *theōria*, is one of the many ways by which the abba shows the interdependence of the practical and contemplative lives.) Perfect *apatheia*, "the health of the soul" (*Prak.* 56), "is had when the spirit begins to see its own light, when it remains in a state of tranquillity in the presence of the images it has during sleep and when it maintains its calm as it beholds the affairs of life" (*Prak.* 64 [Bamberger, pp. 33–34]).[95] Such *apatheia*, as noted above, bears *agapē* as its child.[96] It is also the necessary precondition for pure prayer (*Prayer* 52–55). In the *Kephalaia Gnostica* Evagrius speaks of *apatheia* as the glory and light of soul that make it possible for *nous* to attain its glory and light, that is, *gnōsis* (1.81; cf. 5.75). Within the context of his impressive speculative system, Evagrius's *apatheia*, while dependent on earlier views, especially Clement, shows interesting affinities with the detachment (*Gelassenheit, Abgeschiedenheit*) of the German mystics of a millennium later.[97]

The acquisition of *apatheia* makes possible the transition from the level of *praktikē* to that of *gnostikē*, specifically to the lower stage in which mind gains knowledge of the inner natures (*logoi*) of created things through *theōria physikē*. (This stage also brings a deeper understanding of the scriptures.) The abba does not spend a great deal of time analyzing the contents of this "contemplation of things," which he identifies with the kingdom of heaven, though he does divide this stage into two major parts, the contemplation of corporeal and of incorporeal beings, both considered primarily as mirrors of God.[98] He is anxious to move on to consideration of the higher stage of *theōria theologikē*, the kingdom of God, where *nous* attains "essential knowledge of the Holy Trinity" (*gnōsis ousiados tēs hagias triadas*).[99]

The number and modes of the kinds of contemplation are presented in various ways.[100] Essentially, all *theōria/gnōsis* below that of the Trinity is characterized by multiplicity and movement, the marks of created being. The essential *gnōsis* is realized by *nous* when it has been restored to absolute simplicity: "Naked *nous* is that which through the contemplation which concerns it is united to the science of the Trinity" (*KG* 3.8 [ed. Guillaumont, p. 101]; cf. 3.13, 15). Every other form of contemplation has some kind of determined object at its base — contemplation of the Trinity is unlimited (*KG* 4.87–88). The *nous* that has attained this level can even be spoken of as divine, at least by participation, or what Evagrius would call "reception" (*KG* 4.51; 5.81).

A number of issues arise over the nature and meaning of this *gnōsis* of the Holy Trinity that is the goal of Evagrius's teaching. Three problems stand out: the relation of the Trinity (*hagia trias*) to the divine unity (*monas*) in perfect *gnōsis;* the connection between *nous*'s vision of its own essence and its vision of the Trinity; and finally the issue of whether such *gnōsis* constitutes some form of absolute or indistinct union with God.

Hausherr claimed that despite Evagrius's formulaic use of the expression "essential *gnōsis* of the Trinity," the three divine persons play no real role in his mysticism: "'Holy Trinity' is no more than the Christian name for Divinity, for the 'Monad.'"[101] Bunge, however, has argued against this, showing that while the monk from Pontus makes use of both *henas* and *monas* as philosophical terms for the divine oneness (e.g., *KG* 1.71; 3.61, 72; 4.18, 89; 5.84), the biblical names of Father, Son, and Holy Spirit always remain the ultimate divine designations.[102] Evagrius was a fervent anti-Arian and friend of the Cappadocians, and his trinitarian theology is founded on the nonnumerical Trinity of persons—there is no deeper or prior unity, or God beyond God.[103]

The trinitarian character of Evagrius's mysticism is clearly underlined in several ways. Using John 4:23, he insisted that true prayer is the adoration of the Father in Spirit (i.e., the Holy Spirit) and in Truth (i.e., the Son).[104] Other texts emphasize the trinitarian dimension of the highest form of *theōria* and *gnōsis*. The early *Letter of Faith* says that the contemplation of the Father is not higher or more ultimate than the contemplation of the Word (7 [ed. Courtonne, pp. 29–30]), while the *Letter to Melania* has a presentation of the way in which naked *nous* attains a relationship with each of the divine persons. Just as in the natural order the body reveals the soul, which in turn reveals the *nous*, so *nous* itself functions as a "body" for the Spirit and the Word, who are the "soul" through which the Father works in *nous* (*Ep. ad Mel.* 4 [Parmentier, pp. 10–11]).[105] This is the core of the abba's understanding of *nous*'s character as *imago Dei*, or as image of the perfect Image, that is, the Word (see *KG* 6.34). Citing Col 3:10, he says that the full renewal of the image will come when body, soul, and *nous* will cease to be separate:

> . . . just as the nature of human mind [*nous*] will be united to the Father, as it is his body, so too the names "soul" and "body" will be absorbed in the persons of the Son and Spirit, and will remain continually one nature and three persons of God and his image, as it was before the Incarnation and as it will be again, also after the Incarnation, because of the unanimity of wills. (*Ep. ad Mel.* 5 [Parmentier, p. 12])[106]

A second major issue concerning Evagrius's understanding of essential *gnōsis* of the Trinity involves its relation to the self-knowledge that the naked or purified *nous* acquires of its own inner light. There are texts in which the abba says that mind in coming to behold itself comes to see God.[107] Von Balthasar interpreted these as showing that Evagrius did not rise beyond the level of a natural or philosophical mysticism not unlike that of the Neoplatonists, in which the soul's experience of its pure essence as knower is mistakenly identified with God.[108] But Evagrius also insists on the necessity of grace in the path to essential *gnōsis*,[109] and other texts give *nous*'s self-appropriation a more preparatory role in the path to final *gnōsis*.[110] Even if we were to wish to claim that the self-vision is always copresent with essential *gnōsis* of the Trinity (as the reverse side of the coin, so to speak, since *nous* is the image of the Trinity), such a teaching might be compared with that of Gregory of Nyssa, who saw God as visible in the mirror of the polished soul.[111] (It seems doubtful, however, that Evagrius's teaching is dependent on Gregory.) If the visions are mutual,[112] Evagrius's thought once again would bear interesting comparisons to later mystics, especially to Meister Eckhart, who, by identifying God's ground and the soul's ground, might be said to have fused the contemplation of the essence of the mind with the contemplation of the Trinity.

The third issue concerning essential *gnōsis* is whether or not it implies some kind of identity with God, an indistinct union. Unlike the Macarian homilies, Evagrius never uses the term "mystical union," and even the standard terms for union (*henōsis, koinōnia,* etc.) are largely absent from his vocabulary. But it is clear that essential *gnōsis* involves a "merging" with the Trinity that Evagrius sometimes speaks of in daring fashion. The *Letter to Melania* compares the fall of the *logikoi* from archetypal union with God and their return to it in terms of the image of an "intelligible sea":

> When minds flow back to him like torrents into the sea, he changes them all completely into his own nature, color and taste. They will no longer be many but one in his unending and inseparable unity, because they are united and joined with him. And as in the fusion of rivers with the sea no addition in its nature or variation in its color or taste is to be found, so also in the fusion of minds with the Father no duality of natures or quaternity of persons comes about. (6 [Parmentier, p. 13])

Before the fall, the *logikoi* "were at one in him without distinction." Sin, like the earth that separates the rivers from the sea, divided the *logikoi* from the Father. But the end will be like the beginning, so that ". . . he who observes the making perfect of all intellects is amazed greatly and marvels because he sees all these various distinct knowledges as they merge into one essential and unique knowledge, and that all those become this one, forever" (*Ep. ad Mel.* 12 [Parmentier, p. 20]).

In the *Letter to Melania,* Evagrius distinguishes between the created nature of the *logikoi* as *logikoi* and their eternal existence in the divine mind, so we are not dealing with an inherently divine "inner soul," as is the case in pagan Neoplatonism. Unlike the Trinity, the *logikoi* are not identical with *gnōsis ousiados:* they are always described as merely being "receptive" or "susceptible" of it (e.g., *KG* 2.80; 3.12–13, 32; 4.77; 6.73; *Prak.* 3). Still, Evagrius's affirmation of eventual reunification of the *logikoi* with God suggests a final indistinct union in which the spiritual creation becomes one with its source (cf. *KG* 1.7–8; 2.29). We can then agree with David Ousley when he defines Evagrius's conception of mystical union as "the reception by the pure rational creature of essential knowledge."[113] We must remember, however, that this union is not something naturally owed to *nous* and that it is a reception of the God who is always both one and three. From this perspective as well, Evagrius's thought suggests interesting comparisons with later Christian mystical theories of indistinct union, such as those of Meister Eckhart and his followers.

The claim that Evagrius held to some form of indistinct union between God and the restored *nous* casts light on three important characteristics of his mysticism — apophaticism, intellectualism, and modified esotericism. Like all Christian mystical theorists, Evagrius insisted that God surpasses all human thought, reminding his readers: "Do not theologize inconsiderately and never define the divine. Definitions are proper to created and composed beings" (*Gnost.* 27 [ed. Guillamont, p. 132]).[114] His insistence that the ineffable is to be adored in silence (*Gnost.* 41) echoes a theme found in the Neoplatonists, as well as in his teacher, Gregory of Nazianzen.[115] But Evagrius also develops a distinctive form of apophaticism, especially through his teaching about infinite ignorance. A controversial text in the *Kephalaia Gnostica* can be translated as "blessed is he who has attained unsurpassable ignorance" (3.88 [ed. Guillaumont, p. 134]).[116] This is clarified by a passage in *Praktikos* 87 where Evagrius discusses the diminishment of the passions through ascesis and the reduction of ignorance through *theōria*. He concludes by affirming, "In the matter of ignorance, they say, there is one type which has an end, another which does not" (*Prak.* 87 [ed. Guillaumont, p. 678]).[117] Other texts support the conclusion that Evagrius distinguished between an ignorance of created reality, which would be brought to an end through *theōria physikē*, and an ignorance of the Holy Trinity, which would never end.[118] *Theōria theologikē* is paradoxically at one and the same time infinite *gnōsis* and infinite ignorance, an "agnostic *gnōsis*" that bears an interesting affinity to Gregory of Nyssa's *epektasis*, the inexhaustible movement of the soul into God.[119] In *Kephalaia Gnostica* 1.65, he describes the ultimate unity thus: "There is an indescribable peace and there are nothing but the naked *noes* which are always satisfied in their insatiability" (ed. Guillaumont, pp. 47–49).[120] Thus, while it is true that Evagrius does not develop negative theology through the symbols of cloud and darkness that the Pseudo-Dionysius later utilized,[121] apophaticism is present and powerful in his thought.

Evagrius's agnostic *gnōsis* also is the ground for another apophatic theme he shares with Gregory of Nyssa and later Western mystics such as John Scotus Eriugena.[122] Since *nous* is the true *imago Dei*, the self-knowledge that accompanies essential *gnōsis* of the Trinity has a negative as well as a positive pole. *Kephalaia Gnostica* 2.11 says that we can know the natures of all material things through contemplation, "but our *nous* alone is incomprehensible to us, as is also God its creator. It is not possible for us in effect to comprehend a nature that can receive the Holy Trinity, or to comprehend the Unity, essential *gnōsis*" (ed. Guillaumont, p. 65; cf. *KG* 3.31).

Evagrius, like his master Origen, has been accused of adhering to a rigidly intellectualist form of mysticism. It cannot be denied that his mystical theory exalts the intellect over love and will. Despite his perceptive grasp of the training of all the bodily and emotional forces in the path to gaining *apatheia,* as well as the emphasis he places on *agapē* as the necessary precondition for the higher stages of contemplation, his goal was always the freeing of *nous* from its fallenness and its absorption in the intelligible sea of divinity. This is why he has no place for any form of ecstasy,[123] at least considered as a going outside or beyond *nous.* He believed that on the level of *theōria theologikē,* through pure prayer, we would come to know in a new way—intuitively, perhaps even unconsciously, given the absence of all sensible experience and all concepts.[124] This was not to lose *nous,* however, but to allow it to become its true self, the *logikos* as perfect image and likeness of the Holy Trinity.[125] Evagrius's insistence on ultimate union in the sea of intelligibility does mark him as one of the most intellectualist of Christian mystics. He is far from the stress on the superiority of love we find in Augustine, for example, and he even lacks the "intellectualized affectivity" we have discerned in Origen. Evagrius's intellectualism, however, appears to come from his appropriation of Origen's thought within the context of the desert experience and not from any influence of pagan philosophy.[126]

We have already seen the important role, largely negative, that Gnostic mystical currents of the second century had on the formation of Greek Christian mysticism. Bunge has recently shown how the presence of Gnosticism in Egyptian monasticism at Evagrius's time (well attested by Nag Hammadi) casts important light on the Pontic abba.[127] The anti-Arian deacon of Constantinople became the anti-Gnostic monk of Kellia, seeking to present the ideal of true Christian *gnōsis* to counter the false variety. He attacks those who hold that the body is evil in itself (e.g., *KG* 3.53; 4.60, 62), and he insists on the necessity of grace in the ascent to contemplation.[128] Evagrius also rejects any view that would see the *nous* as naturally divine, as we have seen. In the *Letter of Faith* he distinguishes, much like Origen, between the term "God" as properly applied to the consubstantial Father and Son and the applied use of the term (e.g., Ps 81:6) in referring to those who are "so called because of grace" (3 [ed. Courtonne, p. 25.11–12]).[129]

The debate with Gnosticism is evident also in Evagrius's presentation of the "true Gnostic," that is, the monastic abba as portrayed especially in the *Gnostikos.*[130] Here we find, as with Clement, a form of modified esotericism. Evagrius combines an insistence that the true Gnostic teaches the basic message of salvation to all (e.g., *Gnost.* 12–13) with advice showing that the

Gnostic needs to know how to accommodate his teaching to his audience so that "indifferent matters will not cause scandal." He warns the Gnostic: "Have knowledge of the reasons and laws of circumstances, modes of life and occupations so that you can easily say to each person what is useful for him" (*Gnost.* 15 [ed. Guillaumont, p. 112]).[131] As a general principle this is unexceptionable, but other texts indicate a more exclusive attitude in which it is sometimes necessary to feign ignorance (e.g., *Gnost.* 23) and in which gnostic books (such as the *Kephalaia Gnostica*) should not be made accessible to neophyte monks (*Gnost.* 25).[132]

Evagrius, then, reveals one of the tensions present in the monastic layer of Christian mysticism throughout its history—the uneasy coexistence between the universality of the message of the return to God held out to all and the conviction that the contemplative goal of pure prayer that gains access to essential knowledge of the Trinity at times seems accessible only to advanced monastics who have undergone years of ascetical and theoretical training. As he puts it in one place, "By true prayer a monk becomes another angel (*isangelos;* cf. Luke 20:36), for he ardently longs to see the face of the Father in heaven" (*Prayer*[113] [Bamberger, p. 74]). We must not, however, exaggerate Evagrius's esotericism. He speaks of essential *gnōsis* in all his works, and it seems that what he was most hesitant to reveal to non-gnostics was not so much the goal as the Origenist cosmological framework that enclosed it.[133]

Finally, for Evagrius, the monk who has become like the angels does not lose all connection with and responsibility for his fellow humans or for the rest of God's creation. At the conclusion of a series of beatitudes on pure prayer and the monastic life (*Prayer* 117–23), Evagrius declares, "A monk is one who is separated from all and united with all" (*Prayer* 124).[134] The ritual of dissociation that formed monastic *anachōrēsis* did separate the *monachos* from all, but its goal was to bring the monastic into the divine harmony of the original creation. The achievment of this union gave the monk a new perspective and a new communion with all humans, as well as a new and powerful role in Christianity. This text suggests why the monastic turn was institutionally and spiritually so essential to Christian mysticism in the centuries to come, and why Evagrius's synthesis of the mystical and the monastic elements in early Christianity was also important for the history of mysticism in the West.

Anagogy and Apophaticism:
The Mysticism of Dionysius

Around the year 500 C.E., possibly in Syria, lived a monastic writer whose influence on the Latin West was to be more powerful than any other

Eastern mystic. This still-unidentified figure not only created the term "mystical theology," but also gave systematic expression to a dialectical view of the relation of God and the world that was the fountainhead of speculative mystical systems for at least a thousand years.[135] According to no less an authority than Bonaventure, the spiritual sense of scripture contains three kinds of teaching: doctrinal, moral, and mystical (that is, relating to the union of God and the soul). "The first is especially taught by Augustine, the second especially by Gregory. The third is taught by Dionysius."[136]

Our author adopted the persona of Dionysius the Areopagite, Paul's Athenian convert (Acts 17:34). (Others in his circle also took pseudonymous names from the New Testament, though their leader, the mysterious teacher he calls Hierotheus, did not.)[137] Despite many attempts at identifying this figure, the historical personage of Dionysius (as we will call him rather than the modern appellation "Pseudo-Dionysius") remains a mystery.[138] His writings are also baffling. Written in an idiosyncratic, almost incantatory style filled with neologisms, they are difficult to grasp and controversial. For centuries this Dionysian corpus was treated as a quasi-apostolic authority; but humanists like Lorenzo Valla and Erasmus had begun to doubt its authenticity even before 1520, when Luther publicly attacked it claiming, "Dionysius is most pernicious; he platonizes more than he Christianizes."[139] Many, especially Roman Catholics, continued to defend Dionysius's apostolic authenticity down to the present century, when historical scholarship demonstrated that his use of late Neoplatonic writings, especially those of Proclus, proved that he cannot have written before the latter part of the fifth century C.E.[140]

Luther's complaint about Dionysius's platonizing continues to be heard today, even among serious Dionysian scholars like Jan Vanneste, who see the unknown author as more of a Neoplatonic philosopher than a Christian theologian.[141] Others, e.g., Vladimir Lossky, take a diametrically opposed view, seeing Dionysius as "a Christian thinker disguised as a neo-Platonist, a theologian very much aware of his task, which was to conquer the ground held by neo-Platonism by becoming a master of its philosophical method."[142] Von Balthasar, who has written what is perhaps the most important contemporary theological appraisal of Dionysius, sees his "Christianizing of the Neo-Platonic *milieu* as a side-effect of his own properly theological endeavor," which he describes as "the clear, realized synthesis of truth and beauty, of theology and aesthetics."[143] Other interpreters have adopted a middle ground that recognizes the fundamental Christian inspiration of the Dionysian corpus evident in the transpositions the author made in adapting Neoplatonic categories to the expression of Christian teaching on the Trinity, creation, and the return to God, but also pointing to certain areas that seem theologically problematic or inadequate, most often in Christology.[144]

A further problem relates to the esoteric tone of the Dionysian corpus. A number of passages speak explicitly of the necessity of concealing the mystical secrets of sacred scripture and the sacraments from the unworthy, explaining this esotericism as a part of the economy of salvation in which mysteries can only be gradually revealed to the real "lovers of holiness."[145] Dionysius seems to presuppose that not all believers are or will become such lovers, at least in this life, although all share in the life of the church, within which this love can be truly realized.[146] On the other hand, von Balthasar argues that Dionysius's use of the language of the *disciplina arcani* proceeds not so much from an esotericism wishing to exclude some people as from the desire to find an apt "philological and aesthetic tool" to convey the essential form of his theology—the gradual unveiling of what remains ever mysterious.[147] Dionysius continues to be an enigma and a problem, though one of singular importance in the history of Christian mysticism. In order to provide a sense of what is most important in his contribution to the history of Latin mysticism, we will need to take a glance, if only a cursory one, at the structure of his theological system.[148]

The surviving writings that constitute the core of the Dionysian corpus (it later circulated in the West with important explanatory materials) are four treatises and ten letters, but at least seven other works are mentioned by the author. Many have considered the latter works fictitious, but this need not be the case.[149] *The Divine Names,* the central and longest surviving work, comprises thirteen chapters dealing primarily with the positive or cataphatic theology which ascribes conceptual terms or names to God as creator, though the work also introduces important elements of negative or apophatic theology, especially in chapters 9 and 13.[150] Endre von Ivánka has suggested that this treatise is composed of a series of essays on divine predication based on Plato, Proclus, and the Greek fathers (see fig. 2).[151] Subsequent to *DN* (for abbreviations, see n. 135), Dionysius apparently wrote an important treatise on *Symbolic Theology,* now lost but referred to in his later works.[152] Then he penned the brief but powerful work by which he is best known, *The Mystical Theology,* well translated into Middle English by the author of *The Cloud of Unknowing* under the title *Deonise Hid Divinite.* He summarizes the relation between this treatise and the earlier works as follows:

> In my earlier books my argument traveled downward from the most exalted to the humblest categories. . . . But my argument now rises from what is below up to the transcendent, and the more it climbs, the more language falters, and when it has passed up and beyond the ascent, it will turn silent completely, since it will finally be at one with him who is indescribable. (*MT* 3 [1033C; p. 139])[153]

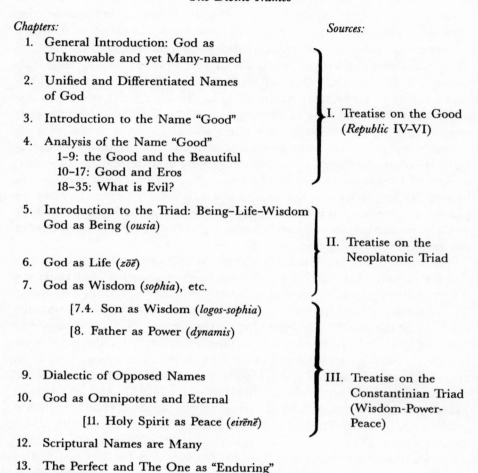

Figure 2
The Divine Names

Chapters:

1. General Introduction: God as Unknowable and yet Many-named

2. Unified and Differentiated Names of God

3. Introduction to the Name "Good"

4. Analysis of the Name "Good"
   1–9: the Good and the Beautiful
   10–17: Good and Eros
   18–35: What is Evil?

5. Introduction to the Triad: Being–Life–Wisdom
   God as Being (*ousia*)

6. God as Life (*zōē*)

7. God as Wisdom (*sophia*), etc.

   [7.4. Son as Wisdom (*logos-sophia*)

   [8. Father as Power (*dynamis*)

9. Dialectic of Opposed Names

10. God as Omnipotent and Eternal

   [11. Holy Spirit as Peace (*eirēnē*)

12. Scriptural Names are Many

13. The Perfect and The One as "Enduring" Names

Sources:

I. Treatise on the Good (*Republic* IV–VI)

II. Treatise on the Neoplatonic Triad

III. Treatise on the Constantinian Triad (Wisdom-Power-Peace)

The lower stages of this upward way form the subject of the two remaining treatises. *The Ecclesiastical Hierarchy* (it might be better called *The Human Hierarchy*) treats of how the church's liturgy and offices function in the anagogic process.[154] *The Celestial Hierarchy* investigates how the scriptural descriptions of the nine choirs of angels are to be understood so that they too may play their part in our uplifting to God. The ten surviving letters, several of some length, are important for grasping interrelations not always evident in the tractates.[155] Reference is also made to "sacred hymns" which do not survive.[156]

The theological center of Dionysius's concern is the exploration of how the utterly unknowable God manifests himself in creation in order that all things may attain union with the unmanifest Source. The Dionysian program is a cosmic one in which the divine Eros (EROS I in terms of our discussion in the previous chapter) refracts itself into the multiple theophanies of the universe, which in turn erotically strive to pass beyond their multiplicity back into simple unity. Although Dionysius considers the role of the intelligent human subject in the return crucial, there is a sense in which his presentation is far more cosmological and "objective" than what we have seen in Origen and especially in Evagrius. There is little theological anthropology as such in his surviving writings, though one is surely implied. Most important are the being, goodness, and beauty of the whole universe. "Any thinking person realizes that the appearances of beauty are the signs of invisible loveliness," as he puts it in *The Celestial Hierarchy* (1 [121D; p. 146]). Dionysius's reflections on the nature of transcendent beauty and his considerations of the necessity and proper use of symbols (see esp. *CH* 1–3; *DN* 9.5; *Ep.* 9) make it easy to understand why he had such an effect on medieval aesthetic theory.[157] Von Balthasar is right in insisting that the whole tenor of Dionysius's theology is aesthetic:

> Denys can be regarded as the most aesthetic of all Christian theologians, because the aesthetic transcendence we know in this world (from the sensible as manifestation to the spiritual as what is manifest) provides the formal schema for understanding theological or mystical transcendence (from the world to God).[158]

The objective quality of the Dionysian writings helps explain several other peculiarities of his thought. Not only is there very little explicit anthropology, but there is also no moral theory since the praxis side of the return process set out in *EH* is concerned with the theurgical use of liturgy and church office, not with the attainment of *apatheia* through exercise of the virtues, as in Evagrius.[159]

Dionysius's attitude toward scripture is also somewhat different from what we have seen in the Greek fathers, at least since the time of Origen. He wrote no biblical commentaries. This is not to say that the scriptures ("divine oracles" is his standard term) are not central to his thinking.[160] He insists that the scriptural authors are the original theologians, whose experience of God guarantees the authenticity of their symbolic and conceptual descriptions of the divine nature.[161] His dependence on scripture as the source for his cataphatic theology, in both its symbolic and its rational aspects, is obvious. A key text in *DN* 2.7 speaks of how *The Theo-logical Outlines* (one of the lost works) treated the "unions and differentia-tions in the divine nature as revealed by scripture," both according to a "true explanation" (*tō alēthei logō*) — that is, cataphatically — and "in a manner that went beyond the workings of the intellect" — that is, apophatically. In this same passage Dionysius affirms that scripture does not reveal the divine nature in itself (nothing can), but only "certain activities apparent to us, activities that deify, cause being, bear life, and give wisdom" (*DN* 2.7 [644D-45B; pp. 63-64]).[162] One gets the sense that Dionysius, despite his dependence on a host of biblical passages, represents a tendency to atomize the biblical text in the service of an overriding systematic concern. Although the Areopagite distanced himself from the actual text of scripture in his concern for methodological issues, he would probably have insisted (as his disciple John the Scot later explicitly claimed) that his method was revealed in the scriptures themselves as the fundamental hermeneutical principle.

Dionysius's relations to earlier Christian authors, especially Origen and the Cappadocians, is scarcely less complex than his connection with the pagan Neoplatonists.[163] There can be no question that he commanded a wide range of both Christian and pagan sources, though the fact that his borrowings from the latter were more direct than from the former has been emphasized by those who view him as more the Neoplatonic philosopher than the Christian mystical theologian. We may gain a vantage point for approaching the problem of platonizing versus christianizing by a brief consideration of how the mysterious Dionysius synthesized the many strands of thought he inherited.

There are a variety of ways in which the Dionysian synthesis can be approached. Like forms of metaphysical scaffolding, Dionysius's structural principles provide handy modes for introducing dense speculation whose originality ultimately escapes such schematization. Among these principles, one that Dionysius often invokes as central to his thought stands out immediately, the Proclean triad of *monē, proodos, epistrophē*. In proposition 35 of his *Elements of Theology,* Proclus expressed the principle thus: "But the effect must either remain simply, or proceed simply, or combine the extreme terms, or combine the mean term with the other two; or else com-bine all three. By exclusion, every effect remains in its cause, proceeds from it, and reverts upon it."[164] This dynamic of *monē* (remaining), *proodos* (pro-ceeding), and *epistrophē* (reverting), a Neoplatonic expansion on Plato's principle of the necessity of mean terms for the connection of opposites (see *Timaeus* 31C), provides what we might call the objective perspective on Dionysius's dialectical view of how the unknown God always remains super-eminently identical with himself (*monē*), while overflowing into differentiation in his effects (*proodos*) in order eventually to regain identity by reversion (*epistrophē*). The "Light beyond all divinity," which is identical with the "Nameless Itself" (*anonymon autēn:* [*DN* 1.6; 596A]), "is at a total remove from every condition, movement, life, imagination, conjecture, name, discourse, thought, conception, being, rest, dwelling, unity, limit, infinity, the totality of existence" — that is, it always remains in itself (*monē*). "And yet, since it is the underpinning of goodness, and by merely being there is the cause of everything, to praise this divinely beneficent Providence you must turn to all of creation" (i.e., by *proodos,* the way of cataphatic theology). Therefore, "all things long for it. The intelligent and rational long for it by way of knowledge (*gnostikos*), the lower strata by way of perception, the remainder by means of stirrings of being alive" (i.e., *epistrophē* apophatically returns all things to the source) (*DN* 1.5 [593CD; p. 54]).[165] This triadic structure can provide a model for understanding the major emphases of the various treatises in the Dionysian corpus. *DN* is primarily concerned with procession, whereas *EH* and *CH* deal with lower stages of reversion. *MT* completes the account of reversion and concludes by saying what little can be said about God in himself through a series of supereminent expressions.

We can also note what may be called a subjective or epistemological perspective on the Dionysian system in which the various kinds of theology and their interaction are understood in relation to levels of apprehension.[166] For Dionysius, of course, the diverse theologies are not separate disciplines but different ways of speaking about God. The symbolic theology depends on sense knowledge; cataphatic theology operates on the level of reason, while modes of apprehension that surpass reason are used in apophatic and mystical theology (see *MT* 1, 3). While this perspective is particularly helpful for understanding the contribution that Dionysius made to the evolution of the term *theologia* in Christian history, he spends little time on epistemology as such in his concern for the objective portrayal of the divine self-unfolding.

We can also suggest a third perspective on Dionysius's system, that of the fundamental distinction between God hidden and God revealed (see esp. *DN* 1.2). Since there is no access to the hidden God save by way of God manifested in creation, all theology begins with the consideration of the God–world relation, the relation that Dionysius presents in distinctive fashion through two of his neologisms — *thearchia* and *hierarchia.*[167]

Letter 2 to Gaius illustrates the distinction between the hidden God and the manifest God (i.e., *Thearchy,* the principle of creation) thus:

> How could it be that he who surpasses everything also transcends the source of divinity (*thearchia*), transcends the source of all goodness? This is possible

if by divinity (*thearchia*) and goodness you mean the substance of the gift which makes [us] good and if you mean the inimitable imitation of him who is beyond divinity and beyond goodness. . . . (*Ep.* 2 [1068A–69A; p. 263])

Thearchy is Dionysius's new term for the triune God, who communicates himself in creation. A passage in *CH* 7, for example, praises the highest ranks of angels for passing on the message "that this Thearchy is a Monad and a tri-hypostatic Unity" whose providence reaches all things and which "transcendentally draws everything into its perennial embrace" (7.4 [212C; p. 166]).[168] Of course, *thearchia* is only one of the many cataphatic names for God, but in coining it Dionysius seems to have expressed his need for a term that would signify the transformation that his Christian under-standing of creation effected in traditional Neoplatonism. *Thearchia* and its correlate *hierarchia* are distinctively Dionysian and eminently creationist: God as the triune Thearchy is the principle of the universe conceived of primarily as hierarchy, that is, a multiplex ordered manifestation of the divine. The powers of purification, illumination, and perfection that make possible the return to God are present in the hierarchies of the created universe only because they are participations in the Thearchy.[169]

While *thearchia* did not really catch on, Dionysius's *hierarchia* proved to be one of the most potent neologisms in the history of Christian thought. The Areopagite provides several definitions of the word, the most important in *CH* 3.1: "In my opinion a hierarchy is a sacred order (*taxis hiera*), a state of understanding (*epistēmē*) and an activity (*energeia*) approximating as closely as possible to the divine" (164D; p. 153). It is "an image of the beauty of God which sacredly works out the mysteries of its own enlightenment," and "a perfect total of all its sacred constituents" (*CH* 3.2 [165B; p. 154]).[170] Since the divine Thearchy is a triunity, the Christian Trinity, every hier-archy must be both one and three in order to fulfill its function as empower-ing trinitarian manifestation (see *EH* 5.1). Each hierarchy comprises a level that perfects, one that enlightens, and one that purifies. And every hierarchy will also contain those who act, those who mediate, and those who are acted upon.

Dionysius tells us little about the legal hierarchy of the law that ruled in the Old Testament times.[171] This prepared the way for the ecclesiastical hierarchy of the New Testament era, which mediates between the material-ity of the legal hierarchy and the spiritual reality of the angelic orders that form the celestial hierarchy. The ecclesiastical hierarchy is the human realm in which the proper interpretation of sacramental rituals performed by liturgists allows the various classes of believers to be divinized. Three orders of sacred agents use three rituals to divinize three groups of Christians, because "the goal of a hierarchy . . . is to enable beings to be as like as possible to God and to be at one with him" (*CH* 3.2 [165A; p. 154]). The sacraments of baptism, Eucharist (*synaxis*), and anointing (*myron*) (*EH* 2-4) are performed by deacons, who purify; priests, who illuminate; and bishops (hierarchs), who perfect (*EH* 5). This is done for the benefit of catechumens, who are being purified; the baptized, who are being enlightened; and the monastics, who are being perfected (*EH* 6).[172] Obviously, Dionysius did not think that all Christians should become monks or bishops — what is divinizing about the hierarchy is not where one stands in it but how one grasps the divine activity manifested in the interrelations of the ordered whole.[173]

The celestial hierarchy functions in a similar way, both with respect to its inner dynamics and its larger meaning. Three groups of angels, each in turn subdivided into three, have been revealed in the symbolic language of the scriptures.[174] The first group or hierarchy is perfectly united to God and consists in the Seraphim as the source of light, the Cherubim who pass it on, and the Thrones who receive it (*CH* 7). In the middle hierarchy, the hierarchy that passes on to the lower what it receives from the higher, we find Dominations, Virtues, and Powers performing similar functions within their respective positions (*CH* 8). Finally, in the lowest hierarchy the "godlike Principalities, Archangels, and Angels" operate according to the same law (*CH* 9). Once again, we note that the function of the celestial hierarchy in our uplifting is not that we try to become angels or even that we reach God through angelic mediation, but that the proper interpretation and understanding of the angels as multiple manifestations of the divine beauty is anagogic and divinizing.[175]

Dionysius's descriptions of his hierarchies cannot help recalling the complex triads of intermediary ontological levels found in late Neoplatonism, especially in Proclus. Here Luther's barb about platonizing more than christianizing returns with renewed insistence. There can be no question that Dionysius is deeply indebted to Neoplatonism in the way he understands both hierarchy and the connection of hierarchy and Thearchy, but a study of *The Divine Names* reveals the inner changes he effected in adapting Athenian Neoplatonism in the service of Christian understanding of creation. His transformations are most evident in two areas: the way he presents divine Goodness as universal Eros, and how he uses the triad Being–Life–Intellect as a real (though still cataphatic) name for the Creator. A study of these moves is critical to any just evaluation of Dionysius's doctrine of creation and the character of his platonizing.

Origen, as we have seen, in adopting the erotic language of the Song of Songs to describe the soul's encounter with Christ came to affirm that God himself is Eros (EROS I). Dionysius, building on both Origen and on the willingness of some Neoplatonists, especially Plotinus and Proclus, to extend eros beyond its role in Plato as a purely intermediate force, created a theory of eros both cosmic and divine that was to be one of his most profound contributions to Christian theology.[176]

Plato held that eros (eros ii, in the sense described in the previous chapter) was acquisitive longing either sexual or spiritual for something not possessed. While eros cannot be ascribed to the gods themselves, it is what makes us desire to be like them—the motive power in the soul's ascent to beauty. But if eros is understood more as the desire to produce beauty than to possess it (and this too is found in Plato), some Neoplatonists extended this line of thinking and came to view eros not only as a force pervading the whole cosmos but also as perhaps applicable to the gods and even the First Principle. Plotinus, as we have seen, concluded that the Good itself "is at once lovable and love and love of himself" (*Enn.* 6.8.15);[177] but he did not develop the implications of this view of the One, nor did he present a full analysis of eros as a cosmic force. Proclus, especially in his *Commentary on the First Alcibiades* advanced such a cosmic analysis by distinguishing between *erōs pronoetikos,* the providential love by which superiors love inferiors on all levels, and *erōs epistreptikos,* the returning love by which inferiors strive to be united with their superiors. Proclus, however, did not identify the First Principle with eros.[178]

In the essay that constitutes the first four chapters of *The Divine Names* Dionysius lays down general principles concerning unified and differentiated divine names before moving on to his main purpose, a treatment of the common and united names (see *DN* 2.11). The first name to be considered, in good Platonic fashion, is "the most important name, 'Good,' which shows forth all the processions of God" (*DN* 3.1 [680B]). In the analysis of the Good that occupies the long chapter *DN* 4, the self-diffusive nature of Goodness for which light is the best symbol (*DN* 4.4–6) and the power of Goodness to move all things as a final cause lead the author to a consideration of the identity of the Good and the Beautiful (*DN* 4.7) and eventually to a detailed discussion of EROS I, considered at once as identical with the Good-Beauty and as the dynamic power by which Thearchy expresses itself in hierarchy. If the Good has a certain priority among the positive names of God, it is precisely because it is understood as Eros or divine "Yearning."

All movement in the hierarchy that is the universe comes from above and is fundamentally erotic. "All things must desire, must yearn for, must love, the Beautiful and the Good. Because of it and for its sake, subordinate is returned to superior, equal keeps company with equal, superior turns providentially to subordinate" (*DN* 4.10 [708A; p. 79]).[179] All of this, of course, can be found in Proclus. What follows is new. "And we may be so bold," Dionysius continues, "as to claim also that the cause of all things loves all things in the superabundance of his goodness, that because of this goodness, he makes all things, brings all things to perfection, holds all things together, returns all things" (*DN* 4.10). The Areopagite concludes with his definition of God as Eros— "Divine Eros is the Good of the Good for the sake of the Good" (*DN* 4.10 [708B; my translation]).[180]

Like Origen before him, Dionysius finds it necessary to defend his equation of *erōs* with the biblical term *agapē*, claiming that they can be used interchangeably because they signify the same divine reality (*DN* 4.11). Eros, however, remains his preferred term, because, as a passage in *CH* 3.4 (141D–144B) suggests, its very materiality and seeming impropriety as an "unlike likeness" make it more effective in the anagogic process. "Real Eros" (*to ontos erōs* or *alēthēs erōs*) is not to be found in physical attraction, which is a mere image, but in "the simplicity of the one divine Eros" (*DN* 4.12 [709C]). In the hierarchical universe eros is any "capacity to effect a unity, an alliance, and a particular commingling in the Beautiful and the Good" (709D). This capacity preexists in the Thearchy and from it is communicated into creation in the cosmic heartbeat of procession and reversion.

Dionysius goes even further in insisting that divine Eros must be ecstatic, producing a situation in which "the lover belongs not to self but to the beloved" (*DN* 4.13 [712A]). But how can God become ecstatic? How can he go out of himself and belong to what he loves? Dionysius's answer penetrates to the root of his understanding of Thearchy:

> It must be said that the very cause of the universe in the beautiful, good superabundance of his benign yearning for all is carried outside of himself in the loving care he has for everything. He is, as it were, beguiled by goodness, by love (*agapē*) and by yearning (*erōs*) and is enticed away from his dwelling place and comes to abide within all things, and he does so by virtue of his supernatural and ecstatic capacity to remain, nevertheless, within himself. (*DN* 4.13 [712AB; p. 82])

In other words, God alone can totally go out of himself in a complete ecstasy of self-giving because he alone has the ability to remain absolutely within himself, utterly transcendent to all things. He loves himself in all things from the very same ground and for the same reason that he loves himself apart from all things. While Dionysius shared a dialectical view of God with his Neoplatonic predecessors, he is the first to express this dialectical understanding primarily in terms of God as Eros.

Eros in Dionysius is not only transcendent but also fully cosmic. Because the Thearchy is totally and perfectly erotic, the hierarchy must be the same.

God is both the object of the yearning of all things to return to him and that very yearning itself as participated in by all levels of the individual hierarchies. "He is yearning on the move, simple, self-moved, self-acting, preexistent in the Good, flowing out from the Good onto all that is and returning once again to the Good" (*DN* 4.14 [712CD; pp. 82–83]). In the circle of love that forms the Dionysian universe we have a God who becomes ecstatic in procession and a universe whose ecstasy is realized in reversion.[181]

To this important transformation of Platonic eros as a way of understanding the relation between God and the universe can be added a second major shift, one that becomes especially clear in *The Divine Names* 5–7, where Dionysius considers the triad of Being–Life–Wisdom (his version of the Neoplatonic triad of Being–Life–Intellect). The work of E. Corsini and S. Gersh, among others, has shown how important Dionysius's alteration of this triad was in the creation of that tradition of Christian Neoplatonism which was central to Maximus the Confessor and John the Scot, and which also had significant repercussions on many later figures.[182]

The Neoplatonic triad of Being–Life–Intellect developed out of Plotinus's analyses of the activities of Nous (e.g., *Enn.* 6.8.16) and had an important history in later Neoplatonism primarily as a way to understand the characteristics of the primary level of emanation from the First Principle, that is, of grasping how plurality is derived from unity.[183] For Proclus *on-zōē–nous* flowed directly from the Unknown One as the supreme triad whose characteristics and activities permeated all subsequent levels of reality in a complex enneadic structure.[184] Proclus and other late Neoplatonists discovered this doctrine in Plato's *Parmenides* by interpreting the negative attributes of the first hypothesis (*Parmenides* 137C–142B) as applying to the One, while ascribing the positive predicates of the second hypothesis (*Parmenides* 142B–157B) to the triad.[185] For Dionysius and his followers, however, to make the first "produced" triad the actual source of all multiplicity seemed to conflict with Christian belief in a Creator who was the direct cause of the universe and all that is within it. As Stephen Gersh puts it, ". . . although the multiplication of the primal unity is also a fundamental problem for Christian Neoplatonists, they attempt to solve it not by the postulation of intermediaries but by locating the source of multiplicity within the First Principle itself."[186]

In chapter 5 of *The Divine Names* Dionysius turns from a consideration of the name "Goodness" to the triad Being–Life–Wisdom (5.1 [816Bff.; pp. 76ff.]),[187] explicitly criticizing pagan (Proclean) formulations in which this triad was considered to be a series of gods who exercise providential activity on lower ranks of reality:

I do not think of the Good as one thing, Being as another, Life and Wisdom as yet other, and I do not claim that there are numerous causes and different Godheads, all differently ranked, superior and inferior, and all producing different effects. No. But I hold that there is one God for all these good processions and that he is the possessor of the divine names of which I speak. . . . (*DN* 5.2 [816C–817A; p. 97])[188]

Applying the dialectic he introduced in *DN* 2.11 concerning how common names of the Thearchy such as "being" ". . . become differentiated in a unified way . . . so that his single existence is said to be manifold by virtue of the fact that it brings so many things to being from itself" (2.11 [649B; p. 66]), Dionysius effects a major turn in the history of Neoplatonism by identifying the primal triad, like Goodness itself, not with the first production but with Thearchy itself cataphatically considered. Of course, this cataphatic identity is not the whole story. Dionysius's dialectical view of God demands that this affirmation always be joined to two other claims. First, he continues to assert that the First Principle as apophatically unknowable also *causes* the triad Being–Life–Wisdom, which, from this perspective, can be viewed in a hierarchical fashion according to which Being is superior to Life and Life in turn exceeds Wisdom.[189] Second, we have a contrasting series of assertions, particularly in Dionysius's attacks on pagan views of the triads as gods, which emphasize that there is no subordination among the terms from the divine perspective insofar as God as transcendent cause precontains them in a unified manner.[190] All three of these forms of assertion must be taken together to grasp the complex mode of Dionysius's adaptation and revision of the Neoplatonic triad.

The significance of this shift is to be seen in terms of the doctrine of creation. It is clear that the Areopagite sees God as the direct and immediate cause of all things as individuals and in all their particular qualities.[191] God does not act *through* intermediaries so that individual material beings have a relation to him only insofar as they participate in higher immaterial paradigms or forms. All things — even material things in their materiality — are good manifestations of the ecstatic divine Eros, whose procession into its effects constitutes the ordered scheme of hierarchies. Every individual thing is a created reflection of the divine mind. In knowing himself, God knows everything, "material things immaterially, divisible things indivisibly, plurality in a single act" (*DN* 7.2 [896B; p. 108]).

Because Dionysius continued to use the metaphors of emanation (as did Albert the Great, Bonaventure, and Thomas Aquinas, among others after him),[192] he has been accused of advancing a view of the God–world relation that fails to give adequate expression to the Christian doctrine of creation by making production a divine necessity and by forcing God to act through intermediaries in order to protect him from direct contact with inferior material existence. Nothing could be further from the truth, as this account has tried to show.[193] Although Dionysius does present a hierarchical view of creation that uses the emanational language of late Neoplatonism, and although he does allow for intermediate causality in the way in which the hierarchies interact within their own orders and in relation to each other,[194] the most important thing in his universe is the direct relation of absolute dependence that each individual reality has to the Thearchy that creates all things.[195] From the human perspective, the understanding of the activities of the hierarchies reveals the immediacy of all creatures to divine Eros. This is the heart of Dionysius's distinctive Christian Neoplatonism.

The Dionysian understanding of mysticism cannot be separated from the dialectical systematics considered above. The objective character of his mysticism has often proved to be a puzzle for those who define mysticism in terms of autobiographical accounts of special experiences of the divine presence.[196] It is not that Dionysius does not appeal to the witness of those who had been granted special experience of God, but he never ascribes this knowledge to himself. Rather it is always spoken of in relation to his teachers, mediate and immediate: Moses and Paul, Carpos and Hierotheus. In this he was adhering to the tradition laid down by his Christian predecessors, who had usually eschewed personal accounts in favor of witnessing to the ecclesial reality of the anagogic life of the believer. This would also better fit the pedagogic character of the corpus which Paul Rorem describes as having "the feel of a leader's manual or guide, intended not for the immediate use of all the faithful but for the guidance of the hierarch who in turn leads others on this spiritual journey."[197] What kind of a spiritual journey does the Dionysian corpus reveal? A description of some basic assumptions and an analysis of Dionysius's key notions will help us to understand its contours.

At the start we must emphasize once again the fundamentally ecclesial and liturgical nature of Dionysian mysticism. The *anagōgē* or uplifting process that returns us to union with God is not a solitary journey of "the alone to the Alone" in the manner of Plotinus, but a process that is accomplished through the interaction of the three essential aspects of the life of the church: (1) the proper understanding of the "holy oracles," (2) in and through the action of the sacred rituals, (3) performed (or received) according to one's place in the ecclesiastical hierarchy. Evagrius had insisted, "If you are a theologian you truly pray," understanding prayer primarily as an individual contemplative exercise. Dionysius would claim that to be a true theologian is to pray liturgically: "The whole theology of the Areopagite is for him a single, sacred liturgical act."[198] Both authors would agree that to be a true theologian one would have to be what later centuries would call a mystic.

A second basic assumption concerns Dionysius's understanding of reversion (*epistrophē*) or uplifting (*anagōgē*).[199] The motifs of ascent and journey that we have seen used by Greek philosophers and Christian writers were always considered to be primarily metaphors for spiritual processes, but in Dionysius the metaphorical character is heightened beyond what we have seen in Origen and Evagrius. Given Dionysius's conception of the whole created hierarchy as an ordered manifestation of Thearchy, one does not really ascend *to* God by passing through various levels of reality as much as one appropriates the significance of the levels as a means of attaining inner union with their source, the hidden God.[200] Augustine, as we shall see, will insist that to go above (*transire*) is really to go within the soul (*intrare*). For Dionysius (less introspective than the bishop of Hippo) uplifting is really more like "instressing" (to borrow a term from Gerard Manley Hopkins).[201]

Finally, we note also by way of basic assumptions the way in which Dionysius uses the qualifier *mystikos* and its equivalents. As we have seen, by the time of Clement of Alexandria the term had already become a Christian possession used to express the secret modes of manifestation of the hidden divine reality in scripture, rite, and prayer.[202] In the writings ascribed to Macarius it had even come to modify union or sharing with God—the earliest appearance of "mystical union" in Christian literature. But it was Dionysius more than anyone who gave the word the importance it has continued to enjoy in Christian thought, using it often and in key contexts in his writings.[203]

The Areopagite, of course, is most noted for creation of the concept "mystical theology" (*theologia mystikē*). This *terminus technicus* signifies not a particular kind of experience but the knowledge (or, better, "super-knowledge") that deals with the mystery of God in himself, the *monē*.[204] Although Dionysius differentiates mystical theology from symbolic and cataphatic theology, these are discriminations of functions not discrete kinds of theology. Hence, it is not incorrect to say that the whole of his thought is mystical insofar as the interaction of all the modes has as its goal attaining union with God in darkness and silence.[205]

Given this fundamentally objective sense, we may ask if Dionysius ever used "mystical" in a more subjective or experiential way. We can point to an important text in *DN* 2.9 as evidence for a move in this direction.[206] Here, in speaking of the doctrine that his teacher Hierotheus acquired either directly from the "holy theologians" (*hieroi theologoi*, i.e., the authors of scripture), or from study of their writings, he speaks of a third and higher type of knowledge in which Hierotheus ". . . was initiated into them [i.e., divine truths] by some more divine inspiration, not only learning the things of God but experiencing them, and through this sympathy with them, if we may say this, having been consummated in initiation into mystical union and faith in them which cannot be taught" (*DN* 2.9 [648B]).[207] The distinction between "knowing by mental effort" (*mathein*) and "knowing by special experience" (*pathein*) used here appears in a famous fragment of Aristotle as a way of describing the knowledge acquired in the mysteries.[208] This aspect is heightened by the use of the term *sympatheia*, used in late Neoplatonism to describe the bonds between the different levels of reality that make theurgic activity possible.[209] Dionysius's qualifier ("if we may say this") hints at another transformation of the Neoplatonic use — "sympathy" for Dionysius is not so much an ontological bond by which material things are manipulated to acquire an access to the upper world as it is an affinity for "reading" the inner meaning of the hierarchies as manifestations of Thearchy.

When we compare these passages on Hierotheus with those in which Dionysius treats his other exemplary mystics, Moses, Paul, and Carpos,[210] a definite pattern emerges. The special experience, knowledge, vision (*theopteia* [*Ep.* 8.6; 1097C]) that these mystics received is described in language often reminiscent of that employed in *The Ecclesiastical Hierarchy* for the celebration of the liturgy. So if Dionysius can be said to include at least elements of a more existential dimension to the term "mystical" (though always ascribed to his teachers and not to himself), this experience is liturgical and ecclesial in setting and context. *The Mystical Theology* is inseparable from *The Ecclesiastical Hierarchy*.[211]

In the first chapter of *MT* Moses appears as the ideal mystic (as he had in Philo and Gregory of Nyssa), the one who undergoes first purification (*katharsis*), then gains contemplation (*theōria*) of the place (not the essence) of God, and finally attains union (*henōsis*).

Here, renouncing all that the mind may conceive, wrapped entirely in the intangible and the invisible, he belongs completely to him who is beyond everything. Here, being neither oneself nor someone else, one is supremely united (*kata to kreitton henoumenos*) by a completely unknowing inactivity of all knowledge, and knows beyond the mind by knowing nothing. (*MT* 1.3 [1001A; p. 137])

This triple pattern, which we have seen adumbrated in Origen and reflected in Evagrius's distinctions between *praktikē* and the two kinds of *theōria*, appears throughout the corpus, especially in the two hierarchies (e.g., *EH* 5.I.3, 7; 6.III.5–6; *CH* 3.2; 7.2–3; 10.1).[212] Over the centuries it was to remain one of the most common ways to understand the mystical itinerary. Dionysius's use of this common triple pattern of purification, illumination, and perfection or union, however, must be viewed according to his understanding of the operation of the diverse modes of theology in the life of the believer.

A well-known passage from *Letter* 9 provides a good starting point:

> Theological tradition has a dual aspect, the ineffable and the mysterious on the one hand, the open and more evident on the other. The one resorts to symbolism and involves initiation. The other is philosophic and employs the method of demonstration. . . . The one uses persuasion and imposes the truthfulness of what is asserted. The other acts and, by means of a mystery which cannot be taught, it puts souls firmly in the presence of God. (*Ep.* 9.1 [1105D; p. 283])[213]

The term "theological tradition" indicates that we are dealing with something broader than what would be called theology today, a reality that might be best described as the total life of the church in which Bible and liturgy are used both positively to teach truths about God and negatively to make the divine mystery present in ways that resist any "demonstration." What cannot be demonstrated can be made present both on the material level of the symbols used by scripture and in the liturgy (the main concern of *Letter* 9), and also, by extension, on the conceptual or intellectual level, where the negation of names and eventually the removal of both affirmation and negation bring the soul to union with the divine mystery.

One of the cornerstones of the Dionysian method is introduced here: the necessity of both affirmation and negation (how can something be negated unless it is first affirmed?). Of course, the negating moment has priority in each stage of this dialectic because of its more direct relation to the divine transcendence. In *CH* 2 Dionysius notes that God is revealed through both similar and dissimilar symbols, understanding the similar symbols as conceptual names like Word, Mind, and Being, while the dissimilar symbols are those drawn from the material world (*CH* 2.3 [140C; p. 149]).[214] But there are also "utterly dissimilar revelations" on the conceptual level, those in which God is described through negations such as "invisible, infinite, ungraspable." Since "God is in no way like the things that have being and we have no knowledge at all of his incomprehensible and ineffable transcendence and invisibility" (140D), the way of negation must be superior to that of affirmation, both on the symbolic level where "incongruities are more suitable for lifting our minds up into the domain of the spiritual than similarities are" (141A), and on the intellectual level as well. "So true negations and the unlike comparisons with their last echoes offer due homage to divine things" (*CH* 2.5 [145A; pp. 152–53]).

All things both reveal and conceal God. The "dissimilar similarity" that constitutes every created manifestation of God is both a similarity to be affirmed and a dissimilarity to be denied.[215] Therefore, the universe is both necessary as an image and impossible as a representation of the God for whom there is no adequate representation.[216] It is only in and through the full appropriation of the cataphatic moment, however — that is, by immersion in the beauty of the universe — that we can dialectically attain the negation of representations necessary for discovering that God is always more than we can conceive.

This dialectic is central to the soul's progressive appropriation of the various functions of what Dionysius calls "the theological tradition." On the symbolic level we find God in the positive symbols of scripture and liturgy at the same time that we begin, through the shock of dissimilar symbols, to recognize that we must surpass the material level to reach the conceptual level of meaning. On the conceptual level, in which we ascribe names to God (as in *DN*) we also begin to learn that all conceptual signification must be abandoned in order to appreciate the real depths of the dissimilarity that leads to God.[217] It is here that Dionysius's special contribution to the history of negative theology is to be found.

In insisting on the superiority of negation over affirmation in all predication relating to God (e.g., *DN* 13.3; *MT* 1-5; *CH* 2.3), Dionysius is careful to distinguish between negation by way of insufficiency and the negation by transcendence that alone is fitting for the divine.[218] Both modes of knowing, however, remain indispensable: "God is therefore known in all things and as distinct from all things. He is known through knowledge (*gnōsis*) and through unknowing" (*agnōsia*) (*DN* 7.3 [872A; pp. 108–9]). This knowing through unknowing is the heart of Dioysius's negative theology.

Jan Vanneste has shown the importance of three terms for understanding Dionysius's apophaticism — *aphairesis, agnōsia,* and *henōsis.*[219] The first two pertain to apophatic theology in the proper sense; the third belongs to the mystical theology that is its goal — that is, what lies beyond both affirmation and negation. *Aphairesis* is best described as "clearing aside" or "negative abstraction," that is, the conceptual analogue to the use of dissimilar symbols found in the operation of consciously stripping away all predicates, however exalted, from God because none of them does justice to his transcendent perfection. Contrasting positive and negative theology in *MT* 2, Dionysius says:

> Now it seems to me that we should praise the denials (*aphaireseis*) quite differently than we do the assertions (*thesesin*). . . . As we climb from the last things up to the most primary we deny all things (*ta panta aphairoumen*) so that

we may unhiddenly know that unknowing (*agnōsian*) which itself is hidden from all those possessed of knowing amid all beings. . . . (1025B; p. 138)

Examples of the exercise of this "aphairetic mode" throughout the corpus are too numerous to cite. Such classic passages as *DN* 7, 9, 13 and *MT* 3 provide a good sense of the method.

Aphairesis leads to *agnōsia,* another important term in Dionysius's mystical vocabulary.[220] For Evagrius Ponticus, "essential gnosis of the Trinity" was the goal; Dionysius, more resolutely apophatic, wishes to negate all knowing. What exactly is this unknowing that the Areopagite praises so highly? Obviously, it is not a "what" at all, not some concept or content that can be described or defined. It is more like a state of mind (if only in a paradoxical way) — the subjective correlative to the objective unknowability of God. It can only be spoken about through paradoxical assertions of contraries: *agnōsia* is the only true *gnōsis* of God. "And this quite positively complete unknowing is knowledge of him who is above everything that is known" (*Ep.* 1 [1065AB; p. 263]),[221]

Dionysius has two ways of speaking about unknowing, as befits his distinction between symbolic and rational theology. Mystical theology in the proper sense lies beyond all images and names and therefore cannot be spoken or written about. But mystical theology *as written* (improperly) is constructed through the aid of symbolic theology and rational theology, which lend the mystical theologian terms from the worlds of symbolic and conceptual discourse that are used in transferred senses in order to suggest what lies beyond all speech. From the world of symbolic discourse Dionysius takes the language of darkness (*skotos, gnophos*), cloud (*nephelē*), and silence (*sigē*) drawn from the account of Moses' ascent to meet God on Sinai (Exodus 19–20) to provide metaphorical descriptions of attaining the hidden God.[222] Moses is the model of one who, breaking free of all seeing, "plunges into the truly mystical darkness of unknowing" (*kai eis ton gnophon tēs agnōsias eisdynei ton ontos mystikon*) (*MT* 1.3 [1001A; my translation]). In appealing to the story of Moses' dark encounter with God, of course, Dionysius was following in a tradition that stretched back to Philo and that had been notably set forth by Gregory of Nyssa.[223] We should note that the mysticism of darkness is not found among pagan Neoplatonists. Indeed, we may even surmise that this distinctively biblical apophaticism serves as a critique of late antique pagan theology with its heavy use of light imagery.[224] Although the Areopagite did not invent the theme of divine darkness, and although he uses it in a primarily objective sense to signify God's utter unknowability, the fact that this unknowability indicates that we attain him only through unknowing (*agnōsia*) means that later, more subjective uses of the Dionysian language, as in the famous *Cloud of Unknowing* of the fourteenth century, are not necessarily illegitimate.[225]

The second mode of using language to suggest what lies beyond it is more complex. Dionysius asserts not only that God is unknowable but that he is "more than unknowable" (*hyperagnostos* [*MT* 1.1; 997A]). What can this mean?

Dionysius teaches that while negation is superior to affirmation in the anagogic process, *both* negation and affirmation need to be surpassed to reach union with God. The Areopagite sometimes, as in *DN* 2.3-4, uses a treatment of "hyper-terms," that is, super-eminent predications such as More-than-Good, More-than-God, More-than-Being (*to hyperagathon, to hypertheon, to hyperousian*) as a way of underlining the point that the divine unified names are "more than ineffable and more than unknowable." This is because within its undifferentiated unity the Trinity holds "the assertion of all things, the denials of all things [and] *that which is beyond every assertion and denial* (*DN* 2.3-4 [640B-641A; pp. 60-61]).[226] That God lies beyond both affirmation and negation is the final message of the great hymn of negations that concludes *The Mystical Theology:*

> It is beyond assertion and denial. We make assertions and denials of what is next to it, but never of it, for it is both beyond every assertion, being the perfect and unique cause of all things, and, by virtue of its preeminently simple and absolute nature, free of every limitation, beyond every limitation; it is also beyond every denial. (5 [1048B; p. 141]; see also 1.2 [1000B])

In arriving at this conclusion, Dionysius often employs what Thomas Tomasic has called "collision statements," that is, dialectical combinations of contrary and even contradictory predicates in relation to God.[227] Sometimes these are negations of paired opposites reminiscent of the first hypothesis of the *Parmenides;*[228] in other places they are affirmations of paired opposites, as in the second hypothesis.[229] Other texts both affirm and deny that contrary and even contradictory predicates can be ascribed to God in a fully dialectical fashion.[230]

Dionysius's intricate use of affirmative, negative, and the three forms of eminent predication just mentioned have occasioned much analysis and discussion. Some have highlighted their relation to the forms of positive and negative predication present in late Neoplatonism;[231] others have sought to evaluate the adequacy of this mode of God-language.[232] More than any other patristic author, Dionysius used language (indeed a very special language of his own) to subvert the claims of language — a position that has remained controversial.

One way to illustrate the logic of Dionysius's various forms of God-language can be illustrated by the following equations:

1. God is x (true, metaphorically).
2. God is not-x (true, anagogically).
3. God is neither x nor not-x (true, unitively).

The third form of predication indicates not "mere" transcendence (which appears under 2), but the form of special eminence that the Areopagite indicated through his more extravagant hyper-terms.[233] Michel Corbin has argued that this form of what he calls "sur-eminence" goes beyond ordinary eminent language to form a redoubling negation according to the form "non-x=more x than the most-x."[234] While this may not be untrue to Dionysius's intentions, it perhaps gives too unilateral a formalization to a mystery the Areopagite wished to signal through the play of a variety of negations.[235]

The issues surrounding the meaning of *agnōsia* should not blind us to the fact that it is not unknowing as such but union (*henōsis*) that is the goal of Dionysian anagogy. It is not easy to determine the relation between the two: is *agnōsia* the threshold to the inner chamber of union, or is it in some way identical with it? Both terms deal with a level of reality that surpasses conceptual language, so the question is somewhat artificial; but Dionysius's use of the terms seems to suggest some differences between them.

The later importance (and sometimes dominance) of the notion of union as a characterization of how the human person achieves an immediate relation to the divine presence is another mark of Dionysius's influence in the later tradition. Of course, union with God was not a new concept, as we have seen in our treatment of the Greek philosophical mystics and the early Greek patristic authors, but once again Dionysius's use of the term gave it a new importance.

Dionysius claimed that his teacher Hierotheus attained "mystical union" with divine things (*DN* 2.9). This is the only place where the Areopagite uses the *terminus technicus* which was to become popular in the modern era,[236] but there are many appearances of *henōsis* and related terms (e.g., *koinōnia*) in relation to the goal of *epistrophē*.[237] In *MT* 1 Dionysius advises "Timothy" to ". . . leave behind everything perceived and understood . . . to strive upward as much as you can to union (*henōsin*) with him who is beyond all being and knowledge."[238] *DN* 7.3 speaks of achieving "the most divine knowledge of God, that which comes through unknowing . . . in a union far beyond the mind" (872B; p. 109).[239] Union should not be separated from the liturgical context within which Dionysius insists that the believer achieves the goal. *EH* 3.1 says that "every sacredly initiating operation draws our fragmented lives together into a one-like divinization. It forges a divine unity out of the divisions among us. It grants us communion and union with the One" (*koinōnian kai henōsin pros ton Hena*) (*EH* 3.I.1 [424CD; p. 209]).[240] In applying the language of union to Moses in *MT* 1.3, Dionysius speaks of being "supremely united by a completely unknowing inactivity (*anenergesia*) of all knowledge" (1001A; p. 137). This term suggests the kind of passivity in the higher stages of union that later mystics often discussed, especially after the sixteenth century; but we should beware of reading back too many of their distinctions into a different thought world.

Despite his numerous uses of *henōsis* and other terms related to union, Dionysius does not expatiate on the nature of union, nor does he, like many later authors, relate it to specific New Testament proof texts that would help to place it within certain broad traditions.[241] One thing is clear, however: union with God is to be thought of in terms of divinization, which "consists of being as much as possible like and in union with God" (*EH* 1.3 [376A; p. 198]).[242] Divinization (generally *theōsis*) is the gift that God bestows on beings endowed with reason and intelligence (*EH* 1.4) through their participation in the hierarchies. "We see our human hierarchy . . . pluralized in a great variety of perceptible symbols lifting us upward hierarchically until we are brought as far as we can be into the unity of divinization" (*EH* 1.2 [373AB; p. 197]).[243]

In identifying union with divinization, Dionysius was tying his new form of dialectical mysticism to what had already become a standard theme in Christian thought. The Areopagite's vocabulary is new, for example, in his description of God as "the Thearchy of those being divinized" (*DN* 1.3 [589C]; cf. 1.4 [376B]), but his doctrine agrees with his Christian predecessors on a crucial issue separating Christian mystical theory from its pagan contemporaries: whether the soul is naturally divine. Even in Origen and Evagrius, who both maintain a prior precosmic creation of intellectual beings, there is a crucial, if not always well-articulated, distinction between real divinity and loaned divinization. Dionysius, on this issue far less Platonic than most other patristic authors, has no place for a prior creation.[244] Thus, his view of the relation of Thearchy and the soul as a part of hierarchy is both greater and less than the predialectical Christian mystics: the soul is divine and can achieve a form of indistinct union with God, but it is divine only as a *manifestation* and is unified and divinized only by God's uplifting eros. Divinization is a gift, not a birthright.[245]

Divinizing union has important relations to two other key terms: *theōria*, a central issue in all Greek patristic mysticism; and *ekstasis*, a less traditional but still important concept.[246] The Areopagite's use of both terms is comprehensible only within the broad framework of his systematics.

For Dionysius *theōria,* or contemplation, was rooted in God himself insofar as the positive name *theos* was thought to derive from *theasthai* ("to behold").[247] *Theōria* is the ability to behold the Thearchy in and through the hierarchy of the creation. On the symbolic level it is the insight into scriptural symbols and liturgical actions by means of which we pass from mere material presentations to inner meanings.[248] On a higher plane, within the ecclesiastical and celestial hierarchies, each level has a *theōria* appropriate to it,[249] and each of these is directed to the yet higher stage of *theōria* where enlightenments concerning the divine names come down from above.[250] But if contemplation of the divine names pertains primarily to illumination, the second stage in the Dionysian itinerary, we may wonder if *theōria* represents something to be overcome on the perfecting level of union that is achieved in the "dazzling darkness of hidden silence" (*MT* 1.1 [997B]). To be sure, Dionysius insists that all sensible and intellectual *theōria* must be forsaken in the passage into darkness; but, paradoxically, even here Dionysius claims that Timothy will strive after "hidden mystical contemplations" (*ta mystika theamata*), that is, things that are seen in not being seen, contemplations that pertain to the *agnōsia* that is the only true *gnōsis* of God.[251] Dionysius's view of contemplation, then, is in perfect conformity with his dialectical view of God. In the words of René Roques: "*Theōria* achieves its completion in an ecstasy that surpasses but does not annihilate it."[252]

Ek-stasis (literally, "standing outside") and forms of the verb *existēmi* ("to go out from") appear only rarely in the corpus but are still important.[253] They may be described as markers signifying the transition to the place where all values are transmuted — both reversed (ignorance becomes knowledge, darkness becomes dazzling) and transcendentalized by passing beyond *both* affirmation and negation. Ecstasy effects this radical rupture through the power of love, the divine eros (*theios erōs*) implanted in the world through the ecstasy of God.[254] Through ecstasy we pass beyond the human condition and become divinized.

As we have seen, Dionysius took the daring step of affirming ecstasy first of God himself, both in terms of *creating ecstasy,* that is, the procession by which God stands outside himself in the eros (EROS I) that constitutes the world (*DN* 4.13 [712A]), and of what we might call the *transcending ecstasy* by which he always remains perfectly in himself and outside all things. *Letter* 9 describes this as a divine inebriation in which God like a drunken lover (see Song 5:1) "stands outside of all good things, being the superfullness of all these things" (*Ep.* 9.5 [1112BC; p. 287]).[255] Driven by the yearning of the *erōs epistreptikos,* which suffuses the universe, the soul strives upward by means of negations, "since this stands the soul outside everything which is correlative to its own finite nature" (*DN* 13.3 [981B; p. 130]). The model for this is Paul, Dionysius's apostolic teacher:

> This is why the great Paul, swept along by his yearning for God and seized of its ecstatic power, had this inspired word to say: "It is no longer I who live, but Christ who lives in me" (Gal 2:20). Paul was truly a lover and, as he says, he was beside himself for God (2 Cor 5:13), possessing not his own life but the life of the One for whom he yearned, as exceptionally beloved. (*DN* 7.13 [712A; p. 82])[256]

Dionysius's conception of union is based on a transcendentalizing of knowing into unknowing and of yearning eros into ecstatic possession.[257] Both love and knowledge have essential roles, though love's is higher. It is true that Dionysius's language of eros is not couched in the sexualized inter-subjective imagery of the Song of Songs, but in the objective analysis of eros as a metaphysical principle. This does not lessen his contribution to the history of love in Western Christian mysticism.

The mention of the Song of Songs does raise one further issue. In Origen, Gregory of Nyssa, and the later mystical commentators on the Song we find great emphasis (differently conceived, to be sure) on the role of Christ, the Divine Lover made flesh, in the soul's return to God. We have been able to discuss Dionysius's mysticism without mention of Christ thus far. What role, if any, does the God-man play for him?

The issue is not about the orthodoxy of Dionysius's Christology (though some have suspected him of Monophysite tendencies), nor is it about failure to mention Jesus the Christ — he appears often in the corpus. The issue is rather how central Jesus' theandric activity is to the process of return. Here, as noted at the outset, there has been considerable difference of opinion. Even scholars sympathetic to Dionysius, such as von Ivánka, Roques, and Rorem, have wondered if his mysticism leaves large enough a place for Christ.[258] Others, such as Lossky, von Balthasar, and Corbin, have insisted that there is a central role for Christ in Dionysian mysticism.[259]

It must be confessed at the outset that neither the procession of the Logos from the Father nor the Incarnation of that Logos in human nature plays the same structural role in Dionysius that it does in his dialectical successors, such as Maximus, John the Scot, and Meister Eckhart. The Areopagite's remarks on Christ are scattered and to some extent unassimilated into his more systematic works, especially *The Divine Names* and *Mystical Theology;* the most important passages occur in *The Ecclesiastical Hierarchy, Celestial Hierarchy,* and in the *Letters.* Dionysius is not without a sense of personal devotion to the God-man, as when he prays that his discourse may be guided "by Christ, by my Christ" at the beginning of *CH* (2.5 [145B]).

But, as we may expect, it is the more objective language of how Jesus functions in the return to God that predominates. A key text is found in *EH* 1.2, where Dionysius calls on "Jesus, the source and perfection of every hierarchy" (1.2 [373B; p. 197]; cf. 1.1 [372B]). Given the importance of the hierarchies in anagogy, this indicates a crucial role for Jesus, though one which Dionysius does not always draw out explicitly. There are texts, however, that demonstrate the role of Jesus in both the celestial and the ecclesiastical hierarchies. In *CH* 7.2 the highest hierarchy of angels is said to be contemplative precisely because they have entered "into communion with Jesus . . . by truly coming close to him in a primary participation" (208C; p. 163; cf. 7.4 [209AB; p. 164]). The sacraments of baptism (*EH* 2.III.6-7 [404AC]), Eucharist (*CH* 1.3 [124A]), and anointing (*EH* 4.III.12 [484D-485A]) all effect participation in Jesus and his saving work, while in *EH* 5.I.5 (505B) the fact that every hierarchy reaches its perfection in Jesus is taken as the ground for the necessity of a "hierarch" in each sacred order. Proposing the life of Jesus for our imitation is also important for Dionysius (e.g., *EH* 7.I.2 [553C]), especially in the *Letters,* where the false monk Demophilus is upbraided for not heeding Jesus' example (*Ep.* 8.1, 4 [1085D-1088A, 1096AC]), and the good hierarch Carpos is presented with a vision of the merciful Jesus that tempers his zeal against sinners (*Ep.* 8.6 [1100C]). Perhaps the most significant aspect of the Areopagite's teaching about Jesus' hierarchical activity is its motive force: love. Again and again, he insists on the Incarnation as a work of divine love,[260] and more tellingly he says that to affirm this truth is to begin to negate the world and thus return to God — "every affirmation regarding Jesus's love for humanity has the force of a negation pointing toward transcendence" (*Ep.* 4 [1072B; p. 264]).

Finally, one other christological component of Dionysius's mysticism deserves consideration. We noted above the dispute over the role of mediation in the Dionysian system. While there can be no question concerning the immediacy of God's creative activity in *proodos,* there is debate over how the divine power continues to be communicated in the hierarchies and over the function of these hierarchies in the ascent. There seems to be some tension between *DN* and *MT* on the one hand, which stress the immediacy of all contact with God, and *EH* and *CH* on the other, which suggest, at least in some texts (e.g., *EH* 6.6 [537C]), a necessity for intermediary activity. Roques has suggested that it is the position of Jesus as the source and perfection of every hierarchy that provides a solution to this tension, though not one explicitly thematized by the Areopagite. Because Christ as God is the head of the celestial hierarchy and as man is the head of the ecclesiatical, the one God-man is the supreme hierarch to whom all are immediately related in attaining union.[261]

Evaluating Dionysius has always been a task dependent on the interpeter's theological stance. Is the mysterious Areopagite a Neoplatonist masquerading as a Christian? Such an extreme view neglects too much evidence to make sense. Is he a misguided Christian thinker who was so overwhelmed by Neoplatonism that he compromised basic biblical beliefs? Many since Luther have thought so, but their case rests on a view of the nature of biblical Christianity that not all Christians have shared. Still, judgments must be made — if not absolute ones, at least those that will try to evaluate how adequate or authentic a given thinker is within a particular situation and what effect his thought has had on the tradition of Christian mysticism.

The importance of the Areopagite lies in the fact that with him theology first became explicitly mystical, that is, he created the categories (including "mystical theology" itself) that enabled later Christian mystics to relate their consciousness of God's presence and the mystery of his absence to the tradition of the apostolic teaching represented by "Dionysius." Our mysterious writer was to remain the master of theology in its mystical incarnations at least in part because later mystics found in his writings the principles by which their lives and experiences could be understood both as expressions of and as essential to the divinizing action of the church's life.

There can be no question of the extent of Dionysius's influence. One measure of the power, or again perhaps of the problematic of his thought, is that there has been very little "pure" Dionysianism in the history of Christianity. From the start his writings were treated much like the Bible itself — as a divine message filled with inner life and mysterious meaning which could never be exhausted, but which needed to be reread in each generation and reinterpreted in the light of new issues. He himself, however, would probably not have been unhappy with this hermeneutical flexibility, since no one knew better the limits of words in the face of the true Mystery. "What is to be said of it remains unsayable; what is to be understood of it remains unknowable" (*Ep.* 3 [1069B; p. 264]).

Conclusion

C HRISTIANITY BEGAN among Jews, but in a milieu already heavily colored by Hellenism. Almost from its origins, the new religion expressed itself in the Greek language and, as it spread to a wider audience, spoke more and more in the Greek of the intelligentsia. This process is especially evident in the history of the mystical elements in Greek patristic thought. The growing importance of terms like *theōria, apatheia,* and *henōsis,* not found in the New Testament (*theōria* occurs once in a nonmystical sense), as well as debates over the proper interpretation of terms like *gnōsis* and *agapē,* which are found in abundance there, provides clear proof of this shift. But to reduce the story of early Christian mysticism to the history of Greek impact on an "original" Christianity (whether this is judged to be a good or a bad thing) would be to misunderstand the history of Christian mysticism.

The Greek fathers, no matter how much they adopted the intellectual categories of the world they were seeking to convert, remained conscious of having to measure and often to modify what they took over on the basis of the belief of the Christian community as enshrined in its authentic scriptures, established teachers, and saving rituals. Of course, they were often not aware of how much cultural baggage they unconsciously carried over from their contemporary milieu into their theology, but this does not negate the importance of their intention to judge all things in the light of Christ — it only indicates the limits of all historical horizons. The ecclesial setting of early Christian mysticism is the great fact that sets it off from contemporary phenomena which often look remarkably similar. The Christians found God not in philosophical speculation and theurgic practice but in and through their life in the tightly knit structure of the *ekklēsia*.

The basic purpose of this first section has been to lay out the foundations of the Western Christian mysticism that is the main subject of these volumes. While these chapters have not tried to tell the full story, they have, at least, suggested that mysticism, when it appears in an identifiable and explicit fashion, as with Origen, is not wholly an innovation in Christianity, but that the great Christian mystics of the third through the fifth centuries c.e. could appeal to a number of elements present in the new religion from its beginnings to justify their views.

The first of these elements was the belief in the new and final presence of God realized in Jesus, the incarnate Logos. The believer's response to this presence was, as we have seen, described in a variety of ways, often by the same author: imitation and following, loving pursuit and marriage, illumination and contemplation, divinization and union. Though understood by different authors in different ways, the christological emphasis of early Christian mysticism is inescapable.

The new and ultimate manifestation of God's presence in Christ reached the faithful in and through the church, as noted above. The "mystical" (a term that originated in paganism, but that had become a Christian possession by the second century) was always "ecclesial" — the hidden or mystical depths of the Bible and the sacraments brought one to a mystical contemplation and even a mystical union with God in Christ. The early Christians rarely spoke of their own experiences of the presence of God. What was important to them was the mystical reality of Christ in the church.

Given these essential bases, it is easy to see how Christian mystics like Origen, Evagrius, and Dionysius came to define themselves over against trends and themes found in the contemporary mystical traditions of Judaism and Greek religious philosophy. If Christian mysticism, like Jewish mysticism, had a strongly exegetical basis, it was unlike Jewish mysticism in rejecting an esoteric reading of the basic texts. The great internal debate of the second century over the nature of saving *gnōsis* led the mainline tradition to reaffirm the universal call to salvation, reject strict esotericism, and leave to future generations the struggle with the modified esotericism and elitism that the existence of various levels of Christian commitment has always presented. Like the Gnostic seers and many Platonist philosophers, the Christian mystics gave considerable attention to how the soul could regain the divine realm from which it had fallen; but, in contrast to them, Christians insisted that the soul's divinity did not belong to it by nature but was a gift of the Good Creator, who is the Father of the Redeemer.

In describing the soul's return, Christian mystics gave greater emphasis to the necessity of divine intervention, gift, or grace than was customary with pagan authors, though, as we saw in chapter 2, something like grace was not unknown to the latter. Finally, the most important Christian mystics, notably Origen and Dionysius, put love (conceived of as *agapē–erōs*) at the center of their thought in a manner beyond anything found in the Platonists. Though consideration of the interlocking roles of love and knowledge in attaining God was a common issue for pagans, Jews, and Christians, the Greek fathers pioneered a new view of mystical love, one that was based on the love that the Savior had implanted in the community and that therefore implied an active concern for others as much as a contemplative and often erotic yearning for Christ.

These notions, to be sure, constitute only the broad contours of an ideal type which each author expressed in differing ways. Still, I believe that they help us to understand why it is legitimate to speak of an early Christian mystical tradition which constitutes the essential foundation for all that was to follow.

PART II

The Beginnings
of Western Mysticism

The Formation
of Latin Christianity

WHAT HAS BEEN set forth to this point, although both important and lengthy, has been the prolegomenon to the story of Western Christian mysticism, understood as that form of mystical expression found in texts written in the Latin language and in the later vernaculars of Western Europe. While it was tempting to give more detailed analyses of many of the figures and issues surveyed in the former chapters, this would have detracted from the main theme of my work. It is now time to turn from the preparations to the actual beginnings, that is, to the writings of the Latin Christian authors of the fourth and early fifth centuries who can be considered the earliest Latin mystics. Their writings, especially the works of Augustine of Hippo, were to remain the cornerstones of Latin mysticism for centuries to come. Before turning to this new Western mysticism that became evident at the end of the fourth century, a brief comment on some of the characteristics of Latin-speaking Christianity will help to shed light on the historical world in which it came to birth.

The great patristic scholar Jean Daniélou structured his three-volume *History of Early Christian Doctrine before the Council of Nicaea* around the three cultures in which Christian faith found expression in its first centuries. "Three worlds went to the making of the Christian Church, three cultures, three visions and expressions of truth — the Jewish, the Hellenistic and the Latin; and each of them produced its own distinctive theology."[1] Although Daniélou's history has been criticized, his insight about the three cultural worlds that shaped the early church is well taken in an era that has begun to recognize, if still

189

grudgingly, the power of the cultural component in every aspect of Christian history.

The image of the united Roman *imperium,* master of the civilized world, tends to mask the major divisions that had always characterized the empire. Rome was the city that had become the world, but how much had the political unity it forced on others really affected local cultural life, especially that of the majority of inhabitants who lived outside the cities or who did not belong to the educated intelligentsia? We shall probably never know, especially since most of our knowledge depends on chance survivals from this educated elite. The Roman upper class, of course, had been philo-Hellenic for centuries. Educated Romans were expected to have mastery of Greek as well as Latin, but the evidence of art styles (given the *basso continuo* of what have been called "sub-antique" traditions),[2] as well as what we can recover of other aspects of local culture, seems to indicate that East and West remained quite different, despite the veneer of a common cosmopolitanism.

The Latin-speaking culture of the western empire, then, maintained its own traits, however much influenced by the hellenization of the Mediterranean culture complex originally created by Alexander's conquests. As the new Christian religion moved into the West, it could not but be colored by this context. This diffusion took place quite early—Paul was writing to Christians at Rome already in the fifties of the first century. The new religion was disseminated by Greek-speaking Jews throughout the cities of the empire, though Gentiles were also soon incorporated. Christianity remained a distinctively urban phenomenon in most places until the fourth century.

Early Christian documents written in the West during the first century or more of Christian existence were uniformly Greek (e.g., *1 Clement; Hermas* and the works of Justin Martyr, which emanate from Rome; and the writings of Irenaeus, which come from Lyons in Gaul). The major Western theologian of the third century, the Roman presbyter Hippolytus (active ca. 200–230), also wrote in Greek. But a Latin-speaking Christianity appears in the last decades of the second century, with the earliest evidence coming from North Africa.[3]

This Latin Christianity was long a parasite on its Greek parent and translations from Greek continued to play a key role in the Latin-speaking church for many centuries.[4] In this, Latin Christians were only repeating the pattern that the Roman elite had cultivated since at least the second century B.C.E. in imitating the cultural riches of Greece. However, just as this imitative origin did not preclude the emergence of a true philosophical culture among Latin speakers,[5] something similar emerged in the history of early Latin Christianity.

The earliest Christian Latin texts, such as the *Acts of the Scillitan Martyrs* (ca. 180 c.e.), the first translations of the Bible into Latin (collectively known as the *Vetus Latina*),[6] and certain obscure and possibly Jewish-Christian treatises, are in general not remarkable. Latin Christianity soon discovered its own voice, most evident in the writings of Tertullian (ca. 160–ca. 217), a North African who joined the Montanist sect late in life.[7] This passionately rigid thinker can scarcely be called a mystic, as a comparison of the treatise that he wrote on prayer (*De oratione*) with that of Origen, will make clear.[8] But one element that would be stressed by Augustine and was later to characterize so much of Western mysticism is already evident in his writings—a sensitivity to introspective experience, a form of subjectivism rare among Greek authors.[9]

The second great figure of early Latin theology was also African. Cyprian, bishop of Carthage, died a martyr's death in 258 c.e. His letters and treatises contain important reflections on how Christians should live in the world and on the ideal of martyrdom discussed in chapter 4 above,[10] but there is little or nothing really mystical in these writings.[11] For example, when the bishop speaks of the union of Christ and his people figured in the mixing of water and wine in the Eucharist (e.g., *Epist.* 63.13.1–3 [*PL* 4:395–96]), he is giving expression to the ecclesiological root of Christian mysticism but not in any way attempting to invite his readers to a deeper personal appropriation of this reality. Later Western mystical authors rarely made extensive use of either of these third-century founders of Latin theology.

Tertullian and Cyprian were typical Roman intellectuals, at home in both Greek and Latin. They were also citizens of an empire that was beginning to show the strains of overextension, internal weakness, barbarian attack, and the host of ills that historians have identified as contributing to the shift in the Roman governmental structure from the relatively flexible principate system founded by Augustus to the rigid dominate of the later empire that took its origin from Diocletian (284–305 c.e.).[12] The latter, an able, if uncultivated, soldier-emperor, was also noted as the last great persecutor. The failure of his systematic attempt to crush the growing power of Christianity was prophetic of the surprising marriage between *christianitas* and *romanitas* that marked the fourth century.

Two great seismic shifts occurred in Christianity in the fourth century. The first, the conversion of the empire to Christianity, has been commented on so often that it is difficult to think of saying anything new about it. Nevertheless, it is remarkable to think that within the span of a single long lifetime, in a political system so impervious to change, an individual could have passed from a situation in which Christianity was a proscribed religion whose profession meant painful death (303 under Diocletian) to one in which it had become the state religion (378 under Theodosius) — and the ancient gods of Rome and their adherents were now the ones proscribed. Rome and Christianity both gained and lost by this epochal decision to wed the fortunes of the great empire and the new religion. Views on how best to describe these gains and losses depend very much on the perspective — religious and/or historical — of the investigator.

Rome was able to retain its traditional symbiosis of what moderns would call the political and religious dimensions of society (and perhaps actually strengthen these by an appeal to a more transcendent God as imperial patron),[13] but only at the expense of embracing a religion whose self-understanding did not allow it to be easily convinced that it was meant to play a role secondary to what any ruler happened to conceive of as the good of the empire. Within the context of the traditional Roman imperial ideal, this tension was bound to result in conflicts, which have continued to enliven Western religious and political history since that time. Although we look in vain for anything like the later distinction between church and state in late antiquity, there were certainly differing attitudes toward the respective roles of priests and rulers. Western Christians welcomed the conversion of the empire as much as did their Eastern counterparts, but they were more open to critical attitudes about imperial control over the church, especially as the emperors' power waned in the West. The *logion* of Jesus — "Give back to Caesar what belongs to Caesar, and to God what belongs to God" (Luke 20:25) — became central to the history of Latin Christianity.

The church's alacrity in accepting the new situation may initially seem surprising. But a survey of the record indicates that most Christians had pursued a policy of accommodation rather than confrontation since the second century, and that they welcomed the conversion to (or at least approval of) Christianity made by the emperor Constantine (313–337 c.e.) as a manifest proof of divine providence. The Christian religion had much to gain from official approval — and not purely in terms of power and wealth. It also had to face a new situation that many later observers have judged ambiguous or even dangerous. The religion of the outcast Jewish preacher who was crucified as a malefactor and whose followers had been usually despised and often persecuted and executed was about to become *the* Roman religion, the state belief of the most powerful world empire. Decisions that Christian leaders had largely been accustomed to making within the confines of their own often squabbling conventicles soon became issues of state politics that called for the intervention of emperors. (Constantine summoned the first general, or ecumenical, council of Christian bishops at Nicaea in 325.) The intense theological divisions that had marked the new religion from the beginning could now be settled with the sword, not just the pen. The fate of Rome, or its successors as "most Christian" states, became hard to distinguish from the destiny of the Christian religion, at least for many believers. We may bewail the problems introduced by these changes (just as some have lamented the changes that overtook Christianity in the second century), but they are part of the story, for both good and ill.

The other major change in the fourth-century Roman Empire has received less notice: the split between the Eastern and Western parts of the empire and consequently between Eastern and Western Christianity.[14] Diocletian's reorganization of the empire was an implicit recognition of the differences between East and West and the difficulties of keeping the two parts under any single head. Constantine thought otherwise, but aside from the last years of his reign and that of Theodosius, the empire was more often split under two rulers in the fourth century than ruled by one all-powerful emperor.[15] After 395, the empire was never again effectively ruled by a single head. The division was abetted by the barbarian invasions, which became critical in the latter fourth century and endemic in the fifth. To be sure, the eastern part of the empire also underwent attack, but the West, with longer frontiers, less population, and more limited resources, was more vulnerable and suffered more lasting harm. The new situation present by the sixth century when a largely barbarian world stood in the midst of the ruins of Rome was to provide an opportunity and a challenge for the Western church, which we shall consider in the next volume.

The political division reflected and encouraged a cultural and religious one. Linguistically, it became increasingly rare to find educated bureaucrats who were equally at home in both Greek and Latin. This was also the case in the church, even as the old Roman aristocracy moved into new positions of power in the Christian hierarchy. Sometime in the mid-fourth century, probably under Damasus, pope from 366 to 384, the Roman church (ever a conservative institution) made the transition to a Latin liturgy. Some of the founders of Latin mysticism, such as Ambrose and Cassian, were still fluent in Greek and much influenced by Greek sources. On the other hand, the extent of Augustine's Greek has been disputed, but no one would claim that he really mastered the language. In 430 (the year of Augustine's death), the bishop of Rome explained that his delay in reacting to the writings of Nestorius that had been forwarded to him was because it took so long to find someone in Rome who could translate them into Latin![16] The long slow split between Eastern and Western Christianity thus first became visible in the fourth century.

The fourth century also saw the development of some of the characteristic institutions of the Western church, especially the Roman papacy and
Western monasticism. The East contained a number of great Christian
centers, or patriarchates, that claimed apostolic foundation (Jerusalem,
Antioch, Alexandria, and later Constantinople). In the West, Rome alone,
which ancient tradition saw as the site of the missionary activities and
martyrdoms of both Peter and Paul, enjoyed this status. Combining the
advantages of both apostolic origin and political accommodation to the
governmental center of the empire, Rome had enjoyed a certain primacy
of prestige among Christian sees since the second century.[17] This was
limited, at best, because on controversial questions such as rebaptism and
penance, it was customary for bishops to act in concert through epistolary
contact or joint meetings in synods and councils. By the third century, a
Roman bishop was upbraided by Cyprian for acting alone — a possible clue
to the beginnings of enhanced claims for Rome's authority.[18]

Constantine's removal of the capital of the empire to his new city of Constantinople on the Bosphorus was both a threat and an opportunity for the
bishops of Rome. The emperor's vast gifts to the Roman church, especially
his building of the great basilica over the traditional burial place of Peter,
gave the Roman bishops special prestige. But the principle of accommodation now favored Constantinople, which presented a threat to Rome's growing sense of its position as the most important Christian center. It was in
reaction to the First Council of Constantinople in 381, which, along with
condemning Arianism, also highlighted the importance of the new capital
as an apostolic see, that the Roman bishop first made use of the term
"primacy" (*primatus*, literally, "the first place") in an official document of
382.[19] Though the Roman bishops of the fourth and early fifth centuries
were not strong leaders, being overshadowed by figures like Hilary,
Ambrose, and Augustine, the seeds of Roman primacy were being sown
during this time, seeds that were to have their full flowering in the pontifi-
cate of Leo I (440–454), who is generally regarded as the earliest major
exponent of Rome's primatial place in the Christian church.

The force that really transformed Western Christianity, however, was the
monasticism that spread westward in the second half of the fourth century.[20] Ascetical tendencies had been present throughout early Christianity,
and the West doubtless had "free-form" monastics of its own before it
received the impulse toward classic forms of monasticism from what later
authors called the *orientale lumen* ("the light from the East"). Exiles during
the time of the Arian troubles (Athanasius twice was sent to the West,
Hilary to the East) spread knowledge of the new form of Christian witness,
but the major source of influence was literary.[21] Augustine's *Confessions*

(8.15) witnesses to the power that the translation of the *Life of Antony* had upon fervent believers looking for a more perfect way of life, and Jerome also made important contributions by disseminating monastic lives and rules to the West.[22] Most important of all perhaps was Cassian, whose writings will be studied in the following chapter.

From the outset, however, Western monasticism was not just a carbon copy of what was found in the East. For one thing, the eremitical life was more difficult to lead in the West (given a generally harsher climate and other dangers) and was considered less of a practical reality, especially for beginners. The solitary hermit remained the ideal, but the cenobite, or monk living in community, was the standard form. This fit well with the other major characteristics of Western monasticism — its tendency toward an urban and often a clerical setting and its close connection with aristocratic and episcopal sponsorship.

The monasticism of the West that became evident ca. 370 sprang not from the movement of peasants and village dwellers out into the desert, as in the East, but from the efforts of bishops and literate upper-class Christians to encourage higher forms of life for themselves and especially for their clergy. Eusebius of Vercelli in the 360s, Ambrose of Milan in the 370s, and Augustine of Hippo in the 390s were just some of the bishops who formed monastic communities among their clergy. Jerome (fortunately never a bishop) spread monastic asceticism among the Roman aristocracy in the 380s as the secretary to Pope Damasus. Paulinus, one of the wealthiest aristocrats of the Western empire, gave away his money and founded a monastery in Campania in 395. He eventually became the bishop of Nola, just as Honoratus, a man of consular rank, founded the monastery of Lerins in southern Gaul shortly after 400 and then became bishop of Arles.

The archetypal figure for this special form of urban, clerical monasticism under episcopal leadership was Martin of Tours (ca. 317–397). This convert became a cleric under Hilary of Poitiers (ca. 315–367), the oldest of the great leaders who shaped Latin Christianity in the second half of the fourth century. While Hilary was in exile during the Arian crisis (356–360), Martin lived as a hermit. After the bishop's return, and at his behest, Martin founded the first Gallic monastic community at Ligugé near Poitiers. In 371 Martin was called to become bishop of Tours, but he continued to live as a monk in a community for clergy which he founded a few miles outside his city (Marmoutier, in Latin *maius monasterium*). Sulpicius Severus, whose *Life of Martin* (*Vita Martini*) and other writings spread the bishop's fame throughout the Latin-speaking West, describes his hero as the perfect combination of wonder-working ascetic and powerful bishop:

What Martin was like, and his greatness, after entering the episcopate, it is beyond my powers to describe. For with unswerving constancy he remained the same man as before. . . . He fully sustained the dignity of the episcopate without forsaking the life and virtues of the monk.

But what is more, Martin, like other Western bishops, also used his monastery as a training ground for the education and formation of the clergy.

There were about eighty disciples there [at Marmoutier], being trained in the pattern of their most beloved master. No one possessed anything of his own; everything was put in the common stock. The buying and selling which is customary with most hermits (*monachi*) was forbidden them. No craft was practiced there except that of the copyist, and that was assigned to the younger men. The older ones were left free for prayer.

After a description of their ascetical practices, Sulpicius concludes his account:

This must be regarded as all the more wonderful because there were so many among them of noble rank, who had been brought up to something quite different before forcing themselves to this lowliness and endurance. Many of them we have since seen as bishops. For what kind of city or church would it be that did not covet a bishop from Martin's monastery? (*Life of Martin* 10)[23]

Although this may be an idealized picture, it captures some of the most distinctive traits of Western monasticism.

Of course, there were critics of monasticism, both within and without the church,[24] but it is remarkable how quickly the monastic form of life came to color Western Christianity on every level. Not least important for our concerns was how monasticism influenced the newly independent Latin spirituality and mysticism.[25] If the great struggle over Pelagianism marks a new level of theological independence and maturity which forms the later Western tradition,[26] the writings of Ambrose, Augustine, Cassian, and others — all of whom can be considered to some degree monastic — mark the true beginnings of Western mysticism. It was a mysticism colored by the monastic life and its ideals of virginity and asceticism, yet also intimately tied to the life of the Christian community, especially because so many of its main spokesmen were bishops.[27]

It will be the task of the two following chapters to analyze the mystical components of this new Latin Christianity of the late fourth and early fifth centuries down to ca. 430, the date of Augustine's death. The first chapter will deal with broad historical context, concentrating on the thought of Ambrose and Cassian. The final chapter will attempt to survey the major lines of Augustine's mysticism.

CHAPTER 6

Early Latin Mysticism

W E KNOW MORE about what it was like to be a Christian in the Latin West in the late fourth century than at any previous time. Our imaginative retrievals are facilitated by the many personal narratives left us. Augustine's *Confessions,* the inexhaustible treasure of late antique literature, is the best known. Hilary of Poitiers has given us an account of his spiritual progress;[1] Jerome is almost too personal at times; and even Ambrose, the most patrician of the Latin fathers, conveys something of his own religious experience, especially in his letters and orations. The extent of the surviving works of these giants of Latin Christianity and the evocative nature of much of what they wrote make the world of the late fourth century surprisingly alive after fifteen hundred years. Even the physical remains of the fourth-century church—its buildings and their decoration—are amply, if imperfectly, present to us.

Later Western Christians looked back on the long lifetime of Augustine (354–430) as the period that laid the foundations of Western theology and mysticism. In the 350s and 360s, when Augustine was displaying his own infant and adolescent signs of the waywardness he later identified as original sin, some Latin thinkers were already beginning the outpouring of Latin theology that reached a flood stage in the decades immediately before and after 400 C.E.

Hilary of Poitiers (ca. 315–367) was a Gallo-Roman aristocrat elected bishop of his native city about 350.[2] It was Hilary's exile to the East for his anti-Arian stance (356–360) that appears to have energized his writing career. Although his twelve-volume *On the Trinity* is his most important work, it is in two of his exegetical writings, the *Commentary on Matthew* (before 356) and especially the *Commentary on the Psalms* (after 360), which made considerable use of Origen, that his most important contributions to Western spirituality are discovered. It would, however, be difficult to speak of Hilary as a mystical author. Despite his favoring of the monastic career of Martin, as noted in the introduction to Part II, he belonged to an older generation which had developed its ideas independently of the three movements that were to be essential to the formation of early Latin mysticism between 360 and 390: monasticism, virginity, and Neoplatonism. The Latin thinkers who engendered this distinctive style of mysticism were each touched by these movements in varying ways.

We have already considered monasticism briefly in the introduction to this part. We must now look at the other two movements that interacted with the monastic wave before analyzing the thought of Ambrose and Cassian, and to a lesser extent other of Augustine's contemporaries. The ideal of virginity as the highest form of Christian life, of course, is easily compatible with, perhaps even inseparable from, monasticism. More surprising was the alliance between a newly born Latin Christian Neoplatonism and monastic fervor. Let us start with Neoplatonism.

Christian Neoplatonism

Latin Neoplatonism of the late fourth century had both pagan and Christian components. The pagan Neoplatonists, of whom Macrobius is the best known, were to have some influence in medieval speculative mysticism, but no direct role in the origins of Latin mysticism.[3] Christian Neoplatonism originated in Rome and Milan about 350 in pagan circles imbued with the thought of Plotinus, as Augustine later recalled in a letter:

> At that time Plotinus's school flourished at Rome and it had many very penetrating and ingenious members. Some of them became corrupted by inquisitiveness into the magic arts, others, recognizing that the Lord Jesus Christ bore the person of that truth and unchanging wisdom they sought to attain, passed over into his army. (*Ep.* 118.5.33 [*PL* 33:448])[4]

The central figure in this passage into Christ's *militia* was Marius Victorinus (ca. 285–ca. 365), a North African rhetor and philosopher who acquired great enough fame in Rome to have his statue erected in the Forum.[5]

Possessed of a broad knowledge of both Plotinus and Porphyry, Victorinus translated some of Plotinus's *Enneads,* Porphyry's *Isagogue* and *On the Return of the Soul* (*De regressu animae*), as well as some of Aristotle's works into Latin.[6] His conversion to Christianity around 355 produced a sensation that Augustine describes in the *Confessions* (8.2.3). In his final years as a Christian, the aged Victorinus produced two important kinds of writings: a group of dense treatises (ca. 357–362) attacking the Arian heresy (these comprise the first speculative trinitarian theology in the West)[7] and a series of commentaries on the Pauline epistles (ca. 362–365), which initiated the fascination with Paul that marked late fourth-century Latin Christianity.[8]

Victorinus's thought was deeply marked by both Plotinus and Porphyry.[9] Pierre Hadot has argued that it was through Victorinus's acquaintance with a possibly Porphyrian commentary on the *Parmenides* that he came to incorporate two key principles of Neoplatonism into Christian theology — the identification of the One with true existence (*esse*)[10] and the use of the triad Being–Life–Intelligence (*esse–vivere–intelligere*) as a tool for understanding the consubstantial Trinity.[11] Victorinus also absorbed a profound negative theology from his Neoplatonic sources insofar as the *esse* that is identified with God the Father is so different from all existence known to us that we can best point to it as nonexistence. "For that which is above the *on* (existent) is the hidden *on* (existent)" (*To Candidus* 14 [ed. Henry and Hadot, pp. 31.11–12]).[12] Although Victorinus showed remarkable originality and penetration in employing these Neoplatonic elements in the service of Nicene orthodoxy, his writings were too difficult and too little known to have real effect. (When it came to trinitarian theology, Augustine's quite different speculative model was to rule the day.) Indeed, it was through the Dionysian adaptation of Proclean understandings of these two Neoplatonic themes, rather than through Victorinus, that they were to enjoy a history in later Western speculative mysticism.[13]

Although the treatises against the Arians are primarily speculative in character, they give evidence of Victorinus's transformation of Neoplatonic ascent in terms of the doctrine of the Trinity. The Holy Spirit, which the African understood as a feminine principle, the "Mother of Jesus,"[14] plays a key role in the knowledge that makes possible our return to God:

> But since you have given us the Spirit, O holy, all-powerful Father, we both have and express a partial knowledge of you. But when we have a total ignorance of you we have knowledge of you. And again through faith we have a perfect knowledge of you when in every word and always we proclaim you to be God the Father, and the Son Jesus Christ our Lord, and the Holy Spirit. (*To Candidus* 32 [ed. Henry and Hadot, pp. 47.4–48.10; trans. Clark, p. 83])[15]

The ascent theme is most clearly expressed in his three hymns to the Trinity, especially the second, which adopts a more personal tone than the others. The underlying motif in this beautiful poem is the Neoplatonic paradigm of the soul's fall and return. The soul has been created in God's image, the supreme life that is the Logos. But it has fallen into a love of the world, God's good creation, but still a distraction away from its true home:

> Have mercy Lord! Have mercy Christ!
> I have loved the world because you made the
> world;
> I am detained in the world because the world
> hates those who are thine.
> Now I hate the world, for I have now
> experienced the Spirit.

Because of this experience of the Spirit, Victorinus says "I know that the return is written in my soul," and he prays that God will give him "wings of faith" (see *Phaedrus* 246CE) to lead him above:

> Have mercy Lord! Have mercy Christ!
> Deep in my heart is the wish to depart
> from the world and earth,
> But without thy support, too feeble are my
> wings to support my wish,
> Give me the wings of faith that I may fly to
> God on high. (*Second Hymn* [ed. Henry
> and Hadot, pp. 291–92; trans.
> Clark, pp. 321–23])[16]

Though it would be difficult on the evidence of this poem and a few passages in his prose works to characterize Victorinus as a mystic, there can be no doubt that his example and his work as a mediator of Neoplatonism played an important role in the birth of Latin mysticism.

Two other, more shadowy figures in the first circle of Christian Latin Neoplatonists deserve mention. Manlius Theodorus was a Neoplatonic philosopher resident in Milan who had considerable influence on the young Augustine.[17] His writings have not survived. The priest Simplicianus, a close friend of Victorinus, instructed the new bishop Ambrose and counseled the convert Augustine. He was to succeed Ambrose in the episcopal seat of Milan.[18] These men were the living links between Ambrose and Augustine and the Neoplatonic tradition whose christianization was begun by Victorinus.

Virginity as a Spiritual Ideal

Christian fascination with virginity as a spiritual ideal goes back to the beginnings of the Jesus movement. In 1 Corinthians 7 the unmarried Paul

responded to a number of queries about marriage and sexuality, underlining the legitimacy of marriage but praising virginity as a higher state
(1 Cor 7:1, 7, 32–34, 38). A *logion* ascribed to Jesus speaks of "eunuchs who
have made themselves that way for the sake of the kingdom of heaven"
(Matt 19:12).[19] Neither Jesus nor Paul made abstention from sexuality a
condition for adherence to the new religion, but some later rigorists (often
called Encratites) are recorded as upholding this view.[20] The complex stages
by which virginity came to play a larger and larger role in Christianity,
finally to be seen by many as a *sine qua non* of the life of perfection, have
been much studied of late, particularly by Peter Brown, who has deftly
uncovered the social meaning of what to most moderns will seem at best
an unusual life choice.[21] In opposition to those who have seen virginity as
springing only from fear of sexuality and involving a perverted mysogyny,
Brown has emphasized the way in which virginity contributed to Christianity's creation of its own social world and also gave women positions of
authority and power otherwise impossible in the ancient world. But the
implications of the ideal of virginity have also usually involved a depreciation of sexuality that has become one of the more ambivalent elements in
the history of Christianity.

It was only in the second half of the fourth century that the leaders of
the Western church came to the conclusion that virginity was an inherently
higher form of life, both in theory *and* in practice. They did so by way of
something like an intellectual revolution. While earlier Christians had
agreed that virginity was theoretically higher than marriage, they had
generally not seen virginity as a style of life that should be actively encouraged, thinking (with Paul) that it was better to marry than to burn (1 Cor
7:9). Indeed, Western Christians seem to have given virginity less importance than did many in the East.

In the second century, Hermas, while himself continent, took virginity
more as an attribute of the church as Christ's body than as a higher life-
style of some Christians.[22] Tertullian, the austere African moralist, was
vehemently opposed to second marriages and thought abstention from
sexual activity conducive to spiritual thoughts,[23] but it would be difficult to
think of his views as more than a minority opinion. Cyprian too valued
virginity, but more for the virgins' symbolic representation of the church's
opposition to the world than as a special form of higher Christian life.[24]
Most Latin Christians in the fourth century probably accepted the pattern
found in much early Christianity—a valuation of virginity, praise of the
virgins found in the church, but a practical acceptance of marriage for good
Christians, both clergy and laity.

There were, of course, rumblings in another direction. A provincial council held at Elvira in Spain in 309 imposed continence on all clergy (canon 33), as well as lifelong excommunication for a variety of mostly sexual sins.[25] But Hilary of Poitiers, the leader of the Nicene West in 350s and 360s, was a married man — in this, typical of his time. The situation changed dramatically in the decades following his death. All the major figures in Latin Christianity between ca. 370 and 430 were avid proponents of the ideal of virginity and wrote extensively on the subject.[26] The fact that they did not necessarily have the same understanding of why virginity was superior to marriage — and why sexuality always involved danger and even sinfulness — does not lessen the fact that their unanimity exercised a powerful gravitational force still evident in Western Christianity.

Of course, voices on the other side were not lacking. Jovinian, a monk active in the last decades of the fourth century, denied that virginity was higher than marriage and doubted the perpetual virginity of Mary. He was attacked by Ambrose, Jerome, and Augustine in various polemical writings.[27] Julian of Eclanum, the real "architect of the Pelagian dogma" in Augustine's view, argued against Augustine's teaching on original sin, affirming that concupiscence was natural to the human condition and that marriage was a basic means of using it productively.[28] But these protests were like straws in the face of the mighty hurricane of praise for virginity orchestrated by the most influential leaders of the Western church. Although most of the clergy continued to marry, following the older pattern for centuries (it was only in the eleventh century that celibacy became mandatory), the alliance forged between the monastic life and the ideal of virginity, which was theoretically strengthened by Neoplatonic attitudes toward the body and sexuality, provided an important part, though not the only part, of the background of the first Latin mysticism. Perhaps no figure, not even Augustine, illustrates this better than Ambrose, bishop of Milan from 374 to 397.

Ambrose of Milan

Ambrose was born around 334 in Trier, scion of an aristocratic Christian family. He grew up in Rome, well trained in rhetoric and law, and followed his father into the Roman bureaucracy, becoming prefect of Liguria and Emilia around 370, with his residence at Milan. This northern Italian city was the sometime capital of the Western empire between 340 and 402, a place of both importance and tension in Ambrose's day because of the struggles between the pro-Arian emperors of Constantine's line and the Nicene majority of the Western church.[29]

When Auxentius, the Arian bishop of Milan, died in late 374, Ambrose, who intervened between the Arians and Nicenes to prevent a riot, was unexpectedly elected bishop by popular acclaim, though still a catechumen. Perhaps he was thought of as a mediator, though this was scarcely to prove the case. The new bishop became famous for his resolute intransigence in the Nicene cause, as well as for his insistence on the independence of the episcopate against any form of imperial pressure. But it is not the career of Ambrose the ecclesiastical politician that interests us here so much as that of Ambrose the preacher, teacher, and writer.[30] Suffice it to say that Ambrose was the leading bishop in the West during the crucial period from 375 until his death in 397.

The new bishop candidly admitted in his work *On Duties,* "I began to teach what I had not myself learnt. I had to be learning and teaching at the same time, since I had no leisure to learn before" (*On Duties* 1.4 [*PL* 16:27C]).[31] Under the guidance of Simplicianus, however, he appears to have read deeply and learned rapidly, perhaps making use of the then unusual practice of "silent reading" (i.e., reading without moving the lips), something that surprised Augustine a decade later (*Conf.* 6.3). Ambrose was perfectly at home with Greek, and it was doubtless in this language that he read widely in Origen and in Philo.[32] He also was familiar with at least some dialogues of Plato (the *Phaedo* and the *Phaedrus*) and was well acquainted with Plotinus and Porphyry.[33]

So much energy has been expended in recent decades on uncovering the broad range of Ambrose's sources, both philosophical and ecclesiastical, that sometimes his unusual literary skill and originality have been lost to view.[34] Certainly, Ambrose is a difficult author, whose style is not always easy to follow, given its imagistic and often almost poetic character; but he is rewarding when studied closely—and he was widely read in the later Western tradition. The immense shadow cast by his convert Augustine should not blind us to his importance.

Ambrose's role in the history of Western mysticism lies in three areas. The first is in his christianization of important elements of Platonic and Neoplatonic thought, especially the theme of the descent and ascent of the soul. Second is his putting the interpretation of the Song of Songs at the center of an ecclesial mysticism (that is, one realized only in and through the church and its sacraments). The third element is his joining of this mysticism to the new emphasis on the ideal of virginity. These elements, while present to some extent throughout the bishop's varied writings, are concentrated in a few texts which will form the basis for our consideration.

The most important of these is the treatise *On Isaac or the Soul* (*De Isaac vel anima*), which is arguably the first great masterpiece of Western mysticism.[35] This is part of a series of treatises giving allegorical readings of the lives of the patriarchs of Genesis (Cain and Abel, Noah, Abraham, Jacob, Joseph), which appear to have been designed to present a typology of the Christian life.[36] The influence of Philo is marked throughout the group, though perhaps less in *On Isaac*. There is still debate over the original format of the work—an issue of some importance for the character of its message. I am convinced that the text is a literary reworking of sermons delivered to the newly baptized probably in 386 or 387; it thus conveys what later ages would think of as an advanced model of the Christian life to neophytes. The importance of this will be taken up below.

Several other treatises of Ambrose are of significance for the mystical element in his thought. (Ambrose, like all patristic authors, never divides mysticism from the other elements in his total theology.) Foremost among these are the works entitled *On Death as a Good* (*De bono mortis*), which seems to be intended to go along with *On Isaac* and was also probably delivered to neophytes about the same time, and *On Flight from the World* (*De fuga saeculi*), which appears to be somewhat later (ca. 391–394).[37] The bishop's liturgical homilies, such as *On the Mysteries* (*De mysteriis* [ca. 390]), and the at times controverted *On the Sacraments* (*De sacramentis* [also ca. 390]), are of some import.[38] Ambrose's works on virginity, especially his *Concerning Virgins* (*De virginibus*, an early work of 377) and his *On Virginity* (*De virginitate* [ca. 393]) are also of value.[39]

Finally, the bishop's expressly exegetical writings must be mentioned. The Latin fathers, no less than their Greek forebears, gave scriptural exegesis, whether in express commentaries or in homilies and treatises, the center stage in their literary production. Ambrose, the avid student of Philo and Origen, was one of the first great spiritual exegetes in the Latin tradition.[40] In interpreting the Old Testament, Ambrose took the Song of Songs as the center of his hermeneutics, but he commented extensively on the other great resource of mystical theology, the Psalms. His *Explanation of Twelve Psalms* (*Explanatio Psalmorum XII*), includes comments on Psalms 1, 35–40, 45, 47–48, and 61, which were given at various times and edited after his death.[41] More important is the *Exposition of Psalm 118* (*Expositio Psalmi CXVIII*), a large group of homilies dated between 386 and 390.[42] Finally, the bishop wrote an extensive work on Luke's Gospel; this commentary is difficult to date.[43]

The importance that Ambrose gave to the work of scriptural commentary may be gauged by a story told about the bishop found in chapter 42 of the life that the deacon Paulinus wrote at Augustine's request in 422. According to this account, Paulinus was taking down the bishop's dictation in early 397, a few days before his final illness confined him to his bed.

. . . he was dictating the 43rd Psalm and I was taking it down and watching him, when suddenly a flame, shaped like a short shield, spread over his head and little by little entered in through his mouth, like someone going into his own house. His face then became as white as snow, but afterwards his features resumed their normal appearance.[44]

The deacon Castus convinced Paulinus that he had witnessed the coming of the Holy Spirit upon the bishop. From the viewpoint of the history of fourth-century mysticism, the fire motif, often found in relation to visionary experiences of the desert fathers,[45] is here applied to the episcopal exegete in his desire to open up the riches of scripture to the Christian congregation.

The theme of the descent and ascent of the soul had deep roots in Plato's dialogues, and ascensions to the heavenly realm were also found in the Jewish heavenly-journey apocalypses, as well as in Paul's account of his rapture in 2 Corinthians 12. Origen had provided a Christian version of the myth of the soul's fall and return in which the Word become flesh through the mediation of the soul of Jesus assumed the central role. Plotinus also gave a detailed account of the soul's descent from its true home through negligence and forgetfulness and its return to the contemplation of *Nous* by means of moral and philosophical *askēsis*. All this has been discussed in former chapters. Though Ambrose is a less-penetrating thinker than either Origen or Plotinus, he deserves study as the first Latin to make this great mystical paradigm available in the West through an original adaptation of Origenist and Plotinian mysticism.[46]

The most detailed presentations are to be found in *On Isaac* and *On Death as a Good*. While the bishop does mention the soul's descent at times, linking it with the "nails" that fix the soul to carnal things, he does not speculate on when, why, or how this fall took place.[47] He is more concerned with the ascent, giving a number of extended discussions heavily dependent on Plotinus, though (as Pierre Courcelle and Pierre Hadot have shown) his Platonic sources have been radically transformed in the service of Christian theological concerns.[48]

On Isaac 4.11 explains the Bride's entry into the king's chamber (Song 1:4) by reference to Paul's account of his rapture to paradise recast in the language of Plotinus's description of his frequent "wakenings" from the body at the beginning of *Ennead* 4.8. The text deserves full citation (with the Plotinian reminiscences italicized):

> Blessed is the soul that enters the inner chambers. For, *rising up from the body she becomes more distant from all*, and she searches and *seeks within herself*, if in any way she can pursue *the divine*. And when she can obtain it, *having passed beyond intelligible things, she is strengthened in it* and fed by it. Such was Paul, who

knew that he had been caught up into paradise but did not know whether he had been caught up in the body or out of the body (2 Cor 12:3-4). For his soul *had risen up from the body,* had withdrawn from the vitals and the bonds of the flesh, and had lifted herself up. And he was alienated from himself and held *within himself* the ineffable words which he had heard and could not reveal, because, as he remarked, it was not permitted to speak such things. (ed. Schenkl, pp. 650.16-651.7; trans. McHugh, pp. 18-19)[49]

Origen was the first to interpret Song 1:4 in terms of Paul's rapture,[50] but Ambrose brings together the autobiographical accounts of Paul and Plotinus through their common element, the emphasis on the loss of the sense of the body. He returns to Paul's account of his *excessus* several times in his writings, showing that he understood it as a paradigm for passing beyond the body to union (*copula spiritualis*) with God.[51]

It is important to note what Ambrose changes or omits as much as what he quotes directly. While he obviously finds Plotinus useful for his emphasis on interiorization (something implied in the Song quotation but not in Paul), and while he incorporates the philosophical notion of "passing beyond intelligible things," Ambrose does not utilize Plotinus's emphasis on the vision of inner beauty (as Augustine was to do), and he changes the Neoplatonist's sense of achieving identity with the divine (*kai toi theoi eis tauton gegenemenos* in *Enn.* 4.8.1 [ed. Armstrong; LC 4:396.5-6]) into a notion of the pursuit of divinity (*divinum illud si qua insequi potest*).

Several subsequent passages in *On Isaac* display similar adaptations of Plotinus and even of Plato to express how the Christian soul (symbolized by Isaac who is also, from another perspective, the Bride of the Song of Songs) returns to God. *On Isaac* 8.65 employs Song 6:11 LXX ("It made me as the chariots of Aminadab") to introduce the Platonic notion of the chariot of the soul (*Phaedrus* 246-47) with its good horses (virtues) and bad horses (vices). In Plato, the charioteer is the soul's rational part (*nous;* see *Phaedrus* 247CD); for Ambrose, "Christ is our master" (*On Isaac* 8.65 [ed. Schenkl, pp. 687.20-688.20]).[52]

Finally, *On Isaac* 8.78-79 contains an important lengthy passage in which Ambrose uses large parts of Plotinus's famous *Ennead* 1.6 ("On Beauty"), the same text that Augustine later used in *Confessions* 9.10 in recounting the vision of Ostia.[53] The soul, cleansed like gold by the fire of love, mounts up to "the Good on which all things depend." Concerning this Good, Ambrose says, "it is our pleasure to approach and to be mingled with it." He continues, "If anyone then has deserved to see that pure and incorporeal Supreme, what else would he have to desire? [a possible reminiscence of *Symposium* 211E]. Indeed, Peter saw the glory of Christ's resurrection and did not wish to descend, for he said, 'Lord, it is good for us to be here'"

(Matt 17:4). It is the *pulcher imago* of the risen Lord that provides us, like Peter, access into the inner world in which the Supreme Good is found. "Let us flee then to our truest Fatherland," Ambrose exclaims, echoing Plotinus.[54] This flight to the heavenly Jerusalem is an ascent of the spirit made on inner feet and with inner eyes which must be cleansed by the practice of the virtues. "For what is seen ought not to be at variance with him who sees, because God has wished that we be conformed to the image of his Son" (citing Rom 8:29) (*On Isaac* 8.79 [ed. Schenkl, pp. 698.21–699.1]).[55] Here, Ambrose has once again brought Plotinus to bear on understanding another of the founding visions of Christian mysticism, the account of the Transfiguration.[56]

Pierre Courcelle has shown how in this, as in so many other passages, the bishop transforms his Platonic and Neoplatonic sources.[57] Naturally, Ambrose removed any traces of the pagan cults and myths that suffuse the original Plotinian text of the *Ennead* "On Beauty," replacing them with a thick web of scriptural quotations and allusions. He avoids Plotinus's teaching on the soul's preexistence in advancing a Christian doctrine of creation and omits any mention of identity with the divine, stressing instead the gift of grace by which we can merit to see God.[58] In identifying Beauty with the Supreme Good and refusing to consider Intelligence as a hypostasis, he replaces the Plotinian hierarchy with the Christian God. Above all, he christologizes the ascent process by seeing it as our growing conformity with Christ.

The treatise *On Death as a Good,* which appears to be a companion piece to *On Isaac,* contains an even larger number of passages based on Plato and Plotinus.[59] Ambrose uses Plato's *Phaedo* throughout this brief work to teach the true attitude toward death: "For the wise man, when he seeks after the divine, frees his soul from the body and forgoes its company" (*On Death as a Good* 3.10 [ed. Schenkl, p. 711.8–10]).[60] He also employs Plotinus to underline the goodness of death in liberating the soul from the body and to caution against letting the soul become mixed with the body.[61] Ambrose's treatise introduced into Latin literature the theme of the three deaths: the natural death, that is, the separation of body and soul, a morally indifferent matter; the penal and evil death that takes place through sin; and the *mors mystica,* that is, the good death by means of which we die to sin by rejecting it (*On Death as a Good* 2.3 [ed. Schenkl, p. 704.10–20]).[62] (This final category, unlike medieval conceptions of the *mors mystica,* is primarily moral not mystical in tone, though it does include an element of sharing in Christ's suffering and death.)

The most important use of Plotinus in this treatise once again displays the bishop's love of fusing Neoplatonic and biblical images to portray the soul's destiny. After an extended evocation, largely biblical in tone, of the necessity of dying to the body to rise to the divine (5.16–17)—"Let us strive for the eternal and fly up to the divine on the wings of love and the oars of charity" (*On Death as a Good* 5.16 [ed. Schenkl, p. 717.23–24; trans. McHugh, p. 82])[63]—Ambrose presents the image of the soul as Jerusalem whose walls are painted, that is, adorned, with virtues (5.18). This image is based on Song of Songs 8:10, where the Bride says, "I am a wall and my breasts are like towers." This is the kind of soul who can enter the garden where the Bridegroom converses with his friends. She even seeks to fly away and be with him above the world.[64]

Following Origen, Ambrose claims that Plato's myth of love's birth in the garden of Zeus (*Symposium* 203BE) was taken from the Song of Songs.[65] The bishop's understanding of the myth, in which Zeus is interpreted as "God and the Mind indifferently," the soul as Venus, and Porus as *logos,* the rational principle of all things, is dependent on Plotinus's distinctive reading found in *Ennead* 3.5.8–9.[66] According to Ambrose, "The soul that cleaves to God entered into the garden of the mind, in which there were an abundance of various virtues and the choicest discourses" (*On Death as a Good* 5.19 [ed. Schenkl, p. 720.16–18; trans. McHugh, pp. 84–85]).[67] This is both the paradise of Genesis containing the tree of life and the tree of the knowledge of good and evil, as well as the flowery garden of Song 4:12–13 and 16 LXX. The garden-soul invites the Word of God to come down to water it so that it may bear the fruit of virtues (Song 5:1–2), "for the soul is united to him in a bond of lawful matrimony" (*On Death as a Good* 5.20 [ed. Schenkl, p. 721.19]).[68]

In the final part of this important passage the bishop analyzes the "good words" (*boni sermones* [Prov 16:24 LXX]) found in the garden, concluding with the "word of more fervent spirit that inebriates like wine and gladdens the heart of man (Ps 103:15), and also the milky word, pure and clear" (*On Death as a Good* 5.20 [ed. Schenkl, pp. 722.20–723.2]).[69] The reference to mystical drunkenness suggested by Song 5:1 allows Ambrose to describe the encounter between the passive soul drunk and oblivious to the world and the active Divine Lover—"and the drunken soul is asleep to the world but awake to God, and therefore, as what follows shows (Song 5:2), God the Word bids her door to be opened to him that he might fill it with his entry" (ibid. [ed. Schenkl, p. 723.7–9]).[70] This is a flight from the world that is also a new birth in and of the Word engendered from the "seeds of the words" he has sown in the soul (*On Death as a Good* 5.21 [ed. Schenkl, p. 723.9–16]).[71]

Each of the mystical themes touched on in the Platonizing passages examined here—the necessity for interiorization, the ascent of the soul, mystical intoxication, and the divine birth in the soul—has deep roots in the tradition and can be found in many places in the bishop of Milan's other writings.[72] To be sure, they possess a profound moral dimension, as pointed out by Ernst Dassmann,[73] because Ambrose the preacher always emphasized the moral meaning of the Christian message. But for our bishop, as well as for his predecessors and followers, moral purification under the Word's inspiration was meant to lead to forms of personal and immediate contact with the Divine Lover, a theme that he found best expressed in the Song of Songs. Ambrosian mysticism, for all its Platonic and Plotinian elements, is centered on the interpretation of the Song.

Ambrose uses the Song throughout his writings, both in the ecclesial and in the personal sense.[74] He is also the first to begin to apply the Song in a special way to Mary conceived of as the ideal lover of the Word.[75] By his method of inserting commentary on the Song into works purportedly dealing with other biblical texts, especially *On Isaac* and the lengthy commentary on Psalm 118, he seems to argue that the Song expresses the inner meaning of all the books of the Bible. Ambrose uses the Song everywhere, even in expressly liturgical homilies such as *On the Mysteries*[76] and in the treatise *On Virgins,* to be considered below. A measure of the importance that sensitive later interpreters saw in his groundbreaking hermeneutic is to be found in the verse-by-verse compendium of his reading put together by the Cistercian William of St. Thierry in the twelfth century.[77]

Ambrose learned much from his predecessors, such as Hippolytus and especially Origen. Like Origen, he mingles the ecclesial reading which sees the Song as an account of the relation between Christ and the church and the personal appropriation which interprets the erotic imagery in terms of the relation of the individual soul and the Word. Although the former reading predominates in the *Exposition of Psalm 118* (which contains some 225 citations and allusions to the Song),[78] the presence of both readings there makes it clear that for the bishop, as for Origen, the ecclesial and the personal readings are inseparable. *On Isaac,* of course, concentrates on the personal sense, but without neglecting the ecclesial (e.g., 4.27; 4.30; 4.36; 5.48; 6.56). The intimate relation between the two is well expressed toward the close of the *Exposition of Psalm 118:*

> There is no one who does not think the marriage of the soul and spirit or of Christ and the church is not blessed. But because the fullness of the Word or of the Holy Spirit flashes forth and gleams and nothing can be compared to it, they [i.e., the friends of the Bride speaking in Song 8:8] wish to put it off so that by the delay both the soul and church can become more perfect. (22.36 [ed. Petschenig, p. 506.4–8])[79]

The genre, purpose, and structure of the treatise *On Isaac* will doubtless be puzzling to the modern reader at first sight.[80] Ambrose opens with an allegorical reading of the marriage of Isaac and Rebekah (Genesis 24) taken as types of Christ and the church (1.1-3.7).[81] Soon (3.7) the bishop shifts the perspective. In the midst of the exegesis of a passage about Rebekah as referring to either the church or the individual soul (Gen 24:60 LXX), Ambrose claims that Isaac, since he too represents a purified soul, can be a Rebekah. An exquisite gender transference takes place here in which Isaac, the male who in Genesis ascetically prepares himself for the coming of Rebekah (here identified with the *mysterium Christi*), is also the female soul (the Bride of the Song), who as Rebekah longing for the sight of the true Isaac (i.e., Christ), exclaims, "Let him kiss me with the kisses of his mouth!" (Song 1:1) (*On Isaac* 3.7 [ed. Schenkl, pp. 646.25-647.4]).[82] While Origen had suggested that the marriage of Isaac and Rebekah was a type of the marriage of the soul and the Word,[83] Ambrose's original melding of Philonian and Origenist exegesis allows him to play off the Genesis and the Song of Songs texts against each other in a manner unprecedented in earlier exegesis.

This interpenetration of the two biblical texts can be seen, for instance, in the two basic itineraries that *On Isaac* presents for understanding the soul's progress to marital union (*copula spiritualis*) with the Word. After a lengthy analysis of Song 1:1-8 in sections 3.8-4.16 of the treatise, Ambrose employs Song 1:9 to return to the story of Isaac and Rebekah in 4.17-22, dwelling on the three wells that Isaac dug (Gen 26:19-22). "Haec doctrina iam mystica est" ("This is already mystical teaching"), he exclaims. The three wells are three kinds of teaching—the moral, the natural, and the mystical—which are also figured in Solomon's three books. Proverbs gives the moral meaning, which cleanses the image of the soul; Ecclesiastes provides the natural meaning, which allows us to transcend the world; and the Song of Songs is the source of the mystical sense where we drink of the abundance of love (*On Isaac* 4.23-25 [ed. Schenkl, pp. 657-59]). This three-fold pattern of spiritual progress, based on Origen's commentary on the Song, was a standard teaching of Ambrose.[84] Because "in the Song of Songs Solomon clearly expressed this triple wisdom," we may take it that the remainder of the treatise *On Isaac* (4.27-8.79) is designed to show how the Song teaches these three forms of wisdom to the Christian community. Later in the work (8.68-70) the three stages of the soul's advance (*institutio, profectus, perfectio*) are also said to be presented in the three passages where the Bride speaks of belonging to her Brother, i.e., her Divine Lover (Song 2:16-17; 6:2; 7:10).

There is, however, another structural pattern found in the *On Isaac*, one that springs more naturally from the Song of Songs itself, not imported from a theoretical imposition of three kinds of knowledge. (These two

organizing principles, like the two essential scriptural bases, are complementary in Ambrose's symbolic theology.) In 6.50 the bishop outlines four
stages of spiritual progression closely bound to the text of the Song.

> First, impatient with love and not bearing the delays of the Word, she asked
> that she might deserve kisses (Song 1:2 LXX). And she deserved to see the
> Beloved and was also led into the King's bedroom (Song 1:4 LXX).
> Second, . . . suddenly the Word left her in the midst of conversation, though
> he was not long gone, for, as she was seeking, he came leaping over the moun-
> tains and bounding over the hills (Song 2:8). . . . Third, . . . although she
> had not found the one she sought in the city, the square and the streets, she
> finally called him back with her prayers and grace so that she was summoned
> closer by the Bridegroom (Song 3:1-4). Fourth, he now wakens her from
> sleep, . . . but while she was opening the door the Word passed by . . . (Song
> 5:2-6). (6.50 [ed. Schenkl, p. 674.4-18])[85]

This itinerary begins with a partial experience of the presence of the Divine
Lover signified through the kiss and the first entry into the bed chamber;
but this is followed by the sudden departure of the Bridegroom, who soon
returns in a new way. The third stage represents the process of purification
the soul must undergo to prove worthy of a further kind of visit, which,
while still imperfect, is deeper and more permanent than what has gone
before. "And she went forth at his word, and finally (through wounds, the
wounds of love), she found and she held the one she sought so as not to lose
him" (*De Isaac* 6.50 [ed. Schenkl, pp. 674.18-675.1]).[86] The emphasis in this
pattern on the experience of presence followed by an absence that increases
the soul's desire and her resolution to purify herself through virtuous practice conforms very well to the actual text of the Song, as Ambrose notes in
a number of places in his commentary.[87] The bishop's recognition of this
pattern may well have influenced his later readers, especially the great
twelfth-century commentators Bernard of Clairvaux and William of St.
Thierry, who also explored the dialectic of presence and absence found in
the Song of Songs.

This pattern also casts light on one of the most remarkable aspects of the
On Isaac. A number of scholars have argued that the treatise is based on
paschal homilies delivered to the newly baptized,[88] though it may seem
surprising that such difficult material presenting so high an ideal should be
given to so neophytic an audience. But this is to judge from a later perspective that would consider the goal of spiritual marriage with Christ in an
elitest and individualized manner. We know from both *On the Mysteries* and
On the Sacraments that Ambrose preached on the sacramental significance of
the Song of Songs to the newly baptized.[89] In *On Isaac* it would seem that
the bishop is suggesting that the first stage of the soul's mystical itinerary

represented by the kisses of the mouth and the entry into the bedchamber has already been experienced in the sacred mysteries of Easter.[90] But this touch of the Word's presence (whose dramatic effects are known to us from many patristic sources) is just the beginning. The Christian life, the bishop implies, consists of a complex game of love in which the Word's coming sometimes revives the soul, but the Word's absence also has a role to play in empowering the soul to the moral effort needed to progress toward a fullness of union not to be attained until the body has been laid aside.

The path of love begins with aggregation into Christ's Body, the church, through baptism, and is nourished by participation in the church's sacramental and liturgical life, especially through reception of the Eucharist.[91] For Ambrose, as for the other patristic mystical authors, there can be no separation between the ecclesial and the mystical readings of the Song. In one of his most remarkable uses of the Song in the *Exposition of Psalm 118*, he begins by noting that the passage applies to "the Church or the just soul" before drawing out the erotic elements with unusual directness:

> Then he [the Bridegroom] does not spurn the prayers and allurements of the Bride, the breasts of the preacher that are dear to him. And he mercifully leads her into the inner part of the house. Finally, playing with unrestrained love (*lascivienti ludens amore*) because he wishes to test the Beloved's feelings — having often gone out to be sought by the Bride, and often gone in to be invited to kiss — he stands behind the wall and looks through the windows, rising up over the lattices (Song 2:9 LXX). [He does this] so that he is not completely outside nor totally inside, and so that he can call the Bride to himself so that they can both enjoy delightful exchanges and both make a burnt offering of love's power with their conversation. (*Expos. Ps. 118* 6.18 [ed. Petschenig, p. 117.16–25])[92]

Ambrose is even willing to apply the images of the Song to specific individuals, although only to dead ones, as when he uses Song 8:5 to refer to Emperor Valentinian II being received into heaven by the angels.[93]

It is obvious that Ambrose's mysticism, especially when viewed from the perspective of its basic scriptural resource, the Song of Songs, is fully ecclesiological with no hint of elitism and esotericism. It is also fundamentally christological. Although *On Isaac* has been described by Gerard Nauroy as "a discourse of an initiatory hermetism,"[94] its message was hidden only to outsiders; those within the Christian community had been given the keys, both scriptural and sacramental, that would unlock the inner meaning. The use of Neoplatonic elements in the formation of this Christ-centered mysticism is evident, but so is their inner transformation.[95] While it is not possible here to discuss all the aspects of how Jesus the Divine Lover functions in Ambrose's thought, we should at least note how personal this devotion is on the part of the bishop of Milan.[96] Christ who is Love in a substantial way unites our souls to himself (*On Isaac* 5.46), so that we can say: "Caritas itaque nostra Christus" ("Our Charity is Christ") (8.75 [ed. Schenkl, p. 694.10–11]).

When we move on to the third area of Ambrose's main contributions to Latin mysticism, however, we may detect tension, or at least a possible qualification of this broad ecclesiological mysticism, which extends to all the baptized the invitation to travel on the path to loving union with Christ. The bishop of Milan, as pointed out above, was not only an ardent defender of the monastic life, but an even more forceful proponent of virginity. According to Peter Brown, Ambrose saw more clearly than anyone else in the West the importance of the alliance of the clergy and the aristocratic women who had elected to dedicate their lives to Christ as virgins and their wealth to the church.[97] This support of virginity may seem to imply a form of elitism, especially when the bishop makes a point of using the Song of Songs to prove the preeminence of virginity. Ambrose is the first in the West to apply the language of the Song directly to the life of female virgins.

The treatise *On Virgins,* in its first two books at least, seems at times like another disguised commentary on the Song. The same is true of the later treatise *On Virginity.* Virginity is a heavenly mode of life, Ambrose claims, brought down to earth through the birth of the Virgin Christ from the Virgin Mary: "Then a Virgin conceived, and the Word became flesh that flesh might become God" (*On Virgins* 1.3.11 [*PL* 16:202C]).[98] This leads Ambrose to stress how Christ is the source of all virginity and also the Spouse of the virgin church: "She is the Virgin who was espoused, the Virgin who gave birth to us, who fed us with her own milk" (*On Virgins* 1.5.22 [*PL* 16:205D]).[99] However, it is Christ as the Divine Lover of individual virgin Christians (especially females) who occupies the center of the bishop's attention. The love relationship between the divine and human lovers is portrayed through frequent evocation of the images and events of the Song, both in the central chapters of book 1 of *On Virgins* (1.6.38–9.53 with sixteen citations) and also at the end of book 2 (2.6.42–43 with four citations).

Cyprian had stressed the special connection between Christian virgins and the virgin church, a bond that is even stronger in Ambrose for whom *integritas,* the unbroken barrier of the virgin body, is the great sign of the boundary between the church and the world.[100] The ideal of virginity was more than a scheme to give the clergy enhanced financial and social control; it was also a complex manifestation of deep ambivalences (not simply negations) about the body and the body's role in the process of salvation that became painfully evident in the late fourth century.

The writings of Ambrose, even more than those of Augustine, were tainted by a suspicion of bodiliness. It is fashionable to blame his Neoplatonism for this, and some influence can scarcely be denied. But concentration on sexuality as the most evident mark of the imperfection of at least our present mode of bodily existence was primarily a Christian creation in which Ambrose played a large part, both in his own right and through his influence on Augustine. Western Christian mysticism, in contrast to its nearest neighbors, the forms of mysticism in Judaism and Islam, which were usually either indifferent to sexual practice or at times even anxious to incorporate it into the mystical path, has often been antisexual, at least from the time of the triumph of the ideal of virginity. Of course, no Christian author excluded the married from the possibility of salvation, and some, as we shall see, thought that attaining Christian perfection was not dependent on the issue of one's marital status. Still, the majority voice in Western Christian mysticism has emphasized the advisability and sometimes the necessity for the virgin state if one is to attain to marriage with the Word in this life. Much of the power of Western mysticism may come from its deliberate eroticizing of the relation between the human virgin and the Divine "Better Bridegroom" (*On Virgins* 1.12.65), as if the absorption of the erotic element into the internal arena becomes more forceful and more total the more it negates all deliberate external expression. On this issue, Ambrose, the first great commentator on the Song of Songs in the Western tradition, was a more influential figure than Augustine, who eschewed any erotic interpretation of the Song.

It is important to be fair to the bishop of Milan. Despite the depreciation of bodily existence that is shot through *On Isaac* and *On Death as a Good,*[101] flesh and the body are not total evils for him. It is the fallen body and its sexual *voluptas* that bother Ambrose.[102] Flesh in the good, unfallen sense is important for the bishop—he insists that it is only through our contact with Christ's virginal flesh that we are saved[103] and that we shall be raised up in transformed flesh on the last day.[104] What is so important about virginity is that it restores this unfallen flesh, at least to some, giving them a foretaste of the untroubled bodily state that all the faithful will eventually enjoy.

Following Paul, he emphasizes that marriage is a good (*On Virgins* 1.6.24-7.35), though a severely limited one. Although he cites a Christian virgin of Antioch confronted with the choice between denying her faith and being committed to a house of prostitution with the observation, "It is preferable to have a virgin mind than a virgin body" (*On Virgins* 2.4.24

[*PL* 16.225]),[105] it is obvious he felt that in less dire situations the virgin body was always superior to one whose integrity had been lost.

Whether or not this stress on virginity introduces a conflicting elitism into his broad ecclesiological mysticism is not a question that Ambrose ever directly addressed to the best of my knowledge. Perhaps he comes closest to an answer in *On Virgins,* when he places virginity's superiority in an eschatological perspective. Here he sets the opposition between sexuality and virginity in absolute fashion: angels preserve chastity; devils lose it — or, "She is a virgin who is the Bride of Christ, a harlot who makes other things gods" (1.8.52 [*PL* 16:214A]).[106] In the present life all must preserve the form of virginity identified with loyalty to Christ if they wish to attain the full angelic virginity promised to the elect at the resurrection (see Matt 22:30: "For at the resurrection men and women do not marry; no, they are like the angels of heaven"). Hence Ambrose concludes by telling virgins, "That which is promised to us is already present to you" (*On Virgins* 1.8.52 [*PL* 16:214A]).[107]

This attempt to study three essential areas of Ambrose's contributions to Western mysticism has largely neglected a number of other themes in which his writings support ideas readily available and more completely developed in other authors. For example, Ambrose does not have an explicit theory of mystical union, though his use of the erotic language of the Song meant that he was more open to using union language about the soul's relation to Christ than Augustine was.[108] (Cassian has more on the nature of union with God, as we shall see.) Like the bishop of Hippo, Ambrose understood God's immediate presence to the soul as involving not only the highest form of love but also some exalted mode of knowing.[109] But, unlike Augustine, he gave little attention to the analysis of this fusion of love and knowledge. Following Origen, he found in the Lucan account of Jesus' preference of Mary over Martha (Luke 10:38–42) a proof of the superiority of the contemplative over the active life, but he has no extensive discussion of the relations of the two.[110] Further, given his knowledge of Origen, it comes as no surprise that he was interested in the interior spiritual senses by which the soul comes to experience the divine presence.[111] Finally, Ambrose's notion of *excessus mentis,* or rapture, briefly discussed in our analysis of his use of Plotinus, would also repay greater scrutiny than can be given here, though there is more on this notion in Augustine.

I have avoided the misleading question whether Ambrose himself can be termed a mystic. Unlike Augustine, he never spoke of his own special experiences of God in the first person. It is also true that the dense and undifferentiated texture of his writings, especially in *On Isaac,* makes it difficult to determine whether particular passages are to be seen primarily as expressing a moral teaching, an eschatological hope or a mystical reality to which his readers are asked to aspire, or perhaps to test against their experience.[112] I do not think it necessary to choose among these options — which is one of the reasons why Ambrose of Milan can be seen as the initiator of so much in classical Latin mysticism.

Jerome

Jerome was born in Dalmatia, perhaps as early as ca. 331 or as late as ca. 347.[113] After receiving an excellent education, he lived as a hermit in Syria for a time (ca. 375–377). He came to Rome as an emissary from Constantinople and served as Pope Damasus's secretary between 382 and 385, spreading the ideal of monastic asceticism, especially among wealthy Roman aristocratic women, such as the widows Marcella and Paula. Jerome's fostering of the ascetic life did not sit well with everyone, and after Damasus's death he and his patron Paula left for the East where they set up a dual monastery at Bethlehem in 385. Here Jerome lived until his death in 419, translating the Bible, writing extensively, quarreling with almost everybody.

Jerome's major contribution to Latin Christianity, of course, was his "Vulgate" translation (Vg), which became the standard Bible of the Western church. But he was also an important translator of Origen (against whom he turned after 393).[114] We have already noted the role he played as a transmitter of monastic texts and ideals to the West. Jerome's defense of monasticism, especially evident throughout his letters,[115] contributed much to the triumph of the monastic ideal in the West.

Like Ambrose, he was also a major proponent of the ideal of virginity, "the apostle of continence," as Ferdinand Cavallera called him.[116] Jerome was not a mystic, either by temperament or training.[117] Though he did make available the resources of Origen's mysticism through his translations and use of Origenist exegesis,[118] it was mainly through his defense of the superiority of the virgin state by an appeal to the Song of Songs that he contributed to later Western mysticism, underlining a theme that we have already seen in Ambrose. The key document is the long letter that he wrote in 384 to the young virgin Eustochium, Paula's daughter.[119]

A comparison of Jerome's use of the Song with Ambrose's in his *On Virgins* is instructive. Jerome's work is far more lively given its satirical bite, but also less balanced than the bishop's, even in Ambrose's most body-negating moments. While Jerome does not condemn marriage, he does insist that it is the result of the Fall (*Ep.* 22.19). About the best he can manage to say of it is "I praise wedlock, I praise marriage; but it is because they produce me virgins" (*Ep.* 222.20 [ed. Wright, p. 94]).[120] Jerome has an obsessive fear about how easily virginity can be lost ("even by a thought" [*Ep.* 22.5]) that is absent in Ambrose, and he is far more direct in his warnings about the sexual dangers of the body (e.g., 22.11–12, 17). Jerome, unlike Ambrose, appeals to his own experience in recounting his sexual temptations in the desert (22.7) and in describing the famous dream in which he was upbraided for being a Ciceronian rather than a Christian (22.30).

The purpose of the letter, however, is to praise virginity rather than to denigrate marriage. Jerome does so by a personalization of the erotic language of the Song in which he invites Eustochium to appropriate the language of the text into her daily life "so that despising the flesh you may be joined to your Bridegroom's embrace" (*Ep.* 22.1 [ed. Wright, p. 54]).[121] The Song is cited some twenty-seven times in the text (as against four times in the parallel *Letter* 130 written some thirty years later). One of the most striking uses occurs when Jerome counsels Eustochium to avoid mixing with the public in order to be open to spiritual encounters with her Divine Lover:

> Let the seclusion of your own chamber ever guard you; ever let the Bridegroom sport with you within (*tecum sponsus ludat intrinsecus*). If you pray, you are speaking with your Spouse: if you read, he is speaking to you. When sleep falls on you, he will come behind the wall and he will put his hand through the hole in the door and will touch your belly (Song 5:4 LXX). And you will awake and rise up and cry: "I am sick with love" (Song 5:8 LXX). (*Ep.* 22.25 [ed. Wright, p. 108])[122]

Although Jerome's troubled sexuality is evident throughout the letter, there is also a devotion to Christ reminiscent in its way of Origen and Ambrose. "Let us love Christ and ever seek his embraces, and everything difficult will seem easy" (*Ep.* 22.40 [ed. Wright, p. 152]).[123]

Other figures of the age of Augustine also made contributions to the emerging mysticism of Latin Christianity. These include well-known saints, such as Martin of Tours, whose life as portrayed by his admirer Sulpicius Severus includes teachings and especially practices (such as Martin's dedication to the ideal of unceasing prayer)[124] that were to have a role in later forms of mysticism. Paulinus of Nola in his letters to the same Sulpicius displays a piety which at times could be characterized as mystical.[125] Other figures, like the little-known Apponius (apparently an early fifth-century cleric) contributed to the spread of Origenist-Ambrosian mystical reading of the Song of Songs.[126] Aside from Augustine (to whom we shall turn in the next chapter), the other major founding figure of Latin mysticism was John Cassian.

John Cassian

Cassian, almost an exact contemporary of Augustine, was born in the East about 360.[127] He was a native Latin speaker, though fluent in Greek. As a young man he joined a monastery near Bethlehem, but he spent most of his Eastern monastic life on long visits to various monasteries in Egypt interviewing the famous abbas of the desert. A convinced Origenist who was much influenced by Evagrius Ponticus, he fled Egypt ca. 400 during the Origenist controversy, going first to John Chrysostom at Constantinople and then on to Rome, where he spent some years. About 415 he settled in southern Gaul at Marseilles, where he founded two monasteries and advised the Gallic bishops about monasticism. His major works were the *Conferences* (*Conlationes*) (ca. 426–429), which present his recollections of what the Eastern fathers had to say about the interior life of both anchorites and cenobites, and the *Institutes of the Coenobites* (*Institutiones*) (ca. 430), which describe the external practices of monks living in community.[128] These writings were the most important links between Eastern and Western monasticism for over a millennium.[129]

The other founders of Western mysticism, Ambrose and Augustine, were devotees of the monastic ideal; Cassian was a monastic *tout court*. His life experience had been a monastic one, and his major writings were directed only to monks. As important leaders of dioceses, both Ambrose and Augustine had obligations to the world of lay Christians, and they played their part in the birth of a distinctive lay spirituality.[130] Cassian had few ties to that world; for him Christian perfection was reserved only for monastics.[131]

Indeed, for Cassian the church was meant to be a monastic institution. He is the earliest witness (*Conl.* 18.5) to the oft-repeated monastic topos that the first Christians in Jerusalem were actually a cenobitic monastic community and that it was the laxity of later ages which allowed for the split between the true monastic Christians and their second-rate lay counterparts. In a sense it is true to say that Cassian thought of monasticism not as an element in a Christian society but as the Christian alternative to society.[132] Much more than Ambrose or Augustine, this transplanted ascetic stands at the beginning of a two-tiered model of Christian spirituality in which higher, mystical perfection, is believed open only to the monastics who have fled the world and who live lives of perfect chastity.

Cassian has often been treated as very much a second-rate author.[133] He is heavily dependent on Evagrius Ponticus,[134] a dependence that may at times mask the skill with which he transformed his Eastern sources into a new linguistic and social milieu. Behind Evagrius stood Origen.[135] Cassian never mentioned either author explicitly (doubtless due to the Origenist controversy), but he did much to convey aspects of their teaching to the West. It is true to say, along with Owen Chadwick, that in the very process of translation, Cassian created new possibilities for a distinctive Western mysticism.[136]

Although Cassian's works are digressive and often treated only as raw material from which to draw evidence for early Western monasticism, in recent years there has been a greater appreciation of his procedures of composition.[137] Cassian may not be as skilled a writer as Ambrose or Augustine, but he is not as superficial and disorganized as has sometimes been implied. He wrote primarily in a practical vein to instruct Western monks in the values and practices of the heroes of the desert. This practical side is seen in his frequent emphasis on the necessity of testing spiritual teaching against experience. While his writing is not meant to be systematic, a system lurks behind it.

The basic structure of Cassian's thought is close to the Evagrian system presented above.[138] *Conference* 14, given by the Abba Nestorius (each conference or group is assigned to a famous Egyptian abba), deals with spiritual knowledge or science (*de spiritali scientia*),[139] dividing it into two parts: "First there is practical, that is, active science, which is perfected in correcting moral actions and purging vices; and second, the theoretical science, which consists in the contemplation of divine things and the grasp of the most sacred meanings [of scripture]" (*Conl.* 14.1 [2:184]).[140] *Scientia actualis* has two basic operations. The first is the negative task of coming to understand and root out the eight principal vices or evil inclinations that Cassian adopted from Evagrius and introduced to the West — gluttony, lust, and avarice (effecting the *concupiscibile,* or desiring power of the soul); anger, sadness, and *acedia* (attacking the *irascibile,* or power of rejection); and finally vainglory and pride (peculiar to the *rationabile,* the soul's reasoning power).[141] Cassian's anthropology is a simplified version of Evagrius, though in keeping with Western interests, he puts stress on monastic perfection as producing the restoration of the soul's likeness to God, especially as we pass from the negative to the positive side of *scientia actualis.*[142]

The positive pole of this practical science is less easily schematized, though Cassian emphasizes humility and discretion as the primary guiding forces in virtuous action.[143] His moral theology is best approached not by attempting to grasp how he views each individual monastic virtue, but by recognizing that it is the acquisition of *puritas cordis* and *caritas* that gives meaning to all moral effort.[144]

In the first conference Abba Moses distinguishes between the *telos* or *finis,* that is, the ultimate end of the monastic life, which is identified as the kingdom of God, and the *scopos,* that is, the direction or aim that enables us to reach the goal. "The end of our profession, as we have said, is the kingdom of God or kingdom of heaven, but its direction (*destinatio*), that is *scopos,* is purity of heart, without which it is impossible for anyone to reach that end" (*Conl.* 1.4 [1:81]).[145] This vocabulary is taken over from Evagrius,[146] but it abandons the desert monk's favorite term, *apatheia,* for the more positive and scriptural connotations of *puritas cordis* (see Matt 5:8). The underlying doctrine is not really different. Evagrius's *apatheia* was far from Stoic forms of indifference. It was essentially a state of tranquillity or detachment ("the health of the soul" [*Praktikos* 56]) achieved through over-coming the eight evil tendencies (*logismoi*).[147] Evagrius claimed that *apatheia* gave birth to *agapē* (*Praktikos* pref.; 81); Cassian brings the two even closer together. While he can describe *puritas cordis* negatively as the avoidance of vices (e.g., *Conl.* 1.6), positively speaking, purity of heart is nothing else but love (". . . puritas cordis, quod est caritas" [*Conl.* 1.7]).[148] The relation between the two is perhaps best expressed in *Institutes* 4.43: "Purity of heart is acquired by the flowering of the virtues, and the perfection of apostolic charity is possessed by means of purity of heart" (ed. Guy, p. 184.16–17).[149]

Matthew 5:8 had promised the vision of God to those who were pure of heart. Hence it was an easy step for Cassian to understand the purity of heart that leads to the kingdom of God in terms of preparation for con-templation. In *Conference* 10.10 (2.90) he describes the purifying activity of his famous formula of unceasing prayer (Ps 69:2) as leading to "invisible and celestial contemplations (*theoriae*) and to that inexpressible fire of prayer experienced by very few."[150] We may take it that charity, contemplation, and union (the latter two will be considered in more detail below) are all correlative terms expressing different but interrelated aspects of the second or theoretical stage of spiritual science.[151]

It may be surprising to note that when Cassian turns to *scientia theoretikē* in *Conference* 14 he describes it not in terms of the two types of contemplation found in Evagrius (i.e., *theōria physikē,* the knowledge of created things, and *theōria theologikē,* knowledge of the divine) but in terms of the proper mode of understanding Scripture. "Theoretical knowledge is divided into two parts, that is, into historical interpretation and spiritual understanding (*intelligentia spiritalis*). . . . There are three types of spiritual knowledge: tropology, allegory, anagogy" (*Conl.* 14.8 [2:189–90]).[152] Cassian goes on to illustrate the famous four senses of scripture in a classic text based on Paul's reading of Abraham's two wives in Galatians 4:22–23. The *historia* is the past historical fact, the *allegoria* is the way in which the two women prefigure the two covenants. "Anagogy climbs up from spiritual mysteries to higher and more sacred celestial secrets," that is, the message that the Jerusalem on high is our true mother (see Gal 4:26–27). Finally, tropology is the moral explanation according to which the two covenants are the practical and theoretical knowledge that instruct the Jerusalem of the soul. Cassian (following Origen) ties his higher science more directly to the biblical text than Evagrius did, and this is borne out by his constant referencing of biblical passages understood in a highly spiritual way. He insists that the proper grasp of the Bible is dependent on moral effort rather than mere study: purity of heart rather than knowledge of the commentators is the key (see *Instit.* 5.34). *Conference* 14.10 uses the image of constant meditation on the scripture eventually forming the ark of the covenant within the soul; that is, the meaning of the Bible becomes connatural.[153]

Cassian makes use of another general pattern, also based on Evagrius and Origen, to structure his account of the monk's progress to perfection. *Conference* 3 of Abba Paphnutius centers on three renunciations:

> The first is that by which we despise all the riches and resources of the world with our bodies. The second that by which we reject former activities, vices and desires of the soul and the flesh; the third that by which we recall our minds from every present visible thing in order to contemplate only what lies ahead and to desire the things that are invisible. (*Conl.* 3.6 [1:145])[154]

These three renunciations, which may be compared with the three motivations for good actions considered in *Conference* 11 (fear of hell, hope of heaven, and love of virtue), portray a broad program of ascent in which the first two comprise the level of *scientia actualis,* while the third embraces *scientia theoretikē.* They are also compared to the three books of Solomon: Proverbs teaches the renunciation of the flesh and earthly things; Ecclesiastes councils the vanity of all creation; and the Song of Songs presents the third renunication "in which the mind transcending everything visible is joined to God's Word by the contemplation of heavenly things" (*Conl.* 3.6). This threefold Origenist theme, which correlates the Song with the highest form of spiritual knowledge, was dear to Ambrose, but Cassian differs from the bishop and from Jerome in making little use of the erotic language of the Song as a instrument for mystical expression.[155]

One final, theological note can be added here. Cassian, as is well known, became the spokesman for those monks who were upset by Augustine's late predestinarian teaching on grace that seemed to deny human freedom and therefore the moral effort of asceticism. *Conference* 13 is taken up with this issue. Cassian has been accused of confusion in his account of the relation of grace and freedom, but this may not be totally fair. He represents the protest of an older, more synergistic view in the face of the rending quarrels that erupted over the teaching of Pelagius. Cassian is no Pelagian (see *Conl.* 13.16); he insists on the necessity of grace for the attainment of purity of heart and perfect charity (e.g., *Conl.* 3.12; 3.15–16; 5.14–15). From the Augustinian perspective, however, he seems to want to have it both ways. Though some texts insist that "the beginning of good will in us is granted by God's inspiration" (*Conl.* 3.19 [1:162]),[156] other passages make it clear that Cassian thought that at least in some cases grace was given to those "who labor and sweat for it" (*Instit.* 12.14 [ed. Guy, p. 468.8–9]).[157]

On the basis of this account of the general structure of Cassian's thought, we can now turn to the interconnected mystical themes that are central to his writing — *oratio, contemplatio, visio,* and *conjunctio.* Prayer is understood as both *oratio* and *contemplatio.* The very structure of the first part of the *Conferences,* which culminates in Abba Isaac's two speeches on prayer, shows how important pure and unceasing prayer was to Cassian.[158] "The entire goal of the monk and the perfection of the heart moves toward continual and uninterrupted perseverance in prayer," as Isaac says at the beginning of *Conference* 9.[159]

In teaching how it is possible for the monk to pray always and thus fulfill the Gospel command (see Luke 18:1; 1 Thess 5:16–18), Cassian's *Conferences* 9 and 10 must be taken together.[160] He begins with a discussion of the goal of prayer (9.2 and 10.5–7; the first four chapters in 10 are taken up with the Anthropomorphite heresy). The goal succinctly announced in the quotation from 9.2 given above is expanded upon in 10.6–7 in one of the monk's more important mystical passages. Since in prayer we see Jesus according to the level of purification we have attained, we see him either in his humble and fleshly state, "or, with the internal gaze of the mind, as glorified and coming in the glory of his majesty" (*Conl.* 10.6 [2:80]).[161] In order to reach such a vision, whose scriptural warrant is found in the Transfiguration, we must withdraw into solitude so that while still dwelling in the body we come to share some likeness of the future state when God will be all in all (1 Cor 15:18). Thus, the goal of prayer is to be absorbed into the loving union that binds the persons of the Trinity, as Cassian says in a passage reminiscent of a text from Origen's *On First Principles:*

> Then will be perfectly fulfilled in us our Savior's prayer when he prayed to his Father for his disciples, "So that the love with which you have loved me may be in them and they in us" (John 17:26), and again, "That they all may be one as you, Father, in me and I in you, and that they may be one in us" (John 17:21). The perfect love with which "he first loved us" (1 John 4:10) will pass into our heart's affection, . . . and that unity which now belongs to the Father and the Son will be transfused into our mind and understanding. . . . (*Conl.* 10.7 [2.81])[162]

This unity, in which whatever we breathe or think or speak about *is* God, is an image or a pledge (*arrha*) of the heavenly state to come. It is the "one unending prayer" (*una et iugis . . . oratio*) which is the goal of the monastic life. Deeply Evagrian as it is, the numerous Johannine references give Cassian's view of unceasing prayer a more christological character than what we find in Evagrius's presentation.[163]

Both conferences deal with the preparation for such perfect prayer (9.3–7; 10.8), and especially with the method by which it is to be attained (9.7–24; 10.9–10). In the more extensive treatment in *Conference* 9, the preparation involves not only freedom from vices but also liberation from distractions and from all earthly concerns.[164] The account of the method of prayer in the two conferences is initially surprising because it seems that rather different methods are advanced. *Conference* 9 provides what is really a small treatise on prayer in general, beginning with a presentation in 9.9–17 of the four kinds of prayer based on 1 Timothy 2:1 (*obsecrationes, orationes, postulationes, gratiarum actiones*). Origen had also analyzed these in his *On Prayer* 14, but he did not see them as progressive, with the prayer of thanksgiving "generated from the consideration of God's benefits and greatness and faithfulness" as the highest form.[165] To illustrate the "higher and more excellent state formed by the contemplation of God and the ardor of charity" (9.18) that follows these four types, Cassian, again like Origen (*On Prayer* 18–30), turns to a commentary on the Lord's Prayer (9.18–24).

In the tenth conference, however, it is another form of prayer, the constant repetition of a single short verse, in this case the form known as the "Deus in adjutorium" taken from Psalm 69:2 ("O God, come to my aid; Lord, make haste to help me"), which is encouraged in order to achieve the goal of ceaseless prayer (10.10–11).[166] Both the Our Father and the "Deus in adjutorium" are described as *formulae* (9.18; 10.10), that is, as scriptural forms of meditation that serve as essential food for the soul in its progress toward the highest stages of prayer. While Cassian stresses the advantages of the latter "monologistic" formula in its ability to concentrate the attention and express the poverty of the human situation, his position seems to be that a variety of modes, methods, and formulas are allowed, but that ones rooted in scripture are preferable.

In both conferences this study of method brings Cassian back to a new and deeper consideration of the goal of prayer in passages that are among the most important for the understanding of his mysticism (9.25–27; 10.11). The controlling image in these texts is fire, *oratio ignita;* the key themes are passivity, rapture (*excessus mentis*), ineffability, and transiency. While earlier passages in *Conference* 9 had mentioned "very fervent and fiery prayers" in connection with thanksgiving (9.15 [2:52]),[167] the level of prayer that Cassian speaks of in 9.25 indicates a higher state of the ineffable "prayer of fire known and experienced by so few" (2:61).[168] This prayer, as the discussions in 9.26–27 and 10.11 indicate, is always a divine gift, one given in a variety of ways that show that Cassian's doctrine of the higher stages of prayer is still a fluid one. Most often, it has its source in compunction, but it finds its expression in "unspeakable joy" and "inexpressible groans" (*ineffabile gaudium, gemitibus inenerrabilibus* [9.27]). It cannot be communicated in words, because it takes place when the combined knowing powers of the soul (*conglobatibus sensibus* [9.25]) pass beyond themselves (inwardly or outwardly) in an *excessus mentis* (9.31; 10.10), or an *excessus cordis* (10.11).[169] The examples given indicate that it is of brief duration, though Cassian does not attempt to describe this aspect in more detail.[170] Such prayer, he says, follows the model given by Jesus (Luke 5:16 and 22:44 are noted). Antony of the desert is also cited, especially his statement "that prayer is not perfect in which the monk is conscious of himself or the fact that he is praying" (*Conl.* 9.31 [2:66]).[171]

The parallel passage in *Conference* 10.11 brings out another dimension of this form of prayer. Here Cassian speaks of praying the Psalms in such a way that they conform perfectly to our own experience. "Receiving the same movement of the heart (*cordis affectus*) in which the Psalm was first sung or written, we become, as it were, its author, anticipating the meaning rather than following it" (2:92).[172] This way of reading or praying the scripture from within is characteristic of the exegetical nature of early Christian mysticism, particularly as we have seen it realized in Origen.[173] Here Cassian says that it prepares for the passage to that kind of pure prayer treated in the previous conference which he now summarizes:

> [This prayer] is not concerned with any consideration of an image, nor characterized by any sound nor set of words. It comes forth from a fiery mental intention through an ineffable rapture of the heart (*excessus cordis*) by means of an inexplicable burst of the spirit. Freed from all sensations and visible concerns, the mind pours itself out to God with unspeakable groans and sighs (Rom 8:26). (*Conl.* 10.11 [2:93])[174]

One other conference sheds further light on Cassian's understanding of mystical prayer and contemplation. In *Conference* 19 Abba John discusses the relationship between the eremitical and the cenobitical lives, arguing that the heights of contemplation can only be reached through the solitary life in the desert, but because of the dangers of this existence for those who have not yet reached perfect purity of heart, it is safer to pursue one's salvation in the midst of the support of the *coenobium*. Cassian claims that only a very few abbas, such as Moses, Paphnutius, and the two Macarii, have been able to combine both types of life (19.9). This extended treatment of the goals and advantages of the two forms of monastic life allows for considerable attention to the ecstatic prayer that is the identifying mark of the hermit, but (as we see on the basis of 9.25–27) need not be totally absent from the life of the monk in community. Abba John admits that while in the desert he was so *frequently* caught up in such raptures that he forgot he was still in the body (19.4),[175] but he allows that as more hermits began to people the wilderness, "the fire of divine contemplation began to grow cold," so that he decided to retreat to the monastery where "what I lose of the heights of contemplation I get back by the submission of obedience" (*Conl.* 19.5 [3:42–43]).[176] John considers the ecstatic prayer he enjoyed in the desert as a means of being united with Christ. As 19.8 declares, the hermit's goal is "to have a mind emptied of all earthly things (as far as human weakness allows) and thus to be united to Christ" (3:46).[177]

It is clear from these conferences that Cassian, like Evagrius, believed that prayer was the essence of the life of perfection and that pure and unceasing prayer provided an immediate access to God's presence as a foretaste of heaven. Though his understanding of what later ages would call mystical prayer is broad and somewhat diffuse, including a variety of experiences (e.g., *Conl.* 9.26) that later theorists would organize into careful but perhaps less flexible categories, Cassian is conscious of the need for some discriminations (e.g., 9.29).

This treatment of his understanding of *oratio* has already exposed a number of the other terms, such as *contemplatio, meditatio,* and *visio,* that are closely allied. Cassian uses *contemplatio* and *theoria* throughout his writings,[178] and he finds these terms interchangeable with the *perfectio caritatis* that is the culmination and heart of all the virtues. "*Theoria,* that is, the contemplation of God, is the one thing in relation to which all the merits of our righteousness and all our virtuous efforts are secondary" (*Conl.* 23.3 [3:141–42]).[179] Contemplation, of course, implies the vision of God, at least in its higher stages, and mention of "the vision of God alone" (*Dei solius intuitus* [*Conl.* 9.17]) appears fairly often in his discussions of prayer and contemplation.[180] Contemplation itself is an elastic term for the monk. Although he specifies various kinds of contemplation in a number of places (sometimes in dependence on Evagrius),[181] his real interest is in contemplation conceived of as the progressive conformation of the soul to God.

Cassian's understanding of the relation of contemplation to action appears mostly in his discussions of the respective advantages of the eremitical and cenobitical forms of monasticism. It is not hard to find passages that express the theoretical supremacy of the eremitical life of contemplation with its goal of ecstatic experience. But in reality things are not that simple. *Conference* 9.25–27 shows that *excessus mentis* can be found in the cenobitical life, and *Conference* 19, as Philip Rousseau has pointed out,[182] indicates that Cassian appears to have realized, at least in his Western situation, that a pure eremitical life was not advisable and that both the solitary and the community forms of monasticism mix action and contemplation, though in differing ways. Cassian did not work out a clear and coherent solution to the relationship of contemplative absorption in God and active love for the monastic brethren (e.g., *Conl.* 24.26), and the issue continued to trouble medieval mystics, especially monastic ones. Perhaps we may take as his basic position something he said about the relation of physical labor to contemplative prayer— "there is a mutual and inseparable link between the two" (*Conl.* 9.2 [2:40]).[183]

As pointed out above, this contemplation or vision of God is also described as a joining or uniting the soul to God.[184] Cassian uses a variety of mostly verb forms in the *Conferences* to indicate the kind of loving union that perfected souls, like Paul, can enjoy: *copulare* (1.14; 10.7), *inhaerere* and *cohaerere* (1.8; 2.2; 3.1; 7.6; 14.4; 23.5), *iungere* and *coniungere* (3.6; 10.7; 23.5; 23.10), *unire* (20.8; 23.11), and *innecti* (6.10). Even though all these passages may not express what later mystics would characterize as an immediate consciousness of God's presence, a passage such as that from *Conference* 10.7 analyzed above shows that Cassian had a definite if not developed doctrine of union with God.

Owen Chadwick has denied that Cassian was really a mystic, claiming that "he was an ascetic theologian who takes his readers to the level of contemplation and there leaves them."[185] But most investigators have wanted to see the monk as some kind of mystic, though their descriptions rarely agree.[186] Abbot Butler claimed that it was Cassian more than Augustine who first domiciled in Latin-speaking lands the form of monastic piety that he identified with "Western mysticism."[187] I would agree that the monk from Marseilles is one of the founders of the Western mystical tradition, though I think that that tradition needs to be more broadly conceived than Butler allowed. The transplanted Easterner's main concern was with conveying to his Latin audience knowledge of the ascetical practices of Egypt, but he does more than leave his readers at the entrance to contemplation. Especially in *Conferences* 9 and 10 he conveys to them something of the inexpressible mystery of more direct contact with God.

At the end of *Conference* 8, Abba Serenus provides a wonderful nautical image for this mystery:

> . . . our brief and simple words have drawn the ship of this Conference to the safe harbor of silence from the deep sea of questions, in which deep indeed, as the breath of the Divine Spirit drives us deeper in, is ever opened up a wider and boundless space reaching beyond the sight of the eye. (*Conl.* 8.25 [2:36-37])[188]

By the time of Cassian's death (probably a few years after Augustine's in 430) the Latin West was largely independent of the Eastern empire. Knowledge of Greek had rapidly disappeared, theological debates (with the exception of the christological controversies) primarily reflected Western preoccupation with grace and freedom, and Latin monasticism was developing on its own. The mounting pressure of the barbarian tide and the growing ineffectiveness of the emperors in far-off Constantinople were signs of a great change in which ancient structures, including ecclesiastical ones, were being slowly and inexorably transformed. With regard to the history of mysticism, it was the new institution of monasticism that would be the main social force for nurturing mystical texts and practices and transmitting them to future generations. This was as true for the writings of Ambrose and Cassian as it was for the great figure of Augustine, to whom we now turn.

CHAPTER 7

Augustine:
The Founding Father

AUGUSTINE WAS BORN in 354, the child of lower middle class North Africans.[1] The influence of his pious Christian mother, Monica, far outweighed that of his pagan father, Patricius. A clever youth, Augustine found education the key to a wider world. By the age of nineteen, this education had already turned him away from a profligate adolescence toward the love of wisdom he discovered through reading Cicero's lost dialogue *Hortensius.* In 383 the young scholar went to Italy, where a bright future awaited him as a teacher of rhetoric in Milan, the Western capital. But the pull of the divine love that he portrayed so movingly in the *Confessions,* acting through a variety of intermediaries, such as the ideal of monasticism, the discovery of the "books of the Platonists," and the preaching of Ambrose, eventually brought him to the famous conversion in the garden described in *Confessions* 8.8–12. There divine grace enabled him to do what the weakness of the fallen will could never achieve: make a decisive choice for Christ that involved not only baptism but also the commitment to adopt a celibate life so typical of the new Christian ideals of perfection. He was baptized by Ambrose on Easter of 387. In autumn of the same year, while awaiting ship at the Roman port of Ostia, he and his mother enjoyed their famous shared experience of the "touching" of God that he described so tantalizingly in *Confessions* 9.10.

Augustine returned to Africa in 391, where he founded a monastic community and was ordained a priest. He plunged into an intense reading of Paul, which profoundly changed his early optimism about human freedom. In 395 he was consecrated bishop of Hippo, where he spent the last thirty-five years of his life caring for his flock and engaging in increasingly acrimonious disputes with the Donatists, and (after ca. 411) with Pelagius and his followers, whose view of Adam's Fall and of the effects of sin on the human condition Augustine came to see as gravely defective.

Augustine was an immensely prolific author — more of his writings survive than can ever be read by most moderns. His roughly eight hundred surviving homilies (many collected into groups devoted to particular books of the Bible) and almost four hundred letters (many really lengthy treatises) constitute the largest part of his oeuvre, but the scores of treatises he left on diverse topics are the most often read parts of this corpus.[2] Since I make no pretense to have read all of Augustine, I note here only those works that I have found essential for understanding his mysticism.

Although some of Augustine's early essays written before 391 (e.g., *On the Greatness of the Soul*) have importance for his mystical thought, the primary resource among his treatises is the *Confessions,* which he wrote between 397 and 401 soon after he had become bishop. At least three of the bishop's five major works are of importance for the study of his mysticism. Most significant are the *Homilies on the Psalms* (*Enarrationes in Psalmos*), partly preached and partly dictated from ca. 391 to possibly as late as 422.[3] They are Augustine's longest and therefore probably least read work, yet they are indispensable for our task. The fifteen books entitled *The Trinity* (ca. 404–420) form Augustine's major contribution to speculative theology, and they also have important ramifications, especially in books 8–15, for his mystical thought.[4] The Gospel of John, ever a favorite text for mystics, was the subject of no fewer than 124 homilies given between ca. 406 and 422 or later.[5] (Also important are the *Homilies on the First Epistle of John,* ten homilies that were apparently delivered at Easter sometime between 413 and 418.)[6]

The other two of Augustine's great works, his *Literal Commentary on Genesis* (*De Genesi ad litteram* [ca. 401–415]), and his *City of God* (*De civitate Dei,* twenty-two books written between 413 and 425) are less directly involved with his mysticism.[7] Nevertheless, book 12 of the former contains an important discussion of the types of visions that became a central *auctoritas* (authoritative text) for medieval mystics, and the *City of God* is helpful for understanding the bishop's attitude toward the contributions and limitations of Platonism, as well as his view of the vision of God in heaven. In addition to these major writings, I shall make use of a selection of letters, sermons, and treatises where helpful, and doubtless there are important texts and passages not cited here that could supplement and enrich what follows.

When Augustine died in 430 at the age of seventy-six, the barbarian Vandals were besieging his episcopal city and the break between Eastern and Western Christianity had become obvious to contemporaries. The bishop of Hippo, the undisputed master of Latin Christian thought, did more than any other figure to shape the new religious world of the next millennium in Western Europe. Disputes over Augustine's thought extend down to the present, though today they are not as sundering as they were in the sixteenth and seventeenth centuries, when Catholics and Protestants both claimed to be his true heirs and when differing camps even within the major divisions of Western Christianity sought to guarantee their legitimacy by appealing to the integrity of their Augustinianism. These debates about what Augustine meant invade almost every aspect of traditional Western theology, so it is not surprising that they extend into the issue of his mysticism.

The question of Augustine's mysticism is not a new one. In his survey of the history of the debate up to 1954, André Mandouze has shown that the issue was raised as early as 1863.[8] Ephraem Hendrikx's famous judgment in 1936 that "Augustine was a great enthusiast but he was no mystic" has been echoed by many.[9] Recently, Gerald Bonner in a 1986 article has doubted the bishop's personal mysticism.[10] Concerning Augustine there are few new debates and perhaps even fewer cases of scholarly consensus in disputed areas.

Disputes over his mysticism, not unlike those noted in relation to other patristic authors, are often "dialogues of the deaf,"[11] in which different understandings of the meaning of mysticism and diverse evaluations of its legitimacy are more important than textual analysis. A priori dichotomies between the Gospel and mysticism (characteristic of some Protestant investigators) or between intellectual philosophy and affective mysticism (on the part of a number of Catholics) make it all too easy to deny that Augustine could be a mystic, or to claim, as H. Meyer did, that Augustine was 98 percent an intellectualist and only 2 percent a mystic![12]

Ephraem Hendrikx, who in 1936 had denied that Augustine was a mystic, in a brief review article he wrote in 1975 surveying forty years of debate on Augustine's relation to mysticism, admitted that the bishop may well have been a mystic, but not in the traditional sense understood by Catholic neoscholastic theology.[13] He and other investigators have quite correctly emphasized that many of the keynotes of traditional understandings of mysticism, such as the notion of personal union with God, are not prominent in Augustine. In the case of the bishop of Hippo, union language seems to be deliberately excluded as a tool for the description of the consciousness of the divine presence in this life, so that if mysticism is to be defined on the basis of the notion of union with God in this life and a clear distinction between acquired and infused contemplation, then

Augustine is certainly not a mystic nor do his writings contain mystical theology in the proper sense. But these definitions of mysticism seem too narrow to do justice to Augustine's thought and are insufficient to grasp the important role that he has had in the history of Western mysticism.

Even Augustine's friends have not always served him well in their attempts to delineate his mysticism. Cuthbert Butler, for example, admitted that the expression "union with God" did not occur in Augustine, but he claimed that "there are passages in which he equivalently expresses the same idea."[14] Fulbert Cayré in his excellent book *La contemplation augustinienne* created unnecessary confusion when he read back a clear scholastic distinction between the natural and supernatural realms into the saint's thought.[15] If nothing else, the critics have taught the defenders to be cautious and above all to be clear.

We do not have to argue that Augustine was a mystic in the sense that such subsequent figures as Bernard of Clairvaux, Meister Eckhart, or Teresa of Avila were in order to vindicate for him an important position in the history of Western mysticism. Nor do we have to prove that he enjoyed a wide variety of mystical experiences, since this issue is secondary to any thinker's role in the mystical tradition. Nor, given the flexible notion of mysticism employed here, do we have to argue that he understood mysticism primarily as a form of union with God.

Augustine's religious genius touched on many fundamental religious issues, of which mysticism is but one. He was a doctrinal and speculative theologian, an educational theorist, a church leader, a monastic founder, a preacher and polemicist—but he was also an author who gave considerable attention to the mystical element in Christianity and to whom almost all later Western mystics appealed. It is in this sense that we can justify calling him not only a mystic, but "the Prince of Mystics" (to use Abbot Butler's term) or "the Father of Christian Mysticism" (to use John Burnaby's).[16]

The main themes of Augustine's mysticism are so enmeshed in his total theology that separating them out always involves a deformation, especially when done on the restricted scale that must be employed in this chapter. While remaining conscious of this danger, I will attempt to lay out the three main building blocks of the bishop's mystical thought and his contribution to later Western mysticism: first, his account of the soul's ascension to contemplative and ecstatic experience of the divine presence; second, the ground for the possibility of this experience in the nature of the human person as the image of the triune God; and third, the necessary role of Christ and the church in attaining this experience.

Such a survey, however extensive, will mean the neglect, to a greater or lesser degree, of many of the key theological ideas with which these three themes are intimately linked.[17] For instance, I will say nothing about Augustine's teaching on the relation of reason and faith, or his important principles for the interpretation of scripture (see especially *On Christian Doctrine*), though we will look at many examples of his spiritual exegesis in practice. The bishop's doctrine of creation will be touched on only with regard to the formation of humanity as the divine image, while his very important teaching on the Fall and on original sin will appear more by implication than by actual consideration. Nor will I deal with his theology of history and all that it implies. Of course, Augustine's teaching on human freedom and grace will require some attention, but only insofar as it becomes visible in the three areas that will concern us. Even the Christology and ecclesiology considered under the third theme will not be a full treatment of all Augustine has to say in these areas. The bishop's moral teaching will appear only sporadically, and his role as a monastic founder will be noted rather than studied.[18] Even with so much left out, Augustine almost overwhelms us with the scope and richness of his teaching.

"Toto Ictu Cordis": The Vision of God

At a culminating point in *Letter* 147, the treatise *On Seeing God* that he wrote for Paulina about 413, Augustine says: "The Lord is spirit (2 Cor 3:17), and so whoever adheres to the Lord is one spirit [with him] (1 Cor 6:17). Hence, the person who is able to see God invisibly can adhere to God incorporeally" (*Ep.* 147.15.37 [*PL* 33:613]).[19] The notion of "seeing God invisibly" gives us an important access to some of the central concerns of Augustine's mysticism. Of course, it is impossible to understand the full depths of what the saint meant by *visio Dei* without eventually considering a series of other terms inextricably bound up with it in the subtle web of Augustinian thought. *Contemplatio* and *sapientia* are the most immediately related words;[20] the crucial notions of *beatitudo, veritas,* and *amor-dilectio* are not far behind. *Visio Dei,* however, was not only often discussed by Augustine, but was also used by the saint in those rare texts in which he speaks of his own experiences of God. As Robert J. O'Connell has put it: "If there is one constant running through all of Augustine's thinking, it is his preoccupation with the question of happiness. . . . But the answer is equally uniform: what makes man happy is the possession of God, a possession achieved by way of vision."[21]

In the seventh book of the *Confessions* Augustine describes an experience (or experiences) that he had at Milan in 386 after reading the "books of the Platonists."[22] The account in general follows a model well known in Plotinus and is artfully presented in three parallel texts (7.10.16–17; 7.17.23; and briefly in recapitulation in 7.20.26).[23] Augustine sets up the first version by noting that the Platonic books clearly taught the eternal birth of the Word from the Father found in the Prologue of John's Gospel, but that they did not know of the Word's taking flesh and dying for our sins. He continues:

> And so, admonished to return to myself, I entered into my inmost parts with you leading me on. I was able to do it because you had become my helper. I entered and saw with my soul's eye (such as it was) an unchanging Light above that same soul's eye, above my mind. . . . He who knows truth knows that light, and he who knows it knows eternity. Love knows it. O Eternal Truth and True Love and Beloved Eternity! You are my God, to you I sigh day and night. . . . And you beat back the weakness of my gaze, powerfully blazing into me, and I trembled with love and dread. And I found myself to be far from you in the land of unlikeness. . . . (*Conf.* 7.10.16 [*PL* 32:742])[24]

The triple pattern described here involves an initial withdrawal from the sense world that often begins from a consideration of the beauty of the universe (*ita gradatim a corporibus ad sentientem per corpus animam, . . . subtrahens se contradicentibus turbis phantasmatum* [7.17.23]). This is followed by an interior movement into the depths of the soul (*intravi in intima mea* [7.10.16]; *inde ad eius* [*anima*] *interiorem vim . . . ad ratiocinantem potentiam* [7.17.23]). Finally, there is a movement above the soul to the vision of God (*et vidi qualicumque oculo animae meae, supra eumdem oculum animae meae, supra mentem meam, lucem incommutabilem* [7.10.16]; *et pervenit ad id quod est in ictu trepidantis aspectus* [7.17.23]).[25]

Though the Plotinian base is important, the differences from Neoplatonic mysticism are equally significant, coming as they do in the midst of Augustine's reflections on just how much, and yet ultimately how little, Neoplatonism approached the fullness of the truth revealed in Christ.[26] Plotinus would doubtless have agreed with Augustine's emphasis on the brevity of the experience and with the emphasis on the shock or "check" encountered by the soul,[27] as *Ennead* 4.8.1 indicates; but he would not have shared Augustine's conviction that the vision was brief and imperfect because of sin, both inherited and personal — the *regio dissimilitudinis* in which the still-unconverted Augustine had exiled himself.[28] For Plotinus, the soul, however fallen, always remains capable of lifting itself up to the vision of God because it is of divine origin; for Augustine, the soul is a fallen creature, bound by both original and individual sin, and hence any such elevation is always a result of God's action in us.

Augustine's emphasis on the necessity of divine intervention if we are to enjoy even such a brief experience (*duce te; et potui quoniam factus es adjutor meus* [7.10.16]) would have appeared strange to Plotinus, though perhaps not his highlighting the role of love in attaining it (*caritas novit eam* [7.10.16];

cf. *Enn.* 6.7.31; 6.9.45–48). Where the bishop decisively parts company with the pagan philosopher is in his insistence that he could not really gain the strength necessary to enjoy God until he had accepted the Incarnate Christ as the mediator between God and humanity (7.18–19.24–25). The christological and, by implication at least, ecclesiological nature of Augustine's mysticism is already evident.

One other dimension of the Milan experience should also be noted, that is, its noetic character. The vision resulted not only in a clear and certain conviction of the existence and goodness of God, but also in a new understanding of both the nature of evil, the problem that had exercised Augustine's mind for so long (7.12–13.18–19), as well as of the manner of existence of all other things (*inspexi caetera infra te* [7.11.17]). God is present in the world as the Truth that regulates all things (7.15.21): whenever we know any truth, we already know the Truth that is God, at least in an implicit way (7.10.16). As Gerald Bonner has pointed out, in Augustine we can never separate accounts of contemplative vision from theory of knowledge.[29]

Even more famous than the vision recounted in book 7 is the description of the Ostia vision at the end of book 9. Paul Henry has provided a deft analysis of the three fundamental elements interwoven in 9.10.23–26: the teaching of the *Enneads,* the influence of scripture, and the concrete dynamism of Christian life found in Monica. Subsequent investigators uncovered even more Plotinian reminiscences,[30] but the evaluation of the significance of this vision remains a perennial issue.[31]

Augustine provides two parallel accounts of the experience, the first in direct discourse as if recounting the event itself, the second his summation of the conversation (or perhaps better monologue) in which he attempts to express its meaning—though in another form, as he candidly admits.[32] The text is too long to give here, but it is important to comment on some of the enrichments that this account adds to what we have already found in the Milan experience.

The first and most significant difference is that the Ostia vision was the shared experience of Augustine and his mother Monica. The presentation of Monica as a soul learned in the Holy Spirit, if not in the wisdom of world, here reaches its fulfillment as the saintly widow shares in the same foretaste of heavenly joy as her philosopher son. It is difficult to conceive of Plotinus, or any other pagan mystic, describing a mystical vision that is at once communal and accessible to a soul not trained in philosophy, especially that of a woman. One cannot but surmise, especially given the "garden" context in which Augustine places the scene,[33] that the bishop is giving a subtle hint that true vision can be achieved only within the saving community of the church of Christ. (The Ostia garden would also have been walled, or enclosed, and in the anti-Donatist propaganda of the years of the writing of the *Confessions* Augustine identified the church with the "enclosed garden" of Song of Songs 4:12.)[34] While the same Plotinian triple pattern of mystical progression is evident in the text,[35] in comparison with the Milan account the Ostia experience is presented in language that is more social in context, as well as both more affective in rhetorical weight and more complex in its appeal to transformed sense experience.[36]

There can be no question that Augustine is describing an experience that is open to symbolization in visual form, as is shown by the mention of *luce corporea* at the beginning of the first version and the stress at the end of the second account that all inferior *visiones* need to be withdrawn. Despite this visual context, within which the analysis is contained, what is remarkable in the two parallel descriptions is the way in which he piles up metaphors taken from the senses of touch and of hearing rather than that of seeing to try to describe what took place.[37] Furthermore, though the Milan account had noted in passing that *caritas* knows the vision, the Ostia account is pervaded by the language of affective intention: (1) "raising ourselves up by a more burning affection to the 'Self-Same' [i.e., God]" (*erigentes nos ardentiore affectu in idipsum*); (2) "we touched her [i.e., Wisdom] slightly with the whole beat of the heart" (*attigimus eum modice toto ictu cordis*); (3) "that we may hear him whom we love in these creatures, though without their interference" (*sed ipsum quem in his amamus, ipsum sine his audiamus* [9.10.24–25]).[38] It is important to note, however, that the brief touch of divine Wisdom which the Ostia text describes is both an *ictus cordis*[39] and a *rapida cogitatio.* Love and knowledge are intertwined in Augustine's mystical consciousness.

These experiences of 386 and 387 are well known. What is less frequently noted is that ten years later, as Augustine the bishop was writing the story of his life, he provided evidence for the continued presence of such brief experiences of vision in the long analysis of *memoria* found in book 10. The search for God "in the fields and broad precincts of memory" (*in campos et lata praetoria memoriae* [10.8.12]) leads beyond memory itself "in the desire to touch you where you can be touched, to cleave to you where such cleaving is possible" (*volens et attingere unde attingi potes, et inhaerere tibi unde inhaerere tibi potest* [10.17.26]). True happiness is rejoicing in God who is Truth (10.22–23.32–33), a God who is paradoxically both within *memoria* insofar as all consciousness of truth is to be found in the mind and yet above memory as its creator (10.24–26.35–37). This analysis culminates in one of Augustine's most noted passages in 10.27.37, the text beginning "Late have I loved you, Beauty so old and so new!" (*Sero te amavi, pulchritudo tam antiqua et tam nova*). While the intention of this lyrical outburst is to stress the distance between God and Augustine the searcher ("You were with me, and I was not with you"; *Mecum eras, et tecum non eram*), the language at the conclusion suggests the kind of synaesthetic brief experiences of divine presence found in the Milan and Ostia accounts. "You have touched me and I am on fire to enjoy your peace" (*PL* 32:795).[40]

This is confirmed by a more direct passage coming near the end of book 10 in which Augustine once again summarizes the threefold Plotinian ascent and speaking in the first person continues:

> And at times you introduce me from within into a wholly unaccustomed state of feeling (*in affectum multum inusitatum*), a kind of sweetness which, were it made perfect in me, would be not of this world, not of this life. But my wretched weights cause me to fall back again and I am swallowed up in the usual run of things. I am held fast; weeping heavily, but heavily held. (*Conf.* 10.40.65 [*PL* 32:807])[41]

Though Augustine discussed the vision of God at length throughout his voluminous writings, only a few other texts unmistakably convey his own experiences. This fact is troubling only to those whose view of the truly mystical is restricted to the autobiographical. Among the fathers, as we have seen, personal descriptions of any form of religious experience are rare. The focus of their work was the teaching and tradition of the church, not their own religious life. Augustine, despite the precious witness of his *Confessions,* is no stranger to this, as a survey of some important treatments of the theme of *visio Dei* in his other writings will show.

For example, in the early work *On the Soul's Greatness* (387–388) the seventh grade of the soul's ascent to God, that is, the "vision and contemplation of Truth," though clearly dependent on the action of Christ (*perventuros per Virtutem Dei atque Sapientiam*) and nourished by the church, is spoken of as both a *mansio,* which suggests a more permanent state than Augustine usually allows later, and as the achievement of "some great and incomparable souls" (*magnae quaedam et incomparabiles animae*), probably Moses, Paul, and John.[42] Though the young Augustine still seems to hold that any vision of truth given in this life is a partial one,[43] here he expresses something of the Neoplatonic confidence about the possibility for perfection on earth present in other early works but later denied.[44] Other texts dating from the period up to about 400 are useful for exploring his views on contemplation and vision, but do not add much to what we have seen in the *Confessions.*[45]

Even after 400, the bishop at times offers a more personal account of the nature of contemplative experience. One important text, dating to ca. 410–412, found in *Sermon* 52, seems to reflect both the kind of mystical experiences presented in the *Confessions* and a new line of thought linking *visio Dei* with the nature of humanity as the *imago Dei.* In the midst of this sermon devoted to the Trinity, Augustine suddenly breaks off to inquire if there is any likeness (*similitudo*) to be found in creatures for the threefold divinity. Unlike the exploration to be conducted in the latter books of *The Trinity*, Augustine's first appeal here is to personal experience of God found in mystical consciousness.[46] Though the language begins in the third person, it soon passes into a first person that seems to be the voice of Augustine rather than the psalmist he is citing: "I spoke in my ecstasy" (*Ego dixi in ecstasi mea* [Ps 30:23]). The same triple pattern of Plotinian *anabasis*, or ascent to God, is obvious: separation from corporeal reality (*abreptus a sensibus corporis*); movement within the soul (*ad te redi, te vide, te inspice, te discute*); and passage above to the divine level (*subreptus in deum; defecisti in divinis*). Also similar is the failure to maintain the elevation (*quod diu ferre non potui*). Because of this inability to maintain lasting contact with the divine light,[47] Augustine is led to suggest that the search for some understanding of the Trinity must begin on a more modest level of the investigation of the nature of the human mind.[48]

The long labors devoted to the writing of *The Trinity* enabled the bishop eventually to bring the two major themes of his theology in this sermon — *visio Dei* and *imago Trinitatis* — into a more intimate relation, as will be studied below. In comparison with his early accounts of vision, however, the text in *Sermon* 52 underlines how the inexpressibility of the experience of ecstasy highlights the unknowability of God — a sign of the modest but significant apophatic element in his thought that becomes evident about 400.[49]

The most striking of the later Augustine's texts on the immediate consciousness of God through vision, found especially in his *Homilies on the Psalms* and *Homilies on John*, are not framed in the first person, but use the voice of the psalmist and the evangelist to present Christian teaching on the mystical goal. Among the many texts in the *Homilies on the Psalms*, I will discuss three of the most informative, the *Homily on Ps.* 26.2.8–11 (an early text from the group preached ca. 392), that on Ps 41.2–10 (ca. 410–14), and finally the *Homily on Ps.* 99.5–6 (delivered in late 412).[50] Along with these passages I will also consider *Homily* 20 on the Gospel of John, which dates either to 413 or more likely to ca. 419.[51] These sermons contain Augustine's mature teaching on the possibility of attaining the vision of God in this life and hence constitute an essential part of his mysticism. In them we hear primarily the voice of the preacher and teacher speaking to and for the whole Christian community.

Before undertaking a brief analysis of these four texts, it is worth noting the character of the audience to which they were preached. Augustine's sermons, like those of Ambrose, were not directed to a spiritual elite, but were given to a general Christian congregation — the average believer in the basilica. (The example of Monica in *Confessions* 9 demonstrates that while Augustine's use of male-gender language is constant, it was not meant to be exclusive.) The bishop's confidence that his message about contemplation was meant for all Christians, and not just for the special few, is consonent with what we have already seen in a number of patristic authors.[52]

Augustine's meditation on vv. 4 and 5 of the Old Latin version of Psalm 26 centers on the meaning of the text, "That I might contemplate the Lord's delight" (*ut contempler delectationem Domini*). Though he uses the passage primarily to stress that true and full contemplation can only be found in heaven when we will be free of earthly toils,[53] this early sermon already contains many of the crucial Augustinian ideas about the relation of vision in this life and vision in the next that will mark his later thought. The first of these is the intimate connection between the *domus Domini,* that is, the heavenly home in which there will be "contemplation of the Good that is unchanging, eternal, always remaining the same" (*contemplatio incommutabilis boni, aeterni, semper eodem modo manentis*), and the *templum Domini,* that is, the Body of his church, which Christ forms out of the faithful and in which he is present as the inner sanctuary (*adytum*). Because "I will become his temple and will be protected by him" (*ero templum eius, et protegar ab eo*) even though I do not yet experience pure contemplation, or delight (*delectatio*) in the Absolute Good that is God, I share in it in this world through my bond with Christ the Head. "He said that he is in us here below, and therefore we are in him there above. . . . What a pledge we have that we are now eternally in heaven with our Head by faith, hope and love — because he is with us on earth until the end of the world by divinity, goodness and unity" (*Hom. on Ps.* 26.2.11 [*PL* 35:205]).[54]

This first text from the *Homilies on the Psalms* leaves open the question of whether or not there is any consciousness of the presence of God in this life by suggesting that this is less important than the real but unconscious union with God that all Christians possess in the Body of Christ. The second two passages from the homilies reaffirm this central truth while exploring the kind of consciousness of divine presence that may be found by believers here below.

The *Homily on Psalm* 41 is justly famous as one of Augustine's greatest mystical texts.[55] Many of the themes seen in the earlier passage are evident, such as the contrast between the *tabernaculum,* or *ecclesia peregrina,* which is our only path to God in this life, and the perfect enjoyment of God to be found in heaven, the *domus Dei mei.*[56] Augustine insists, even more strongly than in his comment on Psalm 26, that all progress toward God can only take place within the church.[57] What is new here is the combination of many of the themes of the *Confessions* with the more ecclesial concerns of Augustine's public preaching.

The most evident of these is the stress given to personal desire, the hunger for God that pervades the *Confessions* and that is suggested by the Psalm text, "As the deer desires the fountains of waters, so does my soul have desire for you, God" (*Quemadmodum desiderat cervus ad fontes aquarum, ita desiderat anima mea ad te, Deus* [Ps 41:1]). The burning thirst that the soul experiences is fundamentally a desire for the illumination of the interior eye — Augustine intertwines the language of love and knowledge as he introduces his theme.[58] The bishop's allegorization of the image of the deer or hart enables him to make two important points about the preparation for interior illumination, namely, that it demands both the destruction of our own vices and also the mutual support found within the Christian community (41.3–4). However, the hart's desire for delight in contemplation (Ps 26:4 is cited) seems frustrated as long as we must live by faith, so that we have no response to the pagan opponent who mockingly asks, "Where is your God?" (see 41.5–6).

This leads Augustine in the latter half of the text (41.7–10) to investigate the question of what kind of vision of God is possible in this life: "I have sought my God in order not only to believe, but also, if possible, to see something [of him]" (*quaesivi etiam ego ipse Deum meum, ut si possem, non tantum crederem, sed aliquid et viderem*). Following the model of the three stages of Plotinian ascent used in the *Confessions,* Augustine insists that God is not to be found in the things of this world, however beautiful and splendid they may be, nor is he discovered even in the interior vision the soul has of itself and of incorporeal realities such as justice. In order for me to "touch" God (*ut eum tangerem*), I cannot remain within myself, but must pass beyond myself in ecstasy, as v. 5 of the Psalm says, "I meditated on these things and poured out my soul above myself" (*Haec meditatus sum, et effudi super me animam meam*). This ecstasy is described as a passage from the tabernacle of the church here on earth to the heavenly *domus Dei.* The ascent is possible only through the agency of the church; indeed, Augustine argues that it is by meditating on the virtues of the saints, the *membra tabernaculi,* that the ecstatic transition comes about, an unusual idea as Butler noted,[59] but one fully in harmony with the indispensably ecclesial nature of Augustine's mystical thought. To give his own words:

> Ascending the tabernacle, the soul comes to the house of God. While it admires the members of the tabernacle it thus is led to the house of God by following a certain sweetness, an indescribable interior hidden pleasure. It is as if a musical instrument sweetly sounded from the house of God, and while walking in the tabernacle he heard the interior sound and, led by its sweetness,

he followed what had sounded, separating himself from every clamor of flesh and blood until he arrived at the house of God. (*Hom. on Ps.* 41.9 [*PL* 36:470])[60]

The enjoyment of the "presence of the face of God" (*vultus praesens Dei*), which Augustine describes here primarily in auditory metaphors, can only be a brief one in this life: "With the fine point of the mind we are able to gaze upon something unchangeable, although hastily and in part" (*acie mentis aliquid incommutabile, etsi perstrictim et raptim, perspicere potuimus*) (*Hom. on Ps.* 41.10 [*PL* 36:471]).[61] This, however, is the lot of the soul as long as it remains in this life — to live in hope of the great reward of which God has given us, at least at times, some brief foretaste.[62]

A brief passage from the *Homily on Psalm* 99 recapitulates the same message and adds valuable corollaries in at least three areas: divine incomprehensibility, God's omnipresence, and the role of love in restoring the divine likeness that makes vision possible. In investigating what the psalmist means by the wordless praise of God implied in v. 2 (*Jubilate Domino universa terra*),[63] Augustine begins by noting how the whole creation gives evidence of God but by no means provides the knowledge that will enable us to speak correctly about him. In order to speak of God we must be able to think of him, and in order to think of him we must draw near to him. Both our ordinary seeing of physical objects and spiritual seeing of God require the attention of the heart, in the case of the latter the "cleansed heart" of Matthew 5:8. But how is sinful humanity to attain the clean heart needed for the vision of God? The first part of Augustine's answer is to insist on the moral purification already emphasized in the comment on Psalm 41; but the bishop now also stresses the inner significance of this, the restoration of the "interior *homo recreatus ad imaginem Dei*" through the progress of *caritas,* especially the love of all humans, both good and evil. "You will draw near to the likeness by the measure you advance in charity, and to the same degree you will begin to perceive God (*sentire Deum*)" (*Hom. on Ps.* 99.5 [*PL* 37:1274]).[64]

What does it mean to "sentire Deum"? It is not that God comes to us as if he had been absent, or even that we "go" to him. God is always present to us and to all things; it is that we, like blind persons, do not have the eyes to see him: "The one you wish to see is not far from you" (*Non est a te longe quod vis videre* [99.5]).[65] We need to become like him in goodness and "loving in thought" (*diligens cogitatione* [99.6]) in order to grasp him. Note that Augustine's language here abandons the spiritual sense of sight to emphasize the other spiritual senses. Only such experiential contact with God can produce the higher form of knowledge that perceives that we can really say nothing about him.

When, as someone who is like him, you begin to draw near and to become fully conscious of God (*persentiscere Deum*),[66] you will experience what to say and what not to say insofar as love grows in you, because "God is Love" (1 John 4:8). Before you had the experience, you used to think you could speak of God. You begin to have the experience, and there you experience that you cannot say what you experience. (*Hom. on Ps.* 99.6 [*PL* 37:1274])[67]

As in the famous passage from *On Christian Doctrine* 1.6.6 in which Augustine summarized his negative theology, the bishop insists here that this experience of the divine inexpressibility does not reduce the grateful soul to silence, but rather to the expression of the *jubilatio* to which the psalmist invites us.[68]

In the important text commenting on John 5:19 in *Homilies on John* 20, Augustine, in order to prove that there can be no separation between the Father and the Son, argues on the basis of mystical vision. Such vision, granted to some, especially to John the Evangelist (see 20.13), demonstrates that no more than brightness can be separated from the sun can we divide the Word from the Father. Demonstrating his case involves a complex repetition (seven different sequences according to Suzanne Poque) of the now familiar Plotinian triple pattern of withdrawal from the body and the physical universe, entry into the mind or soul, and ecstatic passage beyond the self to touch God: "I passed beyond myself that I might touch him" (*Hom. on Jo.* 20.11 [*PL* 35:1562]).[69] What is most remarkable about this text is not only its trinitarian dimension (more will be said about this in the next section) but also the lack of any explicit reference to the experience of the "check" or weakness which causes the soul to fall back from the brief divine vision.[70]

On the basis of this consideration of Augustine's accounts of the vision of God, both those in the first person and those expressed more neutrally in the voice of the exegete and preacher, we may return to the question of Augustine's status as a mystic and mystical theologian. It is customary to say that Augustine was not a mystical theologian in the sense of, say, a John of the Cross, but this statement is only half true. Certainly, the bishop of Hippo did not write sustained expositions of the mystical life, the way that authors since the twelfth century have done. Such expositions imply a scholastic differentiation of theology which neither Augustine nor any other patristic author shared. The great African, like his contemporaries in the Eastern part of the undivided church, saw all theology as mystical in the sense that it was designed to lead the believer into the experience of the presence of God, begun here below in the communal life of the church, but only completed in the glory of heaven. Similarly, while Augustine's thoughts on what later eras would call mystical theology are never given any single definitive exposition, they not only appear throughout his writings, but they are also based upon a coherent, carefully thought-out pattern which has begun to emerge from the texts we have investigated.

Such a pattern conforms quite well with the broad theory of mysticism we have already seen in other patristic authors. Augustine is primarily interested in inviting his flock to a deeper, more intense, even immediate experience of God in this life, which he describes primarily in scriptural terms. Unlike some Greek fathers, he is not much concerned with individual "union" with God. (At best only a very few texts use the language of union in relation to the individual. These will be considered later.) When he does speak of union here below, it is the union of Christ and the church he has in mind.[71] It is difficult not to think that this deliberate avoidance of the language of union in someone who knew Plotinus so well was a conscious choice and an implied criticism of the limitations of non-Christian mystical efforts.

Augustine, like Ambrose, learned much from Plotinus, but it would be a mistake to think of him as a pure Plotinian at any point in his lifetime.[72] Although he continued to use the basic model of Plotinian *anabasis* throughout his career, he employed it within a transformed context of Christian meaning — scriptural, christological, and ecclesiological. The laying out of parallel passages, important as this is for demonstrating lines of influence between the philosopher and the bishop, does not always illuminate this difference. The evidence presented here suggests that there was an evolution in his transformations (Augustine's mind was ever on the move), but it is important to note that even the early Augustine had made major changes in the Plotinian program.

Augustine taught that "to go within is to go above," that is, the "enstatic" movement into the soul's ground would lead to a discovery of the God within who is infinitely more than the soul, and hence to an "ecstatic" movement beyond the self — *Intus Deus altus est*, "The God within is the God above" (*Hom. on Ps.* 130.12 [*PL* 37:1712]).[73] Plotinus too had both enstatic and ecstatic moments in his mystical itinerary, but Augustine and Plotinus had different ideas about the relation of the soul to its source or ground. Augustine's Trinity is not the Plotinian One, however much he benignly interpreted *Nous* as the Christian Word of God (*Conf.* 7.9; *City of God* 10.29). Although the bishop continued to adhere to a view of the "fall of the soul" much influenced by Plotinus (and did so longer than previously admitted, if R. J. O'Connell is correct),[74] his creationist understanding of the radical difference between God and the soul is the root of his rejection of the language of mystical union (*henōsis* and its equivalents). Union is important for Augustine, but only as our union with the Word made flesh — precisely the point where the pagan Platonists went wrong! This loving union we enjoy with all the brethren in the community of the church makes possible the brief experiences of the vision of God that can sometimes be enjoyed in this life.

Augustine's teaching about the *visio Dei* easily leads into many other areas of his theology. Not all of these can be pursued here, but in order to get a fuller picture of his properly mystical teaching, at least two that have appeared in the texts considered above need to be taken up: the role of his theology of the *imago Dei;* and the necessary mediation of the whole Christ in the attainment of *visio Dei.*

Imago Trinitatis: The Trinitarian Basis of Augustine's Mysticism

The notion of humanity as made in the image and likeness of God (Gen 1:26) was the central theme of the theological anthropology of the patristic period and for much of the Middle Ages as well.[75] The importance of Augustine's treatment of this key concept is second to none,[76] though only a few aspects of the mystical implications of his *imago Dei* theology can be presented here.

We have already seen the appearance of the restoration of the *imago* in *Sermon* 52 and in the *Homily on Psalm* 99, and although it does not appear explicitly in the early books of the *Confessions,* the trinitarian character of the *imago* that was so profoundly developed in *The Trinity* was first announced in *Confessions* 13.11.12. Other early works, such as *On the Lord's Sermon on the Mount* (ca. 393–396) also connect the *contemplatio veritatis* with the restoration of the *similitudo Dei.*[77] We can agree with A. Trapé that the "essential task of Augustinian spirituality is the restoration of the image of God in man."[78]

In order to grasp Augustine's reflections on the *imago Dei* theme, even on a superficial level, it is helpful to keep some important distinctions in mind. The first is the difference between the *imago* and the *similitudo* suggested by the Latin translation of Genesis 1:26 (*Faciamus hominem ad imaginem et similitudinem nostram*). For some of the fathers, the *imago* signified the unalterable link between God and the intellectual nature he created, while the *similitudo* was the likeness lost through original sin, but capable of being regained through the grace of Christ. Augustine tended to use the terms more interchangeably, though in his mature thought he distinguished between *similitudo* as any form of likeness between two things and *imago* as a particular kind of likeness by which something both relates to and is expressive of its source. "Certainly, not everything in creatures, which is in some way or other similar to God, is also to be called his image, but that alone to which he himself alone is superior; for the image is only then an expression of God in the full sense when no other nature lies between it and God' (*The Trinity* 11.5.8 [*PL* 42:991]).[79] Some fathers distinguished between the *Verbum,* the only true *Imago Dei,* and the spiritual natures created according to this archetypal model, which are more properly said to be made *ad imaginem* (see Gen 1:26). Augustine recognized that the *Verbum* is the only *Imago* fully equal to the Father and that created spiritual beings become images only through the formative and reformative activity of the second person of the Trinity,[80] but he admitted, following Pauline usage, that it was also proper to speak of human persons in themselves as *imago Dei.*[81] Further, while the early works tend to speak of human nature conceived of as *imago Dei* in a general sense, Augustine's concern in *The Trinity* is to investigate the way in which the human is the *imago trinitatis,* the image that participates in the inner life of the three Persons.[82]

It is possible to describe the *imago Dei* anthropology of the fathers as being expressed in three different forms: that which emphasizes that the image is to be found in the intellectual nature of the subject; that which stresses the freedom of the person as the essential locus; and that which explores the intersubjective character of the image. Augustine insisted that the image resides in the higher dimension of the intellectual subject—"man was made to the image of God in that part of his nature wherein he surpasses the brute beasts; this is, of course, his reason (*ratio*), or mind (*mens*), or intelligence (*intelligentia*), or whatever we wish to call it" (*Lit. Comm. on Gen.* 3.20.30 [*PL* 34:292]).[83] Nevertheless, elements of all three of the modes of understanding the divine image in humanity enter into his full theory, as a glance at *The Trinity* shows.

This great work is far from an arid and abstruse exercise in philosophical theology, however difficult and involved its argumentation is at times. It is also a spiritual, indeed a mystical, document — at times as intensely personal as the *Confessions* themselves. Fulbert Cayré has rightly emphasized its central position in Augustine's mysticism. His analysis (one that does not exclude those aspects of the work which belong more properly to the history of dogmatic and speculative theology) is still suggestive and useful.[84]

The first seven books of the work, which lay out the church's faith in the Trinity, contain important passing reflections on the nature of the *imago,* but it is in the later books (8–15) pertaining to the *intellectus fidei* that Augustine sets out what Eugene Teselle has called "the thoroughly Trinitarian character of the mystical experience."[85] The bishop's aim at understanding, as far as is possible in this life, the supreme mystery of the Christian faith is a spiritual therapy designed to help restore the image of

God in us so that we can more fully share in the experience of the divine presence in this life. As the bishop prays in the magnificent prayer that closes the work: "Grant the power of finding you to the one you have created to find you, and to whom you have more and more given the hope of finding you. May I remember you, understand you, love you. Increase all these things in me until you reform me fully" (*The Trinity* 15.28.51 [*PL* 42:1098]).[86]

As is well known, the later books of *The Trinity* contain two different redactions developing the analogies between the triune God and the image to be found in the human person. Book 8, which apparently belongs to the earlier version of the work written between about 404 and 413, concentrates on the experience of love as the fundamental trinitarian analogy and means of reforming the image in the self. Books 9–15, written between 413 and about 420, form an extended consideration of the *homo interior* as memory, understanding, and will/love. These final books have the same purpose in mind, though they use a different perspective.

A brief glance at the love analogy developed in book 8 and continued over into the beginning of book 9 will demonstrate why the later books of *The Trinity* are just as much mystical texts as the descriptions of Augustine's visionary experiences in the *Confessions*. Book 8, not unlike the three passages we examined from the *Homilies on the Psalms*, shows that it is only by way of love of neighbor that we can love God, and that therefore love alone provides access to the vision of God, both in this life and the next.[87]

Augustine begins his formal treatment in 8.2.3 with a summary of the familiar three stages of the Plotinian ascent to God. The flash of vision, seen with the heart rather than with the eyes, that we experience when we hear the scriptural words "Deus Veritas est" (Wis 9:15), like the contemplative experience described in the *Confessions,* is of short duration.[88] Even when we try to think of God as supreme and unalloyed Goodness, we cannot remain long on this level, though Goodness never departs from us (8.3.4). "If you were able to perceive Absolute Goodness with all other goods removed, you would perceive God; and if you cleave to him in love, you will be immediately made happy" (*si ergo potueris illis detractis per se ipsum perspicere bonum, perspexeris Deum. Et si amore inhaeseris, continuo beatificaberis* [8.3.5]). The problem is that "in order to enjoy the presence of him from whom we are, we must remain steadfast in relation to him and must cleave to him" (*The Trinity* 8.4.6 [*PL* 42:951]).[89] Obviously, as long as we remain in this life it is difficult, or rather impossible, for us to remain absolutely steadfast in relation to God.

Augustine goes on to lay out how it is possible for us through grace to attain an incipient relation to God that can lead to partial vision here below. In order to see God, we must desire him, and in order to desire him we must in some way know him. The faith given to Christians, while it is not the full knowledge given in vision, provides the motive force for the ascent to seeing God (8.4.6). Expanding on what we have already seen in the texts from the *Homilies on the Psalms,* the bishop insists that we know that we love God in faith only through the love that we show to our fellow men, both the love that we have for the virtues of great Christians, like the apostle Paul (cf. *Hom. on Ps.* 41.9), and the love that we show to all persons (8.7.10). Augustine claims that the love of neighbor *is* the love of God: "This is because one who loves his neighbor must necessarily first have love for Love itself. But 'God is Love, and he who abides in Love, abides in God'" (*The Trinity* 8.7.10 [*PL* 42:957]).[90]

Many other passages from Augustine's later works repeat the message that love of our neighbor is love of God. His implied connection between mutual love and the reformation of the image becomes explicit in a text from *Sermon* 90 which brings together progress in loving with the gradual restoration of the image: "And so let charity be nourished so that when nourished it may be perfected. This is how the wedding garment is put on, and thus the image of God to which we were created is sculpted anew by our progress" (*Sermon* 90.10 [*PL* 38:566]).[91]

However, the question remains in what sense this love of neighbor, which is really nothing else than the love of God, is specifically a love that partakes of the Trinity. Augustine tries to answer this in several ways, perhaps none of them totally satisfactory from a speculative point of view.[92] He himself appears not to have found them convincing, since in the second version of the work he did not develop these analogies, but devoted his energies to another form of trinitarian analogy rooted in the three immanent operations of the soul. Still, what the bishop advanced in this inconclusive but pregnant book 8 was to be of importance in the history of Western mysticism, as figures like Richard of St. Victor and Bonaventure were to show. The isometry between love of neighbor/love of God, on the one hand, and vision of God/restoration of the image, on the other, was to be a powerful theme in later centuries.[93]

Even in the later books 9–15 of *The Trinity,* when Augustine turns his attention away from love as the central theme to explore a variety of introspective analogies in the soul for the Trinity,[94] love's special relation to vision remains. The shift in his analogies is meant to place love in a broader, more careful analysis of the nature and activity of the soul as *imago Trinitatis,* and therefore to underline love's role rather than to deny it. As Augustine had insisted in book 8 and throughout his career, we cannot love unless we know, and we cannot know unless we are the kind of subjects capable of knowledge.⁹⁵ All our knowing, every spiritual operation of the human subject, is grounded in the inner life of the Father, Son, and Holy Spirit. This is evident especially in his analysis of *mens* or *memoria*, the intellectual self-consciousness of the subject, which through the production of the inner word, or preconceptual act of understanding,⁹⁶ gives rise to the true knowlege (*notitia, intelligentia*) the subject has of itself. This self-knowledge is the source of the mind's love of itself (*amor, voluntas, intentio*). "There is an image of the Trinity: the mind itself, and its knowledge which is its offspring and the word that comes from it. Love is the third. And these three are one and one substance" (*The Trinity* 9.12.18 [*PL* 42:972]).⁹⁷

Our sharing in the life of the Trinity as knowing and loving subjects is a fact of our existence always present in our minds whether we advert to it or not. Augustine's purpose in writing *The Trinity* was to make his readers conscious that it is the unalterable trinitarian nature of their inner being that makes possible attaining full and perfect vision of the Trinity. This long and difficult text is an invitation to open the interior eye to the triune God already present and active within, and thus to attain vision through the conscious appropriation of the *imago Trinitatis*. This is why Augustine insists that the introspective activity involved in our personal recognition of the trinity within our own consciousness is not meant to be a pure mental exercise in and of itself—it is intended to lead the soul to that participation in divine Wisdom which is not just the recognition that the *mens* does indeed bear the image of the Trinity, but also the conviction that the whole purpose for which this image was created was to attune itself more consciously and more directly to its heavenly source:

> Hence this trinity of the mind is not on that account the image of God because the mind remembers itself, understands itself, and loves itself, but because it can also remember, understand and love him by whom it was made. And when it does so, it becomes wise; but if it does not, even though it remembers itself, knows itself, and loves itself, it is foolish. (*The Trinity* 14.12.15 [*PL* 42:1048])⁹⁸

As elsewhere in his writings, Augustine continues to stress that the activity of reforming the image by deepening our awareness of the Trinity active within us will never be complete in this life: "When the vision of God will be perfect then there will be a perfect likeness to God in the image" (*The Trinity* 14.17.23 [*PL* 42:1055]).⁹⁹ But the process must be begun in this life. What we are striving to do here below, as several texts from the *Homilies on the Psalms* remind us, is to give back to God the coin he originally gave to us, that is, to restore the image given us at our creation.¹⁰⁰

Augustine does not explicitly relate the conscious appropriation of the trinitarian structure of the soul to his Plotinian explorations of the three stages of the soul's ascent to the vision or touching of God. Given the importance of *The Trinity* in his mature thought, however, it is clear that this exploration of the *imago Trinitatis* in the human soul lays bare the onto-logical basis for that knowing and loving which leads to vision. The bishop of Hippo does not present a systematic trinitarian mysticism, though some-thing like this is implied in many passages, especially in books 14 and 15 (e.g., 14.12.15; 15.28.51). He was clearly a major influence on later Western trinitarian mystical thought, such as in William of St. Thierry. Although he did not have access to Gregory of Nyssa's mystical writings, he would have agreed with the Cappadocian that the triune God becomes visible to us in the mirror of the virtuous soul.[101]

In concluding this glance at how Augustine's thought on the *imago Dei* as detailed in *The Trinity* forms an integral part of his mysticism, it is worth noting the role that book 15 plays in the full presentation. Those who have strained their minds to follow some of the most difficult passages in all of Augustine's writings are sometimes disappointed upon getting to book 15 and learning how little they have really learned: "The Trinity itself is one thing, the image of the Trinity in something else is another" (*The Trinity* 15.23.43 [*PL* 42:1090]).[102] This should come as no surprise to those who see the immense speculative effort of the later books of *The Trinity* for what they really were in Augustine's sight—nothing more (though nothing less) than one more brief, and ineluctably temporary and imperfect, attempt to catch a glimpse of the divine reality in this life.

Mediator Dei et Hominum (1 Tim 2:5): The Role of the Whole Christ

One thing that Augustine had discerned as early as 386 (if the evidence of *Conf.* 7.18.24 is to be believed) is that the necessity for the repair of the *imago Dei* might be recognized by a philosopher surveying the human condition, but that it was beyond the power of any fallen soul to do any-thing about it without the intervention of the "Mediator of God and humanity, the man Jesus Christ" (1 Tim 2:5). The bishop always taught that "we can deform God's image in us; we cannot reform it" (*Sermon* 43.3.4 [*PL* 38:225]).[103]

As Goulven Madec puts it: "Augustine considered the doctrine he elabo-rated as integrally Christian, and entirely Christological."[104] Because Christ is divine and human, he functions both as the goal of our journey and as our way there. "His coming indicates his humanity," as Augustine says in one place, "his remaining his divinity. . . . It is his Godhead toward which, his humanity by which, we make progress" (*Hom. on Jn.* 42.8 [*PL*

35:1702]).[105] This emphasis on Christ the mediator is found in all Augustine's writings, from the early treatise *On the Teacher* (389), where the Incarnate Word is the one true (interior) Teacher, to later works, especially the *Homilies on John*, which are replete with references to Christ's mediatorial role.[106] The mystical dimension of Augustine's Christology is not so much concerned with the saving events portrayed in the Gospels (though a devotion to the human Christ is not absent from his teaching),[107] as it is with how the God-man actually effects redemption through his uniting us with him in his Body, the church.

The four texts we have already looked at from the *Homilies on the Psalms* and *Homilies on John* have highlighted the indispensable role of the church in progress toward the *visio Dei*. The same teaching appears throughout the bishop's writings. For instance, in commenting on the Mary–Martha episode (Luke 10:38–42) in *Sermon* 103, Augustine interprets the "one thing" Mary has chosen as the goal of union with the Trinity in heaven, noting: "[The Trinity itself] does not lead us to this one thing unless we many have one heart" (*Sermon* 103.4 [*PL* 38:615]).[108] Since the Fall, the only place on earth where we can find the one heart (*cor unum*) needed to gain this "one thing" is in the church.

The efficacy of the single heart for attaining salvation hinges on its purification, as one of Augustine's favorite scriptural texts, the beatitude "Blessed are the pure of heart, for they shall see God" (Matt 5:8), indicates. It is Christ himself at work in the church who effects this cleansing of the one heart of all his members, according to the bishop's comment on v. 80 of Psalm 118: "The heart of the members and Body of Christ becomes spotless by God's grace through him who is the Body's Head, that is, through Jesus Christ our Lord, through the washing of regeneration" (*Hom. on Ps.* 118.19.7 [*PL* 37:1556]).[109] Thus, the church's saving power comes from its status as the Body of Christ here on earth. The bishop's teaching on the unity of the total Christ, head and members, is the third major block in his mystical teaching.

It would be hard to exaggerate the emphasis that Augustine placed on the doctrine of the Body of Christ.[110] The fundamental exegetical principle that grounds his interpretation of the Psalms, for instance, is that they are the prayer of the *totus Christus*. "His many members, gathered under one Head, our Savior himself, are one single person in the bond of charity and peace. Their voice is often heard in the Psalms as the voice of a single person. Thus one cries out as if he were all, because all are one in the one" (*Hom. on Ps.* 69.1 [*PL* 36:866]).[111] Of course, Augustine also admits that other texts apply solely to the Head, while some passages fit only the Body. In general, however, since it is the one person of the God-man who speaks in the Psalms,[112] any individual Psalm can be spoken of as an "oratio corporis Christi" (*Hom. on Ps.* 118.4.5 [*PL* 37:1511]).[113]

Like many of the fathers, Augustine was interested in the prophetic nature of the Psalms, the way in which they foretold the life of Christ on earth; but he was far more concerned with how they are to be related to the whole Christ, that is, their application to the religious experience of Christians as forming one Body with Christ. Over and over again, he returns to his favorite scriptural proof for this identity, the passage from Acts 9:2 where Christ complains to the persecuting Saul, "Saul, Saul, why do you persecute *me?*"[114]

The unity between Christ and his Body means that by our membership in the church we share in all the *magnalia Christi*, the great mysteries by which the God-man wrought our redemption. This is an ontological bond, a real participation in his life, and not just some form of moral imitation of Christ's good example. In his comment on Psalm 119, Augustine asks how fallen humanity can absorb the solid food of the Word, the second person of the Trinity. Following Paul (1 Cor 2:2), he says this is only possible because the Word has become milk in taking on flesh. He concludes that we must suck what he became for us in order to grow into what he is (*Suge quod pro te factus est, et crescis ad id quod est*) (*Hom. on Ps.* 119.2 [*PL* 37:1599]).[115] This message of God's magnificent generosity as the source of our hope is especially stressed in the *Homilies on Psalms 83–85*, where he summarizes:

> God could have given no greater gift to humanity than to make his Word through whom he founded all things their Head and joining them to him as members so that he might be both Son of God and Son of Man, one God with the Father, one man with men. When we speak to God in prayer, we do not divide the Son; when the Body of the Son prays, it does not separate the Head from itself. Thus, it is the one Savior of his Body, our Lord Jesus Christ the Son of God, who both prays for us, and prays in us and is prayed to by us. (*Hom. on Ps.* 85.1 [*PL* 37:1081])[116]

Augustine was especially enamored of the Johannine text that declares that Christ is the Way, the Truth, and the Life (John 14:6): "We will not err if we make him our goal, because he is the Truth by which we hasten and the Path through which we run" (*Hom. on Ps.* 84.1 [*PL* 37:1069]).[117] But the bishop of Hippo also utilized a full range of scriptural descriptions and metaphors for Christ, both those drawn from the world of natural symbols (where the notion of Christ as the Rock is a favorite),[118] and the world of human activity, where reference to Christ as the healing physician who is also health itself is frequently employed.[119]

The basic consequences of this for Augustine's mystical teaching are two: a strong emphasis on the notion of our divine sonship (and concomitantly the concept of divinization), and an insistence that every activity of the church is really the activity of Christ. Like Irenaeus, Athanasius, and other fathers, Augustine characterizes the ultimate purpose of the Incarnation as the divinization of humanity. "The Son of God was made a partaker of mortality so that mortal man might partake of divinity" (*Hom. on Ps.* 52.6 [*PL* 36:646]).[120] He can thus speak of Christ as "transforming his own into himself" (*transfigurans in se suos*), using a metaphor of eating that calls to mind the image from the seventh book of the *Confessions,* where feeding on the divine food is said to change us into God. (A possible eucharistic implication cannot be ruled out here.)[121]

The Pauline notion of our joint sonship with Christ is evident through-out Augustine's works.[122] What is not so well known is how the bishop drew out of such scriptural texts a distinctive doctrine of deification. Gerald Bonner and others have shown that while the actual terms *deificari* and *deificatus* are relatively rare in Augustine, the reality of his doctrine of deification is beyond question.[123] Unlike the Neoplatonists, however, Augustine did not base deification/divinization on the divine origin of the soul, its natural divinity, which needs only to be awakened to realize its true self. Although the soul of its very essence *participates* in the life of the Trinity, for Augustine deification is not this created participation, but rather the adoptive sonship grounded in it. Christ alone makes it possible for us to become what we were meant to be — fully realized images of the Trinity through our bond with the God-man. Deification is a reality begun in this life through our membership in Christ's Body; it will not be completed until we enter into the joys of heaven. As a text from *Homily on Psalm* 49 puts it:

> It is clear that because he said that humans are gods they are deified from his grace not born from his substance. . . . He who justifies also deifies, because by justification he makes sons of God. . . . If we have been made God's sons, we have also been made gods; but this is by adopting grace, not by nature giving birth. (*Hom. on Ps.* 49.1.2 [*PL* 36:565])[124]

Augustine always insisted that this deifying process never involves any con-fusion of substance between God and humanity, in this life or the next.[125]

Thus the bishop of Hippo, like Origen and Ambrose, placed individual mystical fulfillment, that is, the attainment of a partial vision of God in this life, within the context of the life of the church. For him there was no such thing as a purely private or strictly personal vision. Whatever gift of divine presence we are given here below can be realized only in and through our bond in the Body of Christ.[126] "Let us rejoice and give thanks: we are not only made Christians, but made Christ" (*Ergo gratulemur et agamus gratias, non solum nos christianos factos esse, sed Christum* [*Hom. on Jn.* 21.8]).

Augustinus Mysticus: Some Theoretical Issues

The three doctrinal blocks discussed above (the soul's ascent to vision, the image of the Trinity in the soul, and the ecclesial and christological context of the ascent) are not meant to exhaust the whole of Augustine's mystical teaching. They are intended to show both the inner coherence of the mystical elements in his theology and the areas where he was most influential on later Western mysticism. They also raise again the debate about the nature of the bishop's mysticism. In what sense is he a mystic? In this final section it is important to address the ambiguities involved in the denomination *Augustinus mysticus*.

Augustine, like any Western thinker before the seventeenth century, would not have known what "mysticism" meant. The mystical aspects of his thought were part of a totality oblivious to such compartmentalization. Still, he used the qualifiers *mysticus* and *mystice* frequently,[127] keeping to the primary sense of the Greek root, that is, "hidden" or "secret," referring to the inner significance of anything related to the mystery of salvation. The words are most often used of the deeper meaning of the Bible, such as when he says of certain passages *mystice dicta sunt* (seven times), or speaks of a *mystica significatio* (thirteen times). The persons, rituals, and events of sacred history signified by the biblical text have inner meanings—the ancient patriarchs and prophets "lived mystically" (*Against Faustus* 12.48); Christ's Passion is mystical and his mystical setting (*fixio*) of his cross in our hearts points out the wounds of our sins (*Against Faustus* 33.1; 32.7, 19); anointings of both the Old and the New Testament are often described as "mystical." The eucharistic consecration is a "mystical prayer" (*The Trinity* 3.4.10), and the miracle of the fishes (John 21:9–11) signifies the "blessed, mystical, great church" (*Letter* 252.7). Augustine can even speak generally of *mystica facta et dicta* (*Conf.* 13.20.28), or of *mystica* and a *mysticum aliquid* in the sense of any mystery of Christian belief or practice.

This sense of Christianity as containing an inner dimension in which the believer is called to participate through incorporation into Christ at baptism is the implicit ground of Augustine's "mysticism." Although he represents a less evolved stage in the technical development of the language to describe this element in Christianity (e.g., as compared with Dionysius), his sense of the necessity for all Christians to penetrate into the depths of this mystery in order to find, to touch, and even to see God created the theological foundation upon which more explicit mystical theories were later constructed in Latin Christianity. This view of Augustine as the foundational Western mystic, though still an undifferentiated one, allows us a new approach to some of the specific questions that have been addressed to the meaning and adequacy of the mystical elements in his thought.

Some authors have found Augustine's descriptions and theories of mystical vision confused and inadequate. E. I. Watkin, for example, finds a fundamental conflict between the Platonic category of clear vision which Augustine so often uses and the actual nature of any contact with God which must always take place in obscure intuition, something closer to touch than to sight.[128] Augustine's accounts of the experience of God, however, do not depend on the metaphor of vision alone. Rather, his mingling of the language of vision and metaphors drawn from all the other spiritual senses creates what may be a deliberate confusion in order to convey something of the obscurity of all such encounters. We have investigated several examples of this mingling of the senses (e.g., *Conf.* 10.27.37; *Hom. on Ps.* 41.9). Tactile images are omnipresent in his writings, not only the language of touching (*attingere*), but especially that of clinging and cleaving to, embracing and sticking to, suggested by a favorite Psalm text, *Mihi autem adhaerere Deo bonum est* (Ps 72:28).[129] Another theme that emphasizes the obscurity of consciousness of the immediate presence of God is that of "spiritual drunkenness" (*sacra vel sobria ebrietas*).[130] The most extended development of this is found in the comment on Psalm 35:9, *Inebriabuntur ab ubertate domus tuae* (*Hom. on Ps.* 35:14 [*PL* 36:351–52]).[131] Here Augustine also gives a direct answer to Watkin's criticism. "My brothers, I dare to say that in the matter of the holy words and movements of the heart through which the Truth is proclaimed to us we can neither say what they announce nor think it" (*Hom. on Ps.* 35:19 [*PL* 36:351]).[132] Augustine never thought that our immediate experiences of God in this life could be clearly expressed. The images he used, whether those of vision or of the other spiritual senses, were all strategies meant to suggest and not to circumscribe the inexpressible. Without enunciating a formal theory of the spiritual senses of the soul, as Origen and other Eastern authors had done,[133] his emphasis on a form of synaesthia as helpful in conveying the inexpressible richness of immediate consciousness of the divine presence made an important contribution to the history of Western mysticism.

The bishop of Hippo made frequent use of another set of terms found in scripture to describe the special nature of the direct consciousness of God — *ecstasis* and *excessus*.[134] These words had a long history in later Western Christian mysticism, not least because of their appearance in Augustine.[135] It is not possible to understand what he meant by them without an investigation of the threefold typology of visions that he outlined in several of his writings. Augustine advanced his theory of vision as early as the *Against Adimantus,* written about 393,[136] but it was in the twelfth book of the *Literal Commentary on Genesis,* written ca. 413, that he laid out his full thought on the topic. A contemporary text, *Letter* 147, is also important for relating the general theory of vision to the ecstatic vision of the mystics.[137]

Augustine's major interest in expounding his theory was not so much epistemological as mystical: book 12 of the *Literal Commentary* begins from the puzzle of how to understand the vision of paradise that Paul recounts in 2 Corinthians 12:2–4 (12.1.1–12.5.14), and *Letter* 147 is a response to Paulina's query as to whether the invisible God can be seen with bodily eyes. The bishop's distinction of three kinds of vision: corporeal, spiritual (i.e., imaginative), and intellectual visions is well known (12.6.15–12.7.16; 12.24.51). It is important to note that the threefold distinction is true on two levels, that is, in the kind of visions that we experience in the usual forms of knowing, as well as when the objects of vision are presented by special divine action.[138]

The influence of book 12 of the *Literal Commentary on Genesis* on the history of Western mysticism has been primarily due to its careful description of the state of ecstasy and its claims regarding the possibility of the direct apprehension of God in this life. *Ecstasis,* which may be either the product of natural causes or of some special intervention of grace, is defined as what happens "when . . . the soul's intention is completely turned away or snatched away from the body's senses" (*quando . . . penitus avertitur atque abripitur animi intentio a sensibus corporis* [12.12.25]). In this state the soul sees nothing by means of the senses; it is totally intent on either imaginative or intellectual seeing within. A passage in book 12 discusses God-given raptures, which may be either of the imaginative kind, as John experienced in the Apocalypse, or of an intelligible nature (12.26.53–54).[139] Regarding this highest, infallible type, Augustine says: "There the brightness of the Lord is seen, not through a symbolic or corporeal vision . . . , nor through a spiritual vision . . . , but through a direct vision and not through a dark image, as far as the human mind elevated by the grace of God can receive it" (*Lit. Comm. on Gen.* 12.26.54 [*PL* 34:476]).[140] Two repetitions of the same message later in book 12, one discussing Moses' vision (12.27.55 [*PL* 34:477])[141] and the other showing how intellectual visions involve the sight of both intelligible realities in the soul and the light which is God himself (12.31.59 [*PL* 34:480]),[142] indicate that there can be little doubt that Augustine claimed that direct and in some sense immediate vision of God in this life was possible in a moment of ecstasy. The same teaching is confirmed in *Letter* 147, if in less explicit a fashion.[143]

Some might wish to accuse Augustine of a certain inconsistency here by pointing to the many texts where the bishop seems to say that it is impossible to enjoy the vision of God in this life.[144] But if those passages are seen in the context of the whole of his thought, they are best interpreted as stressing that the perfection of the vision of God remains for the heavenly home. Augustine always insisted that it was only in the life to come that stable beatitude would be attained. Heaven is the land of "vision without defect and love without weariness" (*visio sine defectu et amor sine fastidio*), where "our whole task will be nothing but praising and enjoying God" (*totum negotium nostrum non erit nisi laudare Deum et frui Deo*).[145] Whatever we receive here may differ in intensity (Augustine seems to leave this open) and must differ in duration from this heavenly perfection.

The crucial scriptural proofs for this kind of vision are found in Moses and Paul, but this does not mean that Augustine believed that its manifestation was restricted to them. A text in the *Homilies on John* applies the same to the evangelist,[146] and a variety of other texts, as well as the basic thrust of the whole of the *Homilies on the Psalms,* argue that he thought the experience of the divine presence in this life was something that all Christians were called to share in, if in ways known only to God.[147] One remarkable text from the *Homily on Psalm* 134 (134.6 [*PL* 37:1742]) even indicates that Augustine thought there were some who might even be able to fix their sight on God *diu,* that is, "for some time," while still in this life,[148] though, like most mystics, he more often stressed the brevity of the experience.

Before leaving this topic, one further issue needs to be taken up. Is the vision or experience of which Augustine speaks a mediate or an immediate one? The question has been debated by modern Augustinian scholars, with Cuthbert Butler, Joseph Maréchal, and Paul Henry arguing for an immediate character to at least the highest form of ecstasy, and Fulbert Cayré continuing to insist that all forms of the *visio Dei* are mediated, taking place *per speculum in aenigmate* (1 Cor 13:12).[149] This may be a dispute about terminology in which each side is talking about something rather different; but it is difficult to claim, especially given the texts from book 12 of the *Literal Commentary on Genesis* cited above, that Augustine did not believe that *excessus mentis* granted a direct and immediate contact with God different from anything else to be found here on earth. Though the bishop did not take up the difficult philosophical and theological issues involved in how we are to understand this immediacy, he surely thought that in this life such experience of God was possible.

As noted above, the *visio Dei* can be attained, but only within the *tabernaculum* of the *totus Christus,* that is, the whole God-man. This *visio* involves the restoration of the *imago Dei* to its true original goal, but it is not just an uncovering of a hidden divine spark within, as the Gnostics had held. Our restoration reactivates the powers that were originally intended to lead humanity to God, before their wounding in Adam's sin made this impossible. Through the gift of grace these powers can attain a temporary, direct, and ineffable experience of the presence of the triune God. This experience, one that apparently admits of many degrees, is open to all faithful Christians. This is why Augustine is so insistent on excluding all esotericism from the call to Christian perfection.

The bishop's three sermons commenting on John 16:12–13 (*Homilies on John* 96–98, written 415 or later) form perhaps the most detailed and incisive investigation in patristic writing of the dangers of esotericism.[150] The "many things" that Christ still had to say to the disciples (16:12) which the Spirit will make clear (16:13) are not esoteric secrets revealed by human beings. All true teaching comes not from human teachers but from the Holy Spirit within us (*Hom.* 96.4). The transition from the milk of simple teaching to an increasing diet of the solid food of advanced doctrine (cf. 1 Cor 3:2) is the work of Christ and his Spirit (*Hom.* 97). Though Augustine admits that there must be different levels of appropriation of the Christian message (carnal and spiritual believers), the content is always one and the same. Christ crucified is received as milk by some and solid food by others, "because if they do not hear more, they understand more" (*quia et si non audiunt amplius, intelligunt amplius* [*Hom.* 98.2]). Hence, Augustine concludes, "there seems to be no necessity that some secret teachings are kept silent and hidden from the faithful who are still children in the manner of matters to be spoken privately to the advanced, that is, to the more intelligent" (*Hom. on Jn.* 98.3 [*PL* 35:1881]).[151] While he allows that the spiritual believers need to adapt the message to their audience, the content is uniform.[152]

At least three other questions need to be asked about Augustine's views on the possibility of the immediate consciousness of the divine presence in this life in order to gain a better conception of the scope of his mystical teaching. The first of these deals with the now familiar issue of the relation of this contemplative experience to the life of active love. The second is how this special form of consciousness relates to our ordinary acts of understanding and love, that is, the roles of love and knowledge in the mystical path. The third is a brief look at how Augustine understands the ultimate goal, the perfect vision of the heavenly reward.

We have already seen how Christian thinkers both adopted and transformed the ancient Greek paradigm of the distinction between the *theōria* and *praxis*. What for the Greeks had originally been a difference between two activities constituting two ways of life, the philosophical and the political, in the hands of Christian thinkers, beginning with Clement of Alexandria had become a religious distinction between mystical contemplation of God and the active charity to which Christians were summoned by the Gospel. While the Christians agreed with the Neoplatonists in shifting the meaning of *theōria* away from discursive reasoning in the direction of suprarational insight, they parted company with them in their insistence that the *vita contemplativa* could never dispense with the *vita activa* (to use the Latin terminology).[153] Augustine represents the culmination of this teaching in the fathers and is an important source for later Western thought on the relationship.[154]

The bishop summarizes his views neatly in the *City of God* in commenting on the three modes of life — contemplative, active, and mixed (*otiosus, actuosus, compositus*) — that he knew from Varro:

> As long as faith is preserved, a person can lead any one of these lives and come to the eternal reward. What counts is how he holds to the love of truth and how he weighs the duties of charity. No one should be so contemplative that in his contemplation he does not think of his neighbor's need; no one so active that he does not seek the contemplation of God. (*City of God* 19.19 [*PL* 41:647])[155]

Following the lead of Origen and Ambrose, Augustine frequently presented the relation between the two aspects of the Christian life in terms of scriptural pairs, such as Rachel and Leah from Genesis, the apostles John and Peter, and especially Mary and Martha.[156] His teaching remains constant: both modes of life are good; the contemplative life is the higher because it is more directly related to the heavenly goal (cf. *Hom. on Jn.* 101.5). As long as we are in this life, however, we are always compelled by the gospel command to abandon the delights of contemplation when the demands of active love intercede. Though Augustine understands the *vita activa* as the life of loving service to the neighbor, not as political activity in the state, and although he does not solve all the "ambiguities of action," as Nicholas Lobkowicz terms them (that is, the extent and precise ways in which contemplation should yield to action), his thought "resulted in the notion that 'active life' is a life of Christian perfection, that is, a walk of life *to be defined* in terms of this perfection."[157]

The second issue concerns the way in which Augustine viewed the roles of intellect and love in attaining mystical experience. The bishop of Hippo has sometimes been seen by those who have read him selectively as a resolute intellectualist.[158] Recent writers on his spirituality have more correctly stressed the affectivity that characterizes his mystical theory.[159] There can be no question that Augustine finds both intellect and will essential in the path to and the enjoyment of God; the issue is how best to unravel the distinct roles that these activities of the soul play in this most mysterious but important of journeys.

It would be easy to pile up quotations in which Augustine insists that both love and knowledge are necessary to attain God.[160] It is more important to ascertain just what roles these two activities (not faculties) play in the return to God. The key to the issue is to recognize how Augustine understood the activity of *visio.*

Margaret Miles has recently emphasized that Augustine's theory of sense perception and especially of vision, based upon Platonic models, was not that of passive reception but rather one of interaction in which the primary role is taken by the soul in sending forth a beam of light to make corporeal objects intelligible.[161] In other words, the soul "sees" bodies primarily because it takes an active role in seeing; that is, it emits a beam of light through the eyes that meets the light bathing the external object and succeeds in making the object visible. The organs of sense are necessary, but only as instruments. Following this analogy, Augustine thought of all knowing as a form of active "vision." Whatever the difficulties of this theory on the level of philosophical epistemology, it is the key to understanding how the bishop related love and knowledge in what we can call the mystical epistemology of the *visio Dei.*

Few, if any, patristic authors spoke as often and as profoundly about the nature of love as did Augustine. Love is the soul's weight (*pondus meum amor meus* [*Conf.* 13.9.10]), the soul's foot (*pes amoris* [*Hom. on Ps.* 9.15]), the path by which the soul ascends or descends (*amando ascendis, negligendo descendis* [*Hom. on Ps.* 85.6]). For Augustine, "each person is what he loves" (*talis est quisque, qualis ejus dilectio est* [*Hom. on 1 Jn.* 2.14]). But Augustine always admitted that desire presupposes knowledge. Where does the knowledge come from in the case of the desire for God, who is by definition unknowable? Faith and love provide the answer. In commenting on v. 4 of Psalm 104 (*Quaerite Dominum et confortamini, quaerite faciem ejus semper*) the bishop provides a lapidary response to this question. To be always seeking the face, that is, the presence of the Lord, seems to preclude ever finding him; but what the text really indicates is that he is both already found in faith and still ever sought by hope while in this life. It is *caritas*, the love of God poured out in our hearts, that is the power uniting the two. "Charity both finds him through faith and seeks to have him through appearance (*speciem*), where he is then found in such a way that he satisfies us and is not sought any more" (*Hom. on Ps.* 104.3 [*PL* 37:1391]).[162] The love with which God first loved us (1 John 4:14) enters into our hearts and gives us both a new, if obscure, knowledge of God in faith and a new kind of *desiderium*, or longing for God, that functions as a new eye of the soul, the source of the ray of light that seeks out its ineffable object. This new way of "seeing" is in us, but is not of us; it requires our cooperation, but its operation is from God himself.[163] This is the constant teaching of Augustine, at least in the major works beginning with the *Confessions,* brilliantly expounded in the later books of *The Trinity,* and most richly set out in the *Homilies on the Psalms.*[164]

God "rode far above the fullness of knowledge to show that no one could approach him save by love," as Augustine says in expounding Psalm 17 (*Hom. on Ps.* 17.11 [*PL* 36:149]).[165] The heart must be healed before God can be seen,[166] and this healing is the work of the Holy Spirit, who is Love itself, carried on in the Body of Christ that is the church.[167] The measure of our love is the measure of the vision that we have of God, even here in this life—"the more ardently we love God, the more certainly and calmly do we see him, because we see in God the unchanging form of justice, according to which we judge one ought to live" (*The Trinity* 8.9.13 [*PL* 42:960]).[168] Love leads to the fullness of knowledge, though we can experience this only in a partial way in this life, save for those brief flashes of ecstatic consciousness that God occasionally grants those who ardently desire him.[169]

Love is the "glue" by which we adhere to whatever we truly desire (*The Trinity* 10.8.11), and charity is the true glue that binds us to God (*Hom. on Ps.* 62.17 [*PL* 36:758]). Augustine, as we have seen, spoke of union in terms of the bond that knits all believers into the one Body of Christ,[170] not the union of the individual soul with God. Although his teaching about how the individual soul sees or touches God through love could be (and has been) interpreted as conformable with the *unitas spiritus* mode of understanding mystical union,[171] his general avoidance of the language of union contains an important message about the relation of his mysticism to that of Plotinus.

Given the bishop's knowledge of the great Neoplatonic thinker, especially such texts as *Enneads* 6.4–5, his avoidance of union language seems a deliberate critique, as noted above. Perhaps this implied critique can also cast light on Augustine's qualifications of vision language for describing our consciousness of the presence of God. We have seen how Augustine usually combined the language of spiritual seeing with the invocation of the other spiritual senses, especially hearing, smell, and touch, which have more passive (though never totally passive) connotations. For Augustine, God not only plants (or better "replants") the intention of *caritas* that lifts the soul toward him, but at the journey's goal he also must reveal himself in a free gift of his love. There is nothing foreordained about the meeting; the soul does not discover its inner identity with the One, as in Plotinus. It receives instead the divine disclosure through God's love.[172]

This form of free giving in love might suggest an appeal to the erotic language of the Song of Songs that we have seen in Origen and in Ambrose. But here Augustine surprises us. Though few mystics spoke more often about desire in the *general* sense of a yearning for God, in his mature writings at least, Augustine avoided the use of the erotic language of the love between man and woman to describe the encounters between God and the soul.

We may put this down to the bishop's noted (and often misunderstood) views on the body and on sexuality.[173] From one perspective, Augustine actually took a more positive view of sex than Origen, Ambrose, and Jerome, by admitting that sexuality was not a result of the Fall, that marriage had existed in paradise, and that the root of concupiscence is in the distorted will, not in the sexual urge itself, which is only its most evident manifestation. But from another side, Augustine's growing sense of how deeply sexuality must always labor under the curse of the Fall led him to doubt the advisability of trying to transform this fallen sexuality into a language descriptive of our individual love for the Word. In Peter Brown's words, the later Augustine knew that "sexuality was a disturbingly ageless adversary,"[174] not something that any Christian, even the Christian virgin, could ever feel safe about.

It is true that Augustine the young convert, who had so recently and wrenchingly abandoned an active sex life, did describe something of an erotic relation to God, but through a rather unusual metaphor, one which is couched not in terms of the symbolism of the female Bride of the Song and her love for Christ, but in that of the relation of the male lover to the feminine figure of divine Wisdom (Proverbs 6 and 8). In his *Soliloquies* (Winter, 386) he asks, "What kind of lover of Wisdom are you who longs to see and to hold her naked in a perfectly pure gaze and to embrace her with nothing in between," comparing this dedicated lover to a man "burning with love for a beautiful woman" (*Sol.* 1.13.22 [*PL* 32:881]).[175] A similar passage relating to Wisdom is found in *On Free Choice* (ca. 388).[176] Augustine did not immediately abandon the theme of the lover of Wisdom — it occurs several times in the early *Homilies on the Psalms*.[177] A survey of these texts indicates that what he found most useful in this type of erotic language was the contrast between human eros, in which the male lover wishes to keep the sight and enjoyment of the beautiful female for himself, and the beauty of unclothed divine Wisdom, who offers herself freely and is shared by all her lovers without jealousy.

What is most interesting, however, is the mature Augustine's total neglect of an erotic interpretation of the Song of Songs, an option he certainly knew from Origen and Ambrose. He never commented on the Song, and his treatise *On Virginity* (ca. 401) does not apply the song of love to the female ascetic's relation to Christ.[178] In his rather sparing use of the Song, Augustine adhered to an ecclesial reading: the Bride is always the church, often the church threatened by the Donatist schism.[179]

One of the few places where Augustine does contribute to a major theme in the Song of Songs tradition in Western mysticism is with regard to the important (and nonsexual) theme of the *ordo caritatis* (Song 2:4: *ordinate in me caritatem*). He used this text often, summarizing his teaching in *City of God* 15.22.29: "So it seems to me that a short and good definition of virtue is 'the order of love.' This is why in the Song of Songs, the Bride of Christ, the City of God, sings, 'Order charity in me'" (*PL* 41:467).[180] For Augustine, the order of charity is largely a moral issue, not something that results from the immediate experience of God as it will for many later mystics.[181]

A survey of these ramifications of the relation between love and knowledge in Augustine's thought reveals the truth of Eugene TeSelle's observation that the fundamental issue in Augustine's mysticism is not ecstatic vision as such but the purification of the affections that prepares for it in this life and grants it in the next. In his words, the mystical life for Augustine is "a journey for the affections."[182] The character of journey, the sense of the necessity of constant progress, is one of the most typical notes of Augustine's spiritual teaching, remarked upon by many commentators.[183] "If you were to say, 'That's enough,' you would have been lost," as he puts it in *Sermon* 169.[184]

Unlike some Eastern contemporaries such as Evagrius Ponticus and many later Western Christian mystics, Augustine was not terribly interested in creating itineraries marking out the stages of the soul's ascent to God. Though he often made rather general use of the threefold Plotinian ascent scheme, as we have seen, his mature works are notable for their emphasis on the continuing peregrination of the soul through the confusing welter of history by the power of love, rather than schematic portrayals of the soul's escape from the temporal process.[185] In book 13 of the *Confessions* Augustine presented the *pondus amoris,* pitting self-destructive *cupiditas* against the *caritas* of the Holy Spirit, largely in terms of the rise and fall of the individual soul in the cosmos (cf. *Conf.* 13.7.8–9.10). A detailed study of how Augustine made use of the image of love as a journey shows a more practical and moralizing use of such images in his later works.[186] It is likely that his study of Paul's teaching on the impotence of the will, as well as the annealing fires of the Donatist controversy which revealed to him the importance of the social character of love, were responsible for this shift in his perspective. The later Augustine taught that we journey through history together on the feet of desire (see *City of God* 14.28). Our footsteps toward the goal are our acts of mutual *caritas.*

Finally (and briefly), Augustine's thoughts on this heavenly goal, frequent as they are, tend to be inspiring in individual passages but are repetitive when many texts are taken together.[187] Just as the love that fuels our pilgrimage to God in this life does not preclude real knowledge of him — indeed, rather bestows knowledge far beyond what we might have dreamed of — when desire achieves its goal in heaven, perfect knowledge will follow. But that heavenly knowledge and desire are of the same reality: the God who is love.[188] Augustine's definition of true *Sapientia*, which may be tasted but not swallowed in this life, is "the knowledge and love of him who always is, and never changes, namely God" (*Hom. on Ps.* 135.8 [*PL* 37:1760]).[189] Once again, it would be tedious to pile up references to the many texts, both early and late, which say that the enjoyment of heaven will totally satisfy both our desire for knowledge and for love.[190] The message is clear.

Such a view of heaven may appear static, even boring. Augustine's congregation doubtless felt the same, and the bishop tried to respond to their (and perhaps our) objections. The same text from his comment on Psalm 104 cited above goes on to consider what love and knowledge will possibly have to do in that eternity of fulfillment. Augustine asks if we will be eternally seeking God in heaven because we will eternally be loving him. His answer is that just as we continue to love a friend whom we have present with us in this life, our love of God in heaven will always continue to grow: "As love grows, the search for the one who has been found also increases" (*amore crescente inquisitio crescat inventi*) (*Hom. on Ps.* 104.3 [*PL* 37:1392]).[191] Augustine was too intelligent to try to describe what was beyond even his rhetorical powers to imagine, but he was sure that true love could not be boring.

Augustine's influence on Christian mysticism has been largely in the West. Still, his views on the possibility of attaining a direct and immediate consciousness of the presence of God in this life, as well as the sober Christocentric and ecclesial way in which he presented this mystical goal to the Christian community, were characteristic of many of the great fathers of the fourth century. His insistence that true progress toward God is communal and not individual, that it takes place within the bosom of the church and by means of the exercise of *caritas* toward all, is a message we have heard before. His sense of the fleeting and partial nature of our conscious experiences of the deep reality that Christ and the Spirit are effecting in the whole Body of Christ is also shared by many of the fathers, though they express this, of course, in a variety of ways. There is much in Augustine that is unique — perhaps no personality of sixteen centuries past gives us a better sense that we actually know him. But the bishop of Hippo would be content to be thought of as one "father" among many.

Theoretical Foundations: The Modern Study of Mysticism

Introduction 🔲

I N HIS COMIC NOVEL *Small World*, David Lodge's questing hero, Persse McGarrigle, claims to have written a thesis on T. S. Eliot's influence on Shakespeare, which he explains as follows: "'Well, what I try to show,' said Persse, 'is that we can't avoid reading Shakespeare through the lens of T. S. Eliot's poetry. I mean, who can read *Hamlet* today without thinking of Prufrock.'"[1]

My reasons for including this rather long Appendix in a volume devoted to the study of the foundations of Western mysticism are not unlike those in which Persse defends his unusual choice of topic. Though this volume has been primarily shaped by the historical evidence presented in the preceding chapters, the modern debate over mysticism has also necessarily affected the perspective I have employed.

In the general Introduction I laid out a preliminary and heuristic understanding of mysticism, mentioning some but by no means all of the investigators whose views I have found helpful. Often our approach to an issue is as much the product of what we are trying to avoid or correct — false starts, misunderstandings, omissions — as of what opens our eyes to new possibilities. In my studies of mysticism over the past decade and more, I have tried to read as widely as possible in modern theories of mysticism, though the field is a very extensive one. In teaching the history of mysticism I have also found it profitable to investigate the classics of the modern study of mysticism in terms of criteria both historical and constructive.

There is no general survey of modern theories of mysticism. The few historiographical or critical studies that exist usually examine a rather limited range of literature, especially of a philosophical character. I make no pretense that what is given here is such a general survey: it is an eclectic and personal view, one much stronger in certain areas than in others. Even with this caveat, the three sections of this Appendix cover a wider range of literature on mysticism than other surveys known to me. Hence, it may be of some use, at least for interested students.

In presenting the major figures I have tried, though certainly without perfect success, to give a fair view of their theories, as well as the context in which they wrote, before venturing any criticism. My critiques often concern the clarity and consistency of the authors' views, though I realize that these are not the only values. Other criticisms that reflect my own understanding of mysticism, as set forth in preliminary fashion in the general Introduction, may seem at times rather peremptory, though I hope not unfair.

SECTION I

THEOLOGICAL APPROACHES TO MYSTICISM

In the eleventh book of the *Confessions,* Augustine asks: "What then is time? If no one asks me I know what it is; but if I wish to explain it to someone who asks me, I don't know."[1] Though perhaps not as potent and ancient an issue in the history of thought as the problem of time, the word "mysticism," like "time," is both commonly used and resistant of easy description and definition. Not unlike the related but more general word "religion" (which at least has a much older history),[2] "mysticism" and "mystic" tend to be used with the presumption that others will have at least some grasp of the referent. This may be true, but a glance at the history of the use of the term in modern study demonstrates that this general familiarity masks considerable differences of opinion and usage.

"No word in our language—not even Socialism—has been employed more loosely than 'Mysticism,'" wrote Dean Inge in 1899.[3] "There is probably no more misused word in these our days than 'mysticism,'" echoed Cuthbert Butler in 1923.[4] Things have improved so little in the second half of the century that in 1987 Louis Dupré admitted, "No definition could be both meaningful and sufficiently comprehensive to include all experiences that, at some point or other, have been described as 'mystical.'"[5] Keeping these cautionary maxims in mind, it is still helpful to survey at least some of the understandings of mysticism that have helped shape the construction of these volumes.

"Mysticism" as a noun is a fairly recent creation, the product of early seventeenth-century France, as the researches of Michel de Certeau have shown.[6] In earlier chapters we have already surveyed some aspects of the prehistory of the uses of the Greek adjective *mystikos*,[7] and more will be seen in the volumes to come. Modern academic discussion of the term "mysticism," especially as it affects the English-speaking world, began in earnest toward the end of the nineteenth century.[8] On the basis of a few useful surveys,[9] as well as an admittedly selective reading in a large literature, what follows is meant as an introduction to the issues involved in the modern use of this rich but ambiguous term.

The most significant modern studies of the nature of mysticism have generally proceeded from explicitly theoretical perspectives, however much historical evidence they have employed to support their case. While more or less descriptive historical accounts have not been lacking on the popular level, few of these have made any lasting contribution to scholarship. The theoretical perspectives from which mysticism has been assayed have been multiple, and frequently overlapping. Many of the greatest works do not easily fit under one rubric; some that pretend to advance one perspective may really belong to another. Nevertheless, it may not be totally misleading to characterize the modern study of mysticism under the general headings of (a) theological, (b) philosophical, and (c) comparativist and psychological approaches. The first of these will be the subject of this section; the latter two will be treated in the following sections.

Among the theologians, the study of mysticism has enjoyed diverse evaluations, conditioned at least in part by confessional allegiance. The powerful tradition of German Protestant theology has been on the whole more negative than positive in its evaluation of the place of mysticism, however defined, in the Christian religion, frequently seeing it as an essentially Greek form of religiosity whose emphasis on the inner experience of God is ultimately incompatible with the Gospel message of salvation through faith in the saving word mediated through the church.

Although Friedrich Schleiermacher (1768–1834), the father of modern liberal Protestant theology, certainly gave an important role to what might be called mystical piety, especially in his famous *Speeches on Religion* of 1799, by the end of the nineteenth century continental Protestant theology's antipathy to mysticism's role in Christianity became evident in the work of the dominant theological figure of the era, Albrecht Ritschl (1822–1889), whose three volumes entitled *Christian Doctrine of Justification and Reconciliation* appeared between 1870 and 1874. Ritschl's brief essay *Theologie und Metaphysik,* published in 1881, is the classic expression of the deep division he found between Christian faith and mysticism. "Mysticism therefore is the practice of Neoplatonic metaphysics and this is the theoretical norm of the pretended mystical delight in God. Hence the universal being viewed as God into which the mystic wishes to be mingled is a cheat."[10]

The great historian of theology, Adolf von Harnack (1851–1930) was deeply influenced by Ritschl's thought. He provides a good illustration of this approach to mysticism, one widely influential in Protestant theology down to the present. Harnack had read the mystics with care and in his masterwork, the *History of Dogma* (*Lehrbuch der Dogmengeschichte* [1885–90]), he paid tribute to the spiritual significance of mysticism in the history of Christian theology, especially in the late Middle Ages. But Harnack's overall evaluation of what he understood by mysticism was negative: "Mysticism as a rule is rationalism worked out in a fantastic way, and rationalism is faded mysticism."[11]

Harnack displayed his usual erudition in showing the important role that mysticism played in both Greek Orthodox and Roman Catholic Christianity, but clearly to the detriment of both, since he held that mysticism as such compromised essential elements in the true evangelical faith that had been renewed by Luther. Methodius of Olympus in the third century marks the irruption of the "subjectivity" of monastic mysticism into Christianity.[12] This Eastern type of mysticism, "which bases its hope of redemption on the idea that the God-Logos continually unites himself anew with each individual so as to form a union,"[13] is scarcely what Harnack thought the "essence" of Christianity to be. The notion of the birth of the Logos in the soul of the believer, the key component in what Eastern Christianity refers to as deification (*theōsis*), for Harnack implied pantheism and led to a magical view of the sacraments.[14] No part of the *History of Dogma* is more dated than the sections that display such insensitivity to this central theme of the Greek theological tradition.

Harnack's account of Western Christian mysticism down to the Reformation, found in the fifth and sixth volumes of the *History of Dogma*, is both insightful and puzzling, especially because he does not always clarify how he understood the relation of the Western mystical tradition initiated by Augustine to that of the Christian East, best expressed in the writings of the Pseudo-Dionysius. Though Augustine set aside the ritualistic aspects of mysticism, which Harnack found objectionable in the Greeks,[15] it is not always clear if the bishop of Hippo was subject to the pantheistic tendencies found in the Eastern mystical authors. One of Augustine's foremost medieval disciples, Bernard of Clairvaux, is, however, accused of an "exchange of the historic Christ for the dissolving picture of the ideal," as well as of pantheistic tendencies.[16]

Harnack correctly views Augustine's insistence on the mutuality of contemplative prayer and doctrinal exposition as the foundation for the fusion of scholasticism and mysticism in the High Middle Ages. "Mystic theology and Scholastic theology are one and the same phenomenon, which only present themselves in manifold gradations, according as the subjective or objective interest prevails."[17] On this basis, the extensive discussion of the relation of mysticism to the mendicant orders in chapter 2 of volume 6 occurs under the rubric "On the History of Piety." Here Harnack argues for both the essential unity of all mysticism and for its identification with Catholic piety.[18] His appreciation for the elevation of feeling achieved in late medieval mysticism is tempered throughout by his insistence that all mysticism (even that of Thomas Aquinas!) ends in pantheism and self-deification.[19] Harnack's evaluation of the distinction between mysticism and evangelical faith was well expressed in his famous phrase "a mystic that does not become a Catholic is a dilletante."[20]

The great scholar's influential views can be said to be typical, *mutatis mutandis,* of the attitude to mysticism found in much twentieth-century continental Protestant scholarship. The reaction against the Protestant liberal tradition of Ritschl and Harnack that became evident after World War I (the movement termed neo-orthodoxy in America) did little to change this negative evaluation. The leaders of the new movement, such as Karl Barth and Emil Brunner, saw little good in mysticism.[21] Even Rudolf Bultmann, who departed from Barth in his commitment to a dialogue between the saving word and the insights of existential philosophy, viewed mysticism as a phenomenon more characteristic of Greek religion than of true Christianity.

The attitude taken toward mysticism by Paul Tillich (1886–1965) was more complex.[22] Tillich maintained a lifelong interest in mysticism and spoke of the intuitive awareness of ultimate value and being that is the ground of philosophies of religion as "a type of mystical experience."[23] Despite his frequent kind words about mysticism, however, he criticized any form of "absolute" mysticism that would dissolve individuality, avoid confronting the demonic threats to human existence, and cut itself free from the historical concreteness of positive religion. (Whether Tillich's absolute mysticism was a reality actually present in Christian history, as Harnack had claimed, or only an ideal type more likely to be realized in modern forms of pseudo-mysticism is an open question.)

The scattered nature of Tillich's remarks on mysticism deny him any fundamental role in twentieth-century theories of mysticism, however much sympathy he had for the mystical element in religion. There were, however, two major continental Protestant thinkers who did make substantial contributions to discussion of mysticism in the first part of the century — Ernst Troeltsch (1865–1923) and Albert Schweitzer (1875–1965).

Though originally deeply influenced by Ritschl, Troeltsch had broken with the older liberal theology in many ways by the time he published his masterwork, *The Social Teaching of the Christian Churches* (*Die Soziallehren der christlichen Kirchen und Gruppen*) in 1912. Troeltsch's interpretation of mystical or spiritual religion was unusual in Protestant circles, not only because of the importance that he accorded it as one of the three social forms of Christianity (along with the church type and the sect type),[24] but also because of his claims that this type was best realized when it became sociologically distinct in the Protestantism of the Radical Reformation, and not in either Greek Orthodoxy or medieval Catholicism where it certainly could be found but in a more diffuse fashion.[25]

In *The Social Teaching* Troeltsch claimed that mystical religion is based upon the primacy of direct or immediate religious experience, and thus in the technical sense can be described as an independent religious philosophy present in many concrete religions.[26] This conception may provide a link with the other context within which Troeltsch discussed mysticism, namely, in connection with his theory of the "religious a-priori." In his paper entitled "Psychology and Theory of Knowledge in the Science of Religion," for instance, Troeltsch argued that an adequate science of religion must deal with the mediation between the actualization of the religious a priori in individual psychical phenomena of mystical nature (that is, the "varieties of religious experience" studied by psychologists like William James) and the abstract conception of religion's relation to reason worked out by Immanuel Kant.[27] Though Troeltsch's concept of the religious a priori allowed mysticism an important role, his lack of development of this notion left this role more than a little obscure.

In *The Social Teaching,* however, Troeltsch is primarily interested in the varied concrete manifestations of the mystical or spiritual form of religion as they appear in the history of Christianity from the time of the New Testament down to the triumph of the modern form of spiritual religion which Troeltsch saw as the dominant religious tendency of his time.[28] On the interaction of the three sociological forms, Troeltsch has a perceptive analysis of the reasons why mystics find it easier to live within the church type than do sectarians.[29]

Troeltsch attempted to save mysticism for Protestantism — no mean feat given the views of his teachers and contemporaries in Protestant thought. His insistence on the sociologically embedded nature of mysticism is as important today as it was in 1912, and almost as often forgotten or neglected. The analysis of mysticism presented in *The Social Teaching,* however, is a limited and idiosyncratic one. The only mystics treated in detail are the Protestant radicals from Thomas Müntzer to Nicholas Zinzendorf. Given the way in which Troeltsch defined the inner essence of mystical religion as based on a conscious insistence on the primacy of direct religious experience achieving a sociologically distinct form, this certainly follows; but it has the disadvantage of neglecting those mystics who found their immediate relation to God in forms of objective religious life (such as liturgy and sacraments) and who were not moved to create distinctive forms of religious association. Perhaps there is more to mystical religion than the conscious insistence on the primacy of direct religious experience.

Albert Schweitzer spoke guardedly about at least one central experience in his life that could be described as mystical,[30] but his contribution to the theology of mysticism is not explicitly related to this personal witness. Current fashion has reduced the once prodigious reputation of the Nobel Prize–winning jungle doctor ("the Genius of Humanity," for Winston Churchill) to more modest dimensions. Many think of him as the author of only one important book, *The Quest of the Historical Jesus* (more prosaically entitled in the German original *Vom Reimarus zu Wrede*); but Schweitzer wrote much, including at least one other book of genius, *Die Mystik des Apostels Paulus* (*The Mysticism of Paul the Apostle*), begun in 1906 but not finished until 1929.[31]

Schweitzer's contributions to the study of mysticism were both constructive and historical. The constructive part, best outlined in the second volume of his *Kulturphilosophie* of 1923 (translated as *The Philosophy of Religion*), is of limited value. Like other Protestant thinkers, Schweitzer condemned "mysticisms of identity" that spring from the negation of life and the world, insisting that the affirmation of life and the world could give rise to true ethical mysticism only insofar as such affirmation is based on what he called "elemental thinking." This mode of thought, one concerned with the basic questions in life, grounds the "life-view" (*Lebensanschauung*), an expression of the will that precedes the *Weltanschauung*, or rational and scientific apprehension of the world. It finds its expression in Schweitzer's famous philosophy of "reverence for life." This rational, absolute, and universal reverence for life forms the basis for an ethical mysticism involving union with the infinite will.[32] "Whenever my life devotes itself in any way to life, my finite will-to-live experiences union with the infinite will in which all life is one."[33]

Schweitzer's account of the origin and essence of mysticism has had little effect on contemporary discussion. Given the a priori character of his approach, one can well understand why. Unfortunately, much the same fate has also overtaken Schweitzer's more powerful historical-theological contribution to the study of Christian mysticism in his book on Paul. Whatever one thinks of the validity of his argument, *The Mysticism of Paul the Apostle* is a major work, arguably the most powerful and carefully argued defense of why mysticism was an essential element in early Christianity.

The Mysticism of Paul the Apostle was the second salvo in Schweitzer's consistent eschatological attack on traditional views of Jesus and the early church. The basic argument is designed to show that Paul, like the Jesus of *The Quest of the Historical Jesus,* was "consistently" eschatological in his expectation of the imminent end of the world. For Schweitzer, the hellenization of Christianity that replaced consistent eschatology did not begin with Paul, but with Ignatius of Antioch and the Gospel of John. Their Hellenistic mysticism of "Being-in-the-Logos," however, was basically a misreading of Paul's mysticism of "Being-in-Christ." In the author's words, "Paul was not the Hellenizer of Christianity. But in his eschatological mysticism of the Being-in-Christ he gave it a form in which it could be Hellenized."[34]

In laying out his historical argument, Schweitzer advanced a theory and typology of mysticism not easily identifiable at first glance with that found in *The Philosophy of Religion.* Mysticism is the individual's "feeling himself, while still externally amid the earthly and temporal, to belong to the supernatural and eternal."[35] Primitive mysticism achieves this through magical ceremony, intellectual mysticism through an act of thought made possible by reflection on the relation of the individual to Being itself. The uniqueness of Paul's Christ-mysticism, which for Schweitzer remains the only true Christian mysticism,[36] is that it mixes both primitive and intellectual mysticism without ever becoming a form of God-mysticism. In his negative evaluation of the mysticism of identity with God, Schweitzer rejoins the continental Protestant mainstream: "Pure God-mysticism remains a dead thing."[37] For the jungle doctor, Paul in a sense was the last Christian — his unified eschatological-mystical interpretation of Jesus was subsequently split up among the various divisions of the Christian religion, each carrying off their own treasured pieces of what was once a seamless robe.[38]

This brief account can give little appreciation of the learning and power with which Schweitzer presented his case in *The Mysticism of Paul the Apostle.* It may, however, suggest at least one glaring problem that his view presents. First, even if God-mysticism can be conceived of as basically one thing, Schweitzer never presents the theological grounds upon which he conceives of it as incompatible with Christianity. Like almost all continental Protestant theologians, Schweitzer assumes that God-mysticism always means identity with the divine and is therefore *ipso facto* inconsistent with Christianity's belief in the transcendental distinction between God and the human. The history of Christian mysticism suggests that this picture is far too simple.

English Protestants, especially Anglo-Catholics, have been much more appreciative of the value of mysticism in Christianity than continental Protestants. Several classic works of the past century are worthy of mention, though perhaps more for the influence they have had than for the originality of their theological contributions.

William Ralph Inge (1860–1954), Dean of St. Pauls, wrote several books on mysticism during his long life, the most notable being his *Christian Mysticism,* delivered as the Bampton Lectures in 1899. Inge's interest in mysticism was influenced by the study of Neoplatonism, a topic in which he was a pioneer, though not an uncritical one. The "gloomy Dean" wrote at a time of growing Roman Catholic debate over mysticism, and his book was designed in part to serve as a corrective to Catholic views whose emphasis on negative theology (something he thought entered the Neoplatonic tradition from India) and on what he called "debased supernaturalism" (that is, the concern for extraordinary mystical experiences such as stigmata and levitation) he judged grave dangers to true mysticism.[39] True mysticism, based on the Johannine Logos doctrine, he defined as "the attempt to realise, in thought and feeling, the immanence of the temporal in the eternal, and of the eternal in the temporal."[40] As a form of religion, mysticism is based on the premise that the purified soul, because it partakes of divinity, can finally come to see and perceive the God who is love.[41]

Inge's book proceeds in a basically historical fashion, guided by a broad triple classification of (1) speculative mysticism (largely Platonic in inspiration and based on the principle of supernaturalism), (2) practical and devotional mysticism, which seeks to find God in the world, and (3) nature mysticism, which sees God in all things. Inge's value judgments are often peremptory. Not everyone will be inclined to agree with his dismissal of the Song of Songs— "As to the Song of Solomon, its influence upon Christian Mysticism has been simply deplorable."[42] A whiff of Victorian smugness is detectable in such confident assertions as, "There is no race, I think, in which there is a deeper vein of idealism, and a deeper sense of the mystery of life, than our own."[43] Finally, it is the Dean's lack of understanding of negative, or apophatic mysticism ("the great accident of Christian mysticism," p. 115), as well as his failure to appreciate the role of the erotic element in Christian mysticism, which place the severest limitations on his pioneering account.

No writer on mysticism in English has been more widely read than Evelyn Underhill (1875–1941). Her book *Mysticism,* first published in 1911 and many times reprinted, was the first of many that she dedicated to spreading knowledge of mysticism to a broad public.[44] While Underhill's account is more a historical outline than a profound work of theology or philosophy, she performed a real function in recovering many important mystics who had been forgotten or little studied. Her theological perspective, heavily influenced by her spiritual director, Baron Friedrich von Hügel, was of a high Anglo-Catholic order.

Underhill organized her classic book according to an analytical first part (The Mystic Fact) and a more psychological second part (The Mystic Way).[45] She understood mysticism as "the expression of the innate tendency of the human spirit towards complete harmony with transcendental order, whatever be the theological formula under which that order is understood."[46] This harmony was often described in terms of the category of union with God, though she spoke also of "entering the Presence of God."[47] Underhill reacted against the recently published views of William James (see section 2 below), assigning mysticism a set of characteristics consciously opposed to his.[48]

This Anglican author's interest centered on "the life process of the mystic." The lengthy second part is an extended discussion of the five stages of the mystical itinerary that form a "composite portrait" of a single process of growth.[49] Underhill identifies three symbolic models according to which mystics have attempted to convey information about the ineffable experiences they have enjoyed — the pilgrimage or quest, the soul's marriage, and the alchemical model of transformation.[50] She also analyzes two basic interpenetrating ways of expressing the unitive life that is the goal: deification (the transcendental metaphysical expression), and spiritual marriage (the intimate personal expression).[51] Like the classic Christian mystics she had studied, Underhill insisted that the heights of the mystical path combine both the active and the passive states into a higher synthesis, "the crown of human evolution," as she termed it.[52]

Underhill's florid prose and a certain looseness in her mode of argument make it easy to dismiss her as more journalistic than scholarly. Although *Mysticism* leaves many disputed issues untreated, Underhill's broad acquaintance with the texts of the mystics and her freedom from the prejudices displayed by Inge show why the book has remained a popular introduction for over three quarters of a century. In implying an identification of mysticism with the core of religion, and in explicitly arguing for a transcultural and transreligious unity to the stages of the mystic path, she adopts positions that have been increasingly questioned in recent years. Her lack of sympathy with the more speculative forms of mysticism also constitutes a drawback.

Kenneth Escot Kirk (1886–1954) was Regius Professor of moral and pastoral theology at Oxford before he became bishop of that See in 1937. His 1928 Bampton Lectures were published in 1931 as *The Vision of God:*

The Christian Doctrine of the "Summum Bonum."[53] Kirk's work pertains more directly to the history of Christian ethics than to the study of mysticism, but the contributions it made to the latter are significant, not least because Kirk's holistic approach, which rooted the mystical vision of God in worship (understood broadly as both liturgy and private contemplative practices), is close to the patristic and Eastern Orthodox views.

Kirk's development of a dialectical ethical theory in which the vision of God, the goal of human life and determinant of human conduct, allows the proper balance between the necessary but easily exaggerated ethical tendencies of formalism (expressing demands by means of codes of duties) and rigorism (the need for a disciplined life) is too involved to be detailed here.[54] The true appreciation of the vision of God, he argued, implies no self-centered enjoyment of the experience in itself ("panhedonism," a term Kirk took over from Henri Bremond), but is determined by the priority of divine love and the active call to share this love with others.[55] Like Dean Inge, Bishop Kirk was not sympathetic to the negative theology of the Dionysian tradition, but he paid sincere tribute to the balanced life of active service and contemplative prayer found in Benedict's *Rule*, theoretically set forth by Thomas Aquinas, and revived in the devout humanism of the Catholic Reformation. Kirk's conclusion, one that could be echoed by contemporary Orthodox theologians and also by some Roman Catholic authors, is that "the mystical experience is at once the commonest and the greatest of human accidents. There is not one of us to whom it does not come daily. . . . What Christianity offers, with its fellowship and sacraments, its life of prayer and service, its preaching of the Incarnate Son of God, is the same vision in ever-increasing plenitude."[56] Though a noble sentiment, Kirk's view ends up by identifying the mystical so closely with the religious itself that all distinction seems lost.

Whatever their individual differences, Inge, Underhill, and Kirk all agreed in giving mysticism a value that no continental Protestant theologian shared. Whereas German Protestant scholars saw mysticism, at least God-mysticism or the mysticism of union with God, as essentially world-negating and solipsistic, these Anglicans insisted that true mysticism (which they understood in somewhat different ways) involved an affirmation of the goodness of the world and of the continuity between nature and spirit,[57] as well as the recognition that the mystic life finds its true expression in active love of neighbor. This position implied a rejection, or at least suspicion of the *via negativa*, most marked in Inge and Kirk, less evident in Underhill. Similar tendencies can be seen in a contemporary English Catholic thinker who made a notable contribution to the theology of mysticism, Edward Cuthbert Butler (1858–1934), abbot of Downside.

Butler's *Western Mysticism: The Teaching of Saints Augustine, Gregory and Bernard on Contemplation and the Contemplative Life* first appeared in 1923. Butler was more a historian than a theologian. His book manifests the power of his historical research and the judiciousness of his mind, while displaying some of the weaknesses of his theological outlook. Nevertheless, *Western Mysticism* played an important role in Roman Catholic discussion of mysticism, though more in the English-speaking world than on the Continent.[58]

Butler's work was not well organized. A mixture of detailed textual study of Augustine, Gregory, and Bernard on contemplation, interspersed with more theoretical suggestions about the nature of mysticism in general, the work was reorganized for the second edition of 1926 and prefaced by a lengthy series of "Afterthoughts" that took up, albeit in unsystematic fashion, some of the issues the critics had advanced against the first edition. Butler's return to the "simple practical mysticism" of his three classic Western mystics, however, was an important departure in contemporary Catholic discussion of mysticism, which centered on Teresa of Avila and John of the Cross as witnesses and which looked to the theology of Thomas Aquinas for its theoretical concepts.

Although Butler did speak about mystical union (even mistakenly ascribing the category to Augustine),[59] his understanding of mysticism really focuses on the ancient themes of contemplation and the presence of God. "Contemplation at its highest limit is identical with the mystical experience, and involves the claim of the mystics . . . to an experimental perception of God's Being and Presence."[60] The "Western mysticism" that Butler discerned in his sources he characterized as pre-Dionysian (i.e., largely independent of the negative theology introduced by the Dionysian writings), prescholastic, nonvisionary, indifferent to violent rapture and the lesser "psychophysical concomitants of mystic states," and without undue emphasis on the dangers of diabolical influence.[61] Butler did not intend the "Western mysticism" of his authors to be seen as contradicting the views of the great Spaniards, but he did view it as an important corrective for more dubious forms of mysticism (especially as practiced by women) that began in the thirteenth century. He clearly thought that its sober teaching could serve as a basis for a modern renewal of mysticism which would be open to all believers and not just a spiritual elite. (Butler, like many continental Catholic scholars, insisted that all Christians are in some way called to mystical contemplation.) Such a renewed mysticism would reduce undue emphasis on extraordinary phenomena (Inge's "debased supernaturalism") and would return to the ideal of the mixed life of action and contemplation as the goal of Christian piety.[62]

Butler's views were much criticized in his own days and after. Contemporary Neoscholastics scorned him for not being sufficiently rigorous from a theological point of view (he confessed in response, "I have a feeling that many of the difficulties that have arisen in the discussions under survey are occasioned by undue pressing of theological theories").[63] Subsequent Catholic critics who jettisoned technical scholastic language for a sometimes vague biblicism and appeal to the fathers have unfairly reproached Butler for not breaking with Scholasticism more completely.[64] More judicious appraisers have made clear both the errors in historical method that Butler's anthologizing technique left him open to and also the theological problems involved in his mediating position.[65] Perhaps the most notable of these theological issues occurs in the "Afterthoughts" where his invocation of a distinction between the active "union of uniformity" (as he called it) with God's will and the passive union of conscious direct contact with God allows him to reintroduce a form of the double standard that argues that only some Christians are called to true contemplation.[66] Despite these problems, Butler is still rewarding reading, and his turn to a broader, older, and more "catholic" tradition of mysticism was an important harbinger of things to come.

The most trenchent of Butler's critics were not Protestant or Anglican authors, but his fellow Catholics, especially the continental neoscholastic authors who had been involved in intense theological study of mysticism since the end of the nineteenth century. It is necessary to give a brief, however inadequate, presentation of the importance of this considerable literature for the modern study of mysticism.

Since the Second Vatican Council it has been fashionable, and all too easy, to dismiss the neoscholastic debates of the first part of the century as irrelevant to current theological questions.[67] The narrowness of approach, the frequent polemicism, and the ahistorical mode of argument frequently seem to warrant this dismissal. Nonetheless, many of the issues debated by the Neoscholastics are still of moment, especially in the area of mysticism. There is much to learn from a brief glance at this literature.[68]

The stimulus given Catholic theology by Leo XIII's call for a return to the teaching of St. Thomas Aquinas in his encyclical *Aeterni Patris* of 1879 was the crucial factor in the rise of Neoscholasticism to dominance in Catholic thought. France, the chief center of the Thomist revival, was also the arena for much of the scholastic discussion of the nature of mysticism. The debates revolved around two closely connected questions: (1) Is the call to mystical contemplation a universal one offered to all Christians, or is it a special grace available only to a select few? (2) At what stage in the life of prayer does properly mystical contemplation begin? Implied in both these questions are more basic issues concerning the understanding of grace and the constitution and definition of Christian perfection. How is mystical prayer related to the grace of salvation? If Christian perfection is identified with love of God and love of neighbor, what need is there for a further "mystical" level? Is mystical contemplation in some way necessary in order to attain the heights of perfection? Complicating the debates over these fundamental questions were misunderstandings caused by the use of differing terminologies for the various states of prayer and disagreements about the proper understanding of the authoritative teachers, especially Thomas Aquinas, Teresa of Avila, and John of the Cross.

Augustin-Francois Poulain, S.J. (1836–1919), first published his noted *Des graces d'oraison: Traité de théologie mystique* in 1901 (translated in 1910 as *The Graces of Interior Prayer: A Treatise on Mystical Theology*). This large and influential work went through many subsequent editions.[69] Poulain considered his book to be a descriptive account of the development of prayer from the four degrees of ordinary prayer (chap. 2) through to the four degrees of the prayer of mystical union (chaps. 16–19). He took considerable pains to distinguish true mystical union, which he understood as the felt presence of God by way of "spiritual touch" (chaps. 5–6), from all accompanying phenomena, an important point in helping rescue Catholic thought from the overemphasis on extraordinary mystical experiences, which Dean Inge and others had rightly criticized. Poulain insisted that true mystical prayer is totally beyond any human effort, a purely operative grace passively received without any cooperation on the subject's part.[70] Hence he sharply distinguished between the fourth and final degree of ordinary prayer, the "prayer of simplicity," which he called "acquired contemplation" (a term created in the seventeenth century), and the "infused contemplation" that characterized the stages of mystical union.[71] From this he concluded that there is no universal call to mystical experience; such a call is a special grace over and above what is needed for the Christian perfection necessary to salvation.

Poulain's views in these matters differed sharply from those of Abbe August Saudreau (1859–1942), who in 1896 had published *Les dégres de la vie spirituelle* (*The Degrees of the Spiritual Life* [1907]), and followed this in 1901 with *La vie d'union à Dieu et les moyens d'y arriver* (*The Life of Union with God* [1927]), and in 1903 with *L'état mystique* (*The Mystical State* [1924]). The two French theologians were at one in calling for a return to contemplative prayer, but Saudreau disagreed with Poulain in insisting that mystical contemplation is the normal goal of the Christian life to which all are called, whether or not they actually achieve it in this life. For this reason Saudreau extended the borders of mystical prayer more broadly than Poulain, rejecting the division between acquired and infused contemplation as a late and erroneous reading of the classic mystical teachers.[72] As the debate proceeded, Saudreau also attacked Poulain's claim that the essence of the mystical state rests in some form of direct perception of the divine presence, insisting that the divine presence is ordinarily known only in an indirect fashion.[73]

Four decades of controversy over these issues ensued. The Sulpician Albert Farges (1848–1926) came to Poulain's defense in 1920 with his book *Les phénomènes mystiques distingues de leurs contréfacons humaines et diaboliques* (*Mystical Phenomena Compared with Their Human and Diabolical Counterfeits* [1926]).[74] A number of Jesuit authors, such as A. Bainval, J. de Guibert, and Cardinal Billot, also supported him. Saudreau's side (if not all his positions) attracted the support of the Franciscan Louis de Besse (*La science de la prière* [1903], translated in 1923 as *The Science of Prayer*), the Eudist Emile Lamballe (*La contemplation ou principes de théologie mystique* [1912], translated in 1913 as *Mystical Contemplation*), as well as Jesuits such as M. de la Taille, J. Maréchal, and L. Peeters. The most important proponents of this view, however, proved to be a series of Dominican neo-Thomists, Juan-Gonzalez Arintero (1860–1928), Ambroise Gardeil (1859–1931), and especially Reginald Garrigou-Lagrange (1877–1964).[75]

Arintero's *La evolucion mistica* of 1908 (*The Mystical Evolution in the Development and Vitality of the Church* [1949]) and his *Cuestiones misticas* of 1920 were his major contributions. The Spanish Dominican's emphasis on the ecclesial nature of the universal vocation to mystical prayer was his most notable addition to the literature; his insistence on the errors of opposing viewpoints (which he solemnly affirmed on his deathbed!) were typical of the polemics of the time.[76]

Garrigou-Lagrange (along with L. Mandonnet, the foremost exponent of classical Dominican Thomism of this century) wrote three important works on mysticism: *Perfection chrétienne et contemplation selon saint Thomas d'Aquin et saint Jean de la Croix* (1923), translated in 1937 as *Christian Perfection and Contemplation; L'amour de Dieu et la croix de Jesus* (1929), translated as *The Love of God and the Cross of Jesus* (1947–51); and *Les trois ages de la vie interieur* (1938–39), translated as *The Three Ages of the Interior Life* (1947–48). Garrigou-Lagrange brought much erudition and a clear and powerful mind to the task of showing how St. Thomas and St. John of the Cross were in fundamental agreement on the universality of the call to the mystical life. There can be only one road to Christian perfection, he argued, that which begins with the supernatural gift of faith, advances through the activity of the gifts of the Holy Spirit, and finds its culmination in infused contemplation.[77]

Garrigou-Lagrange's notion of mysticism, like that of Saudreau, did not leave much room for the immediate perception of God at the height of the mystical path, save by way of miraculous exception. Direct and immediate contact with God as the summit of mysticism was argued for on Thomistic grounds by Ambroise Gardeil, Garrigou-Lagrange's teacher, in two volumes issued in 1927 under the title *La structure de l'âme et l'expérience mystique.* Basing himself on John of St. Thomas's interpretation of the Angelic Doctor's view on the immediate relation the soul has to itself in the act of self-knowledge, Gardeil claimed that an analogous direct perception of God by connaturality in infused contemplation was fully conformable with the mind of St. Thomas.[78]

This brief summary of central issues of the debate by no means exhausts the wealth of theological literature devoted to mysticism in France during the early and middle decades of the century.[79] An important contribution came from the pen of the ex-Jesuit, Abbe Henri Bremond (1863–1933), a prolific and influential author elected to the Academie Française in 1923.[80] Bremond was more the literary scholar than the theologian, but his research raised important theological questions. Bremond's great work, the eleven-volume *Histoire littéraire du sentiment religieux en France depuis la fin des guerres de religion jusqu'à nos jours,* published between 1915 and 1933,[81] rediscovered the importance of the spiritual writers of the seventeenth century for French culture and provided a still-unrivaled account of the golden age of French mysticism. Bremond's positions were controversial, especially his support of Fenélon over Bossuet in the dispute over pure love and total abandonment, and his delineation of the opposition between two great parties, the group devoted to the ideal of pure love and that which favored the practice of asceticism.

The attention given to mysticism in France in the 1920s and 1930s was truly remarkable. When one takes into account not only the theological debates briefly sketched here but also the interest of philosophers and psychologists to be studied below, there is perhaps no other period in the present century that has seen such intense concern with mysticism and that has contributed so many significant studies.

The debates over the universality of the mystical call and the discrimination between acquired and infused contemplation, however, were not restricted to France. In Germany, Joseph Zahn in his *Einführung in die christliche Mystik* (1918) sided with Saudreau against Poulain and his followers, while the Benedictine scholar Alois Mager advanced a mediating position in such works as his *Mystik als Lehre und Leben* (1934).[82] The most important German Catholic work on mysticism of the period between the wars, however, came from another direction, one that, like Butler's *Western*

Mysticism, tried to break free from scholastic debates by returning to the age of the fathers.

Anselm Stolz (1900–1942), a German Benedictine, published his *Theologie der Mystik* in 1936. This important work, which was translated into French — but not into English, and is hence surprisingly little known in the English-speaking world — was a forerunner of the return to scripture and the fathers that was to revolutionize Catholic theology in subsequent decades. Stolz agreed with those who insisted that all Christians are called to the mystical life.[83] Where he differed from the neoscholastic views of the French Dominicans and others was in his claim that, since the sixteenth century, mystics had concentrated too much on the psychological investigation of mystical states to the detriment of the objective ground of mysticism in the grace of Christ communicated to believers through the sacraments and the liturgy of the church.[84] In order to understand the *theology* of mysticism, Stolz argued, it was necessary to begin with the scriptures and to study the thought of the great fathers of the East and the West. The Benedictine author did not deny the importance of Teresa and John of the Cross, and he claimed that his views were conformable to the teaching of St. Thomas, but he reversed the order of authorities by seeing the fathers and not the Spaniards as the prime witnesses. In doing so he advanced a theology of mysticism remarkably close to (though not identical with) the ecclesial and sacramental understanding of mysticism found in Eastern Orthodox Christianity and proposed in modern times by such authors as Vladimir Lossky in his *Essai sur la théologie mystique de l'Eglise d'Orient* (1944), translated in 1957 as *The Mystical Theology of the Eastern Church.*

The list of topics treated in *Theologie der Mystik* shows its difference from the standard scholastic treatments. Paul's experience of being rapt to the third heaven (2 Cor 12:1–5) is the starting point for the theology of mysticism, not Teresa's descriptions of the stages of prayer. Scriptural themes like the ascent to heaven, being in Christ, freedom from the power of the devil, and the restoration of the Adamic condition, are given extended discussion. Mysticism is viewed throughout as ecclesial, sacramental, liturgical, and therefore communal in nature. Mystical prayer is seen as a development of the life of grace that is essentially independent of feelings or psychological states.[85] Stolz agrees with those who define mysticism as the experience of God, and he seconds A. Gardeil's account of the direct and immediate nature of this connatural experience;[86] but the core of his position is the claim that "mysticism in the professed sense is a transpsychological experience of being included within the flow of divine life that is given in the sacraments, especially in the Eucharist."[87]

Only two of the many questions that arise from Stolz's important work can be addressed here. The first concerns the problem that many such "objective" and sacramental views of mysticism face: What, if anything, distinguishes Christian mysticism from the Christian life in general?[88] Stolz's answer is a customary one, based on the distinction between foundation and development. The mystical life in its foundation is nothing else than the Christian life; in its restricted sense (the sense in which we call only some Christians true mystics), it is the higher development of that root and foundation.[89] The second issue concerns the relation of Christian mysticism to non-Christian forms of mysticism, an area that had begun to attract considerable attention among Catholic philosophers and subsequently Catholic theologians. Stolz's rooting of mysticism in the life of the church led him to the view that Christian mysticism is not really comparable with other forms of mysticism at all.[90] His answer to Protestant theologians who would dismiss mysticism as a non-Christian diversion from true evangelical faith is to insist that mysticism is the essence of Christianity and that therefore *true* mysticism cannot be found outside it. Merely psychological comparisons of similar Christian and non-Christian "mystical" phenomena tell us nothing about the inner reality. This issue was to continue to be of moment in German Catholic studies of mysticism, as we shall see.

Roman Catholic theological discussion of mysticism since the Second World War has been on the whole less intense than in the first four decades of this century. The great shift in Catholic theology away from the dominant neoscholastic model that began with the rise of "la nouvelle théologie" in France in the 1940s and that witnessed the triumph of the so-called transcendental Thomisms connected with the names of Karl Rahner and Bernard Lonergan in the 1950s and 1960s, was given official encouragement by the abandonment of scholastic language and categories in documents of the Second Vatican Council. The quarter century that has elapsed since the Council has seen some important theological discussion of mysticism, but within the context of a broad range of theological options more concerned with redoing the foundations of theology than with spelling out the implications of these for the understanding of mysticism. Traditional Catholic views of mysticism were bound to be called into question in this challenging new theological world.

Not all Catholic writing on mysticism since 1945 has reflected these new theological views. A case in point can be found in the writings of Dom David Knowles (1896–1974), especially his *The English Mystical Tradition* (1961) and *The Nature of Mysticism* (1966). The former work, a much revised version of a book written in 1928, contains brief chapters introducing

Christian mysticism with lucid accounts of five English mystics. The latter is a short introduction to Christian mysticism written for the collection *The Twentieth Century Encyclopedia of Catholicism.* Knowles's writings on mysticism make no claim to originality, but they do provide clear and competent presentations of the standard neoscholastic view.

A far more important figure — and one more difficult to evaluate in any simple fashion — was the American Cistercian Thomas Merton (1915-1968). Merton was neither a systematic theologian nor a historian, but he was certainly a major spiritual — indeed, mystical — author, as well as a theological essayist of originality and profoundity. His influence, widespread during his lifetime, has shown no signs of abating since his death. Merton's life and writings will need to be taken up in detail when we look at contemporary mystics in the final volume; for now, it must be enough to list some of his most important discussions of the nature of mysticism.

Merton wrote several studies of classic mystical authors, both Christian and non-Christian,[91] as well as a number of works devoted to prayer and contemplation.[92] Some of these were in the form of journals or meditations on the nature and practice of prayer (e.g., *The Sign of Jonas* and *Bread in the Wilderness,* both published in 1953, and *No Man Is an Island* in 1955), while others were more analytic accounts that approach the genre of theological treatises (e.g., *The Ascent to Truth* of 1951, and *New Seeds of Contemplation* of 1962). Besides the materials issued during his lifetime, he left a large body of spiritual and other writings, some of which have subsequently been published. In addition, the extensive interest in Merton has produced more than a few books devoted to aspects of his theory of mysticism.[93]

The most important English-language Catholic theologian of the post-war period, the Canadian Jesuit Bernard Lonergan (1904-1984), wrote little specifically on the issue of mysticism, but Lonergan's project of reorganizing theology through the creation of a more adequate theological method based on critical cognitional theory (i.e., the subject's self-appropriation of what it means to know) has rightly been claimed to offer significant new possibilities for the theology of mysticism.[94] Lonergan's interest in the writings on mysticism of his fellow Jesuit William Johnston showed that he was aware of the importance of the topic, however little direct attention he gave to it.[95] In recent years a series of studies has sought to explore the implications of Lonergan's method for the study of mysticism.[96]

The notion of religious conversion is at the heart of whatever mystical theology might be developed out of the Jesuit's thought. Lonergan's fundamental work, *Insight* (1957) centered on intellectual conversion and largely left religious conversion to one side, but when he turned his attention from general cognitional theory to theological method in *Method in Theology* (1972) it was impossible not to take up the issue of how theology relates to faith defined as the knowledge born of the love experienced in religious conversion.[97] Religious conversion is spoken of both as "being in love with God" and as "the gift of God's love poured out in our hearts" (Rom 5:5).[98] James R. Price argues that the correct way to differentiate religion from mysticism in a Lonerganian perspective is to insist that "being in love with God" (an active experience) is identified with religious consciousness as such, while the inner experience of the reception of God's love is specifically mystical consciousness, that which grounds the mystical life and the theology that reflects upon it.[99] Religious consciousness is intentional insofar as it is directed to God as its goal; it therefore partakes of the mediated differentiations inherent in all intentional drives. Mystical consciousness, on the other hand, is a "mediated return to immediacy" in which a vital intersubjective relationship of union is experienced between God and the human person.[100]

Lonergan does not explicitly discuss the relation between religious and mystical consciousness. Price argues that Lonergan's distinction between consciousness as such and attention to consciousness implies a continuing mutual interaction between the two forms rather than any simple three-stage sequential relation (i.e., from unconscious mysticism defined as the reception of God's love, through mediated religious consciousness, to an explicit awareness of the intersubjective union given in the gift).[101] Such a view bears interesting analogies to Karl Rahner's twofold notion of mysticism, both forms of which can exist in either unthematized or thematized ways (see below); but in the absence of explicit treatment in Lonergan it is difficult to be more precise in comparing the two. Finally, it should be noted that in grounding his notion of mysticism in the structure of human consciousness as such, Lonergan implies that all true mysticism, whatever the differences in its mediated content, is essentially the same in being rooted in the consciousness of our reception of divine love.

One major problem with Lonergan's treatment of mysticism is its lack of development. The very fact that the Canadian said so little about mysticism itself, whereas his disciples have begun to say so much, does not necessarily prove them wrong, but it does give one pause. Certainly, Lonergan's attempt to rebuild theology on the basis of critical cognitional theory would have to be judged a failure if it left no room for the knowing involved in mystical consciousness. Despite the intellectualist cast of his mind, Lonergan never denied that mystical knowing was real knowing — if one that could only be appropriated by those who had undergone religious conversion. But Lonergan himself said little about what this knowing might be. Thus, his own writings do not provide a mystical theology, though they may offer the basis for one. Important elements of Lonergan's theology will enter into the final, more constructive part of my presentation in the last volume of this work.

France, the home of such intense discussion of mysticism among both Catholic theologians and other intellectuals before World War II, has taken a less central role since then. The shift to positive theology, especially to the study of the fathers, was among the great contributions of French theology of the past fifty years. The Jesuit scholar Jean Daniélou (1905–1974) was a leading figure in this return to the sources through his writings and his role as one of the founders of the text series *Sources chrétiennes*. Daniélou's interest in mysticism was not dominated by neoscholastic concerns, but was primarily historical in character.[102] Even those French theologians who pursued more theoretical questions about the nature of mysticism frequently had a different agenda and appealed to a rather different range of sources than their predecessors.

Henri de Lubac, S.J., one of the suspect leaders of "la nouvelle théologie" in the 1940s, but now a cardinal, may be taken as an example. De Lubac wrote little directly on mysticism, though in a preface he contributed to a collection of papers on the topic he advanced a position quite close to that we have seen in Anselm Stolz. Here he argued that Christian mysticism, conceived of as a deeper interiorization of the mystery of faith, is rooted in the scripture, the liturgy, and the sacramental life of the church. It must be carefully distinguished at all times from non-Christian forms.[103]

The relation between Christian and non-Christian mysticism has been one of the key questions in recent Catholic theology of mysticism. Are there forms of true mysticism outside Christianity, or are the striking similarities among mystics of diverse religions really illusory? Louis Gardet, who worked extensively in Islamic as well as Christian mysticism, took a more positive view than de Lubac, distinguishing between the natural mysticism of immanence and the supernatural mysticism that proceeds by way of love and negation, but finding both forms present in Christianity and also at times in other religions.[104] A related issue that confronted those theologians who emphasized the nature of mysticism as open to all Christians who have been given the grace of faith concerned the relation of faith to mystical knowing. Leopold Malévez, S.J., wrote some important studies on this in the 1960s.[105]

Despite these French contributions, it is fair to say that the most significant Catholic writing on mysticism of the recent decades has come from Germany. Karl Rahner, S.J. (1904–1984) was interested in both the historical and constructive dimensions of mysticism throughout his long career.[106]

Rahner has been called the "Doctor mysticus" of the twentieth century.[107] The case has even been made that the whole of his vast theological *oeuvre* is an attempt to mediate between his appropriation of some of the classics of Christian mysticism, especially Bonaventure and Ignatius of Loyola, and the dynamic ontology he developed from his reading of Aquinas, Kant, Hegel, Maréchal, and Heidegger.[108] Rahner's powerful and moving prayers and meditations are further indications of the interaction between the personal and the more theoretical sides of his contributions to the current understanding of mysticism.

The easiest access to Rahner's theology of mysticism is through the selections on this topic to be found in the anthology of his writings published in 1982 under the title *Praxis des Glaubens: Geistliches Lesebuch* (*The Practice of Faith: A Handbook of Contemporary Spirituality* [1983]).[109] These pieces, however, need to be seen within the broad contours of Rahner's total theological program, which is laid out (if only, as he insisted, in introductory fashion) in his *Grundkurs des Glaubens: Einführung in den Begriff des Christentums* of 1976 (*Foundations of Christian Faith: An Introduction to the Idea of Christianity* [1978]), and fleshed out in the numerous studies contained in the seventeen volumes of his *Schriften zur Theologie* (translated as *Theological Investigations*).

The orientation of the finite subject to the infinite mystery of God is the central theme of Rahner's theology. No theologian of the modern era has been a more powerful spokesman of the apophatic tradition —"the night that alone makes our tiny lights visible and enables them to shine forth."[110] For Rahner, God always remains the ultimate mystery, even in the beatific vision. Like Gregory of Nyssa and many other Christian mystics, he holds that progress toward perfection consists in the ever-deepening and more direct awareness of the divine incomprehensibility.

The dogmatic key to Rahner's notion of mysticism rests in his distinction between the transcendental experience (i.e., the a priori openness of the subject to the ultimate mystery) and the supernatural experience in which divine transcendence is no longer a remote and asymptotic goal of the dynamism of the human subject but is communicated to the subject in closeness and immediacy.[111] Rahner insists on the reciprocal unity (not identity) of the experience of God and the experience of the self that is achieved in interpersonal relations: ". . . unity between love of God and love of neighbor is conceivable only on the assumption that the experience of God and the experience of the self are one."[112] On both the transcendental and the supernatural levels (that is, God as question and God as answer), one must always keep in mind the important difference between the experience itself and its subsequent thematization or objectivization in conscious reflection as a mode of categorical thought. Thematization can never capture the fullness of the original experience, but experience calls out for thematizing in order to be communicated to others.[113]

This is the reason why Rahner speaks of mysticism in two ways. On the one hand, "there is the mysticism of everyday life, the discovery of God in all things," that is, the unthematized experience of transcendence at the basis of all human activity.[114] The German Jesuit's theology of grace, the underpinning of the whole discussion from the dogmatic point of view,[115] suggests that this experiential substratum always operates in a mode elevated by grace, that is, one in which God has already answered the call he placed in humanity, though this may not be evident from a psychological consideration of the thematized knowledge of the acts themselves.[116] On the other hand, there are the "special" mystical experiences which Rahner admits can be found both inside and outside Christianity. As far as Christian belief is concerned, these experiences cannot be conceived of as constituting some intermediate state between grace and glory; they are a variety or mode of the experience of grace in faith.[117] Although Rahner is resolute in his opposition to any "elitist" view that would find in mysticism a higher form of Christian perfection beyond the loving service of the neighbor, he does speak of special mystical experiences as a paradigmatic intensification of the experience of God that is open to all.[118] Thus, mystical experience may be *indirectly* higher "inasmuch as the mystical phenomenon (as cause and effect) may be an index of a Christian's acceptance of the grace of God's self-communication proferred him or her in an existentially very intense degree."[119] But Rahner insists that *whether* mystical experience is indeed the height of the normal development of the subject is a question for empirical psychology to judge and is not in the domain of theology as such.[120] This is because the experience under consideration, which Rahner sometimes describes as "Versenkungserfahrungen" or "Versenkungsphänomene" (better translated as "depth experiences" than as "altered states of consciousness" or "experience of suspension of the faculties") are essentially natural phenomena, that is, potentialities of the subject as such, whether elevated by grace or not. If such "Versenkungserfahrungen" are judged by psychology to be a part of the normal maturation process of the subject, then mystical experience in the special sense, whether thematized or not, would be integral to becoming a true human and a true Christian. (Rahner's sympathies seem to lie with this position, just as his view of grace suggests that all "Versenkungserfahrungen," whether within or without Christianity, are not merely natural but are already empowered by grace.)[121]

What is the role of Christ and the church in Rahner's view of special mystical experience? Is Christ merely an addendum to the flight of the soul to God? Though Rahner does not discuss the role of Christ often in speaking of mysticism, in the light of his total theological program there can be no doubt that the Christ event is central for all mystical experience. The historical reality of Jesus as communicated through the life of the church is constitutive of all forms of salvific relation to God. Our relation to Jesus is a unique one in which an *immediate* relation to God is communicated through the mediacy of the incarnate Savior.[122] This is why the German Jesuit insists that "Christ is the 'fruitful model' *per se* for a committed reliance on the mystery of our existence."[123]

It will be evident from this brief survey that Rahner's theology of mysticism offers original and profound answers to some of the basic questions in the modern discussion of mysticism. On the issue of whether mystical experience represents a higher level beyond the ordinary life of faith (the root of many Protestant objections to mysticism) Rahner's answer is "no" theologically and "maybe" psychologically. On the relation of Christian to non-Christian mysticism, he extends his famous thesis concerning the "anonymous Christian" to include the category we can term that of the "anonymous Christian mystic," that is, he believes that some non-Christian forms of mysticism are true expressions of the special experience of God's answer given in Jesus Christ, though not explicitly thematized or known as such.[124]

One crucial ambiguity in Rahner's admittedly selective treatment of mysticism concerns his understanding of special mystical experience. Just what does he mean by "Versenkungserfahrungen"? No extended discussion or typology of such experiences emerges from his writings, although he recognizes the need for "more precise conceptualization" in this area, one in which the contributions of mystics, as well as those of metaphysicians, theologians, and psychologists will all have to be heard.[125] At times, Rahner seems to suggest that the special mystical experiences are to be equated with the extraordinary states described by some Christian mystics; at other times, he speaks of two dimensions of mystical experience conceived analogously according to the models of the traditional *via negativa* and *via eminentiae* and capable of being encountered in everyday life.[126]

Along with this ambiguity, some will also be inclined to wonder if Rahner's claim that empirical psychology has the decisive word in this area does not imply a questionable compartmentalization. To appeal to the necessity of dialogue among various specialists (which Rahner insists upon) is one thing; to say "this is not my task" (which he also does at times) is another. In confronting some of the difficult questions involving the nature of mystical experience, Rahner often seems to throw the ball to another player. Finally, one may wonder if the gap that Rahner creates between experience and its thematization is sometimes so conceived that it hinders attempts to relate the two.[127] Rahner's lack of attention to the ways in which language and other forms of objectification help shape experience itself — even a priori experience — suggest that his account needs broadening in this important area.[128]

Hans Urs von Balthasar (1905–1988), another major voice in contemporary Catholic theology, has also written much on both the historical and constructive investigation of mysticism. Though he and Rahner part company on many issues, they are at one in seeing mysticism as a central issue in theology.

Von Balthasar's early work on mysticism was largely historical in character. At the beginning of his writing career, he produced a trilogy devoted to three great Greek patristic mystical authors, Origen, Gregory of Nyssa, and Maximus the Confessor.[129] Appearing just a few years after Anselm Stolz's groundbreaking book and at the same time that French Catholic scholars were returning to the fathers, von Balthasar's books were a sign of an important shift that was taking place in Catholic theology. Throughout his career, von Balthasar has been interested in modern mystics, writing on Elizabeth of Dijon and on Therese of Lisieux;[130] he also authored an important book on contemplative prayer, *Das betrachtende Gebet* (1955), translated as *Prayer* in 1963.

Von Balthasar's major work, *Herrlichkeit: Eine theologische Ästhetik* (three volumes published in seven parts from 1961; various parts are now available in English under the title *The Glory of the Lord: A Theological Aesthetics*), contains much on mysticism.[131] A full treatment of von Balthasar's views would demand a careful study of this massive and imposing work. Aspects of his treatment, like those of Lonergan and Rahner, will reappear in the last part of the final volume of this work. For the purposes of this brief sketch, we are fortunate that the Swiss theologian has provided a brief summary of his position in a programmatic essay entitled "Zur Ortsbestimmung christlicher Mystik" ("On the Orientation of Christian Mysticism") published in 1974.[132]

In this essay, von Balthasar addresses many of the same issues that we have already seen surfacing in postwar Catholic thought on mysticism in general, especially the question of whether or not all Christians are called to be mystics by the fact of their baptism, and the problem of the relation of Christian to non-Christian mysticism. He begins by distinguishing between the objective coordinate of mysticism found in the revelation of the mystery of Christ and the subjective coordinate expressed in the traditional definition of mysticism as *cognitio Dei experimentalis* ("experiential knowledge of God").[133] Von Balthasar develops his position on mysticism through a quasi-Hegelian argument according to thesis, antithesis, and synthesis.

The thesis of the observed similarity between Christian and at least some forms of non-Christian mysticism is challenged by a theological antithesis that insists on the separation of the two. Von Balthasar recognizes that there are two forms of the antithesis, the Protestant version, which claims that mysticism has nothing to do with Christian faith, and a frequently held Catholic version that only Christian mysticism is true mysticism. His synthesis (only hinted at in this essay) is an original version of the Catholic view that judges the correctness of Christian forms of mysticism according to three theological criteria.[134]

Von Balthasar roots his sense of the distinctiveness of Christian mysticism in the biblical message, especially in the primacy of divine initiative over human effort, the stress on obedience over union as the ultimate religious value,[135] and the uniqueness of the mediation of the Incarnate Word as the expression of the unknowable God. These biblical themes lead him to a relativizing, though not a rejection, of the mysticism found in many classic Christian authors.[136] The synthesis that can appropriate "corrected" views of mysticism into the Christian life operates on these basic criteria: (1) the norm of the supremacy of the reciprocal love of God and neighbor; (2) the necessity for conformity to the pattern of Christ; and (3) the insistence on the continued unknowability of God in and through his manifestation in the Word made flesh.[137] All three of these criteria bear comparison with Rahner's view of mysticism, though von Balthasar displays greater suspicion about mysticism's place in Christianity than does Rahner or most Catholic theologians of the present century. Von Balthasar, like Anselm Stolz or Albert Schweitzer, insists that only Christian mysticism is true mysticism. This strong separation is surely one of the more controversial features of his approach.

The balance sheet of twentieth-century theological study of mysticism presents an uneven picture. Continental Protestant thought, despite the work of Troeltsch and Schweitzer, has maintained the suspicion found in Ritschl and Harnack. English historical theologians, both Anglican and Catholic, contributed much by way of information but less by way of theory. Continental Catholic theology, first in France before World War II and then in Germany mostly after the war, made major contributions but with ambiguous results. The neoscholastic authors took on important issues, but in an overly conceptual and ahistorical way that has relegated most of their tomes to the dusty shelves of libraries. Some consensus did emerge (at least among Catholics) that mysticism was not a special higher or elite form of Christian perfection, but rather a part of the exigence of the life of faith itself, but there was no common agreement on how the dynamics of this were to be understood. More recently, Catholic theologians widened the historical scope of their investigation of Christian mysticism and tried in various ways to reformulate the traditional questions concerning mysticism in the light of the postscholastic era. Both of these new directions are part of the context in which these volumes are being written and will be taken up again in the final volume of *The Presence of God.*

SECTION 2

PHILOSOPHICAL APPROACHES TO MYSTICISM

It is impossible to make a hard and fast discrimination between generally theological approaches to mysticism on the one hand and philosophical and psychological approaches on the other. Some of the works to be considered in this section were written by well-known philosophers from neutral religious positions and would be universally understood as philosophical; others are the work of philosophers or thinkers who wrote more or less directly from a religious viewpoint. Many of these works can be understood as contributions to the theoretical study of the human psyche, and therefore are at once philosophical and psychological in nature. Given the scope of the literature, I will have space to consider only a few of the most significant contributions, but I hope that this will be sufficient to provide a sense of some of the important philosophical issues in the study of mysticism.

Few would argue about beginning a survey of twentieth-century philosophical studies of mysticism with William James (1842–1910), the influential American pragmatist philosopher whose book *The Varieties of Religious Experience* (1902) is one of the classic philosophies of religion of the modern era. The fact that James was successively both professor of psychology and of philosophy at Harvard suggests his importance to both areas of study, as is evident from his account of mysticism in chapters 16 and 17 of *Varieties.*

Among the advantages of James's treatment of mysticism is the fact that it is embedded in an encompassing theory of religion as the lived experience of individuals.[1] For James religion is a "faith-state" consisting of essentially similar feelings and actions coupled with a variable intellectual content or creed. The union with the "more" in the universe that religion effects helps us to overcome our sense of wrongness and empowers us to the strenuous mood that fosters true ethical life.[2] While James does not reduce religion to mysticism, he does claim "that personal religious experience has its root and center in mystical states of consciousness."[3]

The second advantage of James's discussion is the way in which he tries to situate mystical consciousness into a progressive continuum of what he called the "mystical group" and what today many would call altered states of consciousness, though it is not exactly clear in what sense all these should be termed properly mystical states.[4] James prefaced his collection of texts illustrating this continuum with his famous four marks of mystical experience: ineffability, the characteristic of defying expression; noetic quality, that is, the illuminative aspect; and two of lesser importance, transiency and passivity.[5] The second mark, that of mystical experience's noetic quality, highlights one of the essential issues in James's presentation. The Harvard professor obviously places the essence of religion and mystical consciousness primarily on the side of feeling or affect, but he also asserts that mysticism must have noetic content, though this intellectual component should be conceived of in "perceptual," that is, direct and intuitive terms, rather than in the conceptual categories of discursive reasoning.[6] This kind of move is not unlike what many traditional Christian mystics claimed when they said that love itself was a form of knowing; but James, at least here, does not really provide an adequate epistemological analysis of the relation of perceptual and conceptual knowing to buttress this crucial part of his account. In what sense can both kinds of knowing be considered activities of the intellect, or is perceptual knowing only a particular kind of feeling? James's *Varieties* does not give us immediate answers to these questions.

The relationship between affect and thought becomes more complex and problematic as James proceeds. In investigating what the "theoretic drift" of mystical states is, he argues that they point in the direction of the philosophical doctrines of optimism and monism, that is, they foster expanded consciousness and the "overcoming of all the usual barriers between the individual and the Absolute."[7] At first this leads him to posit the universal oneness of all mysticism "hardly altered by differences of clime or creed," a position soon qualified, or perhaps reversed, when he turns his attention to the question of whether mystic states should be considered to have authority for those who do not share them. From this perspective, the varieties of religious and nonreligious contexts within which mysticism has appeared argue against any specific intellectual content to mystic claims. His conclusion deserves quotation in full:

> The fact is that the mystical feeling of enlargement, union, and emancipation has no specific intellectual content whatever of its own. It is capable of forming matrimonial alliances with material furnished by the most diverse philosophies and theologies, provided only that they can find a place in their

framework for its peculiar emotional mood. We have no right, therefore, to invoke its prestige as distinctively in favor of any special belief. . . .[8]

The monist drift of mysticism (and one presumes its optimism too) are the result of "over-beliefs," intellectual and religious systems of thought that are subsequently grafted onto the affective mystical states of consciousness in order to try to communicate them to a wider audience.

It is clear from James's other writings that he thought that the monist over-belief was an incorrect interpretation of mystical experience, because, as Don Browning has put it, it collapsed "any vestige of distance between God and the individual, thereby rendering impossible the partial separatedness, freedom and agency necessary for moral action."[9] Mystical states for James put us in contact with the subconscious self, and the subconscious self in turn is in contact with the vaster world in which God is to be found. What James rejects is the over-beliefs which interpret this God in strictly supernatural fashion and which view the experience of union monistically. His preference (suggested, but not spelled out in his paper on Benjamin Paul Blood) was for a "pluralistic mysticism" consonant with his own view of "piecemeal supernaturalism" and a "finite God."[10]

James has been much criticized for his concentration on the personal and private side of religion to the exclusion of the institutional, which is not to say that he did not have a highly developed social understanding of the human person's relation to God.[11] This lack of attention to the institutional context of religious forms of mysticism is at least part of the reason for some of the ambiguities found in his account, but the fundamental problem is deeper. James's way of distinguishing between the affective state of mystical consciousness and the conceptual over-beliefs of a philosophical and theological nature grafted onto it can scarcely do justice to the complex interactions between experience and interpretation, on the one hand, and feeling and thought, on the other. This also leaves him unable to give serious attention to the more speculative and intellectual forms of mysticism in Western religious history, as John E. Smith notes.[12] Mysticism for James is both cognitive and not cognitive, but we are never sure how.

Baron Friedrich von Hügel (1852–1925), a friend of Ernst Troeltsch and Cuthbert Butler, as well as correspondent with James on mysticism, was one of the most learned men of his time. His two-volume work *The Mystical Element of Religion as Studied in Saint Catherine of Genoa and her Friends*, first published in 1908 and reprinted with a new introduction in 1923, is one of the masterpieces of the modern study of mysticism. Its length, the cumbersomeness of von Hügel's Germanic style, and the puzzling genre of the book, which mingled elements of a philosophy of religion, a historical account of Catherine of Genoa, and a philosophical-theological account of mysticism, make it difficult, though still rewarding, reading. This work was thirty years in the making, and seven years in the writing; von Hügel described it as "an essay on the Philosophy of Mysticism, illustrated by the life of Caterinetta Fiesca Adorna and her friends."[13] Von Hügel's basic contribution is probably best viewed as philosophical, though his philosophy of religion and of mysticism is overtly written from a believer's perspective.

The baron begins his work by identifying the three chief forces in Western civilization as Hellenism, Christianity, and science, powers whose proper harmonious interaction is necessary for the health of society (chap. 1). The second chapter, the major statement of von Hügel's philosophy of religion, uses Christianity to present the three elements found in all religions, elements that he had been helped to develop by reading an early work of William James entitled "Reflex Action and Theism."[14] Religion for von Hügel consists in the interaction of the historical-institutional element related to sense and memory (the Petrine dimension of Christianity), the analytical-speculative element related to reason (the Pauline dimension), and finally the intuitive-emotional element related to will and action (the Johannine dimension). Expressed as Institutionalism, Intellectualism, and Mysticism, these are the three major elements or modalities of religion. Von Hügel insists on their dialectical relationship. Left to themselves each element tends to minimize or suppress the others. The goal of their harmonious interaction is the production of the mature spiritual personality.

Having laid down the elements of his philosophy of religion in part 1, von Hügel turned to the study of Catherine as a test case of the mystical-volitional personality in part 2 (chaps. 3–8). More important for his mystical theory is part 3, "Critical Studies" (chaps. 9–15), where issues raised by the study of Catherine and her circle lead to a detailed, though scarcely complete or systematic, exposition of the nature of mysticism.

The final three chapters contain the heart of von Hügel's argument, though his digressive style allows key issues to emerge almost anywhere in the long book. Von Hügel investigates four "ultimate questions" which flow from the religious positions of Catherine and the other great Christian mystics: (1) the relations between morality, mysticism, philosophy, and religion; (2) mysticism and the limits of human knowledge; (3) mysticism and the nature of evil; and (4) the issue of personality, that is, the relations between the human spirit and the divine Spirit.[15] The discussion of the first issue allows the baron to introduce the presentation of one of the essential themes he felt set his position apart from that of Ritschl, Harnack, and their followers, namely, his emphasis on "inclusive mysticism" over against "exclusive mysticism."[16] Exclusive mysticism is the world-denying variety sprung from the Neoplatonic *via negativa*. Von Hügel criticizes it more discreetly, but no less ardently, than Dean Inge.[17] The higher inclusive mysticism is characterized by a love and appreciation for created reality, the necessity for the soul to transcend all special or ecstatic experiences in the mystical path, a continued occupation with contingent historical reality, and finally the soul's attention to God and Christ alone in the highest recollective stages. Exclusive mysticism has been a dangerous temptation in the history of Christianity; inclusive mysticism demonstrates that mystical religion and morality are closely allied, though by no means identical.[18] (Von Hügel's stress on inclusive mysticism, the dynamic and evolutionary character of his thought, and his insistence that modern religiousness must immerse itself in the material world and its tasks, at times make him sound surprisingly like a younger contemporary, Pierre Teilhard de Chardin.) One can well agree with von Hügel's delineation of the two ideal types or tendencies in the history of Christian mysticism without necessarily following him in placing the root of exclusive mysticism in Neoplatonism's influence on Christianity. This history will attempt to show that the role of Neoplatonism in the development of Christian mysticism is far more varied (and at least at times more positive) than von Hügel, Inge, and others allowed.

Von Hügel's consideration of mysticism and the limits of human knowledge and experience is one of the less successful parts of the work.[19] His unsystematic and murky epistemology does not provide much help for understanding what mystical "knowing" may be. On the third issue, the relation of mysticism to the problem of evil, von Hügel's anti-Platonic stance led him to the position that evil must be treated in terms of will and not only as the privation of being, so that its real, though subordinate, nature can be adequately understood. From this perspective he criticized the excessive optimism of much Christian mysticism.

The relation of mysticism and personality is treated in diffuse fashion in the fourteenth and fifteenth chapters of *The Mystical Element*. These final chapters are provocative, but problematic and obscure, raising as many questions as they answer.[20] Von Hügel's treatment of the relation between pantheism and mysticism allows him to express his option in favor of a form of "panentheism" as representative of the major Christian mystics.[21] This is a highly suggestive view, though in the absence of an evolved metaphysics it is hard to know precisely what kind of "panentheism" von Hügel would have defended.[22] In summarizing the extensive range of issues of the book in the final chapter, von Hügel takes up once more the relations between asceticism and mysticism and mysticism and the scientific habit of thought.

The baron ends by reiterating his emphasis on the necessity of the proper mediation of all three elements of religion — the institutional-historical, the rational-critical, and the mystical-operative — in the development of the mature religious personality.[23]

Along with the epistemological and metaphysical shortcomings of von Hügel's book, there are several important internal ambiguities in the view of religion and mysticism he puts forth. The baron's sense of the richness, dynamism, and dialectical interdependence of the three elements in religion is the source of much of the power of his view of mysticism, and the interdependence of these three elements in the religious personality is a key theme of the work.[24] But von Hügel never really presents us with a developed theory of personality, and the precise contours of the mediation of the three elements is not always clear. The developmental model employed, in which childhood corresponds to sense and memory, youth to question and argument, and maturity to intuition, feeling, and will, seems to imply that the mystical element is the highest of all;[25] but the major thrust of his thought centers on the interdependence and, one would presume, equality of the three. Despite these and other problems, *The Mystical Element of Religion* remains a classic, not least of all because Baron von Hügel, like his friend Ernst Troeltsch, insisted that mysticism does not make sense in itself, but only as one element in concrete religious life. One important conclusion of this (to be developed in these volumes) is that no single figure is ever *just* a mystic — a commonplace observation, perhaps, but one not always taken into account in studying the mystical element in various Christian thinkers.

Other philosophers in the English-speaking world also gave attention to mysticism in the early part of the century. William Ernest Hocking, a student of James and also a Harvard professor, gave a large place to mysticism in his 1912 work *The Meaning of God in Human Experience: A Philosophical Study of Religion.*[26] But not all philosophers were as sympathetic to the claims of mysticism. In 1914 Bertrand Russell published an essay "Mysticism and Logic," later reprinted in the volume *Mysticism and Logic and Other Essays.*[27] According to Russell, the mystical and scientific impulses have been the two motive forces behind the production of metaphysics, and the greatest philosophers, like Heraclitus and Plato, have mingled both elements in their lives and thought. Mysticism for Russell was "little more than a certain intensity and depth of feeling in regard to what is believed about the universe."[28] Important in itself as a motivating force, mysticism is more ambiguous when it seeks to become logical as a metaphysical system which is characterized by a stress on insight as opposed to discursive reason, a belief in the unity of all things, denial of the reality of time, and the teaching that all evil is merely appearance. Russell argues that such mystical philosophy, which originated in Parmenides and dominated the minds of the great metaphysicians down to Hegel and his followers, is wrong on all four counts, though "there is an element of wisdom to be learned from the mystical way of feeling, which does not seem to be attainable in any other way."[29] Russell's attempt to demonstrate the falsity of these four claims was primarily directed at Henri Bergson, a reminder that the most developed philosophical discussion of mysticism in the first four decades of the present century was to be found in the French-speaking and not the English-speaking world.

Rather than starting with Bergson, however, whose explicit writings on mysticism come from late in his career, I shall begin with Joseph Maréchal (1878–1944), a Belgian Jesuit whose earliest writings were in part a reaction to James. Maréchal is today best known as the ancestor of the "transcendental Thomisms" of Bernard Lonergan and Karl Rahner. His five-volume *Le point de départ de la métaphysique* (1927–49) attempted to provide the starting point for a new and more adequate metaphysics by revising the Kantian critique of noumenal knowing through the application of a revised Thomist epistemology based on the dynamism of the act of knowledge.[30] A recent student of Maréchal's view of mysticism, Jure Kristo, has suggested that "he had undertaken both the epistemological issue and the issue of mysticism in view of a more basic concern, namely, the possibility of knowing God."[31]

Maréchal's central essay on the nature of mysticism, entitled "On the Feeling of Presence in Mystics and Non-Mystics," first appeared in 1908 and 1909. In it he not only lays the basis for his many later pieces on the subject, but also briefly (and rather obscurely) announces the fundamental theme of his epistemological program. Subsequent pieces of 1912 ("Empirical Science and Religious Psychology" and "Some Distinctive Features of Christian Mysticism") were collected in 1926 to form the first volume of his *Études sur la psychologie des mystiques*. A series of subsequent papers devoted to both historical and theoretical issues in the investigation of mysticism was published as the second volume of the *Études* in 1937.[32] These two volumes by no means exhaust the riches of the Belgian Jesuit's studies on mysticism.[33]

Maréchal had received a doctorate in biology and studied experimental psychology in Germany. His critical reactions to psychological studies of mysticism, such as those of William James, James Leuba,[34] and Henri Delacroix, are evident throughout his many essays;[35] but his desire for a properly philosophical confrontation with psychology as an empirical approach to the problem of mysticism marks a new beginning in Catholic thought on the subject.

Maréchal the scientist never rejected the legitimacy of psychology's role in the investigation of mystical phenomena. Maréchal the philosopher sought to put such empirical investigation in its proper place. What he objected to in the investigations of Leuba and Delacroix (less so in James) was not the contribution they had made to the investigation of mystical states of consciousness, but their attempt to translate these "scientific facts" into laws and subsume them under an a priori empirical determinism. To put it in his own words, "I hold as certain that the failure of experimental determinism to explain integrally the facts, as much in biology and ordinary psychology as in religious psychology, manifests not only our accidental ignorances, but the partial incompetence of scientific methods."[36] For the Jesuit author, the evidence of increasing mental syntheses presented in empirical psychology suggests (though it cannot prove) the necessity for a philosophical analysis of the nature of human knowing.[37] In confronting the modern situation, however, Maréchal argues that the viewpoint of empirical determinism and that of a philosophical and theological analysis of mystical experience constitute two a priori viewpoints, starting places, or "prejudices" for the study of mysticism.[38] Recognizing the difficulty of convincing an empirical determinist to admit an ontological, let alone a theological, point of view, Maréchal advances two suggestions. The first is that both empirical determinists and philosophers can continue to share research and information on the level of data;[39] the second argues that a philosophical-theological perspective is truer both to the demands of the human structure of knowing and to the data presented in mystical texts.[40] From this perspective, he criticized the tendency of empirical students of mysticism to distort or disregard the evidence, dryly noting, "It is relatively easy to establish a theory explanatory of anything if one arrogates to oneself a discretionary power in dealing with the data of the problem."[41]

Having established the disciplinary location of his approach to mysticism, Maréchal proceeded to outline its theoretical basis, especially in his essay "The Feeling of Presence." As this important but difficult piece shows, he centered his study of mysticism not in the notion of union with God but in the psychological and philosophical investigation of the feeling of presence, that is, the a priori conditions for the possibility of a judgment of presence which is also a judgment of reality.[42] In somewhat tortuous fashion, Maréchal argues that the three fundamental elements in the judgment of reality ("a *certain unity of mind,* realised by the *co-ordination of the representations,* with the *concurrence of the feeling*") cannot be properly harmonized if these elements are viewed as anterior to the judgment, that is, if realism is a secondary phenomenon. "The empirical feeling of presence, the perception of a spatialised reality, is a particular case of *intuition* . . . defined [as] the direct assimilation of a knowing faculty with its object."[43] "The sense brings the subject *in contact with a real thing,* but *does not of itself discern reality.* The criticism of the sense-datum and the true perception of the real spring from a higher faculty—the faculty of 'being,' the *intelligence.*"[44]

For Maréchal the intelligence must be understood as fundamentally intuitive in its drive and finality. He calls it "a *faculty in quest of its intuition* — that is to say, of assimilation with Being, Being pure and simple, sovereignly one." In our ordinary experience, however, intelligence always meets not with Being pure, simple, and one, but with manifold and particular *beings,* and hence it must act constructively and synthetically in eliciting particular judgments of reality as real but limited expressions of its transcendental drive. "The affirmation of reality, then, is nothing else than the expression of the fundamental tendency of the mind to unification in and with the Absolute."[45] It is evident, then, what mystical experience, at least in its culminating point, will be for Maréchal. It is the direct, intuitive, unmediated contact in this life between the intelligence and its goal, the Absolute. In other words, it is "the *intuition of God as present, the feeling of the immediate presence of a Transcendent Being.*"[46]

Despite some obscurity, the basic logic of Maréchal's argument seems clear. Psychological data suggest and epistemological analysis demonstrates the existence of a transcendental dynamism in human knowing (what Bernard Lonergan would later call "the sheer unrestricted desire to know"). This drive, which Maréchal characterizes largely as a movement toward greater unification and integration, posits or demands a Transcendental Object to fulfill it.[47] (Maréchal says that otherwise the human mind would be condemned to perpetual becoming.) Catholic theology teaches and mystical texts witness to the possibility that direct, intuitive contact with this Transcendental Object, that is, God, can be achieved, if rarely, in this life. The special psychological states that characterize the preparation for this intuitive contact can be studied both by the empirical determinist and the believing philosopher and theologian. The former interprets them as the product of unconscious forces of the psyche; the latter, more correctly and with greater fidelity to the sources, understands them as a special gift of grace leading to an intellectual intuition of the immediate presence of God that is not itself subject to psychological investigation.[48]

Maréchal's analysis of the particular features of mysticism paid attention both to Christian mysticism and to comparative study. Recognizing the difficulty of finding any classical definition of mysticism through genus and species, he argued for an understanding of the term that would be comparatively homologous (i.e., searching for similar structures) and philosophically analogous (i.e., arguing for related but more adequate realizations, with Christian mysticism as the prime analogate).[49] He suggested, but did not develop in detail, the argument that the philosophical study of mysticism involves the interaction between the three fundamental themes of metaphysics — God, the self, and the world about us.[50]

From the comparative or descriptive point of view, Maréchal provides a broad definition in his essay "Reflections on the Comparative Study of Mysticism," stating that the mystical in any given environment consists of "a religious experience which is esteemed as superior to the normal: more direct, more intimate or more rare." Mysticism, then, involves three elements: a religious doctrine; certain unusual psychological facts; and a synthesis of the two, or ". . . an interpretation of the psychological facts as a function of the doctrine."[51] Maréchal's various comparisons of mysticisms, however, are not primarily descriptive but are more properly philosophical, analyzing the three components from his Christian philosophical perspective.[52] This accounts for the undisguised Christian "imperialism" in his work, despite the Jesuit's interest in other forms of mysticism and his willingness to admit the operation of mystical grace outside Christianity.[53] Maréchal's analysis of the doctrinal elements of mysticisms led him to distinguish three forms based on their underlying metaphysics: the negative mysticism of liberation found in Manichaeism and Buddhism; positive pantheistic mysticism, as in the Vedanta and Plotinus; and positive theistic mysticism which may be either natural or supernatural.[54]

In studying Christian mysticism, Maréchal carefully distinguished lower from higher mystical states, following a generally Augustinian discrimination of the types of visions.[55] As a monotheistic mystical system, Christian mysticism has three clearly defined grades. First, "integration of the *ego* and its objective content, under the mastery of the idea of a personal God." Second, "the transcendent revelation of God to the soul," frequently with the suspension of all other activities of the soul; and, finally, "a kind of readjustment of the soul's faculties" by which it regains contact with creatures "under the immediate and perceptible influence of God present and acting in the soul."[56] It was the second stage, one which the theological tradition treated under the term "ecstasy," that was the special object of much of Maréchal's historical investigation of Christian mysticism.[57] In his theoretical expositions, the Jesuit argued that ecstasy was a synthesis of empirical negativity characterized by the cessation of conceptual thinking (including consciousness of the dualism of the ego and the non-ego) and transcendental positivity in which the mind is immediately assimilated to

God in the supreme intuition or intellectual union for which it was created.[58]

Maréchal's dense and powerful philosophy of mysticism retains considerable promise for development even today. As the ancestor, however indirectly, of the transcendental Thomist approaches of both Rahner and Lonergan, his move to the epistemological a priori possibilities of mystical contact between the human and the divine Spirit opened up new avenues in Catholic study of mysticism. Maréchal writes, at least in part, as a Christian apologist (this accounts for the somewhat dated tone of his comparisons), but his insights may be open to reformulation from a more ecumenical viewpoint.

Maréchal has been accused of having too intellectual a view of mysticism, of neglecting the affective element in his concentration on "strictly intellectual intuition."[59] It is certainly unfortunate that he never developed an analysis of the role of love in the mystical path, but his basic philosophical position does not exclude it. In the fifth volume of *Le point de départ,* he insisted that reality constitutes not just an object to be known but a value to be desired—the Absolute is the goal of all intellectual and volitional effort.[60] In the *Studies,* he explored the affective context of the judgment of reality, noted that the special standpoint from which he was writing neglected the affective elements,[61] and insisted that in the intuition of Being the soul will realize "at once the supreme unity of speculation and the unmixed possession of love."[62]

Maréchal's theory of mysticism must be judged incomplete. It can also be accused of containing hidden ambiguities and confusions. Just as historians of Thomism have detected a perhaps unresolved confusion in the Belgian Jesuit between a philosophy of essence and a philosophy of existence,[63] contemporary theorists of mysticism may well be unhappy with his rather crude view of the relation between fact or experience and interpretation. Students of mystical texts may also be unsatisfied with the way in which, on the one hand, he insists that his own view of mysticism is supported by the evidence of the mystical texts and, on the other hand, he continues to use popular anthologies of excerpts from classic texts to demonstrate that all Christian mystics give basically the same message. Even greater inconsistency appears in the way in which he is prepared to appeal to the "direct" observation (rather than the theological interpretation) of Christian mystics regarding an imageless vision of God and then turn right around to argue that the theological judgments of a Teresa or a John of the Cross disqualify the legitimacy of empirical deterministic evaluations of such imageless states.[64] Maréchal's weaknesses are evident, but they do not compromise the promise he still offers for contemporary study of mysticism.

The discussion of mysticism in French philosophical circles evident in the first decades of this century grew in intensity in the 1920s and 1930s. Two of the most important French philosophers of the day, Henri Bergson (1859–1941) and Maurice Blondel (1861–1949) made significant contributions.[65]

Blondel's doctoral dissertation published in 1893 under the title *L'Action* proposed a new way of investigating the relation between philosophy and Christianity. He argued that a phenomenology of action could lead to a science of the concrete that would form the basis for a philosophy that would be at once religious and Catholic.[66] Beginning from a critical reflection on the concrete active subject in which Blondel discerned both a "willing will" (*la volonté voulante* — the dynamism common to all willing) and a "willed will" (*la volonté voulue* — the concrete will-act), the French philosopher sought to establish an autonomous but self-limiting philosophy directed to the fundamental issue of human destiny. For Blondel such a philosophy constitutes an appeal — or, perhaps better, a cry — for transcendence, a demonstration of humanity's *need* for the supernatural in general, though not a philosophical *proof* that any determined form of supernatural revelation, such as Christianity, is indeed the answer.[67] Blondel was attacked by rationalist philosophers for illegitimately importing religion into philosophy. He attempted to clarify the relations between Christianity and his new philosophy of action based on what he now called the "method of immanence" in his 1896 *Lettre sur l'apologetique,* a work that provoked intense criticism from conservative Catholic theologians and philosophers. The ensuing controversies, which were affected by the papal condemnation of the Modernist movement in 1907 (Blondel himself was never condemned), were part of the reason why he produced little new systematic work in the early decades of the twentieth century. After his retirement in 1927, Blondel issued major reconsiderations and expansions of his earlier thought in his so-called trilogy (*La Pensée; L'Être et les êtres;* and the second *L'Action* [1934–37]).

Blondel's explicit contribution to the discussion of mysticism appeared in a long essay of 1925 entitled "Le problème de la mystique."[68] Henry Bouillard has shown that this essay was written during a period when Blondel was rethinking important aspects of his philosophy, which may account for some of the problematic aspects of his presentation.[69] In 1922 in his *Le procès de l'intelligence* Blondel had analyzed the relations between mere notional knowledge and real or connatural knowing on the basis of a new appreciation of the Thomistic teaching on connaturality.[70] The essay on mysticism continues this line of thought by seeking to relate mystical knowing to more ordinary forms. Blondel's answer is not unlike Maréchal's, though developed from a different direction. Mysticism is a prolongation of the ordinary Christian life and hence all authentic human actions aim at mystical knowing and through it toward the beatific vision.[71] Connatural knowing, which Blondel insisted had both natural and supernatural modes, was the point of contact.[72]

The deficiencies of all lower forms of human reason indicate that God, if he is ever to be known in this life, can only be known through his self-communication in mystical knowing, a mode of knowledge that is no less reasonable for all that it surpasses inferior modes of rationality. In conformity with the basic thrust of his apologetic philosophy, Blondel says that the natural dynamism of the intellect calls out for unitive mystical knowledge, though the actual reception of the divine mystery remains a supernatural gift.[73] Citing John of the Cross, he resumes themes typical of central traditions in Western Christian mysticism, especially by emphasizing that in the highest mystical states extraordinary ecstatic experiences cease as love and knowledge are unified and subsumed in a harmonious life characterized by "a universal charity which reconciles and hierarchizes without confusion all the phases and degrees [of human existence]."[74] In this state the mystic "suffers actively and acts passively."[75]

Blondel's essay is certainly suggestive, especially in light of its affinities with Maréchal, but it is not as well integrated into the general development of his philosophy of action as it might be. The sharp contrast between notional and real knowing found in this essay and *Le procès de l'intelligence* is one that the author later abandoned, and it is not easy to know how much this might have affected his theory of mysticism because he did not return to the topic.[76] Finally, although his conclusions pick up on some important themes in the history of Christian mysticism, Blondel, unlike Maréchal, did not consciously seek to relate his theory to classic Christian mystical literature.

Henri Bergson, descendant of Polish and English Jews, published his doctoral thesis, *Essais sur les données immediates de la conscience,* in 1889. Given a chair at the Collège de France in 1900, it was the appearance of *L'Évolution creatrice (Creative Evolution)* in 1907 that gave him worldwide fame. Bergson's dynamic evolutionary philosophy burst on the scene with astonishing success, as witnessed both by the placing of his works on the Vatican's *Index of Prohibited Books* in 1914 (supposedly at the behest of Jacques Maritain) and his 1927 Nobel Prize for literature. In 1932, Bergson published his last major work, *Deux sources de la morale et de la religion (The Two Sources of Morality and Religion),* which contains his major discussion of mysticism. After his death, Bergson's prodigious reputation faded as quickly as it had grown; but, although his thought had little direct progeny, it served a useful role in breaking old molds and stimulating a new philosophical generation in France.[77]

As he grew older, Bergson came closer to Catholicism, reportedly refusing baptism at the end of his life to express solidarity with his persecuted people. The increasing religious dimension of his thought is evident in *The Two Sources* where Bergson's fundamental conviction about the centrality of *durée* ("real time," roughly the experience of life in memory) was applied to religion and morality. From this perspective, Bergson came to see mysticism as the direct expression of the evolutionary force at the heart of all reality, the force that he described as the *élan vital*. No twentieth-century thinker has given mysticism a larger role to play both in life in general and in religion — something that may help to explain why Bergson's views in this area have not exercised deep influence on subsequent discussion. If mysticism is virtually the same thing as Bergsonianism, it would seem difficult to make use of his insights on the former without also signing on for the latter.

The importance of Bergson's vitalistic philosophy lay in its attempt to free that great nineteenth-century discovery, evolution, from its mechanistic and deterministic origins. In *The Two Sources,* Bergson advanced this program by attempting to demonstrate, in Leszek Kolakowski's words, "that sociological investigations of religious phenomena and their functions are not only compatible with, but indeed support, a view of religious life as a form of communication with the original *élan* which penetrates the world and coincides with the spirit of the Creator."[78] To the two intermingled kinds of moral obligation discussed in chapter 1 (i.e., the morality of law based on the pressure of society and the morality of the person based on attraction, or creative heroism) correspond two basic types of religion, the static religion analyzed in the second chapter of the work and the dynamic religion that is the subject of the third chapter. Both forms of religion are necessary to the *élan vital* that carries life forward to ever-greater complexity and richness. If the static religious element is that which attaches the person to everyday life and society, it is the dynamic form of religion, or mysticism, which transcendentalizes the subject and society through the subject by allowing a direct, though always mixed, access to life itself, the *élan vital*.[79] Bergson is not notably clear about the relations between dynamic religion and the *élan vital*.[80] The goal of mysticism is not some fixed terminus, but the "creative effort which life itself manifests."[81] This creative effort is also the source of dynamic religion — "We represent religion, then, as the crystallization, brought about by a scientific process of cooling, of what mysticism has poured, while hot, into the soul of man."[82]

Bergson argues for the superiority of Christian mysticism, claiming that neither Greece nor India enjoyed the "complete mysticism" that he identified with "action, creation, love."[83] Like many traditional Christian mystics, as well as his contemporaries Maréchal and Blondel, he saw the heights of mysticism as fusing action and contemplation, or, as he put it, being characterized by "agitation in repose."[84] In a manner that might be described as vaguely Anselmian, he viewed mystical experience's direct contact with the *élan vital* as the basis for a form of intuitive "proof" for the existence of God.[85]

Baron von Hügel took mysticism to be one of the elements of concrete religions; Bergson made mysticism the source and inner reality of all religion. In the face of these bold claims it should not be surprising that Bergson was criticized by philosophers for his lack of analytic rigor, by orthodox Catholic theologians for the pantheism they found in his view of the *élan vital,* and even by Modernists, such as Alfred Loisy, who were rightly or wrongly thought to have applied his evolutionary philosophy to the development of Christianity.[86]

Jacques Maritain (1882–1973), a former student of Bergson, was converted to Catholicism in 1906 and soon became an ardent proponent of Neothomism, which led him into conflict not only with Bergson but also with Blondel.[87] Maritain, along with his contemporary and friend Étienne Gilson (1884–1976), was the premier spokesman for Neothomism in the middle decades of the century. Maritain was fascinated with mysticism throughout his life. His writings on the subject begin with the little book *De la vie d'oraison,* which he wrote with his wife, Raissa, in 1922 (translated as *Prayer and Intelligence* [1928]) and conclude with another joint effort, *Liturgie et contemplation* in 1959. The central studies appeared in the 1930s. The book generally credited with being his philosophical masterwork, *Distinguer pour unir, ou les degrés du savoir (Distinguish to Unite, or The Degrees of Knowledge),* which first appeared in 1932, the same year as Bergson's *The Two Sources,* contains a major treatment of the nature of mystical knowing in its second part. What Maritain attempted to accomplish in this notable work was to mount John of the Cross on the shoulders of Thomas Aquinas in order to present a complete picture of the full range of human modes of knowing.[88] Also important were two essays that first appeared in 1938, "The Natural Mystical Experience and the Void" and "Action and Contemplation."[89]

Maritain's map of the hierarchy of forms of knowledge that provides the basic structure of *The Degrees of Knowledge* is based on Aristotle and Thomas Aquinas, but the French philosopher's use of the schema of three degrees of abstraction differs from that of his predecessors in its direct concern for mystical knowing as the goal of all knowledge.[90] As the powerful opening chapter entitled "The Majesty and Poverty of Metaphysics" shows, true metaphysics calls out for, even if it does not formally demand, mysticism as its completion. "That, then, is the poverty of metaphysics (and yet its majesty, too). It awakens a desire for supreme union, for spiritual possession completed in the order of reality itself and not only in the concept. It cannot satisfy that desire."[91]

Maritain, like Gilson, believed the critical problem that modern philosophy had inherited from Descartes to be a pseudoproblem. His understanding of "critical realism" did not begin from the question, Is there knowledge of reality? but rather from the question, What is the knowledge of reality? because "the pure *cogito,* closed upon itself, can in no sense provide its starting point."[92] The lowest forms of science — that is, "knowledge perfect in its mode"— are the experimental sciences which form the basis for the first level of speculative or properly philosophical science, *physica,* or the philosophy of nature, which investigates the universe of the *sensible real.* Both the experimental sciences and the philosophy of nature exist on the first level of abstraction. The second level, abstraction from matter, is the realm of mathematics, which investigates the universe of the *praeter real;* the third level of abstraction studies the universe of the *transsensible,* beings that exist without matter and the principles of metaphysics. In his sketch of metaphysical knowledge (chapter 5), Maritain distinguishes between the *perinoetic* mode of intellection (knowledge through substitute-signs) found in the empirical sciences, and *dianoetic* intellection, or knowledge of things in their essences found in the philosophy of nature, mathematics, and metaphysics considered as the study of being *qua* being. *Ananoetic* intellection, or knowing by analogy, studies the transintelligible realm of pure spirit.[93] Ananoetic knowing in turn has three degrees: (1) the knowledge of created pure spirits, (2) the knowledge of the existence of God (both of these belong to metaphysics as natural theology), and finally (3) the ananoetic knowledge of faith which comes about by means of a revealed "superanalogy."[94]

In this final stage, which Maritain called uncircumscriptive knowledge, God is better grasped by a knowing that is "no-ing," or a negative theology. It forms the point of contact for the mystical knowledge of God analyzed at length in the second part of *The Degrees of Knowledge* (chapters 6–9). Here Maritain distinguishes, artificially I believe, between a negative theology that is a purely intellectual apophaticism pretending to be mystical (Neoplatonic in origin) and a negative theology that springs from the connaturality of love and is therefore the expression of true mystical experience.[95] (The rigidity of the French philosopher's ardent Thomism made it almost impossible for him to view any other philosophical system according to its own intentions.)

In analyzing Maritain's teaching on mysticism, it may be helpful to distinguish mystical experience, mystical theology, and mystical language. Maritain defines mystical experience as "an experimental knowledge of the deep things of God" or "a possession-giving experience of the Absolute."[96] The primary conditions for this experience in the ontological order are sanctifying grace and the indwelling of the Trinity; in the operational order they are "the gifts of the Holy Ghost and the knowledge by connaturality due to charity."[97] This last condition constitutes the nodal point of Maritain's theory of mysticism — loving connaturality is crucial for his understanding of the phenomenon.[98]

The essay entitled "The Natural Mystical Experience and the Void" is especially helpful in laying out four modes of connaturality: the affective connaturality of the practical moral order, the intellectual connaturality of the scientist and philosopher, the creative connaturality of poetic knowledge, and "connaturality by nescience," which may be either intellectual or affective in nature.[99] Here Maritain goes beyond *The Degrees of Knowledge* in two areas. First, he admits the possibility of a natural mystical experience, that is, "a metaphysical experience of the substantial *esse* of the soul by means of negative, or rather annihilating, intellectual connaturality."[100] This experience, which Maritain associated primarily with Indian mysticism as a form of lived *via negationis*, "attains existence by means of the act of the abolition of everything else." It reaches God in an indirect way, that is, insofar as he gives being to the soul, not as he is in the depths of his own reality. Concerning this natural mystical experience Maritain observes that "inasmuch as it is a purely negative experience, it neither confuses nor distinguishes" the absolute of the soul and the divine Absolute, though philosophical thought in reflecting on the experience runs the danger of monistically identifying the two. The analysis of the four modes of connaturality also allows Maritain to suggest, though not to flesh out, the important observation that the different kinds of connaturality intermingle and interact with each other on both the natural and the supernatural levels inside and outside Christianity.[101] It might be noted in passing that Maritain's discussion of the relation between natural and supernatural mystical experience would bear interesting comparison with Karl Rahner's notion of the natural and supernatural modes of the "depth experience" (*Versenkungsphänomene*), though Maritain would insist on a difference in the content of the experience that Rahner would not share.[102]

Thus, "supernatural mystical contemplation makes use of the connaturality of love in order to know as unknown the Godhead."[103] Basing himself on Thomas Aquinas and John of St. Thomas (the seventeenth-century commentator whom Maritain found the most faithful interpreter of the Angelic Doctor), the French philosopher proceeded to analyze the speculative implications of the connaturality of love in *The Degrees of Knowledge* in considerable detail. He stressed two important elements of traditional teaching on the nature of mystical experience: that mystical experience gives *immediate* contact with God and that this contact unites both love and knowledge. Ever the good Thomist, Maritain distinguished between the absolute immediacy of the beatific vision and the relative immediacy by which God is attained in the connaturality of love. To the mystic, God is no longer known *through* the created effect as an *objectum quod* (i.e., something known in itself and as a means to know something else) but solely by means of (*objectum quo*) the *effectus amoris filialis,* God's loving work in the soul.[104] The union of love with God is, as Maritain insisted, essentially the expression of the gifts of the Holy Spirit at work in the soul. Since the gifts are already inchoatively given to all Christians at baptism, Maritain had no doubts about the universality of the call to mystical contemplation, however varied the ways that the call was responded to and lived out in particular lives.[105]

Maritain's discussion of the nature of union and its relation to love and knowledge in this life and the next is a detailed and illuminating combination of the teaching of Aquinas and John of the Cross. There can, of course, be no question of essential union between God and the soul; the consummated marriage that John of the Cross describes is understood as a loving union of "one spirit" not "one being" (cf. 1 Cor 6:17), "the immaterial intussusception by which the other within me becomes more me than myself."[106] To the *esse intentionale,* the "being of knowledge" in which the knower and known become one thing, there corresponds the "intentional being of love," the ecstatic movement by which the self is alienated in the other.[107] This union involves both love and knowledge, though obviously not the knowledge of reason:

> *Above* nature, *above* reason — yes, that is where John of the Cross leads us: into the supernatural order, into the suprarational denseness of divine wisdom and faith. *Outside* of nature, *outside* of reason — no, he does not want that, he abhors the unreasonable.[108]

According to Maritain's reading of John of the Cross, three things come to pass in this union of spiritual marriage: we come to love God as he loves us because uncreated love becomes the agent of all the soul does; the soul "gives God back to God"; and finally, the soul comes to partake of the very life of the Trinity.[109]

Maritain's understanding of mystical experience (i.e, mystical theology's analysis of mystical experience) is complemented by remarks on both mystical theology as such and mystical language, that is, the forms under which mystics express themselves. The scope and purpose of *The Degrees of Knowledge* required Maritain to give explicit attention to mystical science's place in the map of human sciences, a task addressed at the beginning of chapter 8.[110] If Thomas Aquinas is the doctor of the highest communicable knowledge, the "speculatively practical" science of theology and its teaching on contemplation and union, John of the Cross is the supreme teacher of the "practically practical" science of mystical theology.[111] Their respective teachings are in full accord, though proceeding from different perspectives.[112] Both mystics and mystical theologians need to express themselves in human language, however ultimately incommunicable mystical experience itself may be. Hence Maritain's works also contain some partial and not always satisfactory comments on the nature of mystical language. Since the language of the "practically practical" science must be different from that of a purely speculative or a "speculatively practical" science, he argues that philosophical language speaks about reality "without touching it," whereas "mystical language seeks to divine reality as if by touching it without seeing it."[113] Thus, the predominantly psychological and affective language of the mystics allows for formulas that are theologically incorrect but acceptable, save in the case of those mystics, like Meister Eckhart, who confuse the realms.[114] Unfortunately, the grounds on which Maritain discriminates legitimate separation of languages from illegitimate confusion are not spelled out, so that his examples seem to be based on personal preference rather than argument.

In this area, Maritain seems to employ an extrinsicist theory of the relation of language to thought that has been increasingly criticized in recent years and that seems particularly distorting in the investigation of mystical texts. Maritain's difficulties in dealing with the use of erotic language by the mystics, which he almost grudgingly admits as the most direct analogy to mystical love,[115] are especially puzzling in the case of a thinker who gives affective connaturality such a central role. All in all, it appears that this master of philosophical language found it hard to avoid freezing mystical language within conceptual categories often foreign to it.

It would be tempting, but altogether too easy, to accept Maritain's claim that his theory of mysticism is nothing other than that of Thomas Aquinas and John of the Cross themselves. Much as he tried to be faithful to his two mentors, Maritain was still an interpreter, and philosophers and historians of philosophy today question if his conceptual view of Thomist epistemology is necessarily more faithful to Thomas's intent than the dynamic intentional interpretations initiated by Maréchal and carried forward by Rahner and Lonergan. Still, Maritain's work stands out as the most powerful and systematic study of mysticism that purports to apply the classically recognized "authentic" Catholic teachers, Thomas and John of the Cross, to the issue of mysticism, weaving the two together into a coherent system that impresses as much by its breadth as by its incisive penetration.

An important question to be addressed to this basically Thomist approach, especially because of its abstraction from the issue of historicity, is the extent to which it can do real justice to forms of mysticism that do not fit its mold. Such difficulties are evident throughout Maritain's account, especially in the peremptory judgments advanced about the usefulness of Neoplatonism and in the anomalous role given to Augustine. In the more than fifty years since the appearance of *The Degrees of Knowledge,* Catholic thinkers have come to doubt the absolute validity of a view of philosophical and theological truth that pays so little attention to the historical record — even when presented as powerfully as it was by Jacques Maritain.

Maréchal, Blondel, Bergson, and Maritain are all major names in the modern study of mysticism. Their contributions, which I have grouped under the category of philosophy, must always be seen as part of a broad world of discussion involving literary studies (Bremond), theology (Gardeil, Garrigou-Lagrange, et al.), psychology, history of religions, and a variety of cognate disciplines. Many other scholars noted in their day, such as Henri Delacroix, Jean Baruzi, and Roger Bastide, also contributed to the French discussion of mysticism in the early decades of the twentieth century.[116] The resources presented in these investigations, while outmoded in many particulars, have not always been fully utilized in more recent studies.

Given the intensity of the interest in mysticism in France up to the Second World War, it is somewhat surprising that the past four decades have seen such a marked reduction in original contributions. We have noted some French theological literature devoted to mysticism in these decades; one recent voice that seems best described as philosophical deserves a more extended consideration.

Michel de Certeau, S.J. (1925–1986), is difficult to evaluate as much for the novelty as for the difficulty of his thought. He began his study of mysticism in careful historical fashion by preparing editions and interpretations of important seventeenth-century French mystics, especially Jean-Joseph Surin (1600–1665).[117] This work led him to original insights about how the creation of the term "mysticism" (*la mystique*) in that century marked a basic shift in Western attitudes toward the sacred.[118] De Certeau, who for many years was associated with the Freudian-Lacanian group in Paris, sought to bring the insights of psychoanalysis, semiotics, and linguistics to bear on the theoretical study of mysticism, both in his major book, *La Fable Mystique XVIe–XVIIe Siècle* (1982), as well as in a number of articles.[119] Given the difficulty and unsystematic nature of de Certeau's work, as well as the fact that much still remains unpublished, any summary must be highly provisional.[120] An early general article provides the most accessible introduction to his thought,[121] though *Le Fable Mystique* and other papers are more incisive and original.

De Certeau had little interest in defining mysticism, especially in any transcultural way. His emphasis on the rooting of "mysticisms" in history, language, and culture was meant to underscore particularity and contextuality. "Whatever one thinks of mysticism," he said, "even if one recognizes in it the emergence of a universal or absolute reality, one can only deal with it in relation to a particular cultural and historic situation."[122] Unlike the majority of twentieth-century students, with notable exceptions like Ernst Troeltsch (see above) and Gershom Scholem (to be considered below), de Certeau stressed the way in which mystical experience, though something of profound individual significance in the life of the mystic, was necessarily a social phenomenon in which the mystic always reflects a socioreligious world and in turn affects, even transforms, that world through the creation of new types of discourse and the formation of new religious groups.[123]

Despite his reluctance to define mysticism, de Certeau does discriminate some broad differences between Eastern and Western mysticism and also within Western mysticism itself on the basis of the pivotal change that he holds occurred in the seventeenth century. Speaking of mystical experience in his 1968 article, he says, "that which defines it on the whole in the West is the discovery of an Other as unavoidable or essential. In the East, there would be more the rending of the thin film of consciousness 'in-founded' [*in-fondée*] under the pressure of a reality which encompasses it."[124] Whatever one may think of this generalization, what was more important for de Certeau was the distinction between mysticism "before" and "after" the creation of "la mystique" in the seventeenth century. The two ages of Western mysticism were divided by the seminal period that stretched from Teresa of Avila to Angelus Silesius, when the rapidly changing role of Christianity in European culture made possible the rise of the new "scientific" mysticism.[125] As he puts it:

> Since the sixteenth or seventeenth century one no longer designates as mystical the kind of "wisdom" elevated to the recognition of a mystery already lived and proclaimed in common beliefs, but an experimental knowledge which has slowly detached itself from traditional theology or Church

institutions and which characterizes itself through the consciousness, acquired or received, of a gratified passivity where the self is lost in God.[126]

Two basic consequences of this change to "mysticism" as experimental knowledge grounding a particular science were, first, the creation of a mystical "tradition," that is, the reinterpretation of past thinkers as belonging to something that they never really knew in explicit fashion, and, second, the "psychologization" of the object of study of the new science. Mystical phenomena (an oxymoron, as de Certeau noted) migrated inward in the seventeenth century, away from the liturgical and scriptural context of patristic and medieval Christianity to a situation in which private illumination and unusual psychosomatic experiences became the criteria.[127] This internalization was the source of the analogies that de Certeau discovered between mysticism as a science and modern psychoanalysis.[128] In line with contemporary psychoanalysis and semiotics, he insisted that mystical experience could not be studied in itself but only through mystical language and through the body of the mystic.[129]

De Certeau's thoughts on mystical language and the mystical text are not easy to understand.[130] According to his article entitled "Mystic Speech," mystical experience ". . . has as its essential elements the *ego*, the 'center of the utterance,' and the *present*, the 'source of time.'" But the essence of mystical speech is not the construction of a coherent set of truth statements, but rather the establishment of a dialogical discourse in which the *I* and the *thou* are both put at risk in the situation of speaking — "what is renewed is the relationship between the signifier and the constitution of the subject: do we exist to speak to the other, or to be spoken by him?"[131] Much of the most difficult parts of de Certeau's writings on mysticism were concerned with trying to spell out how the mystical text — the real place of mysticism since the seventeenth century — relates to mystical utterance. How far the Jesuit's thought may be of help here to the ongoing study of mysticism is still an open question. Perhaps the publication of works left behind upon his untimely death may help to clarify his position and make it useful even for those who do not share his abstruse language and adherence to semiotics and Lacanian psychoanalysis.

One further difficulty in de Certeau's approach is evident. While agreeing on the importance of the shift that took place in the seventeenth century, one may well think that de Certeau has made too much of it. Much of what he identifies as mysticism is what Spanish and French mystics immediately before and after this shift said it was. Has de Certeau done nothing more than cast the traditional French neoscholastic obsession with Spanish and French mysticism into a different language? Other forms of Christian mysticism seem to be cited merely as corroborations of a picture of mysticism drawn from an admittedly important but still narrow focus. When these forms would tend to contradict or qualify his view (as in the case of his claim for the essential anti-institutional and disruptive nature of mysticism), he is strangely silent.[132] Despite these reservations, there can be no question that de Certeau's work has opened up new avenues in the debate over mysticism.

On the whole, mysticism has received less direct attention in twentieth-century German philosophy than it has in France. The qualification "direct" is important here, because a case could be made that there are significant resources for the study of mysticism in several of the major German philosophers of this century. Martin Heidegger (1889–1976) has been accused of abandoning philosophy for some form of metaphysical mysticism, and he also did display an interest in some of the great German mystics, such as Meister Eckhart and Angelus Silesius, as is evident in his 1955–56 lectures published as *Der Satz vom Grund.* But Heidegger did not explicitly discuss the history and meaning of mysticism, and, rather than speaking of Heidegger as a mystic or even philosopher of mysticism, it seems better, with John D. Caputo, to note the "mystical element" in his thought.[133] Similarly, Ludwig Wittgenstein (1889–1951) made use of the category of the "mystical" in places in his writings, but the meaning that he gave to the term was peculiar to his own system of thought and, like Heidegger, does not seem to be directly helpful to modern theories of mysticism.[134] Karl Jaspers (1883–1969) expressed an affinity with the thought of such speculative mystics as Plotinus, Meister Eckhart, and Nicholas of Cusa, but the scattered quality of his reflections on mysticism leaves the investigator with the necessity of constructing a possible theory on the basis of an appeal to other resources.[135]

Some recent German thinkers have written directly on the meaning of mysticism. Among these the name of Carl Albrecht, physician, philosopher, and mystic, stands out, though his writing is little known outside Germany.[136] The important contributions of German-speaking scholars to the history of mysticism, especially of medieval Germanic mysticism, will be noted throughout these volumes. In some cases, such as that of Alois M. Haas, recent work has included useful essays on the broader meaning of mysticism.[137]

As we saw, philosophical engagement with mysticism in France during the first four decades of this century was primarily sparked by Christian texts and issues, despite the influence exerted on the field by classic studies of non-Christian mysticism, such as Louis Massignon's *La passion de Husayn*

Ibn Mansūr Hāllāj: martyr mystique de l'Islam (1922).[138] The philosophical discussion of mysticism that has flourished in the Anglo-American world during the last forty years has tended to take its departure from broader comparativist issues and it has been much influenced by the work of historians of religion like Rudolph Otto and R. C. Zaehner.

The issues most discussed in this literature cluster around two broad questions: (1) What is the nature of mystical experience? (2) What, if any, form of knowledge is conveyed by it? In pursuing the nature of mystical experience, these philosophical investigators have tended to concentrate on whether or not all mystical experience, whatever its fundamental characteristics, is of the same nature, that is, whether there is a "common core" to all mysticism. Two other issues directly impinge here. First, the question of typology. If there are various types or kinds of mysticism, as most investigators seem to admit, how are these types to be determined and what effect does the admission of types have on the issue of the "common core"? Are the types really distinct or merely diverse manifestations of a single kind of experience? Second, and more basic, what is the relation between experience and interpretation in mystical accounts? Those who propose some form of common or universal core to mystical experience seem compelled to adopt a position that distinguishes fairly sharply between the original mystical experience and subsequent doctrinal or theological interpretation in order to uphold the underlying unity behind the wide diversity of expression found in mystical texts from around the world. William James can be singled out as the ancestor of this position. More recent investigators have asked how legitimate this distinction really is.

In 1936 A. J. Ayer, in his noted book *Language, Truth and Logic,* reflected the view of many empirical and analytic philosophers in claiming, "If a mystic admits that the object of his vision is something which cannot be described, then he must also admit that he is bound to talk nonsense when he describes it." Hence, ". . . in describing his vision the mystic does not give us any information about the external world; he merely gives us indirect information about the condition of his own mind."[139] Philosophers since the time of William James have wrestled with the issue of the noetic quality of mystical experience—What kind of knowledge is conveyed? What claims does any such knowledge make on the mystic? What claims, if any, might it make on others? These issues are made more difficult because of the insistence of so many mystics that their experience cannot really be communicated: that is, by definition mystical experience is ineffable and only capable of indirect communication through paradoxical language. Is the mystical experience really ineffable? If so, how does this affect claims that it conveys some kind of knowledge? These interrelated issues have framed a complex, if somewhat inbred, body of philosophical literature in English during the past forty years.

A convenient place to begin is with a much-cited book first published in 1960, W. T. Stace's *Mysticism and Philosophy*.[140] The issues of the universal core and the noetic claims of mystical experience are to the fore throughout Stace's account. Although Stace (1886–1967) considered himself both an empiricist and an analyst, he wished to argue against both Bertrand Russell and A. J. Ayer that mystical experience is not merely an emotional or subjective state. Although he confesses that he is not an expert in "any of the cultural areas of mysticism,"[141] in opposition to comparativists like R. C. Zaehner, he defends the universal or common core of mysticism, while still admitting two distinct types.[142] The presupposition on which he argues his case (directly in the latter issue, indirectly in the former) is "that it is important as well as possible to make a distinction between a mystical experience itself and the conceptual interpretations which may be put upon it."[143] Just as the possibility of mistaken identity or illusion makes it necessary to distinguish between sense experience in general and its conceptual interpretation, the distinction between mystical experience and its interpretation is the all-important sword that cuts the Gordian knot. But this distinction, which at first glance seems a commonsense one, involves presuppositions and thorny problems in epistemology that have continued to be debated. Even abstracting from the possibility or validity of some form of a distinction (not separation) between experience and interpretation, one can still ask if Stace's understanding of the distinction is convincing. From this perspective, a look at the crucial second chapter of *Mysticism and Philosophy* displays both theoretical and historical shortcomings.

Although Stace admits concerning sense experience in general and mystical experience in particular that "it is probably impossible in both cases to isolate 'pure' experience,"[144] in practice he proceeds as if this were not the case as he gathers excerpts from mystical texts to argue for seven common characteristics of the two basic forms or species of the genus mysticism — the extrovertive and introvertive types (terms taken over from R. Otto).[145] Stace provides no criteria for investigating the relation between experience and interpretation in mystical accounts, just as he displays no sensitivity to the historical and contextual variations among his texts. He never takes up the question of whether it is possible for language and conceptual systems of belief to help to shape experience as well as to be utilized in its interpretation, so that his implied basis for distinguishing experience and interpretation seems to be that any term that is religiously distinctive (e.g., God, Trinity, Christ, Buddha, nirvana) is always subsequent interpretation, and any term that is not (e.g., unity, indifferentiation, light, inmost spirit) is "uninterpreted description."[146] This arbitrary way of proceeding involves at least three errors. It not only begins by withdrawing the mystical text from its cultural and religious context in order to pull it to pieces virtually line by line in order to save the core and discard the rest, but second, it also remains totally oblivious to the profound differences that even such supposedly descriptive terms as "pure spirit" and "indistinction" have in diverse languages and religious contexts. Finally, if good hermeneutics involves interpreting the part in terms of the whole, Stace's argument by excerpt constitutes a classic exercise in misreading.[147]

Having established a "general sense of unity" as "the very inner essence of all mystical experience,"[148] Stace takes up in chapter 3 the question of the objective reference of mysticism. On the basis of his identification of the criterion of objectivity with orderliness (i.e., obedience to the laws of nature), his position is that mystical experience is properly neither subjective nor objective, but *transsubjective* in the sense that although it is unanimous in its universal manifestations, because it is the experience of undifferentiated unity, it cannot be judged to be either *in* or *out* of harmony with the natural order.[149] The conviction of objectivity possessed by the mystics is the result of their passing beyond the individual self into the pure unity of the Universal Self, the "Vacuum-Plenum," which Stace is prepared to argue can legitimately be called God.[150]

The case for mysticism's transsubjective nature leads the author in chapters 5 and 6 to a discussion of how the paradoxical and ineffable character of mystical language reflects its noetic if not objective claims. Rather than apologize or seek to mitigate the force of the paradoxes found in mystical texts,[151] Stace insists that mystical language must be nonlogical because mystical experience itself is not logical. "There can be no logic in an experience in which there is no multiplicity."[152] When mystics say that their experiences are ineffable what they really mean is that words cannot be used during the experience itself, but that the *remembrance* of the experience of transsubjective unity allows the mystic to make use of words not only metaphorically but even literally to describe it subsequently.[153] The mystics themselves (not being good philosophers) do not recognize this, confusing paradoxicality (the literally true description of the contradictory mystical experience) with ineffability (the supposed inability to describe it). Here Stace's argument comes full circle. Though he denies other explanations of mystical ineffability on the basis of the logical difficulties involved in any doctrine of what he calls "absolute" ineffability,[154] it is difficult to see how Stace's mystic could ever find words adequate to express the remembrance of the experience of undifferentiated unity. Indeed, how can the mystic ever remember "it" if, by definition, undifferentiated unity is not an "it" at all, that is, "it" does not fall within the world of logical discrimination? How can the mystic—let alone the investigator—know which terms reflect this totally unknown experience best, and which are merely theological interpretations? More subtle accounts of the interaction between experience and language might be able to suggest at least partial answers to these problems. Stace can only avoid them.[155]

Many of the issues that Stace investigated also surface in other philosophical accounts of mysticism in recent Anglo-American thought. Richard M. Gale, in reaction to an earlier position of Stace, argued against the ineffability of mystical experiences and affirmed their subjectivity.[156] J. N. Findlay in a 1966 lecture entitled "The Logic of Mysticism" attacked Stace's account of the universal core as "a rag-bag of empirical features" and disagreed with his view of the transsubjective nature of mystical claims.[157] Galen K. Pletcher argued that the mystics' use of paradoxical or contradictory language was not so much a departure from all logic as an indication of the deficiencies of our present conceptual systems (though not all possible ones).[158] These interventions make it clear that concern for the meaning of mystical language, especially in its paradoxical forms, has remained an important feature of the discussion.[159]

Perhaps the most central issue in the ongoing English-language philosophical debate has been that of the relation between mystical experience and its interpretation. In the decade of the 1970s several authors, such as Bruce Garside and Terence Penelhum, questioned whether the differences among mystics could be easily accounted for on the basis of a fairly simple distinction between experience and interpretation.[160] John Hick supported the idea of the unity of mystical experience as the inner essence of religion, but on different grounds from that found in Stace.[161] Recognizing the deficiencies of Stace's handling of this problem, other investigators sought to provide more nuanced treatments of the experience–interpretation relationship without abandoning the distinction as the key to determining the nature of mysticism.

Among these attempts we can note a series of papers by Ninian Smart, a scholar who is both a philosopher and a historian of religion.[162] Beginning from a distinction based upon N. Söderblom and R. Otto between numinous and mystical religious experiences, Smart advanced a phenomenology of mysticism as part of a broader theory of religion. Although he remains in essential agreement with Stace that mystical experience is the same wherever it is found, he differs from Stace both in his characterization of the core of mysticism and in the more subtle way he accounts for the relation between the experience and interpretation. In numinous forms of religion the difference between subject and object remains, whereas mysticism as inner contemplative quest aims at a state of "consciousness-purity" or "void" in which the subject–object polarity disappears, and in which there are no mental images or sense of time, only a sublime intensity of feeling.[163]

Smart admits that in concrete religions the numinous and mystical types are generally intermingled,[164] and that it is necessary for bare consciousness-purity to be tied to a religious context in order for it to have meaning. Thus, Smart is willing to go beyond Stace in admitting that "experiences are always in some degree interpreted."[165] Indeed, he accepts the fact that religious systems of belief with their highly "ramified" or doctrinal language help to shape mystical experience as well as being used to communicate it to other believers. Smart's important paper entitled "Interpretation and Mystical Experience" lays out four ways in which interpretations get built into accounts of mystical experience, distinguishing between "high" and "low" levels of "ramification" (crudely determined according to the rule "how many propositions are presupposed as true by the description in question"), as well as *auto*-interpretation and *hetero*-interpretation, depending on whether the interpreter shares the belief perspective of the mystic or writes from the point of view of another system.[166] Smart concludes: "It would seem to be a sound principle to try to seek a low hetero-interpretation coinciding well with a low auto-interpretation. In this way an agreed phenomenological account of experience will be arrived at, and this will facilitate the attempt to distinguish experience from interpretation."[167]

Though Smart's optimistic projection provides criteria lacking in Stace, one can still wonder if it is not subject to the same difficulties. In practice, it seems extremely difficult if not impossible to separate the different terms and propositions of mystical texts into highly and lowly ramified levels, and Smart's own admission that systems of belief precondition the experience as well as being used to express it seems to undercut the distinction. Furthermore, Smart's assertion that "the higher the degree of ramification, the less is the description guaranteed by the experience itself,"[168] reverses the almost universal claims of the mystics that their experience provides them with clear and undoubted verification of the specific, or ramified, beliefs of their traditions. The mystics may be mistaken in this, but Smart's theory of mysticism does not give us much help in dealing with this universal "delusion."

Finally, we may note that Smart, like other recent authors, has been concerned with the question of the incomprehensibility of mystical experience and the paradoxicality of the language used to describe it. With regard to the former, he insists that to say that mystical experience is ineffable or incomprehensible is really to say that it is not *totally* comprehensible. The rhetorical and even the dialectical paradoxes of mystical texts are a form of *askēsis*, a "performative transcendence" of "performatively using words to sketch expression beyond their conventional limits."[169] Thus, he admits a noetic content to mysticism, though this must be seen as a knowing by acquaintance,[170] not propositional knowing. Smart's remarks in these areas, though perceptive, are not highly developed. In the end, a deep ambiguity also pervades his central claim for the identity of all mystical experience as "consciousness-purity." At times this position is presented as merely a possibility against those like R. C. Zaehner who have argued for a multiplicity of kinds of mysticism. At other times it seems to be a given implied in his understanding of the experience–intepretation distinction.[171]

In his 1978 paper "Understanding Religious Experience," Smart warned that "there are limits upon the philosophical discussion of mysticism in the abstract."[172] Despite this salutary reminder, the most recent contributions to the Anglo-American philosophical views of mysticism have been largely critical studies of the inner consistency of theories of mysticism whose treatment of mystical texts evidences a form of "proof-texting" that pays little attention to context, original language, and other textual issues which any form of sound hermeneutics demands. Two recent survey books illustrate this tendency: William Wainwright's *Mysticism* (1981), and Philip Almond's *Mystical Experience and Religious Doctrine* (1982). Both are useful for providing surveys of the recent philosophical debates, and both also seek to make constructive contributions; but the increasingly internecine nature of the debates witnessed to in these volumes, as well as the secondary role that actual mystical texts play in their arguments, leaves their contributions ambiguous at best.

Wainwright's basic concern is with the cognitive claims implied in mystical experience.[173] The purpose of the book is "to show that there are good reasons for crediting at least some mystical intuitions, and thus for believing that there are realms of being or types of reality hidden from ordinary consciousness."[174] Though his argument usually concerns theistic mystical consciousness, he does not wish to exclude the validity of other types of mysticism. Mystical experience for Wainwright is a unitary state which is noetic but lacking in specific empirical content. Although he sides with those who affirm the necessity of sharply distinguishing mystical experience from its interpretation,[175] Wainwright criticizes Stace and constructs a typology close to that of the comparativist R. C. Zaehner. Wainwright's mitigated defense of some form of "common core" of mystical experience and of the possibility of cross-cultural typology is typical of his mode of argument, which frequently consists of a detailed negative argument showing that the case against a position has not been definitively proven (e.g., "no adequate reasons have been provided for asserting that mystical experiences cannot be described, or that a cross-cultural typology of mystical experience is impossible"),[176] followed by a shift to a positive position advanced more as a possibility than as a fully worked out argument, as in the case of his complex and questionable typological sketch.[177] The large gap between a mode of argumentation based on "it has not been shown that it is impossible that" and "it has been demonstrated that such is the case" affects most of the positions he adopts.

Wainwright's third chapter deals with the cognitive claims of mysticism. While I believe that he is right in his view that it is mere assumption to say (as Ayer and others would) that "no experience can be cognitive which is unlike sense experience in very many important respects,"[178] Wainwright's attempt to defend the cognitive nature of mystical experience waffles between what we might call "a posteriori" validations based on the genuineness of the mystic's experience as evidenced in his or her life, character, and conformity with religious traditions (tests that have always been central in Christian verification of a mystic's authenticity) and more problematic "a priori" validations concerning the reality of the object of mystical experience. Here Wainwright seems to be implying a kind of natural theology and proof for the existence of God that is never clearly spelled out.[179] The epistemology he adopts denies that there can be such a thing as intuitive knowledge and apparently treats God as any other entity to be known. Hence, he criticizes Maritain, Maréchal, and others in insisting that mystical knowing must always be conceptual if it is to be really cognitive.[180] On this basis, Wainwright proceeds to attack aspects of some earlier theories of mysticism, such as Stace's views on mystical paradoxicality and Roman Catholic views (especially Maritain's) on the mediated immediacy of mystical knowledge.[181] In sum, Wainwright's book is more useful for laying out some of the problems implied in other accounts than for setting any coherent agenda of its own.

Much the same can be said for Philip Almond's book, which is also primarily an examination of some recent views of mysticism, especially those of S. Radhakrishnan, R. C. Zaehner, N. Smart, W. T. Stace and R. Otto.[182] Almond's aim is not only to suggest a more adequate classification of mystical experience, but also to show that the appeal to mystical experience cannot solve the problem of the conflicting truth claims among religions, as some have argued.[183] Almond's view of the matter, though more subtle than those of Stace and Smart, is still a variation on the common core theory. This becomes clear in the second part of his brief book, a consideration of five different "models" of the relationship of experience and interpretation in the study of mysticism.

Almond's five models have considerable historiographical usefulness, though one can disagree with his placement of some of the theories he discusses. According to Model 1 (M1) all mystical experience is the same,[184] while in M2 (represented by thinkers like Underhill, Radhakrishnan, and Smart) mystical experience is always the same but the interpretations of it vary according to the religious and philosophical frameworks employed. M3 believes that there are a small number of types of mysticism which transcend religious barriers, a view ascribed to Otto and Zaehner, and less helpfully to Stace, whose two types really seem to meld into one. M4, a category Almond says is only implicit in some students of mysticism, holds that there are as many kinds of mystical experience as there are paradigmatic expressions, that is, expressions which refer to the central focus, aim, or nature of the experience.[185] Since all these models, in Almond's view, fail to bridge the gap between experience and interpretation, he advances a case for an M5, a view combining insights from M2 and M4 with the recent work of Steven Katz and others.[186] Building on a distinction first suggested by Peter Moore between retrospective, reflexive, and incorporated interpretations of experience, Almond argues that there are as many varieties of mystical experience as there are incorporated interpretations of it.[187] He finds that this model, suggested by authors like B. Garside and S. Katz, provides a more adequate way of dealing with the relation between experience and interpretation and allows for an interaction in which religious interpretation can both shape mystical experience and yet still be open to be changed and transformed by it.[188] Nevertheless, Almond also wishes to argue that there are "higher" mystical experiences in which there are *no* incorporated interpretations at all, where the basic datum of the experience, at least as a limit situation, is a "contentless" experience beyond the subject–object dichotomy. Here he seems to take back with one hand what he had given with the other, a point not lost on his critics.[189] His arguments, especially the textual ones, for the existence of such contentless states are not convincing,[190] and the epistemological basis upon which the case could be argued is not really spelled out.

Almond, as we have seen, made use of the writings of both Peter Moore and Steven Katz to work out his position. In 1978 Katz and Moore contributed important papers to a volume edited by Katz under the title *Mysticism and Philosophical Analysis*. Though the ten authors in this collection by no means represent a single point of view, Katz's focal piece, "Language, Epistemology and Mysticism," as well as the essays by Moore, R. Gimello and others, constitute an important challenge to the understanding of the nature of mystical experience and its noetic claims that had been developed in recent Anglo-American philosophy.

The key to Katz's position is his insistence that there is no such thing as an unmediated experience — "*all* experience is processed through, organized by, and makes itself available to us in extremely complex epistemological ways."[191] On the basis of this unexceptionable premise, Katz has little trouble in showing the inconsistencies and shortcomings of many classic accounts, from William James through Zaehner, Stace, and others. Katz reminds us that mystical experiences are above all religiously specific experiences: Buddhists have Buddhist mystical experiences; Jews Jewish ones; and Christians have mystical experiences relating to Christ. In their haste to find the common core of mysticism, the philosophical and comparativist scholars of our ecumenical age have played down the specific elements in mystical texts, which in almost every case outweigh the rare words and themes that in English translation *sound* the same to naïve ears. Katz's critical agenda is designed not only to emphasize the religious plurality of mysticism, but also to question the commonly received view that mystical language is by definition ineffable and paradoxical.[192] While his concerns in this essay are largely negative (one might say almost nominalistic at times), he does not preclude all comparative philosophical possibilities.[193]

Katz's defense of the contextual nature of all mystical experience is echoed by a number of the other essays in *Mysticism and Philosophical Analysis*. Notable among these is that by Peter Moore entitled "Mystical Experience, Mystical Doctrine, Mystical Technique." Moore agrees with Katz in denying the absolute nature of mystical ineffability and insisting that the "mystic's doctrinal background should . . . be seen as a key to his experience rather than a door which shuts us off from it."[194] He also advances a more detailed version of his earlier scheme of three modes of interpretation utilized by Almond, distinguishing retrospective, reflexive, and two kinds of incorporated interpretation (reflected and assimilated) from the "raw experience," that is, the features of the experience unaffected by prior beliefs.[195] Moore's short essay lays out an interesting and original program that would probably require a book for its full delineation.

Other essays in the volume echo Katz's central point about the religious specificity of mystical experience,[196] further explore the question of the possible meaning of the ineffability of mystical language,[197] or investigate basic issues in the epistemology of mysticism.[198] A subsequent companion volume entitled *Mysticism and Religious Traditions* published in 1983 provides some concrete illustrations of the advantages of a religiously-contextual approach to the study of mysticism.[199]

Two themes seem to dominate these recent philosophical discussions of mysticism in the English-speaking world.[200] The first is the ongoing debate specifically addressed to the issues raised by Katz in his essay, the second is the wider question of renewed interest in the contextual study of mysticism in general. Katz's attack on the notion of a common core of mystical experience, as well as his denial that mystical language is really ineffable or paradoxical in the way that most mystics seem to suggest, seemed to hit a nerve in contemporary philosophy of mysticism, as the variety of discussions and criticisms of his views demonstrate. William Wainwright, as we have seen, was not convinced by Katz, though the brevity of his response leads one to wonder if he really comes to grips with Katz's argument.[201] Philip Almond used Katz, but in a way that Katz took issue with.[202] Three subsequent critiques of Katz's views from diverse philosophical positions are more substantive.

James R. Price III, writing from the perspective of Lonerganian cognitional analysis, praises the turn to the subject in Katz's recognition of the mediated nature of all mystical experience, but he insists that such a turn must be a *critical* turn to a theory of knowing which allows for the possibility of a judgment regarding the correctness or adequacy of interpretations of experience, something he finds lacking in Katz's view.[203] In a later piece Price further develops his view of a more adequate cognitional theory for the investigation of mysticism. Criticizing the typological approach to the cross-cultural analysis of mysticism that has been so influential since the time of Rudolf Otto, Price analyzes the twin principles behind such typologizing as (1) the distinction between the inner and the outer in human experience, and (2) the assumption that mystical data are to be understood as (a) the object or content of consciousness, and (b) analyzable according to the metaphysical and doctrinal language employed by the mystics.[204] Price's Lonerganian suggestion, illustrated by a brief comparative example, is that a shift to the horizon of interiority which attends to the operations of consciousness rather than its object or content is the necessary ground for an explanatory and not merely descriptive account of mysticism. This call for a "critical grammar of mystical interiority" is provocative and deserves further work, though one can wonder if it would work equally well with all mystical texts, especially those that do not directly witness to the subject's cognitive states.

Two other recent criticisms of Katz deserve mention. Anthony M. Perovich, noting a similarity between Katz's unqualified contextualism applied to the philosophy of mysticism and the unqualified contextual views of the philosophy of science advanced by Thomas Kuhn and Paul Feyerabend, argues for a "qualified" contextualism based on the thesis that "*some* (not *all*) beliefs shape experience" — a position that does not exclude the possibility of at least some shared mystical experience.[205] Perovich's further suggestion, that a shift from problems of meaning to problems of reference would be of assistance in the investigation of mysticism, seems less helpful, at least on the basis of the example he gives.[206] Wayne Proudfoot in the chapter devoted to mysticism in his book *Religious Experience* (1985) also takes issue with Katz, especially with regard to the issue of the ineffable, paradoxical, and noetic nature of mystical experience. Proudfoot maintains that ineffability and paradoxicality, far from being a category mistake on the part of mystics, are a priori conditions for the identification of an experience as mystical, functioning as prescriptive grammatical rules or "placeholders."[207] He goes on to criticize Katz's attack on the noetic quality of mystical experience, noting that a sense of objectivity is an integral part of the mystic's claims and therefore must enter into any comparative evaluation.[208]

These and other reactions to Katz's position show that there are serious reasons for holding that this form of what might be called "mystical nominalism," based on an unqualified contextualism, needs to be modified in the direction of a position that will both recognize the mediated aspects of all mystical experience and still not preclude the possibility of comparison (recall that Katz himself seems to suggest this at the end of his programmatic essay). There is obviously no agreement on the epistemological basis upon which a more cautious and more adequate comparativism based on a qualified contextualism should be constructed.

The return to the contextual study of mysticism emphasized in the work of Katz and his colleagues also finds an echo in the writings of a number of other recent students of mysticism of diverse philosophical and theological perspectives. Among these the names of Louis Dupré and Ewert Cousins stand out.[209]

Dupré, a philosopher of religion, has been increasingly occupied with the study of mysticism since the publication of his general study of religion, *The Other Dimension,* in 1972.[210] Dupré possesses a good knowledge of world mystical traditions,[211] and has done extensive work with such Christian mystics as John Ruusbroec.[212] Describing mysticism in broad terms as essentially a passively infused experience of transcendence,[213] Dupré's writings on mysticism have been especially insightful in two areas: first, with regard to the experience of the self in theistic mysticism; and, second, the role of mysticism in the modern secular world. For Dupré, the mystics are those special individuals who have immediate access to the deepest core of the self, where the laws of ordinary consciousness are suspended and the soul comes to have direct knowledge of its self-transcendence and transcendence of the world.[214] He agrees with Maritain that this new awareness is a cognitive state in which the mystic attains "a direct, although negative, knowledge of ultimate selfhood, an immediate awareness of presence to oneself and to the transcendent source of self."[215] In accordance with the teaching of Meister Eckhart and John Ruusbroec, he holds that in this self-awareness the soul comes to realize the ground of its identity with God. Dupré has also investigated the possible role of mysticism in secular modern society, where the direct experience of the sacred is for the most part no longer available.[216] He argues that the mystical sense of the divine absence, such as the desert of Eckhart, provides a point of contact between classical Christian mysticism and the wasteland of modern atheism. Even the believer "who shares in fact, if not in principle, the practical atheism of his entire culture, is left no choice but to vitalize this negative experience and to confront his feeling of God's absence" in order to encounter the transcendent.[217] It is only through this willingness, Dupré contends, that the modern believer can overcome secular atheism and come to recognize "a transcendent dimension in a fundamental engagement to a world and a human community at once totally autonomous and totally dependent."[218]

Ewert Cousins has written extensively on Franciscan mysticism, especially the thought of Bonaventure,[219] and he has recently worked in the comparative study of spirituality. An example of his approach can be found in his monograph *Global Spirituality: Toward the Meeting of Mystical Paths*, which resumes some earlier papers.[220] Though the larger part of this slim volume consists of a study of St. Francis, Bonaventure, and Eckhart as representatives of distinctive but complementary forms of Christian mysticism, Cousins's study is informed by a phenomenological method designed to facilitate cross-cultural collaborative work in the study of mysticism.[221] For Cousins, as for most modern interpreters, the fundamental object of the study of mysticism remains mystical experience, but Cousins realizes that this can only be approached through the mystical text, whose penetration demands careful literary and historical study. The crucial stage in Cousins's method, however, consists of a phenomenological analysis of mystical experience that explores the structures of consciousness revealed in the text through the cultivation of the faculty of empathy by which "we can extend our consciousness so that it enters into the consciousness of another and perceives reality from the perspective of the other's experience."[222] Only on the basis of such empathetic phenomenology does Cousins believe we will be able to answer such questions as whether all mystical experience is one and the same and whether it has a true intellectual content. Cousins's volume contains an illustration of his method by way of a comparative analysis of the objective and subjective correlatives of the mysticism of Bonaventure and Meister Eckhart. Promising as this analysis is, the full implications of this form of empathetic and intentional methodology—another illustration of the contemporary turn toward the mystical subject—demands a more careful theoretical formulation and a broader application to non-Christian mystics before its value can be really assessed.

The intense recent discussion of mysticism in the English-language world is an important part of the context within which these volumes are being written. While not abandoning hopes for a determination of the essence of mysticism that could be used on a broad comparative level, contemporary thinkers have emphasized the necessity for more careful attention to the contextual rooting and linguistic shaping of all mysticism. These salutary developments, however, also call out for critical cognitional and epistemological programs, as many of the great investigators of the past made clear. While a direct return to these classic epistemologies seems impossible today, the example they offer of the necessity for critical theory is still a salutary one.

SECTION 3

COMPARATIVIST AND PSYCHOLOGICAL APPROACHES TO MYSTICISM

Modern philosophical, and even theological, treatments of mysticism have been increasingly influenced by the work of historians of religion and other comparativists, as the first two sections of this Appendix have shown. From the time of William James and his contemporaries, psychological investigation of the nature of the special states of consciousness associated with mysticism has also become part of the agenda that philosophical and even theological investigators neglect to their peril. Therefore, attention needs to be given to the contribution of some of the classics of the comparativist and psychological study of mysticism. These are broad fields of research, and my own limitations will account for the brevity of this third section, which will survey these aspects of the methodological context for contemporary research in mysticism.

The pioneers of the academic study of the history of religions at the turn of the century were much interested in mysticism. For example, Nathan Söderblom (1866–1931), the founder of the Swedish school of the history of religions, distinguished between impersonal and personal forms of communion with the deity in the two main types of what he identified as the "highest religion."[1] In his work *The Nature of Revelation* (Swedish original

1903) Söderblom spoke of these as the mysticism of personality and the mysticism of infinity. In his Gifford Lectures for 1931, published as *The Living God,* Söderblom used more psychological terminology, distinguishing between the spontaneous mysticism of will or feeling exemplified in Luther and the cultivated mysticism of Ignatius Loyola.[2] Edvard Lehmann (1862–1930), his Danish contemporary, wrote one of the earliest attempts at a comparativist survey of mysticism in 1904, *Mystik i Hedensgab og Kristendom* (translated as *Mysticism in Heathendom and Christendom* [1910]). Lehmann's knowledge of different mystical traditions was admirable for its time, but his understanding of the phenomenon was problematic both because of the vagueness of his presentation and because of his evident animosity toward many forms of mysticism.[3] Both Söderblom and Lehmann were Protestant clergymen whose considerable knowledge of Eastern religions did not mask the Protestant agenda of their comparativist studies. The same was also true of two of their contemporaries whose writings on mysticism continue to have great influence today.

Rudolf Otto (1869–1937), along with William James and Baron von Hügel, is one of the most important contributers to the theory of religion of the present century. Otto was a professor of Theology at Göttingen, Breslau, and Marburg. His best-known books, *Das Heilige* (1917), translated in 1923 as *The Idea of the Holy,* and *Mysticism East and West* (1932) were comparativist studies whose mastery of and sympathy for non-Christian, especially Oriental religions, were still deeply colored by their author's neo-Kantianism and liberal Protestantism. Even so, *The Idea of the Holy* took a different direction from that advocated by Otto's contemporary, Karl Barth. Following in the tradition of Friedrich Schleiermacher, Otto insisted that Christianity, though the highest religion, was still a *form* of religion, not something that stood outside it. The investigation of religion as a comparative and phenomenological enterprise was not only important in itself, but had significant theological implications.[4]

Otto's main concern was to rescue religion from the reductionists, that is, to vindicate its role as an a priori category of feeling, prior to, but not independent of, rational explanation. The essence of religion is to be found in the prerational feeling of the "numinous" that is to be understood as the "creature consciousness" or "creaturehood" humans experience in the presence of the *mysterium tremendum,* the transcendent source experienced as the "Wholly Other."[5] Otto's evocation of the Wholly Other is passionate and powerful, if not always totally clear.

In *The Idea of the Holy,* Otto comes close to identifying mysticism if not with the core at least with the acme or goal of religion. The aspect of the numinous expressed by the Latin word *tremendum* signifies both unapproach-ability (*tremor*) and overpoweringness (*majestas*). Mysticism is found when the unapproachability element recedes and the overpowering force of the numinous induces the human subject to see it as the sole reality and thus to seek self-annihilation.[6] As the "identification of the personal self with the transcendent Reality,"[7] mysticism is also related to the *mysterium*, that is, the numinous experienced as the Wholly Other. Insofar as the numinous is Wholly Other,[8] it gives rise to the mystical sense of the "beyond" (Greek *epekeina*) that leads the mystic to oppose Being itself to the numinous con-ceived of as nothingness or as void and emptiness.[9] But since it also remains "uniquely attractive and *fascinating*," the numinous becomes the mystical "overabounding" (*das Überschwengliche*) in which the subject tries to identify itself with "the mysterious."[10] In a later footnote, Otto summarizes (albiet obscurely) his view of mysticism as follows: "As a provisional definition of mysticism I would suggest that, while sharing the nature of religion, it shows a preponderance of its non-rational elements and an over-stressing of them in respect to the 'over-abounding' aspect of the 'numen.'"[11]

In autumn of 1924, Otto delivered the Haskell Lectures at Oberlin College, subsequently expanded and published as *Mysticism East and West*. The book was important for several reasons: (1) as a development and sometimes qualification of Otto's view of the relation of mysticism to religion in general; (2) as an interesting comparison of classic mystics from different traditions, Meister Eckhart and Shankara; and (3) as the work that popularized the cross-cultural typological study of mysticism. *Mysticism East and West* lacks the passion of *The Idea of the Holy* and is not always easy reading, but these deficiences have not prevented it from having a contin-uing role even in the most recent discussions of mysticism.

Otto spoke vaguely of "a uniform nature of mysticism," but he also insisted that in mysticism, as in any sphere of spiritual life, the variations that spring from different attitudes toward the numinous were the most important object of study.[12] In defining the general character of mysticism in this book, Otto seems to go beyond the position advanced in *The Idea of the Holy*. Mysticism is still a reaction to the numinous, but rather than being the prolongation or acme of the numinous experience itself, it is now con-trasted with theism as one of the two major kinds of numinous experience. The contrast is based on the character of the object. "It is clear that Godhead as an immanent principle is different from and means something other than the transcendent God. . . . The point of departure and the essential distinction is not that the mystic has another and new relationship to God, but that he has a different God."[13] The advantage that Otto accrues from this position is that it enables him to vindicate, as truly mystical, phenomena such as Yoga and aspects of Buddhism that are indifferent to God in their concentration on the inner numinous nature of the soul.[14] The disadvantage is that in the case of Christian mystics, at least, most have insisted that the God they experience is both transcendent and immanent — not two different beings! Meister Eckhart, Otto's test case, made the dialectic of transcendence and immanence the cornerstone of his thought.

On the basis of this questionable view that the immanent God of the mystics is "another God," Otto advanced his well-known typology of mysticism in which the two highest interpenetrating forms, identified as the outward way, or mysticism of unifying vision, and the inward way, or mysticism of introspection, are contrasted with three lower forms, those of the illuminists; the emotionalists, and the nature mystics.[15] The introspective mystic sinks "down into the self in order to reach intuition, and here in the inmost depth of the self to find the Infinite, or God, or Brahman."[16] The extrovertive mystic "looks upon the world of things in its multiplicity, and in contrast to this leaps to an 'intuition' or a 'knowledge,'" that is, the recognition of the unity of all things that eventually leads to seeing the vital immanence of the One in everything.[17] What makes Eckhart and Shankara such important figures for Otto is that they combine both higher forms of mysticism in ways that are distinctively Western and Eastern.[18]

This is not the place to evaluate the adequacy of Otto's interpretation of his two major figures,[19] but we must note some of the questions that can be raised about the general theory. Otto's categories are ambiguous in several respects. First of all, the inward and outward forms of mysticism, which might suggest a distinction between God within and God without, should not be confused with the immanence/transcendence distinction that differentiates the mystical from the theistic. Outward mysticism for Otto still seeks an immanent God, while theism's God is totally other — a distinction which may seem peculiar to many. Second, Otto insists that the two types of *religion* (i.e., mystical and theistic) are intermingled in his test-case "theistic" mystics. (Eckhart and Shankara were believers whose God was both immanent and transcendent.) Thus, Otto has to put back into his two subjects the transcendent/theistic element which was denied by his original division between the immanent and the transcendent God — another indication that the original distinction is in need of revision. Finally, if we accept the view that mystical language describes not so much the content of mystical experience (something the mystics always held was incommunicable) as the transformative process of mystical knowing, as a number of recent investigators have argued,[20] Otto's cross-cultural typologies based on content would collapse. Thus, while Otto's *Mysticism East and West* remains one of the more insightful comparisons between mystics from different traditions, the theoretical structure that grounds it has serious problems.

Friedrich Heiler (1892–1967) was born a Catholic but joined the Lutheran Church in 1919 shortly after the appearance of his best-known work, *Das Gebet* (1918), translated as *Prayer* (1932). He later was professor of the History of Religions at Marburg and was active in the ecumenical movement. Heiler was much influenced by Baron von Hügel and Nathan Söderblom, and the keystone of his thought was the sharp distinction between mystical and prophetic religion.[21] Mystical religion is "that form of intercourse with God in which the world and the self are absolutely denied, in which human personality is dissolved, disappears and is absorbed in the infinity of the Godhead."[22] Prayer, which Heiler defined as "a living communion of the religious man with God, conceived as personal and present in experience, a communion which reflects the forms of the social relations of humanity,"[23] appears in both mystical and prophetic religion. Nevertheless, mysticism's denial of the life impulse, its exaltation of private experience over authority, its "feminine passivity," static idea of God, moral and societal indifferentism, individualism, monism — and a host of other ills — make it the polar opposite of prophetism and mean that its view of prayer is radically other than that found in the religion of prophetic revelation.[24] Although *Prayer* remains a useful source of information because of Heiler's prolific learning (much of this found in the notes not available in the English version), the artificiality of its polarized types of religion renders it *in fine* no more than a dated if "powerful essay in propaganda for the classic North-Atlantic Protestant understanding of human nature."[25] Later papers of Heiler, however, took a more positive view of the role of contemplative mysticism in Christian history.[26]

Protestant comparativists like Söderblom, Otto, and Heiler viewed mysticism in opposition to evangelical and prophetic religion (or true Christianity), along much the same lines as the continental Protestant theologians discussed in section 1. Other comparativists adopted a different approach in seeking to identify the inner unity behind the diversity of concrete religions rather than to discover the ideal polar opposites whose interactions were needed to ensure religion's proper Hegelian evolution. The most evident exemplification of this latter approach, sometimes spoken of as the "perennial philosophy" after a well-known work of Aldous Huxley,[27] has included a number of scholars who tend to conceive of the underlying message of all religions in a vaguely "mystical" way identified with the inner experience of the Absolute.

The Indian philosopher Sarvepalli Radhakrishnan (1888–1975) is an older representative of this viewpoint, as can be seen from the many writings that he devoted to "the religion of the spirit."[28] More recently, this position has been advanced by the Swiss comparativist Frithjof Schuon through his distinction between the esoteric and exoteric aspects of religion.[29] Other scholars who have followed this line include Huston Smith and Seyyed Hossein Nasr.[30] In identifying the essence of religion with the mystical, broadly and often very vaguely conceived, this approach encounters many of the same difficulties found in philosophical views like those of Henri Bergson.

The interest of another new discipline of the modern era, that of empirical psychology, parallels at least chronologically the contribution of the comparativists, and even slightly antedates it. When William James published his *Varieties of Religious Experience* in 1902, he was already able to make use of an extensive literature, especially by French investigators, on the abnormal states of consciousness that nineteenth-century Catholic theology had all too often identified with the essence of the mystical. What seemed manifest proofs of supernatural intervention to these Catholic theologians all too easily became test cases of "hysteria" for the early scientific psychologists. This unhappy confrontation may help explain the tensions and often hostile relations between psychological studies of mysticism and more traditional theological approaches during the present century. There were, to be sure, those who sought to bring together both perspectives, such as James and Maréchal among older investigators, and de Certeau more recently. Their success has been limited.[31]

Characteristic of the earliest phase of English-language interest in the psychology of mysticism was the work of James H. Leuba (1868–1946), a Swiss-born American psychologist who was active between the 1890s and the 1930s. Leuba was an atheist and a critic of religion whose major work, *The Psychology of Religious Mysticism* (1925), brought together papers and projects begun with the author's 1896 dissertation. Leuba's reductionist approach to mysticism emphasized the sexual motivations lurking beneath the accounts of the classic Christian mystics. Freud's famous question "What do women want?" was echoed in the title of the fifth chapter of this work: "What do the Christian Mystics Want?" Leuba's crude presentation of the answer, doubtless shocking in its day, seems rather simple and trite today.[32] Contemporary students of mysticism, both theological and philosophical, are well aware of the sexual component in any human experience; but they continue to doubt that this is all there is to mysticism.

Contemporary with Leuba among French psychologists was Henri Delacroix, briefly mentioned in section 2. His 1908 work *Études d'histoire et de psychologie du mysticisme* provoked some discussion among French philosophical students of mysticism. Among the older American psychologists of religion, the relation of mysticism to hysteria and hypnosis was a major topic, as the work of George Albert Coe, James Bissett Pratt, Robert H. Thouless, and others shows.[33]

Debate over psychology's relation to mysticism in the first half of this century cannot avoid the views of Sigmund Freud (1856–1939). Freud wrote little about mysticism, but he wrote just enough (and ambivalently enough) to spark a considerable debate, something not unusual where Freud is concerned. At first glance, Freud's attitude seems totally negative, at least as evidenced in his late work *Civilization and its Discontents* (1930), where he sees mystical desire for contact with the divine as a regression to the earliest postnatal stage of development, a stage characterized by a narcissistic union of mother and child in which the infant does not distinguish the ego from the external world.[34] His overt comments on the meaning of the "oceanic feeling" that his friend Romain Rolland, a French novelist and mystic, had claimed constituted the essence of religion may, however, mask a deeper ambivalence.[35]

Freud paid tribute to Rolland as a representative of the difference between higher, mystical religion and the religion of the common people he had attacked in *The Future of an Illusion* (1927). In his letters to Rolland, Freud admitted the complexity of the nature of mystical experience and the tentative character of his own analysis.[36] There may be hints in these letters and even in the first chapter of *Civilization and its Discontents* that transient forms of mystical experience can have a positive, cathartic value. Of course, even if there are the germs of a more positive view of mysticism in Freud, there can be no question of any transcendental dimension to mystical consciousness. On the whole, Freud clearly emphasized the regressive aspects of all religion and this is the view that has become canonical in the Freudian school,[37] although some recent pyschoanalysts have begun to suggest other possibilities.[38]

Carl Gustav Jung (1875–1961), the other great name in the development of twentieth-century analytic psychology, wrote little directly on mysticism, though his thought has had great influence on many contemporary students of religion. Several of Jung's disciples, notably Erich Neumann (1905–1960), attempted to relate Jungian thought to mysticism more directly. Neumann's paper "Mystical Man," first given at the Sixteenth Eranos Conference in 1948, is a provoking essay, though one that has not had much effect on recent study of mysticism, to judge by its neglect in the literature.

Neumann's view of the mystical is thoroughly psychological: "For us the mystical is rather a fundamental category of human experience which, pyschologically speaking, manifests itself wherever consciousness is not yet, or is no longer, centered around the ego."[39] Mysticism for Neumann moves throughout the entire development of the individuation process, from the "uroborous" stage, in which the ego is still one with the non-ego (not unlike Freud's understanding of the regressive nature of "oceanic feeling"), through the development of the ego toward its encounter with the "numinous transpersonal."[40] The overcoming of the antithesis between the ego with its customary structures and the numinous understood as the depth dimension of consciousness (the non-ego) transforms and merges both partners and thus produces, momentarily, or by way of lasting transformation, the truly individuated self. Therefore, *homo mysticus,* in Neumann's terminology, is the definition and goal of all human life.

Neumann's development of the mystical synthesis through its various stages is heavily dependent on the Jungian model of self-integration and is difficult to square with any traditional mystical model. The adaptation of this psychological perspective demands a concerted lack of attention to the particularities of the historical record that historians, and even theologians, will find hard to accept. The Jungian view of mysticism, at least as advanced by Neumann, is something like Bergsonianism: in making the mystical the essence of all human striving it seems to make it at once too general, and yet also too particular as the captive of a specific psychological hermeneutic.

The figures dealt with thus far for the most part did the major part of their creative work in the first third of the present century. The past fifty or more years of comparativist and psychological study of mysticism are more difficult to summarize if only because they stand closer to us in time.

The comparativists and historians of religion most active in the middle of the present century (roughly 1935–1970) were also interested in mysticism, though none of the major theorists, such as Gerardus van der Leeuw (1890–1950), Joachim Wach (1898–1955), and Mircea Eliade (1907–1986), wrote major works on the topic. Van der Leeuw's *Phänomenologie der Religion* (1933) was translated into English in 1938 as *Religion in Essence and Manifestation.* The book treats mysticism as one of the forms of inward action demonstrating the reciprocal operation of the subject and object of religion, the dipolarity upon which the Dutch scholar based his phenomenological approach.[41] Joachim Wach, who began his career in Germany but taught in the United States from 1935 to 1955, studied with both Heiler and Otto. His work *The Sociology of Religion* (1944) has some observations on the social forms compatible with the radical individualism he thought of as the fundamental characteristic of mysticism, a view which displays his training in German Protestant thought.[42]

Mircea Eliade, who taught first in Paris (1946–1956), and then in Chicago (1956–1986), contributed major works early in his career on two important non-Western religious forms that have often been described as mystical, or at least related to mysticism: *Yoga: Immortality and Freedom* (first published in French in 1948), and *Shamanism: Archaic Techniques of Ecstasy* (French original 1951). Eliade's large *oeuvre* contains papers and contributions devoted to descriptions of particular aspects of comparative mysticism,[43] but neither his early synchronic survey, *Patterns of Comparative Religion* (French original 1948; English 1958), nor his unfinished diachronic work, *A History of Religious Ideas* (French original 1976–83; English 1978–85) contains independent theoretical discussions of the nature of mysticism.[44] Perhaps Eliade's overriding interest in the primordial origins of religion led to a certain lack of attention to the more developed forms of mysticism in the strict sense among the high religions of the West.[45]

Other historians of religion of the middle part of the century also contributed to the study of mysticism, though none in ways that seem to have had a decisive influence. Ernst Arbman, professor of comparative religion at Stockholm from 1937 to 1958, died before the publication of his three-volume compilation entitled *Ecstasy or Religious Trance* (1963–70). Despite Arbman's wide reading, the work is too disorganized, prolix, and unreadable to be of much value. Arbman's interest in religious ecstasy has continued in Scandinavian history of religions.[46] Ernst Benz (1907–1978), another Marburg historian of religion, wrote many papers devoted to comparative mystical themes, especially for the Eranos Conferences, the meetings of the group influenced by Jung which have been held every summer at Ascona since 1933. In 1969 Benz published a large comparativist study on visionary experience, *Die Vision: Erfahrungsformen und Bilderwelt.*

Arguably the most impressive insights into the comparative study of mysticism made during the middle years of the century came from the pen of the premier scholar of Jewish mysticism, Gershom Scholem (1897–1982).[47] Scholem's groundbreaking contributions to the study of Jewish mysticism rest on a host of articles and three major books: *Major Trends in Jewish Mysticism* (mostly given as lectures in 1938 and first published in 1941); *Sabbatai Sevi: The Mystical Messiah* (Hebrew original 1956; English 1973); and *Origins of the Kabbalah* (German original 1962; English 1987). The first chapter of *Major Trends* and two important essays summarize Scholem's general theory of mysticism.

The Jewish scholar's interpretation of mysticism was tied to a view of religion that seems to have been largely shaped by German philosophy. Warning against overly speculative definitions of the term, he insisted that "there is no mysticism as such, there is only the mysticism of a particular religious system, Christian, Islamic, Jewish mysticism, and so on."[48] Quoting the Quaker scholar Rufus Jones, who defined mysticism as "the type of religion which puts emphasis on immediate awareness of relation with God,"[49] Scholem refused to restrict mysticism to the experience of union with God (*unio mystica*), a salutary suggestion, though one perhaps more conditioned by his questionable exclusion of any kind of union from Jewish mysticism than by theoretical reasons.[50] Above all, Scholem emphasized that "mysticism is a definite stage in the historical development of religion and makes its appearance under certain well-defined conditions," that is, during particular moments in the evolution of religious consciousness.[51]

Scholem's theory of the evolution of religion involved three general stages: (1) the mythical foundation when no gap existed between the gods and humanity; (2) the creative or classical phase in which the breakthrough to institutional religion destroyed the undifferentiated harmony of God, man, and universe to establish a polarity in which God addressed and demanded service from humans; and finally (3) the romantic stage in which mysticism revived mythical thought and strove to win back the original unity "in a new upsurge of the religious consciousness."[52] This stage frequently arose in conjunction with new religious impulses that did not break with the inherited values of the institutional religion, but that valorized and deepened them on the basis of the "direct contact between the individual and God" that is the basis of mysticism.[53]

This theory of the place of mysticism in the evolution of religion led to original reflections on the social role of mysticism, a much-neglected area, as Scholem observed. Against those who claimed that mysticism is always inherently radical and at least potentially revolutionary in relation to established religion because of its claims to direct access to God, Scholem advanced a more nuanced dialectical view of the relation between mysticism and society. "All mysticism has two contradictory or complementary aspects: the one conservative, the other revolutionary."[54] Though the mystic begins with a personal quest for God that takes him or her far from human society, mysticism as a historical phenomenon comes about only when and insofar as the mystic returns to society in order to communicate or to give form to the originally formless message. Here the dialectical character of mysticism's relation to its societal context becomes manifest. The mystic must speak the language of the tradition in order to be understood at all, but in doing so she or he is confronted by certain choices and problems. Insofar as the mystic identifies the source of the mystical communication with the original revelation grounding the tradition, mysticism can serve as a conservative force renewing and strengthening that tradition, as Scholem argued it generally had in the history of Judaism.[55] If the mystic, in situations of conflict with religious authority,[56] comes to value the source of mystical revelation higher than the founding revelation of the tradition and thus finds it increasingly difficult to use the inherited religious language to interpret the new message, then the revolutionary power of mysticism will burst forth, either as mystical nihilism, some form of sectarianism based on an invisible church, or as a force in combination with messianism (e.g., the Sabbatian movement, or Thomas Müntzer).[57]

Scholem's analysis of the social dynamics of mysticism is more convincing than nondialectical views, even if one can question his overemphasis on the private and formless nature of the original mystical revelation. Such revelation is prepared for and mediated by the beliefs and practices of the institutional element of any religion and therefore, at least in principle, can have a public component from its origins. On a more general level, we can ask if Scholem was correct in seeing mysticism as primarily a particular historical stage rather than a constant element or possibility in religion. Why can't a religion begin on the mystical level? Alternatively, why can't concrete existing religions display a continuing interaction between classical and romantic elements throughout their recorded history? Scholem's important insights about the dialectical nature of mysticism need to be reconsidered on the basis of a more detailed and critical theory of religions in their full historical development.

It is not out of place here to consider another Jewish author, who, like Gershom Scholem, fled Germany to settle in Israel (though only for part of his academic career). Hans Jonas (1903–), who studied under Rudolf Bultmann, advanced the intellectual traditions of the *religionsgeschichtliche Schule* in the study of Gnosticism and other religious and mystical movements of late antiquity, though from a philosophical perspective influenced by his studies with Martin Heidegger. Only two parts of his major work, *Gnosis und spätantike Geist,* were published (1934, 1954). In the second volume, subtitled *Von der Mythologie zur mystischen Philosophie,* Jonas presented an account of the origins of Western mysticism that can be described as both comparativist and philosophical. He later summarized his thesis in a memorable paper delivered to the American Academy of Religion in 1968 and subsequently published in the *Journal of Religion* under the title "Myth and Mysticism."[58]

Jonas based his historical reconstruction on an existentialist analysis of the ways in which objectifications of existential realizations of subjectivity are constructed.[59] He insisted on the irreducible mutuality of spirit and world in the objectification process: "The entire world is spiritualized through a spirit made worldly."[60] Both myth and mysticism are related expressions of the inner existential ground of the subject, "a total attitude toward being, whose theoretical explication is its own urgent concern."[61] Myth is the objective representation of this "way of being in the world" and is generally prior in time to the mystical objectification, "which may appear as an internalized version of the same motif."[62] The historical development of the inner relations between myth and mysticism is quite complex, at least in Western religious history, as Jonas illustrates through his consideration of mystery cults, Gnosticism, and mystical theory as found in Origen and Plotinus.[63] Following a basic theme of ancient religion, the doctrine of the emanation of the soul presented as a process of descent and ascent, Jonas shows how by a form of "psychologization" the eschatological or salvational myth of the Hellenistic world gave rise first to the Gnostic myth, which he considers an intermediary stage, and eventually to mystical philosophy and mysticism. As he puts it, "With this transposition of a mythological scheme into the inwardness of the person, with the translation of its objective stages into subjective phases of self-performable experience whose culmination has the form of *ecstasis* or mystic union, gnostic myth passes into mysticism (Neoplatonic and monastic). . . ."[64]

In classical antiquity, a secondary mediating factor that made possible the movement of objective mythic structure back into its existential ground via mystical theory was found in the mystery cults in which the ritual or sacramental performance of the myth, especially in its later more spiritualized interpretations, created the basic categories and images later used by mystical thought — catharsis, ecstasy, union, perfection, and the like.[65] Building on this highly original account, Jonas presents an important critique of the usual view that mystical theory is nothing more than a secondary reflection and projection of mystical "experience." He sees this as putting the cart before the horse — rather, theoretical objectification precedes as an a priori condition for the possibility of mystical experience! The explicit theory or "primal objectification" of the existential stance

> . . . furnishes the horizon for its evidential experiences and specifies them in advance. It inspires the search for them, fastens them, and legitimates them. Without antecedent dogmatics there would be no valid mysticism. And mysticism, let it be noted, wants to be "valid," namely, more than a revel in feeling.[66]

In a few pages Jonas's brilliant paper manages to give a synoptic theory of the development of early Western mysticism, as well as an original insight into the relation between experience and theory in mysticism in general. Still, experts in the religion of late antiquity may question the rather murky philosophical presuppositions of his historical reconstruction, and comparativists may wonder if his insistence that dogmatics *must* precede "valid mysticism" is too one-sided a view of the intricate ways within which forms of religious experience and theoretical systems mediate the ongoing development of mystical traditions.

Among the comparativist contributions to the study of mysticism in the past generation the name of Robert Charles Zaehner (1913–1974), Spalding Professor of Eastern Religions and Ethics at Oxford, stands out. His *Mysticism Sacred and Profane* (1957) remains, along with Evelyn Underhill's *Mysticism,* perhaps the most read English work on the subject in this century.

A convert to Roman Catholicism, Zaehner's approach to mysticism, while well grounded in the languages and texts of several traditions, especially Persian and Hindu, was scarcely a disinterested one. For Zaehner comparative studies need not be nonjudgmental, and the grounds for his own judgments were clearly formed by his Catholic beliefs and to a lesser extent by his interest in Jungian psychology. Virtually every major treatment of mysticism in recent years has discussed Zaehner's book, and for at least three reasons. First, the work is engaging and clearly written (something that cannot be said for many books on the subject). Second, Zaehner challenged the prevailing view of the unity of mystical experience by advancing a classification of three discrete types of mysticism — nature mysticism, monistic mysticism, and theistic mysticism. Third, the very title of *Mysticism Sacred and Profane* reflected a new context for the study of mysticism, the beginnings of the search by disaffected Western intellectuals for ecstatic experiences through experiments with drugs and/or a turn to Eastern religions and meditational techniques.

In 1954 Aldous Huxley, one of the foremost English men of letters of the day, issued an essay entitled *The Doors of Perception,* in which he recounted his experiments with the American Indian hallucinogen peyote, claiming that with its help he had attained contemplation at its height, "but not yet in its fullness."[67] Huxley's experience was a warning of things to come, things which Zaehner abhorred. In *Mysticism Sacred and Profane* Zaehner attacked Huxley's "platitudinous premise" that every form of preternatural experience is necessarily a mystical one, arguing that there is an essential difference between nature mysticism and forms of religious mysticism.[68]

Confining himself to "praeternatural experiences in which sense perception and discursive thought are transcended in an immediate apperception of a unity or union which is apprehended as lying beyond and transcending the multiplicity of the world as we know it,"[69] Zaehner identified his three distinct kinds of mysticism. "First is the experience which tells you that you are all and that all is you," the nature mysticism he calls "pan-en-henism." The second type "is to experience one's soul as being the Absolute, and not to experience the phenomenal world at all." "Thirdly there is the normal type of Christian mystical experience in which the soul feels itself to be united with God by love."[70] Although union is the essence or keynote of all three types of mysticism,[71] there is a crucial divide between union with Nature, in part or in whole, and the two higher forms of union, the union of pure self-isolation and loving union with God, both of which exclude the phenomenal world.[72]

Oddly enough, given his judgment on the value of the three kinds of experience, Zaehner's book is most successful in its discussion of nature mysticism, especially in relation to Proust and Rimbaud (chaps. 3-5). In turning to the higher mystical forms of monism (chaps. 6-8) and theism (chap. 9), the arbitrariness of his views, the selective nature of his evidence, and the irruption of sudden theological evaluations,[73] render his argument methodologically unsystematic and at times delightfully idiosyncratic. One evident theoretical problem is Zaehner's rigid views of monism and theism, views that leave no room for dialectical mysticisms that affirm both identity and distinction between the human and the divine.[74]

It is important to note that Zaehner's analysis of mysticism implies a rather different view of the relation of experience to the mystical text from what we have seen in most contemporary philosophical discussion. The Oxford don begins from the premise that different descriptions imply different experiences, a position criticized by those whose starting point is the conviction that all mystical texts are merely interpretations of an experience that *must* be the same.[75] One can, of course, take Zaehner's approach a step further and ask why he restricts the kinds of mysticism to three, when the descriptions within and across traditions seem to point to a much greater diversity. Further, Zaehner's assertion of the superiority of theistic mysticism has been much criticized, even by some fellow Catholics.[76] Claims of this sort, when advanced by Catholic philosophers like Maréchal and Maritain, or theologians like Stolz or von Balthasar, are not unexpected. Coming from a comparativist like Zaehner, they have been treated as somehow less appropriate.[77]

The most interesting recent comparativist work on mysticism has tended to be concerned with specific traditions rather than with the construction of general theories.[78] Thus, the works of Annemarie Schimmel on Islamic mysticism have been widely read, and not just by students of Islamic mysticism.[79] From a more philosophical perspective, Toshihiko Izutsu's *Sufism and Taoism: A Comparative Study of Key Philosophical Concepts* (1983) has been praised. During this past generation, the growing interest in mysticism has also produced numerous introductions to and anthologies of world mysticism,[80] works which may serve a useful function for the general reader but which rarely make significant new contributions to the theory of mysticism. (Anthologies of Christian mysticism have also been popular.)[81]

In concluding this brief section, it is necessary to take a very partial look at some recent contributions to the study of mysticism from the area of psychology. Here the most interesting materials, at least for those outside the camp of professional psychology, appear to have come from investigators who have combined an interest in altered states of consciousness with broad humanistic concerns about the place of mysticism in modern culture.

The study of ecstasy and other altered states of consciousness has attracted many, both from the camp of professional psychologists and from a wider group of authors. An example of the latter would be the 1961 book of Marghanita Laski, *Ecstasy: A Study of some Secular and Religious Experiences.* Laski, a novelist, became so fascinated with the subject of ecstasy that she decided to write a descriptive account based on a questionnaire she distributed to a number of friends (sixty-three responses were tabulated), as well as a series of excerpts from literary and religious texts. This lengthy but readable book is devoted to what she identifies as "a range of experiences characterized by being joyful, transitory, unexpected, rare, valued, and extraordinary to the point of often seeming as if derived from some praeternatural source."[82] Laski's work is one of the most detailed treatments of the nature of ecstasy, but it is marred by the rather vague and unprofessional nature of her original questionnaire, as well as by some a priori assumptions about the relation of experience and interpretation.[83] More overtly psychological in character is the book of Ben-Ami Scharfstein, *Mystical Experience* (1973), though it adds little that is original and is far less readable than Laski.[84]

Empirical research into altered states of consciousness has been a growing field in recent decades. Not all such research is directed to mysticism, but a number of significant recent studies have addressed the nature of meditation and mystical experience in general. What follows is a perhaps random sampling of some of these studies.

Arthur J. Deikman's paper "Deautomatization and the Mystic Experience" (1966) distinguishes three kinds of accounts of mystic experiences and two basic techniques involved in all mystical exercises, contemplation and renunciation. Deikman interprets such experiences as a "deautomatization of the psychological structures that organize, limit, select and interpret perceptual stimuli," seeking to show the relation between the traditional techniques of religious practices and modern psychological studies of deautomatizing.[85] By "reinvesting actions and percepts with attention," the mystic gains "in sensory intensity and richness at the expense of abstract categorization and differentiation."[86] The alternate modes of consciousness thus produced may be regressive, as Freud thought, or they may be "the result of the operation of a new perceptual capacity responsive to dimensions of the stimulus array previously ignored or blocked from awareness."[87] Deikman concludes the paper by noting that it is not within the purview of the psychologist to settle the question of the possibility of a transcendental source for some of these experiences. In his more recent book, however, *The Observing Self: Mysticism and Psychotherapy,* he argues for an easy rapprochement between a "religionless mysticism" and psychotherapy in a way that is more troubling for anyone with knowledge of the intimate relation between mysticism and religious practices in the history of humanity.[88]

Claudio Naranjo and Robert E. Ornstein provide another example of contemporary psychological interest in mysticism in their joint work *On the Psychology of Mysticism* (1971). Their expressed aim is to bring together the empirical-experiential mode of human understanding found in the East and the empirical-experimental one found in the West (the historian can only envy such ability to generalize!).[89] The survey of electroencephalogram (EEG) research on altered states of consciousness, both laboratory experiments and Eastern meditation techniques, is more interesting than the highly dubious historical generalizations found in this volume.[90] Experimental evidence seems to indicate that "continuous repetition of the same stimulus may be considered the equivalent of no stimulus at all," so that many traditional meditation practices that aim to produce a negative state of awareness through forms of concentrated attention seem to be examples of what can be called "practical applied psychology."[91] This analysis also uncovers how the detachment encouraged by such techniques and forms of meditation aims at a state of increased receptivity or expanded awareness in which the subject exists "totally in the moment," something not unlike the traditional Christian understanding of the union between action and contemplation.[92]

One final example of a recent psychological perspective on mysticism is that of Stanislav Grof, a Czech psychiatrist working in the United States who has done extensive research on the role of psychedelic drugs, especially LSD, in exploring the dimensions of human consciousness.[93] Grof distinguishes the psychodynamic experiences relating to the individual's history, the four basic perinatal experiences common to all human consciousness, and the transpersonal experiences in which the ego is surpassed in a variety of ways, including the mystical. Like Deikman, he brackets the question of the source of transpersonal experiences. As he puts it in his book *Beyond Death:*

The psychodynamic level draws from the individual's history and is clearly biographical in origin and nature. Perinatal experiences seem to represent a frontier between personal and trans-individual, as is reflected by their deep association with biological birth and death. The transpersonal realm, then, reflects the connections between the individual and cosmos mediated through channels which seem at present to be beyond our comprehension.[94]

Deikman, Naranjo and Ornstein, and Grof are cited here as examples of trends evident since about 1960 which have enabled psychologists and psychiatrists of various backgrounds to take a new look at mystical states of consciousness as part of a broad concern for investigating alternatives to mechanistic and deterministic views of human life. This concern is evident not only in individual authors but also in various symposia and collections of papers. In 1969, for example, Charles E. Tart edited a volume of papers under the title *Altered States of Consciousness,* summarizing works in the 1950s and 1960s in this area. This anthology (which includes papers by Ornstein and Deikman) evidences the fascination of modern Western psychology with Eastern meditational techniques, especially Zen and Yoga.[95]

The most-studied meditational technique in recent years has been the Yoga-based system of Transcendental Meditation (TM), popularized on a worldwide basis in recent decades by the Maharishi Mahesh Yogi and his disciples. A large compilation of papers devoted to TM was published in 1977 edited by David Orme-Johnson and John Farrow as *Scientific Research on the Transcendental Meditation Program: Collected Papers,* vol. 1. Since this volume was issued under the auspices of the controversial TM movement itself, some have doubted its impartiality. Nevertheless, a number of its offerings provide some indication of recent experimental attempts to correlate meditational states with empirically verifiable changes in brain functions, especially with increase in alpha-wave activity.[96] A more general collection of papers edited by Philip R. Lee and others under the title *Symposium on Consciousness* (1976) contains several offerings devoted to meditation and mysticism by major recent invesigators, such as Deikman, Ornstein, and Tart.

At the beginning of the century, Ernst Troeltsch in his 1904 essay "Psychology and Theory of Knowledge in the Science of Religion" noted concerning the modern science of religion that "it demands, above all, empirical knowledge of the phenomenon; but it demands this only in order, on the basis of this knowledge, to be able to answer the question of the amount of truth. But this leads to an entirely different problem, that of the theory of knowledge, which has its own conditions of solution. It is impossible to stop at merely empirical psychology."[97] Joseph Maréchal, as we have seen, argued a similar case, though from a different epistemological perspective, in his 1912 essay "Empirical Science and Religious Psychology."[98] Sigmund Freud, of course, would not have agreed, nor would many of his fellow psychologists and psychoanalysts. Some recent psychological investigators of mysticism, however, have been willing to go further, at least to the extent of seeing mystical states as more than mere regressions or repressions of sexuality, even bracketing the question of a possible transcendental source for some of the observable changes in brain patterns and the other physiological transmutations empirically connected with contemplative and meditational techniques. Others continue to insist that the mounting evidence that these changes can be induced through nonreligious means, especially through drugs, indicates that we are dealing with nothing more than little-understood operations of the natural human psyche.

In answering this claim philosophers and theologians of mysticism would tend to respond that epistemological issues do not belong to the category of questions that can be settled on the basis of empirical evidence alone, however interesting and important such evidence may be. The stand-off between empiricism and transempirical epistemology is as strong now as it was at the beginning of the century. Even those, like myself, who are convinced that a purely empirical reading of mystical texts from a reductive psychological perspective has only an ambiguous contribution to make to the present study of mysticism, cannot but be troubled by the lack of conversation between psychological investigators and those involved in studying the history and theory of mystical traditions. Both sides seem equally at fault in this unrealized conversation.

Notes ▣

General Introduction

1. M.-D. Chenu, *Nature, Man and Society in the Twelfth Century* (Chicago: University of Chicago Press, 1969), p. xx.

2. *The Life of Teresa of Jesus: The Autobiography of St. Teresa of Avila*, trans. and ed. E. Allison Peers (Garden City, NY: Doubleday Image Books, 1960), 1.10 (p. 119).

3. Evelyn Underhill, *Mysticism: A Study in the Nature and Development of Man's Spiritual Consciousness* (12th ed.; Cleveland and New York: World, 1965), p. 83, but see p. 95 for a qualification.

4. It might be suggested that Hans Urs von Balthasar's threefold distinction of *Mystik* as experience of God, *Mystologie* as categorical reflection and writing upon it, and *Mystagogie* as theoretical-practical instruction directed to the experience is more helpful than the usual twofold distinction, as long as the intimate relation of the three is not forgotten. See Werner Beierwaltes, Hans Urs von Balthasar, Alois M. Haas, *Grundfragen der Mystik* (Einsiedeln: Johannes Verlag, 1974), p. 52. For a consideration of von Balthasar's view of mysticism, see Appendix, section 1, pp. 289–90.

5. Such a view is traditional in Catholic theology to anyone who considers what Thomas Aquinas has to say about the nature of "sacra doctrina" in q. 1 of the first part of the *Summa theologiae*. "Sacra doctrina" is necessary for salvation, and therefore must be a part of the lived experience of every saving action, but it is also a true science insofar as it involves the subject's progressively greater grasp of the truth in dependence on the teaching of the most veracious Teacher.

6. Henri-Irenée Marrou, *The Meaning of History* (Baltimore and Dublin: Helicon, 1966), p. 131: "The historian begins by posing a question to himself. . . . The increase of knowledge is achieved by that dialectical movement described as circular—or better yet as spiral—in which the historian goes successively from the object of his study to the document that is its instrument, reciprocally. The question which started the whole process in motion does not maintain its original identity, but in contact with the documentary data it is continuously changing."

7. For a more detailed study of von Hügel's *The Mystical Element of Religion*, see Appendix, section 2, pp. 293–96.

8. There is no really adequate history of the originally Greek qualifier *mystikos* and its various derivatives. For a survey of the early uses, see Louis Bouyer, "Mysticism: An Essay on the History of the Word," in *Understanding Mysticism*, ed. Richard Woods (Garden City, NY: Doubleday Image Books, 1980), pp. 42–55. On the creation of

"mysticism" as a substantive and the significance of this in the history of mysticism, see Michel de Certeau, "'Mystique' au XVIIe siècle: Le problème du langage 'mystique,'" in *L'Homme devant Dieu: Mélanges offerts au Père Henri de Lubac*, 3 vols. (Paris: Aubier, 1964) 2:267-91. For more on de Certeau's studies of mystical hermeneutics, see Appendix, section 2, pp. 310-13.

9. For a sketch of some of the medieval varieties of understanding mystical union, see my paper "Love, Knowledge and *Unio Mystica* in the Western Christian Tradition," in *Mystical Union and Monotheistic Faith: An Ecumenical Dialogue*, ed. Moshe Idel and Bernard McGinn (New York: Macmillan, 1989), pp. 59-86, 203-19 (notes).

10. Joseph Maréchal's major works on mysticism are discussed in Appendix, section 2, pp. 297-302.

11. I have already presented some elements of this broad understanding of mysticism in my paper on "Love, Knowledge and *Unio Mystica*"; and in an essay entitled "Eriugena Mysticus," in *Giovanni Scoto nel suo tempo: L'Organizzazione del sapere nel età carolingia*, Atti del XXIV Convegno storico internazionale. Accademia Tudertina. Centro di Studi sulla spiritualità medievale (Spoleto: Centro Italiano di studi sull'alto medioevo, 1989), pp. 235-60 (esp. pp. 236-39).

12. A number of recent discussions of mysticism have suggested a shift to the language of consciousness, especially those of some of the followers of Bernard Lonergan; see Appendix, section 1, pp. 283-85.

13. *The Cloud of Unknowing*, edited with an Introduction by James Walsh, CWS (New York: Paulist, 1981), chaps. 68-69 (pp. 252-53).

14. *The Notebooks of Simone Weil*, trans. Arthur Wills, 2 vols. (London: Routledge & Kegan Paul, 1976) 1:239-40.

15. The following paragraph has been adapted from my paper "Eriugena Mysticus," pp. 238-39 (see n. 11).

16. For Maritain's theory of mysticism, see Appendix, section 2, pp. 305-10.

17. See Bernard Lonergan, *Method in Theology* (New York: Herder, 1972), pp. 77, 273, 340-42.

Introduction to Part I

1. The exegetical character of Christian mysticism, a major theme of these volumes, has been surprisingly neglected in many standard works on mysticism. For some useful remarks, see "Écriture sainte et vie spirituelle," *DS* 4:128-278; and Sandra M. Schneiders, "Scripture and Spirituality," in *Christian Spirituality: Origins to the Twelfth Century*, ed. Bernard McGinn and John Meyendorff, WS 16 (New York: Crossroad, 1986), pp. 1-20.

2. See A. J. Festugière's classic work, *Contemplation et vie contemplative selon Platon* (Paris: Vrin, 1936).

3. Among older works, the most useful remains Marcel Viller and Karl Rahner, *Aszese und Mystik in der Väterzeit: Ein Abriss* (Freiburg: Herder, 1939). More recently, see Louis Bouyer, *The Spirituality of the New Testament and the Fathers*, vol. 1 of *A History of Christian Spirituality* (New York: Seabury, 1982; French original, 1960); Andrew Louth, *The Origins of the Christian Mystical Tradition: From Plato to Denys* (Oxford: Clarendon, 1981); and *Christian Spirituality: Origins to the Twelfth Century*, WS 16.

4. See the discussion in Appendix, section 1, pp. 267-69.

5. F. Heiler, "Contemplation in Christian Mysticism," in *Spiritual Disciplines: Papers from the Eranos Yearbooks* (New York: Pantheon, 1960), p. 192.

Chapter 1

I wish to thank David Satran for reading this chapter and making several valuable suggestions. Part of the discussion of the apocalyptic literature above reflects materials delivered in my 1988 Haskell Lectures, "Endtime and Eternity: Biblical Apocalyptic and the Western

Tradition," given at Oberlin College. Some of it appears in an expanded form in my essay "The Apocalypse and Apocalyptic Literature," in *The Apocalypse in the Middle Ages,* ed. Richard K. Emmerson and Bernard McGinn (Ithaca: Cornell University Press, 1992) (to appear).

1. Michael Stone, *Scriptures, Sects and Visions: A Profile of Judaism from Ezra to the Jewish Revolts* (Philadelphia: Fortress, 1980), p. 18. The terms Judaism (*ioudaismos*) and Hellenism (*hellenismos*) first occur in the deuterocanonical work 2 Maccabees from the late second century B.C.E. (see 2:21 and 4:13).

2. See V. Tcherikover, *Hellenistic Civilization and the Jews* (New York: Atheneum, 1970); Martin Hengel, *Judaism and Hellenism,* 2 vols. (Philadelphia: Fortress, 1974); John J. Collins, *Between Athens and Jerusalem: Jewish Identity in the Hellenistic Diaspora* (New York: Crossroad, 1983). On the Hellenistic mingling of cultures, see also Arnaldo Momigliano, *Alien Wisdom: The Limits of Hellenization* (Cambridge: Cambridge University Press, 1975).

3. See Stone, *Scriptures, Sects and Visions,* pp. 112–16; Isaiah Gafni, "The Historical Background," in *Jewish Writings of the Second Temple Period,* ed. Michael E. Stone, Compendia Rerum Iudaicarum ad Novum Testamentum, Section 2 (Philadelphia: Fortress, 1984), p. 3.

4. The literature on apocalypses and their content is immense. For a brief survey, see Ithamar Gruenwald, "Jewish Apocalypticism to the Rabbinic Period," in *The Encyclopedia of Religion,* ed. Mircea Eliade (New York: Macmillan, 1987) 1:336–42. Longer recent accounts are John J. Collins, *The Apocalyptic Imagination: An Introduction to the Jewish Matrix of Christianity* (New York: Crossroad, 1984); and Michael E. Stone, "Apocalyptic Literature," in *Jewish Writings of the Second Temple Period,* pp. 383–440.

5. For a brief account of apocalyptic eschatology, see Bernard McGinn, "Early Apocalypticism: The ongoing debate," in *The Apocalypse in English Renaissance thought and literature,* ed. C. A. Patrides and Joseph Wittreich (Ithaca: Cornell University Press, 1984), pp. 2–39.

6. See M. E. Stone, "Lists of Revealed Things in Apocalyptic Literature," in *Magnalia Dei: The Mighty Acts of God,* ed. F. M. Cross et al. (Garden City, NY: Doubleday, 1976), pp. 414–52.

7. John J. Collins, ed., in *Apocalypse: Morphology of a Genre,* Semeia 14 (Missoula, MT: Scholars Press, 1979), p. 9. This definition has been criticized by E. P. Sanders, "The Genre of Palestinian Jewish Apocalypses," in *Apocalypticism in the Mediterranean World and the Near East,* ed. David Hellholm (Tübingen: Mohr, 1983), pp. 447–59; see also in the same volume Lars Hartman, "Survey of the Problem of Apocalyptic Genre," pp. 329–43.

8. Collins, in *Apocalypse: Morphology,* pp. 12–19.

9. For a brief description of the formation of the canon of the Hebrew Bible and references to further literature, see Joel Rosenberg, "Biblical Tradition: Literature and Spirit in Ancient Israel," in *Jewish Spirituality: From the Bible through the Middle Ages,* ed. Arthur Green, WS 13 (New York: Crossroad, 1986), pp. 82–85.

10. See Michael Fishbane, *Biblical Interpretation in Ancient Israel* (Oxford: Clarendon, 1985).

11. Stone, *Scriptures, Sects and Visions,* p. 24 (cf. p. 116). See also M. E. Stone, "Eschatology, Remythologization and Cosmic Aporia," in *The Origins and Diversity of Axial Age Civilizations,* ed. S. N. Eisenstadt (Albany: SUNY Press, 1986), pp. 242–45.

12. James L. Kugel and Rowan A. Greer, *Early Biblical Interpretation* (Philadelphia: Westminster, 1986), p. 13.

13. For a brief introduction to the Greek roots of Christian spiritual reading of scripture, see Robert M. Grant, *The Letter and the Spirit* (New York: Macmillan, 1957), chaps. 1–2. A more detailed history of Greek allegory and its influence on Christians and Jews can be found in Jean Pépin's classic work, *Mythe et allégorie: Les origines grecques et les contestations judéochrétiennes* (Paris: Aubier, 1958).

14. This translation is from *Philo of Alexandria,* translations and introduction by David Winston, CWS (New York: Paulist, 1981), p. 79.

15. M. E. Stone, "Apocalyptic—Vision or Hallucination?" *Milla wa-Milla* 13 (1973), pp. 53–54.

16. For a survey of recent literature, see the section "Pseudepigraphy, Inspiration and Esotericism," in Stone's "Apocalyptic Literature," pp. 427–33.

17. Jacob Neusner, "Varieties of Judaism in the Formative Age," in *Jewish Spirituality*, ed. Green, p. 176.

18. An extensive literature has been devoted to *1 Enoch* in recent years. For an introduction, see Stone, "Apocalyptic Literature," pp. 395–406.

19. Trans. E. Isaac in *Apocalyptic Literature and Testaments*, vol. 1 of *The Old Testament Pseudepigrapha*, ed. James H. Charlesworth, 2 vols. (Garden City, NY: Doubleday, 1983, 1985). All translations from Second Temple literature will be taken from this collection unless otherwise noted.

20. Alan F. Segal, "Heavenly Ascent in Hellenistic Judaism, Early Christianity and their Environment," in *Aufstieg und Niedergang der römischen Welt, II. Prinzipat* (Berlin and New York: de Gruyter, 1980), 23.2, p. 1388.

21. Ioan Petru Culianu, *Psychanodia I: A Survey of the Evidence concerning the Ascension of the Soul and its Relevance* (Leiden: Brill, 1983), pp. 5–15.

22. Morton Smith, "Ascent to the Heavens and the Beginning of Christianity," *Eranos Yearbook* 50 (1981), p. 405.

23. The classic account is that of Wilhelm Bousset, "Die Himmelsreise der Seele," *Archiv für Religionswissenschaft* 4 (1901): 136–69, 229–73.

24. John S. Hanson, "Dreams and Visions in the Graeco-Roman World and Early Christianity," in *Aufstieg und Niedergang, Prinzipat*, 23.2, p. 1409.

25. See esp. Culianu, *Psychanodia*, chaps. 2 and 3; and his "Introduction," in *Expériences de l'Extase: Extase, Ascension et Récit visionnaire de l'Hellenisme au Moyen Âge* (Paris: Payot, 1984). See also Segal, "Heavenly Ascent," pp. 1334–51.

26. Culianu, *Expériences de l'Extase*, pp. 19–21.

27. E.g., M. E. Stone, "Apocalyptic—Vision or Hallucination?" pp. 47–56; Susan Niditch, "The Visionary," in *Ideal Figures in Ancient Judaism*, ed. George W. E. Nickelsburg and John J. Collins (Chico: Scholars Press, 1980), pp. 153–79; Christopher Rowland, *The Open Heaven: A Study of Apocalyptic in Judaism and Early Christianity* (New York: Crossroad, 1982), esp. pp. 78–123, 358–402; Martha Himmelfarb, "From Prophecy to Apocalypse: The *Book of Watchers* and Tours of Heaven," in *Jewish Spirituality*, ed. Green, pp. 145–65.

28. The most detailed of these is found in *2 Enoch* 22 after an ascent through seven heavens. The dating of this text is much disputed, but the work may well be Jewish of the first century C.E. For others, see, e.g., *Apocalypse of Moses* 37–39, *Apocalypse of Abraham* 15–32, *3 Baruch* 6–9, and the Parables of *1 Enoch* 70–71.

29. See Jon D. Levenson, "The Jerusalem Temple in Devotional and Visionary Experience," in *Jewish Spirituality*, ed. Green, pp. 32–61; idem, *Sinai and Zion* (Minneapolis: Winston-Seabury, 1985), chap. 2. For a general introduction to the history of theophanies in the Hebrew Bible, see James Barr, "Theophany and Anthropomorphism in the Old Testament," in *Congress Volume: Oxford 1959*, Supplements to *Vetus Testamentum* 7 (Leiden: Brill, 1960), pp. 31–38.

30. Levenson, "Jerusalem Temple," pp. 43–51.

31. On the meaning of this vision, see Moshe Greenberg, *Ezechiel 1–20*, The Anchor Bible 22 (Garden City, NY: Doubleday, 1983), pp. 37–59.

32. See Himmelfarb, "From Prophecy to Apocalypse," pp. 150–51.

33. Gershom Scholem, *Major Trends in Jewish Mysticism* (New York: Schocken, 1961), pp. 43–45.

34. David Halperin distinguishes four Jewish types of ascension account along with Paul's autobiographical narrative in 2 Corinthians 12 ("Heavenly Ascension in Ancient Judaism: The Nature of the Experience," in *Society of Biblical Literature 1987 Seminar Papers*, ed. K. H. Richards [Atlanta: Scholars Press, 1987], pp. 218–20).

35. Rowland, *Open Heaven*, pp. 214–47.

36. Both Rowland (*Open Heaven*, pp. 232–34) and Himmelfarb ("From Prophecy to

Apocalypse," pp. 153–54) are willing to describe them as mystical, as is I. Gruenwald, who entitles the second chapter of his *Apocalyptic and Merkavah Mysticism* (Leiden: Brill, 1980) "The Mystical Elements in Apocalyptic" (pp. 29–72). Halperin, on the basis of the fact that a journey through seven heavens cannot be "objectively" real to any post-Copernican, seeks for explanations in Freudian psychology without any recognition that this understanding of the world is also conditioned by its historical and cultural context (Halperin, "Heavenly Ascension," pp. 220–30; see also D. Halperin, "Ascension or Invasion: Implications of the Heavenly Journey in Ancient Judaism," *Religion* 18 [1988]: 47–67). As Martha Himmelfarb reminds us, "mystical visions are not independent of the visionary's assumptions about the world" ("From Prophecy to Apocalypse," p. 153).

37. Gruenwald, "Jewish Apocalypticism to the Rabbinic Period," p. 340.

38. See Himmelfarb, "From Prophecy to Apocalypse," pp. 161–62.

39. Stone, "Eschatology, Remythologization and Cosmic Aporia," p. 246.

40. John J. Collins, "Apocalyptic Eschatology as the Transcendence of Death," *Catholic Biblical Quarterly* 36 (1974): 21–43.

41. Bousset, "Die Himmelsreise der Seele," p. 136.

42. Kugel, *Early Biblical Interpretation,* p. 45.

43. E.g., A. J. Festugière, *Personal Religion among the Greeks* (Berkeley: University of California Press, 1954), chaps. 3 and 7; Franz Cumont, *Astrology and Religion among the Greeks and Romans* (1912; reprint, New York: Dover, 1960). For a recent survey, see Jean Pépin, "Cosmic Piety," in *Classical Mediterranean Spirituality: Egyptian, Greek, Roman,* ed A. H. Armstrong, WS 15 (New York: Crossroad, 1986), pp. 408–35.

44. See John J. Collins, "Cosmos and Salvation: Jewish Wisdom and Apocalyptic in the Hellenistic World," *History of Religions* 17 (1977): 121–42.

45. For comparisons between Wisdom and Philo, see David Winston, *The Wisdom of Solomon,* The Anchor Bible 43 (Garden City, NY: Doubleday, 1979), pp. 59–63 (whose translation I am using here). See also his "Philo and the Contemplative Life," in *Jewish Spirituality,* ed. Green, pp. 206–7.

46. On this, see Kugel, *Early Biblical Interpretation,* pp. 44–51.

47. For "cosmic paranoia," see Jonathan Z. Smith, "Birth Upside Down or Right Side Up?" *History of Religions* 9 (1970), p. 295.

48. See esp. Walter Schmithals, *The Apocalyptic Movement: Introduction and Interpretation* (Nashville: Abingdon, 1975), pp. 89–110; Francis Fallon, "The Gnostic Apocalypses," in *Apocalypse: Morphology,* pp. 123–58; and esp. George MacRae, "Apocalyptic Eschatology in Gnosticism," in *Apocalypticism in the Mediterranean World and the Near East,* ed. Hellholm, pp. 317–25.

49. Culianu, *Psychanodia,* p. 21; see also his *Expériences de l'Extase,* chap. 2, "Demonisation du cosmos et dualisme gnostique."

50. Gruenwald, *Apocalyptic and Merkavah Mysticism.*

51. A reminiscence does seem to appear in the first-century c.e. Jewish apocalypse 4 Ezra 5:24–26.

52. *Tosefta Sanhedrin* 12.10, as translated in *Song of Songs: A New Translation with Introduction and Commentary,* by Marvin H. Pope, The Anchor Bible 7C (Garden City, NY: Doubleday, 1977), p. 19.

53. The oldest account appears to be that found in the Tosefta Ḥagigah 2.2–3. For a translation and commentary, see Louis Jacobs, *Jewish Mystical Traditions* (New York: Schocken, 1978), pp. 21–25. Recently, Peter Schaefer has denied that this text originally had a mystical meaning, though he admits a subsequent mystical interpretation. See his "New Testament and Hekhalot Literature: The Journey into Heaven in Paul and in Merkabah Mysticism," *Journal of Jewish Studies* 35 (1984), pp. 24–32.

54. G. Scholem, *Jewish Gnosticism, Merkabah Mysticism, and Talmudic Tradition* (New York: Jewish Theological Seminary of America, 1965), pp. 36–42; S. Lieberman, "Mishnath Shir ha-Shirim," republished in the same volume on pp. 118–26; Joseph Dan, *Three Types of Ancient*

Jewish Mysticism, The Seventh Annual Louis Feinberg Memorial Lecture in Judaic Studies (Cincinnati: University of Cincinnati Press, 1984), pp. 9–11; idem, "The Religious Experience of the 'Merkavah,'" in *Jewish Spirituality,* ed. Green, pp. 292–96.

55. Dan, following Scholem and Lieberman, believes that the *Shi'ur Qomah* is directly tied to a mystical exegesis based on the Song of Songs and that the text dates from the second century C.E. Martin Samuel Cohen doubts the directness of the tie to the Song and dates the text tentatively to the sixth century C.E. (*The Shi'ur Qomah: Liturgy and Theurgy in Pre-Kabbalistic Jewish Mysticism* [Lanham, MD: University Press of America, 1983], pp. 21–31, 65).

56. Dan, *Three Types,* p. 9.

57. The relation between Origen's reading and that of the rabbis has been studied by Ephraim E. Urbach, "The Homiletic Interpretations of the Sages and the Expositions of Origen on Canticles, and the Jewish-Christian Disputation," *Scripta Hierosolymitana* 22 (1971): 247–75. See also Nicholas de Lange, *Origen and the Jews* (Cambridge: Cambridge University Press, 1976).

58. Urbach, "Homiletic Interpretations," p. 252; and Scholem, *Jewish Gnosticism,* pp. 38–40.

Chapter 2

I would like to thank David Satran and David Tracy for reading an earlier version of this chapter and for making helpful suggestions. I also wish to note that given the background nature of this and the following three chapters, I will not always provide the original, largely Greek, texts in the notes, but only quote essential phrases where needed in the text and notes. Titles of ancient texts will be given in English unless otherwise noted.

1. On this text, see the discussion in Robert M. Grant, *The Early Christian Doctrine of God* (Charlottesville: University Press of Virginia, 1966), pp. 18–22. In *Dialogue* 8, Justin's goal is to "become acquainted with Christ, and after being initiated (or made perfect—*teleiō genomenō*), live the blessed life."

2. *Sayings of the Desert Fathers* (Alphabetical Collection) (*PG* 65:313). I am using the translation of Benedicta Ward, *The Sayings of the Desert Fathers: The Alphabetical Collection* (London: Mowbrays, 1975), p. 135. A. J. Festugière cites the story as a way of illustrating the contrast between pagan mysticism and Christian charity, but without noting the ambiguity of the elders' approval of the pagan priest's observations (*L'Enfant d'Agrigente* [Paris: Plon, 1950], pp. 127–28). It is interesting to note the combination of the language of contemplation (*theōria*) and revelation (*apokalypsis*) in this account.

3. This is evident from the fact that by far the longest entry in the *DS* is the great, multiauthor article "Contemplation" in *DS* 2:1643–2193.

4. Andre Jean Festugière, *Contemplation et vie contemplative selon Platon* (Paris: Vrin, 1936), p. 5.

5. See Appendix, section 1, pp. 267–69.

6. Esp. "Mystique païenne et charité," and "Ascése et contemplation," in Festugière, *L'Enfant d'Agrigente,* pp. 127–48.

7. A. J. Festugière, *Personal Religion among the Greeks* (Berkeley and Los Angeles: University of California Press, 1954), p. 2: "But Plato is not an isolated prodigy in the history of Greek religion. If he left his mark on all that came after, he himself bears the mark of all that went before."

8. Ugo Bianchi, "Initiation, Mystères, Gnose (Pour l'histoire de la mystique dans la paganisme greco-oriental)," in *Initiation,* ed. C. J. Bleeker (Leiden: Brill, 1975), pp. 154–71; idem, "Osservazioni storico-religiose sul concetto di mistica," in *Mistica e Misticismo Oggi* (Rome: Passionisti, 1979), pp. 225–33.

9. Unless otherwise noted, I will make use of the text and translations of Plato found in the twelve-volume edition of the LC.

10. As recognized in Paul Friedlander, *Plato: An Introduction* (New York: Harper, 1958), chap. 1.

11. On this mediating function, see Ernst Hoffmann, *Platonismus und Mystik im Altertum: Sitzungsberichte der Heidelberge Akademie der Wissenschaften. Philosophisch-historische Klasse, 1934-35.* 2 Abhandlung (Heidelberg: Carl Winter, 1935), pp. 7-8, 22-25.

12. Peter Manchester, "The Religious Experience of Time and Eternity," in *Classical Mediterranean Spirituality: Egyptian, Greek, Roman,* ed. A. H. Armstrong, WS 15 (New York: Crossroad, 1986), p. 393.

13. See E. R. Dodds, *The Greeks and the Irrational* (Berkeley: University of California Press, 1963), pp. 207-35. Plato criticized the traditional gods in *Laws* 10 and elsewhere, but never advocated a complete break with traditional religion. For a succinct summary of his views, see Daniel Babut, *La religion des philosophes grecs* (Paris: Presses universitaires de France, 1974), pp. 75-104.

14. Festugière, *Personal Religion,* chap. 3; the citation is from p. 46.

15. For a critique of Christianity's ambivalence toward accepting the holiness of the cosmos, see A. H. Armstrong, "St. Augustine and Christian Platonism," in *Plotinian and Christian Studies* (London: Variorum Reprints, 1979), XI, esp. pp. 14-24.

16. *Symposium* 209E: *telea kai epoptika.* Plato uses the language of the mystery cults in other places to describe the mystical goal; see *Symposium* 210E; *Phaedrus* 249C, 250B, etc. See Éduard des Places, "Platon et la langue des mystères," in *Études platoniciennes* (Leiden: Brill, 1981), pp. 83-98. On Diotima, see David M. Halperin, "Why is Diotima a Woman? Platonic *Eros* and the Figuration of Gender," in *Before Sexuality: The Construction of Erotic Experience in the Ancient Greek World,* ed. David M. Halperin et al. (Princeton: Princeton University Press, 1990), pp. 257-308.

17. *Symposium* 212A: *theophilei* (my translation).

18. Anders Nygren, *Agape and Eros* (Philadelphia: Westminster, 1953), pp. 175-81.

19. As pointed out by R. A. Markus, "The Dialectic of Eros in Platos's Symposium," *Downside Review* 73 (1955): 219-30.

20. E.g., Irving Singer is too quick in affirming an impersonal understanding of love union in Plato (*The Nature of Love: 1, Plato to Luther* [2nd ed.; Chicago: University of Chicago Press, 1984], pp. 67-70).

21. See Festugière, *Contemplation,* p. 205.

22. E.g., Singer, *The Nature of Love,* p. 73; A. H. Armstrong, "Platonic Mysticism," *The Dublin Review* 216 (1945), pp. 133-34.

23. Festugière, *Contemplation,* p. 220: "*Voir,* quand il s'agit des relations entre intellect et l'etre, ne peut signifier qu'une union immédiate, supérieure et à la production d'une image et à la production d'un concept, une union d'ordre mystique"; see pp. 208-9, 217-19, 260-62, 266, 288, 343, 452, etc. For an alternative view, see Richard Sorabji, "Myths about nonpropositional thought," in *Language and Logos: Studies in ancient Greek philosophy presented to G. E. L. Owens,* ed. Malcolm Schofield and Martha Nussbaum (Cambridge: Cambridge University Press, 1982), pp. 299-301.

24. On the relation between love and knowledge, both in the gradual ascent of *theōria* and in its culmination, see Festugière, *Contemplation,* pp. 288-357 (esp. 288-90).

25. R. Arnou in "Contemplation," *DS* 2:1723 (my translation).

26. E.g., *Republic,* books 4, 10; *Timaeus* 69B-70A and 89E-90D. The literature on Plato's varying views of the soul is vast. For an introduction, see T. M. Robinson, *Plato's Psychology* (Toronto: University of Toronto Press, 1970).

27. Subsequently, in *Phaedrus* 255CE the reciprocal action of the "stream of beauty" back upon the beloved is also analyzed. The importance of the initiatory role of the "shock of beauty" is not undercut by Plato's views, as contrasted with those of Aristotle, on the active nature of sense perception. For Plato, vision is always synergistic, that is, it results from the confluence of the stream of light issuing from the eye with that which proceeds from the visible object (see *Timaeus* 45C).

28. See Martha C. Nussbaum, *The Fragility of goodness: Luck and ethics in Greek tragedy and philosophy* (Cambridge: Cambridge University Press, 1986), chap. 7. In chap. 6 Nussbaum sees Alcibiades as advancing a similar view in the final speech of the *Symposium*. Plato's two views of love have also been insightfully treated by Julia Kristeva, *Tales of Love* (New York: Columbia University Press, 1987), pp. 72-76. See also A. W. Price, *Love and Friendship in Plato and Aristotle* (Oxford: Clarendon, 1990), chaps. 2-3.

29. The "eye of the soul" (see *Republic* 519B and 533D) is one of Plato's most influential mystical images. For a survey of the history, see "Oculus (Animae, Cordis, Mentis, etc.)," *DS* 11:591-601.

30. See Pierre Hadot, "Forms of Life and Forms of Discourse in Ancient Philosophy," *Critical Inquiry* 16 (1990): 483-505.

31. As pointed out by Andrew Louth, *The Origins of the Christian Mystical Tradition: Plato to Denys* (Oxford: Clarendon, 1981), pp. 3-7.

32. For a seminal study of the symbolization of humanity's fallenness, see Paul Ricoeur, *The Symbolism of Evil* (New York: Harper & Row, 1967).

33. Festugière, "Mystique païenne et charité," in *L'Enfant d'Agrigente*, p. 131. On the importance of *exaiphnēs* as a paradoxical temporal/a-temporal category in Western thought, see W. Beierwaltes, *"Exaiphnēs* oder: Die Paradoxie des Augenblicks," *Philosophisches Jahrbuch* 74 (1966-67): 271-83.

34. For a summary, see "Ascése, Ascetisme," *DS* 1:936-1010, esp. "Section II: L'Ascése païenne," by M. Olphe-Galliard (cols. 941-60).

35. E.g., *Phaedo* 62B, 65E-67D, 82E-83E; *Cratylus* 400C; *Gorgias* 493AC; and *Thaeatetus* 176B. On this aspect of Plato's thought, see the important articles of Pierre Courcelle: "Tradition platonicienne et traditions chrétiennes du corps-prison (Phédon 62B; Cratyle 400C)," *Revue des études latines* 43 (1963): 6-43; "L'âme en cage," in *Parusia: Studien zur Philosophie Platons und zur Problemgeschichte des Platonismus. Festgabe für Johannes Hirschberger*, ed. Kurt Flasch (Frankfurt: Minerva, 1965), pp. 103-16; "Le corps-tombeau (Platon, Gorgias 493A; Cratyle 400C; Phédre 250C)," *Revue des études anciennes* 68 (1966): 101-22; and "Grab der Seele," *Reallexikon für Antike und Christentum*, ed. T. Klauser et al. (Stuttgart: Hiersemann, 1950-) 12:455-67. On this issue, see also R. Ferwerda, "The Meaning of the Word *Sōma* (Body) in the Axial Age: An Interpretation of Plato's Cratylus 400C," in *The Origins and Diversity of Axial Age Civilizations,* ed. S. N. Eisenstadt (Albany: SUNY Press, 1986), pp. 111-24.

36. E.g., Festugière, "Ascése et contemplation," in *L'Enfant d'Agrigente,* pp. 134-48; T. Camelot, "Hellénisme (et spiritualité patristique)," *DS* 7:149-56, 162-64.

37. The apophatic element in Plato's thought has been studied by many scholars; see esp. Festugière, *Contemplation*, pp. 227-29, 262; idem, *Le révélation d'Hermès Trismégiste*, vol. 4, *Le Dieu inconnu et la Gnose* (Paris: Gabalda, 1954), pp. 79-91, which reviews the key texts.

38. Stephen Gersh, *Middle Platonism and Neoplatonism: The Latin Tradition,* 2 vols. (Notre Dame: University of Notre Dame Press, 1986), 1:266-72 and passim. For a useful introduction to Greek apophaticism, see R. T. Wallis, "The Spiritual Importance of Not Knowing," in *Classical Mediterranean Spirituality,* ed. Armstrong, pp. 460-80. See also Christian Guerard, "La théologie negative dans l'apophatisme grec," *Revue des sciences philosophiques et théologiques* 68 (1984): 183-200, which concentrates on the Neoplatonic materials.

39. On the interpretation of this text, see A. D. Nock, "The Exegesis of Timaeus 28C," *Vigiliae Christianae* 16 (1982): 79-86.

40. *Symposium* 509B: *ouk ousias ontos tou agathou, all' epi epekeina tēs ousias* (my translation).

41. Among those favored by the Neoplatonists were several elliptic passages in *Letter 2* (312E-313A; 314AC).

42. For a survey of some typical modern interpretations, see W. G. Runciman, "Plato's *Parmenides,*" an article first published in 1959 and reprinted in *Studies in Plato's Metaphysics,* ed. R. E. Allen (London: Routledge & Kegan Paul, 1967), pp. 149-84.

43. E.g., E. R. Dodds, "The *Parmenides* of Plato and the Origin of the Neoplatonic 'One,'" *Classical Quarterly* 22 (1928): 129–42; C. J. de Vogel, "On the Platonic Character of Neoplatonism and the Neoplatonic Character of Platonism," *Mind* 62 (1953): 43–64; Jean Trouillard, "Le 'Parménide' de Platon et son interprétation néoplatonicienne," in *Études Néoplatoniciennes* (Neuchâtel: A La Baconnière, 1973), pp. 9–26; H.-G. Gadamer, "Plato's Parmenides and its Influence," *Dionysius* 7 (1983): 3–16; Gersh, *Middle Platonism and Neoplatonism,* "Introduction," in 1:1–50; etc. For an introduction to "henology" in the Greek tradition, see W. Beierwaltes, "Hen," *Reallexikon für Antike und Christentum* 12:445–72. For the Neoplatonic interpretations of the hypotheses, see the summary remarks in the "Introduction," in *Proclus: Théologie Platonicienne,* ed. H. D. Saffrey and L. G. Westerink (Paris: Belles Lettres, 1968) 1:LXXV–LXXXIX.

44. If the One exists, then (a) it lacks both members of contrary predicates (137C–142B); (b) it possesses both members of such predicates (142B–157B); and (c) other things possess such predicates (157B–159B); and (d) other things lack them (159B–160B).

45. If the One does not exist, then (a) it possesses contrary predicates (160B–163B); (b) it lacks such predicates (163B–164B); or (c) other things possess contrary predicates (164B–165E); and (d) other things lack such predicates (165E–166B).

46. Some modern interpreters contend that the purpose of the first hypothesis is to prove the impossibility of the One conceived of apart from being and real existence and that the demonstration of a different kind of "One" begins with the second hypothesis. See, e.g., F. M. Cornford, *Plato and Parmenides* (Indianapolis: Bobbs-Merrill, n.d.), pp. 107, 112, 131–35.

47. Aristotle in book 1 of the *Metaphysics* (987b–988a) says Plato held that the One "is the cause of the essence of Forms," but also that Plato considered the One to be a substance (*ousia*).

48. Dodds, "The *Parmenides* of Plato and the Origin of Neoplatonic 'One,'" p. 141; see also Festugière, *Contemplation,* p. 128.

49. Festugière, *Contemplation,* p. 261: "Or c'est le *sentiment de présence,* redisons-le, qui fait le marque propre de la *theōria.*" Cf. pp. 187, 208–9, 223, 262–66, 288, 343, 452.

50. The axiom that like is known by like is first found in fragment 109 of Empedocles. For an explicit statement in Plato, see *Timaeus* 45B–46A.

51. A. J. Festugière, *L'Ideal religieux des grecs et l'Évangile* (Paris: Gabalda, 1932), pp. 39–41, 43; idem, *Personal Religion,* pp. 42–45.

52. For an overview of divinization, see "Divinisation," in *DS* 3:1370–1459 (cols. 1373–74 discuss Plato).

53. The most detailed defense of Plato the mystic is to be found in the various works of A. J. Festugière, but other scholars, such as R. Arnou (see n. 25) and U. Bianchi (see n. 8), also consider Plato to be a mystic. Among those who deny Plato the title of mystic, see Armstrong, "Platonic Mysticism," pp. 133–36, 140–41; P. Merlan, "Greek Philosophy from Plato to Plotinus," in *The Cambridge History of Later Greek and Early Medieval Philosophy,* ed. A. H. Armstrong (Cambridge: Cambridge University Press, 1967), p. 30; Wallis, "The Spiritual Importance of Not Knowing," p. 4.

54. E.g., Festugière, *L'Ideal religieux des grecs,* pp. 188–89. In his *La révélation d'Hermès Trismégiste* (4:138–39), Festugière points out a source for confusion about Plato and in the Platonic tradition in the fact that the word *nous* is used both to designate an organ of rational consciousness and an organ of mystical intuition.

55. See P. Merlan, *Monopsychism, Mysticism, Metaconscious* (The Hague: Nijhoff, 1963), pp. 17–21, 81–84; Moshe Idel, "Abraham Abulafia and Unio Mystica," in *Studies in Ecstatic Kabbalah* (Albany: SUNY Press, 1988), pp. 5–10.

56. Armstrong, "Platonic Mysticism," pp. 140–41; Bianchi, "Initiation, Mystères, Gnose," p. 171.

57. For a bibliography, see Heinrich Dörrie, "Bibliographischer Bericht über den Stand der Forschung zum Mittleren und Neueren Platonismus," in Dörrie, *Platonica Minora*

(Munich: Fink, 1976), pp. 524–48 (up to 1974). There are full bibliographies in Gersh's *Middle Platonism and Neoplatonism*. General accounts in English include the provocative but partial study in P. Merlan's *From Plato to Neoplatonism* (3rd ed.; The Hague: Nijhoff, 1968), and many of the papers in *The Cambridge History of Later Greek and Early Medieval Philosophy*, as well as the important contributions in *Classical Mediterranean Spirituality*, ed. Armstrong.

58. This is the argument of Gersh's "Introduction," in *Middle Platonism and Neoplatonism*, esp. pp. 45–47.

59. The most important of these is John Dillon, *The Middle Platonists: 80 B.C. to A.D. 200* (Ithaca: Cornell University Press, 1977). See also Robert M. Berchman, *From Philo to Origen: Middle Platonism in Transition* (Chico, CA: Scholars Press, 1984).

60. See Pierre Hadot, "Théologie, exégèse, révélation, écriture, dans la philosophie grecque," in *Centre d'études des religions du livre: Les régles de l'interprétation*, ed. Michel Tardieu (Paris: Cerf, 1987), pp. 13–34.

61. In pursuing these representatives of the Platonic tradition, we will neglect other dimensions of classical mystical piety whose influence on Christianity was at best distant. Among these are the rationalist or intellectualist mysticism of union with the Self-thinking Thought developed in the Neoaristotelian tradition (on which, see Merlan, *Monopsychism*, pp. 17–25, 30–37, etc.), and the cosmic or astral mysticism first described by F. Cumont, "Le mysticisme astral dans l'antiquité," *Bulletin de l'Académie Royale de Belgique: Classe des Lettres* 5 (1909): 256–86.

62. See A. Solignac, "Philon d'Alexandrie II. Influence sur les pères de l'église," *DS* 12:1366–74. Eusebius's account of Philo in his *Church History* 2.17–18 had much to do with spreading his reputation among Christians.

63. David Winston, *Logos and Mystical Theology in Philo of Alexandria* (Cincinnati: Hebrew Union College Press, 1985), p. 13.

64. The most detailed study remains Jean Pépin, *Mythe et allégorie: Les origines grecques et les contestations judéo-chrétiennes* (Paris: Aubier, 1957), which treats of Philo on pp. 231–42.

65. The most convenient edition of Philo is to be found in LC, edited by F. H. Colson and G. H. Whitaker for the Greek (vols. 1–9) and Ralph Marcus for the two volumes of the Philo *Supplement* containing the *Questions and Answers on Genesis* and the *Questions and Answers on Exodus*, whose complete text survives only in Armenian. All Greek passages will be cited from this edition by volume and page (e.g., LC 1:24). The traditional Latin titles will be used. The translations, unless otherwise noted, will be taken from the excellent anthology *Philo of Alexandria: The Contemplative Life, the Giants and Selections*, translated and introduced by David Winston, CWS (New York: Paulist, 1981). On Philo's exegesis, see also H. A. Wolfson, *Philo*, 2 vols. (Cambridge, MA: Harvard University Press, 1947) 1:66–71.

66. Winston, *Logos and Mystical Theology*, p. 36.

67. V. Nikiprowetzky, "Philon d'Alexandrie, I, La personne et l'oeuvre," *DS* 12:1352–66.

68. Erwin Goodenough, *By Light, Light: The Mystic Gospel of Hellenistic Judaism* (New Haven: Yale University Press, 1935). For Winston's defenses of this position, besides his already mentioned *Logos and Mystical Theology*, see the "Introduction" in his anthology *Philo of Alexandria*, pp. 21–35; "Philo and the Contemplative Life," in *Jewish Spirituality: From the Bible through the Middle Ages*, ed. Arthur Green, WS 13 (New York: Crossroad, 1986), pp. 198–231; and "Was Philo a Mystic?" in *Studies in Jewish Mysticism*, ed. Joseph Dan and Frank Talmadge (Cambridge, MA: Harvard University Press, 1982), pp. 15–41. For another recent exposition of Philo's mysticism, see chap. 2, "Philo," in Louth, *Origins of the Christian Mystical Tradition*, pp. 18–35. For Philo's place in Middle Platonism, see Dillon, *Middle Platonists*, pp. 139–83.

69. On this, see Louth, *Origins of the Christian Mystical Tradition*, p. 19; and esp. Henry Chadwick, "Philo," in *The Cambridge History of Later Greek and Early Medieval Philosophy*, pp. 141, 144, 148–49.

70. Eusebius cites Philo as a witness to the Christian understanding of the Logos in his *Preparation for the Gospel* 7.12–13.

71. See chapter 1, pp. 18–19. The Septuagint had sometimes rendered the Hebrew "word of God" as *Logos*, as in Ps 33:6: *tō logō Kyriou hoi ouranoi estereōthēsan.*

72. On the intradeical interpretation of the Ideas, see Audrey Rich, "The Platonic Ideas as the Thoughts of God," *Mnemosyne*, Series IV.7 (1954): 123–33; H. A. Wolfson, "Extradeical and Intradeical Interpretations of the Platonic Ideas," in *Religious Philosophy: A Group of Essays* (Cambridge, MA: Belknap Press, 1961), pp. 27–68; and B. McGinn, "Platonic and Christian: The Case of the Divine Ideas," in *Of Scholars, Savants and their Texts: Studies in Philosophy and Religious Thought: Essays in Honor of Arthur Hyman*, ed. Ruth Link-Salinger (New York: Peter Lang, 1989), pp. 163–73.

73. On the roots of Philo's negative theology, see John M. Dillon, "The Transcendence of God in Philo: Some Possible Sources," and the attendant discussion in *The Center for Hermeneutical Studies in Hellenistic and Modern Culture: Protocol of the Sixteenth Colloquy: 20 April 1975* (Berkeley, 1975).

74. See the exegesis of this verse in *Quod deterius potiori insidiari soleat* 159–60 (Winston, pp. 132–33). God can be characterized alternately as *to ontos on* (i.e., "the really Existent"), as in *Heres* 187, or as *to on* ("the Existent"), as in *De vita contemplativa* 2. Cf. *De posteritate Caini* 167–69 (Winston, pp. 124–25).

75. These passages can be found in Winston, *Philo*, pp. 141–42, and 172, though for the latter I have adopted the translation found in the LC 2:263.

76. See *Quod Deus sit immutabilis* 31–32 (Winston, p. 108). In *De opificio mundi* 25 the second world is said to be an image of the Logos.

77. See also *Quaestiones et Solutiones in Exodum* 2.124. "The Intelligible World is nothing else than the Divine Logos already in the act of building the cosmos" (*De opificio mundi* 24 [Winston, p. 100]).

78. In a fragment cited by Eusebius, *Preparation for the Gospel* 7.13.

79. Winston, "Philo and the Contemplative Life," p. 209.

80. For some representative texts on these two powers, see *Quis rerum divinarum* 166, *De cherubim* 27–28, *De Abrahamo* 121–25, *De fuga et inventione* 95. In *De sacrificiis Abeli et Caini* 60, Philo refers to the "sacred story [or perhaps 'mystic speech': *to hieron . . . mystēn logon*] that unveils to us the truth of the Uncreated and his potencies" (LC 2:139).

81. See the exegesis of Gen 1:27 in *Op.* 69–71, where the image is affirmed as residing in *nous*, which is created according to the Mind of the Universe as its archetype.

82. Augustine's interpretation in *The Trinity* 12.13.20 is different in identifying the serpent with the sense faculty, the woman with lower reason and the man with upper reason, but he explicitly notes other Christians who, like Philo, saw the woman as sense and the man as mind. Cf. Ambrose, *On Paradise* 15.73 (*PL* 14:311).

83. On this see Goodenough, *By Light, Light*, chaps. 4–9 (esp. the summary on pp. 238–43); see also Winston, "Philo and the Contemplative Life," pp. 213–15.

84. Cf. *Abr.* 58 (LC 6:32).

85. This treatise is edited in LC 9:103–69; see the translation in Winston, *Philo*, pp. 41–57. For a summary text on the role of asceticism, see *Mig.* 1–4, 7–12 (Winston, pp. 167–68).

86. See the passages in Winston, *Philo*, pp. 165–67 on this, especially *De plantatione* 23–27.

87. For other texts on ecstasy in Philo, see Winston, *Philo*, pp. 53, 153–54, 266.

88. See Louth, *Origins of the Christian Mystical Tradition*, pp. 25–26.

89. See Hans Lewy, *SOBRIA EBRIETAS: Untersuchungen zur Geschichte der Antiken Mystik.* Beihefte zur *Zeitschrift für die neutestamentliche Wissenschaft* 9 (Giessen: Töpelmann, 1929), pp. 3–41, for Philo's role in the creation and dissemination of this theme.

90. Winston, "Introduction," *Philo*, p. 21. This position seems to be supported by texts like *De praemiis et poenis* 40 (LC 8:334; Winston, p. 128), which distinguish between a vision of the Father who saves showing *that* he is and a vision showing *what* he is (this latter being beyond human abilities). However, it is by no means clear that the former vision is to be identified with the Logos and the latter with the unknowable Father.

91. Any such contact with God, of course, transcends reason and can only be attained in vision, as *Leg.* 4-6 makes clear.

92. E.g., *Plant.* 64 (LC 3:244) speaks of knowing the One, the Uncreated (*apoginoskon hēn monon oide kai gnorizei to ageneton*); *Fug.* 92 (LC 5:58-60) asserts that the mind in perfect solitude "will cleave in purity and without distraction to the Alone Existent" (Winston, p. 171); *De ebrietate* 152 (LC 3:398) has the mind hastening to the "most glorious and loveliest of visions—the Vision of the Uncreated" (*pros tēn tou agenetou pagkalon kai aoidimon thean epeixthenai*); and *De legatione ad Gaium* 5 (LC 10:4) speaks of the "souls that have transcended all things created and have been trained to behold the uncreated and divine, the primally Good . . ." (Winston, p. 143).

93. *Post.* 12 (LC 2:334): "He bids them 'cleave to him' (Deut 30:20), bringing out by the use of this word how constant and continuous and unbroken is the concord and union (*harmonias kai henōseōs*) that comes through making God our own" (Winston, p. 34). See also *Quaestiones et Solutiones in Genesin* 4.188 (LC *Suppl.* 1:473), which speaks of the wise man as striving "as far as possible, to unite the created with the uncreated and the mortal with the immortal. . . ."

94. E.g., *Som.* 1.71 (Winston, p. 172).

95. E.g., ibid., 2.233.

96. On this, see *Gig.* 54 (Winston, pp. 68-69), as well as *Vita Moysis* 1.159-60 (Winston, pp. 269-70), *De mutatione nominum* 7-9 (Winston, pp. 141-42), and *Post.* 13-15. There is a considerable literature on Moses as a "divine man" (*theios anēr*): see, e.g., Wayne A. Meeks, "Moses as God and King," in *Religions in Antiquity*, ed. Jacob Neusner (Leiden: Brill, 1968), pp. 354-71; and D. T. Runia, "God and Man in Philo of Alexandria," *Journal of Theological Studies* 39 (1988): 48-75.

97. Wolfson, *Philo* 2:87-93; Winston, "Introduction," *Philo*, pp. 27-30; idem, "Philo and the Contemplative Life," pp. 223-25; idem, *Logos and Mystical Theology*, pp. 45-46, 53-54.

98. E. g., *Spec. leg.* 3.1-6 (Winston, pp. 75-76).

99. E.g., *Mig.* 34-35 (Winston, p. 76), *Cher.* 27 (LC 2:24).

100. Goodenough, *By Light, Light*, p. 7. For a critique of this, see A. D. Nock, "The Question of Jewish Mysteries," *Gnomon* 13 (1937): 156-65.

101. H. Jonas, *Von der Mythologie zur mystischen Philosophie* (Göttingen: Vandenhoeck & Ruprecht, 1954), chap. 3 (pp. 70-121). For Jonas's view, see below, Appendix, section 3, pp. 336-38.

102. Jonas, *Mythologie*, pp. 119-21.

103. Two useful recent surveys are Kurt Rudolph, "Mystery Religions," in *The Encyclopedia of Religion*, ed. M. Eliade (New York: Macmillan, 1987) 10:230-39; and Walter Burkert, *Ancient Mystery Cults* (Cambridge, MA: Harvard University Press, 1987). Both writers insist that these groups are better termed cults than churches or religions. Rudolph defines the mysteries as "special initiation ceremonies that are esoteric in character and often connected with the yearly agricultural cycle. Usually they involve the destiny of the divine powers being venerated and the communication of religious wisdom that enables the initiates to conquer death" (p. 231). Burkert sees them as a personal, but not necessarily as a spiritual or salvational form of religion (p. 87).

104. Bianchi, "Initiation, Mystères, Gnose," pp. 154-71; cf. Dario Sabbatucci, *Saggio sul misticismo greco* (Rome: Edizioni dell'Ateneo, 1965), pp. 18-22, 36.

105. Burkert, *Ancient Mystery Cults*, p. 7; cf. p. 113.

106. Ibid., p. 90; cf. pp. 112-14, on the ecstatic character of the mysteries of Dionysius and the *Magna Mater.*

107. Albrecht Dieterich, *Eine Mithrasliturgie* (3rd ed.; Leipzig: Teubner, 1923), pp. 92-212; see esp. the summary on pp. 208-12 (quotation is from p. 208). The text that Dieterich described as a Mithras liturgy is now known to be a private magical treatise; see Hans Dieter Betz, *The Greek Magical Papyri in Translation* (Chicago: University of Chicago Press, 1986), pp. 48-54.

108. See Hans Jonas, "Myth and Mysticism: A Study of Objectification and Interiorization in Religious Thought," *Journal of Religion* 49 (1969): 315–29.

109. See Burkert, *Ancient Mystery Cults,* chap. 3, "Theologia and Mysteries: Myth, Allegory and Platonism," pp. 66–88; and Rudolph, "Mystery Religions," pp. 237–38.

110. Rudolph, "Mystery Religions," p. 237.

111. Pierre Hadot, "Neoplatonist Spirituality, I, Plotinus and Porphyry," in *Classical Mediterranean Spirituality,* ed. Armstrong, pp. 236–39.

112. Hans Lewy, *Chaldaean Oracles and Theurgy: Mysticism, Magic and Platonism in the Later
Roman Empire* (Cairo: Institut français d'archéologie orientale, 1956). A revised edition by
M. Tardieu appeared in Paris in 1978.

113. H.-D. Saffrey, "Les Néoplatoniciens et les Oracles Chaldaïques," *Revue des études
augustiniennes* 27 (1981): 209–25; and Hadot, "Théologie, exégèse, révélation," pp. 26–34.

114. Lewy, *Chaldaean Oracles and Theurgy,* pp. 420–21, 435.

115. Ibid., pp. 165ff., 366–75.

116. For recent surveys of these writings (now enriched by the discoveries at Nag
Hammadi), see Garth Fowden, *The Egyptian Hermes: A historical approach to the late pagan mind*
(Cambridge: Cambridge University Press, 1987); and Jean-Pierre Mahé, "Hermes Tris-
megistos," in *The Encyclopedia of Religion* 6:287–93. The fundamental book remains A. J.
Festugière, *La révélation d'Hermès Trismégiste,* 4 vols. (Paris: Gabalda, 1950–54). On the history
of the influence of the *Hermetica,* see Antoine Faivre, "Hermetism," in *The Encyclopedia of
Religion* 6:293–302; and the classic work of Frances Yates, *Giordano Bruno and the Hermetic
Tradition* (Chicago: University of Chicago Press, 1964).

117. Mahé, "Hermes Trismegistos," p. 289.

118. *Corpus Hermeticum,* vol. 1, ed. A. D. Nock with a translation by A. J. Festugière (Paris:
Collection Budè, 1960), Treatise X, 4b–6 (pp. 114–16). Wallis describes the text as the
"clearest anticipation" of Plotinus's view of mystical union ("The Spiritual Importance of Not
Knowing," p. 468).

119. One noted text occurs in *Asclepius* 20 (*Corpus Hermeticum* 2:320–21), where God, who
is both *unus et omnia,* is described in dialectical fashion as both *innominis* and *omninominis.*
The God of the *Asclepius* is thus both transcendent and immanent, as in many later
dialectical mystics, though the materialistic tone to this immanence, probably derived from
Stoic sources, would not be acceptable to most Christians. For a recent detailed analysis of
the *Asclepius,* see Gersh, *Middle Platonism and Neoplatonism* 1:332–87.

120. Wallis provides an excellent brief analysis of these five types of second-century
apophaticism ("The Spiritual Importance of Not Knowing," pp. 465–70).

121. Numenius, frag. 2, as found in Eusebius, *Preparation for the Gospel* 11.22, and critically
edited by Édouard des Places, *Numenius: Fragments* (Paris: Collection Budè, 1973), pp. 43–44.
I have used the translation of Edwin Hamilton Gifford, *Eusebius: Preparation for the Gospel*
(1903; reprint, Grand Rapids: Baker, 1981) 2:587. On the negative theology of Numenius
and other Neopythagoreans, see esp. the studies of John Whittaker collected in *Studies in
Platonism and Patristic Thought* (London: Variorum, 1984).

122. A. J. Festugière, *Hermétisme et mystique païenne* (Paris: Aubier-Montaigne, 1967),
pp. 13–27.

123. Ibid., pp. 23–24.

124. E. R. Dodds ties Plotinus's pessimism and other expressions of negative views of the
world, both pagan and Christian, to "an endogenous neurosis, an index of intense and widespread guilt-feelings" in late antiquity (*Pagan and Christian in an Age of Anxiety* [Cambridge:
Cambridge University Press, 1965], pp. 10, 26–36). This widely discussed interpretation has
been criticized for too facile an application of modern psychological categories to distant and
different social worlds.

125. Joseph Maréchal, *Études sur la psychologie des mystiques,* 2 vols. (Bruges: C. Beyaert,
1937) vol. 2, chap. 7, "Le 'Seul à Seul' avec Dieu dans l'extase, d'après Plotin," pp. 51–87;
René Arnou, *Le désir de Dieu dans la philosophie de Plotin* (2nd ed.; Rome: Gregorian

University, 1967; 1st ed. 1921); A. H. Armstrong, *The Architecture of the Intelligible Universe in the Philosophy of Plotinus* (Cambridge: Cambridge University Press, 1940); idem, "Plotinus," in *The Cambridge History of Later Greek and Early Medieval Philosophy,* ed. Armstrong, pp. 195–268; idem, "Platonic Mysticism"; and many other studies, esp. those collected in A. H. Armstrong, *Plotinian and Christian Studies* (London: Variorum Reprints, 1979); Jean Trouillard, *La procession plotinienne* (Paris: Presses universitaires de France, 1955); idem, "Raison et mystique chez Plotin," *Revue des études augustiniennes* 20 (1974): 3–14; Pierre Hadot, *Plotin ou la simplicité du regard* (Paris: Études Augustiniennes, 1973); idem, "Les niveaux de conscience dans les états mystiques selon Plotin," *Journal de psychologie normale et pathologique* 77 (1980): 243–65; idem, "L'Union de l'âme avec l'intellect divin dans l'expérience mystique plotinienne," in *Proclus et son influence: Actes du Colloque de Neuchâtel. Juin, 1985,* ed. G. Boss and G. Seel (Neuchâtel: Éditions du Grand Mich, 1986), pp. 3–27; idem, "Neoplatonist Spirituality, I, Plotinus and Porphyry," pp. 230–49 (largely based on the former article); Werner Beierwaltes, *Denken des Einen: Studien zur Neuplatonischen Philosophie und ihrer Wirkungsgeschichte* (Frankfurt: Klostermann, 1985); idem, "Plotins philosophische Mystik," in *Grundfragen christlicher Mystik,* ed. Margot Schmidt and Dieter R. Bauer (Stuttgart-Bad Cannstaat: Froomann-Holzboog, 1987), pp. 39–49. Most recently, see John Peter Kenney, *Mystical Monotheism* (Hanover, NH: Brown University Press, 1991), chap. 3.

126. In *Plotinus,* with an English translation by A. H. Armstrong, LC (Cambridge, MA: Harvard University Press, 1966–88), 7 vols. Armstrong's text is basically that of the *editio minor* of P. Henry and H. R. Schwyzer, *Plotini Opera,* 3 vols. (Oxford: Clarendon, 1964–83). All citations will be of Armstrong's text unless otherwise noted. I will cite according to volume and page (e.g., LC 1:70–71 for the passage above and its translation). Porphyry is here speaking of a five-year period ca. 263–268 C.E.

127. Dominic O'Meara, "À propos d'un témoignage sur l'expérience mystique de Plotin (*Enn.* IV 8 [6], 1, 1–11)," *Mnemosyne* 27 (1974): 238–44. Also on this passage, see Gerard J. P. O'Daly, "The Presence of the One in Plotinus," in *Plotino e il Neoplatonismo in Oriente e in Occidente* (Rome: Accademia Nazionale dei Lincei, Quaderno 198, 1974), pp. 159–69.

128. See O'Meara, "À propos d'un témoignage," p. 244: "Cet état mystique de Plotin ne semble pas non plus constituer un moment exceptionnel interrompant la continuité de la vie d'ici-bas; ce serait plutôt l'expérience de l'état primaire de l'âme, rendue discontinue par le rapport qui existe entre l'âme et le corps." For other texts on union with the Intellect, see, e.g., 5.3.4 and 6; 5.8.10–11. On this type of union, see Hadot, "L'Union de l'âme avec l'intellect divin," pp. 12–17.

129. See the excellent analysis of this passage by Hadot, "Les niveaux de conscience," pp. 256–65.

130. In this case I have utilized the translation of Elmer O'Brien, S.J., *The Essential Plotinus* (New York: Mentor Books, 1964), p. 86. On this passage, see Clyde Lee Miller, "Union with the One: Ennead 6,9,8–11," *The New Scholasticism* 51 (1977): 182–95. For the distinction between two kinds of union in Plotinus, see 6.7.35.

131. A. H. Armstrong argues that "experience of divine presence is the starting-point, not the conclusion, of Plotinus' thinking," in his interesting paper, "Tradition, Reason and Experience in the Thought of Plotinus," in *Plotino e il Neoplatonismo in Oriente e in Occidente,* pp. 171–94 (the quotation is from p. 183).

132. For the terms "One-Many" and "One and Many," see 5.1.8. Although qualified and corrected by subsequent work, Armstrong's *Architecture of the Intelligible Universe* remains a good introduction to the roots of Plotinus's thought in previous Greek philosophy.

133. Emanation is described in terms of metaphors of the diffusion of light (e.g., 1.7.1; 5.1.6; 5.3.12), or of the action of fire, perfume, or snow (e.g., 5.1.6).

134. E.g., Emile Bréhier, *The Philosophy of Plotinus* (Chicago: University of Chicago Press, 1958); and Werner Beierwaltes, "Henosis, I, Einung mit dem Einen oder der Aufhebung des Bildes: Plotins Mystik," in *Denken des Einen,* pp. 123–47. See also R. T. Wallis, "NOUS as Experience," in *The Significance of Neoplatonism,* ed. R. Baine Harris (Norfolk, VA: Old

Dominion University Press, 1976), pp. 121–53; and Louth, *Origins of the Christian Mystical Tradition,* chap. 3, Plotinus (pp. 36–51).

135. O'Daly, "The Presence of the One," p. 164.

136. Michael Sells ("Apophasis in Plotinus: A Critical Approach," *Harvard Theological Review* 78 [1985]: 47–65) also argues for a mystical dialectic in Plotinus (e.g., pp. 53–54, 64).

137. For a pioneering study of Plotinus's influence on some Western authors, see Paul Henry, S.J., *Plotin et l'Occident* (Louvain: Spicilegium Sacrum Lovaniense, 1934).

138. For the text of *Enn.* 1.6, see LC 1:232–63. Like Plato, Plotinus frequently speaks in a negative way about the evil nature of this material world and the necessity of flight from it (e.g., 1.2.1; 1.8.1–5), but his attack on the Gnostics in 2.9 and elsewhere shows a more optimistic side to his traditional Hellenic piety and the role that physical beauty plays in the soul's ascent (2.9.16–17).

139. On purification, see Jean Trouillard, *La purification plotinienne* (Paris: Presses universitaires de France, 1955).

140. *Enn.* 1.6 is echoed in Augustine's *Confessions* (e.g., 1.18 and 8.8) and elsewhere. For the relation between Plotinus and Augustine, see chapter 7 below, pp. 242–43.

141. On the role of love in Plotinus's mysticism no work has surpassed the seminal study of René Arnou, *Le désir de Dieu dans la philosophie de Plotin.* For some comments that attempt to fit Plotinus into the perspective of debates on the relation of love and knowledge in Western Christian mysticism, see B. McGinn, "Love, Knowledge and *Unio Mystica* in the Western Christian Tradition," in *Mystical Union and Monotheistic Faith: An Ecumenical Dialogue,* ed. M. Idel and B. McGinn (New York: Macmillan, 1989), p. 61.

142. This is why A. Nygren can deny that there is any descending love in Plotinus akin to the "Christian" agape—though this is only half the story (*Agape and Eros,* pp. 195–96).

143. See W. Beierwaltes, "Love of Beauty and Love of God," in *Classical Mediterranean Spirituality,* ed. Armstrong, pp. 303–6.

144. Here I make use of the translation of Stephen MacKenna, *Plotinus: The Enneads* (London: Faber & Faber, 1956), p. 589. Note the appearance of the theme of "sober drunkenness" first found in Philo. On Plotinus's use, see Lewy, *SOBRIA EBRIETAS,* pp. 103–5.

145. On *Nous erōn,* see *Enn.* 5.5.8; 6.7.32; and 6.9.11; cf. Hadot, "Neoplatonist Spirituality, I, Plotinus and Porphyry," pp. 244–46, whose translation of 6.9.9 I am using here.

146. Bréhier, *Philosophy of Plotinus,* p. 192.

147. Beierwaltes, "Henosis," in *Denken des Einen,* pp. 127, and 147, where the quotation is found. A similar point is made by M. Sells, who in speaking of references to Nous proceeding from the One says, "But the language reference is not *fully* itself until it turns towards its source in intuition (gazing inward), in insight into the pre-predication, the unlimited" ("Apophasis in Plotinus," p. 64).

148. Much has been written on Plotinus's apophaticism. Besides the studies of Beierwaltes, Sells, and Wallis already referred to, see A. H. Armstrong, "The Escape of the One: An investigation of some possibilities of apophatic theology imperfectly realised in the West," and "Negative Theology," both reprinted in *Plotinian and Christian Studies.*

149. E.g., *Enn.* 1.7.1; 2.4.16; 3.9.9; 5.4.1; 5.5.5–6; 6.7.40; 6.8.19; etc.

150. See *Enn.* 3.8.11; 5.3.3 and 10; 5.6.2–3; 5.8.1; 6.7.35; 6.8.16; 6.9.3; etc.

151. See the excellent analysis of these texts in Sells, "Apophasis in Plotinus," pp. 52–60.

152. Bréhier, *Philosophy of Plotinus,* p. 189.

153. The quotations from *Enn.* 6.8 are drawn from the MacKenna translation.

154. See *Enn.* 6.9.6 for another ascription of some kind of thinking (in this case *noēsis*) to the One; cf. 6.8.18.

155. See the discussion of Intellect and the One in Gersh, *Middle Platonism and Neoplatonism* 2:690–92; and Sells, "Apophasis in Plotinus," pp. 55–57.

156. The intimate relations between the One and Nous have been studied by Hadot ("L'Union de l'âme avec l'intellect divin") and Sells ("Apophasis in Plotinus").

157. The circle is one of Plotinus's favorite images; see, e.g., *Enn.* 1.7.1; 3.8.8; 3.9.4; 4.3.17;

4.4.16; 5.1.11; 5.5.5; 6.9.8 and 10; etc. See Beierwaltes, "Henosis," pp. 138–39; and T. G. Sinnige, "Metaphysical and Personal Religion in Plotinus," in *Kephalaion*, ed. J. Mansfeld and L. M. de Rijk (Assen: Van Gorcum, 1975), pp. 147–54.

158. Armstrong, however, denies this reading, holding that the subject of *heōra* is the non-reflexive *auto* referring here to Intellect. He thus translates, "Because by its return to it it sees: and this seeing is Intellect" (LC 5:34–35 n.1).

159. Hadot puts it thus: "L'âme, au sommet de l'expérience mystique, coincide avec l'extase amoureuse dans laquelle nait la Pensée" ("L'Union de l'âme avec l'intellect divin," p. 26). Cf. Sells, "Apophasis in Plotinus," pp. 55–56.

160. This passage reminds us of Meister Eckhart's call for the stripping away (*abegeschei-denheit*) of all created particular reality (*esse hoc et hoc*) in order to reach the ground of reality, the *esse absolutum* of God.

161. Dialectical language is especially strong in the latter part of *Enn.* 6.8: e.g., the Supreme is simultaneously seeker and sought (6.8.15), everywhere and nowhere (6.8.16), within and without (6.8.18), etc. Thus the One violates the rule of contradiction because it is both x and not-x (cf. *Parmenides*, Hypothesis 2), and also because it is neither x nor not-x (cf. *Parmenides*, Hypothesis 1). On the language of immanence and transcendence in Plotinus, see the survey in Arnou, *Le désir de Dieu*, pp. 157–91.

162. The translations from *Enn.* 6.9, unless otherwise noted, will be from O'Brien, *The Essential Plotinus*, pp. 73–88 (in this case slightly modified).

163. The stress on the direct presence of the One as the best way of expressing the mystic's relation to it appears also in *Enn.* 3.8.10; 6.7.34; 6.9.7 and 8, etc. See J. Trouillard, "La présence de Dieu selon Plotin," *Revue de metaphysique et de morale* 59 (1954): 38–45; O'Daly, "The Presence of the One."

164. Plotinus's preference for metaphors of touch even over those of seeing has been noted by J. Trouillard ("Raison et mystique," pp. 5–6).

165. The phrase is that of Clyde Lee Miller whose article "Union with the One: Ennead 6,9,8–11," is an excellent study of this text (quotation from p. 187).

166. See Arnou, *Le désir de Dieu*, pp. 195–201, on introversion as leading to divinization. Trouillard puts it well: "La transcendance néoplatonicienne n'est jamais exteriorité, mais anteriorité génératrice, point de départ inépuisable" ("Raison et mystique," p. 5).

167. On the cosmic dance in Plotinus, see James Miller, *Measures of Wisdom: The Cosmic Dance in Classical and Christian Antiquity* (Toronto: University of Toronto Press, 1986), chap. 4, esp. pp. 220–32.

168. On the identity of seer and seen, see, e.g., *Enn.* 6.7.35–36; 6.9.5. O'Daly, relying on passages like 4.8.1, where Plotinus speaks of the arising out of the body "into myself" (*eis emauton*), argues for the survival of the self in mystical union (see "The Presence of the One," pp. 159–63). However, he does not sufficiently stress that the "self" that survives is not the self of our ordinary experience but the unfallen transcendent self.

169. Hadot, "Les niveaux de conscience," pp. 255–56. See also his "Neoplatonist Spirituality, I, Plotinus and Porphyry," p. 233: "To be present to the self, to be conscious of the real self, is thus to be present to God." Julia Kristeva is good on this aspect of Plotinus's thought. She summarizes: "Plotinus knew that the soul is always already in an other, but it can emerge from its solitude, its nothingness, its possible downfall, by means of an amorous return to the Single Source. After having been barely sketched out, the soul's otherness is thus reintegrated into the mystical, initiatory path of nondualistic Platonism" ("Narcissus: The New Insanity," in *Tales of Love*, pp. 120–21).

170. In most places Plotinus uses the word in a broader sense (e.g., *Enn.* 5.3.7; 6.7.17). The claims for Plotinus's originality in applying *ekstasis* to mystical union made by Dodds (*Pagan and Christian*, pp. 70–72) rest on a questionable nonmystical reading of Philo's use of the term. For a treatment of Plotinian ecstasy, see Beierwaltes, "Henosis," pp. 140–42.

171. Trouillard, "Raison et mystique," p. 5.

172. Among the most important texts for both the productive and reductive aspects of

Plotinus's view of contemplation is *Enn.* 3.8, "On Nature and Contemplation and the One." Among other important treatments, see 1.6.7–9; 4.4.2; 5.3.14 and 17; 5.5.7–8; 5.8.10–11; 6.7.34–36; 6.8.10–11 and 15; and 6.9.4, 7 and 10–11.

173. See Arnou, "Contemplation," *DS* 2:1727–38.

174. Ibid., col. 1731.

175. On the suddenness of the presence of the One in Plotinus, see John M. Rist, *Plotinus: The Road to Reality* (Cambridge: Cambridge University Press, 1967), pp. 224–25.

176. Arnou, "Contemplation," cols. 1732–37.

177. Beierwaltes, "Henosis," in *Denken des Einen*, pp. 123–47.

178. Plotinus attacks the pantheism of the Stoics in *Enn.* 3.8.9.

179. Rist, *Plotinus*, p. 219. Rist's defense of a theistic reading of Plotinus's mysticism according to R. C. Zaehner's categories is not convincing.

180. See W. Beierwaltes, "Reflexion und Einung: Zur Mystik Plotins," in *Grundfragen der Mystik* (Einsiedeln: Johannes, 1974): "Den Eifer, der sich auf die Frage konzentriert, ob Plotins Mystik ausschliesslich 'monistisch' (und damit etwa der indischen Mystik nahestehend), 'theistisch' oder aber 'pantheistisch' sei, halte ich für müssig" (p. 9).

181. On *tautotēs*, see *Enn.* 3.8.8; 4.8.1.

182. See the convenient lists of these terms in Rist, *Plotinus,* p. 226; cf. Arnou, "Contemplation," cols. 1733–35.

183. See, e.g., Trouillard, "Raison et mystique," p. 12; Beierwaltes, "Henosis," in *Denken des Einen*, pp. 143–47; Hadot, "L'Union de l'âme avec l'intellect divin," p. 27; Louth, *Origins of the Christian Mystical Tradition,* p. 48; O'Daly, "The Presence of the One," pp. 159–63.

184. For some well-balanced observations, see A. H. Armstrong, "Salvation, Plotinian and Christian," reprinted in *Plotinian and Christian Studies.*

185. See, e.g., *Enn.* 3.8.6; 5.3.17; and esp. 5.5.8, where we read: "So one must not chase after it [the vision of the Beautiful], but wait quietly until it appears, preparing oneself to contemplate it, as the eye awaits the rising of the sun" (LC 5:178–79). On the role of "grace" in Plotinus, see Armstrong, "Tradition, Reason and Experience," pp. 186, 191.

186. Armstrong, "Tradition, Reason and Experience," p. 189.

187. Note the remark of Armstrong: "To the Christian, a very great deal that Plotinus says about Intellect and higher soul seems to be true, but true not about something that we are or have by nature but about something which God has, and is giving us by grace in conforming us to the likeness of his Son . . ." ("Salvation, Plotinian and Christian," p. 135).

188. For a survey of Neoplatonism, the best book is R. T. Wallis, *Neoplatonism* (New York: Scribner, 1972); important aspects of the speculative development of late Neoplatonism have been illuminated in Stephen Gersh, *From Iamblichus to Eriugena: An Investigation of the Prehistory and Evolution of the Pseudo-Dionysian Tradition* (Leiden: Brill, 1978).

189. The qualification "cryptoproclean" is taken from Edward Booth, whose *Aristotelian Aporetic Ontology in Islamic and Christian Thinkers* (Cambridge: Cambridge University Press, 1983) is one of the more substantive contributions to this aspect of Greek influence on Western thought. See my review in *Journal of Religion* 67 (1987): 95–97.

190. The translation of Porphyry's *Isagoge*, or introduction to logic, into Latin was one of the decisive philosophical events of the millennium.

191. For an English introduction to these fragments, see Wallis, *Neoplatonism,* pp. 114–18.

192. P. Hadot, *Porphyre et Victorinus,* 2 vols. (Paris: Études Augustiniennes, 1958) 2:106–7 (my translation).

193. See P. Hadot, "L'être et l'étant dans la Néoplatonisme," in *Études Néoplatoniciennes,* pp. 27–41; idem, "Dieu comme acte d'être dans le néoplatonisme," in *Dieu et l'être: Exégèses d'Éxode 3,14 et de Coran 20,11–24* (Paris: Études Augustiniennes, 1978), pp. 58–63. J. M. Rist, in his important article "Mysticism and Transcendence in Later Neoplatonism," *Hermes* 92 (1964), pp. 220–25, argues that Porphyry's difference from his master may have been due to the influence of the Chaldean Oracles.

194. For a brief sketch of the thought of Marius Victorinus, see chapter 6 below, pp. 198–200.

195. Hadot, *Porphyre et Victorinus* 2:110–13.

196. Iamblichus, fragment 65 on *Timaeus* 38A in *Iamblichi Chalcidiensis in Platonis Dialogos Commentariorum Fragmenta,* ed. John M. Dillon (Leiden: Brill, 1973), p. 178 (cf. the discussion on pp. 36–37).

197. Rist, "Mysticism and Transcendence in Later Neoplatonism," p. 220. Wallis also wonders how often mystical union was attained in post-Porphyrian Neoplatonism ("The Spiritual Importance of Not Knowing," pp. 476–77).

198. The best introduction in English to Proclus's mysticism is H. D. Saffrey, "Neoplatonist Spirituality, II, From Iamblichus to Proclus and Damascius," in *Classical Mediterranean Spirituality,* ed. Armstrong, pp. 250–65. Modern studies of Proclus have given ample attention to mysticism, e.g., Werner Beierwaltes, *Proklos: Grundzüge seiner Metaphysik* (Frankfurt: Klostermann, 1965), pp. 277–329; Jean Trouillard, *L'un et l'âme selon Proclos* (Paris: Belles Lettres, 1972); idem, *La mystagogie de Proclos* (Paris: Belles Lettres, 1982); idem, "Théologie négative et psychogonie chez Proclus," in *Plotino e il Neoplatonismo in Oriente e in Occidente,* pp. 253–64.

199. On Proclus's four modes of exegesis outlined in his *Theologia Platonica* 1.4, see Hadot, "Théologie, exégèse, révélation," pp. 30–34.

200. See Saffrey, "Neoplatonist Spirituality, II," pp. 250–52. On *epistēmē* as *gymnasia,* see A. H. Armstrong, "The Negative Theology of Nous in Later Neoplatonism," in *Platonismus und Christentum: Festschrift für Heinrich Dörrie, Jahrbuch für Antike und Christentum, Ergänzungsband 10,* ed. H.-D. Blume and F. Mann (Münster: Aschendorff, 1983), p. 36.

201. Trans. Saffrey, "Neoplatonist Spirituality, II," p. 252. Proclus uses the term *mystikos* more frequently than earlier Neoplatonists such as Plotinus, who employs it only once to refer to the hidden meaning of cult statues (*Enn.* 3.6.19, line 27). See, e.g., the reference to "mystic visions" (*mystika thaemata*) in *Theologia Platonica* 3.18.

202. The *Theologia Platonica* in six books is being edited by H. D. Saffrey and L. G. Westerink, *Proclus: Théologie Platonicienne* (Paris: Belles Lettres, 1968–), 5 vols thus far.

203. Trans. Saffrey, "Neoplatonist Spirituality, II," p. 254.

204. *Proclus: The Elements of Theology,* ed. and trans. E. R. Dodds (2nd ed.; Oxford: Clarendon, 1963), p. 39. S. Gersh stresses how this law enables Proclus and his followers to see "the structure of reality as a continuous series of causes and effects in which each term is related dynamically to the previous one: it 'remains' in its prior (manifests an element of identity with it), it 'proceeds' (manifests an element of difference), and it 'reverts' (strives to re-establish the identity)" (*From Iamblichus to Eriugena,* p. 125).

205. *Elements of Theology,* p. 93 (translation slightly modified).

206. Ibid., p. 123.

207. Gersh, *From Iamblichus to Eriugena,* pp. 11, 155–56, 166, making use of E. Corsini, *Il trattato 'De Divinis Nominibus' dello Pseudo-Dionigi e i commenti neoplatonici al Parmenide* (Turin: G. Giappichelli, 1962).

208. On this, see chapter 5 below, pp. 168–69.

209. For a brief introduction, see Wallis, *Neoplatonism,* pp. 146–58. The One itself, of course, is imparticipable.

210. *Proclus: Alcibiades I. A Translation and Commentary,* by William O'Neill (The Hague: Nijhoff, 1965), #51 (pp. 32–33).

211. Ibid., #52 (p. 34).

212. Ibid., #56 (p. 37).

213. Ibid., #117, 122 (pp. 77, 80).

214. *In Parm.* 6, 1074: *apotemaxi zousi gar hai kataphaseis to onta* (see following note).

215. The surviving Greek text commenting down to *Parm.* 141E was edited by V. Cousin with a translation into French by A. E. Chaignet (Paris, 1900–1903). The Latin text commenting on 141E–142A was first edited by R. Klibansky and C. Labowsky as vol. 3 of the

Plato Latinus, along with a translation of E. Anscombe (London: Warburg Institute, 1953). This is the edition used here. Recently, an edition of the full Latin translation has appeared, *Proclus: Commentaire sur le Parménide de Platon. Traduction de Guillaume de Moerbeke,* ed. Carlos Steel, 2 vols. (Leiden/Leuven: Brill, 1982–85), as well as a translation of the Greek text into English by Glenn Morrow and John Dillon, *Proclus's Commentary on Plato's Parmenides* (Princeton: Princeton University Press, 1987).

216. See Klibansky and Labowsky, *Plato Latinus* 3:34–35, for the text and the translation.

217. Ibid., pp. 36, 52.

218. Ibid., pp. 40, 44, 62.

219. Ibid., p. 70: dicte abnegationes non sunt circa unum, sed de uno.

220. Ibid., p. 72.

221. Ibid., p. 54 (text), p. 55 (trans.). On the relation between negation and the soul's autoconstitution, see Trouillard, "Théologie négative et pyschogonie."

222. See also *In Parm.* 6, 1079–81. On this "hypernégation mystique," see Guerard, "La théologie négative dans l'apophatisme grec," pp. 197–99; idem, "Le théorie des Hénades et la mystique de Proclus," *Dionysius* 6 (1982): 73–82.

223. See Laura Westra, "Proclus' Ascent of the Soul towards the One in the *Elements of Theology:* Is It Plotinian?" in *Proclus et son influence,* pp. 129–43. A. H. Armstrong stresses this difference between Plotinus and the later Neoplatonists in "Tradition, Reason and Experience," pp. 188–91.

224. See the treatment of Rist, who distinguishes three stages in the ascent: (1) ascent to Nous; (2) ascent to the "flower of Nous" where union with the participated One or Being of the first triad takes place; and finally (3) ascent to the "flower of the whole soul" (see *De Philosophia Chaldaica,* chap. 4), which unites us to the imparticipable One.

225. See Klibansky and Labowsky, *Plato Latinus* 3:44–46. I have slightly modified the translation of E. Anscombe here.

226. A text from book 1 of the *Timaeus* commentary, cited by Saffrey, "Neoplatonist Spirituality, II," p. 256.

227. See Klibansky and Labowsky, *Plato Latinus* 3:76–77): Nam per negari et ipse removit [omnes] abnegationes. Silentio autem conclusit eam que de ipso theoriam. On the negation of negation in Proclus, see Beierwaltes, *Proklos,* pp. 395–98; and Trouillard, *L'un et l'âme selon Proclos,* pp. 86–89, 97.

228. See especially chapter 5 below, pp. 162–82.

Chapter 3

1. Studies of early Christian writings, especially of those documents that form the canonical New Testament, are legion. For one recent major introduction, see Helmut Koester, *Introduction to the New Testament,* 2 vols. (Philadelphia: Fortress, 1982). For an overall study of the history of early Christianity, see W. H. C. Frend, *The Rise of Christianity* (Philadelphia: Fortress, 1984). In citing from the New Testament, I will make use of the Jerusalem Bible, unless otherwise noted.

2. For a demonstration of this, see Marguerite Harl, "Le langage de l'expérience religieuse chez les pères grecs," *Rivista di storia e letteratura religiosa* 15 (1977): 5–34.

3. Irenaeus (ca. 180 C.E.) already contrasts the old covenant of the law and the new covenant of the gospel, though both were produced by the same God and Father (*Against Heresies* 4.9.1). On the formation of the Christian Bible, see Rowan A. Greer, *Early Biblical Interpretation* (Philadelphia: Westminster, 1986), part 2.

4. For a summary of Friedrich von Hügel's teaching on mysticism as an element in religion, see Appendix, section 2, pp. 293–96.

5. A survey of some of the debates about the existence of a New Testament mysticism can be found in the Appendix, section 1, pp. 267–72 and 281–82. Among the Catholic studies that argue this case are, Anselm Stolz, *Theologie der Mystik* (Regensburg: Pustet,

1936); Joseph Huby, *Mystiques paulinienne et johannique* (Paris: Desclée, 1946); Alfred Wikenhauser, *Pauline Mysticism* (Herder: New York, 1955); and Louis Bouyer, *The Spirituality of the New Testament and the Fathers,* vol. 1 of *A History of Christian Spirituality* (New York: Seabury, 1982), chaps. 2–10. For a survey of the issue of mysticism in the Bible, see François Vandenbroucke, "Die Ursprunglichkeit der biblischen Mystik," in *Gott in Welt: Festgabe für Karl Rahner,* 2 vols. (Freiburg: Herder, 1964) 1:463–91.

6. Stolz (*Theologie der Mystik,* pp. 41–46), Huby (*Mystiques paulinienne et johannique,* pp. 8–9, 25–26), and Wikenhauser (*Pauline Mysticism,* pp. 104–5) all make use of such distinctions, arguing for the presence of explicit and objective mysticism in at least some elements of the New Testament.

7. E.g., André Jean Festugière, *L'Enfant d'Agrigente* (Paris: Plon, 1950). This is also suggested by Andrew Louth, who in his book *The Origins of the Christian Mystical Tradition: From Plato to Denys* (Oxford: Clarendon, 1981) says nothing about scripture.

8. For Schweitzer's views, see Appendix, section 1, pp. 271–72.

9. Some recent historians and exegetes have begun to argue that recognizing the importance of the historical-critical method does not necessarily imply a denial of the role of spiritual interpretation; see, e.g., Henri Crouzel, "Spiritual Exegesis," in *Encyclopedia of Theology: The Concise Sacramentum Mundi,* ed. Karl Rahner (New York: Seabury, 1975), pp. 126–33; and Sandra Schneiders, "Scripture and Spirituality," in *Christian Spirituality: Origins to the Twelfth Century,* ed. Bernard McGinn and John Meyendorff, WS 16 (New York: Crossroad, 1986), pp. 1–20.

10. For an introduction to the genres of the New Testament, see David E. Aune, *The New Testament in Its Literary Environment* (Philadelphia: Westminster, 1987). Other materials about Jesus (apart from the Gospel of John, to be considered below) are found in some of the apocryphal gospels and in a number of early Christian writers.

11. For a historical-critical study of the importance of this element in the New Testament, see Hans Dieter Betz, *Die Nachfolge und Nachahmung Jesu in Neuen Testament* (Tübingen: Mohr, 1967). The distinction that some have drawn between "following after Christ" (*Nachfolge*) as authentically New Testament and "imitating Christ's virtues" (*Nachahmung*) as a posterior development seems anachronistic.

12. For an introduction to the history of the important theme of the imitation of Christ in Christian spirituality, see the multiauthor article "Imitation du Christ" in *DS* 7:1536–97.

13. Eduard Norden, noting that the rare verb *episkiazein* occurs only in one other place in the New Testament, Luke's account of the Incarnation (Luke 1:35), argued that the author intended it to convey a mystical ecstasy (*Die Geburt des Kindes* [Leipzig: Teubner, 1924], pp. 92–99).

14. Kenneth E. Kirk, *The Vision of God: The Christian Doctrine of the "Summum Bonum"* (1932; reprint, Cambridge: James Clarke, 1977), on which see Appendix, section 1, pp. 274–75.

15. On Clement's exegesis, see Jean Daniélou, *Gospel Message and Hellenistic Christianity* (Philadelphia: Westminster, 1973), chap. 10; see the treatment of Clement in the following chapter (pp. 101–8).

16. E.g., as in the *Gospel of Mary;* see Elaine Pagels, *The Gnostic Gospels* (New York: Vintage Books, 1981), pp. 76–81.

17. For a history of the patristic uses of this passage, see Daniel A. Csányi, "OPTIMA PARS: Die Auslegungsgeschichte von Lk. 10, 38–42 bei den Kirchenvätern der ersten vier Jahrhunderte," *Studia Monastica* 2 (1960): 5–78.

18. A long tradition of modern critical study of the New Testament, represented by Johannes Weiss in the last century and Albert Schweitzer in our own, viewed Jesus himself as an apocalyptic preacher. More recent biblical scholarship has tended to distance the historical Jesus from apocalypticism, arguing that although he made use of apocalyptic motifs in his preaching, his conception of the kingdom of God was more immanent than imminent.

19. There is general agreement that the Pastoral letters ascribed to Paul (1 and 2 Timothy

and Titus) are products of the emergent church of the early second century. Many hold that 2 Thessalonians, Ephesians, and Colossians are not products of Paul's pen, but were written by his followers in the generation after his death. For a brief discussion, see Norman Perrin, *The New Testament: An Introduction* (New York: Harcourt, Brace, Jovanovich, 1974), chaps. 5 and 6.

20. Stolz, *Theologie der Mystik,* esp. pp. 26–46, 64, 77–78, 92–93, and 144–46. On the interpretation of Paul's writings in the early church, see M. F. Wiles, *The Divine Apostle* (Cambridge: Cambridge University Press, 1967).

21. See James Tabor, *Things Unutterable: Paul's Ascent to Paradise in its Greco-Roman, Judaic and Early Christian Contexts* (Lanham, MD: University Press of America, 1986); Peter Schaefer, "New Testament and Hekhalot Literature: The Journey into Heaven in Paul and in Merkavah Mysticism," *Journal of Jewish Studies* 35 (1984): 19–35.

22. Tabor, *Things Unutterable,* p. 117.

23. For the importance of this text in the apophatic mysticism of the fathers, see Harl, "Le langage de l'expérience religieuse," pp. 9–10.

24. On the importance of the visionary element in early Christianity, see Christopher Rowland, *The Open Heaven: A Study of Apocalyptic in Judaism and Early Christianity* (New York: Crossroad, 1982).

25. Schweitzer, *The Mysticism of Paul the Apostle* (London: A. & C. Black, 1931). For a summary of Schweitzer's view of Paul's eschatological "Christ-mysticism" as contrasted with the Hellenistic "Logos-mysticism" found in John and Ignatius, see Appendix, section 1, pp. 271–72.

26. For a recent exegetical survey of 1 Corinthians 13, see Hans Conzelmann, *1 Corinthians,* Hermeneia (Philadelphia: Fortress, 1975), pp. 217–31. On the face-to-face vision of v. 12, Conzelmann argues that Paul is thinking in eschatological, not mystical, terms, though he admits that the passage is open to a mystical or Gnostic interpretation.

27. Philo appears to use the word in this sense in *Legum allegoria* 3.101, and Tertullian translates it as *contemplantes* in *Against Marcion* 5.11. On this passage, see Jacques Dupont, "Le chrétien, miroir de la gloire divine d'après II Cor., iii, 18," *Revue biblique* 56 (1949): 392–411.

28. See Vandenbroucke, "Die Ursprunglichkeit der biblischen Mystik," pp. 474–76, for a list.

29. On the history of *agapē,* a classic, but I believe flawed, work is that of Anders Nygren, *Agape and Eros* (Philadelphia: Westminster, 1953). For the New Testament use, the most complete study is Ceslaus Spicq, *Agape in the New Testament,* 3 vols. (St. Louis: Herder, 1962–66). See also Gottfried Quell and Ethelbert Stauffer, *Love: Bible Key Words from Gerhard Kittel's Theologisches Wörterbuch zum Neuen Testament,* Vol. 1 (London: A. & C. Black, 1949).

30. For Paul on *agapē,* see Spicq, *Agape,* vol. 2.

31. See G. Adolf Deissmann, *Die Neutestamentliche Formel "in Christo Jesu"* (Marburg, 1893); see also his *Paul: A Study in Social and Religious History* (New York: Harper & Row, 1926). The theme was studied by Schweitzer (*Mysticism of Paul,* pp. 122–29) and especially by Wikenhauser (*Pauline Mysticism,* chaps. 1–2).

32. Schweitzer, *Mysticism of Paul,* chap. 5, esp. pp. 96–99. We should note that Paul uses the formula "in God" three times (Rom 2:17; 5:11; 1 Thess 2:2), and he twice speaks of God being in us (1 Cor 14:25; 2 Cor 6:16), but these uses do not have any mystical implications.

33. See Conzelmann, *1 Corinthians,* p. 112.

34. For some consideration of later Western uses of this text in mystical contexts, see Bernard McGinn, "Love, Knowledge and *Unio Mystica* in the Western Christian Tradition," in *Mystical Union and Monotheistic Faith: An Ecumenical Dialogue,* ed. Moshe Idel and Bernard McGinn (New York: Macmillan, 1989), pp. 59–86.

35. This is evident, e.g., by the way in which the reference to the three heavens is discussed by Augustine and Bonaventure in their treatments of visions; see Augustine, *Literal Commentary on Genesis* 12.1–5; and Bonaventure, *Collationes on the Hexaemeron* 9.9–10.

36. See, e.g., Schweitzer, *Mysticism of Paul,* chap. 13; Huby, *Mystiques paulinienne et*

johannique, book 2; André Feuillet, *Johannine Studies* (Staten Island: Alba House, 1964), pp. 169–80; L. William Countryman, *The Mystical Way in the Fourth Gospel: Crossing over into God* (Philadelphia: Fortress, 1987).

37. E.g., C. H. Dodd, *The Interpretation of the Fourth Gospel* (Cambridge: Cambridge University Press, 1960), pp. 187–200.

38. E.g., Rudolf Bultmann, *The Gospel of John: A Commentary* (Philadelphia: Fortress, 1971), pp. 380–83, 404, 427, 536, 613–14, 621; see also Bultmann's "Die Eschatologie des Johannes-Evangeliums," in *Glauben und Verstehen: Gesammelte Aufsätze* (Tübingen: Mohr, 1933), 1:134–52.

39. See Raymond E. Brown, *Community of the Beloved Disciple* (New York: Paulist, 1979).

40. On the Johannine writings, see especially the massive commentaries by Raymond E. Brown: *The Gospel according to John,* Anchor Bible 29, 29A (Garden City, NY: Doubleday, 1966, 1970); *The Epistles of John,* Anchor Bible 30 (Garden City, NY: Doubleday, 1982); see also Ernst Haenchen, *John 1 and 2,* Hermeneia (Philadelphia: Fortress, 1984).

41. On the early exegesis of John, see M. F. Wiles, *The Spiritual Gospel: The Interpretation of the Fourth Gospel in the Early Church* (Cambridge: Cambridge University Press, 1960).

42. See Countryman, *Mystical Way,* p. 2: "Conversion, baptism, and reception of the Eucharist lead on without a break (though not by any sort of inevitability) to mystical enlightenment and union." See also pp. 124–26, 131–32.

43. See Arthur Droge, "The Status of Peter in the Fourth Gospel: A Note on John 18:10–11," *Journal of Biblical Literature* 109 (1990): 307–11.

44. See chapter 4 below, pp. 89–99.

45. Helpful in this connection is the section "Knowledge of God" in Dodd, *Interpretation of the Fourth Gospel,* pp. 151–69. See also the survey of Johannine verbs of seeing (*blepein, theasthai, theōrein, idein, horan*) in Brown, *Gospel of John* 1:501–3.

46. See Dodd, *Interpretation of the Fourth Gospel,* pp. 10–73, for extended comparisons with the *Hermetica* and Philo.

47. On *agapē* in John, see Spicq, *Agape,* vol. 3. For a brief survey of the words *agapē, agapan; philein,* see Brown, *Gospel of John* 1:497–99.

48. Of course, many other passages in the New Testament also support this teaching, e.g., the account of the Last Judgment in Matt 25:31–46.

49. On union in John, see Dodd, *Interpretation of the Fourth Gospel,* pp. 187–201; David L. Mealand, "The Language of Mystical Union in the Johannine Writings," *Downside Review* 19 (1977): 19–34; Countryman, *Mystical Way,* passim.

50. On the use of the verb *menein* in John, see Brown, *Gospel of John* 1:510–12.

51. On *koinōnia,* see Brown, *Epistles of John,* p. 170.

52. See Countryman, *Mystical Way,* p. 7.

53. For the text of Ignatius, I will use that of Kirsopp Lake in *The Apostolic Fathers I,* LC (Cambridge, MA: Harvard University Press, 1975). The translation will be that of William R. Schoedel (*Ignatius of Antioch: A Commentary on the Letters of Ignatius of Antioch,* Hermeneia [Philadelphia: Fortress, 1985]), whose commentary has been very helpful. The seven letters will be abbreviated as follows: *Ephesians (Eph.), Magnesians (Mag.), Trallians (Tr.), Romans (Rom.), Philadelphians (Phil.), Smyrnaeans (Smyr.),* and *Polycarp (Pol.).*

54. Schweitzer, *Mysticism of Paul,* pp. 339–44, emphasizing *Mag.* 12.2.

55. Frederick Augustus Schilling, *The Mysticism of Ignatius of Antioch* (Philadelphia: University of Pennsylvania Press, 1932); T. Preiss, "La mystique de l'imitation du Christ et de l'unité chez Ignace d'Antioche," *Revue d'histoire et de philosophie religieuses* 18 (1938): 197–241 (esp. pp. 227–29, 237–41).

56. Bouyer says that Ignatius "expressed in pure and burning terms this mysticism of primitive Christian gnosis" (*The Spirituality of the New Testament and the Fathers,* p. 183; see also pp. 182–84, 194–204). V. Corwin sees union with the Father becoming a central mystical category in Ignatius (*St. Ignatius and Christianity at Antioch,* Yale Publications in Religion 1 [New Haven: Yale University Press, 1960], e.g., pp. 247–66).

57. E.g., *Eph.* 8.2; 10.3; 11.1–2; 12.2; 20.2; *Mag.* 6.2; *Tr.* 1.1; 9.2; 13.2–3; *Rom.* 1.1; 2.2; *Phil.* 10.1–2; 11.2; *Pol.* 8.3.

58. E.g., *Eph.* 15.3; *Mag.* 12.1; *Rom.* 6.3.

59. E.g., *Eph.* 1.1; 6.2; *Mag.* 3.1, 14; *Tr.* 4.1; 8.2; *Pol.* 1.1; 6.1.

60. According to Schoedel, "Ignatius does not exploit the mystical possibilities of such language. His conception of the relation between God and human beings revolves not about identification but about communion within the context of the solidarity of the group" (*Ignatius*, p. 19). Of course, the latter may also be capable of grounding a type of mysticism, in my view.

61. Ibid., p. 105, commenting on *Mag.* 1.1. Other texts, such as *Eph.* 15.3, which Schoedel dismisses as not being on a "high mystical plane," seem to me at least capable of a mystical reading.

62. For a discussion, see Schoedel, *Ignatius*, pp. 28–29.

63. For some other appearances, see *Eph.* 12.2; *Mag.* 14.1; *Tr.* 13.3; *Smyr.* 11.1; *Pol.* 7.1.

64. Cf. *Eph.* 10.1 and *Tr.* 5.2 for the other general uses.

65. Even Schoedel, who in general opposes a mystical reading of Ignatius, admits, "The expression 'to attain God,' then, takes its place with others in the letters that describe the relations between God and human beings in terms of a deep communion verging on or passing over into mysticism" (*Ignatius*, p. 29; cf. p. 18).

66. E.g., *Martyrdom of Saint Polycarp* 2, which speaks of the martyrs holding converse with Christ present during their sufferings and mentions both visions (chap. 5) and auditions (chap. 9) given to Polycarp. Visions and ecstasies are also described in the *Martyrdom of Saints Perpetua and Felicitas* 4, 11–13, 20. For an edition and translation of these texts, see Herbert Musurillo, *The Acts of the Christian Martyrs* (Oxford: Clarendon, 1979). To be sure, not every form of visionary experience is to be equated with mysticism, but there are many close connections between the two forms of religious life.

67. Cf. *Eph.* 1.1; 18.1–2; *Tr.* 10.1. On imitation in the letters, see Willard M. Swartley, "The Imitatio Christi in the Ignatian Letters," *Vigiliae Christianae* 27 (1973): 81–103.

68. See the comment on this passage in Schoedel, *Ignatius*, pp. 184–87.

69. The literature on martyrdom is large. For a broad historical background, see W. H. C. Frend, *Martyrdom and Persecution: A Study of a Conflict from the Maccabees to Donatus* (New York: New York University Press, 1967); Hans von Campenhausen, *Die Idee des Martyriums in der alten Kirche* (2nd ed.; Göttingen: Vandenhoeck & Ruprecht, 1964). For martyrdom as an ideal of perfection, see Marcel Viller and Karl Rahner, *Aszese und Mystik in der Väterzeit: Ein Abriss* (Freiberg: Herder, 1939), chap. 2 (resuming a number of earlier studies by Viller); Bouyer, *The Spirituality of the New Testament and the Fathers*, chap. 8; Michele Pellegrino, "L'imitation du Christ dans les actes des martyrs," *La vie spirituelle* 98 (1958): 38–54; Willy Rordorf, "Martyre, II, Théologie et spiritualité du martyre," *DS* 10:726–32.

70. Viller and Rahner, *Aszese und Mystik*, pp. 33–36.

71. *Martyrdom of Perpetua and Felicitas* 15 (edition and translation of Musurillo, *Acts of the Christian Martyrs*, pp. 122–25).

72. Festugière, *L'Enfant d'Agrigente*, pp. 127–33 ("Mystique païenne et charité"), pp. 134–48 ("Ascèse et contemplation").

Chapter 4

In this and the following chapter I wish to express a special debt of thanks to Robert L. Wilken, who read both chapters with care and made a number of valuable suggestions.

1. This is a point that recent histories of early Christianity have made clear; see, e.g., Robert M. Grant, *From Augustus to Constantine* (New York: Harper & Row, 1970); W. H. C. Frend, *The Rise of Christianity* (Philadelphia: Fortress, 1984). For methodological remarks on this trend and its limits, see Robert L. Wilken, "Diversity and Unity in Early Christianity," *The Second Century* 1 (1981): 101–11.

2. Histories of early Christian spirituality, both ascetic and mystical, are many. I have found two of the oldest the most helpful: Anselm Stolz, *Theologie der Mystik* (Regensburg: Pustet, 1936); and Marcel Viller and Karl Rahner, *Aszese und Mystik in der Väterzeit: Ein Abriss* (Freiburg: Herder, 1939). Among other attempts at surveys, note Gustave Bardy, *La vie spirituelle d'après les pères des trois premiers siècles,* ed. A. Hamman, 2 vols. (Tournai: Desclée, 1968); and the articles of Arrigo Levasti on Clement, Origen, Gregory of Nyssa, Evagrius, and the Pseudo-Macarius published in *Rivista di Ascetica e Mistica* 12-14 (1967-69). Also useful are the surveys of Irenée Hausherr, such as "Les grands courants de la spiritualité orientale," *Orientalia Christiana Periodica* 1 (1935): 114-38; idem, "Le spiritualité des premières generations chrétiennes," in *La mystique et les mystiques,* ed. A. Rivier (Paris: Desclée, 1965), pp. 409-61. Important, despite its at times idiosyncratic viewpoint, is Louis Bouyer, *The Spirituality of the New Testament and the Fathers,* vol. 1 of *A History of Christian Spirituality* (New York: Seabury, 1982; originally published in 1960 in French as vol. 1 in Aubier's *Histoire de la Spiritualité chrétienne*). The most recent treatments are Andrew Louth, *The Origins of the Christian Mystical Tradition: From Plato to Denys* (Oxford: Clarendon, 1981); Olivier Clement, *Sources: Les mystiques chrétiens des origines. Textes et commentaires* (Paris: Stock, 1982), a collection of texts and comments; and *Christian Spirituality: Origins to the Twelfth Century,* ed. Bernard McGinn and John Meyendorff, WS 16 (New York: Crossroad, 1986). For a bibliographic survey of French contributions to the field from ca. 1945 to 1959 (a period of great importance), see F. Refoulé, O.P., "La doctrine spirituelle des Pères de l'église," *La vie spirituelle* 102 (1960): 310-26.

3. The notion of perfection is central to Viller and Rahner, *Aszese und Mystik;* see also R. Newton Flew, *The Idea of Perfection in Christian Theology* (London: Oxford University Press, 1934), chaps. 1-10; also, "Perfection chrétienne, II, Pères et prémiers moines," *DS* 12:1081-1118.

The most detailed treatment of divinization is Jules Gross, *La divinisation du chrétien d'après les péres grecs* (Paris: Gabalda, 1938); see also M. Lot-Borodine, *La deification de l'homme d'après les pères grecs* (Paris: Cerf, 1970), as well as the insightful review of the original appearance of this work in article form by M.-D. Chenu, "La deification dans la tradition spirituelle de l'Orient," *La vie spirituelle* 43 (1935): [91]-[107]. For other surveys of the theme of divinization, see "Divinisation," *DS* 3:1370-98 (patristic period); and, on the negative side, Ben Drewery, "Deification," in *Christian Spirituality: Essays in Honour of Gordon Rupp,* ed. Peter Brooks (London: SCM, 1975), pp. 35-62. The notion of divinization is intimately connected to that of participation (Platonic *methexis*), for whose influence on the fathers, see Friedrich Normann, *Teilhabe—ein Schlüsselwort der Vätertheologie* (Münster: Aschendorff, 1978).

The role of Platonic contemplation is the major theme in Louth, *Origins,* and it has been exhaustively studied in the article "Contemplation" in *DS* 2:1762-1911 for the Greek fathers. For an overview, see Louis Bouyer, "Die mystische Kontemplation bei den Vätern," in *Weisheit Gottes—Weisheit der Welt: Festschrift für Joseph Kardinal Ratzinger zum 60. Geburtstag,* ed. W. Baier et al., 2 vols. (St. Ottilien: EOS Verlag, 1987) 1:637-49.

The contrast between true and false gnosis is stressed by Bouyer, *Spirituality,* esp. chaps. 9-12. See also Pierre-Thomas Camelot, "Gnose chrétienne," in *DS* 6:509-23.

On the vision of God, see esp. K. E. Kirk, *The Vision of God: The Christian Doctrine of the "Summum Bonum"* (1932; reprint, Cambridge: James Clarke, 1977); Vladimir Lossky, *The Vision of God* (London: Faith Press, 1963).

The theme of divine birth and its relation to *theōria* is the subject of an interesting paper by Dietmar Mieth: "Gottesschau und Gottesgeburt: Zwei Typen Christlicher Gotteserfahrung in der Tradition," *Freiburger Zeitschrift für Philosophie und Theologie* 27 (1980): 204-23. For the patristic treatment of birthing, see H. Rahner, "Die Gottesgeburt: Die Lehre der Kirchenväter von der Geburt Christi aus dem Herzen der Gläubigen," in *Symbole der Kirche: Die Ekklesiologie der Väter* (Salzburg: Müller, 1964), pp. 13-87; and "Naissance divine (mystique de la)" in *DS* 11:24-28.

Divine likeness has been studied by Hubert Merki, *HOMOIOSIS THEOU: Von der platonischen Angleichung an Gott zur Gottähnlichkeit bei Gregor von Nyssa* (Freiburg: Paulusverlag, 1952), part 1, of which pp. 1–91 deal with the background to Gregory's use.

For background on the enjoyment of God, see "Fruitio Dei" in *DS* 5:1546–52, which treats only of the Latin fathers, and the more inclusive treatment of J. Haussleiter, "Fruitio Dei," *Reallexikon für Antike und Christentum* 8:538–55.

For an overview of prayer in the patristic period, see "Prière, III, Dans la tradition chrétienne," *DS* 12:2247–71. The most important study of the development of the "Jesus" form of continual prayer from its patristic roots is also available in English in Irenée Hausherr, *The Name of Jesus* (Kalamazoo: Cistercian Publications, 1978).

For the notion of ecstasy, see the excellent article "Extase," in *DS* 4:2087–2109, for the Greek fathers.

Union with God, though often seen as the hallmark of true mysticism, has, to the best of my knowledge, not been the subject of monographic study by patristic scholars.

4. For an introduction, see "Imitation du Christ" in *DS* 7:1536–1601 (1563–71 on patristic uses). See also M. Pellegrino, "L'imitation du Christ dans les actes des martyrs," *La vie spirituelle* 98 (1958): 38–54; and T. Preiss, "La mystique de l'imitation du Christ et de l'unité chez Ignace d'Antioche," *Revue d'histoire et de philosophie religieuses* 18 (1938): 197–241.

5. The study of Greek patristic mysticism has been especially enriched by the long series of monographs by Walther Völker, including (in historical order): *Fortschritt und Vollendung bei Philo von Alexandrien* (Leipzig: Hinrichs, 1938); *Die wahre Gnostiker nach Clemens Alexandrinus* (Berlin: Akademie-Verlag, 1952); *Das Vollkommenheitsideal des Origenes* (Tübingen: Mohr, 1931); *Gregor von Nyssa als Mystiker* (Wiesbaden: F. Steiner, 1955); *Kontemplation und Ekstase bei Pseudo-Dionysius Areopagita* (Wiesbaden: F. Steiner, 1958); *Scala Paradisi: Eine Studie zu Johannes Climacus und zugleich eine Vorstudie zu Symeon dem Neuen Theologen* (Wiesbaden: F. Steiner, 1968); *Maximus Konfessor als Meister des geistlichen Lebens* (Wiesbaden: F. Steiner, 1965); and *Praxis und Theoria bei Symeon dem Neuen Theologen* (Wiesbaden: F. Steiner, 1974).

6. For an introduction to the formative role of scripture in Christian mysticism, see the important article "Écriture sainte et vie spirituelle" in *DS* 4:128–278 (132–69 for the patristic period).

7. This is why the earliest use of the adjective *mystikos* ("hidden, secret") in Christianity is to describe the deeper, Christological meaning, of the text. Clement of Alexandria, for instance, speaks of a "mystical interpretation" (*tēn mystikēn hermēneian*) in *Stromateis* 5.6 (*PG* 9:64A). For a survey of early uses (many of which will be considered in this and the following chapter), see Louis Bouyer, "Mysticism: An Essay on the History of the Word," in *Understanding Mysticism*, ed. Richard Woods (Garden City, NY: Doubleday Image Books, 1980), pp. 42–55.

8. Self-definition as a key aspect of the whole religious world of the time was the subject of a major symposium held in 1978 and published in three volumes as *Jewish and Christian Self-Definition*, ed. E. P. Sanders et al. (Philadelphia: Fortress, 1980–82).

9. Justin Martyr in his *Apology* 1 and 2 is well known for expressing a positive attitude toward Greek philosophers (e.g., 1.5, 8, 20, 44, 46, 59–60; 2.8, 10, 13). Other apologists, such as Tatian, are more negative.

10. The most recent study is Robert M. Grant, *Greek Apologists of the Second Century* (Philadelphia: Westminster, 1988).

11. The literature on the relation between Christianity and classical philosophy is large. Two useful and balanced introductions can be found in A. H. Armstrong and R. A. Markus, *Christian Faith and Greek Philosophy* (London: Darton, Longman & Todd, 1960); and Henry Chadwick, *Early Christian Thought and the Classical Tradition: Studies in Justin, Clement, and Origen* (New York: Oxford University Press, 1966). Among other studies, see the noted treatment of René Arnou, "Platonisme des Pères," *Dictionnaire de théologie catholique* 12:2258–2392; and P.-T. Camelot, "Hellenisme (et spiritualité patristique)," *DS* 7:145–64. For a recent

summary, see A. H. Armstrong, "The Self-Definition of Christianity in Relation to Later Platonism," in *Jewish and Christian Self-Definition,* ed. Sanders et al., 1:74–99.

12. W. R. Inge, *Christian Mysticism* (London: Methuen, 1899), p. 82.

13. A. von Harnack, *History of Dogma,* 7 vols. (New York: Dover, 1961) 1:227–28, 253. See p. 17 for the famous declaration "Dogma in its conception and development is a work of the Greek spirit on the soil of the Gospel."

14. Hans Jonas, *Gnosis und spätantike Geist,* 2 vols. (Göttingen: Vandenhoeck & Ruprecht, 1934, 1954). Jonas's major research was done prior to the Nag Hammadi discoveries, but he included some reactions to these in his book *The Gnostic Religion: The Message of the Alien God and the Beginnings of Christianity* (Boston: Beacon, 1958).

15. For a brief account of these discoveries and their complex history, see Kurt Rudolph, *Gnosis,* trans. R. McL. Wilson (San Francisco: Harper & Row, 1983), pp. 34–52.

16. For reflections on these two approaches, see Hans Jonas, "Gnosticism, Existentialism, and Nihilism," in *Gnostic Religion,* pp. 320–40; and Gilles Quispel, "Gnosis and Psychology," in *The Rediscovery of Gnosticism,* vol. 1, *The School of Valentinus,* ed. Bentley Layton (Leiden: Brill, 1980), pp. 17–31.

17. For a salutary critique of neo-Gnostic misreadings of Gnosticism, see Pheme Perkins, *The Gnostic Dialogue: The Early Church and the Crisis of Gnosticism* (New York: Paulist, 1980), pp. 205–17.

18. E.g., Morton Smith emphasizes the differences among the groups (largely Platonic in inspiration) who seem to have used the term for self-identification and the various kinds of Christians to whom Irenaeus and others applied the term ("The History of the Term Gnostikos," in *The Rediscovery of Gnosticism,* vol. 2, *Sethian Gnosticism,* ed. Bentley Layton [Leiden: Brill, 1981], pp. 796–807).

19. For a recent formulation of these questions, see Bentley Layton, *The Gnostic Scriptures* (Garden City, NY: Doubleday, 1987), p. xii.

20. On Jonas's theories, see the discussion in chapter 2, p. 42, and the summary in Appendix, section 3, pp. 336–38.

21. Thus, Jacques Ménard says: "Phenomenologically speaking, true Gnosis could easily be defined as being a mystical theology of the identification of God with the Self. . . . [Various Gnostic texts] all expound a mystical religion, according to which man is divine emanation through his own Intellect and through his own *nous* . . ." ("Normative Self-Definition in Gnosticism," in *Jewish and Christian Self-Definition,* ed. Sanders et al., 1:149). Robert M. Grant says that "some Gnostics joined Neoplatonists like Plotinus by enjoying mystical experience here and now" ("Gnostic Spirituality," in *Christian Spirituality: Origins to the Twelfth Century,* ed. McGinn and Meyendorff, 56). Bentley Layton in *Gnostic Scriptures* gives the most detailed recent exposition of Gnostic mysticism, as we shall see below (though he does not say what he means by mysticism).

22. For an overview of recent discussion on Gnosticism and its origins, see R. van den Broek ("The Present State of Gnostic Studies," *Vigiliae Christianae* 37 [1983]: 41–71), who argues for a possible Jewish origin (pp. 60–61, 66).

23. Ibid., p. 71.

24. *Gospel of Philip* 85 (Layton, *Gnostic Scriptures,* p. 346).

25. This position was advanced by Robert M. Grant (*Gnosticism and Early Christianity* [New York: Harper & Row, 1959], pp. 13–38), but was later retracted. More recent work has also suggested possible Jewish sources, but without specifying the failure of apocalyptic hopes as the explanation.

26. Plotinus, *Ennead* 2.9.6 (LC 2:242–43). Plotinus's attack on the Gnostics comes as the conclusion of one of the most important treatises in his works, the great treatment of contemplation comprising *Enneads* 3.8; 5.8; 5.5; and 2.9 (chronologically #30–33 of his writings, but artificially split up by Porphyry when he prepared his master's writings for publication). On Plotinus's knowledge of and opposition to Gnosticism, see Porphyry, *Vita Plotini* 16.

27. Rudolph, *Gnosis,* p. 54.

28. Jonas speaks of the general religious climate of which Gnosticism is the chief representative as one centering on "a dualistic transcendent religion of salvation" (*Gnostic Religion,* pp. 31–32). Grant says, "It is a religion of saving knowledge, and the knowledge is essentially self-knowledge, recognition of the divine element which constitutes the true self" (*Gnosticism and Early Christianity,* p. 10). Rudolph says, "We shall not go far wrong to see in it a dualistic religion, consisting of several schools and movements, which took up a definitely negative attitude toward the world and the society of the time, and proclaimed a deliverance ('redemption') of man precisely from the restraints of earthly existence through 'insight' into his essential relationship . . . with a supramundane realm of freedom and rest" (*Gnosis,* p. 2). (Rudolph fleshes this out in the second section of his book, pp. 53–272, entitled "Nature and Structure.")

29. Rudolph, *Gnosis,* p. 308.

30. Early anthologies, such as that of R. M. Grant (*Gnosticism* [New York: Harper & Row, 1961]), are still useful; but the most up-to-date anthologies are *The Nag Hammadi Library,* ed. James M. Robinson (New York: Harper & Row, 1977), which translates all the Nag Hammadi texts; and B. Layton, *Gnostic Scriptures,* which contains most of the Nag Hammadi material, as well as other important texts along with an extensive apparatus. All quotations will be taken from Layton unless otherwise noted.

31. For some case studies in Gnostic mythology, see G. Stroumsa, *Another Seed: Studies in Gnostic Mythology* (Leiden: Brill, 1984).

32. Especially important here have been the studies of Ugo Bianchi, e.g., *Il dualismo religioso: Saggio storico ed etnologico* (Rome: L'Erma di Bretschneider, 1958). More recently, see the work of Ioan Culianu, *I Miti dei Dualismi Occidentali: Dai sistemi gnostici al mondo moderno* (Milan: Jaca, 1989).

33. See Ptolemy, *Letter to Flora* 33.7.9 (Layton, *Gnostic Scriptures,* p. 314), and Layton's comments on p. 303. For more on Valentinus and Valentinianism, see vol. 1 of the Yale Symposium published as *The Rediscovery of Gnosticism* (see nn. 16 and 18).

34. Irenaeus recognized the differences between Valentinians and other Gnostics on the role of Christ (*Against Heresies* 3.18.6). See Elaine Pagels, "Gnostic and Orthodox Views of Christ's Passion: Paradigms for Christians' Response to Persecution?" in *Rediscovery of Gnosticism* 1:262–88.

35. Layton, *Gnostic Scriptures,* pp. xv–xvi, 121, 141, 220, 359–60.

36. A similar negative theology can be found in the *Apocryphon of John* (Codex II) 2:26–4:24 (Layton, *Gnostic Scriptures,* pp. 29–30).

37. It appears that it is the Invisible One and not his offspring who is being addressed, though the hymn as a whole is to Barbelo.

38. "Such a person becomes a god and has withdrawn into God" (Layton, *Gnostic Scriptures,* p. 133). Cf. *Zost.* 53:20.

39. Some passages seem to reflect an early stage of the famous Neoplatonic triad of Being–Life–Intelligence, e.g., *Allogenes* 59:9–24. See van den Broek, "Present State," pp. 65–66.

40. For a discussion of the background and importance of the all-encompassing God who is contained by none, see W. R. Schoedel, "Gnostic Monism and the Gospel of Truth," in *Rediscovery of Gnosticism* 1:379–90. The *Gospel of Truth* is certainly far from the dualism of the "classic" forms of the Gnostic myth, but whether or not we should call it monistic is another question.

41. Cf. *Gospel of Philip* 39 (61:36–62:5).

42. The Greek *Acts of John* was edited by M. Bonnet, *Acta apostolorum apocrypha* II.1 (Leipzig: Teubner, 1896; reprint, Hildesheim: Olms, 1959); it is translated in Edgar Hennecke, *New Testament Apocrypha,* ed. Wilhelm Schneemelcher, trans. R. McL. Wilson (Philadelphia: Westminster, 1965) 2:215–58 (the hymn is on pp. 227–32). The *Acts* may have been written in the second century in Asia Minor. The hymn refers to the Ogdoad, the primeval first group of eight emanations found in the Valentinian myth but also in other

Gnostic texts. Gilles Quispel claims that the text is Valentinian ("Valentinian Gnosticism and the Apocryphon of John," in *Rediscovery of Gnosticism* 1:126–29).

43. *Epistle to Rheginus,* esp. 48:33–49:8: "It [spiritual resurrection] is what stands at rest: And the revealing of what truly exists."

44. Cf. *Gos. Phil.* 96 (78:25–79:13) and 102 (82:23–24).

45. Layton, *Gnostic Scriptures,* p. xvi.

46. "Jesus said, 'Whoever drinks from my mouth will become like me; I, too, will become that person, and to that person the obscure things will be shown'" (Layton, *Gnostic Scriptures,* p. 398).

47. See G. Stroumsa, "Ascèse et gnose: Aux origines de la spiritualité monastique," *Revue Thomiste* 81 (1981): 557–73. According to Grant ("Gnostic Spirituality," p. 54): "Almost all Gnostics, whether ascetic or libertine, were deeply concerned about human sexuality and its problems." I have deliberately refrained from entering into the complex area of whether and to what extent Gnostic dualism may have issued into forms of erotic behavior that were accorded spiritual value. See my remarks on this issue in "The Language of Love in Jewish and Christian Mysticism," in *Mysticism and Language,* ed. Steven Katz (New York: Oxford University Press, 1991) (to appear). Accusations of sexual impropriety, of course, were central to the orthodox polemic against Gnosticism.

48. On the complexities of this issue, see Peter Brown, *The Body and Society: Men, Women, and Sexual Renunciation in Early Christianity* (New York: Columbia University Press, 1988).

49. Justin refers to the lost treatise he wrote against the Gnostics (*Apology* 1.26).

50. See the discussion at the beginning of chapter 2.

51. Rudolph says, "It is just this opposition of 'faith' and 'knowledge' which was one of the central themes in the debates of the Church with the gnostic heresy" (*Gnosis,* p. 56).

52. "Cedat curiositas fidei, cedat gloria saluti; certe aut non obstrepant aut quiescunt; adversus regulam nihil scire omnia scire est."

53. Helpful in this connection is Elaine H. Pagels, "Visions, Appearances, and Apostolic Authority: Gnostic and Orthodox Traditions," in *Gnosis: Festschrift für Hans Jonas,* ed. B. Aland (Göttingen: Vandenhoeck & Ruprecht, 1978), pp. 415–30.

54. See Herbert Musurillo, *The Acts of the Christian Martyrs* (Oxford: Clarendon, 1979), pp. 6, 8, 110–12, 114–22.

55. E.g., Origen, *Homily on the Song of Songs* 1.7; see the treatment below, pp. 123–24.

56. See the discussion in the Appendix, section 3, pp. 334–36.

57. Bouyer, *Spirituality,* chaps. 9–12.

58. Much work has been done on Gnostic exegesis in recent years; see esp. Elaine Pagels, *The Johannine Gospel in Gnostic Exegesis* (Nashville: Abingdon, 1973); eadem, *The Gnostic Paul: Gnostic Exegesis of the Pauline Letters* (Philadelphia: Westminster, 1975).

59. According to Layton, "obscurity is not a mark of our distance from classical antiquity but rather a function of the esoteric character of gnostic life in a closed, and sometimes persecuted, religious sect that was defiantly sure of its superiority to the rest of humanity" (*Gnostic Scriptures,* p. 17).

60. This text is discusssed in more detail in chapter 7, p. 256.

61. See esp. Hans Urs von Balthasar, *The Glory of the Lord,* vol. 2, *Studies in Theological Styles: Clerical Styles* (New York: Crossroad, 1984), pp. 31–94, who admits that "Gnosis was the opponent Christian thought needed in order to fully find itself" (p. 32).

62. For a detailed study of the text, see Edward Baert, "Le thème de la vision de Dieu chez S. Justin, Clement d'Alexandrie et S. Grégoire de Nysse," *Freiburger Zeitschrift für Philosophie und Theologie* 12 (1965): 440–55.

63. *Dialogue* 4.1: *Ē ton theon anthrōpou nous opsetai pote me hagia pneumati kekosmemenos.* Baert argues that Justin restricts vision of God to the next life ("Le thème de la vision," 433, 455), but the text, despite the shift from present to future tense, leaves open the question whether or not *some* vision is possible to the God-endowed soul here below.

64. See Baert, "La thème de la vision," p. 439.

65. "Gloria enim Dei vivens homo, vita autem hominis visio Dei (*horasis theou*, according to the retroversion to the Greek).

66. Von Balthasar, *Glory of the Lord* 2:45; cf. pp. 46–47, 75–76. On the theme of the vision of God in Irenaeus, see Real Tremblay, *La manifestation et la vision de Dieu selon saint Irenée de Lyon* (Münster: Aschendorff, 1978).

67. Nicholas Gendle, O.P., "St. Irenaeus as a Mystical Theologian," *The Thomist* 39 (1975): 185–97.

68. E.g., Valentinus, Fragment H (Layton, *Gnostic Scriptures*, p. 245); and in the *Excerpts from Theodotus* 56.5, preserved by Clement of Alexandria. The text also appears in several second-century documents that appear to come from Asia Minor, e.g., *Gospel of Thomas* 27, and *Acts of Paul* 3.5.

69. Among the "orthodox" fathers, Matt 5.8 first appears in Theophilus of Antioch, *To Autolycus* 1.2, where the verb has already been changed to the more Platonic-sounding *theōrein*. Shortly after, Irenaeus uses it in *Against Heresies* 4.9.2 and 4.20.5.

70. According to the *Biblia Patristica*, 4 vols. (Paris: CNRS, 1975–), Clement refers to the text eighteen times (1:232–33), whereas Origen uses it no fewer than fifty-five times (3:230–31).

71. There are brief references to the doctrine in Justin (*Oration to the Greeks* 5) and in Theophilus (*To Autolycus* 2.24). Irenaeus has a number of important treatments, e.g., *Against Heresies* 3.19.1; 4.38.4; 5. pref.; and 5.9.2.

72. Arrigo Levasti, "Clemente Alessandrino, iniziatore della Mistica cristiana," *Rivista di Ascetica e Mistica* 12 (1967): 127–47.

73. E.g., Drewery, "Deification," pp. 41–44, 54–55 (see n. 3 above).

74. John Chapman, "Mysticism," in *Encyclopedia of Religion and Ethics*, ed. J. Hastings (New York: Scribner, 1908–) 9:91. The most important modern monograph on Clement's mysticism agrees: P.-T. Camelot, *Foi et gnose: Introduction à l'étude de la connaissance mystique chez Clement d'Alexandrie* (Paris: Vrin, 1945), p. 137.

75. For a list of Clement's uses of *mystikos* and related forms, see the "Wort- und Sachregister" in vol. 4 of the edition of Clement by Otto Stählin in the GCS (4th ed.; Berlin: Akademie-Verlag, 1985). References to Clement will be to this edition, noting the title, book, chapter, and section, and (in parentheses) the Stählin volume, page, and, when necessary, line numbers.

76. On Christ, the one teacher, see *Stromateis* 7.2.6 (3:6).

77. *The Excerpta ex Theodoto of Clement of Alexandria*, edited with a translation by Robert Pierce Casey (London: Christophers, 1934), p. 41.

78. See the comments on this text in Casey, *Excerpta ex Theodoto*, pp. 25–26.

79. Camelot's treatment of this tension is excellent; see *Foi et gnose*, pp. 43–48, 87–88, 92–95 and esp. 141–42.

80. My renderings of Clement are generally taken from the translations in *ANF* 2, but for book 7 of *Stromateis* I have used the version found in *Alexandrian Christianity*, ed. Henry Chadwick (Philadelphia: Westminster, 1954). At times I have preferred to make my own translations.

81. Besides Camelot, many of the standard treatments of patristic spirituality are helpful on Clement, esp. Viller and Rahner, *Aszese und Mystik*, pp. 61–71; Bouyer, *Spirituality*, chap. 11; Levasti, "Clemente Alessandrino"; and Baert, "Le thème de la vision," pp. 460–80.

82. *Ho philalēthes Platōn hoion theophoroumenos;* cf. *Strom.* 2.19.100, where Clement comments on how both Moses and Plato teach that humanity can become like God. For other praise of Plato, see, e.g., *Strom.* 4.25.155; 5.1.7.

83. Camelot, *Foi et gnose*, p. 58.

84. Citing Plato; cf. *Strom.* 2.21, which refers to other philosophers. Clement sometimes uses the older term *epopteia* for contemplative vision, as in *Paed.* 1.7.54 (1:122.9), and even combines the two in *Strom.* 5.10.66, where he contrasts the milk (cf. 1 Cor 3:1–3) of catechetical instruction with the meat, or solid food, of contemplation: "And the meat is

visionary contemplation (*epoptikē theōria*), the flesh and the blood of the Word, that is, the comprehension of divine power and being. . . . The meat and drink of the Divine Logos is the gnosis of the divine being" (2:370.15-21, my translation).

85. On this text, see Baert, "Le thème de la vision," pp. 472-73. For another important text on *theōria*, see *Strom.* 4.22.136 (2:308).

86. Also citing Matt 5:8.

87. See, e.g., *Strom.* 7.3.14 (3:10.30), which speaks of "being enlightened into an indissoluble unity" (*henōsin adiakriton*). *Strom.* 7.7.44 (3:33.19-20) says that the Gnostic "is united [*henōtai*] to the Spirit through the love that knows no bounds." In 7.11.68 (3:49.12-20) the fellowship that lies in unity has its roots in the God who is truly one.

88. In *Strom.* 7.14.88 (3:62.28-30) we find Clement using 1 Cor 6.17, later the favorite text of mystics to express loving union of wills: "he that is joined to the Lord after a different kind of union [*to diaphoron tēs synodou*], in spirit, is a spiritual body."

89. For an overview, somewhat dated, see G. Bardy, "Apatheia," *DS* 1:727-46 (729-31 on Clement).

90. Brown, *Body and Society*, pp. 130-31.

91. *Strom.* 6.9.71-79 (2:467-71). For some other important passages, see, e.g., 2.20.110; 7.2.10; 7.9.52-54, etc.

92. Nicholas Lobkowicz, *Theory and Practice: History of a Concept from Aristotle to Marx* (Notre Dame: University of Notre Dame Press, 1967), p. 59.

93. On this, see Lobkowicz, *Theory*, chap. 5. What follows summarizes Lobkowicz's presentation of the Greek philosophical tradition in chaps. 1-4.

94. . . . *nai phēmi, ho logos ho tou theou anthrōpos genomenos, hina de kai sy para anthrōpou mathes, te pote ara anthrōpos genetai theos.*

95. . . . *ouranio didaskalia theopoion anthrōpon.*

96. Citing Plato.

97. The theme of likeness to God is found throughout book 7, e.g., 1.3; 3.13; 3.16; 5.29; 10.57; 11.68; 14.84; 14.85; 16.95.

98. E.g., *Strom.* 5.10.65 (2:369-70) quotes Plato's *Letter 2* (312D and 314BC) together with 1 Cor 2:6-7. On Clement's use of negative and "veiled" language, see Marguerite Harl, "Le langage de l'expérience religieuse chez les pères grecs," *Rivista di storia e letteratura religiosa* 10 (1977), pp. 10-12.

99. E.g., *Strom.* 5.11.71 (2:374); 5.12.81-82 (2:380-81); 5.6.38-40 (2:351-54, a famous passage on Christ as high priest). On Clement's use of Moses' ascent into the cloud as an entry into apophatic knowing, see *Strom.* 2.2.5-6 (2:115-16).

100. See also *Paed.* 1.7.57 (1:124), where the Word is identified with the face of God seen by Jacob in Gen 32:29.

101. See, e.g., Drewery, "Deification," pp. 41-44 and 51-55; G. W. Butterworth, "The Deification of Man in Clement of Alexandria," *Journal of Theological Studies* 17 (1916): 157-69.

102. See the judicious evaluation of Camelot, *Foi et gnose*, pp. 137-43.

103. I refrain from entering into the question of whether or not Clement himself ever enjoyed mystical experiences. There is a discussion of the various views in Camelot, *Foi et gnose*, pp. 134-43; he wisely decides that we cannot answer the question—nor is the answer of real importance for Clement's place in this history.

104. The literature on Origen is large. For general introductions, see Henri Crouzel, *Origen: The Life and Thought of the First Great Theologian* (San Francisco: Harper & Row, 1989); and Joseph Wilson Trigg, *Origen: The Bible and Philosophy in the Third-Century Church* (Atlanta: John Knox, 1983). The sixth book of Eusebius's *Church History* contains an extensive biography of Origen. The most complete account of Origen's life is P. Nautin, *Origène: Sa vie et son oeuvre* (Paris: Beauchesne, 1977).

105. I have used the translation of P. Salmond in *ANF* 6:28.

106. The most complete editions of Origen's works, more of which survive in Latin translation than in the original Greek, are found in *PG*, vols. 13-17, and in the twelve

volumes of the GCS devoted to his works. Numerous volumes of Origen's works with excellent apparatus have also been published in the SC. All three editions will be used here.

107. Henri de Lubac's studies of Origen's exegesis are still useful reading, especially his *Histoire et Esprit: L'Intelligence de l'Écriture d'après Origène* (Paris: Aubier, 1950). The best English introduction is Karen Jo Torjesen, *Hermeneutical Procedure and Theological Method in Origen's Exegesis* (Berlin: de Gruyter, 1986). See also E. Klostermann, "Formen der exegetischen Arbeiten des Origenes," *Theologische Literaturzeitung* 72 (1947): 203–8.

108. The thirty-two books of the *Commentary*, of which only nine survive complete and two in parts, extend down to John 13:33. The most recent edition (not complete) is by C. Blanc in SC 120, 157, 222, and 290. There are partial English translations by A. Menzies in *ANF* 10, and R. Heine in FC 80 (1989). To be recommended for its helpful apparatus is the Italian translation of E. Corsini in *Commento al Vangelo di Giovanni di Origene* (Turin: Tipografia Torinese, 1968).

109. The critical edition is by W. Baehrens in GCS 33 (vol. 8 of the Origen series). All references here will be to this edition by page and line number. There is an excellent English translation with extensive comment by R. P. Lawson, *Origen: The Song of Songs. Commentary and Homilies*, ACW No. 26 (Westminster: Newman, 1957), whose translation I will use unless otherwise noted.

110. Crouzel emphasizes the interaction of these three aspects of his thought (*Origen*, p. 267).

111. See H. Crouzel, "Origène, précurseur du monachisme," in *Théologie de la vie monastique* (Paris: Aubier, 1961), pp. 15–38.

112. Crouzel, *Origen*, pp. 167–68, 266.

113. Recent scholarship is rightly critical of some older views that saw Origen more as a philosopher than as a churchman, e.g., Hans Jonas, "Die origenistische Spekulation und die Mystik," *Theologische Zeitschrift* 5 (1949): 24–45.

114. *On First Principles* has been most recently edited by H. Crouzel and M. Simonetti in SC 252, 253, 268, and 269. I will use the translation of G. W. Butterworth, *Origen: On First Principles* (New York: Harper & Row, 1966), unless otherwise noted (see pp. 277–78 for this passage).

115. Torjesen, *Hermeneutical Procedure*, pp. 39–41, 130–38.

116. Ibid., pp. 113–18, on the modes of the presence of the Logos.

117. See Crouzel, *Origen*, pp. 79–80, on the lack of distinction.

118. *Comm. on Mt.* 10.14 (GCS 40 [Origen 10]:17.13–14), as translated by Torjesen, *Hermeneutical Procedure*, p. 144 (see her discussion pp. 143–47). Cf. *Comm. on Jn.* 10.3 (10) (SC 157:386), which says that the discrepancies among the Gospels are to be solved "through anagogy" (*dia tēs anagogēs*).

119. *Per largissima enim spatia intelligentiae mysticae et spiritalis equitabo.*

120. Much has been written on the subject of Origen's relation to Platonism. Some describe him as the summation of Middle Platonism, e.g., Robert M. Berchman, *From Philo to Origen: Middle Platonism in Transition*, Brown Judaic Studies 69 (Chico, CA: Scholars Press, 1984). But most recent studies have stressed how much Origen's thought represents a Christian adaptation and critique of a more diffuse Platonic tradition, e.g., the papers of J. Dillon and C. Kannengiesser in *Origen of Alexandria: His World and his Legacy*, ed. C. Kannengiesser and W. Petersen (Notre Dame: University of Notre Dame Press, 1988), pp. 213–49. The most detailed study on the issue is still that of Hal Koch, *Pronoia und Paideusis: Studien über Origenes und sein Verhältnis zum Platonismus* (Berlin: de Gruyter, 1932), though he perhaps "platonizes" Origen too much.

121. On divine goodness, see, e.g., *De prin.* 1.7.1; 2.9.6.

122. On participation in Origen, see David Balas, "The Idea of Participation in the Structure of Origen's Thought: Christian Transposition of a Theme of the Platonic Tradition," in *Origeniana: Premier colloque intérnational des études origéniennes* (Bari: Istituto di Letteratura Cristiana Antica, 1975), pp. 257–75.

123. E.g., *Against Celsus* 6.64; 7.38; *Comm. on Jn.* 2.28 (172–74); 13.21 (123); 19.6 (37). *De prin.* 1.1.5 is one of Origen's longer treatments of divine unknowability.

124. Against his pagan opponent, Celsus, Origen stresses not so much the absolute unknowability of the Father as the ability of the Logos to reveal him; see, e.g., *Against Celsus* 6.65 (cf. 6.17 on Moses' meeting with God in relative, not absolute, darkness).

125. *De prin.* 1.2 is a key text. On this issue, see Crouzel, *Origen*, 186–92, 203.

126. See *De prin.* 1.7.1; Crouzel, *Origen*, p. 191.

127. SC 7bis: 28.14–18; Heine, FC 80:49. The fundamental book on this aspect of Origen's teaching is H. Crouzel, *Théologie de l'image de Dieu chez Origène* (Paris: Aubier, 1957), esp. pp. 147–79, 217–45.

128. Origen seems to have interpreted Genesis 2 as referring to this prior heavenly creation and the fall from it; see Crouzel, *Origen*, pp. 91, 94.

129. Patricia Cox, "'In My Father's House Are Many Dwelling Places': *Ktisma* in Origen's *De principiis*," *Anglican Theological Review* 62 (1980), p. 333.

130. For brief accounts of Origen's trichotomous anthropology, see Crouzel, *Origen*, pp. 87–92; and Brown, *Body and Society*, pp. 163–68.

131. Brown, *Body and Society*, p. 165.

132. See *Comm. on Jn.* 20.22 (20), and *Hom. on Gen.* 1.13 (6) for representative texts on *imago Dei.*

133. SC 7bis: 62.85–86; Heine, FC 80:66: Semper ergo intuemur istam imaginem Dei, ut possimus ad eius similitudinem reformari. As Henri Crouzel puts it (*Origen*, p. 98): "The trichotomic scheme, through the theme of spiritual struggle, controls the ascetic and moral teaching. The theology of the image of God, at the root of the possibility of knowing God, is the foundation of the whole of Origen's mysticism."

134. It is usually said that the soul of Christ is the only unfallen intellect from the first creation, but Crouzel assembles texts to indicate that Origen thought there might be others (*Origen*, p. 211).

135. See *De prin.* 1.6.1–2 for a classic exposition; cf. 1.6.4; 3.5.6–7; 3.6.3; etc. See Crouzel, *Origen*, p. 205.

136. The problem of Origen's views on the return of all things to God, the most controversial part of his theology, does not need to be solved here in order to discuss his mysticism. For a benign interpretation, see Crouzel, *Origen*, pp. 257–66.

137. There have been many studies of Origen's mysticism since the monograph of Walther Völker, *Das Vollkommenheitsideal des Origenes.* Among the most important are A. Lieske, *Die Theologie des Logosmystik bei Origenes* (Münster: Aschendorff, 1938); H. Urs von Balthasar, *Origenes: Geist und Feuer. Ein Aufbau aus seiner Schriften* (Salzburg: Otto Müller, 1938; the second edition has been translated by Robert J. Daly, S.J., as *Origen: Spirit and Fire* [Washington, DC: Catholic University of America Press, 1984]); Frederic Bertrand, *Mystique de Jésus chez Origène* (Paris: Aubier, 1951); and esp. Henri Crouzel, *Origène et la "connaissance mystique"* (Bruges-Paris: Desclée, 1961), as well as part 3 of his *Origen.* Among the most useful articles are Henri-Charles Puech, "Un livre récent sur la mystique d'Origène," *Revue d'histoire et de philosophie religieuse* 13 (1933): 508–36 (a review of Völker); Jean Daniélou, "Les sources bibliques de la mystique d'Origène," *Revue d'ascétique et de la mystique* 23 (1947): 126–41, which may be found in English as part 4 of Daniélou's *Origen* (New York: Sheed & Ward, 1955), pp. 293–309; C. W. Macleod, "Allegory and Mysticism in Origen and Gregory of Nyssa," *Journal of Theological Studies* n.s. 22 (1972): 362–79; and esp. M. Harl, "Le langage de l'expérience religieuse chez les pères grecs," *Rivista di storia e letteratura religiosa* 15 (1977): 5–34; and Henri Crouzel, "Origène," *DS* 11:933–61.

138. On Origen's *theologia ascendens* and its relation to Platonism, see von Balthasar, *Spirit and Fire*, pp. 7–13, 17–19. Origen argued that Plato's teaching about the descent from and ascent to vision of the divine realities was borrowed from the Jewish prophets; see *Against Celsus* 6.19–20.

139. See esp. *De prin.* 4.3.

140. For a presentation of these metaphors, see the Introduction by Rowan A. Greer, *Origen: An Exhortation to Martyrdom, Prayer and Selected Works*, CWS (New York: Paulist Press, 1979), pp. 18–22. Daniélou stresses the unity of the doctrine achieved through many symbols ("Les sources bibliques," p. 128).

141. See the recently discovered work *Peri Pascha* (*On the Passover*), parts of which are translated in von Balthasar, *Spirit and Fire*, pp. 368–70.

142. On the soul's journey, see the evocative remarks in Cox, "'In My Father's House,'" pp. 329, 332–33.

143. Harl, "Le langage," p. 8.

144. SC 7bis: 256.36–37: Quae leguntur mystica sunt, in allegoricis exponendis sunt sacramentis.

145. Harl, "Le langage," pp. 12–16.

146. See the consideration of this text in Macleod, "Allegory and Mysticism," p. 371.

147. The phrase is that of Cox, "'In My Father's House,'" p. 336.

148. Harl, "Le langage," p. 26 (my translation).

149. Ibid., p. 33 (my translation).

150. Pierre Hadot, "Les divisions des parties de la philosophie dans l'Antiquité," *Museum Helveticum* 36 (1979): 218–31.

151. On the three sciences and stages in the Christian itinerary, see Louth, *Origins*, pp. 56–61; and Karl Rahner, "The 'Spiritual Senses' according to Origen," in *Theological Investigations* (New York: Seabury, 1979) 16:92–94.

152. I will make use of the translation found in Greer, *Origen*, pp. 245–69. For an analysis of the text, see Daniélou, "Les sources bibliques," pp. 131–37.

153. The role of the demons in Origen's spirituality can scarcely be overemphasized — "There is not a sin accomplished without them," as *Hom. on Num.* 27.8 puts it. Origen insists that temptation always remains in this life, but in the higher stages as a protection and defense against pride — see stages 17 (Ressa), 28–29 (Galgad and Tabitha), 32 (the desert of Sin) and 35 (Dibongad).

154. Daniélou notes this as another indication of Origen's distance from strong apophaticism ("Les sources bibliques," p. 131).

155. Crouzel, *Origen*, pp. 121–30.

156. The overarching symbol is that of the ancient *hieros gamos*, the marriage between a god and a human. Origen does not use this pagan term, but he does speak of a *pneumatikos gamos* between Christ and the soul. See the texts surveyed in Völker, *Das Vollkommenheitsideal*, p. 105 n. 1.

157. For a further development of my approach, see B. McGinn, "The Language of Love in Jewish and Christian Mysticism," in *Mysticism and Language*, ed. Katz (to appear).

158. The most powerful example would be that of Sigmund Freud, whose attitude toward mysticism, however, was more complex than simple sublimation (see Appendix, section 3, p. 332). For a simple application, though one explicitly invoking Freud, see James Leuba, *The Psychology of Religious Mysticism* (London: Routledge & Kegan Paul, 1972).

159. This is the thesis of Irving Singer's challenging book, *The Nature of Love: 1, From Plato to Luther* (2nd ed.; Chicago: University of Chicago Press, 1984), e.g., p. 151.

160. Simone Weil, *The Notebooks of Simone Weil*, trans. Arthur Wills, 2 vols. (London: Routledge & Kegan Paul, 1976) 2:472.

161. Anders Nygren, *Agape and Eros* (Philadelphia: Westminster, 1953), pp. 349–53, 368–92.

162. For some aspects of this development, see John M. Rist, *Eros and Psyche: Studies in Plato, Plotinus and Origen* (Toronto: University of Toronto Press, 1975).

163. The most noted of these passages is to be found in *Hom. on Ezek.* 6.6 (GCS 33 [Origen 8:384–85]), where it is asserted "Deus non est impassibilis"; cf. *Comm. on Mt.* 10.23.

164. Von Balthasar, *Spirit and Fire*, pp. 11–12.

165. For an introduction to Origen's place in the tradition of Song of Songs commentaries, see E. Ann Matter, *The Voice of My Beloved: The Song of Songs in Western Medieval Christianity* (Philadelphia: University of Pennsylvania Press, 1990), chap. 2. See also Patricia Cox, "'Pleasure of the Text, Text of Pleasure': Origen's *Commentary on the Song of Songs," Journal of the American Academy of Religion* 54 (1986): 241–53.

166. See *Comm. on Song* prol. (ed. 62 and 63–64; Lawson, pp. 22–23 and 24–25).

167. Brown, *Body and Society*, pp. 170–77.

168. On Origen's relation to Jewish exegesis, see Ephraim E. Urbach, "The Homiletic Interpretations of the Sages and the Expositions of Origen on Canticles, and the Jewish-Christian Disputation," *Scripta Hierosolymitana* 22 (1971): 247–75; and Nicholas de Lange, *Origen and the Jews* (Cambridge: Cambridge University Press, 1976).

169. On the prohibition against the carnal-minded reading the Song, see 62.5–22.

170. Karl Rahner was the first to point out Origen's importance in this regard in a paper published in German in 1932 and available in abbreviated form in English as "The 'Spiritual Senses' according to Origen," *Theological Investigations* 16:81–103. Origen developed his doctrine in dependence on Clement's interpretation of Prov 2:5 (and to a lesser extent Exod 28:3), as shown by Marguerite Harl, "La 'bouche' et le 'coeur' de l'apôtre: deux images bibliques du 'sens divin' de l'homme ('Proverbes' 2,5) chez Origène," in *Forma Futuri: Studi in Onore del Cardinale Michele Pellegrino* (Turin: Bottega d'Erasmo, 1975), pp. 17–42.

171. The treatment of the spiritual senses pervades Origen's writings. Among the classic presentations, *De prin.* 1.1.9 stands out: "For the names and organs of sense are often applied to the soul, so that we speak of seeing with eyes of the heart, that is, of drawing some intellectual conclusions by means of the faculty of intelligence. So too we speak of hearing with the ears when we discern the deeper meaning of some statement. So too we speak of the soul as being able to use teeth, when it eats and consumes the bread of life who comes down from heaven. In a similar way we speak of it as using all the other bodily organs, which are transferred from their corporeal significance and applied to the faculties of the soul; as Solomon says, 'You will find a divine sense' (Prov 2:5)." Among other appearances, note *De prin.* 1.1.7; *Hom. on Lev.* 3.3; 31.7; *Hom. on Ezek.* 11.1; *Comm. on Jn.* 10.40; 13.24; *Comm. on Lk.* frgs. 53, 57; *Comm. on Rom.* 4.5; *Against Celsus* 1.48; 7.34; and esp. *Comm. on Song* 2 (ed. 167ff.); and the *Dialogue with Heracleides* 15–24 (SC 67:88–102).

172. Rahner's phrase in "Spiritual Senses," p. 97.

173. See *Against Celsus* 1.48 (GCS Origen 2:98.22): *aisthēsai ouk aisthētē*.

174. Brown, *Body and Society*, p. 172. I am reminded of the statement by Lulu Lamartine in Louise Erdrich's novel *Love Medicine:* "How come we've got these bodies. They are such frail supports for what we feel."

175. See Cox, "'Pleasure of Text,'" on how the text itself as "actively erotic" transforms the reader, though her interpretation minimizes the anthropological referent.

176. For some examples, see *Comm. on Song* bks. 1.4; 2.9; 3.14; and *Hom.* 1.3.

177. For an analysis of these five steps in relation to the comment on Song 1:1 (ed. 89–92; Lawson, pp. 58–62), see Torjesen, *Hermeneutical Procedure*, pp. 54–57.

178. On the importance of the image of the interior mouth, which is both open to God and then ready for preaching, see Harl, "La 'bouche' et le 'coeur,'" pp. 35–42.

179. On the *hēgemonikon* in Origen, see Karl Rahner, "Coeur de Jesus chez Origène?" *Revue d'ascétique et de la mystique* 15 (1934): 171–74.

180. *Comm. on Song* bk. 2 (ed. 168–70 [the passages cited can be found on 169.5–7, and 170.13–15]; Lawson, pp. 163–66, with helpful notes on pp. 341–42). For a slightly different treatment of the same text, see *Hom. on Song* 2.3 (ed. 45–46; Lawson, pp. 287–88).

181. H. Crouzel, "Origines patristiques d'un thème mystique: Le trait et la blessure d'amour chez Origène," in *Kyriakon: Festschrift Johannes Quasten*, ed. P. Granfield and J. Jungmann, 2 vols. (Münster: Aschendorff, 1970) 1:311–19; briefly summarized in his *Origen*, pp. 123–24.

182. See also the treatment in *Hom. on Song* 2.8 (ed. 53–54; Lawson, p. 297).

183. For a treatment of "touching" Jesus, see Bertrand, *Mystique de Jésus,* pp. 121–40.

184. Est quidam spiritualis amplexus atque utinam contingat, ut et meam sponsam artior sponsi amplexus includat, ut et ego quoque possim dicere, quod in hoc eodem libro scriptum est: "sinistra eius sub capite meo, et dextra eius complexabitur me." For another individual treatment, see *Hom. on Song* 2.9.

185. Saepe, Deus testis est, sponsum mihi adventare conspexi et mecum esse quam plurimum; quo subito recedente invenire non potui, quod quaerebam. Rursum igitur desiderio eius adventum et nonnumquam iterum venit; et cum apparuerit meisque fuerit manibus comprehensus, rursus elabitur et, cum fuerit elapsus, a me rursus inquiritur. . . ." For other important texts on the dialectic of the presence and the absence of the Groom, which bring out the exegetical context of the experience of illumination from the Word, see the comments on Song 2:8 and 2:9 in *Comm. on Song* bk. 3 (ed. 202.1–204.1; Lawson, pp. 211–13; and ed. 216–23; Lawson, pp. 229–38). Origen often speaks of the Word's visitation of the soul in connection with exegetical activity, e.g., *Comm. on Jn.* 6.52 (272) (SC 157:336); *Sermon on Mt.* 38 (GCS Origen 11:72.11ff.); *Frg. in Lk.* 151 (GCS Origen 9:287.10 ff.).

186. Harl, "Le langage," pp. 24–25.

187. The most extensive treatment of gnosis in Origen remains that of Völker, *Das Vollkommenheitsideal,* chap. 2 (pp. 76–144). But gnosis should not be isolated from Origen's other terms that indicate higher modes of knowing, as Crouzel argues in *Origène et la "connaissance mystique,"* pp. 375–98.

188. For differing views of elitism and esotericism in Origen's thought, compare Crouzel, *Origen,* pp. 104, 114–15, and Trigg, *Origen,* pp. 238–39, with von Balthasar, *Spirit and Fire,* pp. 17–20. On the relation of the two classes of believers, see Crouzel, *Origène et la "connaissance mystique,"* pp. 474–95.

189. Crouzel, *Origen,* p. 116.

190. Besides the texts from Origen's reading of the Song surveyed above, see, e.g., *Hom. on Isa.* 5.2 (GCS Origen 8:264–65). On this issue, see Bertrand (*Mystique de Jésus*), who emphasizes Origen's pioneering role.

191. Commenting on Matt 12:46–50.

192. For other appearances of this theme in Origen's writings, see, e.g., *Hom. on Gen.* 3.7 (GCS Origen 6:49–50); *Hom. on Ex.* 10.3 (GCS Origen 6:248); *Hom. on Lev.* 12.7 (GCS Origen 6:466); *Hom. on Jer.* 9.1 (GCS Origen 3:64); *Hom. on Song* 2.6 (GCS Origen 8:51); etc. The most detailed study is that of Hugo Rahner, "Die Gottesgeburt," in *Symbole der Kirche,* pp. 29–35 (see n.3).

193. *Hom. on Jer.* 9.4 (GCS Origen 3:70.11ff.) insists that the just man is born of God and gives birth to God within himself in every good work he performs (a teaching close to that later advanced by Meister Eckhart).

194. On the relation of love and knowledge in Plotinus, see chapter 2, pp. 47–50; on Augustine, see chapter 7, pp. 257–62.

195. Of course, for Origen the analogy remains a partial one, because elsewhere he insists that Adam did not know Eve in paradise but only after the Fall. See frg. 29 on 1 Corinthians, as discussed in Brown, *Body and Society,* p. 175.

196. John Eudes Bamberger, with more justice, speaks of him as "a remarkable mystic and a great intellectual" ("The Personality of Origen: Problems in Psychohistory," *Monastic Studies* 16 [1985], p. 54).

197. E.g., *Against Celsus* 7.10; *Comm. on Jn.* 1.30 (208).

198. Harl, "Le langage," pp. 6–7, 12–16.

199. Von Balthasar, *Spirit and Fire,* p. 10.

200. Ibid., p. 12. For a selection of texts on the God-Fire, see pp. 325–30.

201. H. Chadwick, ed., *Alexandrian Christianity,* p. 186.

202. Origen comments twice on Song 2:4b: *Comm. on Song* bk. 3 (ed. 196–91; Lawson, pp. 187–95), and *Hom. on Song* 2.8 (ed. 52–53; Lawson, pp. 294–96).

203. See Lobkowicz, *Theory and Practice,* chap. 5. For a sketch of Origen's views, see Rahner, "Spiritual Senses," pp. 90–92.

204. Origen does not give *apatheia* as large a role as Clement did, emphasizing rather the necessity for constant struggle as long as we are in the flesh; but see, e.g., *Hom. on 1 Kings* 1.4 (GCS Origen 3:5–7); and *Select. on Ps.* passim (e.g., *PG* 12:1085b, 1672c). A lengthy, but controversial, treatment is to be found in Völker, *Das Vollkommenheitsideal,* pp. 44–62.

205. *In Lk.* frg. 39 (GCS Origen 9:251–52); cf. *Comm. on Jn.* frg. 80 (GCS Origen 4:547). See Daniel Csányi, "OPTIMA PARS: Die Auslegungsgeschichte von Lk. 10.36–42 bei den Kirchenvätern," *Studia Monastica* 2 (1960): 5–78 (pp. 10–27 on Origen).

206. For a study of the interdependence of action and contemplation, see Völker, *Das Vollkommenheitsideal,* chap. 3, pp. 145–96.

207. Origen's doctrine of grace and its necessity appears especially in the surviving Latin abridgment of his great *Comm. on Rom.,* e.g., 4.5 (*PG* 14:974–75). He also insisted on it in countering Celsus's arguments, e.g., *Against Celsus* 7.33, 42.

208. For a sketch of Origen's teaching on the church and the sacraments, see Crouzel, *Origen,* chap. 12 (pp. 219–33).

209. Tertullian's *On Prayer* was written for catechumens about 200 C.E. Origen's treatise, edited in GCS Origen 2:297–403, has been translated several times. I will use the version of Greer in *Origen,* pp. 81–170. To be recommended is the introduction by Henry Chadwick to his translation in *Alexandrian Christianity,* pp. 180–237, which includes a comparison with Tertullian (pp. 224–30).

210. The *Exhortation to Martyrdom* was edited in GCS Origen 2:1–47. I will make use of the translation in Greer, *Origen,* pp. 41–79. For Origen's hankering after the "good old days" of persecution, see *Hom. on Jer.* 4.3.

211. On the difference between the "oppositional" *passiones* of the martyr accounts and the "gradational" character of the desert *vitae patrum,* see Alison Goddard Elliot, *Roads to Paradise: Reading the Lives of the Early Saints* (Hanover: University Press of New England, 1987), e.g., pp. 19–24.

212. For Origen's teaching on contemplation, see Lossky, *Vision of God,* pp. 48–58; and esp. Crouzel, *Origène et la "connaissance mystique,"* notably pp. 496–536.

213. See *Comm. on Song* bk. 3 (ed. 231; Lawson, p. 250).

214. A classic discussion of this is *De prin.* 1.1.9.

215. The John commentary, as might be expected, is rich in its expositions of how the Incarnate Word reveals the Father; see, e.g., *Comm. on Jn.* 2.8. (61) (SC 120:242–44); *Comm. on Jn.* 19.6 (35–36) and 20.7 (46–48) (SC 290:66–68 and 178–80); cf. *Against Celsus* 6.65.

216. E.g., *ekstasis* occurs in *Hom. on Num.* 27.12 (GCS Origen 7:275.17–22) and *Comm. on Song* bk. 2 (ed. 140.3–11); *enthysiasmos* can be found in *Comm. on Jn.* 1.30 (206) (SC 120:160–62); sobria vel sacra ebrietas (*methē theia*) occurs in *Comm. on Jn.* 1.30 (206), and *Comm. on Song* bk. 3 (ed. 184–86). On the latter term, see Hans Lewy, *SOBRIA EBRIETAS: Untersuchungen zur Geschichte der antiken Mystik* (Giessen: A. Töpelmann, 1929), pp. 119–28.

217. Völker (*Das Vollkommenheitsideal,* pp. 139–44) interpreted such texts as referring to rapture, a position controverted by Puech ("Un livre recent," pp. 526–33), Daniélou ("Les sources bibliques," pp. 135–36), and others. Note also Origen's attack on the ecstasy of the Pythian seer in *Against Celsus* 7.3–4.

218. GCS Origen 6:196.24–25; Heine, FC 80:291; cf. *Comm. on Jn.* 2.2–3 (17–19) (SC 120:216–20).

219. See *Comm. on Jn.* 19.4 (22) (SC 290:58.12). On *henōsis* in Plotinus, see chapter 2, pp. 52–54; on Dionysius, chapter 5, pp. 170–74.

220. Völker suggests some form of indistinct union (*Das Vollkommenheitsideal,* pp. 127–29), but this contradicts Origen's understanding of creation and his attack on Stoic views of the absorption of all into God (e.g., *Against Celsus* 6.71). For a more accurate treatment, see Crouzel, *Origène et la "connaissance mystique,"* pp. 443–96; and, more briefly, *Origen,* pp. 260–62.

221. Origen uses 1 Cor 6:17 three other times in the commentary to refer to the union of Christ and the soul (52.22–23; 85.19–25; and 103.12–17); and no fewer than forty-two other times in his writings (cf. *Biblia Patristica* 3:392–93).

222. E.g., *Comm. on Jn.* 20.7 (46–48) (SC 290:178–80). On this issue, see Völker, *Das Vollkommenheitsideal*, p. 110; and Crouzel, *Origène et la "connaissance mystique,"* pp. 496–507.

223. E.g., *Comm. on Jn.* 1.29 (189–93) (SC 120:154–56).

224. See, e.g., Crouzel, *Origen*, pp. 118–19, 176; Rahner, "Spiritual Senses," pp. 96–97; Greer, "Introduction," in *Origen*, pp. 24–25; etc.

225. Von Balthasar, *Spirit and Fire*, p. 2.

226. Among the most judicious accounts of Origen's relation to Platonism are those of Henry Chadwick, *Early Christian Thought and the Classical Tradition*, pp. 100–123; and "Christian Platonism in Origen and Augustine," in *Origeniana Tertia* (Rome: Edizioni dell'Ateneo, 1985), pp. 217–30.

227. Controversial issues, of course, always remain. For example, Daniélou accuses Origen of being "mal degagée" from the Platonic view of the natural divinity of the soul ("Les sources bibliques," pp. 130–31), a criticism repeated by Louth (*Origins*, p. 197). This seems to me an exaggeration, because even though the soul is preexistent for the Alexandrian, he always insists that it is not naturally divine.

Chapter 5

1. The fact that some early monastic groups in Egypt and Syria were interested in Gnostic texts (the Nag Hammadi library appears to have been a monastic collection) strengthens this case.

2. Strong esotericism, of a true Gnostic variety, is rare, though it can be found in Syria in texts such as the *Book of the Holy Hierotheus*. Modified esotericism, such as in Evagrius Ponticus, will be discussed below.

3. To give but one example, the famous Abba Macarius, the most noted of all wonder-working ascetics, was told by a voice that he had not reached the perfection of two married women living in the city. Seeking them out, he was so impressed by their humility and peaceableness that he exclaimed: "Truly, it is not whether you are a virgin or a married woman, a monk or a man in the world: God gives his Holy Spirit to everyone, according to their earnestness of purpose" (*Sayings of the Fathers* [*Verba Seniorum*] 20.17, as translated by Owen Chadwick, *Western Asceticism* [Philadelphia: Westminster, 1958], p. 188). On the issue of perfection outside the monastic life, see M. Viller and K. Rahner, *Aszese und Mystik in der Väterzeit: Ein Abriss* (Freiburg: Herder, 1939), pp. 72–73.

4. On this text see E. A. Judge, "The Earliest Use of Monachos for Monk (P. Coll. Youtie) and the Origins of Monasticism," *Jahrbuch für Antike und Christentum* 20 (1977), pp. 72–73.

5. Karl Heussi, *Der Ursprung des Mönchtums* (Tübingen: Mohr, 1936) is still of value on this issue. In the account that follows, I will make use of my article "Christian Monasticism," in *The Encyclopedia of Religion*, ed. Mircea Eliade (New York: Macmillan, 1987) 10:44–50. Two multiauthor surveys are helpful: "Monachesimo," in *Dizionario degli Istituti di Perfezione*, ed. Guerrino Pelliccia and Giancarlo Rocca (Rome: Edizioni Paoline, 1973) 5:1672–1742; and "Monachisme," *DS* 10:1524–1617.

6. See esp. Peter Brown, *The Making of Late Antiquity* (Cambridge, MA: Harvard University Press, 1978), esp. chaps. 3–4.

7. Peter Brown, *The Body and Society: Men, Women, and Sexual Renunciation in Early Christianity* (New York: Columbia University Press, 1988); chaps. 11–12 deal specifically with the early desert ascetics.

8. On this important document (as well as a survey of early uses of the term *monachos*), see Judge, "Earliest Use," pp. 72–89.

9. See Alison Goddard Elliot, *Roads to Paradise: Reading the Lives of the Early Saints* (Hanover: University Press of New England, 1987), pp. 90–91.

10. For a Freudian interpretation, see E. R. Dodds, *Pagan and Christian in an Age of Anxiety* (Cambridge: Cambridge University Press, 1965). More recently, Robert Kirschner, "The Vocation of Holiness in Late Antiquity," *Vigiliae Christianae* 38 (1984): 105–24.

11. On how the monk succeeded the martyr, see Edward E. Malone, *The Monk and the Martyr* (Washington: Catholic University Press, 1950).

12. Peter Brown, "The Rise and Function of the Holy Man in Late Antiquity," *Journal of Roman Studies* 61 (1971), p. 91.

13. Antony appears as one early abba among others in the "Alphabetical Collection" of the *Apophthegmata Patrum* (*Sayings of the Fathers;* Greek text in *PG* 65:75–88). In addition, there are seven remarkable letters ascribed to Antony (complete text surviving only in Latin and Georgian, with parts in Coptic and Syriac), which are deeply imbued with an Origenist spirit. (For a translation, see Derwas Chitty, *The Letters of St. Antony the Great* [Fairacres, Oxford: SLG Press, 1977].) The other major source is the famous *Vita Antonii* (*Life of Antony*) described in the following note.

14. The *Vita Antonii* is the first great hagiographical masterpiece in Christian literature. The standard Greek text ascribed to Athanasius appears in *PG* 26:837–976, and has been translated by Robert C. Gregg, *Athanasius: The Life of Antony and the Letter to Marcellinus,* CWS (New York: Paulist Press, 1980). Two fourth-century Latin translations exist, as well as a Syriac text and a later Coptic translation of the Greek. R. Draguet, the editor of the Syriac version, followed by T. D. Barnes, has argued that this text is actually closer to the lost Coptic original (not by Athanasius in their view) than the standard Greek version. See T. D. Barnes, "Angel of Light or Mystic Initiate? The Problem of the *Life of Antony,*" *Journal of Theological Studies* n.s. 37 (1986): 353–68. Literature on Antony is extensive; see, e.g., B. Steidle, ed., *Antonius Magnus Eremita 356–1956* (Rome: Studia Anselmiana 38, 1956). I will use the Gregg translation.

15. The Greek of this key phrase, echoing Hellenic ideas of mystical initiation, is *hōsper ek tinos adytou memystagogēmenos kai theophoroumenos* (*PG* 26:864C). Barnes argues that the Syriac represents a more primitive and less hellenized picture — ". . . when he came out like a man who rises from the depths of the earth, they saw his face as that of an *angel of light*" (see 2 Cor 11:14) ("Angel of Light," pp. 360–62).

16. An Origenist anthropology stressing the role of the *nous,* or "intellectual substance," is also found in the Letters, e.g., Letter 3, 4, and 6 (trans. Chitty, pp. 9, 12–13, 17, 21–22, etc.).

17. On these collections, see Wilhelm Bousset, *Apophthegmata: Studien zur Geschichte des ältesten Mönchtums* (Tübingen: Mohr, 1923); and Jean-Claude Guy, *Recherches sur la tradition grecque des "Apophthegmata Patrum"* (Brussels: Société des Bollandistes, 1962). Also see the dissertation of Ruth F. Frazer, "The Morphology of Desert Wisdom in the 'Apophthegmata Patrum'" (Ph.D., University of Chicago, 1977).

18. This text, traditionally known as the *Verba Seniorum,* is most readily accessible as books 5 and 6 of the collection of materials about early monastic saints edited by the Jesuit Heribert Rosweyde in 1615 under the title of *Vitae Patrum* (reprinted in *PL* 73:855–1022). For a translation (expanded and revised in consultation with older manuscripts), see Chadwick, *Western Asceticism,* pp. 37–189. Two other important collections of stories about the saints of the desert conveyed this material to Western Christianity: Rufinus's translation of the *Historia Monachorum in Aegypto,* whose Greek original dates to 394 (*PL* 21:387–462; English translation by Norman Russell, *The Lives of the Desert Fathers* [Kalamazoo: Cistercian Publications, 1981]); and Palladius's *Historia Lausiaca,* written about 420 and soon translated into Latin (*PL* 74:249–382 [two versions]; English translation by Robert T. Meyer, *Palladius: The Lausiac History,* ACW 34 [Westminster: Newman Press, 1965]).

19. The text is available in *PG* 65:71–440 and has been translated by Benedicta Ward, *The Sayings of the Desert Fathers: The Alphabetical Collection* (London: Mowbrays, 1975), which

includes a useful index (pp. 213–19) showing the relationship between materials in the two collections.

20. On the instrumental character of monastic asceticism as compared with Gnostic asceticism, see G. Stroumsa, "Ascèse et gnose: Aux origines de la spiritualité monastique," *Revue Thomiste* 81 (1981): 557–73.

21. See Joseph T. Lienhard, "On 'Discernment of Spirits' in the Early Church," *Theological Studies* 41 (1980), pp. 520–21.

22. *Alphabetical Collection*, Macarius 32 (Ward, p. 113): "They said of Abba Macarius the Great that he became, as it is written, a god upon earth, because, just as God protects the world, so Abba Macarius would cover the faults which he saw, as though he did not see them; and those which he heard, as though he did not hear them." See Brown, *Making of Late Antiquity*, pp. 96–97.

23. In 20.5 the Abba Sisois's face shines like the sun.

24. First Greek Life, chap. 12, as found in *Pachomian Koinonia*, translated by Armand Vieilleux, 3 vols. (Kalamazoo: Cistercian Publications, 1980–82) 1:305.

25. The remains of the First Sahidic Life are translated in *Pachomian Koinonia* 1:425–41.

26. The various versions of the *Pachomian Rule* (Coptic fragments and a more complete Latin translation of Jerome) are available in English in *Pachomian Koinonia* 2:141–83.

27. See Jean Leclercq, "Monachesimo: I, Fenomenologia del monachesimo," in *Dizionario degli Istituti di Perfezione* 5:1673–84.

28. These works are currently available in English. See *Gregory of Nyssa: The Life of Moses*, trans. Everett Ferguson and Abraham Malherbe, CWS (New York: Paulist Press, 1978); *Saint Gregory of Nyssa: Commentary on the Song of Songs*, trans. Casimir McCambley (Brookline, MA: Hellenic College Press, 1987); and *St. Gregory of Nyssa: The Lord's Prayer. The Beatitudes*, trans. Hilda C. Graef, ACW 18 (Westminster: Newman, 1954).

29. Along with Daniélou's book *Platonisme et théologie mystique: Doctrine spirituelle de Saint Grégoire de Nysse* (Paris: Aubier, 1944), see Hans Urs von Balthasar, *Présence et pensée: Essai sur la philosophie religieuse de Grégoire de Nysse* (Paris: Beauchesne, 1942); Hubert Merki, *HOMOIOSIS THEOU: Von der platonischen Angleichung an Gott zur Gottähnlichkeit bei Gregor von Nyssa* (Freiburg: Herder, 1952); Walther Völker, *Gregor von Nyssa als Mystiker* (Wiesbaden: F. Steiner, 1955); Ekkehard Mühlenberg, *Die Unendlichkeit Gottes bei Gregor von Nyssa: Gregors Kritik am Gottesbegriff der klassischen Metaphysik* (Göttingen: Vandenhoeck & Ruprecht, 1965); David L. Balas, *METOYSIA THEOU: Man's Participation in God's Perfections according to Saint Gregory of Nyssa*, Studia Anselmiana 55 (Rome: Herder, 1966); and Ronald E. Heine, *Perfection in the Virtuous Life: A Study in the Relationship Between Edification and Polemical Theology in Gregory of Nyssa's De Vita Moysis* (Philadelphia: Philadelphia Patristic Foundation, 1975). It is not possible here to list important articles, but see especially H. Crouzel, "Grégoire de Nysse est-il le fondateur de la théologie mystique?" *Revue d'ascétique et de la mystique* 33 (1957): 189–202.

30. My thanks to Robert Wilken for helping me to see the importance of this issue for subsequent mysticism.

31. On God's limits, see *De prin.* 2.9.1 and 4.4.8 in passages preserved in the Greek condemnation of Origen, but omitted by Rufinus (see G. W. Butterworth, *Origen on First Principles* [New York: Harper & Row, 1966], pp. 129, 323).

32. See M. Harl, "Recherches sur l'origenisme d'Origène: La 'satieté' (*koros*) de la contemplation comme motif de la chute des âmes," *Studia Patristica* 8 (1966): 373–405.

33. On this break, see Heine, *Perfection in the Virtuous Life*, chap. 2.

34. In *Grégoire de Nysse: La vie de Moïse*, ed. Jean Daniélou, SC 1bis (Paris: Cerf, 1955), pp. 107–9. I have used the translation of Malherbe and Ferguson, *The Life of Moses*, pp. 115–16, with the exception of the last sentence, where I give a more literal version of the Greek: *Kai touto estin ontos to idein ton theon to mēdepote tēs epithymias koron heurein* (p. 109.1–3).

35. On Gregory's role in the evolution of apophatic theology leading to Dionysius, see Henri-Charles Puech, "La Ténèbre mystique chez le Pseudo-Denys l'Aréopagite," originally

published in 1938, and available in H.-C. Puech, *En quete de la Gnose,* 2 vols. (Paris: Gallimard, 1978) 1:119–41.

36. See *Gregorii Nysseni Opera,* ed. Werner Jaeger; *Gregorii Nysseni in Canticum Canticorum,* ed. Hermann Langerbeck, vol. 6 (Leiden: Brill, 1960), pp. 353–54. I have used the translation of McCambley, *Commentary on the Song of Songs,* p. 218.

37. Ed. Langerbeck, *Gregorii Nysseni,* p. 182; trans. McCambley, *Commentary on the Song,* p. 131. I have investigated Gregory's exegesis of the Song in more detail in my paper "Tropics of Desire: Mystical Interpretations of the Song of Songs in Christian Exegesis" (to appear).

38. The Macarian *Homilies* appear to have been known to Cassian and therefore had at least some indirect effect on early Western mysticism. They were translated into Latin ca. 1300 by Angelo da Clareno, but this version does not appear to have been much read. The sixteenth-century translation, however, was eagerly read, especially by Lutheran pietists such as John Arndt, John Gerhard, and Gottfried Arnold, and by many later Protestants including the Wesleys. For an introduction, see V. Desprez, "Pseudo-Macaire (Syméon). III. Influence," *DS* 10:39–43.

39. On the considerable complications of the "Macarian" corpus, communicated through four different Greek manuscript collections, see Vincent Desprez, "Pseudo-Macaire (Syméon). I. L'Oeuvre, l'auteur et son milieu," *DS* 10:20–27, as well as the "Introduction" to his *Pseudo-Macaire: Oeuvres Spirituelles I,* SC 275 (Paris: Cerf, 1980), an edition and translation of Collection III (pp. 13–69). I will cite the *Spiritual Homilies* (which form Collection II) in the most recent edition, *Die 50 Geistlichen Homilien des Makarios,* ed. Hermann Dörries, Erich Klostermann, and Matthias Kroeger, Patristische Texte und Studien 4 (Berlin: de Gruyter, 1964). The most recent translation is that of George A. Maloney, S.J., *Intoxicated with God* (Denville, NJ: Dimension Books, 1978).

40. On the Messalians, see A. Guillaumont, "Messaliens," *DS* 10:1074–83; and John Meyendorff, "Messalianism or Anti-Messalianism? A Fresh Look at the 'Macarian' Problem," in *Kyriakon: Festschrift Johannes Quasten,* ed. P. Granfield and J. Jungmann, 2 vols. (Münster: Aschendorff, 1975) 2:585–90.

41. Theodoret of Cyrus, *Church History* 4.11.2 (*PG* 83:429b); I use the translation of J. Quasten, *Patrology,* 3 vols. (Westminster: Newman, 1950–60) 3:164.

42. On Messalian teaching, see the excellent summary in Guillaumont, *DS* 10:1079–82.

43. L. Villecourt, "La date et l'origine des homilies spirituelles attribuées à Macaire," *Comptes-rendus de l'académie des inscriptions et belles-lettres* (1920): 250–58; H. Dörries, *Symeon von Mesopotamien: Die Überlieferung der Messalianischen Makarios-Schriften,* Texte und Untersuchungen 95.1 (Leipzig: J. C. Hinrichs, 1948).

44. Meyendorff, "Messalianism or Anti-Messalianism?" p. 589.

45. E.g., L. Bouyer, *The Spirituality of the New Testament and the Fathers,* vol. 1 of *A History of Christian Spirituality* (New York: Seabury, 1982), pp. 369–80.

46. Meyendorff, "Messalianism or Anti-Messalianism?" p. 590. For a summary of the doctrine of the *Spiritual Homilies,* see Mariette Canivet, "Pseudo-Macaire (Syméon). II. Doctrine," *DS* 10:27–38.

47. Gilles Quispel, "Sein und Gestalt," in *Studies in Mysticism and Religion presented to Gershom G. Scholem* (Jerusalem: Magnes Press, 1967), pp. 191–95. For a more complete exposition, see G. Quispel, *Makarius, das Thomasevangelium und das Lied von der Perle* (Leiden: Brill, 1967).

48. E.g., *Hom.* 10.2: *kai tou hagiou pneumatos tou arretou kai mystikēs koinōnias* (Dörries, *Die 50 Geistlichen Homilien,* p. 93.23–24); *Hom.* 15.2: *ho epouranios nymphios Christos pros tēn heautou mystikēn kai theian koinōnian* (Dörries, p. 127.15–16); *Hom.* 47:17: *eis tēn hagian kai mystikēn kai achranton koinōnian tou gamou* (Dörries, p. 312.237–38). For *synousia mystikē,* see, e.g., *Ep.* 2 (*PG* 34:416d). Note that Macarius understands such mystical union according to the loving union of wills of the Divine Groom and human bride. For Macarius's doctrine of mystical union, see Louis Bouyer, "Die mystische Kontemplation bei den Vätern," in *Weisheit Gottes —*

Weisheit der Welt: Festschrift für Joseph Kardinal Ratzinger zum 60. Geburtstag, ed. W. Baier et al., 2 vols. (St. Ottilien: EOS Verlag, 1987) 1:642.

49. Meyendorff, "Messalianism or Anti-Messalianism?" p. 586.

50. For general introductions to Evagrius, see Viller and Rahner, *Aszese und Mystik,* pp. 97–109; Bouyer, *Spirituality,* pp. 380–94; A. Louth, *The Origins of the Christian Mystical Tradition: From Plato to Denys* (Oxford: Clarendon, 1981), pp. 100–113; and especially the more detailed investigations of A. and C. Guillaumont, "Évagre le Pontique," *DS* 4:1731–44; and John Eudes Bamberger, "Introduction," *Evagrius Ponticus: The Praktikos. Chapters on Prayer* (Spencer: Cistercian Publications, 1970), pp. xxiii–xciv. I am also indebted to two dissertations: David Alan Ousley, "Evagrius' Theology of Prayer and the Spiritual Life" (University of Chicago, 1979); and Michael Wallace O'Laughlin, "Origenism in the Desert: Anthropology and Integration in Evagrius Ponticus" (Harvard University, 1987). (My thanks to Charles Kannengiesser for bringing the latter to my attention.)

51. Bouyer, *Spirituality,* p. 381.

52. On Evagrius's place in Egyptian monasticism, see Gabriel Bunge, "Évagre le Pontique et les deux Macaire," *Irenikon* 56 (1983): 215–27, 323–60.

53. Much has been written on the complex story of Origenism and its condemnations. The best study of Evagrius's role is A. Guillaumont, *Les "Kephalaia Gnostica" d'Évagre le Pontique et l'histoire d'origenisme chez les Grecs et chez les Syriens* (Paris: Seuil, 1962). More recently, see Jon F. Dechow, *Dogma and Mysticism in Early Christianity: Epiphanius of Cyprus and the Legacy of Origen,* North American Patristic Society Patristic Monograph Series 13 (Macon, GA: Mercer University Press, 1988).

54. See the survey in Dechow, *Dogma and Mysticism,* pp. 139–79.

55. E.g., Palladius, *Lausiac History* 11, on Ammonius.

56. The propositions can be found in J. B. Mansi, *Sacrorum conciliorum nova et amplissima collectio* 9:395–400; Dechow, *Dogma and Mysticism,* pp. 449–60, has a translation of both condemnations. For the relation of the canons to Evagrius's writings, see Guillaumont, *Les "Kephalia Gnostica,"* pp. 147, 153–59.

57. The *Praktikos* and *Gnostikos* have been edited by Antoine and Claire Guillaumont in SC 170–71 (1971) and SC 356 (1989) respectively. For the former, I will use the English translation by Bamberger in *The Praktikos and Chapters on Prayer* (1971); for the latter I will translate from the SC edition. The *Kephalaia Gnostica* has been edited by A. Guillaumont, *Les six centuries des "Kephalaia Gnostica" d'Évagre le Pontique,* Patrologia Orientalis 28.1 (Paris: Firmin-Didot, 1958) along with a French translation. This includes the six centuries, but not the sixty-chapter supplements, which may not have been put together by Evagrius himself. For translations from the *Kephalaia Gnostica* (hereafter abbreviated *KG*) I have relied on Guillaumont's French versions compared with the translations available in the theses of Ousley and O'Laughlin (see n. 50).

58. There is no critical edition of the Greek text of *De Oratione* (*Prayer*), which is available in *PG* 79:1165–1200, under the name of Nilus, and in an improved version in I. Hausherr, *Leçons d'un contemplatif* (Paris: Beauchesne, 1960). It is available in English in Bamberger, *Praktikos and Chapters on Prayer,* which version I will use unless otherwise noted. Given the emphasis in *Prayer* on the purity and formlessness of its highest stages, it is quite possible that the treatise was written against monastic Anthropomorphites, and perhaps may even have sparked the famous controversy of 400.

59. See M. J. Rondeau, "Le commentaire sur les Psaumes d'Évagre le Pontique," *Orientalia Christiana Periodica* 26 (1960): 307–48. The neglect of Evagrius's exegetical works has probably led to an undervaluation of the scriptural foundations of his thought, as G. Bunge notes in claiming: "The starting point of Evagrius's thought is always scripture, the word that reveals the God in three Persons, and not the postulates of any philosophy" ("The 'Spiritual Prayer': On the Trinitarian Mysticism of Evagrius of Pontus," *Monastic Studies* 17 [1986], p. 196).

60. The Greek original of the *Letter of Faith* (*Ep. fid.*) survived as *Letter* 8 of Basil. I will

use the edition of Yves Courtonne, *Saint Basile. Lettres I* (Paris: Belles Lettres, 1957), pp. 22–37. The *Letter to Melania (Ep. ad Mel.)*, an exceptionally important text, survives in Syriac and was edited partly by E. Frankenberg and partly by G. Vitestam. I will use the English version of M. Parmentier, "Evagrius of Pontus' 'Letter to Melania,'" *Bijdragen, tijdschrift voor filosofie en theologie* 46 (1985): 2–38. On the letter, see chap. 2 of O'Laughlin's "Origenism in the Desert."

61. Gennadius of Marseilles translated the *Gnostikos* and the *Antirrhetikos* into Latin, but these versions are lost. *The Mirror of Monks and Nuns,* one of Evagrius's minor works, survives in a translation of Rufinus (*PG* 40:1277–86) and another version. On the Latin versions of Evagrius and their influence, see J. Leclercq's "Preface" in Bamberger, *Praktikos,* pp. xiii–xix.

62. For the genre, see I. Hausherr, "Centuries," *DS* 2:416–18; and Bamberger, *Praktikos,* pp. lxvii–lxx.

63. H. Urs von Balthasar, "Metaphysik und Mystik des Evagrius Pontikos," *Zeitschrift für Aszese und Mystik* 14 (1939): 31–47; Eng. trans., "The Metaphysics and Mystical Theology of Evagrius," *Monastic Studies* 3 (1965): 183–95 (the quotation is on p. 193).

64. See von Balthasar, "Metaphysics and Mystical Theology," p. 195; von Balthasar affirms: "Evagrius remains standing at the stage of world denial, at the pre-Christian stage of thought." For von Balthasar's view of mysticism, see Appendix, section 1, pp. 289–90.

65. I. Hausherr, "Ignorance infinie," *Orientalia Christiana Periodica* 2 (1936), esp. pp. 357–59.

66. Karl Rahner, "Die geistliche Lehre des Evagrius Ponticus," *Zeitschrift für Aszese und Mystik* 8 (1933): 31–47; Bamberger, "Introduction," *Praktikos;* Guillaumont, "Évagre le Pontique," *DS* 4:1731–44; idem, "Un philosophe au desert: Évagre le Pontique," *Revue de l'histoire des religions* 181 (1972): 29–56. Among the recent studies of G. Bunge the most important is "The 'Spiritual Prayer': On the Trinitarian Mysticism of Evagrius of Pontus," *Monastic Studies* 17 (1986): 191–208. See also his "Origenismus–Gnostizimus: Zum geistesgeschichtlichen Standort des Evagrios Pontikos," *Vigiliae Christianae* 40 (1986): 24–54; and *Geistliche Vaterschaft: Christliche Gnosis bei Evagrios Pontikos* (Regensburg: Friedrich Pustet, 1988).

67. For general expressions of this dynamic of fall and return, see, e.g., *KG* 1.40; 6.75; and *Ep. ad Mel.* 6 (Parmentier, pp. 12–14). *KG* 2.17 on the return (*apokatastasis*) formed the partial basis for Anathema 14 of the condemnations of 553.

68. *KG* 2.64 (ed. Guillaumont, p. 87). These translations will generally be from the S2, considered the more authentic version, unless otherwise noted. See the whole of *KG* 2.64–77 for important remarks on the two creations.

69. *KG* 4.58: "God, when he created the *logikoi,* was in nothing; but when he created corporeal nature and the worlds that arise in it, he was in his Christ." Cf. *KG* 6.20.

70. See *Gnostikos* 40 (ed. Guillaumont, pp. 164–65).

71. This standard Platonic understanding (e.g., *Timaeus* 89E–90D) of the divisions or powers of the soul appears often in Evagrius, e.g., *Praktikos* 86, 89.

72. *Nous* is one of the most difficult terms in Evagrius's vocabulary. At times it seems synonymous with *logikos* (*nous* 1 in fig. 1, e.g., *KG* 1.65); more often it is used to identify the highest dimension of the soul (*nous* 2 in fig. 1). *Nous,* when it is free of passions, is pure light, as we are told in *KG* 5.15.

73. See esp. *KG* 1.68; cf. *KG* 5.11.

74. The best expositions of Evagrius's anthropology are to be found in the dissertations of Ousley ("Evagrius' Theology of Prayer," esp. 142–65) and O'Laughlin ("Origenism in the Desert").

75. Cf. *Gnostikos* 1–3; *KG* 5.65.

76. Plato (*Statesman* 258E–259A) was the first to divide the sciences into *praktikē epistēmē* and *gnostikē epistēmē* (Aristotle preferred the term *theoretikē* for the latter). Clement, as we have seen, used the term *gnostikos* widely, while Origen generally avoided it.

77. E.g., *Gnostikos* 18–21.

78. Cf. *Praktikos* 84: "The goal of the ascetic life is charity; the goal of contemplative

knowledge is theology. The beginnings of each are faith and contemplation of nature respectively" (Bamberger, *Praktikos,* p. 37).

79. As claimed by A. Guillaumont, "Évagre," *DS* 4:1741: "a été décisive sur la formation de la doctrine ascétique chrétienne. . . ."

80. While Evagrius may make use of elements from Greek—especially Stoic—ethics and certainly Origen and the tradition of the desert abbas, it is the originality of his system and perceptions that is most striking. For some general background, see the articles of H. Bacht, "Logismos," *DS* 9:955–58; and A. Solignac, "Péchés capitaux," *DS* 12:853–62. See also Ousley, "Evagrius' Theology of Prayer," pp. 171–97.

81. *Praktikos* 48: "The demons strive against men of the world chiefly through their deeds, but in the case of monks for the most part by means of thoughts, since the desert deprives them of such affairs" (Bamberger, p. 29). While the demons are most evident on the level of *praktikē,* it is clear from such texts as *Praktikos* 84 and *KG* 1.10 that there are demons at work on each level of the return. Evagrius's teaching is a summation of much to be found in both Origen and the early desert abbas; see A. and C. Guillaumont, "Démon," *DS* 3:196–205; and Bamberger, *Praktikos,* pp. 4–10.

82. The basic discussion of the *logismoi* can be found in *Praktikos* 6–14; 15–56 contain an expanded discussion on how to deal with them.

83. On Evagrius's place in the evolution of this important theme, see Lienhard, "On 'Discernment of Spirits,'" pp. 522–24.

84. For a survey of Evagrius's Christology and its condemnation, see François Refoulé, "La Christologie d'Évagre et l'origenisme," *Orientalia Christiana Periodica* 27 (1961): 221–66.

85. See A. Guillaumont, "Évagre le Pontique," in "Contemplation III.1.2D," *DS* 2:1775–85, for an introduction; see also Rahner, "Die geistliche Lehre."

86. Guillaumont notes that while the two terms are not perfectly identical in practice it is impossible to separate them (*DS* 2:1776–77). See also Ousley, "Evagrius' Theology of Prayer," pp. 229–60. While *gnōsis* is generally used in relation to the Trinity, in *KG* 5.84 Evagrius speaks of "contemplation of the Holy Trinity" (ed. Guillaumont, p. 213). *KG* 4.90 says that the *gnōsis* of God does not belong to a "dialectical" soul but to a "seeing" soul.

87. Perhaps the best description of the intimate relations of the three terms is to be found in *Prayer* 86: "Knowledge! [*gnōsis*] The great possession of man. It is a fellow-worker with prayer, acting to awaken the power of thought to contemplate the divine knowledge" (Bamberger, p. 69).

88. On Evagrius's understanding of prayer, see Ousley, "Evagrius' Theology of Prayer," chap. 4, esp. pp. 262–73.

89. See *Prayer* 117, 120, 153. In general, the sections *Prayer* 55–73 and 117–20 repay careful study on these issues.

90. E.g., Guillaumont in *DS* 2:1783–84.

91. Bamberger, *Praktikos,* p. 46.

92. See *KG* 2.4 (ed. Guillaumont, pp. 61–63): "Although the transformations are numerous we have received knowledge of only four. . . . The first is, as we said, the passage from evil to virtue; the second is that from *apatheia* to second, [that is] natural contemplation. The third is the passage from that to the knowledge that concerns the *logikoi,* and the fourth is the passage from all things to the knowledge of the Holy Trinity."

93. Cf. *Prak.* 81.

94. *Prak.* 60; cf. 53, 83. See "Apatheia," *DS* 1:734–36. Evagrius himself did not use the term "purity of heart" as synonymous with *apatheia,* the way that his disciple Cassian did; but Cassian's rendering is not a misconception. For a history of the term, see Juana Raasch, "The Monastic Concept of Purity of Heart and its Sources," *Studia Monastica* 8–12 (1966–70), with a treatment of Evagrius and his school in 12 (1970), pp. 31–34.

95. See the entire section 63–69, treating of the signs of *apatheia.* On *apatheia* in Evagrius, see Bamberger, *Praktikos,* pp. lxxxii–lxxxvii. Bamberger defines Evagrius's *apatheia* as "deep

calm arising from full and harmonious integration of the emotional life, under the influence of love" (p. lxxxiv).

96. *Agapē* is defined in *KG* 1.86 (ed. Guillaumont, p. 57) as "the superior state of the rational soul in which it cannot love any worldly thing more than the knowledge of God." Cf. *Prak.* 89. Especially important for Evagrius's idea of *agapē* is *Letter* 56.3-9 as translated (German) in Bunge, *Geistliche Vaterschaft,* pp. 41-43.

97. As noted by Rahner, "Die geistliche Lehre," pp. 25-26.

98. For a study, see Rahner, "Die geistliche Lehre," pp. 31-34. It is on this level that Evagrius appropriates most of Origen's teaching on the spiritual senses (e.g., *KG* 1.33-34, 37; 2.35), though K. Rahner argues that the "spiritual eye" has a transcendentalized role even in the contemplation of the Trinity. See K. Rahner, "The 'Spiritual Senses' according to Origen," *Theological Investigations* (New York: Seabury, 1979) 16:97-100.

99. For the distinction between the kingdom of heaven and the kingdom of God, see *Prak.* 2-3; *KG* 2.40; *Ep. fid.* 12. On the higher mode of contemplation, see, e.g., *KG* 2.2-3; 3.42; 5.40.

100. E.g., *KG* 1.27 speaks of five principal kinds of contemplation, while *KG* 1.70 presents five different levels of contemplator — from God himself down to one who has just attained *apatheia.* Other texts (e.g., *KG* 1.74 and 5.52) speak of three levels of *gnōsis* or *theōria.* For a discussion, see Rahner, "Die geistliche Lehre," pp. 30-31; and Guillaumont, *DS* 2:1777-78.

101. I. Hausherr, "Le Traité de l'Oraison d'Évagre le Pontique (Pseudo Nil)," *Revue d'ascétique et de la mystique* 15 (1934), p. 117.

102. Bunge, "Spiritual Prayer," pp. 191-94.

103. On the nonnumerical nature of the Trinity, see *KG* 6.10-13.

104. *Prayer* 58-59; see Bunge, "Spiritual Prayer," pp. 196-98.

105. Given Evagrius's anti-Arianism, we must presume that the analogy he is suggesting is an operational one, not one indicating different levels of reality.

106. This important, if enigmatic, text seems to suggest a relation to all three persons through loving oneness of willing that might be compared with later trinitarian mystics, especially William of St. Thierry. Cf. *Ep. ad Mel.* 6: ". . . in the unification of the rational beings with God the Father, they will be one nature in three persons, without addition or subtraction" (Parmentier, p. 13). On the trinitarian nature of Evagrius's mysticism, see Bunge, "Spiritual Prayer," pp. 201-2; Rahner, "Die geistliche Lehre," pp. 36-37.

107. E.g., *KG* 1.74; 6.87; cf. 3.6 (in S1 version, however).

108. Von Balthasar, "Metaphysics and Mystical Theology," pp. 191-92.

109. On grace in Evagrius, see Ousley, "Evagrius' Theology of Prayer," pp. 197-203; for texts, see *Prak.* 58, 66; *Gnost.* 43; *Prayer* 58, 62-63, 65, 78; and *KG* 1.37, 79; 5.77; 6.60; etc.

110. E.g., *Prak.* 64; *Gnost.* 45, citing Basil, though not to be found in any surviving Basil text (see the note by Guillaumont in SC 356, pp. 179-81).

111. For the comparison, see Guillaumont in *DS* 2:1782.

112. Rahner claims this is so: "Trinitätsschau und Schau des Wesens des eigenen Geistes scheinen für E. zwei Seiten desselben Erlebnisses zu sein" ("Die geistliche Lehre," p. 37).

113. Ousley, "Evagrius' Theology of Prayer," p. 349.

114. Cf. *Prayer* 4; *KG* 5.26, 51, 62-63.

115. See the note in the edition of the *Gnostikos* (SC 356, p. 169). For background on this theme, see J. Souilhé, "Le silence mystique," *Revue d'ascétique et de la mystique* 4 (1923): 128-40.

116. In the S1 version; the S2 version reads "unsurpassable *gnōsis*" (p. 135). On the meaning of this and related texts, see Hausherr, "Ignorance infinie," pp. 351-62; and Ousley, "Evagrius' Theology of Prayer," pp. 250-59, 270-72.

117. *Tēs de agnōsias tēs men einai peras, tēs de me einai phasi.*

118. See *KG* 1.71; 3.63. On the bad form of ignorance, see *KG* 4.29.

119. Guillaumont speculates that Basil and Gregory of Nazianzen are more likely sources than Gregory of Nyssa (*Praktikos,* pp. 679-80 [note to #87]).

120. On this text, see O'Laughlin, "Origenism in the Desert," p. 186.

121. Hausherr showed that later interpretations of Evagrius by Maximus the Confessor and others which read him in the light of the negative theology of the Pseudo-Dionysius were mistaken, but this should not preclude a recognition of his distinctive apophaticism ("Ignorance infinie").

122. On this tradition, see B. McGinn, "The Negative Element in the Anthropology of John the Scot," *Jean Scot Érigène et l'histoire de la philosophie* (Paris: CNRS, 1977), pp. 315–25.

123. Hausherr ("Ignorance infinie," p. 357) and Guillaumont (in *DS* 2:1784) note the absence of ecstasy in Evagrius.

124. See *Prayer* 117: "Happy is the spirit that attains to perfect formlessness at the time of prayer" (Bamberger, p. 75); and *Prayer* 120: "Happy is the spirit that attains to complete unconsciousness of all sensible experience at the time of prayer" (ibid.).

125. Some texts seem to distinguish between image and likeness, identifying the image with *nous*'s natural likeness to God and the likeness with what is gained through supernatural life; other texts seem to use the two more interchangeably speaking of both the image (e.g., *KG* 3.32) and the likeness (e.g., *KG* 6.73) as what is capable of receiving the divine unity. The absence of the Greek text here makes it difficult to reconstruct Evagrius's teaching.

126. On Evagrius's intellectualism, I agree with Ousley that it is better to use it as a descriptive than a judgmental term; see "Evagrius' Theology of the Spiritual Life," pp. 165–67.

127. Bunge, "Origenismus—Gnostizismus"; idem, *Geistliche Vaterschaft*, esp. pp. 55–64.

128. On grace in Evagrius, see n. 109 above.

129. *All' hoi men kata charin onomazontai.* . . .

130. See Bunge, *Geistliche Vaterschaft*, pp. 40–44; and Guillaumont, "Introduction," in *Gnostikos* (SC 356), pp. 29–40.

131. For other texts suggesting the different levels of knowledge appropriate for different groups, see, e.g., *KG* 4.6; 6.65.

132. See *Gnost.* 36, which counsels that the Origenist view of the end or universal return should not be revealed to seculars and young monks. For other texts that emphasize that pearls should not be cast before swine, see esp. *Prak.* pref. (Bamberger, p. 15); and *Ep. ad Mel.* 4 (Parmentier, p. 11).

133. A point brought out by O'Laughlin, "Origenism in the Desert," pp. 245–48.

134. *Monachos estin ho pantōn choristheis kai pasi synermosmenos* (my translation). Cf. *Prayer* 125, which explains the second part by saying, "A monk is a man who considers himself one with all men because he seems constantly to see himself in every man" (Bamberger, p. 76).

135. The Dionysian writings consist of four treatises and ten letters: *The Divine Names* (*DN*), *The Mystical Theology* (*MT*), *The Celestial Hierarchy* (*CH*), *The Ecclesiastical Hierarchy* (*EH*), and *The Letters* (*Ep.*). They appear in *PG* 3 in the edition of B. Corderius. (A new critical edition by A. M. Ritter, G. Heil, and B. Suchla is forthcoming.) A key tool for the investigation of the Dionysian corpus and its history is the line-by-line edition of the text and major Latin translations (along with valuable indices) done by Philippe Chevallier, *Dionysiaca*, 2 vols. (Paris: Desclée, 1937). A good recent translation exists: *Pseudo-Dionysius: The Complete Works*, trans. Colm Luibheid et al., CWS (New York: Paulist, 1987). Unless otherwise noted, this translation will be used throughout. For direct quotations, reference will be made to the abbreviated title, followed by chapter and section number, with the Migne column number and the page of the CWS translation in parentheses, e.g., *DN* 4.12 (709B; p. 81).

136. Bonaventure, *The Reduction of the Arts to Theology* (*S. Bonaventurae Opera Omnia* 5:321): Primum maxime docet Augustinus, secundum maxime docet Gregorius, tertium vero docet Dionysius.

137. Many scholars have considered Hierotheus to be a fiction, but others argue that references to him and summaries of his teaching (e.g., *DN* 2.9–10; 3.2; 4.15–17; *CH* 6.2; *EH* 2.1; 3.1) indicate that he was a real person. He is not to be confused with the author of the Syriac *Book of the Holy Hierotheos*, a quasi-Gnostic treatise written by Stephan bar Soudaili

in the early sixth century, which shows knowledge of the Dionysian writings. See A. Guillaumont, "Étienne bar Soudaili," *DS* 4:1481–88; and I. Hausherr, "L'influence du 'Livre de Saint Hierothée,'" *Études de spiritualité orientale*, Orientalia Christiana Analecta (Rome: Pontificium Institutum Studiorum Orientalium, 1969), pp. 23–58.

138. For a survey of attempts to identify the author, see R. Roques, "Denys l'Aréopagite (Le Pseudo-)," *DS* 3:249–57; and, more fully, idem, "La question dionysienne," in his *Structures théologiques de la Gnôse à Richard de Saint-Victor* (Paris: Presses universitaires de France, 1962), pp. 63–91.

139. Martin Luther, *Babylonian Captivity of the Church* (*Weimarer Ausgabe* 6, 562).

140. Proof of the dependence on Proclus was worked out independently by J. Stiglmayr and H. Koch, who published their studies in 1895. More recently, see H.-D. Saffrey, "New Objective Links between the Pseudo-Dionysius and Proclus," in *Neoplatonism and Christian Thought*, ed. Dominic J. O'Meara (Albany: SUNY Press, 1982), pp. 64–74.

141. See Jan Vanneste, *Le mystère de Dieu: Essai sur la structure rationelle de la doctrine mystique du Pseudo-Dionysius l'Aréopagite* (Brussels: Desclée, 1959), e.g., pp. 21 and 221; and esp. idem, "Is the Mysticism of the Pseudo-Dionysius Genuine?" *International Philosophical Quarterly* 3 (1963): 286–306. Similar views have been expressed by Ronald F. Hathaway, *Hierarchy and the Definition of Order in the Letters of Pseudo-Dionysius* (The Hague: Nijhoff, 1969). Eberhard Jüngel has attacked Dionysian emphasis on silence as a miscontruction of Christian theology of the word (*God as the Mystery of the World* [Grand Rapids: Eerdmans, 1983], pp. 250–61). (For an answer to Jüngel, see Michel Corbin, "Négation et transcendance dans l'oeuvre de Denys," *Revue des sciences philosophiques et théologiques* 69 [1985]: 41–76.)

142. Vladimir Lossky, *The Vision of God* (London: Faith Press, 1963), pp. 99–100, building on two previous papers: "La théologie négative dans la doctrine de Denys l'Aréopagite," *Revue des sciences philosophiques et théologiques* 28 (1939): 204–21; and "La notion des 'analogies' chez Denys le Pseudo-Aréopagite," *Archives d'histoire doctrinal et littéraire du moyen âge* 5 (1930): 279–309. Similar arguments have been advanced by Endre von Ivánka in *Plato Christianus: Übernahme und Umgestaltung des Platonismus durch die Väter* (Einsiedeln: Johannes Verlag, 1964), esp. pp. 262–89; idem, "La signification historique du 'Corpus Areopageticum,'" *Recherches des sciences religieuses* 36 (1949), pp. 15–19. See also Bouyer, *Spirituality*, pp. 399–401. Dionysius himself mentions that he was accused of being a parricide for using Greek ideas against the Greeks (see *Ep.* 7.2).

143. H. Urs von Balthasar, *The Glory of the Lord*, vol. 2, *Studies in Theological Style: Clerical Styles* (New York: Crossroad, 1984), pp. 144–210 ("Denys"); quotation from pp. 148–49.

144. E.g., René Roques, *L'univers dionysien: Structure hierarchique du monde selon le Pseudo-Denys* (2nd ed.; Paris: Cerf, 1983); idem, *Structures théologiques* mentioned above. See also Bernard Brons, *Gott und die Seienden: Untersuchungen zum Verhältnis von neuplatonischer Metaphysik und christlichen Tradition bei Dionysius Areopagita* (Göttingen: Vandenhoeck & Ruprecht, 1976), e.g., p. 327. On Dionysius's relation to Neoplatonism, see E. Corsini, *Il trattato 'De Divinis Nominibus' dello Pseudo-Dionigi e i commenti neoplatonici al Parmenide* (Turin: Giappichelli, 1962); and esp. Stephen Gersh, *From Iamblichus to Eriugena: An Investigation of the Prehistory and Evolution of the Pseudo-Dionysian Tradition* (Leiden: Brill, 1978).

145. See esp. *Ep.* 9.1 (1105C–8B); *CH* 2, 5 (140AB, 145A); *EH* 1.4 (376C); 4.III.2 (476BC).

146. On this point, see Charles André Bernard, "La doctrine mystique de Denys l'Aréopagite," *Gregorianum* 68 (1987), p. 564.

147. Von Balthasar, *Glory of the Lord*, 2:152–54.

148. For a general introduction to his thought and influence, the long, multiauthor article, "Denys l'Aréopagite" (*DS* 3:244–429) is still indispensable. Besides the treatments in introductions to spirituality (e.g., Viller and Rahner, Bouyer, Louth), see also I. P. Sheldon-Williams, "The pseudo-Dionysius," in *The Cambridge History of Later Greek and Early Medieval Philosophy*, ed. A. H. Armstrong (Cambridge: Cambridge University Press, 1967), pp. 457–72; and Paul Rorem, "The Uplifting Spirituality of Pseudo-Dionysius," in *Christian*

Spirituality: Origins to the Twelfth Century, ed. Bernard McGinn and John Meyendorff, WS 16 (New York: Crossroad, 1986), pp. 132–51. The most recent introduction is Andrew Louth, *Denys the Areopagite* (Wilton, CT: Morehouse-Barlow, 1989). Two important works for Dionysius's mysticism are Walther Völker, *Kontemplation und Ekstase bei Pseudo-Dionysius Areopagita* (Wiesbaden: F. Steiner, 1958); and Paul Rorem, *Biblical and Liturgical Symbols within the Pseudo-Dionysian Synthesis* (Toronto: Pontifical Institute of Mediaeval Studies, 1984).

149. For accounts of the works in their order in the corpus, see Roques, *Structures théologiques,* pp. 132–34; and von Balthasar, *Glory of the Lord* 2:154–64.

150. *DN* presupposes the existence of at least four earlier works: (1) *The Theological Outlines,* or *Theological Representations,* a cataphatic introduction dealing with scriptural names for God and the God-Man; (2) *On the Properties and Orders of Angels,* apparently a different work from the *CH,* or perhaps an earlier version of it; (3) *On the Soul;* and (4) *On the Just Divine Judgment.*

151. See von Ivánka, *Plato Christianus,* pp. 228–42. For a different view of the structure, see von Balthasar, *Glory of the Lord* 2:189–90.

152. E.g., *DN* 1.8 (597B; p. 57); *MT* 3 (1033B; p. 141); *CH* 15.6 (336A; p. 187); *Ep.* 9.1, 6 (1104B, 1113B; pp. 280, 288).

153. On the place of this treatise in the corpus, see P. Rorem, "The Place of *The Mystical Theology* in the Pseudo-Dionysian Corpus," *Dionysius* 4 (1980): 87–98.

154. On this work, see esp. *Dionysius the Pseudo-Areopagite: The Ecclesiastical Hierarchy,* translated and annotated by Thomas L. Campbell (Lanham, MD: University Press of America, 1981).

155. On the letters, see Hathaway, *Hierarchy and the Definition of Order,* which includes a translation and detailed study.

156. E.g., *CH* 7.4 (212B; p. 166). In *EH,* which appears to be the last of the surviving treatises, there is also reference to a work *On the Intelligibles and Objects of Sense* (e.g., *EH* 1.2).

157. See, e.g., Otto von Simson, *The Gothic Cathedral* (New York: Harper & Row, 1964).

158. Von Balthasar, *Glory of the Lord* 2:168; cf. 2:154.

159. A point noted by Sheldon-Williams, "The pseudo-Dionysius," p. 459.

160. On the Dionysian use of scripture, see Roques, *L'univers dionysien,* pp. 210–25; and esp. Rorem, *Biblical and Liturgical Symbols.*

161. See Theresia Benedicta a Cruce [Edith Stein], "Ways to Know God: The 'Symbolic Theology' of Dionysius the Areopagite and its Factual Presuppositions," *The Thomist* 9 (1946), p. 401.

162. Dionysius's distinction between the unknowable divine nature and the manifested activities (*energeiai*) has been read by V. Lossky and others as equivalent to the later Byzantine (especially Palamite) distinction between the divine essence and energies. Lossky's reading is certainly exaggerated, as shown by S. Gersh ("Ideas and Energies in Pseudo-Dionysius the Areopagite," in *Studia Patristica* 15, ed. E. A. Livingstone [Berlin: Akademie Verlag, 1984], pp. 297–300), who emphasizes the background in the history of later Neoplatonism. From the viewpoint of the history of Christian thought, Dionysius's innovation may well have been developed from the Cappadocian emphasis on our accessibility to divine actions and inaccessibility to God's nature; see, e.g., Gregory of Nyssa, *To Ablabius* (*PG* 45:119–29; translated in W. G. Rusch, *The Trinitarian Controversy* [Philadelphia: Fortress, 1980], pp. 152–56).

163. Of particular importance for Dionysius's relation to earlier Greek fathers are Völker, *Kontemplation und Ekstase;* von Ivánka, *Plato Christianus;* and Roques, "A propos des sources du Pseudo-Denys," in *Structures theologiques,* pp. 226–40.

164. *Proclus: The Elements of Theology,* a revised text by E. R. Dodds (2nd ed.; Oxford: Clarendon, 1963), p. 39.

165. For some other appearances of the triad, see, e.g., *CH* 1.1 (120B); *EH* 3.III.3 (429AB); *DN* 4.14 (712CD); *MT* 3 (1033C); etc. A detailed study can be found in Gersh, *From Iamblichus to Eriugena,* pp. 217–29.

166. On the modes of theology in Dionysius, see Roques, "Les 'théologies' dionysiennes: notions, fonctions et implications," in *Structures théologiques,* pp. 135–50.

167. The classic study of *hierarchia* in Dionysius is Roques's *L'univers dionysien,* which also considers *thearchia* (pp. 111–15). On this theme, see also Bernard, "La doctrine mystique," pp. 533–37; and von Balthasar, *Glory of the Lord* 2:201–2. Chevallier (*Dionysiaca* 2:1585) lists forty-seven appearances of *thearchia* and ninety appearances of *hierarchia* (p. 1592).

168. I have altered the first part of the translation of C. Luibhead (*Pseudo-Dionysius*) to bring out the technical trinitarian vocabulary of the original. On Thearchy, see, e.g., *DN* 1.2 (588CD); 1.4 (693B).

169. *EH* 5.I.7 (508D; p. 239): "The divinity (*thearchia*) first purifies those minds which it reaches and then illuminates them. Following on their illumination it perfects them in a perfect conformity to God. This being so, it is clear that the hierarchy, as an image of the divine, is divided into distinctive orders and powers in order to reveal that the activities of the divinity are preeminent for the utter holiness and purity, permanence and distinctiveness of their orders." Cf. *CH* 3.3 (168A). For a study of the Dionysian understanding of participation, see Dom Placid Spearritt, "The Soul's Participation in God according to Pseudo-Dionysius," *Downside Review* 88 (1970): 378–92.

170. See also *EH* 1.3 (373C; p. 197).

171. On the legal hierarchy, see *EH* 3.III.4 (432B); 5.I.2 (501BD); *Ep.* 8 (1089C); and the discussion in Roques, *L'univers dionysien,* pp. 171–74.

172. See the summary in *EH* 7.III.5–6 (536D–37C; pp. 248–49).

173. Von Balthasar, *Glory of the Lord* 2:201–2.

174. *CH* 6.2 (200D) says that the division comes from Hierotheus.

175. This is especially clear in *CH* 15.1 (328A; p. 182): "So now, if you will, the eye of our intelligence is going to relax the effort by which it tries to reach the solitary heights of contemplation befitting the angels. We must come down to the plains of distinction and multiplicity, to the many variegated forms and shapes adopted by the angels. Then, once more, we will take off from these images, and will, by retracing, rise up again to the simplicity of the heavenly minds."

176. For background, see Gabriel Horn, "Amour et extase d'après Denys l'Aréopagite," *Revue d'ascétique et de la mystique* 6 (1925): 278–89; John M. Rist, "A Note on Eros and Agape in Pseudo-Dionysius," *Vigiliae Christianae* 20 (1966): 235–43; and Bernard, "La doctrine mystique," pp. 552–54. I have made use in what follows of parts of my unpublished paper "God as Eros: Reflections on Cosmic Love in the Christian Tradition."

177. Discussed in chapter 2, pp. 47–48.

178. See the discussion of Proclus in chapter 2, p. 59.

179. Cf. *PG* 3:711A, 713AB.

180. *Esto kai ho theios erōs agathos agathou dia to agathon.* See Rist, "Note," pp. 239–41.

181. See Horn, "Amour et extase," esp. pp. 284–88.

182. See Corsini, *Il trattato 'De Divinis Nominibus,'* e.g., pp. 42–44, 115ff., 156ff.; and Gersh, *From Iamblichus to Eriugena,* e.g., pp. 17–23, 152–66, 190, etc.

183. See chapter 2, pp. 56–58.

184. E.g., *Elements of Theology* props. 92, 103.

185. E. Corsini was the first to demonstrate this important shift.

186. Gersh, *Iamblichus to Eriugena,* p. 138.

187. Dionysius generally uses Wisdom (*sophia*) for the third member, most likely for scriptural reasons, but *DN* 7.2 (869A) speaks of the divine intellect (*theios nous*).

188. See the similar critique in *DN* 11.7 (953D); cf. 1.3 (589BC).

189. See esp. *DN* 5.4–6 (817C–820D). In *DN* 11.6 (953C–956B) Dionysius distinguishes between terms like "life itself," which are ascribed to God insofar as they are drawn from creatures, and terms like "subsistence of life itself," which indicate God's transcendence of all things, including the primaries. Edward Booth describes the former as "corresponding powers given forth providentially to be participated in by creatures, since God in himself

is imparticipable" (*Aristotelian Aporetic Ontology in Islamic and Christian Thinkers* [Cambridge: Cambridge University Press, 1983], p. 79).

190. On the tension between these two kinds of claims, see Gersh, *Iamblichus to Eriugena*, pp. 158–65.

191. See Booth, *Aporetic Ontology*, pp. 76–80.

192. See Gersh, *Iamblichus to Eriugena*, p. 207 n. 18, and p. 217, for examples.

193. On the creationist ontology of Dionysius, see, e.g., von Ivánka, *Plato Christianus*, pp. 262–89; Louth, *Origins*, pp. 176–77; Booth, *Aporetic Ontology*, pp. 76–80; and esp. Gersh, *Iamblichus to Eriugena*, pp. 20–23, 204–6, 227–29, 283–88. Also helpful is O. Semmelroth, "Gottes geeinte Vielheit: Zur Gotteslehre des Ps.-Dionysius Areopagita," *Scholastik* 25 (1950), pp. 393–94.

194. The question of creation in Dionysius continues to elicit varied judgments. Roques, while underlining the removal of intermediaries between God and creatures (e.g., *L'univers dionysien*, pp. 77–81, 111–15), still finds that Dionysius maintains an important role for both descending and ascending mediation (pp. 101–11). Jean Pépin contrasts Dionysius with Augustine on the necessity for mediation between God and the soul ("Univers dionysien et univers augustinien," in *Aspects de la dialectique: Recherches de philosophie II* [Paris: Desclée, 1956], esp. pp. 196, 205–8), but Pépin's view neglects Dionysius's continued insistence on a direct relation between God and each created being.

195. This seems to be the reason why Dionysius consciously avoids associating the angelic hierarchies with Being–Life–Wisdom lest they seem to mediate these attributes to lower realities. See Gersh, *Iamblichus to Eriugena*, pp. 172–77.

196. Among general students of mysticism this is evident, for instance, in W. R. Inge, *Christian Mysticism* (London: Methuen, 1899), pp. 104–10. Among students of Dionysius a classic example is Vanneste, "Is the Mysticism of Pseudo-Dionysius Genuine?"

197. Rorem, *Biblical and Liturgical Symbols*, p. 149.

198. Von Balthasar, *Glory of the Lord* 2:153.

199. On the equivalence of the two, see, e.g., *CH* 9.2 (260B); 15.4 (333B).

200. This is well put by Louth: ". . . ascent means a more perfect union with the divine energy (or will) which establishes one in the hierarchy. So one 'ascends' into the hierarchy rather than up it" (*Origins*, p. 171).

201. "The verb 'instress' in GMH's spiritual writings has the special meaning of the soul's spiritual energy caused by and co-operating with God's creative activity. . . . To instress the mind is to spiritualize a sensory image, turning a simple apprehension into a judgement" (Christopher Devlin, S.J., *The Sermons and Devotional Writings of Gerard Manley Hopkins* [Oxford: Oxford University Press, 1959], pp. 283–84).

202. See chapter 4, p. 102. For the history of the term, see Louis Bouyer, "Mysticism: An Essay on the History of the Word," in *Understanding Mysticism*, ed. Richard Woods (Garden City, NY: Doubleday Image Books, 1980), pp. 42–55; idem, "Die mystische Kontemplation bei den Vätern."

203. For a list of twenty-six appearances, see Chevallier, *Dionysiaca* 2:1634.

204. See Bernard, "La doctrine mystique," p. 525.

205. See Rorem, "Uplifting Spirituality," pp. 132–33, 136.

206. Bouyer has rightly drawn attention to the following texts (*Spirituality*, pp. 410–16), but he goes too far in claiming that in Dionysius we have "the first *habitual* [my italics] use of the word to designate an interior experience" (p. 410).

207. *Eite kai ek tinos emyēthē theioteras epipnoias, ou monon mathōn, alla kai pathōn ta theia; kak tēs pros auta sympatheias, ei outō chrē phanai, pros tēn adidakton auton kai mystikēn apotelestheis henōsin kai pistin.* I have used the translation of Bouyer (*Spirituality*, p. 410) as preferable to that of Luibhead (*Pseudo-Dionysius*). Subsequent passages echo this: *DN* 3.2 (681D–684A) speaks of Hierotheus as "experiencing communion with the things hymned" (*kai tēn ta pros ta hymnou-mena koinōnian*); and *DN* 3.3 (684A) says that he knows "mystical things" (*ta mystika*) hidden from the multitude.

208. Aristotle frg. 15 (see W. D. Ross, *Aristotelis fragmenta selecta*, vol. 12 in *The Works of Aristotle*, ed. W. D. Ross [Oxford: Clarendon, 1908–31], p. 84): "Those who are being initiated are not required to grasp anything with the understanding (*mathein*), but to have a certain inner experience (*pathein*), and so to be put in a particular frame of mind, presuming that they are capable of this frame of mind in the first place." See Werner Jaeger, *Aristotle* (Oxford: Clarendon, 1948), p. 160; see also M. Harl, "Le langage de l'expérience religieuse chez les pères grecs," *Rivista di storia e letteratura religiosa* 15 (1977), pp. 6–7, 12–16.

209. On *sympatheia* in Proclus, see, e.g., *Elements of Theology* prop. 140 (ed. Dodds, p. 124). For the influence of late Neoplatonic theurgy on Dionysius, see P. E. Rorem, "Iamblichus and the Anagogical Method in Pseudo-Dionysian Liturgical Theology," in *Studia Patristica*, vol. 18, ed. E. A. Livingstone (Oxford and New York: Pergamon, 1982), pp. 453–60.

210. Moses is treated especially in *MT* 1 (1000C–1001A); Paul in *DN* 4.13 (712A) and *Ep.* 5 (1073A–1076A); and Carpos in *Ep.* 8.6 (1097B–1100D). For a careful analysis of most of these texts, as well as those relating to Hierotheus, see Rorem, *Biblical and Liturgical Symbols*, pp. 133–42.

211. This aspect has been stressed by Bouyer (*Spirituality*, pp. 411–12) and Rorem (*Biblical and Liturgical Symbols*, pp. 140–42).

212. See Roques, *L'univers dionysien*, pp. 94–101.

213. See Rorem, *Biblical and Liturgical Symbols*, pp. 50–52.

214. The suggested division is too simple, for, as *DN* 9.7 (916A; p. 118) reminds us, "the very same things are both similar and dissimilar to God," that is, all things are both like and unlike God, though in varying degrees.

215. Rorem, "Uplifting Spirituality," p. 136.

216. See von Balthasar, *Glory of the Lord* 2:169, 178–84.

217. See Sheldon-Williams, "The pseudo-Dionysius," p. 463.

218. *DN* 7.2 (869A; p. 107): ". . . when we talk of God as being without mind and without perception, this is to be taken in the sense of what he has in superabundance and not as a defect"; cf. *MT* 4 (1040D).

219. Vanneste, *Le mystère de Dieu*, passim, esp. pp. 218–24, for a summary. Also useful for Dionysius's negative theology is Lossky, "La théologie négative dans la doctrine de Denys l'Aréopagite."

220. See Chevallier, *Dionysiaca* 2:1586, for a list of thirteen appearances of *agnōsia*.

221. Vanneste, *Le mystère de Dieu*, p. 170.

222. See esp. *MT* 1.1 (997B–1000A); 1.3 (1000C); 2 (1025AB); 3 (1033B); also *Ep.* 1 (1065A); 5 (1073A).

223. See pp. 141–42 above, noting the important paper of Henri-Charles Puech, "La Ténèbre mystique chez le Pseudo-Denys l'Aréopagite." Cf. Vanneste, *Le mystère de Dieu*, pp. 161–81; and especially Roques, "Contemplation, extase et ténèbre mystique chez le Pseudo-Denys," *DS* 2:1885–1911. *MT* 1.3 should be compared with Gregory of Nyssa's *Life of Moses* 2.162–69, in *Grégoire de Nysse. La vie de Moïse* (SC 1bis: 80–84).

224. Following the suggestion of Puech, "La Ténèbre mystique," p. 140.

225. Puech recognizes both the objective and the subjective poles of the Dionysian darkness ("La Ténèbre mystique," pp. 122, 125), though he emphasizes that Dionysius is not giving an account of his own experience (pp. 129–33, 141).

226. I have altered the translation somewhat and supplied the emphasis. On God as beyond both affirmation and negation, see Corbin, "Négation et transcendance," pp. 47, 58–63, 69. See also J.-L. Marion, *L'idole et la distance* (Paris: Grasset, 1977).

227. See Thomas Michael Tomasic, "The Logical Function of Metaphor and Oppositional Coincidence in the Pseudo-Dionysius and Johannes Scottus Eriugena," *Journal of Religion* 68 (1988), pp. 364–66.

228. E.g., *MT* 5 (1048A; p. 141): "It is not . . . greatness or smallness, equality or inequality, similarity or dissimilarity. . . . It falls neither within the predicate of nonbeing nor of being." Cf. *DN* 13.3 (981A).

229. E.g., *DN* 9.1-10 (909B-917A); cf. 13.2 (980A).

230. E.g., *DN* 5.10 (825B; p. 103): "He is at rest and astir, is neither resting nor striving . . ."; *DN* 7.3 (872A; p. 109): "He is all things in all things and he is no thing among things. He is known to all from all things and he is known to no one from anything"; *Ep.* 9.3 (1109D; p. 286): "Always at rest and on the move it is never at rest or on the move. . ."; cf. *DN* 13.3 (980C).

231. See esp. Gersh, *From Iamblichus to Eriugena,* and the literature cited there.

232. E.g., the divergent evaluations of Jüngel and von Balthasar (see nn. 141 and 143).

233. E.g., *hyperagnōstos* in *DN* 1.5 (593B) and *MT* 1.1 (997A); *hyperochitos* in *Ep.* 1 (1065A); *hyperphaēs* in *DN* 1.8 (597A).

234. Corbin, "Négation et transcendance," pp. 58-59, 69.

235. One indication of this is that Dionysius gives no special emphasis to the negation of negation (as contrasted with the negation of both negation and affirmation), although this was present in Proclus and appropriated by later mystics in the tradition of dialectical Neoplatonism, especially Meister Eckhart.

236. See my remarks in *Mystical Union and Monotheistic Faith,* ed. M. Idel and B. McGinn (New York: Macmillan, 1989), pp. 185-93.

237. The term *henōsis* appears no fewer than fifty-eight times in Dionysius (see Chevallier, *Dionysiaca* 2:1590), but it is not always used in the sense of mystical union; *koinōnia* is used fifty-nine times, but in a wide variety of senses. On union in Dionyius, see esp. Vanneste, *Le mystère de Dieu,* chap. 4.

238. *MT* 1.1 (997B; p. 135 with my changes in the translation).

239. Cf. *DN* 13.3 (981B), which speaks of the soul "being joined" (*synappousan*) to God. Other occurrences of *henōsis* in a mystical sense can be found in *DN* 1.1 (588A); 1.4 (589D); 1.5 (592C); 3.1 (680B); 4.11 (*di'henōseos agnōstou,* 708D); 11:2 (949D-952A); *CH* 1.2 (121B); *EH* 2.I.1 (392A); 2.III.4 (400C); 3.III.3 (429A); *Ep.* 10 (1117B).

240. For more on the Eucharist and union, see *EH* 3.III.7-9 (436D-437C).

241. I have tried to specify two broad traditions in medieval ideas of union, *unitas spiritus* (using 1 Cor 6:17), and *unitas indistinctionis* (employing a number of Johannine texts for a scriptural base), in my essay in *Mystical Union and Monotheistic Faith,* pp. 59-86. The dynamics of Dionysius's system of thought suggest a position close to the *unitas indistinctionis* later found in Eckhart and his followers.

242. Union, divinization, and imitation of God are linked in *CH* 12.3 (293B); cf. *DN* 8.5 (893A).

243. On divinization in Dionysius, see Bouyer, *Spirituality,* pp. 416-21; and *DS* 4:1385-87.

244. A point emphasized by von Balthasar (*Glory of the Lord* 2:161-62).

245. See esp. Roques in *DS* 2:1898.

246. Two scholars have devoted considerable attention to these issues: Völker, *Kontemplation und Ekstase;* and Roques, "Contemplation chez les orientaux chrétiens. E. Le Pseudo-Denys L'Aréopagite," *DS* 2:1785-87; idem, "Contemplation, extase et ténèbre mystique chez le Pseudo-Denys," *DS* 2:1885-1911 (partly reprinted in *Structures théologiques,* pp. 151-63).

247. E.g., *DN* 12.2 (969C).

248. This is most evident in the key texts devoted to symbolic theology, such as *CH* 2 and *Ep.* 9; but in *EH* it is significant that the title given to the deeper penetration of the meaning of each sacrament is *theōria* (e.g., 397A, 428A, 473A, 509C, 533C, 556D).

249. See Roques, *DS* 2:1890-91.

250. *DN* 1.2 (588CD; p. 50): ". . . the Good is not absolutely incommunicable to everything. By itself it generously reveals a firm, transcendent beam, granting enlightenments proportionate to each being, and thereby draws minds upward to its permitted contemplation, to participation and to the state of becoming like it."

251. See Sheldon-Williams, "The pseudo-Dionysius," pp. 469-70. This helps explain texts such as *DN* 1.4 (592BC), which discuss the vision of God to be enjoyed in heaven. On the importance of this passage for Byzantine theology, see Lossky, *Vision of God,* pp. 103-4.

252. Roques, *DS* 2:1886.

253. *Ekstasis* appears only four times, and the adjective *ekstatikos* three, all in the same three important places, *DN* 4.13 (712AB); *MT* 1.1 (1000A); and *Ep.* 9.5 (1112BC). On *existēmi*, see esp. *DN* 11.2 (952A). For studies of ecstasy in Dionysius, see Völker, *Kontemplation und Ekstase*, chap. 3; and Roques in *DS* 2:1895-1911.

254. On the relation between eros and ecstasy, see Roques, *DS* 2:1900-1902.

255. This casts light on an unusual passage in *CH* 13.4 (305B), where Thearchy (not the mystic) is described as enjoying "unknown union with its own hiddenness."

256. *MT* 1.1 (1001A) also emphasizes the mystic's self-abandonment, though without the language of eros.

257. See Roques, *DS* 2:1984-95.

258. E.g., von Ivánka, *Plato Christianus,* pp. 285-86; Roques, *L'univers dionysien,* pp. 327-29; idem, *Structures théologiques,* pp. 235-36; Rorem, "Uplifting Spirituality," p. 144.

259. See Lossky, "La notion des 'analogies' chez Denys," p. 307; von Balthasar, *Glory of the Lord* 2:192-93, 208-10; Corbin, "Négation et transcendance," pp. 65-75.

260. E.g., *DN* 1.4 (592B); 2.10 (648D-649A); *CH* 4.4 (181B); *EH* 3.III.11-13 (441A-443C); 5.III.5 (512C); *Ep.* 3 (1069B).

261. Roques, *DS* 2:1908-10.

Introduction to Part II

1. Jean Daniélou, *The Theology of Jewish Christianity* (Chicago: Regnery, 1964), p. 1.

2. See, e.g., Ernst Kitzinger, *Early Medieval Art* (Bloomington: Indiana University Press, 1966), pp. 7-12.

3. For an introduction, see "Latine (Église)," in *DS* 9:330-82.

4. For a survey of the importance of translations, see Jean Gribomont, "The Translations of Jerome and Rufinus," in *Patrology,* Vol. 4, *The Golden Age of Latin Patristic Literature from the Council of Nicea to the Council of Chalcedon,* ed. Angelo di Berardino with an introduction by Johannes Quasten (Westminster: Christian Classics, 1987), pp. 195-212, on the translations prior to Jerome and Rufinus. (Hereafter this work will be referred to as *Patrology* 4.)

5. On the intellectual history of the Roman *imperium,* see esp. C. N. Cochrane, *Christianity and Classical Culture: A Study of Thought and Action from Augustus to Augustine* (New York: Oxford University Press, 1967).

6. There was no single "Old Latin" (*Vetus Latina*) version of the Bible; differing texts were available in different places, especially North Africa, southern Gaul, and later Rome. Tertullian is the earliest witness, so the oldest versions antedate 200 C.E.

7. On Tertullian, see J. Daniélou, *The Origins of Latin Christianity* (Philadelphia: Westminster, 1977), esp. chaps. 14-15.

8. For a comparison of Tertullian's commentary with Origen's, see *Alexandrian Christianity,* ed. Henry Chadwick (Philadelphia: Westminster, 1954), pp. 224-30.

9. Daniélou, *Origins,* pp. 341, 404.

10. For Cyprian on martyrdom, see esp. S. Deleani, *Christum sequi: Étude d'un thème dans l'oeuvre de Saint Cyprien* (Paris: Études Augustiniennes, 1979), pp. 84-111.

11. This despite a few studies that have attempted to find a mystical element in the martyr-bishop, e.g., A. d'Alès, "Le mysticisme de Saint Cyprien," *Revue d'ascétique et de la mystique* 2 (1921): 256-67.

12. A standard, if now somewhat old, treatment is that of A. H. M. Jones, *The Later Roman Empire 284-602: A Social, Economic, and Administrative Survey,* 2 vols. (Norman: University of Oklahoma Press, 1964).

13. See H. I. Marrou, "L'idée de Dieu et la divinité du Roi," *La regalità sacra* (Leiden: Brill, 1959), pp. 478-80.

14. For a survey, see Adalbert Hamman, "The Turnabout of the Fourth Century," in *Patrology* 4:1-32.

15. Between 305 (the death of Diocletian) and the death of Theodosius in 395, only twenty-two years saw a commonly ruled empire. On the precipitous decline of Greek in the West during the first third of the fifth century, see Pierre Courcelle, *Late Latin Writers and their Greek Sources* (Cambridge, MA: Harvard University Press, 1969), pp. 147–48.

16. See Hamman, "Turnabout," p. 6.

17. On the interplay of apostolicity and accommodation, see Francis Dvornik, *Byzantium and the Roman Primacy* (New York: Fordham University Press, 1966). The most famous second-century text on Rome's preeminence is to be found in Irenaeus's *Against Heresies* 3.2–3.

18. See Cyprian *Epist.* 75.16–17, attacking the Roman bishop Stephen.

19. The Roman Synod of 382, held under Damasus, declared: ". . . the Holy Roman Church is preferred to the other churches as if it were the one dwelling of Christ. By the evangelical voice of the Lord our Savior it has gained the primacy, 'You are Peter and upon this rock I will build my church and the gates of hell will not prevail against it.' . . . The fellowship of the most holy Paul the Apostle, the 'vessel of election,' has also been added to this" (*PL* 13:374).

20. For the history of early Western monasticism, see R. Lorenz, "Die Anfänge des abendländisches Mönchtums in 4. Jahrhundert," *Zeitschrift für Kirchengeschichte* 77 (1966): 1–66; Joseph T. Lienhard, *Paulinus of Nola and Early Western Monasticism* (Cologne/Bonn: Peter Hanstein, 1977); and Philip Rousseau, *Ascetics, Authority and the Church in the Age of Jerome and Cassian* (Oxford: Oxford University Press, 1978).

21. Rousseau is helpful on this aspect of early Western monasticism, e.g., *Ascetics, Authority and the Church*, pp. 1–2, 93–95.

22. On Jerome as translator, see Gribomont, *Patrology* 4:212–31, and pp. 237–38 for his *Lives of the Hermits*.

23. I have used the translation of F. R. Hoare, whose *The Western Fathers* (New York: Harper & Row, 1965) contains the lives of Martin, Ambrose, Augustine, Honoratus, and Germanus of Auxerre. See pp. 24–25 for this text.

24. For a survey of Western opposition to monasticism, see Lienhard, *Paulinus of Nola*, chap. 7.

25. Many aspects of this new piety, its relation to episcopal power, and its social dynamics cannot be considered here. Among the most sensitive studies are the numerous writings of Peter Brown: see esp. *Religion and Society in the Age of Saint Augustine* (New York: Harper & Row, 1972); *The Cult of the Saints: Its Rise and Function in Latin Christianity* (Chicago: University of Chicago Press, 1981); *Society and the Holy in Late Antiquity* (Berkeley: University of California Press, 1982); and *The Body and Society: Men, Women, and Sexual Renunciation in Early Christianity* (New York: Columbia University Press, 1988).

26. Hamman, "Turnabout," p. 29.

27. See Rousseau, *Ascetics, Authority and the Church*, p. 79: "Christians of the West in the fourth century developed a particular style of religious enthusiasm, and a much greater readiness to link a life of dedication, more or less monastic, to the needs and anxieties of the Church as a whole."

Chapter 6

1. Hilary of Poitiers, *De trinitate* 1.1–16 (*PL* 10:25–37). In this and the following chapter the Latin titles for works will be cited in the notes in order to facilitate reference to the Bibliography.

2. For a brief introduction to the major Eastern and Western fathers of the fourth century, see Charles Kannengiesser, "The Spiritual Message of the Great Fathers," in *Christian Spirituality: Origins to the Twelfth Century*, ed. Bernard McGinn and John Meyendorff, WS 16 (New York: Crossroad, 1986), pp. 61–88.

3. The best introduction to pagan Latin Neoplatonism is Stephen Gersh, *Middle Platonism*

and Neoplatonism: The Latin Tradition, 2 vols. (Notre Dame: University of Notre Dame Press, 1986).

4. Tunc Plotini schola Romae floruit, habuitque condiscipulos, multos acutissimos et solertissimos viros. Sed aliqui eorum magicarum artium curiositate depravati sunt, aliqui Dominum nostrum Jesus Christum ipsius veritatis atque sapientiae incommutabilis, quam conabantur attingere, cognoscentes gestare personam, in ejus militiam transierunt. No single study of the formation of Latin Christian Neoplatonism exists, though much valuable material may be found in Paul Henry, *Plotin et l'Occident* (Louvain: Spicilegium Sacrum Lovaniense, 1934); and Pierre Courcelle, *Late Latin Writers and their Greek Sources* (Cambridge, MA: Harvard University Press, 1969). For a brief introduction, see Peter Brown, "The Platonists," chap. 9 in *Augustine of Hippo: A Biography* (Berkeley: University of California Press, 1967).

5. Victorinus is one of the major discoveries of recent patristic studies. Among the most important treatments are Pierre Hadot, *Porphyre et Victorinus,* 2 vols. (Paris: Études Augustiniennes, 1968); idem, *Marius Victorinus: Recherches sur sa vie et ses sources* (Paris: Études Augustiniennes, 1971). For a recent English survey, see Mary T. Clark, "Introduction," in *Marius Victorinus: Theological Treatises on the Trinity,* FC 69 (Washington, DC: Catholic University Press, 1981), pp. 3–44.

6. On these translations, see Henry, *Plotin et l'Occident,* pp. 44–62, 79–82; and Courcelle, *Late Latin Writers,* pp. 173–82.

7. These treatises have been edited by Paul Henry and Pierre Hadot in *Marii Victorini Opera,* CSEL 83.1 (Vienna: Hoelder-Pichler-Tempsky, 1971), and have been translated into English by Mary Clark, *Marius Victorinus.*

8. Ambrosiaster, Jerome, Augustine, and Pelagius were all to comment on Paul in the decades that followed.

9. See Mary T. Clark, "The Neoplatonism of Marius Victorinus the Christian," in *Neoplatonism and Early Christian Thought: Essays in Honour of A. H. Armstrong,* ed. H. J. Blumenthal and R. A. Markus (London: Variorum, 1981), pp. 153–59; idem, "A Neoplatonic Commentary on the Christian Trinity: Marius Victorinus," in *Neoplatonism and Christian Thought,* ed. Dominic J. O'Meara (Albany: SUNY Press, 1982), pp. 24–33.

10. E.g., *Adversus Arium* IA.19 (ed. Henry and Hadot, pp. 84–85).

11. E.g., *Adversus Arium* IB.52; III.4; IV.16–18 and esp. 21 (ed. Henry and Hadot, pp. 148, 197–99, 248–53, 257–58). Hadot has clearly shown Victorinus's dependence on the anonymous commentary (*Porphyre et Victorinus*), but his argument that the commentary is Porphyrian has not been universally accepted.

12. Quod enim supra *on* est, absconditum *on* est (trans. Clark, *Marius Victorinus,* p. 71). For other passages on negative theology, see *Adversus Arium* IB.49–50; IV.19 (ed. Henry and Hadot, pp. 143–46, 253–55).

13. See chapter 5, pp. 168–70.

14. See *Adversus Arium* IB.56–58 (ed. Henry and Hadot, pp. 155–58). Victorinus also holds that the Logos is androgynous.

15. Sed quoniam dedisti spiritum nobis, sancte omnipotens pater, partilem de te cognoscentiam et habemus et dicimus, omnigenus autem ignorantiam de te habentes cognoscentiam de te habemus et rursus per fidem perfectam de te cognoscentiam habemus te patrem deum et filium Iesum Christum dominum nostrum et sanctum spiritum in omni verbo semper confitentes.

16. The translation is slightly altered.
Miserere domine! Miserere Christe!
Amavi mundum, quia tu mundum feceras;
Detentus mundo sum, dum invidet mundus tuis;
Nunc odi mundum, quia nunc percepi spiritum. . . .
Miserere domine! Miserere Christe!
Velle mihi adiacet mundum et terras linquere,

Sed inbecilla pluma est, velle sine subsidio tuo,
Da fidei pennas, ut volem sursum deo.

See the discussion of this hymn in Hadot, *Marius Victorinus,* pp. 280–81.

17. Augustine dedicated his early treatise *De beata vita* (ca. 386) to him. On Theodorus (toward whom Augustine later cooled), see Courcelle, *Late Latin Writers,* pp. 134–40.

18. On Simplicianus, see Augustine, *Conf.* 8.2.3; Ambrose, *Ep.* 65; and Gennadius, *De scriptoribus ecclesiasticis* 36 (*PL* 58:1078C).

19. For a summary of biblical teaching, see Lucien Legrand, *The Biblical Doctrine of Virginity* (New York: Sheed & Ward, 1963).

20. See Henry Chadwick, "Enkrateia," in *Reallexikon für Antike und Christentum* 5:343–65.

21. See Peter Brown, *The Body and Society: Men, Women, and Sexual Renunciation in Early Christianity* (New York: Columbia University Press, 1988); idem, "The Notion of Virginity in the Early Church," in *Christian Spirituality: Origins to the Twelfth Century,* pp. 427–43.

22. Brown, *Body and Society,* pp. 69–72.

23. See Tertullian's treatises *Ad uxorem, De exhortatione castitatis, De monogamia,* and *De velandis virginibus.* For a brief summary, see Brown, *Body and Society,* pp. 76–82.

24. Cyprian's writings on the subject, especially his *De habitu virginum,* are discussed in Brown, *Body and Society,* pp. 192–95.

25. On this synod, see Samuel Laeuchli, *Power and Sexuality: The Emergence of Canon Law at the Synod of Elvira* (Philadelphia: Temple University Press, 1972).

26. Ambrose's writings on virginity include *De virginibus, De virginitate, De viduis, De institutione virginis,* and *Exhortatio virginis.* One should also look at the bishop's *Epistolae* 41 and 42. Jerome's most famous works on virginity are his *Epistola* 22 (*Ad Eustochium*), *Epistola* 130, and the polemical treatises *Contra Helvidium, Adversus Jovinianum,* and *Contra Vigilantium.* In the case of Augustine, see *De bono coniugale, De sancta virginitate, De continentia,* and, of course, the *Confessiones.* For Cassian's views, see *Conlationes* 4, 12, and 22, and *Institutiones* 6. Of course, others also wrote on these topics during the period.

27. On Jovinian, see David G. Hunter, "Resistance to the Virginal Ideal in Late Fourth-Century Rome: The Case of Jovinian," *Theological Studies* 48 (1987): 45–64.

28. See Augustine, *Contra Julianum* 6.11.36 (*PL* 44:842). On Julian's battle with Augustine, see Brown, *Body and Society,* pp. 408–19; idem, *Augustine of Hippo,* chap. 32.

29. For an interesting account of Milan in Ambrose's time, see Richard Krautheimer, *Three Christian Capitals: Topography and Politics* (Berkeley: University of California Press, 1983).

30. Among the many accounts of Ambrose's life in English, the most complete is still that of F. Homes Dudden, *The Life and Times of St. Ambrose,* 2 vols. (Oxford: Clarendon, 1935).

31. Itaque factum est ut prius docere inciperem, quam discere; discendum igitur mihi simul et docendum est, quoniam non vacavit ante discere.

32. Much has been written about Ambrose's relation to Philo. The most detailed work is H. Savon, *Saint Ambroise devant l'exégèse de Philon le Juif,* 2 vols. (Paris: Études Augustiniennes, 1977). For a brief introduction, see "Philon chez les Pères," *DS* 12:1371–72. Surprisingly less is available on Ambrose's debt to Origen, but see K. Baus, "Das Nachwirken des Origenes in der Christusfrömmigkeit des heiligen Ambrosius," *Römische Quartalschrift für christliche Altertumskunde und für Kirchengeschichte* 49 (1954): 21–55.

33. Ambrose's relation to Plotinus, to Porphyry, and to Plato has been the subject of important detailed studies by P. Courcelle and P. Hadot, which will be referred to below. H. Dörries argued for a Porphyrian basis to Ambrose's view of the soul's ascent, but this has not met with acceptance ("Das fünffach gestufte Mysterium," originally published in 1964 and later reprinted in his *Platonica Minora* [Munich: Fink, 1976], pp. 474–90). For the whole question of Ambrose's relation to philosophy (too large to be pursued here), see Goulven Madec, *Saint Ambroise et la philosophie* (Paris: Études Augustiniennes, 1974).

34. Ambrose's originality, despite his use of disparate sources, has been well defended by Gerard Nauroy, "La structure du *De Isaac vel Anima* et la cohérence de l'allegorese d'Ambroise

de Milan," *Revue des études latines* 63 (1985): 210–36, esp. pp. 214–15. There are some interesting remarks about Ambrose's imagistic and poetic style in Maria Tajo, "Un confronto tra S. Ambrogio e S. Agostino a proposito dell'esegesi del Cantico dei Cantici," *Revue des études augustiniennes* 7 (1961): 144–51. The best study, however, is Jacques Fontaine, "Prose et poésie: L'interférence des genres et des styles dans la création littéraire d'Ambroise de Milan," in *Ambrosius Episcopus,* ed. Giuseppe Lazzati, 2 vols. (Milan: Università Cattolica del Sacro Cuore, 1976), 1:124–70.

35. The critical edition of *De Isaac* is to be found in *Sancti Ambrosii Opera,* ed. Carolus Schenkl, CSEL 32.1 (Vienna: Tempsky-Freytag, 1897), pp. 639–700 (citations will be from this edition by page and line number for direct quotations). There is a translation in Michael P. McHugh, trans., *St. Ambrose: Seven Exegetical Works,* FC 65 (Washington, DC: Catholic University Press, 1972), pp. 10–65.

36. See A. Solignac, "Latine (Église) IV. Traits distinctifs de la spiritualité," *DS* 9:362–63.

37. *De bono mortis* was edited by C. Schenkl in CSEL 32.1 (pp. 701–53), and is translated in McHugh, *St. Ambrose,* pp. 70–113. *De fuga saeculi* was edited by Schenkl in CSEL 32.2, pp. 163–207, and is translated in McHugh, *St. Ambrose,* pp. 281–323.

38. *De mysteriis* was a series of homilies given to the neophytes and published ca. 390. *De sacramentis,* whose Ambrosian authorship has been doubted, is probably a stenographic record of these or similar homilies of the bishop. The texts have been edited by B. Botte in SC 25bis (Paris: Cerf, 1961). There is an English translation by T. Thompson and J. H. Srawley, *St. Ambrose: On the Sacraments and On the Mysteries* (London: SPCK, 1950).

39. Ambrose's *De virginibus* is most conveniently found in *PL* 16:197–244. It is translated in *NPNF,* 2nd series 10:363–87. *De virginitate* is in *PL* 16:279–316.

40. On Ambrose as exegete, see L. F. Pizzolato, *La dottrina esegetica di San Ambrogio* (Milan: Università Cattolica del Sacro Cuore, 1978).

41. *Explanatio Psalmorum XII,* ed. M. Petschenig, CSEL 64.6 (Vienna: Tempsky-Freytag, 1919).

42. *Expositio Psalmi CXVIII,* ed. M. Petschenig, CSEL 62.5 (Vienna: Tempsky-Freytag, 1913).

43. The *Tractatus in Evangelio secundum Lucam* appears in CSEL 32.4, but I will make use of the more recent critical edition, *Ambroise de Milan: Traité sur l'Évangile de S. Luc,* ed. Gabriel Tissot, SC 45, 52 (Paris: Cerf, 1956, 1958).

44. Paulinus's *Vita Ambrosii* appears in *PL* 14:27–46. I am quoting from the English translation of F. R. Hoare, *The Western Fathers* (New York: Sheed & Ward, 1954), p. 180.

45. See chapter 5, pp. 115–18.

46. For a good characterization, see P. Hadot, "XXIX. Patristique Latine," *École pratique des hauts études. Ve Section. Sciences religieuses. Annuaire 1965–66* (Paris: Sorbonne, 1965), pp. 151–52.

47. E.g., *De bono mortis* 5.16 (ed. Schenkl, p. 718.8–10): Sic quoque et anima nostra caveat ad haec mundana descendere. Laqueus in auro, viscum est in argento, nexus in praedio, clavis in amore. . . . Cf. *De virg.* 16.99 (*PL* 16:291C); and *In Luc.* 4.65 (SC 45, p. 177). On these texts, see P. Courcelle, "Nouveaux aspects du Platonisme chez saint Ambroise," *Revue des études latines* 34 (1956), p. 225.

48. P. Courcelle, "Plotin et saint Ambroise," *Revue de philologie* 76 (1950): 31–45, which is largely identical with chap. 3 ("Aux sermons d'Ambroise: La decouverte de néo-platonisme chrétien," in his *Recherches sur les Confessions de saint Augustin* (Paris: Boccard, 1950), pp. 106–38. (See also his "Nouveaux aspects du Platonisme.") P. Hadot summarized and extended Courcelle's findings in "Platon et Plotin dans trois sermons de saint Ambroise," *Revue des études latines* 34 (1956): 202–20. For a summary of Ambrose's use of Plotinus, see Madec, *S. Ambroise et la philosophie,* pp. 61–71.

49. Beata anima quaecumque ingreditur penetralia. nam ea insurgens de corpore ab omnibus fit remotior atque intra semet ipsam divinum illud si qua insequi possit scrutatur et quaerit. quod cum potuerit conprehendere, ea quae sunt intelligibilia supergressa in illo

confirmatur atque eo pascitur. talis erat Paulus, qui sciebat se raptum in paradisum, sed sive extra corpus raptum sive in corpore nesciebat. adsurrexerat enim anima eius de corpore et se a visceribus et vinculis carnis abduxerat atque elevaverat, factusque a se ipso alienus intra semet ipsum tenuit verba ineffabilia, quae audivit, et vulgare non potuit, quia advertit ea loqui homini non licere. The translation is slightly altered. See the discussion of this text in Hadot, "Platon et Plotin," p. 205.

50. Origen, *Comm. on Song* bk. 1.5 (GCS 33, p. 109).

51. For other references to Paul's rapture, see, e.g., *Expos. Ps. 118* 4.2 (ed. Petschenig, pp. 68–69); and *De paradiso* 1 (*PL* 14:291). For other discussions of *mentis excessum* in Ambrose, which he likens to *spiritualis ebrietas*, see *Expos. Ps. 118* 13.24 (ed. Petschenig, p. 295), and *De fide* 5.19.237 (CSEL 78, p. 307). There is a discussion of Ambrose's teaching on rapture in Ernst Dassmann, *Die Frömmigkeit des Kirchenvaters Ambrosius von Mailand* (Münster: Aschendorff, 1965), the most helpful volume on Ambrose's piety (see pp. 188–96). I believe that Dassmann mutes the mystical dimensions too severely.

52. See Hadot, "Platon et Plotin," pp. 208–9. The parallel between the chariot of Aminadab and Plato's chariot occurs elsewhere in Ambrose, e.g., *Expos. Ps. 118* 2.34–35 (ed. Petschenig, pp. 40–41). *Phaedrus* 246–47 is used also in Ambrose's *De virginitate* 17.109 (*PL* 16:294AB). On the bishop's knowledge of the *Phaedrus*, see Courcelle, "Nouveaux aspects," pp. 226–32.

53. *De Isaac* 8.78–79 (ed. Schenkl, pp. 696.21–699.4). I have slightly altered the translation of McHugh, pp. 62–64, in what follows.

54. *Enn.* 1.6.8 (ed. Armstrong; LC 1:256.16–17), quoting *Iliad* 2.140. Augustine cites the same passage in *De civ. Dei* 9.17.

55. Quod enim videtur non debet dissonare ab eo qui videt, quoniam conformes nos deus imaginis voluit esse filii sui. What follows in *De Isaac* 8.79 (ed. Schenkl, p. 699.11–17) depends on *Enn.* 1.7.1. For more on the reformation of the image, see *De Isaac* 8.74–75 (ed. Schenkl, pp. 693–94).

56. Ambrose also discusses the Transfiguration in *In Luc.* 7.17–18 (SC 52, pp. 14–15), which emphasizes the limitations of Peter's experience (and therefore of any experience of God while we are still in the body): Sed non capit humana condicio in hoc corruptibili, in hoc mortali corpore facere tabernaculum deo. On this passage, see Dassmann, *Die Frömmigkeit*, p. 196.

57. Courcelle, *Recherches*, pp. 109–17. Courcelle also discusses Ambrose's use of *Enn.* 1.6.8 in the *Epistula ad Irenaeum* 29.8 (*PL* 16:1058A).

58. Grace is also stressed in *De fuga saeculi* 1.1 (CSEL 32.2, p. 163).

59. *De Isaac* 8.79 (ed. Schenkl, p. 699.11–17) ends with a reminiscence of *Enn.* 1.7.1–2, while the *De bono mortis* 1.1 (ed. Schenkl, p. 703.1–10) begins with a paraphrase of *Enn.* 1.7.3, thus showing the close relationship between the two treatises.

60. Sapiens enim cum illud divinum requirit, absoluit animam suam corpore et eius ablegat contubernium. . . . (see *Phaedo* 64C). A list of other correspondences to the *Phaedo*, based on Hadot, "Platon et Plotin," pp. 210–20, follows: 3.8–12 (see *Phaedo* 64A–66B passim); 5.16 (see *Phaedo* 82E–83D); 9.38–42 (see *Phaedo* 79CD, 106AB); and 10.45–11.51 (see *Phaedo* 114C, 80D, 63B).

61. *De bono mortis* 4.13–14, using *Enn.* 1.7.3; and 6.25–7.27, employing *Enn.* 1.1.3–4.

62. The three forms of death occur in a number of Ambrosian texts, e.g., *In Luc.* 7.35 (SC 52, p. 21); *De excessu fratris Satyri* 2.36–37 (*PL* 16:1382–83); *De paradiso* 45 (*PL* 14:313). Ambrose appears to have adopted the tripartition from Origen, *Dialogue with Heracleides* 168–70. For more on this theme, see Dassmann, *Die Frömmigkeit*, pp. 181–84.

63. Contendamus ad illud aeternum, ad illud divinum evolemus pinnis dilectionis et remigio caritatis. On the image of the wings of the soul in Ambrose's predecessors, see Adhémer d'Alès, "Les ailes de l'âme," *Ephemerides theologicae lovanienses* 10 (1933): 63–72. On Ambrose's ascent imagery in general, see R. T. Otten, "Caritas and the Ascent Motif in the

Exegetical Works of St. Ambrose," *Studia Patristica*, vol. 8, ed. F. L. Cross, Texte und Untersuchungen 93 (Berlin: Akademie Verlag, 1966), pp. 442–48.

64. *De bono mortis* 5.17–18 (ed. Schenkl, pp. 719–20), a passage close to Ambrose's *Hexaemeron* 6.49 (*PL* 14:277C).

65. Origen (*Against Celsus* 4.39) avers that Plato probably took the myth from Genesis, noting that he had already discussed this in his (now lost) commentary on Genesis. W. Wilbrand was the first to note the Origen connection ("Ambrosius und Platon," *Römische Quartalschrift für christliche Altertumskunde und für Kirchengeschichte* 25 [1911], pp. 44*–46*).

66. See Courcelle, *Recherches*, pp. 120–22.

67. Eo quod anima deo adhaerens in hortum mentis ingressa sit, in quo esset abundantia diversarum virtutum floresque sermonum.

68. Cui anima legitimo quodam conubii foedere copulatur. Ambrose discusses the *copula spiritualis* between Christ and the soul in several places in *De Isaac*, e.g., 6.51; 8.73 (ed. Schenkl, pp. 675.5–8, 692.17–21). For further remarks, see Baus, "Das Nachwirken des Origenes," pp. 41–44.

69. Est etiam ferventioris spiritus sermo, qui inebriat sicut vinum et cor hominis laetificat, est etiam lacteus sermo, purus et candidus.

70. Atque inebriata saeculo dormiebat, vigilabat deo, et ideo, sicut posteriora docent, aperiri sibi deus verbum eius ianuam postulabat, ut eam suo repleret ingressu. On Ambrose's interpretation of Song 5:2–3, see Tajo, "Un confronto tra S. Ambrogio e San Agostino," pp. 138–40.

71. Here Ambrose reaffirms that Plato took his understanding of the myth from the Song.

72. The importance of interiorization, especially the theme of the "inner man," in Ambrose has been studied by Goulven Madec, "L'homme interieur selon saint Ambroise," in *Ambroise de Milan: XVIe centenaire de son élection épiscopale*, ed. Yves-Marie Duval (Paris: Études Augustiniennes, 1974), pp. 283–308. See also Wolfgang Seibel, *Fleisch und Geist beim heiligen Ambrosius* (Munich: Karl Zink, 1958); and P. Courcelle, "Saint Ambroise devant le précepte delphique," in *Forma Futuri: Studi in Onore del Cardinale Michele Pellegrino* (Turin: Bottego d'Erasmo, 1975), pp. 179–88.

There are numerous texts on the ascent to God in the Psalms commentaries, e.g., *Expos. Ps. 118* 14.38 (ed. Petschenig, pp. 323–24). For a survey of texts, see Otten, "Caritas and the Ascent Motif."

Ambrose makes frequent use of the ancient theme of *sobria ebrietas*, which, as we have seen, goes back to Philo. See, e.g., *De Isaac* 5.49; 6.50; the hymn "Splendor paternae gloriae" (*PL* 16:1411); *Expos. Ps. 118* 13.24; 15.28; 21.4; etc.; *De sac.* 5.17. In *Hexaemeron* 3.17.72 (*PL* 14:200A) the believer is described as "mane ergo plantatus in domo domini . . . ut inebrieris in Christo." For a discussion, see Hans Lewy, *SOBRIA EBRIETAS: Untersuchungen zur Geschichte der antiken Mystik*, Beihefte zur *Zeitschrift für die neutestamentliche Wissenschaft* 9 (Giessen: Töpelmann, 1929), pp. 146–57; "Ivresse spirituelle," *DS* 7:2312–37 (2317–18 on Ambrose).

Ambrose's use of the theme of the birth of God in the soul has been studied by Hugo Rahner, "Die Gottesgeburt: Die Lehre der Kirchenväter von der Geburt Christi aus dem Herzen der Kirche und der Gläubigen," in *Symbole der Kirche: Die Ekklesiologie der Väter* (Salzburg: Müller, 1964), pp. 56–59; and Dassmann, *Die Frömmigkeit*, pp. 184–89 (both authors overstress, in my view, a purely moral interpretation). For some representative texts, see *Explan. in Ps.* 47.10 (ed. Petschenig, pp. 353–54); and *Expos. Ps. 118* 12.16 (ed. Petschenig, p. 260).

73. Dassmann emphasizes the moral interpretation of many of these themes (*Die Frömmigkeit*, pp. 183–84, 188, 190–91, 196); but he also allows for a possible mystical dimension (see p. 198).

74. For Ambrose's use of the Song of Songs, see Solange Sagot, "Le 'Cantique des cantiques' dans le 'De Isaac' d'Ambroise de Milan," *Recherches augustiniennes* 16 (1981): 3–57; Dassmann, *Die Frömmigkeit*, pp. 135–214 (chap. 3, "Veni, Sponsa Mea!"); Franca Ela

Consolino, *"VENI HUC A LIBANO:* La *SPONSA* del Cantico dei Cantici come modello per le vergini negli scritti esortatori di Ambrogio," *Athenaeum* n.s. 62 (1984): 399–415; and esp. Friedrich Ohly, *Hohelied-Studien: Grundzüge einer Geschichte der Hoheliedauslegung des Abendlandes bis um 1200* (Wiesbaden: F. Steiner, 1958), pp. 32–46. Ohly (p. 33) says that Ambrose commented on all but about ten verses of the 117 in the Song.

75. E.g., *De instit. virg.* 14.87–88 (*PL* 16:340–41).

76. On the use of the Song in this text, see Dassmann, *Die Frömmigkeit,* pp. 161–64, 171.

77. William of St. Thierry, *Super Cantica Canticorum ex operibus Sancti Ambrosii* (*PL* 15:1849–85). Ohly argues that Ambrose's special mode of reading the Song as the "dramatische Selbstauslegung des Wortes" was not revived until twelfth-century mystical commentators (*Hohelied-Studien,* pp. 43–46).

78. See the list of references in CSEL 62.5, pp. 521–23. For a few representative texts, see *Expos. Ps. 118* 1.4; 1.16; and esp. 6.5–25 (ed. Petschenig, pp. 7, 16, 110–21).

79. Nemo est enim qui copulam vel animae et spiritus vel Christi et ecclesiae non beatam putet. sed quia plenitudo verbi et spiritus sancti vibrat et fulget et nihil est quod ei possit aequari, ideo differe desiderant, ut illa dilatione vel anima vel ecclesia possit esse perfectior.

80. On Christian understandings of Isaac, see Jean Daniélou, "La typologie d'Isaac dans le christianisme primitif," *Biblica* 28 (1947): 363–93 (389–92 on Ambrose).

81. The opening section of *De Isaac* includes a discussion of the soul's nature in 2.3–6 (ed. Schenkl, pp. 643–46). See Madec, *S. Ambroise et la philosophie,* pp. 318–23, for aspects of Ambrose's teaching on the soul.

82. Ergo vel anima patriarchae videns mysterium Christi, videns Rebeccam venientem cum vasis aureis et argenteis tamquam ecclesiam cum populo nationum mirata pulchritudinem verbi et sacramentum eius dicit: osculetur me ab osculis oris sui vel Rebecca videns verum Isaac, verum illud gaudium, veram laetitiam desiderat osculari. See the excellent analysis of Nauroy, "La structure du *De Isaac vel anima,*" pp. 222–26.

83. See *Homilia in Genesim* 10.5 (GCS 29, p. 99.17–23). On the relations between Origen's commentary and Ambrose, see Roberto Palla, "Tema del *Commento* Origeniano *al Cantico dei Cantici* nel *De Isaac* di Ambrogio," *Annali della Scuola Normale Superiore di Pisa* 9 (1979), pp. 570–72.

84. See Origen *Comm. on Song* prol. (GCS 33, p. 75.6–23). Ambrose uses the pattern in *De Isaac* 8.68 (ed. Schenkl, p. 690.8–24); *Expos. Ps. 118* 1.3 (ed. Petschenig, p. 6.11–23); *Explan. in Ps.* 36 1.2 (ed. Petschenig, pp. 70.10–71.26), which notes that the Psalms include all the senses too; and *In Luc.* prol. 2–5 (SC 45, pp. 40–43), according the same privilege to the Gospel (but using a tripartition closer to Cicero's division of the sciences). On this important category in Ambrose's thought, see S. Sagot, "La triple sagesse dans le *De Isaac vel anima:* Essai sur les procédes de composition de saint Ambroise," in *Ambroise de Milan: XVIe centenaire de son élection épiscopale,* pp. 67–114; as well as Dassmann, *Die Frömmigkeit,* pp. 172–73; and Nauroy, "La structure du *De Isaac vel anima,*" pp. 228–36.

85. Primum etenim caritatis impatiens et verbi moras non ferens rogabat, ut oscula mereretur, et meruit desideratum videre, introducta quoque est in cubiculum regis. secundo . . . , et subito verbum ei de medio sermone discessit, quaerenti tamen non diu abfuit, sed saliens super montes et transiliens super colles advenit. . . . tertio . . . , in civitate et foro et plateis quaesitum non repperisset, aliquando orationibus suis gratiaque revocavit, adeo ut etiam propius vocaretur a sponso. quarto, ipsa iam ab eo dormiens excitatur, . . . dum aperit ostium, transivit verbum. . . . This fourfold pattern is emphasized by Dassmann, *Die Frömmigkeit,* pp. 172–80.

86. Et ipsa exivit in verbo eius et per vulnera requisitum, sed vulnera caritatis vix tandem invenit et tenuit, ut postea non amitteret. . . . Although the notion of the wound of love (Song 2:4) appears in Hilary of Poitiers (e.g., *In Ps.* 119.16 in *PL* 9:649–50), it was Ambrose who first made extensive use of this Origenist theme, especially in *Expos. Ps. 118,* e.g., 5.18; 6.6; 6.18; and esp. 15.39 (ed. Petschenig, pp. 90, 111, 117, 351). See also *De Isaac* 4.30 (ed. Schenkl, p. 661).

87. E.g., *De Isaac,* 4.14 (ed. Schenkl, p. 652.20-24). Hadot puts it well: "Ce sermon [*De Isaac*] est, pour l'essentiel, un commentaire du *Cantique des Cantiques* et decrit les mouvements de l'âme qui se rapproche ou s'eloigne du Verbe divin" ("Platon et Plotin," p. 203).

88. E.g., Dassmann, *Die Frömmigkeit,* p. 88; and Nauroy, "La structure du *De Isaac vel anima,*" p. 234.

89. *De mysteriis* 7.35-41 (a purely ecclesial reading), and *De mysteriis* 9.55-58 and *De sacramentis* 2.5-3.17 (passages that mingle the ecclesial and the personal readings).

90. The necessary starting place in baptism for the soul's ascent has been stressed by Otten, "Caritas and the Ascent Motif," pp. 443-44.

91. E.g., *In Luc.* 6.72-73 (SC 45, p. 254); cf. Dassmann, *Die Frömmigkeit,* pp. 170-71.

92. Deinde preces sponsae blanditiasque non spreverit dilecta sibi ubera praedicantis atque in interiora domus eam benignus induxerit, denique tamquam lascivienti ludens amore, quia vellet pertemptare sensus amantis, saepe egressus, ut quaereretur a sponsa, saepe regressus, ut invitaretur ad oscula, adstiterit post parietem, prospexerit per fenetras eminens super retia, ut non totus abesset nec quasi totus intraret et ipse ad se sponsam vocaret, ut veniendi ad se invicem fierent gratiora commercia amorisque vim mutuis adolerent sermonibus. On this passage, see Dassmann, *Die Frömmigkeit,* pp. 146-47.

93. *De obitu Valentiniani* 77 (*PL* 16:1442BC). There is considerable use of the Song in this text, on which see Ohly, *Hohelied-Studien,* pp. 39-41.

94. See Nauroy, "La structure du *De Isaac vel anima,*" p. 235.

95. Dassmann puts it well, despite his tendency to avoid the term mysticism in speaking of Ambrose: "Aus einer uberwiegend philosophisch-ethisch bestimmten Frömmigkeit wird Jesusfrömmigkeit" (*Die Frömmigkeit,* p. 200).

96. See, e.g., *De Isaac* 5.46; 8.72-77 (ed. Schenkl, pp. 670-71, 692-95); *Expos. Ps. 118* 8.7; 22.28-30 (ed. Petschenig, pp. 152-53, 502-4); *In Luc.* 1.7 (SC 45, pp. 49-50); and *De virginitate* 13.77 (*PL* 16:299CD).

97. Brown, *Body and Society,* pp. 342-45.

98. Tunc in utero virgo concepit, et Verbum caro factum est, ut caro fieret Deus. Ambrose's stress on Christ's virgin birth is found throughout his writings, e.g., *In Luc.* 2.43; 2.56-57 (SC 45, pp. 92, 97-98); *Expos. Ps. 118* 6.23 (ed. Petschenig, p. 120); *Explan. in Ps.* 37.5 (ed. Petschenig, pp. 139-40); *De sac.* 53 (SC 25 bis, pp. 186-88).

99. Virgo est ergo quae nupsit, virgo quae nos suo utero portavit, virgo quae genuit, virgo quae proprio lacte nutrivit.

100. Brown, *Body and Society,* pp. 346-47, 353-55, 363-64.

101. E.g., *De Isaac* 2.5; 3.6; *De bono mortis* 3.10; 3.12; 5.16; 6.25; 9.40.

102. This is especially evident in the letter that he wrote to the church at Vercelli about 396 condemning some followers of Jovinian; see *Ep.* 63.7-14, 32-33, 71-74 (*PL* 16:1242-44, 1249-50, 1260-61).

103. See Brown, *Body and Society,* pp. 350-53.

104. For Ambrose on the resurrection of the body, see Dudden, *Ambrose of Milan* 2:665-68.

105. Tolerabilius est mentem virginem quam carnem habere.

106. Virgo est quae Deo nubet; meretrix, quae deos fecit.

107. Quod nobis promittitur, vobis praesto est.

108. In *De Isaac* 7.59 (ed. Schenkl, p. 683) Ambrose applies the notion of *unitas spiritus* to the soul's perfection in itself rather than to its union with the Word, the later standard practice. Elsewhere, he tends to use the language of *copula, iungere,* or *miscere* to describe the union between the Word and the soul, e.g., *De Isaac* 4.14; 5.46; 6.51; 6.72-73; 8.78.

109. On the union of love and knowledge, see, e.g., *Expos. Ps. 118* 12.1 (ed. Petschenig, p. 252); and *De Isaac* 4.23 (ed. Schenkl, p. 657). See also Dassmann, *Die Frömmigkeit,* pp. 199-200. The notion of the presence of the Word appears often in *De Isaac,* e.g., 5.47; 6.53; 7.57; 7.62 (ed. Schenkl, pp. 671.7-672.7, 677.16-20, 681.19-20, 686.17-21).

110. *In Luc.* 7.85-86 (SC 52, pp. 36-37). See Dassmann, *Die Frömmigkeit,* pp. 157-58; and D. Csányi, "OPTIMA PARS: Die Auslegungsgeschichte von Lk. 10, 38-42 bei den

Kirchenvätern der ersten vier Jahrhunderte," *Studia Monastica* 2 (1960), pp. 54–58.

111. E.g., *Explan. in Ps.* 37.27; 40.39 (ed. Petschenig, pp. 156, 256); also *De Spirito Sancto* II.7.66–68 (CSEL 79, pp. 112–13). On this, see Madec, "L'homme interieur," pp. 284–88.

112. Dassmann, *Die Frömmigkeit,* p. 174.

113. The standard biography of Jerome is J. N. D. Kelley, *Jerome: His Life, Writings and Controversies* (New York: Harper & Row, 1975).

114. For an overview of Jerome's translation of the Bible, see Jean Gribomont in *Patrology* 4:221–27. Gribomont also lists the translations of Origen completed by Jerome and Rufinus on pp. 229–30.

115. See, e.g., *Epp.* 14, 22, 53, and 58 (to Paulinus of Nola), 66, 108, 118, 122, 145, etc. The standard edition of Jerome's letters is by I. Hilberg in CSEL 54 in 3 volumes (1910–18).

116. F. Cavallera, "Saint Jerome et la vie parfaite," *Revue d'ascétique et de la mystique* 2 (1921): 101–27 (see p. 105). This is still perhaps the best introduction to Jerome's spirituality. On his views of sex and the body, see chap. 18 of P. Brown's *Body and Society,* pp. 366–86.

117. I would disagree with scholars who have tried to characterize Jerome as a mystic, e.g., Paul Antin, "Saint Jerome Directeur mystique," *Revue d'histoire de la spiritualité* 48 (1972): 25–30.

118. See, e.g., *Ep.* 18, the earliest of Jerome's exegetical letters (ca. 381), which contains an Origenist exposition of the vision found in Isaiah 6.

119. This letter, like many of Jerome's missives, was obviously meant to be a public document. It was written at about the same time that he was translating Origen's *Homilies on the Song* for his ascetic circle. I will cite it according to the text and translation of F. A. Wright based on Hilberg's text and found in *St. Jerome: Select Letters,* trans. by F. A. Wright, LC (Cambridge, MA: Harvard University Press, 1980), pp. 52–158. For background, see Kelley, *Jerome,* chap. 10, pp. 91–103.

120. Laudo nuptias, laudo coniugium, sed quia mihi virgines generant. For Jerome's attitude toward the flesh, see the revealing comment in *Ep.* 84.8.

121. . . . [c]arne contempta sponsi iungaris amplexibus. Later (*Ep.* 22.21) Jerome says that since Christ's birth from a virgin the gift of virginity has been poured out more abundantly on women than on men. On Jerome's changing ideas about the relations between the sexes, see P. Brown, who argues for an Origenist a-sexual view of male–female adepts at this stage in Jerome's career (*Body and Society,* pp. 368–71), and a more rigidly defined sexual view after the break with Origen (pp. 381–84).

122. Semper te cubiculi tui secreta custodiant, semper tecum sponsus ludat te intrinsecus. Oras: loqueris ad sponsum; legis: ille tibi loquitur, et, cum te somnus oppresserit, veniet post parietem et mittet manum suam per foramen et tanget ventrem tuum, et tremefacta consurges et dices: "Vulnerata caritatis ego sum." . . .

123. Amemus et nos Christum, semper eius quaeramus amplexus, et facile videbitur omne difficile. The passage continues with a reference to the wound of love (*iaculo illius vulnerati*) reminiscent of Origen's use of Isa 49:2.

124. Sulpicius Severus, *Vita Martini* 26.4 (SC 133, p. 314).

125. E.g., Paulinus of Nola, *Ep.* 28 (*PL* 61:308–12).

126. This commentary, which includes both an ecclesial and a more personal reading, was written ca. 398–404 and sometimes circulated under Jerome's name. It has recently been edited by B. de Vregille and L. Neyrans in CC 19 (Turnhout: Brepols, 1986).

127. Concerning Cassian, see especially the excellent article of Michel Olphe-Galliard, "Cassien (Jean)," *DS* 2:214–76, summarizing a number of earlier studies. See also Owen Chadwick, *John Cassian: A Study in Primitive Monasticism* (Cambridge: Cambridge University Press, 1950), an interesting though at times prejudiced study; and more recently, Philip Rousseau, *Ascetics, Authority and the Church in the Age of Jerome and Cassian* (Oxford: Oxford University Press, 1978).

128. Cassian's major works will be cited according to the editions found in the SC. For the *Conlationes,* see *Jean Cassien: Conférences,* ed. E. Pichery, SC 42, 54, 64 (Paris: Cerf,

1955–59). They will be cited according to conference and chapter number with the volume and page number in parentheses, e.g., *Conl.* 4.2 (1:168). Several partial translations of the *Conferences* exist, but I have preferred to make my own. The *Institutes* will be cited according to *Jean Cassien: Institutions Coenobitiques*, ed. J.-C. Guy, SC 109 (Paris: Cerf, 1965). Cassian's other work was a treatise in seven books, *De incarnatione Domini contra Nestorium*, written at the request of his friend the deacon Leo, later Pope Leo I.

129. O. Chadwick characterizes the monk's contribution thus: "Cassian bequeathed to Latin Christianity the idea that the spiritual life was a science in which prayer reigned: that it was possible to analyse temptations and the nature of sin: that the methods of prayers and mortification were neither haphazard nor individual, but ordered according to established experience" (*Cassian*, p. 18).

130. See Jacques Fontaine, "The Practice of Christian Life: The Birth of the Laity," in *Christian Spirituality: Origins to Twelfth Century*, pp. 453–91.

131. On the role of perfection in Cassian's works, see "Perfection chrétienne," *DS* 12:1111–13. For his attitude toward the laity, see *DS* 2:231; and toward the church in general, A. de Vogüe, "Monachisme et Église dans la pensée de Cassien," in *Théologie de la vie monastique* (Paris: Aubier, 1961), pp. 213–40. In *Conl.* 14.7 Cassian tellingly includes the story of a layman who surpassed the holy Abba John in sanctity, but only because he lived as a monk (i.e., in chastity with his wife).

132. Peter Munz, in an idiosyncratic article, has stressed this point ("John Cassian," *Journal of Ecclesiastical History* 1 [1960], p. 20).

133. E.g., M. Olphe-Galliard describes him as "un excellent vulgarisateur" (*DS* 2:225).

134. The connection between Cassian and Evagrius has been studied by Salvatore Marsili, *Giovanni Cassiano ed Evagrio Pontico: Dottrina sulla carità e contemplazione*, Studia Anselmiana 5 (Rome: Herder, 1936). He collects fifty-one passages in Cassian that show close affinities with Evagrian texts (pp. 87–103), and studies seven areas of mutual influence (pp. 103–49). Despite the criticism of some reviewers (e.g., B. Capelle, in *Revue d'histoire écclesiastique* 35 [1939], p. 554), Marsili's conclusions have been generally accepted.

135. Marsili studies some textual parallels (not all convincing) between Origen and Cassian (*Giovanni Cassiano*, pp. 150–58).

136. O. Chadwick, *John Cassian*, pp. 87–88.

137. See A. de Vogüe, "Pour comprendre Cassien: Un survol des Conférences," *Collectanea Cisterciensia* 39 (1977): 250–72.

138. See chapter 5, pp. 144–57.

139. *Spiritalis* is one of Cassian's favorite words. He speaks of *spiritalis vita* (e.g., *Conl.* 16.5; 17.2, 5; *Instit.* 12.27); *spiritalis profectus* (*Instit.* 10.6); and *spiritalis agon*, or *certamen* (e.g., *Conl.* 2.11; *Instit.* 5.21; 11.19). *Mysticus* is less frequently used, almost always traditionally, that is, relating to the deeper sense of scripture, e.g., *Conl.* 4.6; 7.5; 22.5; 24.1; *Instit.* 3.9; 7.15.

140. . . . [p]rima *praktike*, id est actualis, quae emendatione morum et vitiorum purgatione perficitur: altera *theoretike*, quae in contemplatione divinarum rerum et sacratissimorum sensuum cognitione consistit. For an extensive introduction to Cassian based on this division, see Olphe-Galliard, "Cassien (Jean)," *DS* 2:235–66.

141. *Conl.* 8 (1:188–217) gives the general theory, while *Instit.* 5–12 provides detailed descriptions of each sin. As simplified by Gregory the Great into the seven deadly sins, this aspect of desert moral practice was to have a remarkable history. For an introduction, see Morton Bloomfield, *The Seven Deadly Sins* (East Lansing: Michigan State University Press, 1952); and "Péchés capitaux," *DS* 12:853–62.

142. On Cassian's treatment of humanity as the *imago et similitudo Dei*, see Olphe-Galliard, "Cassien (Jean)," *DS* 2:227–29.

143. See *Conl.* 2. On the role of discernment in Cassian, see Joseph Lienhard, "On 'Discernment of Spirits' in the Early Church," *Theological Studies* 41 (1980), pp. 525–26.

144. On *caritas* in Cassian, see Marsili, *Giovanni Cassiano*, pp. 6–73. On *puritas cordis* there is a large literature. The background is surveyed in J. Raasch, "The Monastic Concept of

Purity of Heart and its Sources," *Studia Monastica* 8 (1966): 7–33 and 183–213; 10 (1968): 7–55; 11 (1969): 269–314; and 12 (1970): 7–41. More useful for Cassian are O. Chadwick, *John Cassian,* pp. 91–93; Olphe-Galliard, "Cassien (Jean)," *DS* 2:247–49; and Nicholas Groves, "*Mundicia cordis:* A Study of the Theme of Purity of Heart in Hugh of Pontigny and the Fathers of the Undivided Church," in *One Yet Two: Monastic Traditions East and West,* ed. M. Basil Pennington (Kalamazoo, MI: Cistercian Publications, 1976), pp. 304–31 (pp. 314–18 on Cassian).

145. Finis quidem nostrae professionis ut diximus regnum dei seu regnum caelorum est, destinatio vero, id est scopos, puritas cordis, sine qua ad illum finem inpossibile est quempiam pervenire. See the whole discussion in *Conl.* 1.2–5 (1:79–83); cf. *Instit.* 5.15 (ed. Guy, p. 214).

146. See the discussion and texts assembled by Marsili, *Giovanni Cassiano,* pp. 38–41, 93.

147. On Evagrius's teaching, see chapter 5, pp. 148–49.

148. O. Chadwick considers *puritas cordis* to be the negative side of *caritas* (*John Cassian,* p. 95), while Munz argues that they are successive ("John Cassian," pp. 6–7). Cassian seems to have aspects of both views.

149. Pullulatione virtutum puritas cordis adquiritur. Puritate cordis apostolicae caritatis perfectio possidetur. Perfect purity of heart entails absolute chastity (see the strange story in *Conl.* 15.10), as well as forgetfulness of past sins (*Conl.* 20.7). For a more Evagrian characterization of *puritas cordis* as "inperturbatae mentis constantiam et inmobilem patientiae . . . firmitatem," see *Conl.* 19.11 (3:48).

150. . . . [a]d illas invisibiles theorias caelestesque perducet atque ad illum ineffabilem ac perpaucis expertum provehet orationis ardorem.

151. On the relation of union, charity, and contemplation, see Marsili, *Giovanni Cassiano,* pp. 41, 65–73, and such texts as *Conl.* 1.8; 10.6–7; 11.6; 18.8.

152. Theoretike vero in duas dividitur partes, id est in historicam interpretationem et intelligentiam spiritalem. . . . Spiritalis autem scientiae genera sunt tria, tropologia, allegoria, anagoge. . . .

153. Compare this with the text on praying the Psalms as if we were their authors in *Conl.* 10.11 (see below n. 172).

154. Prima est qua corporaliter universas divitias mundi facultatesque contemnimus, secunda qua mores ac vitia affectusque pristinos animi carnisque respuimus, tertia qua mentem nostram de praesentibus universis ac visibilibus evocantes futura tantummodo contemplamur et ea quae sunt invisibilia concupiscimus. On these renunciations, see Olphe-Galliard, "Cassien (Jean)," *DS* 2:256–57. Marsili discusses the sources in Evagrius (*Giovanni Cassiano,* pp. 95–96, 116–21).

155. Use of the Song in an erotic sense is rare, but see *Conl.* 6.10 (1:232), where Song 2:6 indicates the soul's union with Christ, and *Conl.* 3.12 and *Instit.* 5.18. *Conl.* 16.14 (2:233–34) discusses the *ordo caritatis* of Song 2:4 LXX.

156. Initium voluntatis bonae nobis domino inspirante concedi. . . . Cf. *Conl.* 3.15 and 13.3.

157. . . . [l]aborantibus tantum ac desudantibus. Cf. *Conl.* 13.17–18. On this conference, see O. Chadwick, *John Cassian,* pp. 126–34.

158. For Evagrius's teaching on prayer, see above, chapter 5, pp. 150–57. Marsili studies Cassian's use of Evagrius on prayer (*Giovanni Cassiano,* pp. 145–49) For Cassian's doctrine, see "Prière III. Dans la tradition chrétienne," *DS* 12:2266–69; O. Chadwick, *John Cassian,* pp. 141–48; and especially Columba Stewart, "John Cassian on Unceasing Prayer," *Monastic Studies* 15 (1984): 159–76. For an excellent overview, see Kilian McDonnell, "Prayer in the Ancient Western Tradition," *Worship* 55 (1981): 34–61.

159. *Conl.* 9.1 (2:40): Omnis monachi finis cordisque perfectio ad iugem atque indisruptam orationis perseverantiam tendit.

160. Stewart has analyzed their structure and I have profited from his description ("John Cassian on Unceasing Prayer," pp. 163–73).

161. Vel glorificatum et in majestatis suae gloria venientem internis obtutibus animae pervideri.

162. Tunc enim perfecte consummabitur in nobis illa nostri salvatoris oratio, qua pro suis discipulis oravit ad patrem dicens: ut dilectio qua dilexisti me in eis sit et ipsi in nobis, et iterum, ut omnes unum sint, sicut tu pater in me et ego in te, ut et ipsi in nobis unum sint, quando illa dei perfecta dilectio, qua prior nos ille dilexit, in nostri quoque transierit cordis affectum. . . . [i]llaque unitas quae nunc est patris cum filio et filii cum patre in nostrum fuerit sensum mentemque transfusa. . . . G. Marsili has shown the dependence of this text on Origen's *De prin.* 3.6.3 (*Giovanni Cassiano*, pp. 155–56).

163. See Stewart, "John Cassian on Unceasing Prayer," p. 166.

164. *Conl.* 4.2–3 discusses three roots of distraction in prayer.

165. *Conl.* 9.15 (2:52–53).

166. Such prayer, termed *monologistos* (single-formulated), was well known in the East, where it eventually gave rise to the Jesus-Prayer. See Adalbert de Vogüe, "De Jean Cassien à John Main: Réflexions sur la méditation chrétienne," *Collectanea Cisterciensia* 47 (1985): 179–81.

167. . . . [f]erventissimas saepissime novimus preces ignitasque prodire . . . in modum cuiusdam incomprehensibilis ac rapacissimae flammae. . . .

168. . . . [i]gneam ac perpaucis cognitam vel expertam, immo ut proprius dixerim ineffabilem orationem. . . .

169. The notion of *excessus mentis,* which Cassian, like his contemporaries, found in scripture (e.g., Pss 30:23; 67:28; Acts 10:10; 11:5), is found in other places in his writings, e.g., *Conl.* 4.5; 12.12; and the passages from *Conl.* 19 discussed below. See also *Instit.* 2.10.1–2; 3.3.4; 3.3.7. See the remarks in McDonnell, "Prayer," p. 60; and "Extase," in *DS* 4:2109–10. M. Olphe-Galliard in "Cassien (Jean)," *DS* 2:264 seems to me to limit *excessus* too much by saying that it is purely the result of a process of internalization. On the relation of *oratio ignita* and *excessus,* see Marsili, *Giovanni Cassiano,* pp. 33–37.

170. O. Chadwick uses the brevity of the prayer to indicate that we are not dealing with mystical states properly (judging on the basis apparently of the teaching of the Spanish mystics), but such brevity of higher experiences was the standard teaching among the classic medieval mystics, such as Gregory and Bernard (*John Cassian,* pp. 141–47).

171. . . . [n]on est, inquit [Antony], perfecta oratio, in qua se monachus vel hoc ipsum quod orat intellegat.

172. Eundem namque recipientes cordis affectum, quo quisque decantatus vel conscriptus est psalmus, velut auctores eius facti praecedemus magis intellectum ipsius quam sequemur. . . .

173. See chapter 4, pp. 111–12.

174. . . . [q]uae non solum nullius imaginis occupatur intuitu, sed etiam nulla vocis, nulla verborum prosecutione distinguitur, ignita vero mentis intentione per ineffabilem cordis excessum inexplebili spiritus alacritate profertur, quamque mens extra omnes sensus ac visibiles effecta materies gemitibus inenarrabilibus atque suspiriis profundit ad deum. The final section of the twin conferences (9.28–36; 10.12–14) deal with more practical considerations concerning prayer and will not be taken up here.

175. *Conl.* 19.4 (3:41): Itaque pio domini nostri munere memini me in huiusmodi raptum frequenter excessum. . . . The term *excessus* characterized as *caelestis* and *spiritalis* occurs three more times in John's account in 19.4–5 (3:41–43).

176. . . . [i]gnem illum divinae contemplationis frigere fecisset . . . quod mihi de illa theoretica sublimitate subtrahitur, hac oboedientiae subiectione pensetur.

177. Heremitae vero perfectio est exutam mentem a cunctis habere terrenis eamque, quantum humana inbeccilitas valet, sic unire cum Christo.

178. For some important uses, see, e.g., *Conl.* 1.8 (citing the Mary–Martha paradigm); 1.13; 1.15 (an important text on the various kinds of contemplation); 3.7; 14.9; 23.5, 19; and

Instit. 8.16; 10.3; 11.8. For Cassian's use of Mary and Martha from Luke 10, see Csányi, "OPTIMA PARS," pp. 59–64.

179. Una ergo est theoria, id est contemplatio dei, cuius merito omnia justificationum merita, universa virtutum studia postponuntur. (This passage goes on to refer to Mary and Martha of Luke 10:41–42.)

180. On *visio dei* and *intuitus dei* in Cassian, see, e.g., *Conl.* 1.10; 1.14–15; 5.6; 12.13; 14.9, etc.; also *Instit.* 6.16–17. For the vocabulary and its roots in Evagrius, see Marsili, *Giovanni Cassiano,* pp. 61–65, 93, and 107.

181. See Marsili, *Giovanni Cassiano,* pp. 121–26. The text considered here from *Conl.* 9.18 is close to Evagrius *Prayer* 54 (see Marsili, *Giovanni Cassiano,* p. 99).

182. Rousseau, *Ascetics, Authority and the Church,* pp. 177–82; and idem, "Cassian, Contemplation and the Coenobitic Life," *Journal of Ecclesiastical History* 26 (1975): 113–26.

183. Et est inter alterutrum reciproca et quaedam inseparabilisque conjunctio. Cf. *Instit.* 2.14.

184. While Cassian does not have a highly developed doctrine regarding union, it is a mistake to say (as I once did) that "he does not dwell on union with God." See B. McGinn, "Love, Knowledge and *Unio mystica* in the Western Christian Tradition," in *Mystical Union and Monotheistic Faith,* p. 62. On union with God in Cassian, see "Cassien (Jean)," *DS* 2:228–29, 233, 265; and Marsili, *Giovanni Cassiano,* pp. 65–73.

185. O. Chadwick, *John Cassian,* p. 139.

186. M. Olphe-Galliard wants to see him as propounding "une mystique intellectualiste," presumably like Origen and Evagrius, but this does not account for Cassian's restricted speculative interests and the changes he made in his sources ("Cassien [Jean]," *DS* 2:225–29). Munz views him as a self-naughting mystic, in an Eckhartian (almost Buddhist) mode — surely a misconstrual ("John Cassian," pp. 6–7).

187. C. Butler, *Western Mysticism: The Teaching of Saints Augustine, Gregory and Bernard on Contemplation and the Contemplative Life* (New York: Dutton, 1923), p. 190.

188. . . . [d]e profundissimo quaestionum pelago cumbam conlationis huiusce ad tutissimum silentii portum conpendium nostrae rusticitatis adtraxit. In quo quidem profundo quanto nos interius divini spiritus introduxerit flatus, tanto diffusior praecedens oculorum aciem semper aperietur immensitas.

Chapter 7

An early version of this chapter was presented as a Master's Theme at the International Patristic Conference at Oxford in 1987. I have profited from several suggestions received then, but special thanks are due to J. Patout Burns, who read the paper with care and offered numerous helpful comments.

1. The best biography of Augustine remains Peter Brown's *Augustine of Hippo: A Biography* (Berkeley: University of California Press, 1967). The literature on Augustine is immense. Some helpful bibliographies are T. van Bavel and F. van der Zande, *Répertoire bibliographique de Saint Augustin, 1950–60* (The Hague: Nijhoff, 1963); and Carl Andresen, *Bibliographia Augustiniana* (Darmstadt: Wissenschaftliche Buchgesellschaft, 1973). More recent bibliographical materials can be gleaned from the annual lists published in the *Revue des études augustiniennes.* Two recent major scholarly tools for research on Augustine are the *Augustinus-Lexikon,* ed. Cornelius Mayer et al. (Basel: Schwabe, 1986–), and the *Thesaurus Augustinianus* (Turnhout: CEDOC [Brepols], 1988).

2. For a recent introduction to Augustine's writings, see Agostino Trapé, "VI. Saint Augustine," in Johannes Quasten, *Patrology,* 4 vols. (Westminster: Christian Classics, 1983–86) 4:342–462. The best listing of editions is that found in the *Clavis Patrum Latinorum: Editio altera,* ed. E. Dekkers and E. Gaar (The Hague: Nijhoff, 1961). I will cite all works of Augustine in the most readily available edition, the Maurist text found in *PL* 32–47. All translations are my own unless otherwise noted.

3. The *Enarrationes in Psalmos* are found in *PL* 36–37. For a chart indicating one system of the dating of these sermons, see *St. Augustine on the Psalms,* translated and annotated by Dame Scholastica Hebgin and Dame Felicitas Corrigan, ACW 29 (Westminster: Newman, 1960), pp. 17–19. On the chronology of Augustine's writings, see Anne-Marie La Bonnardière, *Recherches de chronologie augustinienne* (Paris: Études Augustiniennes, 1965). There is no complete translation of this work into English, the fullest being that found in *NPNF,* First Series, Vol. 8.

4. The *De Trinitate* may be found in *PL* 42:819–1098. There is a good English version, *Saint Augustine: The Trinity,* trans. Stephen McKenna, FC 45 (Washington: Catholic University, 1963). Considerable dispute still exists about aspects of the dating of the work, on which see Robert J. O'Connell, *The Origin of the Soul in Augustine's Later Works* (New York: Fordham University, 1987), Introduction.

5. *In Johannis Evangelium Tractatus CXXIV* is in *PL* 35:1379–1976. There is an English translation in *NPNF,* First Series, Vol. 7.

6. The commentary on 1 John, *In Epistolam Joannis ad Parthos Tractatus Decem,* is in *PL* 35:1977–2062. For a translation, see *Augustine: Later Works,* ed. John Burnaby (Philadelphia: Westminster, 1955), pp. 251–348.

7. *De Genesi ad litteram* is in *PL* 34:245–486. See the excellent annotated translation, *St. Augustine: The Literal Meaning of Genesis,* by John Hammond Taylor, ACW 41–42 (New York: Paulist, 1982). The *De civitate Dei* (of which there are numerous translations) is in *PL* 41:13–804.

8. A. Mandouze, "Où en est la question de la mystique augustinienne?" *Augustinus Magister* (3 vols.; Paris: L'Année théologique augustinienne, 1954) 3:103–68.

9. Ephraem Hendrikx, *Augustins Verhältnis zur Mystik* (Würzburg: Augustinus Verlag, 1936), p. 176. Earlier, Dean Inge had denied that Augustine should be called a mystic (*Christian Mysticism* [London: Methuen, 1899], p. 128). Similar judgments can be found in M. Heim, *Der Enthusiasmus in den Konfessionen des hl. Augustins* (Würzburg: Augustinus Verlag, 1941); R. Lorenz, "Fruitio Dei bei Augustin," *Zeitschrift für Kirchengeschichte* 63 (1950–51): 75–132; Hans Meyer, "War Augustin Intellektualist oder Mystiker?" *Augustinus Magister* 3:429–37.

10. G. Bonner, "Augustine's Conception of Deification," *Journal of Theological Studies* n.s. 37 (1986), p. 382.

11. Mandouze, "Où en est la question?" p. 153.

12. H. Meyer as quoted in Mandouze, "Où en est la question?" p. 166.

13. E. Hendrikx, "Augustins Verhältnis zur Mystik: Ein Rückblick," in *Scientia Augustiniana: Festschrift Adolar Zumkeller* (Würzburg: Augustinus Verlag, 1975), pp. 107–111.

14. Cuthbert Butler, *Western Mysticism: The Teaching of Saints Augustine, Gregory and Bernard on Contemplation and the Contemplative Life* (New York: Dutton, 1923), p. 62. John Burnaby in *Amor Dei: A Study of the Religion of St. Augustine* (London: Stoddard & Houghton, 1938), also made considerable use of the language of union in describing Augustine's mysticism without noting the important distinction between what is possible in this life and what will take place in that to come (cf. pp. 176–77, 179, 314).

15. F. Cayré, *La contemplation augustinienne: Principes de spiritualité et de théologie* (2nd ed.; Paris: Desclée, 1954). For some examples of this problematic approach, see pp. 117, 121, 125, 248, and 267. A similar anachronism can be found in other studies devoted to Augustine's mysticism, e.g., E. I. Watkin, "The Mysticism of St. Augustine," in *St. Augustine: His Life and Thought* (Cleveland and New York: Meridian, 1957), pp. 105–19; and Gerald Bonner, "The Spirituality of St. Augustine and its influence on Western mysticism," *Sobornost* 4 (1982), p. 153.

16. Butler, *Western Mysticism,* p. 24; Burnaby, *Amor Dei,* p. 23. More recently Henry Chadwick has claimed, "The aspirations of all western mystics have never escaped his influence, above all because of the centrality of the love of God in his thinking" (*Augustine* [Oxford: Oxford University Press, 1986], p. 2). Among recent studies of Augustine's

mysticism in English, note Rowan Williams, *Christian Spirituality* (Atlanta: John Knox, 1979), chap. 4; and Andrew Louth, *The Origins of the Christian Mystical Tradition* (Oxford: Clarendon, 1981), chap. 7; David N. Bell, *The Image and Likeness: The Augustinian Spirituality of William of St. Thierry* (Kalamazoo, MI: Cistercian Publications, 1984), chaps. 1 and 2; Bonner, "The Spirituality of St. Augustine"; Eugene Teselle, "Augustine," in *An Introduction to the Medieval Mystics of Europe,* ed. Paul Szarmach (Albany: SUNY, 1984), pp. 19-35; A. Trapé, "Saint Augustine: Spiritual Doctrine," in *Patrology* 4:453-62; and Vittorino Grossi, "La spiritualità agostiniana," *Le grandi scuole della spiritualità cristiana* (Rome: Teresianum, 1984), pp. 159-206.

17. Among the most helpful general books on Augustine's thought are Etienne Gilson, *The Christian Philosophy of St. Augustine* (New York: Random House, 1960); and E. Teselle, *Augustine the Theologian* (New York: Herder & Herder, 1970).

18. For Augustine as a monastic figure, see Adolar Zumkeller, *Augustine's Ideal of the Religious Life* (New York: Fordham University Press, 1986); and George Lawless, *Augustine of Hippo and His Monastic Rule* (Oxford: Clarendon, 1987).

19. Dominus enim spiritus est, unde qui adhaeret Domino unus spiritus est. Proinde qui potest Deum invisibiliter videre, ipse Deo potest incorporaliter adhaerere.

20. Cayré identifies the vision of God with contemplation (*La contemplation augustinienne,* p. 133), which is in turn defined as the act through which we recognize God present in the gift of *sapientia* (p. 269). On the role of *sapientia* in Augustine, see Goulven Madec, "Christus, scientia et sapientia nostra: Le principe de cohérence de la doctrine augustinienne," *Recherches augustiniennes* 10 (1975): 77-85.

21. Robert J. O'Connell, S.J., *St. Augustine's Early Theory of Man, A.D. 386-391* (Cambridge, MA: Belknap Press, 1968), p. 205.

22. For an overview of the older debates over Augustine's relation to Neoplatonism, see John J. O'Meara, "Augustine and Neoplatonism," *Recherches augustiniennes* 1 (1958): 91-111. Since the 1950s extensive research by P. Courcelle, P. Hadot, A. Mandouze, J. O'Meara, R. J. O'Connell, and others has demonstrated Augustine's extensive knowledge of Plotinus (certainly *Enn.* 1.6; 4.3-5; 5.1; 5.8; 6.4-5), and also Porphyry. At least part of this acquaintance was mediated through Ambrose.

23. Among the many studies of these famous texts (*PL* 32:742-47), see Paul Henry, *La vision d'Ostie: Sa place dans la vie et l'oeuvre de Saint Augustin* (Paris: Vrin, 1938); Eng. version, *The Path to Transcendence: From Philosophy to Mysticism in Saint Augustine,* trans. Francis F. Burch (Philadelphia: Pickwick Press, 1981), pp. 82-97; Pierre Courcelle, *Recherches sur les Confessions de Saint Augustin* (Paris: Boccard, 1950), pp. 157-67; and O'Connell, *Augustine's Early Theory of Man,* pp. 43-51, 205-23. There is a detailed comparison of the Milan and Ostia experiences in André Mandouze, *Saint Augustin: L'aventure de la raison et de la grace* (Paris: Études Augustiniennes, 1968), pp. 684-99. For a comparison of this and other ascent texts in Augustine and their relation to Plotinus, see Suzanne Poque, "L'expression de l'anabase plotinienne dans la prédication de saint Augustin et ses sources," *Recherches augustiniennes* 10 (1975): 187-215. A contemporary witness to the Milan experience may be found in *Ep.* 4.2 (*PL* 33:66), written to Nebridius from Cassiciacum in 387.

24. Et inde admonitus redire ad memetipsum, intravi in intima mea, duce te; et potui, quoniam factus es adjutor meus. Intravi, et vidi qualicumque oculo animae meae, supra eumdem oculum animae meae, supra mentem meam, lucem incommutabilem. . . . Qui novit veritatem, novit eam; et qui novit eam, novit aeternitatem. Charitas novit eam. O aeterna veritas, et vera charitas, et chara aeternitas! tu es Deus meus; tibi suspiro die ac nocte. . . . Et reverberasti infirmitatem aspectus mei, radians in me vehementer, et contremui amore et horrore; et inveni longe me esse a te in regione dissimilitudinis. . . .

25. *Enn.* 1.6, a text certainly known by Augustine, is a clear presentation of the triple pattern. In addition, investigators have detected the influence of numerous other key Plotinian texts on this section of the *Conf.,* e.g., 5.3; 5.8; 6.4-5; 6.9. On the importance of the triple pattern in Augustine, see Poque, "L'expression de l'anabase plotinienne"; and

Vernon J. Burke, "Augustine of Hippo: The Approach of the Soul to God," in *The Spirituality of Western Christendom,* ed. E. Rozanne Elder (Kalamazoo, MI: Cistercian Publications, 1976), pp. 6–9.

26. See the comment by Mandouze, *Saint Augustin: L'aventure,* p. 503: "Et c'est ainsi qu'Augustin converti Platon, et non l'inverse."

27. Et reverberasti infirmitatem aspectus mei (7.10.16); sed aciem figere non evalui, et repercussa infirmitate redditus solitis (7.17.23); et repulsus sensi quid per tenebras animae meae contemplari non sinerer (7.20.26). Most recently, see Thomas Finan, "A Mystic in Milan. *'Reverberasti Revisited,'"* in *From Augustine to Eriugena: Essays on Neoplatonism and Christianity in Honor of John O'Meara,* ed. F. X. Martin and J. A. Richmond (Washington, DC: Catholic University Press, 1991), pp. 77–91.

28. Much has been written on the famous *regio dissimilitudinis;* for a bibliography, see B. McGinn, *The Golden Chain* (Washington: Cistercian Publications, 1972), pp. 133–34 n. 132.

29. Bonner, "Spirituality of St. Augustine," p. 148. On the objects of vision in these passages, see O'Connell, *Augustine's Early Theory of Man,* pp. 210–17.

30. A. Mandouze identifies fourteen biblical references in the text and no fewer than twenty-one Plotinian ones ("L'extase d'Ostie," in *Augustinus Magister* 1:67–84).

31. Henry, *Path to Transcendence,* chaps. 2–6, and the debate over his views summarized in Mandouze, "Où en est la question?" pp. 113–17. Also see Courcelle, *Recherches sur les Confessions,* pp. 222–26; Teselle, "Augustine," pp. 20–22; and Louth, *Origins,* pp. 134–41.

32. *Conf.* 9.10.26 *(PL* 32:775): Dicebam talia etsi non isto modo et his verbis.

33. The shared, communal nature of sin (both original and personal) and of the process of conversion and ascent to God portrayed in the *Confessions* is frequently presented under "garden" symbols that cannot help but recall the happiness and subsequent guilt of Adam and Eve (e.g., *Conf.* 2.4.9–2.10.18, the pear tree incident; and 8.8.19–8.12.30, the conversion scene). For some reflections on this, see Robert J. O'Connell, *St. Augustine's Confessions: The Odyssey of a Soul* (Cambridge, MA: Belknap Press, 1969), pp. 115–19.

34. For the church as the walled garden of Song 4:12, see *De baptismo* 5.27; 6.29; 7.51. I owe this suggestion to J. Patout Burns.

35. In the first account: (1) perambulavimus gradatim cuncta corporalia; (2) et adhuc ascendebamus interius cogitando; (3) et venimus in mentes nostras et transcendimus eas. In the second account: (1) the continued repetition of the "silencing" of all created reality (si cui sileat tumultus carnis, etc.); (2) et ipsa anima sileat; (3) et transeat se non se cogitando.

36. For these reasons I tend to doubt those investigators who see no real difference between the accounts in *Conf.* 7 and 9, e.g., Mandouze, *Saint Augustin: L'aventure,* p. 697.

37. Metaphors of touching are found in both accounts: (1) attingeremus regionem ubertatis indeficientis, . . . attigimus eum (9.10.24); (2) attigimus aeternam Sapientiam (9.10.25). Metaphors of hearing are implied in the first account by the return to human words from the soundless Word of God, and explicit in the second account through the stress on the necessity for the silence of all creation: ut audiamus verbum eius (9.10.26).

38. On the affectivity of the Ostia account, see Williams, *Christian Spirituality,* p. 74.

39. The precise meaning of *ictus* ("blow, beat, effort") in this context has been discussed in the secondary literature; see, e.g., Mandouze, "L'extase d'Ostie," p. 73 n. 3; Teselle, "Augustine," p. 332 n. 18.

40. Vocasti, et clamasti, et rupisti surdidatem meam [auditory images]. Corucasti, splenduisti, et fugasti caecitatem meam [visual images]. Fragasti, et duxi spiritum, et anhelo tibi [olfactory images]. Gustavi, et esurio, et sitio [tasting images]. Tetigisti me, et exarsi in pacem tuam [tactile images].

41. Et aliquando intromittis me in affectum multum inusitatum introrsus ad nescio quam dulcedinem, quae si perficiatur in me, nescio quid erit quod vita ista non erit. Sed recido in haec aerumnosis ponderibus, et resorbeor solitis, et teneor, et multum fleo, sed multum teneor. It might also be argued, though with more difficulty, that a passage in book 11.9.11

referring to action of *Sapientia* also describes such an experience.

42. *De quantitate animae* 33.76 (*PL* 32:1076–77). On this text, see Cayré, *La contemplation augustinienne,* pp. 69–74.

43. *De quan. an.* 33.76 (*PL* 32:1077): Tanta autem in contemplanda veritate voluptas est, quantacumque ex parte eam quisque contemplari potest.

44. See the comments on the *Soliloquies* 1.7.14 in *Retractationes* 1.4.3 (*PL* 32:590). On this change, see Cayré, *La contemplation augustinienne,* pp. 48–51, 135–36. Texts like *De consensu evangelistarum* 4.10.20 (ca. 400) declare that all experience of divine light in this life is transitory; and *De Trin.* 4.15.20 attacks Platonic pretensions of auto-salvation. For Augustine's later views on the Platonists, see *De civ. Dei* 8.4–12; 10.23–32.

45. For some illustrative texts, see *De libero arbitrio* 2.16.42 (*PL* 32:1264); *De ordine* 2.20.51 (*PL* 32:1019); *De sermone Domini in monte* 1.3.10 (*PL* 34:1233–34); *Contra Faustum* 12.42; 22.52–58 (*PL* 42:276–77, 432–37); *De consensu evangelistarum* 1.5 (*PL* 34:1046); and *Sermo* 7.7 (*PL* 38:66).

46. See *Sermo* 52.6.16–17 (*PL* 38:360–61). The key text begins: Et forte verba quisquam nostrum, cui fulgor veritatis aliqua mentem quasi coruscatione perstringit, potest dicere verba illa: 'Ego dixi in ecstasi mea.' See Mandouze, *Saint Augustin: L'aventure,* pp. 659–61; and Poque, "L'expression de l'anabase," pp. 191–92.

47. *Sermo* 52.6.16 (*PL* 38:360): . . . pervenisse spirituali quodam contactu ad illam incommutabilem lucem, eamque infirmitatem conspectus ferre non valuisse.

48. *Sermo* 52.6.17 (*PL* 38:361): De Trinitate ineffabilis Majestatis loquebaris; et quia defecisti in divinis, tuamque infirmitatem debita humilitate confessus es, ad humana venisti; ibi discute. For a treatment of this text, see Bell, *Image and Likeness,* pp. 44–46.

49. *Sermo* 52.6.16 (*PL* 38:360): Quid ergo dicamus, fratres, de Deo? Si enim quod vis dicere, si cepisti, non est Deus: si comprehendere potuisti, aliud pro Deo comprehendisti. . . . Hoc ergo non est, si comprehendisti; si autem hoc est, non comprehendisti. For similar texts, see *De Trin.* 5.3.4; 7.4.7; *Sermo* 122.5; *Ep.* 120.3.13. As early as *De doct. christ.* 1.6.6, written ca. 397 (*PL* 34:21), Augustine had meditated on the paradoxes of speaking about God. Though he never systematically pursued the apophatic way, there are important elements of negative theology in his thought, on which see V. Lossky, "Les éléments de 'Théologie négative' dans la pensée de saint Augustin," in *Augustinus Magister* 1:575–81.

50. These three texts can be found in *PL* 36:202–5, 466–71; 37:1274–75.

51. *Tr. in Jo.* 20.11–13 (*PL* 35:1562–64). This text, along with *En. in Ps.* 41, are studied in Mandouze, *Saint Augustin: L'aventure,* pp. 662–63; and Poque, "L'expression de l'anabase," pp. 192–95 and 205–9.

52. The implication that all should aspire to contemplative vision in this life is made explicit in several texts, e.g., *Ep.* 120.1.4 (*PL* 33:454). On this, see Trapé, "VI. Saint Augustine," p. 455; and Butler, *Western Mysticism,* pp. 208–10.

53. Augustine constantly insists that the fullness of vision is to be found only in the next life. For a few representative texts in his preaching, cf. *Enn. in Pss.* 43.4; 48.1.5; *Tr. in Jo.* 124.5.

54. Se dixit in nobis esse his deorsum: ergo et nos in illo sumus ibi sursum. . . . Ecce quale pignus habemus, unde et nos fide et spe et caritate cum capite nostro sumus in coelo in aeternum: quia et ipsum divinitate, bonitate, unitate nobiscum est in terra usque in consummationem saeculi.

55. See especially the treatment in Butler, *Western Mysticism,* pp. 26–36.

56. *En. in Ps.* 41.9 (*PL* 36:469–70). A similar emphasis on God's presence in the temple of the church is to be found in *Epp.* 187.12.35 and 13.38 (*PL* 33:845–47).

57. *En. in Ps.* 41, passim, e.g., . . . in tabernaculo invenitur via per quam venitur ad domum . . . ; Nam extra locum tabernaculi errabo quaerens Deum meum; Ascendens tabernaculum, pervenit ad domum Dei.

58. *En. in Ps.* 41.2 (*PL* 36:465): Eia, fratres, aviditatem meam capite, desiderium hoc mecum communicate: simul amemus, simul in hac siti exardescamus, simul ad fontem

intelligendi curramus; Si et fons est, et lumen est; merito et intellectus est, quia et satiat animam avidam sciendi. Lumen hoc desidera, quemdam fontem, quoddam lumen quale non norunt oculi tui; cui lumini videndo oculus interior praeparatur, cui fonti hauriendo sitis interior inardescit. The thirst for God is found elsewhere in the *Enn. in Pss.*, e.g., 62.5-6; 106.9.

59. Butler, *Western Mysticism,* p. 33.

60. Ascendens tabernaculum, pervenit ad domum Dei. Tamen dum miratur membra tabernaculi, ita perductus est ad domum Dei, quamdam dulcedinem sequendo, interiorem nescio quam et occultam voluptatem, tamquam de domo Dei sonaret suaviter aliquod organum: et cum ille ambularet in tabernaculo, audito quodam interiore sono, ductus dulcedine, sequens quod sonabat, adstrahens se ad omni strepitu carnis et sanguinis, pervenit usque ad domum Dei.

61. Immediately below, it is described as "quo sic rapta sum quasi per transitum."

62. Another important early mystical text, *En. in Ps.* 145.5-7 (*PL* 37:1887-89), preached about 395, also echoes some of these themes.

63. For another treatment of this theme, see *En. in Ps.* 32.2.1.8 (*PL* 36:283).

64. Quantum accedis ad similitudinem, tantum proficis in caritate, et tanto incipis sentire Deum.

65. The relation between divine omnipresence and human consciousness is also discussed in *Epp.* 187.3.7 and 5.16 (*PL* 33:834-35, 837-38); and in *En. in Ps.* 138.10-13 (*PL* 37:1790-92). On Augustine's view of the divine presence, see S. Grabowski, "St. Augustine and the Presence of God," *Theological Studies* 13 (1952): 336-58.

66. The word *persentiscere* is also found in *Conf.* 10.37.60 (*PL* 32:805).

67. Et cum accedere coeperis similis, et persentiscere Deum, quantum in te caritas crescit, quia et caritas Deus est, senties quiddam quod dicebas, et non dicebas. Ante enim quam sentires, dicere te putabas Deum: incipis sentire, et ibi sentis dici non posse quod sentis. Immediately below we read: Modicum ipsum quod sentire possum ex parte in aenigmate per speculum jam explicare non possum.

68. See *De doct. christ.* 1.6.6 (*PL* 34:21). The theme of the *iubilus* or *iubilatio* as expressing a joy "quae verbis explicare non possit" is frequent in the *Enn. in Pss.*, e.g., 26.13; 32.8; 46.7; 65.2; 88.16-17; 94.3; 97.4. For this aspect of Augustine's theology, see *DS* 8:1472-73.

69. Transcendi me, ut illum tangerem (Augustine also quotes Ps 41:4-5 here).

70. Poque puts emphasis on this ("L'expression de l'anabase," pp. 206-15), arguing that the new "victorious" attitude is due to the influence of Basil's *Homily* 15 (*PG* 31:465), though this is scarcely a compelling argument.

71. E.g., *En. in Ps.* 27.2 (*PL* 36:211); and *En. in Ps.* 101.2.8 (*PL* 37:1309). Related texts may be found in *De Trin.* 6.7; 8.5; *De civ. Dei* 10.5; and *Ep.* 118.15. Augustine does at times make use of the language of union to describe the joys of heaven, e.g., *De Trin.* 4.7.11 (*PL* 42:895-96).

72. Mandouze rightly complains of the vicious circle which consists of finding Augustine at once too "Plotinian" to be a mystic who is a true Christian and not mystical enough in the Plotinian sense to be a Christian who is truly mystical ("L'extase d'Ostie," p. 84).

73. The relation of introversion and ecstatic ascent appears in *Conf.* 3.6; 4.12; and 7.10, and is succinctly formulated in *De vera religione* 39.72 (*PL* 34:154). For comments on the relation of *enstasis* and *ecstasis* in the major visionary texts, see Mandouze, *Saint Augustin: L'aventure,* pp. 689-93.

74. O'Connell, *Origin of the Soul.*

75. For an introduction, see "The Human Person as Image of God. I. Eastern Christianity (Lars Thunberg). II. Western Christianity (Bernard McGinn)," in *Christian Spirituality: Origins to Twelfth Century,* ed. Bernard McGinn and John Meyendorff, WS 16 (New York: Crossroad, 1985), pp. 291-330.

76. Literature on Augustine's theology of the image of God is extensive; see esp. John Edward Sullivan, *The Image of God: The Doctrine of St. Augustine and its Influence* (Dubuque,

IA: Priory Press, 1963); Gerhart B. Ladner, *The Idea of Reform: Its Impact on Christian Thought and Action in the Age of the Fathers* (Cambridge, MA: Harvard University Press, 1959), chap. 5; Cayré, *La contemplation augustinienne*, chap. 4; Bell, *Image and Likeness*, chap. 1; J. Heijke, "St. Augustine's Comments on 'Imago Dei.' (An anthology from all his works exclusive of the De Trinitate)," *Classical Folia: Supplement III* (April, 1960).

77. *De Sermone Domini in Monte* 1.3.10 (*PL* 34:1234).

78. Trapé, "VI. Saint Augustine," p. 454.

79. Non sane omne quod est in creaturis aliquo modo simile est Deo, etiam ejus imago dicenda est: sed illa sola qua superior ipse solus est. Ea quippe de illo prorsus exprimitur, inter quam et ipsum nulla interjecta natura est. Cf. *De diversis quaestionibus 83*, q. 74 (*PL* 40:85–86).

80. On creation and recreation through the *Verbum*, see, e.g., *En. in Ps.* 142:17 (*PL* 37:1855).

81. On the *Verbum* as the perfect *imago*, see, e.g., *De Gen. lib. imperf.* 16.57 (*PL* 34:242), an early text using the language of *similitudo; De vera rel.* 44.82 (*PL* 34:159); *Ep.* 9.8.9 (*PL* 38:82); and *De Trin.* 6.10.11 (*PL* 42:931). On the legitimacy of speaking of the human as the *imago Dei* made to the image of the whole Trinity, a key text is *De Trin.* 7.6.12 (*PL* 42:946).

82. For a sketch of the "unitarian" and "trinitarian" models, see Sullivan, *Image of God*, chaps. 2 and 4.

83. . . . [u]t videlicet intelligamus in eo factum hominem ad imaginem Dei, in quo irrationalibus animantibus antecellit. Id autem est ipsa ratio, vel mens, vel intelligentia, vel si quo alio vocabulo commodius appellatur. The intellectual character of the *imago Dei* not only involves the mind's ability to comprehend reality, but it also can embrace its inability to grasp what lies beyond understanding, that is, its being an image *of God*, as Augustine notes in *De symbolo* 1.2 (*PL* 40:628): ideo mens ipso non potest comprehendi nec a se ipsa, ubi est imago Dei.

84. Cayré, *La contemplation augustinienne*, esp. chap. 4. Also useful is Bell, *Image and Likeness*, chap. 1; Louth, *Origins*, pp. 146–58; and Oliver O'Donovan, *The Problem of Self-Love in St. Augustine* (New Haven: Yale University Press, 1980), pp. 75–92.

85. Teselle, "Augustine," p. 31.

86. Tu da quaerendi vires, qui invenire te fecisti, et magis magisque inveniendi te spem dedisti. . . . Meminerem tui, intelligam te, diligam te. Auge in me ista, donec me reformes ad integrum.

87. On the mystical character of book 8, see also the "Note Complémentaire 5: Mysticisme et théologie trinitaire" in *Oeuvres de Saint Augustin. 16. La Trinité (Livres VIII–XV)*, ed. P. Agaësse and J. Moingt (Paris: Desclée, 1955), pp. 574–75.

88. *De Trin.* 8.2.3 (*PL* 42:949): Ecce in ipso primo ictu quo velut coruscatione perstringeris, cum dicitur, Veritas, mane si potes.

89. Sed dilectione standum est ad illud et inhaerendum illi, ut praesente perfruamur a quo sumus.

90. Sed et hoc ideo, quia et qui proximum diligit, consequens est ut et ipsam praecipue dilectionem diligit. "Deus," autem, "dilectio est, et qui manet in dilectione, in Deo manet." This theme of the identity of love of God and love of neighbor is frequent in the *Tr. in 1 Jn.* (e.g., 5.7–9; 9.10).

91. Sic caritas nutriatur, ut nutriata perficitur: sic vestis nuptialis induatur: sic imago Dei ad quam creati sumus, proficiendo resculpatur.

92. Three forms of trinitarian analogy based on love are briefly explored: (1) the notion of loving love, loving something that itself loves, and the love we have of it precisely because it loves (Quia cum diligimus caritatem, aliquid diligentem diligimus, propter hoc ipsum quia diligit aliquid [8.8.12]); (2) the lover, that which is loved, and love (Ecce tria sunt: amans, et quod amatur, et amor [8.10.14]); and finally, a more subjective version of (2) in which Augustine dwells on the intersubjective experience of love, that is, (3) I love, what I love, and that love itself (ego, et quod amo, et ipse amor [9.2.2]). It is this last that provides

the bridge to the more extended introspective analyses of the *imago* that begin in 9.3.3 with the statement "Mens enim amare se ipsam non potest, nisi etiam se noverit: nam quomodo amat quod nescit?" (*PL* 42:962). See M. Nedoncelle, "L'intersubjectivité humaine est-elle pour saint Augustine une image de la Trinité?," in *Augustinus Magister* 1:595–602.

93. On love of neighbor in Augustine, see O'Donovan, *Problem of Self-Love,* chap. 5; and Gustave Combes, *La charité d'après Saint Augustin* (Paris: Desclée, 1934), part 4.

94. For a list of the analogies of the Trinity in books 8–14, see Cayré, *La contemplation augustinienne,* p. 113 n. 1.

95. Being created in the image of God is the necessary condition both for the reception of grace (e.g., *Sermo* 26.1.4) and for the heavenly reward of the vision of God (e.g., *De civ. Dei* 13.22.32).

96. The *verbum interius* (see, e.g., 9.11.16–18) is the knowledge, or self-awareness, of the subject as subject, not as object or content. See Bernard J. Lonergan, "Introduction," in *Verbum: Word and Idea in Aquinas* (Notre Dame: University of Notre Dame Press, 1967), pp. x–xiii.

97. Et est quaedam imago Trinitatis, ipsa mens, et notitia ejus, quod est proles ejus ac de se ipsa verbum ejus, et amor tertius, et haec tria unum atque una substantia. For other important passages on the equality of the three operations in the subject's consciousness, the nodal point of the trinitarian analogy, see, e.g., 14.5.7; 14.6.8; 14.7.10; 15.12.22.

98. Haec igitur trinitas mentis non propterea Dei est imago, quia sui meminit mens, et intelligit ac diligit se: sed quia potest etiam meminisse, et intelligere, et amare quo facta est. Cf. 14.19.26.

99. In hac quippe imagine tunc perfecta erit Dei similitudo quando Dei perfecta erit visio. Cf. *De Trin.* 15.6.10. For some texts on the relation between the *imago Dei* and the *visio Dei,* see J. Heijke, "Augustine's Comments on the 'Imago Dei,'" ##80, 95, 109, 135.

100. *En. in Ps.* 102.3 (*PL* 37:1318); cf. *Enn. in Pss.* 4.8; 115.8 (*PL* 36:81; 37:1494).

101. For Gregory of Nyssa's teaching on God becoming visible in the mirror of the soul, see chapter 5, p. 141.

102. Aliud est itaque trinitas ipsa res, aliud imago trinitatis in re alia. This is the essential message of the whole last part of book 15 beginning with 15.15.24.

103. Imaginem in nobis Dei deformare potuimus, reformare non possumus.

104. Madec, "Christus, scientia et sapientia nostra," p. 78.

105. Adventus ejus, humanitas ejus: mansio ejus, divinitas ejus: divinitas ejus quo imus, humanitas ejus qua imus.

106. For a collection of texts, see M. Comeau, "Le Christ, chemin et terme de l'ascension spirituelle, d'après saint Augustin," *Recherches de science religieuses* 40 (1952): 80–89.

107. Augustine does at times display devotion to the humanity of the Redeemer (e.g., *Tr. in Jo.* 26.4), being in this a predecessor of the later medieval *amor carnalis Christi.*

108. Ad hoc unum [the Trinity] non nos perducit, nisi multi habeamus cor unum.

109. Fit ergo cor immaculatum membrorum et corporis Christi, gratia Dei per ipsum corporis caput, hoc est per Jesum Christum Dominum nostrum.

110. Augustine's teaching on the Body of Christ has been much studied, especially since the work of Emile Mersch (*The Whole Christ* [Milwaukee: Bruce, 1938], pp. 384–440) first revealed its importance. For some further accounts, see S. Grabowski, "Saint Augustine and the Doctrine of the Mystical Body of Christ," *Theological Studies* 7 (1946): 72–125; G. Philips, "L'influence du Christ-Chef sur son corps mystique suivant saint Augustin," in *Augustinus Magister* 2:805–16; Antonio Piolanti, "Il mistero del 'Cristo totale' in s. Agostino," in *Augustinus Magister* 3:453–69; and *DS* 7:1049–53.

111. Multa enim membra ejus, sub uno capite ipso Salvatore nostro caritatis et pacis vinculo colligata, . . . unus homo sunt: et ipsorum et unius hominis vox plerumque in Psalmis auditur; et sic clamat unus tamquam omnes, quia omnes in uno unus sunt. *En. in Ps.* 65.18 says, "corpus Christi loquitur, unitas Christi loquitur" (*PL* 36:798). Cf. *Hom. in Jo.* 12.9.

112. *En. in Ps.* 117.3 (*PL* 37:1496).

113. Cf. *En. in Ps.* 30.3.1 (*PL* 36:248).

114. E.g., *Enn. in Pss.* 26.2.11; 30.2.3; 32.2.2; 37.6; 39.4; 52.1; 54.3; 69.3 (to cite only examples from the first half of the psalter).

115. Cf. *Enn. in Pss.* 130.13; 131.24 (*PL* 37:1714, 1727).

116. Nullum majus donum praestare posset Deus hominibus, quam ut Verbum suum per quod condidit omnia, faceret illis caput, et illos ei tamquam membra coaptaret; ut esset Filius Dei et filius hominis, unus Deus cum Patre, unus homo cum hominibus: ut et quando loquimur ad Deum deprecantes, non inde Filium separemus; et quando precatur corpus Filii, non a se separet caput suum; sitque ipse unus salvator corporis sui Dominus noster Jesus Christus Filius Dei, qui et oret pro nobis, et oret in nobis, et oretur a nobis. A similar passage may be found in *En. in Ps.* 90.2.1 (*PL* 37:1159–60).

117. In illum si intendamus, non errabimus; quia ipse est Veritas quo festinamus, et ipse est Via per quam curramus. Cf. *En. in Ps.* 66.5 (*PL* 36:807); and *En. in Ps.* 141.9 (*PL* 37:1838).

118. On Christ as Rock (and alternately Cornerstone), see, e.g., *Enn. in Pss.* 96.11; 113.1.11; 117.17; 136.21–22; 140.18.

119. See esp. *En. in Ps.* 102.5–6 (*PL* 37:1319–21).

120. Filius enim Dei particeps mortalitatis effectus est, ut mortalis homo fiat particeps divinitatis. An equivalent text can be found in *En. in Ps.* 118.19.6 (*PL* 37:1556). See also *Enn. in Pss.* 102.22; 29.2.1, on the role of Christ as mediator.

121. *En. in Ps.* 32.2.2 (*PL* 36:278); cf. *Conf.* 7.10.16: Cibus sum grandium; cresce, et manducabimus me. Nec tu in me mutabis, sicut cibum carnis tuae, sed tu mutaberis in me (*PL* 32:742). The *Enarratio* text was actually written before that of the *Conf.*

122. For a few representative texts in the *Enarrationes*, see 52.6; 84.7; 102.19; 124.10; 136.1; 139.7; etc.

123. See Victorino Capanaga, "La deificacion en la soteriologia agustiniana," in *Augustinus Magister* 2:745–54; and Bonner, "Augustine's Concept of Deification," pp. 369–86.

124. Manifestum est ergo, quia homines dixit deos, ex gratia sua deificatos, non de substantia sua natos. . . . Qui autem justificat, ipse deificat, quia justificando filios Dei facit. . . . Si filii Dei facti sumus, et dii facti sumus; sed hoc gratiae est adoptantis non naturae generantis. Among the other key texts are *Sermo* 166.4.4; *Sermo* 192.1.1; *Sermo* 344.1; *In Ep. ad Gal.* 30.6; *Ep.* 140.4.10; *De civ. Dei* 9.23; and *Tr. in Jo.* 48.9.

125. E.g., *De mor. ecc. cath.* 1.12.20 (*PL* 32:1320); *De Trin.* 6.3.4 (*PL* 42:926); *De nat. et grat.* 33.37 (*PL* 44:265).

126. Among the key texts on this, see *De civ. Dei* 11.2.

127. According to the *Thesaurus Augustinianus*, Augustine uses the term 124 times, especially often in the *Contra Faustum* (ca. 397–398).

128. Watkin, "Mysticism of St. Augustine," pp. 114–17.

129. A host of texts in the *Enarrationes* take up this theme, e.g., *Enn. in Pss.* 5.1; 18.1.15; 37.28; 62.13; 72.34. Cf. *De ver. rel.* 3.3; 47.90; 55.113 (*PL* 34:124, 162–63, 172). "Adhaerere" is used both of this life and the next.

130. See Hans Lewy, *SOBRIA EBRIETAS: Untersuchungen zur Geschichte der antiken Mystik.* Beihefte zur *Zeitschrift für die neutestamentliche Wissenschaft* 9 (Giessen: Töpelmann, 1929). See pp. 157–64 for Augustine.

131. For other appearances, see *Contra Faustum* 12.42 (*PL* 42:276–77); *Sermones* 34.1.2; 225.4 (*PL* 38:210, 1098); and *En. in Pss.* 74.11, etc. The changing of the water of the Old Testament into the wine of Christ is also spoken of as an "inebriatio"; see *Tr. in Jo.* 8.3; 9.3–5.

132. Audere dicere, fratres mei, etiam de sanctis linguis et cordibus, per quas nobis veritas nuntiata est, nec dici potest quod annuntiabunt, nec cogitari.

133. For the development of the doctrine of the spiritual senses, see chapter 4, pp. 121–24, and the literature cited there. Little has been written on Augustine's teaching. The only

study known to me is P.-L. Landsberg, "Les sens spirituels chez saint Augustin," *Dieu vivant* 11 (1948): 83–105.

134. According to the *Thesaurus Augustinianus, ecstasis* appears eighty-seven times in Augustine's writings. It is used for a variety of modes of alienation from ordinary sense experience (even extreme fear). *Excessus* (sixty-three appearances) is employed in three different ways: (a) generalized, as excess or overflowing of any kind; (b) pejoratively, of the excess of concupiscence or sin (most often in the *Contra Julianum*); and (c) positively, of the mystical *excessus mentis* (twenty-four times). This last is often equated with *ecstasis*. The verbal form *excedere* occurs sixty-nine times, of which twenty uses are more or less mystical. Fourteen of these quote 2 Cor 5:13: "sive enim mente excedimus Deo."

135. *Excessus (mentis)* appears in Pss 30:23; 67:28; 115:11; and in Acts 10:10 and 11:5 in texts that could at least suggest mystical experience. These are to be linked with 2 Cor 5:13: "sive enim mente excedimus Deo." *Exstasis* is found in Ps 30:1 and Acts 3:10. Among the most important uses in Augustine are those of *De gen. ad lit.* 8.25.47; 12.12.26 (*PL* 34:391, 464); *Epp.* 120.11; 147.13.31 (*PL* 33:457, 610); *Sermo* 52.6.16 (*PL* 38:360). Particularly important are the appearances in the *Enn. in Pss.* 30.1.1; 30.2.1–3; 34.2.6; 37.12; 67.36 (*PL* 36:226, 230, 338, 405, 834–35); 34.2.6 (*PL* 36:338); and *En. in Ps.* 119.2 (*PL* 37:1598). For background, see "Extase," *DS* 4:2045–2189. A large literature has been devoted to the meaning of these terms; see Butler, *Western Mysticism,* pp. 60–61, 71–78; Bell, *Image and Likeness,* pp. 86–87; and esp. J. Maréchal, "La vision de Dieu au sommet de la contemplation d'après saint Augustin," *Nouvelle Revue théologique* 57 (1930): 89–109, 191–214.

136. See *Contra Adimantum* 28.2 (*PL* 42:171–72).

137. *De Gen. ad lit.* 12 (*PL* 34:453–86); *Ep.* 147 (*PL* 33:596–622).

138. The initial discussion of the three kinds of vision (12.6.15–12.7.16) clearly pertains to our natural ways of knowing, but in 12.26.53–54, where the discussion is of imaginative and intellectual raptures that take place "divinae admonitionis est et adjutori" (*PL* 34:476), the knowing is divinely given. The distinction is also clear in 12.31.59 (*PL* 34:479), where in discussing the kinds of objects seen in intellectual vision, Augustine uses the phrase "ut omnia *vel in se vel in illo* veraciter intellecta conspiciat." The "in se" refers to normal intellectual vision; the "in illo" to mystical vision in God, whether in this life or in the next.

139. An earlier text in *De Gen. ad lit.* (8.25.47 [*PL* 34:391]) used the term *ecstasis* only of the second type, that is, spiritual vision; 12.12.26 (*PL* 34:464) also uses it in this way. But on the evidence of 12.12.25 (*PL* 34:463), which speaks of two kinds of *ecstasis,* and 12.26.53 (*PL* 34:476), which discusses two types of *raptus,* it is clear that Augustine thought that both spiritual and intellectual visions could involve *ecstasis.*

140. Ibi videtur claritas Domini, non per visionem significantem, vel corporalem . . . , sive spiritualem . . . : sed per speciem, non per aenigmata, quantum eam capere mens humana potest, secundum assumentis Dei gratiam, ut os ad os loquatur ei quem dignum tali Deus colloquio fecerit, non os corporis, sed mentis.

141. [Moses] videre Deum . . . , sed in ea substantia qua Deus est, nulla assumpta corporali creatura, quae mortalis carnis sensibus praesentetur . . . , sed per speciem suam, quantum eam capere creatura rationalis et intellectualis potest. . . .

142. Cum ergo illuc rapitur, et a carnalibus subtracta sensibus, illi visioni expressius praesentatur non spatiis localibus, sed modo quodam suo, etiam supra se videt illud, quo adjuta videt quidquid etiam in se intelligendo videt. Cf. *Conf.* 7.10.16.

143. *Ep.* 147 insists that God cannot be seen by either corporeal or ordinary mental vision, and that most of the visions of God spoken of in the Old Testament were imaginative visions (7.19–8.20). In this matter, Augustine is using Ambrose, on which see Basil Studer, *Zur Theophanie-Exegese Augustins* (Rome: Herder, 1971). But in 13.31–32 (*PL* 33:610) Augustine admits that Moses and Paul enjoyed the normally impossible vision of the divine substance in this life, though this took place in ecstasy ". . . quia necesse est abstrahi ab hac vita mentem quando in illius ineffabilitatem visionis assumitur." See also 18.45 on how God's *pax* and *claritas* (the Son) and *caritas* (the Holy Spirit) make this possible.

144. Texts that seem to suggest that vision is not possible in this life include the following: *Sermo* 255.5.5 (*PL* 38:1188); *De Trin.* 4.7.11 (*PL* 42:895-96); *De civ. Dei* 22.29-30 (*PL* 41:796-804); *Enn. in Pss.* 36.1.12; 37.28; 43.5 (*PL* 36:362-63, 411-12; 484-85).

145. Combining *Enn. in Pss.* 85.11 and 86.9 (*PL* 37:1089 and 1107). Texts on the joys of heaven are frequent in the *Enarrationes.*

146. *Tr. in Jo.* 36.5 (*PL* 35:1666); cf. *De cons. ev.* 1.7; 4.20 (*PL* 34:1045, 1227-28).

147. For a collection of texts arguing that Augustine held that contemplation was open to all, see Butler, *Western Mysticism,* pp. 208-10; and Burnaby, *Amor Dei,* pp. 64-65.

148. Sed etsi est aliquis, sicut fieri potest, et valde potest, acie mentis fortior me, et contuitum cordis sui diu figit in eo quod est; laudet ille ut potest, et quomodo nos possumus, laudet. On this and related texts, see Poque, "L'expression de l'anabase," pp. 56-57; and Bell, *Image and Likeness,* pp. 80-81.

149. Maréchal, "La vision de Dieu," pp. 191-213; Henry, *Path to Transcendence,* pp. 106-8; Butler, *Western Mysticism,* pp. 78-88; Cayré, *La contemplation augustinienne,* pp. 129-30, 171, 193-95.

150. *Tr. in Jo.* 96-98 (*PL* 35:1873-85). See B. Capelle, "Le progrès de la connaissance religieuse d'après s. Augustin," *Recherches de théologie ancienne et médiévale* 2 (1930): 410-19.

151. Nulla videtur esse necessitas, ut aliqua secreta doctrinae taceantur, et abscondantur fidelibus parvulis, seorsum dicenda majoribus, hoc est intelligentioribus. . . .

152. Augustine concludes in *Tr. in Jo.* 98.8 (*PL* 35:1885) with an attack on false revelations, specifically the well-known "Apocalypse of Paul," for having the temerity to pretend to reveal what the apostle said were "unutterable things" (2 Cor 12:4).

153. For an excellent summary of this development, see Nicholas Lobkowicz, *Theory and Practice: History of a Concept from Aristotle to Marx* (Notre Dame: University of Notre Dame Press, 1967), chaps. 1-5.

154. For Augustine's teaching on contemplation and action, see Butler, *Western Mysticism,* pp. 195-210; Lobkowicz, *Theory and Practice,* pp. 63-68; and G. O'Daly and L. Verheijen, "Actio-contemplatio," *Augustinus-Lexikon* 1:58-63.

155. . . . [s]alva fide quisque possit in quolibet earum vitam ducere, et ad sempiterna praemia pervenire; interest tamen quod amore teneat veritatis, quod officio charitatis impendat. Nec sic quisque debet esse otiosus, ut in eodem otio utilitatem non cogitet proximi; nec sic actuosus, ut contemplationem non requirat Dei. Cf. *Ep.* 48 (*PL* 33:187-89).

156. On Rachel and Leah, see, e.g., *Contra Faustum* 22.53-54; and *De cons. ev.* 1.5.8. On John and Peter, see, e.g., *Tr. in Jo.* 124.5-7. On Mary and Martha, se, e.g., *Sermones* 103.5; 104.4; 169.17; 179.4, 255; *De Trin.* 1.10.20; for a complete survey on Mary and Martha, see D. Csányi, "OPTIMA PARS: Die Auslegungsgeschichte von Lk. 10, 38-42 bei den Kirchenvätern der ersten vier Jahrhunderte," *Studia Monastica* 2 (1960), pp. 65-74.

157. Lobkowicz, *Theory and Practice,* p. 68.

158. E.g., Hans Meyer, "War Augustin Intellektualist oder Mystiker?" in *Augustinus Magister* 3:429-37.

159. E.g., Bonner, "Spirituality of Augustine," p. 149; Teselle, "Augustine," pp. 28-30. For Augustine's teaching on love, see esp. Burnaby, *Amor Dei;* Combes, *La charité d'après Saint Augustine;* and O'Donovan, *Problem of Self-Love;* and Isabelle Bochet, *Saint Augustin et le désir de Dieu* (Paris: Études Augustiniennes, 1982). For a brief recent introduction, see D. Dideberg, "Amor," *Augustinus-Lexikon* 1:294-300.

160. To cite just one of the most lapidary texts, *Ep.* 92.3 (*PL* 33:319): Et tanto efficimur similiores illi, quanto magis in eius cognitione et caritate proficimus.

161. M. Miles, "Vision: The Eye of the Body and the Eye of the Mind in Saint Augustine's *De Trinitate* and *Confessions," Journal of Religion* 63 (1983): 125-42. This is well brought out by the analysis of sensation in the *De Gen. ad lit.,* e.g., 3.4.6-3.5.7; 7.19.25-7.20.26; 12.16.32-33, etc.

162. Caritas autem et invenit eum per fidem, et eum quaerit habere per speciem: ubi tunc sic invenietur, ut sufficiat nobis, et ulterius non quaeratur.

163. I would disagree here with Miles's formulation that in spiritual vision "the initiative remains with the viewer" ("Vision," p. 130), a position she later qualifies in the light of texts like *De Trin.* 15.17.31. For another text on the priority of God's love, see *En. in Ps.* 118.27.6 (*PL* 37:1582).

164. Some scholars (e.g., Burnaby, *Amor Dei,* pp. 80–82, 143) have argued that the central role of love is not yet clearly presented in the early works of the Cassiciacum period.

165. Et exaltatus est super plenitudinem scientiae, ut nemo ad eum pervenit, nisi per caritatem. Cf. *Contra Faustum* 32.18 (*PL* 42:507): Nemo intratur in veritatem nisi per caritatem.

166. See especially the beautiful passage in *En. in Ps.* 39.21 (*PL* 36:447).

167. See *Tr. in 1 Jo.* 6.8–9 (*PL* 35:2024–25) on love as the sign of the Holy Spirit's presence in us. Also see the passage in *En. in Ps.* 98.4 (*PL* 37:1260–61) on how love as the fulfillment of the law grants the fullness of knowledge. Augustine goes on to say that every soul is a true Sion ("id est, visio et contemplatio") which strives to fix its attention on the divine light, but that Sion is most properly the church in which all live together in the Love that is God.

168. . . . [u]t quanto flagrantius diligimus Deum, tanto certius sereniusque videamus; quia in Deo conspicimus incommutabilem formam justitiae, secundum quam hominem vivere oportet judicamus. On love and desire as the measure of our vision of God both here and hereafter, see *Tr. in 1 Jo.* 4.5–6 (*PL* 35:2008–9); and also *Ep.* 155.13 (*PL* 33:672): Imus autem non ambulando, sed amando. Quem [God] tanto habebimus praesentiorem, quanto eumdem amorem quo in eum tendimus, potuerimus habere puriorem.

169. E.g., *En. in Ps.* 79.2 (*PL* 36:1022): Sit in te caritas et necesse est plenitudo scientiae consequatur. Quid enim nescit qui caritatem scit, quandoquidem dictum est: "Deus caritas est?" Another text comes close to the "amor ipse notitia est" formula that became classic with Gregory the Great: Haec meditatio amantis est cogitatio . . . (*En. in Ps.* 118.19.4 [*PL* 37:1555]). On the thirty-two homilies on Psalm 118, an important anti-Pelagian summary of Augustine's spiritual teaching, see C. Kannengiesser, "Enarratio in psalmum CXVIII: Science de la révélation et progrès spirituel," *Recherches augustiniennes* 2 (1962): 359–81.

170. An especially fine formulation of this is *De Trin.* 4.1.11 (*PL* 42:895–96): . . . cum multa membra intueremur praecessisse nos caput unum; in quo nunc per fidem mundati, et tunc per speciem redintegrati, et per Mediatorem Deo reconciliati heareamus uni, fruamur uno, permaneamus unum. Cf. *Tr. in Jo.* 27.6 (*PL* 35:1618); and *Tr. in 1 Jo.* 10.3 (*PL* 35:2055–56).

171. There are a few texts, e.g., *De Trin.* 6.3.4 (*PL* 42:926) and *Ep.* 238.12–13 (*PL* 33:1042–43), which discuss how we become one with God, citing the classic scriptural basis, 1 Cor 6:17. On the *unitas spiritus* mode of understanding union with God, see B. McGinn, "Love, Knowledge and *Unio Mystica* in the Western Christian Tradition," in *Mystical Union and Monotheistic Faith,* ed. M. Idel and B. McGinn (New York: Macmillan, 1989), pp. 59–86.

172. My thanks to J. Patout Burns for helping me to clarify this point.

173. On Augustine on the body and sexuality, see Peter Brown, *The Body and Society: Men, Women, and Sexual Renunciation in Early Christianity* (New York: Columbia University Press, 1988), chap. 19; and, most recently, G. Stroumsa, "*Caro salutis cardo:* Shaping the Person in Early Christian Thought," *History of Religions* 30 (1990): 25–50.

174. Brown, *Body and Society,* p. 419.

175. Nunc illud quaerimus, qualis sis amator sapientiae, quam castissimo conspectu atque amplexu, nullo interposito velamento quasi nudam videre ac tenere desideras. . . . An vero si alicujus pulchrae feminae amore flagrans. . . .

176. *De lib. arbit.* 2.14.37 (*PL* 32:1261). These neglected texts have been studied by Nicholas Perella, *The Kiss Sacred and Profane* (Berkeley: University of California Press, 1969), pp. 46–48.

177. E.g., *En. in Pss.* 32.2.7; 33.2.6; 35.5 (*PL* 37:282–83, 310–11, 344). *Homily* 32 dates to 392 or before; *Homily* 33 to the early years of his episcopacy. Only *Homily* 35, the most bland, is later (ca. 412?).

178. *De virg.* 54–55 (*PL* 40:427–28), the only passage that emphasizes the love of Christian virgin for her Divine Lover, studiously avoids using the Song.

179. A.-M. La Bonnardière shows that Augustine used the Song seventy-four times, mostly in connection with baptism ("Le Cantique des Cantiques dans l'oeuvre de saint Augustin," *Revue des études augustiniennes* 1 [1955]: 225–37).

180. Unde mihi videtur quod definitio brevis et vera virtutis, ordo est amoris; propter quod et in sancto Cantico Canticorum cantat sponsa Christi, civitas Dei: "ordinate in me caritatem."

181. This emerges from a survey of the some of the other uses, e.g., *De doct. christ.* 1.27.28; *Ep.* 190; *Sermones* 37.16.23; 100.2.2; 344.2.

182. Teselle, "Augustine," pp. 27–28.

183. E.g., ibid.; Cayré, *La contemplation augustinienne,* p. 75; O'Donovan, *Problem of Self-Love,* p. 150; Bell, *Image and Likeness,* p. 77.

184. *Sermo* 169.18 (*PL* 38:926): Si autem dixeris "sufficit," et peristi.

185. See Miles, "Vision," p. 136, for reflections on the transition from spatial to temporal and historical metaphors in Augustine's thought.

186. As in the many passages in Augustine which speak of love or *affectus* as the "space" in which or the "steps" by which the soul journeys, e.g., *De mor. ecc. cath.* 1.11.18; *De musica* 6.13.40; *Ep.* 155.13; *De Trin.* 14.17.23; and *Enn. in Pss.* 6.9; 85.6; 94.2; 119.2.

187. Just to note a few of the texts in the *Enarrationes in Psalmos* on the joys of heaven will be suggestive; cf. 36.1.12; 66.10; 83.8; 84.7; 85.8, 20–22; 86.8–9; 87.13; 117.22; 122.4; 124.3–4; 136.16; 144.2, 11; 149.9–10, etc.

188. See the important discussion in *En. in Ps.* 149.4 (*PL* 37:1951): Est quaedam visio hujus temporis; erit altera visio futuri temporis: visio quae modo est, per fidem est; visio quae futura est per speciem erit. Si credimus, videmus; si amamus, videmus. Quid videmus? Deum.

189. . . . [n]on incongruenter intelligimus sapientiam in cognitione et dilectione ejus quod semper est atque incommutabiliter manet, quod est Deus.

190. E.g., *De ver. rel.* 31.58 (*PL* 34:148).

191. Cf. *Sermo* 170.9 (*PL* 38:931), which says "Satietas erit insatiabilis." For further remarks, see Bell, *Image and Likeness,* p. 77.

Introduction to Appendix

1. David Lodge, *Small World: An Academic Romance* (New York: Macmillan, 1984), p. 52.

Appendix: Section I

I wish to thank Louis Dupré, who read this and the other sections of the Appendix and made valuable suggestions.

1. Augustine, *Confessions* 11.14.17 (*PL* 32:816): Quid est ergo tempus? Si nemo ex me quaerat, scio; si quaerenti explicare velim, nescio.

2. See Michel Despland, *La religion en occident: Evolution des idées et du vecu* (Montreal: Fides, 1979).

3. W. R. Inge, *Christian Mysticism* (London: Methuen, 1899), p. 3. Appendix A (pp. 335–48) lists no fewer than twenty-six definitions.

4. Cuthbert Butler, *Western Mysticism: The Teaching of Saints Augustine, Gregory and Bernard on Contemplation and the Contemplative Life* (New York: Dutton, 1923), p. 2.

5. Louis Dupré, "Mysticism," in *The Encyclopedia of Religion,* ed. Mircea Eliade (New York: Macmillan, 1987) 10:245.

6. Michel de Certeau, "'Mystique' au XVIIe siècle: Le problème du langage 'mystique,'" in *L'Homme devant Dieu: Mélanges offerts au Père Henri du Lubac,* 3 vols. (Paris: Aubier, 1964) 2:267–91.

7. Among the studies of the evolution of the term, see esp. Louis Bouyer, "Mysticism:

An Essay on the History of the Word," in *Understanding Mysticism,* ed. Richard Woods, O.P. (Garden City, NY: Image Books, 1980), pp. 42–55 (this essay was originally published in French in 1952).

8. In the Germanic world, serious modern treatment of mysticism began with Catholic Romantics such as Johann Joseph von Görres, whose four-volume *Christliche Mystik* appeared between 1836 and 1842, and theologians like Johann Sebastian Drey, whose article "Über das Verhältnis des Mysticismus zum Katholicismus" was published in the *Theologische Quartalschrift* in 1831.

9. Among the most useful, if partial, surveys of literature are Augustin Leonard, "Recherches phénoménologiques autour de l'expérience mystique," *La vie spirituelle: Supplement* 23 (Nov. 1952): 430–94; and Fritz-Dieter Maas, *Mystik im Gespräch: Materialen zur Mystik-Diskussion in der katholischen und evangelischen Theologie Deutschlands nach dem ersten Weltkrieg* (Würzburg: Echter, 1972). More recent historiography has tended to concentrate on philosophical treatments. See, e.g., Peter Moore, "Recent Studies on Mysticism: A Critical Survey," *Religion* 3 (1973): 146–56; idem, "Notes and Comments: A Recent Study of Mysticism," *Heythrop Journal* 25 (1984): 178–83; Steven Katz, "Review Article: Recent Work on Mysticism," *History of Religions* 25 (1985–86): 76–86; and esp. William J. Wainwright, *Mysticism: A Study of its Nature, Cognitive Value and Moral Implications* (Madison: University of Wisconsin Press, 1981). Individual studies will be referred to below.

10. Albrecht Ritschl, *Theologie und Metaphysik* (2nd ed.; Bonn: Marcus, 1887), pp. 27–28: "Die Mystik also ist die Praxis der neuplatonischen Metaphysik und diese ist die theoretische Norm des prätendirten mystischen Genusses Gottes. Dass nun das allgemeine Sein, in welchem der Mystiker zu zerschmelzen wunscht, als Gott angesehen wird, ist eine Erschleichung." Ritschl's opposition to mysticism is evident also in his *Geschichte der Pietismus,* 3 vols. (Bonn: Marcus, 1880–86). (My thanks to my colleague Brian Gerrish for drawing my attention to these texts.)

11. Adolf Harnack, *History of Dogma* (an unabridged republication of the 1900 translation of the 3rd German ed.; 7 vols. bound as 4; New York: Dover, 1961). See 4:271 n. 3.

12. Ibid. 3:109–10, 270; 4:280.

13. Ibid. 4:222.

14. Ibid. 4:240, 271, 279, 335–39; 5:278.

15. Ibid. 5:238.

16. Ibid. 6:12–14.

17. Ibid. 6:27.

18. Ibid. 6:100. He describes the characteristics of mysticism as individualism, "feeling," pantheistic metaphysic, ascetic views, and the resolution of Christology into the birth of Christ in the soul, and "Illuminism." In the absence of more detailed discussion, it is difficult to know what Harnack meant by all these notes and how far they are true of all Christian mysticism.

19. Ibid. 6:103–6.

20. Ibid. 6:99.

21. Emil Brunner's most noted attack on mysticism came in his book *Die Mystik und das Wort* (Tübingen: Mohr, 1928), where he claims "Der Gegensatz zwischen reformatorischer und mystiker Frömmigkeit ist anerkannt, was wollen wir mehr?" (p. iii). For Barth's more nuanced, though essentially negative views, see A. Kemmer, "Die Mystik in Karl Barths *Kirchliche Dogmatik,*" *Freiburger Zeitschrift für Philosophie und Theologie* 7 (1960): 3–25.

22. On Tillich's view of mysticism, see James R. Horne, "Tillich's Rejection of Absolute Mysticism," *Journal of Religion* 58 (1978), p. 130. A more recent Protestant systematician who has taken a positive interest in mysticism is Jürgen Moltmann; see his "The Theology of Mystical Experience," in *Experiences of God* (Philadelphia: Fortress, 1980), pp. 55–80.

23. Paul Tillich, *Systematic Theology,* 3 vols. (Chicago: University of Chicago Press, 1967) 1:9: "The theological concepts of both idealists and naturalists are rooted in a 'mystical a-priori,' an awareness of something that transcends the cleavage between subject and object."

24. Ernst Troeltsch, *The Social Teaching of the Christian Churches,* 2 vols. (New York: Harper & Row, 1960) 2:733, 743, 799–800, 993.

25. Ibid., pp. 691–93, 740–41, 744–46.

26. Ibid., pp. 734–38, 749–50, 791–92.

27. See, e.g., E. Troeltsch, *Psychologie und Erkenntnislehre in der Religionswissenschaft,* translated as "Main Problems of the Philosophy of Religion: Psychology and Theory of Knowledge in the Science of Religion," in *Congress of Arts and Science: Universal Exposition, St. Louis, 1904,* ed. Howard J. Rogers, 2 vols. (Boston and New York: Houghton, Mifflin, 1905) 1, esp. pp. 286–88. (My thanks to Brian Gerrish, who first drew my attention to this aspect of Troeltsch's teaching, one that deserves more consideration than the brief mention given here.)

28. Troeltsch, *Social Teaching,* pp. 797–800, 996–97. "In general, however, the modern educated classes understand nothing but mysticism" (p. 798).

29. Ibid., pp. 747, 753.

30. Schweitzer's account of the special experience of the reverence for life that he had on the Ogoaue River in 1915 would fit most definitions of a mystical experience.

31. On Schweitzer's mysticism, see esp. Henry Clark, *The Ethical Mysticism of Albert Schweitzer* (Boston: Beacon, 1962).

32. Ibid., pp. 32–37, for a brief sketch of "ethical mysticism."

33. Albert Schweitzer, *The Philosophy of Civilization* (New York: Macmillan, 1950), p. 246.

34. Albert Schweitzer, *The Mysticism of Paul the Apostle* (London: A. and C. Black, 1931), p. ix.

35. Ibid., p. 1.

36. Ibid., see chap. 14, esp. pp. 378–79, 391–92.

37. Ibid., p. 379.

38. Ibid., pp. 291–92, 395–96.

39. William Ralph Inge, *Christian Mysticism* (London: Methuen, 1899), pp. 98, 106, 110–17, on the dangers of the *via negativa;* and viii–ix, 142, 243–44, on debased supernaturalism.

40. Ibid., p. 5.

41. Ibid., pp. 6–8.

42. Ibid., p. 43; cf. pp. 369–72.

43. Ibid., p. 197; cf. pp. 200, 294.

44. Among Underhill's other early works on mysticism, were *The Mystic Way* (London: J. M. Dent and Sons; New York: E. P. Dutton, 1913), *Practical Mysticism* (New York: E. P. Dutton, 1914), and *The Essentials of Mysticism* (New York: E. P. Dutton, 1920).

45. A later work, *The Mystics of the Church* (London: James Clarke, 1925) was arranged in chronological order.

46. Evelyn Underhill, *Mysticism: A Study in the Nature and Development of Man's Spiritual Consciousness* (Cleveland and New York: World, 1965), p. xiv.

47. Ibid., e.g., pp. 73, 81, 170; see chap. 10 for union, and p. 94 for presence language.

48. Ibid., pp. 81ff. The characteristics are four: (1) mysticism is practical not theoretical; (2) mysticism is entirely a spiritual activity; (3) its method is love; and (4) it entails a psychological experience of the whole self. A later corollary is that mysticism is never self-seeking (pp. 92–93). On James's characteristics, see below, p. 292.

49. Ibid., pp. 168–71, for an outline.

50. Ibid., pp. 126–48.

51. Ibid., pp. 415–32.

52. Ibid., p. 448.

53. A second and revised edition appeared in 1932, and an abridged edition (closer to the lectures as originally delivered) came out in 1934. Since this last is the only edition currently in print, I will cite from it, though it lacks the full apparatus. See K. E. Kirk, *The Vision of God* (Cambridge: James Clarke, 1977).

54. Ibid., pp. 4–6 for an introduction, and chaps. 3 and 4 for the development.

55. Ibid., pp. 49–50, 90, 120, 180–82, 192, etc.

56. Ibid., p. 194.

57. On this, see Margaret Furse, "Mysticism: Classic Modern Interpreters and their Premise of Continuity," *Anglican Theological Review* 60 (1978): 180–73, surveying Inge, Underhill, and von Hügel.

58. For the context, as well as an insightful critique, see Rowan Williams, "Butler's *Western Mysticism:* Towards an Assessment," *Downside Review* 102 (1984): 197–215. Cf. David Knowles, "Edward Cuthbert Butler, 1858–1934," in *The Historian and Character* (Cambridge: Cambridge University Press, 1963), pp. 264–362.

59. Cuthbert Butler, *Western Mysticism,* pp. 62–64.

60. Ibid., p. 278; cf. p. 3, and also p. xliii in the "Afterthoughts" to the second edition.

61. Ibid., pp. 179–89, for these notes.

62. Ibid., pp. 190–91, 276–77, 290–93.

63. Butler, "Afterthoughts," p. lvii.

64. E.g., Abbot Benedetto Calati, "Western Mysticism," *Downside Review* 98 (1980): 201–13.

65. See Williams, "Butler's *Western Mysticism,*" pp. 199–202.

66. Butler, "Afterthoughts," pp. xli–xlii, liv–lv. See Williams, "Butler's *Western Mysticism,*" p. 210.

67. For a perceptive survey, see Gerald A. McCool, S.J., "Twentieth-Century Scholasticism," in *Celebrating the Medieval Heritage: A Colloquy on the Thought of Aquinas and Bonaventure,* ed. David Tracy (*The Journal of Religion* 58 [1978], Supplement): S198–S221.

68. There is no adequate history of this debate in English. One survey of some of the earlier literature is to be found in Joseph Maréchal, "Sur les cimes de l'oraison: Quelques opinions récentes de théologiens," *Nouvelle revue théologique* 56 (1929): 107–27, 177–206. Much can also be learned from the multiauthor article "Contemplation" in *DS* 2, esp. 2058–2194. In addition, see the *DS* entries on a number of the major figures involved, such as J.-G. Arintero, A. Farges, A. Gardeil, R. Garrigou-Lagrange, A. Poulain, etc. The long paraphrases of some positions found in Ernst Arbman, *Ecstasy or Religious Trance,* 3 vols. (Uppsala: Appelberg, 1963), vol. 1, under the title "The Mystical Christian Contemplation in Modern Catholic Theological Discussion: A Critical Review" (pp. 416–546), must be used with caution. On the crucial issue of infused contemplation, see Robert B. Eiten, S.J., "Recent Theological Opinion on Infused Contemplation," *Theological Studies* 2 (1941): 89–100.

69. I will cite from the English version of the 10th (posthumous) ed. of 1922 with an important introduction by J.-V. Bainvel, S.J., *The Graces of Interior Prayer* (reprint, Westminster, VT: Celtic Cross Books, 1978).

70. Ibid., chap. 1, pp. 1–6.

71. Ibid., chap. 4, on acquired and infused contemplation.

72. A. Saudreau, *The Mystical State* (London: Burnes, Oates and Washbourne, 1924), chap. 12 and Appendix 1. For Saudreau's own summary of his views on contemplation, see *DS* 2:2159–71.

73. See Butler, "Afterthoughts," pp. xliii–xlvii, on this aspect of the quarrel. In *The Mystical State,* chaps. 8–10, Saudreau identifies the essence of the mystical state as a superior though confused knowledge and love communicated by God himself (p. 65). Consciousness of direct contact between God and the soul he thinks a possible though very rare gift, as in the case of John of the Cross's "divine touches" (pp. 95–96).

74. Note especially the fourteen chapters of the revised second edition of 1923 which deal with various issues in the debate, e.g., chap. 14, "Is Infused Contemplation Accessible to All?" See *Mystical Phenomena* (London: Burnes, Oates and Washbourne, 1926), pp. 299–314.

75. Others also contributed, e.g., Donatien Joret, O.P., *La contemplation mystique d'après S. Thomas d'Aquin* (Paris: Desclée, 1923).

76. The "Biographical Note" to the English translation contains the following account:

"Shortly before his death, the holy friar made this statement about his teaching and writing: 'Within a few hours I shall be brought before the tribunal of God, and I assure you that our teachings concerning contemplation are the true doctrines and that they represent the traditional Christian teaching; but the contrary doctrines are deviations which serve only to mislead souls.'" See John G. Arintero, *The Mystical Evolution in the Development and Vitality of the Church,* 2 vols. (St. Louis: Herder, 1950) 1:xiii.

77. R. Garrigou-Lagrange, O.P., *Christian Perfection and Contemplation according to St. Thomas Aquinas and St. John of the Cross* (St. Louis: Herder, 1951), pp. 127-29. For a summary of the Dominican's views on contemplation, see the article devoted to him in *DS* 6:128-34, as well as his treatment "La contemplation dans l'école dominicaine" in *DS* 2:2067-80.

78. Also see Gardeil's posthumous series of articles "L'expérience mystique dans le cadre des missions divins," *La vie spirituelle: Supplement, 1932* (June): 129-46; (July): 1-21; (September): 65-76; and (October): 1-28.

79. Among the important contributors were, for instance, Maurice de la Taille, S.J., "L'oraison contemplative," *Recherches de science religieuse* 9 (1919): 273-92; Adolphe Tanquerey, *Précis de théologie ascetique et mystique* (Paris: Desclée, 1923-24), translated as *The Spiritual Life: A Treatise on Ascetical and Mystical Theology* (1930); Joseph de Guibert, S.J., *Études de théologie mystique* (Toulouse: L'Apostolat de la prière, 1930); and the Carmelite Gabriele di Santa Maria Maddalena, *La contemplation acquise* (Paris, 1949).

80. See the sympathetic, if critical, article by J. de Guibert in *DS* 2:1928-38.

81. There is an English translation of the first three volumes, Henri Bremond, *A Literary History of Religious Thought in France from the Wars of Religion down to our own Times* (London: SPCK, 1928-36).

82. On Mager's work and on the German discussion in general, see the full account in Maas, *Mystik im Gespräch.*

83. Anselm Stolz, *Theologie der Mystik* (Regensburg: Pustet, 1936), pp. 41-43, 57-58, 250.

84. On the psychologizing changes that took place in the sixteenth century, see *Theologie der Mystik,* pp. 19, 133-35, 140-43.

85. Ibid., pp. 136-37, 175-76, 189-90, 245, 248.

86. Ibid., pp. 153, 168-74; cf. pp. 151-52 on the possibility of unmediated knowledge of God.

87. Ibid., p. 246. On the nature of this transpsychological experience, see chap. 9, pp. 175-92.

88. M.-D. Chenu, in his review "Une théologie de la vie mystique," summarized thus, "La vie mystique n'est autre, en son fond, que la vie chrétienne" (*La vie spirituelle* 50 [1937]: [49]).

89. Stolz, *Theologie der Mystik,* pp. 248-51.

90. Ibid., pp. 246-47.

91. See the series of papers "The Transforming Union in St. Bernard and St. John of the Cross," *Collectanea Ordinis Cisterciensium Reformatorum* 10 (1948): 107-17; 11 (1949): 41-52, 352-61; 12 (1950): 25-38; and the studies in *Mystics and Zen Masters* (New York: Farrar, Straus, Giroux, 1967).

92. E.g., *The Climate of Monastic Prayer* (Washington, DC: Cistercian Publications, 1969), also published by Herder under the title *Contemplative Prayer: Contemplation in the World of Action* (New York: Herder & Herder, 1969); and the papers "The Inner Experience: Notes on Contemplation (I)-(VIII)," *Cistercian Studies* 18 (1983): 3-15, 121-34, 201-16, 288-300; 19 (1984): 62-76, 139-50, 267-82, 336-43.

93. Among these works, see Raymond Bailey, *Thomas Merton on Mysticism* (Garden City, NY: Doubleday, 1974); and William H. Shannon, *Thomas Merton's Dark Path: The Inner Experience of a Contemplative* (New York: Farrar, Straus, Giroux, 1981). More recently, see Anne E. Carr, *A Search for Wisdom and Spirit: Thomas Merton's Theology of the Self* (Notre Dame: University of Notre Dame Press, 1988).

94. Bernard J. F. Lonergan, S.J., *Insight: A Study of Human Understanding* (London and New York: Longmans, 1957); idem, *Method in Theology* (New York: Herder & Herder, 1972).

Scattered comments can also be found in Lonergan's occasional papers found in *Collection,* ed. F. E. Crowe, S.J. (New York: Herder & Herder, 1967); *A Second Collection,* ed. William J. Ryan, S.J., and Bernard J. Tyrrell, S.J. (Philadelphia: Westminster, 1974); and *A Third Collection,* ed. F. E. Crowe, S.J. (New York: Paulist, 1985).

95. William Johnston, S.J., *The Still Point: Reflections on Zen and Christian Mysticism* (New York: Harper & Row, 1971); idem, *The Inner Eye of Love: Mysticism and Religion* (New York: Harper & Row, 1978); idem, *Christian Mysticism Today* (San Francisco: Harper & Row, 1984).

96. E.g., Anthony J. Kelly, "Is Lonergan's *Method* Adequate to Christian Mystery?" *The Thomist* 39 (1975): 437–70; Harvey D. Egan, S.J., *What are They Saying about Mysticism?* (New York: Paulist, 1982); Vernon J. Gregson, Jr., *Lonergan, Spirituality and the Meeting of Religions* (Lanham, MD: University Press of America, 1985); Tad Dunne, S.J., *Lonergan and Spirituality: Towards a Spiritual Integration* (Chicago: Loyola University Press, 1985); and especially James Robertson Price III, "The Objectivity of Mystical Truth Claims," *The Thomist* 49 (1985): 81–98; idem, "Lonergan and the Foundations of a Contemporary Mystical Theology" (unpublished). I thank James Price for allowing me to use this helpful paper.

97. Lonergan, *Method in Theology,* p. 115.

98. Ibid., pp. 105–7.

99. J. R. Price, "Lonergan and the Foundations," pp. 6–11 (typescript).

100. Lonergan, *Method in Theology,* pp. 29, 77, and esp. 340–42.

101. Price, "Lonergan and the Foundations," pp. 11–18, 24 (typescript).

102. E.g., Jean Daniélou, S.J., *Platonisme et théologie mystique: Doctrine spirituelle de Saint Grégoire de Nysse* (Paris: Éditions Montaigne, 1944).

103. Henri de Lubac, S.J., "Preface," in *La mystique et les mystiques,* ed. A. Ravier, S.J. (Paris: Desclée, 1965), pp. 7–39.

104. Louis Gardet, *La mystique* (Paris: Presses universitaires de France, 1970); "Théologie de la mystique," *Revue Thomiste* 71 (1971): 571–88; "Expérience du soi, expérience des profundeurs de Dieu," *Revue Thomiste* 78 (1978): 357–84; and L. Gardet and Olivier Lacombe, *L'expérience du soi: Étude de mystique comparée* (Paris: Desclée, 1981).

105. L. Malévez, S.J., "Théologie contemplative et théologie discursive," *Nouvelle revue théologique* 88 (1964): 225–49; "Connaissance discursive et connaissance mystique des mystères du salut," in *L'homme devant Dieu: Mélanges de Lubac* 3:167–83.

106. Early in his career, Rahner translated and edited M. Viller's work on patristic asceticism and mysticism into German; see M. Viller and K. Rahner, *Aszese und Mystik in der Väterzeit: Ein Abriss* (Freiburg im Breisgau: Herder, 1939). A number of Rahner's early writings dealt with the history of mysticism. These later were reprinted in the seventeen volumes of his *Schriften zur Theologie,* which, for the sake of convenience, will be cited according to the twenty-volume English translation under the title of *Theological Investigations* (various publishers and places of publication, 1961–1986; hereafter abbreviated as *TI* with volume number). See, e.g., "The 'Spiritual Senses' according to Origen," *TI* 16:81–103 (originally published in 1932); "The Doctrine of the 'Spiritual Senses' in the Middle Ages," *TI* 16:104–34 (originally published in 1933); "The Ignatian Mysticism of Joy in the World," *TI* 3:277–93 (originally published in 1937). See also K. Rahner, *Visions and Prophecies* (London: Burns & Oates, 1963).

107. See "Translator's Foreword," by Harvey D. Egan, S.J., in Karl Rahner, *I Remember: An Autobiographical Interview with Meinhold Krauss* (New York: Crossroad, 1985), p. 3.

108. On this point, see esp. the detailed study of Klaus P. Fischer, *Der Mensch als Geheimnis: Die Anthropologie Karl Rahners* (Freiburg: Herder, 1974). (I am grateful to Anne Carr for having brought this book to my attention.)

109. K. Rahner, *The Practice of Faith* (New York: Crossroad, 1983) ##10–15 (pp. 57–84). The most important of these pieces is #14, "The Theology of Mysticism," originally published as the "Vorwort" to Carl Albrecht, *Das mystische Wort,* ed. Hans A. Fischer-Barnicol (Mainz: Matthias-Grünewald, 1974), pp. vii–xiv (this is also available in a different translation in *TI* 17:90–99). These selections, however, do not include all of Rahner's significant

theoretical pieces on mysticism. At least two others need to be added: "Reflections on the Problem of the Gradual Ascent to Christian Perfection," in *TI* 3:3–23; and "Experience of Transcendence from the Standpoint of Catholic Dogmatics," in *TI* 18:173–88 (a brief excerpt from this is found in *The Practice of Faith*, pp. 69–70).

110. Rahner, *Practice of Faith*, p. 78. On Rahner's apophatic theology, see esp. the three papers in part 4 of *TI* 16 under the title "Questions about God" (pp. 227–50). Cf. "The Concept of Mystery in Catholic Theology" in *TI* 4:36–73.

111. K. Rahner, *Foundations of Christian Faith* (New York: Crossroad, 1978), pp. 19–23, 34–35, 119–30, 170–75.

112. See Rahner, "Experience of Self and Experience of God" in *TI* 13:122–32 (the quotation is from p. 128). Cf. "The Experience of God Today" in *TI* 11:149–65 (my thanks to Anne Carr for reminding me of the importance of these pieces for a full view of Rahner's theory of mysticism).

113. A detailed exposition of this in relation to mysticism is found in "Experience of Transcendence from the Standpoint of Christian Dogmatics," pp. 177–81.

114. Rahner, *Practice of Faith*, p. 84; cf. pp. 69–70, 78, 80–84.

115. See Rahner, "Concerning the Relationship between Nature and Grace," in *TI* 1:297–318.

116. Rahner, *Practice of Faith*, pp. 75–77.

117. Ibid., pp. 69, 72–73.

118. Ibid., p. 60; and "Experience of Transcendence," pp. 174, 176. On the intensification of religious acts, see Rahner, "Reflections on the Problem of the Gradual Ascent," pp. 20–21.

119. Rahner, *Practice of Faith*, p. 77.

120. Ibid., pp. 70, 77; cf. Rahner, "Experience of Transcendence," p. 184; and "Reflections on the Problem of Gradual Ascent," pp. 22–23.

121. The final thesis of the essay "Experience of Transcendence" (pp. 184–88) may qualify this, because here Rahner seems to accept the hypothetical possibility of a natural mysticism.

122. Rahner, "Experience of Transcendence," pp. 179–81, 186.

123. Rahner, *Practice of Faith*, p. 61.

124. The most extended discussion is in Rahner, "Experience of Transcendence," pp. 181–84.

125. Rahner, *Practice of Faith*, pp. 71–72.

126. Ibid., pp. 80–81; and "Experience of Transcendence," p. 186.

127. See Rahner, "Experience of Transcendence," pp. 177–79, for some problematic passages.

128. For some suggestions along this line, see Paul Ricoeur, "Response to Rahner," in *Celebrating the Medieval Heritage*, pp. S126–S131.

129. The trilogy began with an anthology of Origen's writings, *Origenes, Geist und Feuer: Ein Aufbau aus seiner Schriften* (Salzburg: Otto Müller, 1938), translated as *Origen, Spirit and Fire: A Thematic Anthology of His Writings* (1984). Appearing subsequently were *Kosmische Liturgie: Maximus der Bekenner* (Freiburg im Breisgau: Herder, 1941); and *Présence et pensée: Étude sur la philosophie religieuse de Grégoire de Nysse* (Paris: Beauchesne, 1942). Von Balthasar wrote a second book on Origen, *Parole et mystère chez Origène* (Paris: Cerf, 1957).

130. E.g., *Schwestern im Geist: Therese von Lisieux und Elisabeth von Dijon* (2nd ed.; Einsiedeln: Johannes-Verlag, 1970).

131. Hans Urs von Balthasar, *The Glory of the Lord* (New York: Crossroad; San Francisco: Ignatius, 1982, 1984, 1986). For an extended review, see Louis Dupré in *Theological Studies* 49 (1988): 299–318.

132. This essay may be found in the volume *Grundfragen der Mystik* (Einsiedeln: Johannes-Verlag, 1974), pp. 37–71. See also *The Glory of the Lord: I, Seeing the Form*, "Mysticism within the Church," pp. 407–17.

133. Von Balthasar, *Grundfragen*, pp. 42–44.

134. Ibid., pp. 51–52.

135. Von Balthasar denies that a mysticism of radical union is compatible with Christianity, e.g., *The Glory of the Lord* 1:378.

136. Von Balthasar, *Grundfragen*, pp. 57–65.

137. Ibid., pp. 66–70.

Appendix: Section II

1. On this, see John E. Smith, "William James's Account of Mysticism: A Critical Appraisal," in *Mysticism and Religious Traditions*, ed. Steven T. Katz (New York: Oxford, 1983), p. 247. Smith claims that James was the first to use the term "religious experience" in a technical sense (p. 277 n. 3). For a recent study of the evolution and meaning of the term, see Wayne Proudfoot, *Religious Experience* (Berkeley: University of California Press, 1985).

2. William James, *The Varieties of Religious Experience: A Study in Human Nature* (New York: Collier-Macmillan, 1961), pp. 390–402. See also the five characteristics of religious life on p. 377. On the important issue of the relation between mysticism and religion in general to ethics, see Don Browning, "William James's Philosophy of Mysticism," *Journal of Religion* 59 (1979): 56–70.

3. James, *Varieties*, p. 299.

4. Ibid., pp. 301–14. James returned to this in one of his last papers, "A Suggestion about Mysticism," now available in *Understanding Mysticism*, ed. Richard T. Woods, O.P. (Garden City, NY: Doubleday, 1980), pp. 215–22.

5. James, *Varieties*, pp. 299–301.

6. In his description of his own mystical experiences in "A Suggestion about Mysticism" (p. 217), James says, "The mode of consciousness was perceptual, not conceptual. . . ." On the relation of the perceptual and the conceptual in James, see Smith, "William James's Account of Mysticism," p. 259.

7. James, *Varieties*, pp. 326–31. The quote is on p. 329.

8. Ibid., pp. 333–34.

9. Browning, "William James's Philosophy of Mysticism," p. 67 (see the whole discussion on pp. 63–68, 70). On over-beliefs, see James, *Varieties*, pp. 397–98.

10. William James, "A Pluralistic Mystic," *Hibbert Journal* 8 (1910): 739–59. On piecemeal supernaturalism, see James, *Varieties*, pp. 403–8.

11. One of the earliest critics was Friedrich von Hügel in a letter of 1909 discovered and edited by James Luther Adams, "Letter from Friedrich von Hügel to William James," *Downside Review* 98 (1980): 214–36; see esp. pp. 230, 234. For a more recent criticism, see Smith, "William James's Account of Mysticism," pp. 247–48, 275–77.

12. Smith, "William James's Account of Mysticism," pp. 264, 272–75, though I am not happy with the term "rationalistic mysticism."

13. Baron Friedrich von Hügel, *The Mystical Element of Religion*, 2 vols. (London: James Clarke & J. M. Dent, 1961), Preface to the First Edition, 1:xxiii.

14. Von Hügel paid tribute to James's influence; see *Mystical Element* 1:51 n. 1. For further remarks, see Adams, "Letter from Friedrich von Hügel," pp. 218–19.

15. Von Hügel, *Mystical Element* 2:259.

16. On inclusive and exclusive mysticism, see *Mystical Element* 2:264–65, 283, 290–93, 305–9, 351, 366, etc. In an earlier article von Hügel had used the term "pure mysticism" for exclusive mysticism. See "Experience and Transcendence," *Dublin Review* 29 (1906): 357–79.

17. E.g., von Hügel, *Mystical Element* 2:287–90, 351–53.

18. Ibid. 2:272–75, for the relation between mysticism and morality.

19. Ibid. 2:275–90.

20. In his letter to James, von Hügel advised the Harvard professor to read pp. 341–96

of the last chapter, adding "which I well know, alas, to be, in parts, still very obscure" (Adams, "Letter from Friedrich von Hügel," p. 229).

21. Von Hügel, *Mystical Element* 2:336–37.

22. Neoscholastic reviewers, such as Léonce de Grandmaison ("L'élément mystique dans la religion," *Recherches de science religieuse* 1 [1910]: 180–208), were quick to point out the lack of an evolved metaphysics in von Hügel's book, as well as to criticize the universal call to mysticism implied in his view.

23. Von Hügel, *Mystical Element* 2:387–96.

24. Ibid. 1:72–73, 76–77, 86, 229, 232–34, 242–43; 2:336, 383–86.

25. Ibid. 1:50–53; 2:290–91.

26. On Hocking's view of mysticism, see Richard Woods, "Mysticism, Protestantism and Ecumenism: The Spiritual Theology of W. E. Hocking," in *Western Spirituality: Historical Roots, Ecumenical Roots,* ed. M. Fox (Santa Fe: Bear, 1981), pp. 414–35.

27. Bertrand Russell, *Mysticism and Logic and Other Essays* (London: Allen & Unwin, 1956), pp. 1–32.

28. Ibid., p. 3.

29. Ibid., p. 11.

30. For a translation of parts of this work, see *A Maréchal Reader,* ed. and trans. Joseph Donceel, S.J. (New York: Herder & Herder, 1970). For the place of Maréchal in twentieth-century Thomism, see Helen James John, *The Thomist Spectrum* (New York: Fordham University Press, 1966), pp. 139–49.

31. Jure Kristo, "Human Cognition and Mystical Knowledge: Joseph Maréchal's Analysis of Mystical Experience," *Mélanges de science religieuse* 37 (1980), p. 58. Treatment of Maréchal's view of mysticism has been limited. Besides Kristo's article, see Filippo Liverziani, *Dinamismo intelletuale ed esperienza mistica nel pensiero di Joseph Maréchal* (Rome: Liber, 1974).

32. The three central papers of vol. 1 of Joseph Maréchal's *Études sur la psychologie des mystiques,* 2 vols. (Bruges: C. Beyaert, 1926, 1937) have been translated by Algar Thorold under the title *Studies in the Psychology of the Mystics* (Albany: Magi Books, 1964). The same volume includes the first three of the seven papers and three long appendixes of vol. 2.

33. Among Maréchal's other important papers, see esp. "Note d'enseignement théologique: La notion d'extase, d'après l'enseignement traditionnel des mystiques et des théologiens," *Nouvelle revue théologique* 64 (1937): 986–98; and the posthumous essay "Vraie et fausse mystique" in *Nouvelle revue de théologie* 67 (1945): 275–95.

34. James Leuba's book *The Psychology of Religious Mysticism* (New York: Harcourt, Brace, 1929) was based upon a series of essays stretching back to 1902. Maréchal's devastating attack, "Professor Leuba as a Psychologist of Mysticism," from vol. 2 of *Études* can be found in *Studies in the Psychology of the Mystics,* pp. 219–38.

35. Maréchal was one of the early Catholic respondents to Freud's psychology; see "Les lignes essentielles du Freudisme," *Nouvelle revue théologique* 52 (1925): 537–51, 577–605; 53 (1926): 13–50.

36. Maréchal, *Studies,* p. 40. For attacks on empirical determinism, see pp. 31, 35–43, 125–30, 217–38.

37. Ibid., p. 307.

38. Ibid., pp. 51–52, 195.

39. Ibid., pp. 52–53.

40. E.g., ibid., p. 195: "Our apriorism, open minded enough not to exclude a transcendental experience, is as good as any other; and it permits us to respect the letter of the mystical writings."

41. Ibid., p. 190.

42. Ibid., pp. 57–77, esp. p. 60.

43. Ibid., p. 92 for the three elements, and subsequently p. 98.

44. Ibid., p. 99.

45. Ibid., p. 101. For Maréchal's doctrine of the dynamism of the intelligence's drive to the pure intuition of being see pp. 26, 42, 50–51, 86, 100–101, 133–34, 154–55, 196–97, 290. This teaching is expanded in the fifth volume of Maréchal, *Le point de départ*, 5 vols. (Bruges: C. Beyaert, 1922–49).

46. Maréchal, *Studies*, pp. 102, 103.

47. Jure Kristo has criticized Maréchal's objectivizing of God as the term of mystical knowing (Kristo, "Human Cognition and Mystical Knowledge," pp. 60, 66–72).

48. Maréchal, *Studies*, p. 111.

49. Ibid., pp. 124, 286–87; Maréchal, "Vrai et fausse mystique," pp. 275–83.

50. Maréchal, *Studies*, p. 290; "Vrai et fausse mystique," pp. 278–81. For a post-Maréchalian development of this perspective through the use of transcendental "horizon analysis," see Jure Kristo, "The Interpretation of Religious Experience: What Do Mystics Intend When They Talk about Their Experiences?" *Journal of Religion* 62 (1982): 21–38.

51. This important essay, based on a conference given at Louvain, first appeared in the second volume of the *Études* (see Maréchal, *Studies*, pp. 285–344). The quotation is on p. 288.

52. The most detailed comparison is found in "Reflections on the Comparative Study," in Maréchal, *Studies*, pp. 289–339; but see also "The Feeling of Presence," in *Studies*, pp. 111–18.

53. See "The Problem of Mystical Grace in Islam," in *Studies*, pp. 241–81; and "Le 'Seul à Seul' avec Dieu dans l'extase d'après Plotin," in *Études* 2:51–87.

54. Maréchal, *Studies*, p. 303. On natural and supernatural theistic mysticism, see p. 133.

55. Ibid., pp. 155–80.

56. Ibid., p. 322. In "Some Distinctive Features of Christian Mysticism," *Studies*, pp. 199–203, Maréchal discusses six characteristics of Christian mysticism in terms of its specific doctrinal content.

57. The 1914 article "L'intuition de Dieu dans la mystique chrétienne," as well as the long papers on the teaching of Augustine and Aquinas, are all available in vol. 2 of Maréchal's *Études*, though not in the English translation. See also "Note d'enseignement théologique: La notion d'extase, d'après l'enseignement traditionnel des mystiques et des théologiens" (see n. 33).

58. See Maréchal, *Studies*, pp. 118–23, 190–95, 338–39.

59. The intellectualist emphasis is evident in *Studies*, p. 196; cf. pp. 121, 131, 134. For an early critique, see Jacques Maritain, *Redeeming the Time* (London· G. Bles, 1944), p. 233.

60. Maréchal, *Le point de départ* 5:305–6, 311–13, 344, etc.

61. See Maréchal, *Studies*, pp. 81–91, 122.

62. Ibid., p. 154; cf. p. 187. See also the letter of explanation that Maréchal wrote in 1943 available in *Mélanges Joseph Maréchal* (Paris and Brussels: Desclée, 1950) 1:372–73.

63. See Helen John, *Thomist Spectrum*, pp. 140–43.

64. Compare Maréchal, *Studies*, pp. 122–23, 127–28.

65. For a general introduction to the two, as well as a good account of modern French philosophy, see Frederick Copleston, S.J., *A History of Philosophy*, 9 vols. (Garden City, NY: Doubleday, 1977) 9.2: chaps. 9–11. For a general sketch of French discussion of mysticism in the first three decades of the twentieth century, see Emile Poulat, *Critique et mystique: Autour de Loisy ou la conscience catholique et l'esprit moderne* (Paris: Le Centurion, 1984), chap. 8, "L'Humanité polie par la mystique," pp. 255–306 (my thanks to Paul Lachance for bringing this useful work to my attention). Also see Jacques Colette, "Mystique et philosophie," *Revue des sciences philosophiques et théologiques* 70 (1986): 329–48.

66. For a general account of Blondel in English, see Henry Bouillard, *Blondel and Christianity* (Washington: Corpus, 1970). On the issue of mysticism, see George S. Worgul, Jr., "M. Blondel and the Problem of Mysticism," *Ephemerides theologiae lovanienses* 71 (1985): 100–122.

67. See Copleston, *History of Philosophy* 9.2:19–24; and Bouillard, *Blondel*, pp. 23–24.

68. M. Blondel, "Le problème de la mystique," was published in *La nouvelle journée* in 1925 and was reissued as no. 8 of the *Cahiers de la nouvelle journée* (Paris: Bloud & Gay, 1929) under the title *Qu'est-ce que la mystique?* In the 1929 edition, which I shall cite, it occupies pp. 1–63.

69. Bouillard, *Blondel*, pp. 33–35.

70. Blondel, *Le procès de l'intelligence* was originally published in *La nouvelle journée* in 1921 and was reprinted as a separate volume (Paris: Bloud & Gay, 1922). Blondel had been influenced by Pierre Rousselot's *L'Intellectualisme de S. Thomas d'Aquin* (Paris: Beauchesne, 1908).

71. See Blondel, "Le problème de la mystique," pp. 18–19, 44–45, 53, on mysticism as a prolongation of the ordinary Christian life, and pp. 42, 58–59, more particularly on the continuity between mystical knowing and the lower forms.

72. Ibid., pp. 30, 36–37, 40.

73. Ibid., pp. 52–53, 62.

74. Ibid., p. 56: ". . . elle est en cette universelle charité qui concilie et hierarchise, sans confusion, toutes les phases et tous les degrés." See the whole section on pp. 53–57, as well as the discussion in Worgul, "Blondel and the Problem of Mysticism," pp. 116–19.

75. Blondel, "Le problème de la mystique," p. 62: "il souffre activement et agit passivement." See the striking description of the mystic on pp. 61–63, beginning, "Le mystique, lui, est la vivante et féconde conciliation de la liberté et la authorité, de la vie interieure la plus independante et de la communion sociale le plus efficace et la plus disciplinée."

76. Bouillard, *Blondel*, pp. 34–36.

77. Besides Copleston's clear account in vol. 9 of *A History of Philosophy*, see Leszek Kolakowski, *Bergson* (Oxford and New York: Oxford University Press, 1985). On Bergson's philosophy of morality, religion and mysticism, see also Jacques Maritain's revealing study, "The Bergsonian Philosophy of Morality and Religion," in *Redeeming the Time* (London: G. Bles, 1944), pp. 74–100.

78. Kolakowski, *Bergson*, p. 73.

79. Henri Bergson, *The Two Sources of Morality and Religion* (Notre Dame: University of Notre Dame Press, 1977), pp. 210–14.

80. On this question, see Kolakowski, *Bergson*, pp. 81–85.

81. Bergson, *The Two Sources*, p. 220. He goes on to say, "This effort is of God, if it is not God himself."

82. Ibid., p. 238.

83. Ibid., p. 225.

84. Ibid., p. 231.

85. Ibid., pp. 240–56.

86. Alfred Loisy (1857–1940), excommunicated as a Modernist in 1908, was Professor of the History of Religions at the Collège de France from 1909 to 1930. He attacked Bergson's *Two Sources* in his polemical work *Y a-t-il deux sources de la religion et de la morale?* (Paris: E. Nourrey, 1934). For situating this debate within the context of modern French discussions of mysticism, see Poulat, *Critique et mystique*, chap. 8.

87. Jacques Maritain's first published work in 1913 was a book highly critical of Bergson, *La philosophie bergsonienne* (in English as *Bergsonian Philosophy and Thomism* [New York: Greenwood Press, 1955]. His essay on Bergson's *Two Sources* (see n. 77) was far more positive in distinguishing between Bergson's faulty conceptualization and the basic correctness of his intention. Maritain criticized Blondel's *Le procès de l'intelligence* in "L'intelligence d'après M. Maurice Blondel," *Revue de philosophie* 30 (1923): 333–64, 484–511.

88. I will cite from Gerald B. Phelan's English translation of the fourth French edition, *Distinguish to Unite, or The Degrees of Knowledge* (New York: Scribner, 1959). The work contains both a critique of Bergson's views of mysticism for "thoroughgoing Pelagianism" (see pp. 288–300 n. 1), as well as an attack on Blondel's view of mysticism in Appendix 6, "Some Clarifications" (pp. 451–55).

89. I shall cite these from the English translations. Jacques Maritain, "Action and

Contemplation" in *Scholasticism and Politics* (New York: Macmillan, 1940), pp. 170-93; idem, "The Natural Mystical Experience and the Void" in *Redeeming the Time* (London: G. Bles, 1944), pp. 225-55.

90. To quote Henry Bars, "It [i.e., Maritain's ontology of mystical experience] is a question of situating mystical experience in the hierarchy of approaches which lead the human spirit towards the possession of Truth . . . ," in "Maritain's Contributions to an Understanding of Mystical Experience," in *Jacques Maritain, the Man and his Achievement,* ed. Joseph William Evans (New York: Sheed & Ward, 1963), p. 116.

91. Maritain, *Degrees,* p. 7; see pp. 277-80, where Maritain denies that metaphysics can demand mystical experience.

92. Ibid., p. 75, in the important chapter 3, entitled "Critical Realism." See Copleston, *History of Philosophy* 9.2:48-49.

93. Maritain, *Degrees,* pp. 202-20.

94. Ibid., pp. 220-44.

95. Ibid., pp. 236-41.

96. Ibid., p. 247, for the first definition; the second is found in idem, "Natural Mystical Experience and the Void," p. 225 (hereafter cited as "Void").

97. Maritain, *Degrees,* p. 254.

98. It is interesting to note how large, but diverse, a role the notion of connaturality played in French Catholic discussion of mysticism at this time. Blondel appears to have discovered the importance of mysticism through his reading of Rousselot on intellectual connaturality. Maréchal made connaturality a key to the development of his dynamic Thomist epistemology and was criticized by Maritain for neglecting the affective connaturality which is the true center of mysticism. Maritain summarized his own understanding of connatural knowing in a paper published in 1951 entitled "On Knowledge through Connaturality" (see Jacques and Raissa Maritain, *Oeuvres completes* [Paris: Editions Saint-Paul] 9:980-1001).

99. Maritain, "Void," pp. 226-35.

100. Ibid., p. 240; see the detailed analysis on pp. 241-48, from which the quotations that follow are drawn. Such natural mystical experience had been denied in *Degrees,* pp. 268-77. Maritain always admitted the possibility of supernatural mystical experience outside Christianity; see *Degrees,* pp. 272-75; "Void," pp. 252-53.

101. Maritain, "Void," pp. 248-49; cf. "Action and Contemplation," pp. 188-90.

102. See pp. 287-88 above. On natural mystical experience in Maritain, see Bars, "Maritain's Contributions," pp. 119-25.

103. Maritain, "Void," p. 242.

104. Maritain, *Degrees,* pp. 260-65, and 448-50 (a discussion of Gardeil's views on this issue).

105. Ibid., pp. 345-46; "Action and Contemplation," pp. 184-90.

106. Maritain, *Degrees,* p. 368.

107. Ibid., pp. 368-72.

108. Ibid., p. 350 (see the whole passage on pp. 349-51); cf. pp. 258, 287, 338, 356-57.

109. Ibid., pp. 373-81; cf. pp. 465-67. Maritain attacks Eckhart's understanding of our share in the life of the Trinity (p. 376 n. 2).

110. Maritain, *Degrees,* chapter 7, "Augustinian Wisdom," forms an uneasy prologue, in which Augustine is relegated to the more diffuse category of "wisdom" rather than the precisely developed category of mystical science.

111. Maritain, *Degrees,* pp. 310-19; cf. Bars, "Maritain's Contribution," pp. 114-15.

112. Maritain, *Degrees,* p. 338.

113. Ibid., p. 326.

114. Ibid., pp. 326-27, 336-37.

115. Ibid. , pp. 7, 282-83; cf. "Void," pp. 235-36.

116. Henri Delacroix (1873-1937) wrote his thesis on Eckhart (*Essai sur la mysticisme*

speculatif en Allemagne au XIVe siècle [Paris: Alcan, 1900]) and also published a work entitled *Études d'histoire et de psychologie du mysticisme: Les grands mystiques chrétiens* (Paris: Alcan, 1908), which treats Teresa of Avila, Madame Guyon, and Henry Suso. For Jean Baruzi, see *Saint Jean de la Croix et le problème de l'expérience mystique* (Paris: Alcan, 1924); see also Baruzi, H. Delacroix, M. Laberthoniere, and E. LeRoy, "Saint Jean de la Croix et le problème de la valeur noétique de l'expérience mystique," *Bulletin de la Société française de Philosophie* (1925), as well as Baruzi's paper "Introduction à des recherches sur le langage mystique," *Recherches philosophiques* 1 (1931–32): 66–82. Baruzi was criticized by Maritain in *Degrees*, pp. 8–10. Finally, see Roger Bastide, *Les problèmes de la vie mystique* (Paris: Colin, 1931).

117. See de Certeau's editions of Pierre Favre, *Memorial* (Paris, 1960); and Jean-Joseph Surin, *Guide spirituel* (Paris, 1963), and idem, *Correspondence* (Paris, 1966).

118. First sketched in Michel de Certeau, "'Mystique' au XVIIe siècle: Le problème du langage mystique,'" in *L'Homme devant Dieu: Mélanges offerts au Père Henri de Lubac*, 3 vols. (Paris: Aubier, 1964) 2:267–91.

119. Michel de Certeau, *La Fable Mystique XVIe–XVIIe Siècle* (Paris: Gallimard, 1982) was to form the first of three volumes. Among the most important articles, see M. de Certeau, "Histoire et Mystique," *Revue d'histoire de spiritualité* 48 (1972): 69–82; "L'Enonciation mystique," *Revue de science religieuse* 64 (1976): 183–215 (available in English as "Mystic Speech," in Michel de Certeau, *Heterologies: Discourse on the Other* [Minneapolis: University of Minnesota Press, 1986], pp. 80–100); and "Historicités mystiques," *Revue de science religieuse* 73 (1985): 325–54.

120. Little has been written about de Certeau's work thus far; but see Guy Petitdemange, "L'invention du commencement: *La Fable Mystique*, de Michel de Certeau. Première lecture," *Revue de science religieuse* 71 (1983): 497–520; and Antoine Lion, "Le discours blessé: Sur le langage mystique selon Michel de Certeau," *Revue des sciences philosophiques et religieuses* 71 (1987): 405–19.

121. Michel de Certeau, "Mystique," *Encyclopaedia universalis* (Paris: Encyclopaedia universalis de France, 1968) 11:521–26. (I will make use of an unpublished translation by Paul Lachance and George York. My thanks to the translators for allowing me to use this manuscript.)

122. Ibid., p. 522.

123. Ibid., pp. 524–25; de Certeau, "Historicités mystiques," pp. 342–47; *La Fable Mystique*, pp. 37–43.

124. De Certeau, "Mystique," p. 524.

125. See, e.g., de Certeau, *La Fable Mystique*, pp. 28–29, 101–208; idem, "Mystic Speech," pp. 82–83.

126. De Certeau, "Mystique," p. 522.

127. Ibid., pp. 522–23.

128. See de Certeau, *La Fable Mystique*, pp. 15–18, for some general remarks on the relation.

129. On the role of the mystic's body, see de Certeau, *La Fable Mystique*, pp. 12–15.

130. See Lion, "Le discours blessé," pp. 413–19, for some helpful comments.

131. De Certeau, "Mystic Speech," pp. 90–91.

132. E.g., de Certeau, "Mystique," pp. 525–26; idem, "Historicités mystiques," pp. 329–31.

133. John D. Caputo, *The Mystical Element in Heidegger's Thought* (Athens, OH: Ohio University Press, 1978), esp. p. 239, where he characterizes this "mystical element" in the following way: "It consists in this: that Heidegger has appropriated the structural relationship between the soul and God which is found in Meister Eckhart's mysticism in order to articulate the relationship in his own work between thought and Being. . . . Mysticism, then, is one of the 'models' for 'thinking,' but thinking is not a species of mysticism."

134. This is evident from the essay of E. Zemach, "Wittgenstein's Philosophy of the Mystical," *Review of Metaphysics* 18 (1964): 38–57. Cf. Ronald Burr, "Wittgenstein's Later

Language Philosophy and Some Issues in the Philosophy of Mysticism," *International Journal for Philosophy of Religion* 7 (1976): 261–87.

135. See the paper of Alan M. Olson, "Jasper's Critique of Mysticism," *Journal of the American Academy of Religion* 51 (1983): 251–66.

136. Carl Albrecht, *Das mystischen Erkennen: Gnoseologie und philosophische Relevanz der mystischen Relation* (Bremen: Schunemann, 1958); idem, *Das mystische Wort: Erleben und Sprechen in Versunkenheit* (Mainz: Matthias Grünewald, 1974). For another contribution, see August Brunner, *Der Schritt über die Grenzen: Wesen und Sinn der Mystik* (Würzburg: Echter Verlag, 1972).

137. Alois M. Haas, "Was ist Mystik?" in *Abendländische Mystik im Mittelalter: Symposion Kloster Engelberg 1984,* ed. Kurt Ruh (Stuttgart: Metzler, 1986), pp. 319–42. See also the paper of Dietmar Mieth, "Gottesschau und Gottesgeburt: Zwei Typen christlicher Gotteserfahrung in der Tradition," *Freiburger Zeitschrift für Philosophie und Theologie* 27 (1980): 204–23.

138. L. Massignon (1883–1962), *La passion de Husayn Ibn Mansūr Hāllāj: martyr mystique de l'Islam,* was first published in two volumes. An enlarged edition in four volumes appeared in 1975. This has been translated into English by Herbert Mason under the title *The Passion of al-Hallaj: Mystic and Martyr of Islam,* 4 vols. (Princeton: Princeton University Press, 1982).

139. Alfred Jules Ayer, *Language, Truth and Logic* (New York: Dover, 1952), pp. 118–19.

140. W. T. Stace, *Mysticism and Philosophy* (New York and London: Macmillan, 1960). Stace also published an anthology of mystical texts under the title *The Teaching of the Mystics* (New York: New American Library, 1960), as well as a number of other papers on the topic.

141. Stace, *Mysticism and Philosophy,* p. 7.

142. Ibid., pp. 35–38.

143. Ibid., p. 31.

144. Ibid.

145. Ibid., pp. 131–33. The common characteristics of extrovertive mystical experiences are unifying vision (all things are one), concrete apprehension of the One as life in all things, a sense of objectivity and reality, blessedness and peace, feeling of the holy, paradoxicality, and alleged ineffability. The common characteristics of the higher form of introvertive mystical experience toward which the extrovertive tends are pure or unitary consciousness, nonspatiality and nontemporality, a sense of objectivity and reality, blessedness and peace, feeling of the holy, paradoxicality, and alleged ineffability. On both types as universal, see *Mysticism and Philosophy,* p. 62.

146. Ibid., p. 94.

147. It would be tedious to detail all the examples of this. For a few of the more conspicuous cases under (1), see *Mysticism and Philosophy,* pp. 88, 94–95, 97 n. 44 on the alleged "point-by-point" identity of passages from the Mandukya Upanishad and Jan van Ruusbroec; under (2) pp. 100–103 where Eckhart and John of the Cross are said to have had the same experience despite their difference of language; and under (3) p. 107 for the assertion that the appearance of the term "Nothing" in mystical texts always signifies an experience of the undifferentiated void.

148. Stace, *Mysticism and Philosophy,* p. 132.

149. Ibid., pp. 137–45.

150. Ibid., pp. 153–54, 158–59, 161–82, 194–204. The view of God implied here is described as pantheism in chap. 4, understood as "identity in difference" and contrasted with pure monism and the mistaken dualism of the monotheistic religions. What Stace calls pantheism, other investigators, such as Baron von Hügel, would term "panentheism."

151. Stace dismisses four mitigating theories on pp. 253–68 of *Mysticism and Philosophy.*

152. Ibid., pp. 268–70, where he denies that any higher logic, such as Hegel's "identity of opposites," applies in this realm.

153. Ibid., pp. 295–306.

154. Ibid., pp. 291, 294.

155. For a recent detailed critique of Stace's referential theory of mysticism (i.e., his

attempt to identify mystical experience through an analysis of mystical texts), see Christer Norrman, *Mystical Experiences and Scientific Method* (Stockholm: Almqvist & Wiksell, 1986).

156. Richard M. Gale, "Mysticism and Philosophy," *Journal of Philosophy* 57 (1960): 471–81.

157. J. N. Findlay, "The Logic of Mysticism," in *Ascent to the Absolute: Metaphysical Papers and Letters* (London: Allen & Unwin, 1970), pp. 162–83 (the quotation is on p. 170).

158. Galen K. Pletcher, "Mysticism, Contradiction, and Ineffability," *American Philosophical Quarterly* 10 (1973): 201–11. Pletcher acknowledges a debt to Paul Henle, "Mysticism and Semantics," *Philosophy and Phenomenological Research* 9 (1949): 116–22.

159. See, e.g., Charles Morris, "Mysticism and its Language," in *Writings on the General Theory of Signs* (Paris: Mouton, 1971), pp. 456–63.

160. Bruce Garside, "Language and the Interpretation of Mystical Experience," *International Journal for the Philosophy of Religion* 3 (1972): 93–102; Terence Penelhum, "Unity and Diversity in the Interpretation of Mysticism," in *Mystics and Scholars: The Calgary Conference on Mysticism 1976*, ed. Harold Coward and Terence Penelhum, *Sciences Religieuses: Supplements* 13, pp. 71–81.

161. Hick's neo-Kantian distinction between the unity of the mystical noumenon and the diversity of the phenomena can be found in his essay "Mystical Experience as Cognition," in *Mystics and Scholars*, pp. 41–56 (see pp. 61, 83–84 for clarifications).

162. Ninian Smart, "Mystical Experience," *Sophia* 1 (1962): 19–26; idem, "Interpretation and Mystical Experience," *Religious Studies* 1 (1965): 75–87; idem, "The Exploration of Mysticism," in *Mystics and Scholars*, pp. 63–69; idem, "Understanding Religious Experience," in *Mysticism and Philosophical Analysis*, ed. Steven T. Katz (New York: Oxford University Press, 1978), pp. 10–21; idem, "The Purification of Consciousness and the Negative Path," in *Mysticism and Religious Traditions*, ed. Steven T. Katz (New York: Oxford University Press, 1983), pp. 117–29. See also his historical overview, "Mysticism, History of," in *The Encyclopedia of Philosophy*, ed. Paul Edwards (New York: Macmillan, 1967) 5:419–29.

163. The term "consciousness-purity" appears only recently in Smart's writings ("The Purification of Consciousness and the Negative Path," pp. 117–20, 123, 124–25) as a more precise characterization of his earlier thought. This leaves somewhat ambiguous Smart's view on how far extrovertive types of mysticism, especially the "panenhenic" forms of nature mysticism, can be said to be mystical at all. Philip Almond criticizes Smart for this exclusion (*Mystical Experience and Religious Doctrine* [Berlin and New York: Mouton, 1982], pp. 44–45 and 65–68), but in his article "Mysticism, History of," Smart rather confusingly says of panenhenic feelings: "These neither coincide with prophetic experiences nor strictly with those of introvertive mysticism, but since they sometimes occur in conjunction with the latter, it is convenient to treat them as mystical" (p. 420).

164. Smart's early book *Reasons and Faiths* (London: Routledge & Kegan Paul, 1958) was concerned with spelling out various forms of religion on the basis of such interactions.

165. Smart, "Understanding Religious Experience," p. 14; cf. "Purification of Consciousness," pp. 126–28.

166. Smart, "Interpretation and Mystical Experience," as reprinted in *Understanding Mysticism*, ed. Richard Woods (Garden City, NY: Doubleday, 1980), pp. 81–84.

167. Ibid., p. 84.

168. Ibid., p. 83.

169. Smart, "Understanding Religious Experience," pp. 17–20 (quotation on p. 18); cf. "Purification of Consciousness," pp. 120–24. Smart's notion of the *askēsis* of performative transcendence is not unlike Augustine's view of the function of ineffable language in *De doctrina christiana* 1.6.

170. Smart, "Purification of Consciousness," p. 123.

171. Contrast the possibility language of Smart's "Interpretation and Mystical Experience," pp. 89–91, with the concluding pages (pp. 124–28) of his "Purification of Consciousness."

172. Smart, "Understanding Religious Experience," p. 15.

173. William J. Wainwright, *Mysticism: A Study of its Nature, Cognitive Value and Moral Implications* (Madison: University of Wisconsin Press, 1981). In these remarks on Wainwright I will draw in part on my review in *Journal of Religion* 65 (1985): 306-7.

174. Wainwright, *Mysticism,* p. 233.

175. Wainwright criticizes scholars like B. Garside and S. Katz (see below) who have attacked the experience-interpretation distinction (*Mysticism,* pp. 18-22).

176. Ibid., p. 27.

177. Ibid., pp. 33-40, where four types of extrovertive mysticism which take the external world as object are divided from two separate forms of introvertive mysticism, the monistic mysticism of pure empty consciousness and the dualistic theistic mysticism of mutual love with God.

178. Ibid., p. 102.

179. Ibid., pp. 96-102.

180. Ibid., pp. 117-27.

181. Ibid., pp. 139-59, for the former, and pp. 160-84, for the latter. The book closes with a chapter entitled "Mysticism and Morality" (pp. 198-231), another topic much discussed in recent Anglo-American philosophical treatments.

182. Philip C. Almond, *Mystical Experience and Religious Doctrine: An Investigation of the Study of Mysticism in World Religions* (Berlin and New York: Mouton, 1982).

183. Ibid., pp. vii, 3-7, 185-86.

184. Almond places James in this category (p. 129), which does not do justice to the full range of his views.

185. Ibid., p. 148.

186. See ibid., chap. 8, pp. 157-86.

187. Ibid., pp. 162-63. Retrospective interpretation comes after the experience, reflexive during it, and incorporated interpretation precedes and shapes it. See Peter Moore, "Recent Studies of Mysticism: A Critical Survey," *Religion* 3 (1973): 147-48.

188. See Almond's remarks on the relation and possible conflicts between incorporated and retrospective interpretations (*Mystical Experience,* pp. 167-68, 182-83).

189. Peter Moore, "A Recent Study of Mysticism," *Heythrop Journal* 25 (1984): 178-83; Steven Katz, "Recent Work on Mysticism," *History of Religions* 25 (1985/86): 77-78.

190. Almond, *Mystical Experience,* pp. 175-80. This is especially true of his unconvincing attempt to argue for a similarity between John of the Cross and Eastern forms of contentless experience.

191. Steven T. Katz, ed., *Mysticism and Philosophical Analysis* (New York: Oxford University Press, 1978), p. 26.

192. Ibid., pp. 54-56.

193. The end of Katz's essay explicitly says that "further fundamental epistemological research into the conditions of mystical experience has to be undertaken in order to lay bare the skeleton of such experience in so far as this is possible" (*Mystical and Philosophical Analysis,* p. 66).

194. Ibid., p. 111; cf. pp. 102-7 for a discussion of the relation between mystical "ineffability" and the types of mystical writing.

195. Ibid., pp. 108-110.

196. E.g., Robert Gimello, "Mysticism and Meditation," in *Mysticism and Philosophical Analysis,* ed. Katz, pp. 170-99; see esp. p. 193.

197. E.g., Renford Bambrough, "Intuition and the Inexpressible," in *Mysticism and Philosophical Analysis,* ed. Katz, pp. 200-213.

198. The most important of these is the interesting essay of Frederick Streng, "Language and Mystical Awareness," in *Mysticism,* ed. Katz, pp. 141-69, which argues that different mystical epistemologies are conditioned by different soteriological expectations.

199. *Mysticism and Religious Traditions,* ed. Steven T. Katz (New York: Oxford University

Press, 1983); see esp. the essays by Katz, Schimmel, Cousins, and Carman. The essays by Smart and Smith in this volume have been noted earlier.

200. For comments on the current Anglo-American philosophical debate on mysticism from a continental perspective, see de Certeau, "Historicités mystiques," pp. 347-50.

201. Wainwright, *Mysticism,* pp. 19-22.

202. See Katz, "Recent Work on Mysticism," pp. 77-78.

203. James Robertson Price III, "The Objectivity of Mystical Truth Claims," *The Thomist* 49 (1985): 81-98.

204. James Price, "Typologies and Cross-Cultural Analysis of Mysticism: A Critique," in *Religion and Culture: Essays in Honor of Bernard Lonergan,* ed. T. Fallon and B. Riley (Albany: State University of New York Press, 1987), pp. 181-80; see esp. pp. 182-83.

205. Anthony N. Perovich, "Mysticism and the Philosophy of Science," *Journal of Religion* 65 (1985): 63-82, esp. p. 71.

206. Ibid., pp. 69, 75-82.

207. Wayne Proudfoot, *Religious Experience* (Berkeley: University of California Press, 1985), pp. 124-36.

208. Ibid., pp. 136-54. See esp. pp. 138-39, where Proudfoot introduces the important distinction between two senses of the term mystical experience: "(1) a simple description of certain mental and/or physiological states. . . , or (2) not a simple description but, like *miracle,* a phrase that includes among the rules for its proper application an explanatory commitment — namely, the judgment that whatever physiological or mental states are being identified as mystical could not be accounted for in naturalistic terms." His argument proceeds on the basis that mystical experience is mostly used in the latter sense.

209. Another example of a balanced approach which pays attention to context can be found in Walter Principe, "Mysticism: Its Meaning and Varieties," in *Mystics and Scholars,* ed. Coward and Penelhum, pp. 1-15.

210. Louis Dupré, *The Other Dimension: A Search for the Meaning of Religious Attitudes* (Garden City, NY: Doubleday, 1972); see chap. 9, "The Mystical Vision."

211. See Louis Dupré, "Mysticism" in *The Encyclopedia of Religion,* ed. Mircea Eliade (New York: Macmillan, 1987) 10:245-61; idem, *"Unio mystica:* the State and the Experience," in *Mystical Union and Monotheistic Faith: An Ecumenical Dialogue,* ed. Moshe Idel and Bernard McGinn (New York: Macmillan, 1989), pp. 3-23.

212. Louis Dupré, *The Common Life: The Origins of Trinitarian Mysticism and its Development by Jan Ruusbroec* (New York: Crossroad, 1984).

213. Louis Dupré, *The Deeper Self: An Introduction to Christian Mysticism* (New York: Crossroad, 1981), pp. 19-22.

214. See Louis Dupré, *Transcendent Selfhood: The Loss and Recovery of the Inner Life* (New York: Seabury, 1976), chap. 8, "The Mystical Experience of the Self" (pp. 92-104).

215. Ibid., p. 102.

216. Louis Dupré, "Spiritual Life in a Secular Age," *Daedalus* 111 (1982): 21-31.

217. Ibid., p. 27.

218. Ibid., p. 31.

219. See esp. Ewert Cousins, *Bonaventure and the Coincidence of Opposites* (Chicago: Franciscan Herald Press, 1978).

220. Ewert Cousins, *Global Spirituality: Toward the Meeting of Mystical Paths* (Madras: University of Madras, Radhakrishnan Institute for Advanced Study in Philosophy, 1985).

221. Cousins pays tribute to a research seminar on mysticism conducted by Peter Berger in 1978 as formative of his approach. Papers offered in this seminar were later published as *The Other Side of God: A Polarity in World Religions,* ed. Peter L. Berger (Garden City, NY: Doubleday, 1981). Cousins's own paper, "Francis of Assisi and Bonaventure: Mysticism and Theological Interpretation" (pp. 74-103) is summarized in his *Global Spirituality.*

222. Cousins, *Global Spirituality,* p. 24.

Appendix: Section III

1. Nathan Söderblom, "Communion with Deity (Introductory)," *Encyclopaedia of Religion and Ethics*, ed. James Hastings (New York: Scribner, 1911) 3:736–40.

2. N. Söderblom, *The Nature of Revelation* (Philadelphia: Fortress, 1966), pp. 81–97; idem, *The Living God* (Oxford: Oxford University Press, 1933), p. 348.

3. Lehmann's understanding of mysticism as "oneness of the human soul with the Divine Being" implied for him the complete obliteration of both divine and human personality; see Edvard Lehmann, *Mysticism in Heathendom and Christendom* (London: Luzac, 1910), p. 7.

4. For an introduction to Otto, see Joachim Wach, *Types of Religious Experience: Christian and Non-Christian* (Chicago: University of Chicago Press, 1951), pp. 209–27; and Theodore M. Ludwig, "Rudolf Otto," *The Encyclopedia of Religion*, ed. Mircea Eliade (New York: Macmillan, 1987) 11:139–41. For an evaluation of Otto on mysticism, see Philip C. Almond, *Mystical Experience and Religious Doctrine* (Berlin and New York: Mouton, 1982), pp. 92–119.

5. Rudolf Otto, *The Idea of the Holy* (London: Penguin, 1959), pp. 24–25, 35.

6. Ibid., pp. 26–39, esp. pp. 34–37.

7. Ibid., p. 36.

8. Otto's citation from Augustine *Confessions* 2.9.1 on p. 42 n. 1 hints that the numinous cannot be "wholly" Wholly Other, as many critics have noted. The discussion of the "Wholly Other" occupies pp. 39–53.

9. Otto, *Idea of the Holy*, pp. 40–44, 106.

10. Ibid., pp. 45–53.

11. Ibid., p. 101 n. 1.

12. Rudolf Otto, *Mysticism East and West* (New York: Macmillan, 1970), pp. 5, 14, 157.

13. Ibid., p. 158. Thus, as P. Almond notes (*Mystical Experience*, pp. 113, 116–17), for Otto there are really three types of numinous experience: theistic, introvertive mystical, and extrovertive mystical.

14. Otto, *Mysticism East and West*, pp. 159–62. See Almond, *Mystical Experience*, p. 118.

15. Otto, *Mysticism East and West*, chaps. 5 and 6.

16. Ibid., p. 59.

17. Ibid., pp. 61–71, where Otto describes three progressive forms of extrovertive mysticism.

18. Ibid., pp. 161–79; cf. pp. 275–82, on the intertwining of the two types.

19. Otto's presentation of Eckhart contains many valuable insights, though his interpretation of the German Dominican as a "Gothic man" struggling to be free of the toils of scholasticism is quite chauvinist (e.g., pp. 185–88, 204, 249, etc.).

20. See, e.g., Almond, *Mystical Experience*, pp. 103–4; Frederick Streng, "Language and Mystical Awareness," in *Mysticism and Philosophical Analysis*, ed. Steven T. Katz (New York: Oxford University Press, 1978), p. 162; James R. Price III, "Typologies and the Cross-Cultural Analysis of Mysticism: A Critique," in *Religion and Culture: Essays in Honor of Bernard Lonergan*, ed. T. Fallon and B. Riley (Albany: State University of New York Press, 1987), pp. 182–83.

21. On Heiler, see Rowan Williams, "The Prophetic and the Mystical: Heiler Revisited," *New Blackfriars* 64 (1983): 330–44.

22. Friedrich Heiler, *Prayer: A Study in the History and Psychology of Religion* (London: Oxford University Press, 1932), p. 136. For a brief summary of Heiler's view of mysticism, see his *Die Bedeutung der Mystik für die Weltreligionen* (Munich, 1919).

23. Heiler, *Prayer*, p. 358.

24. For these contrasts, see *Prayer*, pp. 142–71.

25. Williams, "Heiler Revisited," p. 333.

26. Friedrich Heiler, "Contemplation in Christian Mysticism," in *Spiritual Disciplines: Papers from the Eranos Yearbooks* (New York: Pantheon, 1960), pp. 186–238 (first given in 1933).

27. Aldous Huxley, *The Perennial Philosophy* (New York: Harper, 1945).

28. See Almond, *Mystical Experience,* pp. 11–22, for a brief account of his views.

29. Esp. Frithjof Schuon, *The Transcendent Unity of Religions* (Wheaton, IL: Theosophical Publishing House, 1984).

30. E.g., Huston Smith, *Forgotten Truth: The Primordial Tradition* (New York: Harper, 1976). Seyyed Hossein Nasr, *Knowledge and the Sacred* (New York: Crossroad, 1981).

31. General surveys of psychological views of mysticism are sorely lacking. For some comments, see Daniel Merkur, "Unitive Experiences and the State of Trance," in *Mystical Union and Monotheistic Faith,* ed. Moshe Idel and Bernard McGinn (New York: Macmillan, 1989), pp. 125–53. A collection of reprinted papers on this topic may be found in *Understanding Mysticism,* ed. Richard Woods, O.P. (Garden City, NY: Doubleday, 1980), part 4.

32. James H. Leuba, *The Psychology of Religious Mysticism* (London: Routledge & Kegan Paul, 1972), p. 138: "The thesis which we shall maintain is that the delights said by our great mystics to transcend everything which the world and the senses can procure, involve some activity of the sexual organs."

33. On these authors, see D. Merkur, "Unitive Experiences and Trance," pp. 127–29.

34. E.g., Sigmund Freud, *Civilization and its Discontents,* trans. James Strachey (New York: Norton, 1961), chaps. 1 and 2.

35. For the relation of Freud and Rolland, I am indebted to William Parsons for allowing me to read his unpublished paper "Psychoanalysis and Mysticism: The Freud–Romain Rolland Correspondence."

36. Ernst Freud, ed., *The Letters of Sigmund Freud* (New York: Basic Books, 1960), pp. 389, 392–93.

37. For an example, see J. Moussaieff Masson, *The Oceanic Feeling: The Origins of Religion in Ancient India* (Dordrecht, Boston, and London: Reidel, 1980), esp. chaps. 2–4.

38. E.g., Sudhir Kakar, *The Inner World* (Delhi: Oxford, 1980).

39. Erich Neumann, "Mystical Man," in *The Mystic Vision: Papers from the Eranos Yearbooks* (Princeton: Princeton University Press, 1968), p. 378.

40. Ibid., pp. 379–80.

41. G. van der Leeuw, *Religion in Essence and Manifestation,* 2 vols. (New York: Harper, 1963) 2:493–508.

42. Joachim Wach, *The Sociology of Religion* (Chicago: University of Chicago Press, 1944), pp. 162–65.

43. E.g., Mircea Eliade, "Experiences of the Mystic Light," in *The Two and the One* (New York: Harper, 1965), pp. 19–77 (originally given as a paper at the Eranos Conference in 1957); and idem, "Sense Experience and Mystical Experience among Primitives," in *Myths, Dreams and Mysteries* (London: Harvill, 1960), pp. 73–98.

44. Volume 3 of Mircea Eliade, *A History of Religious Ideas* (Chicago: University of Chicago Press, 1985) discusses medieval Islamic, Jewish, and Christian mysticism (chaps. 35–37).

45. I owe this suggestion to Moshe Idel.

46. E.g., the papers in *Religious Ecstasy,* ed. Nils G. Holm (Stockholm: Almqvist & Wiksell, 1981).

47. On Scholem, see David Biale, *Gershom Scholem: Kabbalah and Counter History* (Cambridge, MA: Harvard University Press, 1979).

48. Gershom Scholem, *Major Trends in Jewish Mysticism* (New York: Schocken, 1961), p. 6.

49. Scholem, *Major Trends,* p. 4. The quotation is from Rufus M. Jones, *Studies in Mystical Religion* (New York: Macmillan, 1909), p. xv. Scholem adopts the same position in defining the mystic as "a man who has been favored with an immediate, and to him real, experience of the divine, of ultimate reality, or who at least strives to attain such experience" in "Religious Authority and Mysticism," *On the Kabbalah and its Symbolism* (New York: Schocken, 1965), p. 5.

50. For a corrective to Scholem on this issue, see Moshe Idel, *Kabbalah: New Perspectives* (New Haven: Yale University Press, 1988), chap. 4; and idem, "Universalization and

Integration: Two Conceptions of Mystical Union in Jewish Mysticism," in *Mystical Union and Monotheistic Faith*, pp. 27–57.

51. Scholem, *Major Trends*, p. 7.

52. Ibid., pp. 8–9. In his important essay "Mysticism and Society," *Diogenes* 58 (1967), p. 8, Scholem cites the Jewish philosopher Leo Baeck (1873–1956) as the source of his terminology.

53. In "Religious Authority and Mysticism," pp. 9–11, on the basis of the difference between the classical and the romantic stages of religion, Scholem distinguished between the prophet with his clear message and the mystic with his formless one, a distinction that seems somewhat arbitrary.

54. Scholem, "Religious Authority and Mysticism," p. 7; cf. idem, "Mysticism and Society," pp. 9, 15–16.

55. Three ancillary issues arise in the wake of the central problem of the identity of source: (1) the success of the mystic in transforming traditional images to express mystical revelation; (2) the reception the mystic receives from religious authorities; and (3) the nature of the mystic's social activities — conservative or radical. See Scholem, "Mysticism and Society," pp. 8–13, for a discussion of these. In "Religious Authority and Mysticism," pp. 11–15, Scholem lays stress on the importance of mystical exegesis of the foundational texts.

56. Scholem discusses the frequently circumstantial nature of such conflicts ("Religious Authority and Mysticism," pp. 23–25).

57. Scholem, "Mysticism and Society," pp. 21–24; and "Religious Authority and Mysticism," pp. 11, 27–29.

58. Hans Jonas, "Myth and Mysticism: A Study of Objectification and Interiorization in Religious Thought," *Journal of Religion* 49 (1969): 315–29.

59. These are not spelled out in Jonas's "Myth and Mysticism," and are only briefly discussed at the beginning of volume 2 of his *Gnosis und spätantike Geist: Von der Mythologie zur mystischen Philosophie* (Göttingen: Vandenhoeck & Ruprecht, 1954), pp. 1–23. On Jonas's approach to religion, see also his paper "Gnosticism, Existentialism, Nihilism," reprinted as an epilogue to the second edition of his book *The Gnostic Religion* (Boston: Beacon, 1963), pp. 320–40.

60. Jonas, *Von der Mythologie zur mystischen Philosophie*, p. 7: "So ist die ganze Welt vergeistert — durch den verweltlichen Geist."

61. Jonas, "Myth and Mysticism," p. 328.

62. Ibid., p. 315; cf. pp. 317–18, 326–29. See also *Von der Mythologie zur mystischen Philosophie*, pp. 1–9.

63. Missing in the article is a consideration of Philo, who receives extensive treatment in *Von der Mythologie zur mystischen Philosophie*, chap. 3 (pp. 70–121).

64. Jonas, "Myth and Mysticism," p. 317. The connection between mystical philosophy and gnostic myth, however, need not be a genetic one: ". . . they are analogical formulations sprung from the same source in a certain temporal order" (p. 318; cf. p. 320).

65. Ibid., pp. 320–24. "Through the cultic conjunction of *mythos* and *praxis* the transcendent finds a way to become immanent before the mind discovers the way for itself" (p. 324).

66. Ibid., p. 328.

67. Aldous Huxley, *The Doors of Perception* (New York: Harper, 1954), p. 41.

68. R. C. Zaehner, *Mysticism Sacred and Profane: An Inquiry into some Varieties of Praeternatural Experience* (New York: Oxford University Press, 1961). See the "Introduction" and chaps. 1 and 2 for the attack on Huxley. In "Appendix B" (pp. 212–26) Zaehner gives an account of his own clinically observed experience with mescalin in 1955. The drug induced a state of farcical hilarity rather than a natural mystical experience. A subsequent work of Zaehner, *Drugs, Mysticism and Make-Believe* (London: Collins, 1972), also dealt with these issues.

69. Zaehner, *Mysticism Sacred and Profane*, pp. 198–99.

70. Ibid., pp. 28–29; see the summary on p. 168.

71. Ibid., pp. 32–33, 144.

72. In a later work, *Concordant Discord* (Oxford: Clarendon, 1970), p. 202, Zaehner appears to qualify the sharp break between panenhenic and monistic mysticism by seeing the latter as the fruit of the convergence of the two elements of the former, transcendence of space and transcendence of time. It is not fully clear how these two categories relate to the understanding of panenhenic mysticism in *Mysticism Sacred and Profane* as containing elements of "positive inflation" and "integration" (p. 118).

73. E.g., Zaehner, *Mysticism Sacred and Profane*, pp. 194–95, 203–5.

74. The same problem is also evident in Zaehner's last paper on mysticism, "Mysticism without Love," *Religious Studies* 10 (1974): 257–64.

75. See W. T. Stace, *Mysticism and Philosophy* (London: Macmillan, 1960), pp. 35–36, 337–38; Ninian Smart, "Understanding Religious Experience," in *Mysticism and Philosophical Analysis*, pp. 13–15; and to a lesser extent Almond, *Mystical Experience*, pp. 23–42.

76. E.g., E. I. Watkin, "Mysticism and the Supernatural," *The Month* 18 (1957): 274–81. Watkin was a frequent contributer on mystical issues to *The Month* and other English Catholic journals. His two books in the area are *The Philosophy of Mysticism* (London: Grant Richards, 1920); and *Poets and Mystics* (London: Sheed & Ward, 1953).

77. S. Katz praises Zaehner for going beyond common-core typologies, but also criticizes him for not going far enough due to his Catholic agenda (*Mysticism and Philosophical Analysis*, pp. 31–32).

78. Recent attempts at general statements have not been impressive: e.g., Frits Staal's *Exploring Mysticism* (Berkeley: University of California Press, 1975), which is based on the questionable dual premises of the "irrationality" of Western religion and the necessity for the elimination of all theological explanations that mystics have given to the experiences.

79. E.g., Annemarie Schimmel, *Mystical Dimensions of Islam* (Chapel Hill: University of North Carolina Press, 1975); and idem, *As through a Veil: Mystical Poetry in Islam* (New York: Columbia University Press, 1982).

80. The best of these is Sidney Spencer, *Mysticism in World Religion* (Baltimore: Penguin, 1963). Less successful are F. C. Happold, *Mysticism: A Study and an Anthology* (Harmondsworth: Penguin, 1963); Geoffrey Parrinder, *Mysticism in the World's Religions* (New York: Oxford University Press, 1976); and Robert J. Ellwood, *Mysticism and Religion* (Englewood Cliffs, NJ: Prentice-Hall, 1980).

81. See Elmer J. O'Brien, S.J., *Varieties of Mystic Experience* (New York: Mentor, 1964); and Louis Dupré and James A. Wiseman, O.S.B., *Light from Light: An Anthology of Christian Mysticism* (New York: Paulist, 1988).

82. Marghanita Laski, *Ecstasy* (Bloomington: Indiana University Press, 1962), p. 5. Laski divides ecstasies into the following types: (1) withdrawal types; and (2) intensity types of three kinds (purification, knowledge, union). See pp. 369–74.

83. Laski's claim that there is little difference between her secular respondents and her religious texts stems from a priori adherence to the principle that religious elements in the descriptions are "over-beliefs" that can be safely excised without doing damage to the description itself.

84. Ben-Ami Scharfstein, *Mystical Experience* (Indianapolis and New York: Bobbs Merrill, 1973); see esp. chap. 10, "Eleven Quintessences of the Mystic State."

85. Arthur J. Deikman, M.D., "Deautomatization and the Mystic Experience," *Psychiatry* 29 (1966): 324–38. Reprinted in *Understanding Mysticism*, ed. Woods, pp. 240–60, from which I will quote (the quotation is on p. 247).

86. Ibid., pp. 248–51.

87. Ibid., p. 258. For reports on Deikman's experiments with induced meditation, see Arthur J. Deikman, "Experimental Meditation," *Journal of Nervous and Mental Diseases* 136 (1963): 329–43; and idem, "Implications of Experimentally Induced Contemplative Meditation," *Journal of Nervous and Mental Diseases* 142 (1966): 101–16.

88. Arthur J. Deikman, M.D., *The Observing Self: Mysticism and Psychotherapy* (Boston: Beacon, 1982).

89. Claudio Naranjo and Robert E. Ornstein, *On the Psychology of Mysticism* (New York: Viking, 1971), pp. 137, 233.

90. See esp. ibid., pp. 164–87.

91. Ibid., p. 169.

92. Ibid., pp. 210–12. Ornstein describes the detachment as "an attempt to reach a similar state [of expanded awareness] within by separating the state itself from the stimuli that usually trigger it, and by the conjoint practice of concentrating on parts of the nervous system that produce this experience" (pp. 211–12).

93. E.g., S. Grof and C. Grof, *Beyond Death* (London: Thames & Hudson, 1980); and S. Grof, "East and West: Ancient Wisdom and Modern Science," in *Ancient Wisdom and Modern Science,* ed. Stanislov Grof and Marjorie Livingston Valier (Albany: State University of New York Press, 1984), pp. 3–23.

94. Grof and Grof, *Beyond Death,* p. 88; cf. S. Grof, "Ancient Wisdom," pp. 18–21, on transpersonal experiences.

95. Charles E. Tart, ed., *Altered States of Consciousness* (New York: Wiley, 1969).

96. David Orme-Johnson and John Farrow, eds., *Scientific Research on the Transcendental Meditation Program: Collected Papers,* vol. 1 (Seelisburg, Switzerland: Maharishi European Research University Press, 1977). My thanks to Robert K. C. Forman for his comments on this volume, which I have not seen.

97. Ernst Troeltsch, "Main Problems of the Philosophy of Religion: Psychology and Theory of Knowledge in the Science of Religion," in *Congress of Arts and Science: Universal Exposition, St. Louis 1904,* ed. Howard J. Rogers, 2 vols. (Boston and New York: Houghton, Mifflin, 1905) 1:277.

98. See above, p. 298.

Bibliography

Primary Texts

Acts of John. In *Acta apostolorum apocrypha,* II. Edited by M. Bonnet. Leipzig: Teubner, 1896. Reprint, Hildesheim, 1959.

Acts of the Christian Martyrs. Edited and translated by Herbert Musurillo. Oxford: Clarendon, 1979.

Ambrose. *De bono mortis.* In *Sancti Ambrosii Opera,* edited by Carolus Schenkl. CSEL 32.1, 701–53. Vienna: Tempsky-Freytag, 1897.

———. *De fuga saeculi.* In *Sancti Ambrosii Opera,* edited by Carolus Schenkl. CSEL 32.2, 163–207. Vienna: Tempsky-Freytag, 1897.

———. *De Isaac vel anima.* In *Sancti Ambrosii Opera,* edited by Carolus Schenkl. CSEL 32.1, 639–700. Vienna: Tempsky-Freytag, 1897.

———. *De mysteriis.* Edited by B. Botte. SC 25bis. Paris: Cerf, 1961.

———. *De sacramentis.* Edited by B. Botte. SC 25bis. Paris: Cerf, 1961.

———. *Explanatio Psalmorum XII.* Edited by M. Petschenig. CSEL 64.6. Vienna: Tempsky-Freytag, 1919.

———. *Expositio evangelii secundum Lucam.* Edited by Carolus Schenkl. CSEL 32.4. Also in *Ambroise de Milan, Traite sur l'Evangile de S. Luc.,* edited by Gabriel Tissot. SC 45 and 52. Paris: Cerf, 1956, 1958.

———. *Expositio Psalmi CXVIII.* Edited by M. Petschenig. CSEL 62.5. Vienna: Tempsky-Freitag, 1913.

———. *Opera Omnia. PL* 14–16.

(Ambrose. *St. Ambrose: Seven Exegetical Works.* Translated by Michael P. McHugh. FC 65. Washington, DC: Catholic University Press, 1972).

(Thompson, T., and J. H. Srawley. *St. Ambrose: On the Sacraments and On the Mysteries.* London: SPCK, 1950).

Anthony. *The Letters of St. Antony the Great.* Translated by Derwas Chitty. Fairacres, Oxford: SLG Press, 1977.

Apophthegmata Patrum: 1, *Alphabeticon. PG* 65:71–440.

(*The Sayings of the Desert Fathers: The Alphabetical Collection.* Translated by Benedicta Ward. SLG. London: Mowbrays, 1975.)

Apophthegmata Patrum: 2, *Verba Seniorum. PL* 73:855–1022.
(*The Sayings of the Fathers.* In *Western Asceticism,* translated by Owen Chadwick. Philadelphia: Westminster, 1958.)
Apponius. *In Canticum Canticorum expositio.* Edited by B. de Vregille and L. Neyrans. CC 19. Turnhout: Brepols, 1986.
Athanasius. *Vita Antonii. PG* 26:837–976.
(Athanasius. *Athanasius: The Life of Antony and the Letter to Marcellinus.* Translated by Robert C. Gregg. CWS. New York: Paulist, 1980.)
Augustine. *Opera Omnia. PL* 32–47.
(Augustine. *Expositions on the Book of Psalms.* Edited by Philip Schaff. *NFPF,* First series 8.)
(Augustine. *Homilies on the Gospel of John.* Edited by Philip Schaff. *NFPF,* First series 7.)
(*Augustine. Later Works.* Edited by John Burnaby. Philadelphia: Westminster, 1955.)
(Augustine. *Saint Augustine: The Literal Meaning of Genesis.* Annotated translation by John Hammond Taylor. ACW 41–42. New York: Paulist, 1982.)
(Augustine. *Saint Augustine: The Trinity.* Translated by Stephen McKenna. FC 45. Washington, DC: Catholic University Press, 1963.
(*St. Augustine on the Psalms.* Translation and annotation by Scholastica Hebgin and Felicitas Corrigan. ACW 29. Westminster: Newman, 1960.
Cassian. *Conlationes.* In *Jean Cassien: Conferences,* edited by E. Pichery. SC 42, 54, 64. Paris: Cerf, 1955, 1958, 1959.
———. *Institutiones.* In *Jean Cassien: Institutions Coenobitiques,* edited by J.-C. Guy. SC 109. Paris: Cerf, 1965.
Clement of Alexandria. *Excerpta ex Theodoto.* In *The Excerpta ex Theodoto of Clement of Alexandria,* edited and with introduction by Robert Pierce Casey. London: Christophers, 1934.
———. *Die Werke.* Edited by Otto Stählin. 4th ed. GCS. 4 vols. Berlin: Akademie Verlag, 1985.
(Clement of Alexandria. *Works.* Translated in *ANF* 2:163–605.
Corpus Hermeticum. Edited by A. D. Nock with a translation by A. J. Festugière. 4 vols. Paris: Collection Budé, 1945–54.
Cyprian. *De habitu virginum. PL* 4:451–78.
———. *Epistolae. PL* 4:193–452.
Evagrius Ponticus. *De Oratione. PG* 79:1165–1200. Also available in I. Hausherr, *Leçons d'un contemplatif.* Paris: Beauchesne, 1960.
———. *Epistola ad Melaniam.* Translated in "Evagrius of Pontus' 'Letter to Melania,'" by M. Parmentier. *Bijdragen, tijdschrift voor filosofie en theologie* 46 (1985): 2–38.
———. *Epistola Fidei.* Survived as Letter 8 of Basil. In *Saint Basile: Lettres I,* edited by Yves Courtonne. Paris: Belles Lettres, 1957.
———. *Gnostikos.* Edited by Antoine and Claire Guillaumont. SC 356. Paris: Cerf, 1989.
———. *Kephalaia Gnostica.* In *Les six centuries des "Kephalaia Gnostica" d'Evagre le Pontique,* edited by Antoine Guillaumont. *Patrologia Orientalis* 28.1. Paris: Firmin-Didot, 1958.
———. *Praktikos.* Edited by Antoine and Claire Guillaumont. SC 170, 171. Paris: Cerf, 1971.
(Bamberger, John Eudes. *Evagrius Ponticus: The Praktikos. Chapters on Prayer.* Spencer, MA: Cistercian Publications, 1970.)
Gennadius. *De scriptoribus ecclesiasticis. PL* 58:1053–1120.

The Gnostic Scriptures. Edited by Bentley Layton. Garden City, NY: Doubleday, 1987.

Gregory of Nyssa. *Ad Ablabium. PG* 45:119–29.

———. *Grégoire de Nysse: La vie de Moïse.* Edited by Jean Daniélou. SC 1 bis. Paris: Cerf, 1955.

———. *Gregorii Nysseni in Canticum Canticorum.* Edited by Herman Langerbeck. Vol. 6 in *Gregorii Nysseni Opera,* edited by Werner Jaeger. Leiden: Brill, 1960.

———. *Gregorii Nysseni Opera.* Edited by Werner Jaeger. 10 vols. with supplement. Leiden: Brill, 1958–1990.

(Gregory of Nyssa, Saint. *Commentary on the Song of Songs.* Translated by Casimir McCambley. OCSO. Brookline, MA: Hellenic College Press, 1987.

(Gregory of Nyssa. *The Life of Moses.* Translated by Everett Ferguson and Abraham Malherbe. CWS. New York: Paulist, 1978.

(Gregory of Nyssa, St. *The Lord's Prayer. The Beatitudes.* Translated by Hilda C. Graef. ACW 18. Westminster: Newman, 1954.

Hilary of Poitiers. *Commentarius in Evangelium Matthaei. PL* 9:917–1078.

———. *Tractatus super psalmos. PL* 9:231–890.

———. *De trinitate. PL* 10:9–472.

Ignatius of Antioch. *Ignatius, Works.* In *The Apostolic Fathers I,* edited by Kirsopp Lake. LC. Cambridge, MA: Harvard University Press, 1975.

(Ignatius of Antioch. *A Commentary on the Letter of Ignatius of Antioch.* Translated by William R. Schoedel. Hermeneia. Philadephia: Fortress, 1985.)

Irenaeus. *Adversus haereses.* Edited by Adelin Rousseau and Louis Doutreleau. SC 100, 152, 153, 210, 211, 263, 264, 293, 294. Paris: Cerf, 1952–82..

Jerome. *Epistolae.* In CSEL 54–56, edited by I. Hilberg. Vienna: Tempsky-Freytag, 1910–18.

———. *Letters.* In *St. Jerome: Select Letters.* Translated by F. A. Wright. LC 262. Cambridge, MA: Harvard University Press, 1980.

Justin Martyr. *Opera Omnia. PG* 6:229–800.

Macarius (Pseudo). *Die 50 Geistlichen Homilien des Makarios.* Edited by Hermann Dörries, Erich Klostermann, and Matthias Kroeger. Patristische Texte und Studien 4. Berlin: de Gruyter, 1964.

———. *Pseudo-Macaire: Oeuvres Spirituelles I.* Edited by Vincent Desprez. SC 275. Paris: Cerf, 1980.

(Maloney, George A., S.J. *Intoxicated with God.* Denville, NJ: Dimension Books, 1978.)

Marius Victorinus. *Marii Victorini Opera.* Edited by Paul Henry and Pierre Hadot. CSEL 83.1. Vienna: Holder-Pichler-Tempsky, 1971.

(Marius Victorinus. *Theological Treatises on the Trinity.* Translated by Mary T. Clark. FC 69. Washington, DC: Catholic University Press, 1981.)

The Nag Hammadi Library. Edited by James M. Robinson. New York: Harper & Row, 1977.

Numenius. *Fragments.* Edited by Édouard des Places. Paris: Collection Budé, 1973.

The Old Testament Pseudepigrapha. Edited by James H. Charlesworth. 2 vols. Garden City, NY: Doubleday, 1983.

Origen. *Commentaria in Epistolam B. Pauli ad Romanos. PG* 14:837–1292.

———. *Commentarium in Evangelium Ioannis.* Edited by Cecile Blanc. SC 120, 157, 222, 290. Paris: Cerf, 1964–. Also in GCS Origen series 4.

———. *De principiis.* Edited by H. Crouzel and M. Simonetti. SC 252, 253, 268, 269, 312. Paris: Cerf, 1978–84.

——. *Entretien d'Origene avec Héraclide.* Edited by Jean Scherer. SC 67. Paris: Cerf, 1960.

——. *Homiliae in Genesim.* Edited by Louis Doutreleau. SC 7bis. Paris: Cerf, 1976.

——. *Opera Omnia.* GCS Origen series 1–12. See also *PG* 12–17.

——. *Selecta in Psalmos. PG* 12:1053–1686.

(Butterworth, G. W. *Origen: On First Principles.* New York: Harper & Row, 1966.)

(Corsini, E. *Commento al Vangelo di Giovanni di Origene.* Turin: Tipografia Torinese, 1968.)

(Greer, Rowan A. *Origen: An Exhortation to Martyrdom. Prayer and Selected Works.* CWS. New York: Paulist, 1979.)

(Lawson, R. P. *Origen: The Song of Songs. Commentary and Homilies.* ACW 26. Westminster: Newman, 1957.)

Pachomius. *Pachomian Koinonia.* Translated by Armand Vielleux. 3 vols. Kalamazoo, MI: Cistercian Publications, 1980–82.

Palladius. *Historia Lausiaca. PL* 74:249–382.

(Palladius. *Palladius. The Lausiac History.* Translated by Robert T. Meyer. ACW 34. Westminster: Newman, 1965.)

Paulinus of Nola. *Epistolae. PL* 61:153–438.

Paulinus Notarius. *Vita Ambrosii. PL* 14:29–50.

Philo. *Philo: Works.* Translated by F. H. Colson and G. H. Whitaker. LC. 10 vols. New York: G. Putnam's Sons, 1929–62. *Works. Philo Supplement.* Translated by Ralph Marcus. LC. 2 vols. Cambridge, MA: Harvard University Press, 1953.

(Winston, David, trans. and intro. *Philo of Alexandria: The Contemplative Life, the Giants and Selections.* CWS. New York: Paulist, 1981.)

Plato. *Plato: Works.* Translated by Harold North Fowler et al. LC. 12 vols. Cambridge, MA: Harvard University Press.

Plotinus. *Enneads.* In *Plotinus,* with English translation by A. H. Armstrong. LC. 7 vols. Cambridge, MA: Harvard University Press, 1966–88.

——. *Plotini Opera.* Edited by P. Henry and H. R. Schwyzer. 3 vols. Oxford: Clarendon, 1964–83.

(MacKenna, Stephen. *Plotinus: The Enneads.* London: Faber & Faber, 1956.)

Porphyry. Fragments of *Commentary on Parmenides.* In *Porphyre et Victorinus,* edited by Pierre Hadot. 2 vols. Paris: Etudes Augustiniennes, 1958.

——. *Vita Plotini.* In *Plotinus,* with English translation by A. H. Armstrong. LC. Cambridge, MA: Harvard University Press. Vol. 1, 2–85.

Proclus. *Alcibiades I: A Translation and Commentary.* Translation and commentary by William O'Neill. The Hague: Nijhoff, 1965.

——. *Commentary on the Parmenides of Plato.* Greek text down to *Parm.* 141E, edited by V. Cousin with a translation into French by A. E. Chaignet. Paris, 1900–1903. Latin text commenting on 141E–142A, in *Plato Latinus,* edited by R. Klibansky and C. Labowsky, translated by E. Anscombe, vol. 3. London: Warburg Institute, 1953. Full Latin translation in *Proclus, Commentaire sur le Parmenide de Platon: Traduction de Guillaume de Moerbeke,* edited by Carlos Steel. 2 vols. Leiden and Leuven: Brill, 1982–85.

——. *The Elements of Theology.* Edited and translated by E. R. Dodds. 2nd ed. Oxford: Clarendon, 1963.

——. *Theologia platonica.* In *Proclus: Théologie Platonicienne,* edited by H. D. Saffrey and L. G. Westerink. 5 vols. thus far. Paris: Belles Lettres, 1968–.

(Proclus. *Proclus's Commentary on Plato's Parmenides.* Translated by Glenn Morrow and John Dillon. Princeton, NJ: Princeton University Press, 1987.)

Pseudo Dionysius. *De coelesti hierarchia.* Edited by René Roques et al. SC 58bis. Paris: Cerf, 1970.

------. *Dionysiaca.* Edited by Philippe Chevallier. 2 vols. Paris: Desclée, 1937.

------. *Opera Omnia. PG* 3.

    (Campbell, Thomas L., trans. and ed. *Dionysius the Pseudo-Areopagite: The Ecclesiastical Hierarchy.* Lanham, MD: University Press of America, 1981.)

    (Pseudo-Dionysius. *The Complete Works.* Translated by Colm Luibheid et al. CWS. New York: Paulist, 1987.)

Rufinus. *Historia Monachorum in Aegypto. PL* 21:387–462.

    (Rufinus. *Historia Monachorum.* In *The Lives of the Desert Fathers,* translated by Norman Russell. Kalamazoo, MI: Cistercian Publications, 1981.)

Sacrorum conciliorum nova et amplissima collectio. Edited by J. D. Mansi. 53 vols. Reprint. Graz: Akademische Druck und Verlagsanstalt, 1960–61.

Sulpicius Severus. *Vita Martini.* Edited by Jacques Fontaine. SC 133–135. Paris: Cerf, 1967–69.

    (Hoare, Frederick Russell. *The Western Fathers.* New York: Harper & Row, 1965.)

Tertullian. *De exhortatione castitatis. PL* 2:963–80.

------. *De oratione. PL* 1:1243–1304.

------. *De virginibus velandis. PL* 2:935–64.

William of St. Thierry. *Super Cantica Canticorum ex operibus Sancti Ambrosii. PL* 15:1849–85.

Wisdom of Solomon. In *The Wisdom of Solomon,* edited with commentary by David Winston. Anchor Bible 43. Garden City, NY: Doubleday, 1979.

Secondary Works

Adams, James Luther. "Letter from Friedrich von Hügel to William James." *Downside Review* 98 (1980): 214–36.

Agaesse, Paul, and Theodore Koehler. "Fruitio Dei." *DS* 5:1546–69.

Albrecht, Carl. *Das mystischen Erkennen: Gnoseologie und philosophische Relevanz der mystischen Relation.* Bremen: Schunemann, 1958.

------. *Das mystische Wort: Erleben und Sprechen in Versunkenheit.* Edited by Hans A. Fischer-Barnicol. Mainz: Matthias Grünewald, 1974.

Almond, Philip. *Mystical Experience and Religious Doctrine: An Investigation of the Study of Mysticism in World Religions.* Berlin and New York: Mouton, 1982.

Andresen, Carl. *Bibliographia Augustiniana.* Darmstadt: Wissenschaftliche Buchgesellschaft, 1973.

Antin, Paul. "Saint Jerome Directeur mystique." *Revue d'histoire de la spiritualité* 48 (1972): 25–30.

Arbman, Ernst. *Ecstasy or Religious Trance.* 3 vols. Uppsala: Appelberg, 1963–70.

Arintero, John G. *The Mystical Evolution in the Development and Vitality of the Church.* 2 vols. St. Louis: Herder, 1950.

Armstrong, A. Hilary. *The Architecture of the Intelligible Universe in the Philosophy of Plotinus.* Cambridge: Cambridge University Press, 1940.

------. *The Cambridge History of Later Greek and Early Medieval Philosophy.* Cambridge: Cambridge University Press, 1967.

------. "The Negative Theology of Nous in Later Neoplatonism." In *Platonismus und Christentum: Festschrift für Heinrich Dörrie. Jahrbuch für Antike und Christentum,*

Ergänzungsband 10, edited by H.-D. Blume and F. Mann, 31–27. Münster: Aschendorff, 1983.

———. "Platonic Mysticism." *The Dublin Review* 216 (1945): 130–43.

———. *Plotinian and Christian Studies.* London: Variorum Reprints, 1979.

———. "Plotinus." In *The Cambridge History of Later Greek and Early Medieval Philosophy,* 195–268. Cambridge: Cambridge University Press, 1967.

———. "The Self-Definition of Christianity in Relation to Later Platonism." In *Jewish and Christian Self-Definition,* edited by E. P. Sanders et al., 1:74–99. Philadelphia: Fortress, 1980–83.

———. "Tradition, Reason and Experience in the Thought of Plotinus." In *Plotino e il Neoplatonismo in Oriente e in Occidente,* 171–94. Accademia Normali dei Lincei, Quaderno 198. Rome, 1974.

———, ed. *Classical Mediterranean Spirituality: Egyptian, Greek, Roman.* WS 15. New York: Crossroad, 1986.

———, and R. A. Markus. *Christian Faith and Greek Philosophy.* London: Darton, Longman & Todd, 1960.

Arnou, René. *Le désir de Dieu dans la philosophie de Plotin.* 2nd ed. Rome: Gregorian University, 1967.

———. "Platonisme des Pères." *Dictionnaire de théologie catholique,* 15 vols. 12:2258–2392. Paris: Letouzey et Ané, 1909–50.

Aune, David E. *The New Testament in Its Literary Environment.* Philadelphia: Westminster, 1987.

Ayer, Alfred Jules. *Language, Truth and Logic.* New York: Dover, 1952.

Babut, Daniel. *La Religion des philosophes grecs.* Paris: Presses universitaires de France, 1974.

Bacht, H. "Logismos." *DS* 9:955–58.

Baert, Edward. "Le thème de la vision de Dieu chez S. Justin, Clement d'Alexandrie et S. Grégoire de Nysse." *Freiburger Zeitschrift für Philosophie und Theologie* 12 (1965): 440–55.

Bailey, Raymond. *Thomas Merton on Mysticism.* Garden City, NY: Doubleday, 1974.

Balas, David L. "The Idea of Participation in the Structure of Origen's Thought: Christian Transposition of a Theme of the Platonic Tradition." In *Origeniana: Premier colloque intérnational des études origéniennes,* 257–75. Bari: Istituto di Letteratura Cristiana Antica, 1975.

———. *METOYSIA THEOU: Man's Participation in God's Perfections according to Saint Gregory of Nyssa.* Studia Anselmiana 55. Rome: Herder, 1966.

Bamberger, John Eudes. "The Personality of Origen: Probings in Psychohistory." *Monastic Studies* 16 (1985): 51–62.

Bambrough, Renford. "Intuition and the Inexpressible." In *Mysticism and Philosophical Analysis,* edited by Steven T. Katz, 200–213. New York: Oxford University Press, 1978.

Bardy, G. "Apatheia." *DS* 1:727–46.

———. *La vie spirituelle d'après les pères des trois premiers siècles,* edited by A. Hamman. 2 vols. Tournai: Desclée, 1968.

Barnes, T. D. "Angel of Light or Mystic Initiate? The Problem of the *Life of Antony.*" *Journal of Theological Studies* n.s. 37 (1986): 353–68.

Barr, James. "Theophany and Anthropomorphism in the Old Testament." In

Congress Volume: Oxford 1959, 31–38. Supplements to *Vetus Testamentum* 7. Leiden: Brill, 1960.

Bars, Henry. "Maritain's Contributions to an Understanding of Mystical Experience." In *Jacques Maritain, the Man and his Achievement,* edited by Joseph William Evans. New York: Sheed & Ward, 1963.

Baruzi, Jean. "Introduction à des recherches sur le langage mystique." *Recherches philosophiques* 1 (1931–32): 66–82.

———. *Saint Jean de la Croix et le problème de l'expérience mystique.* Paris: Alcan, 1931.

———, H. Delacroix, M. Laberthoniere, and E. LeRoy. "Saint Jean de la Croix et le problème de la valeur noetique de l'expérience mystique." *Bulletin de la Société française de Philosophie,* 1925.

Bastide, Roger. *Les problèmes de la vie mystique.* Paris: Colin, 1931.

Baus, K. "Das Nachwirken des Origenes in der Christusfrömmigkeit des heiligen Ambrosius." *Römische Quartalschrift für christliche Altertumskunde und für Kirchengeschichte* 49 (1954): 21–55.

Beierwaltes, Werner. *Denken des Einen: Studien zur Neuplatonischen Philosophie und ihrer Wirkungsgeschichte.* Frankfurt: Klostermann, 1985.

———. *"Exaiphnēs* oder: Die Paradoxie des Augenblicks." *Philosophisches Jahrbuch* 74 (1966–67): 271–83.

———. "Hen." In *Reallexikon für Antike und Christentum,* edited by Theodor Klauser et al., 12:445–72. Stuttgart: Anton Hiersemann, 1950–.

———. "Love of Beauty and Love of God." In *Classical Mediterranean Spirituality: Egyptian, Greek, Roman,* edited by A. H. Armstrong, 293–313. WS 15. New York: Crossroad, 1986.

———. "Plotins philosophische Mystik." In *Grundfragen christlicher Mystik,* edited by Margot Schmidt and Dieter R. Bauer, 39–49. Stuttgart and Bad Cannstaat: Froomann-Holzboog, 1987.

———. *Proklos: Grundzüge seiner Metaphysik.* Frankfurt: Klostermann, 1965.

———. "Reflexion und Einung: Zur Mystik Plotins." In *Grundfragen der Mystik,* 7–36. Einsiedeln: Johannes, 1974.

Bell, David N. *The Image and Likeness: The Augustinian Spirituality of William of St. Thierry.* Kalamazoo, MI: Cistercian Publications, 1984.

Benz, Ernst. *Die Vision: Erfahrungsformen und Bilderwelt.* Stuttgart: E. Klett, 1969.

Berchman, Robert M. *From Philo to Origen: Middle Platonism in Transition.* Chico, CA: Scholars Press, 1984.

Berger, Peter L., ed. *The Other Side of God: A Polarity in World Religions.* Garden City, NY: Doubleday, 1981.

Bergson, Henri. *The Two Sources of Morality and Religion.* Notre Dame: University of Notre Dame Press, 1977.

Bernard, Charles André. "Le doctrine mystique de Denys l'Aréopagite." *Gregorianum* 68 (1987): 523–66.

Bertrand, Frederic. *Mystique de Jésus chez Origène.* Paris: Aubier, 1951.

Betz, Hans Dieter. *The Greek Magical Papyri in Translation.* Chicago: University of Chicago Press, 1986.

———. *Die Nachfolge und Nachahmung Jesu in Neuen Testament.* Tübingen: Mohr, 1967.

Biale, David. *Gershom Scholem: Kabbalah and Counter-history.* Cambridge, MA: Harvard University Press, 1979.

Bianchi, Ugo. *Il dualismo religioso: Saggio storico ed etnologico.* Rome: L'Erma di Bretschneider, 1958.

———. "Initiation, Mystères, Gnose (Pour l'histoire de la mystique dans la paganisme greco-oriental)." In *Initiation,* edited by C. J. Bleeker, 154–71. Leiden: Brill, 1975.

———. "Osservazioni storico-religiose sul concetto di mistica." In *Mistica e Misticismo Oggi,* 225–33. Rome: Passionisti, 1979.

Biblia Patristica. 4 vols. Paris: CNRS, 1975–.

Blondel, Maurice. *L'Action: Essai d'une critique de la vie et d'une science de la pratique.* Paris: Alcan, 1895.

———. *L'Être et les êtres.* Paris: Alcan, 1935.

———. *Lettre sur l'apologetique.* 1896. Eng. trans. *The Letter on Apologetics and History and Dogma.* Translated by Alexander Dru and Illtyel Trethowan. London: Harvill Press, 1964.

———. *La Pensée.* Paris: Alcan, 1934.

———. "Le problème de la mystique." *La nouvelle journée,* 1925. Reissued as "Qu'est-ce que la mystique." In *Cahiers de la nouvelle journée,* no. 8, 1–63. Paris: Bloud & Gay, 1929.

———. "Le procès de l'intelligence." *La nouvelle journée,* 1921. Reissued as *Le procès de l'intelligence.* Paris: Bloud & Gay, 1922.

Bloomfield, Morton. *The Seven Deadly Sins.* East Lansing: Michigan State University Press, 1952.

Bochet, Isabelle. *Saint Augustin et le désir de Dieu.* Paris: Études Augustiniennes, 1982.

Bonner, Gerald. "Augustine's Conception of Deification." *Journal of Theological Studies* n.s. 37 (1986): 369–86.

———. "The Spirituality of St. Augustine and its influence on Western mysticism." *Sobornost* 4 (1982): 143–62.

Booth, Edward. *Aristotelian Aporetic Ontology in Islamic and Christian Thinkers.* Cambridge: Cambridge University Press, 1983.

Bouillard, Henry. *Blondel and Christianity.* Washington: Corpus, 1970.

Bousset, Wilhelm. *Apophthegmata: Studien zur Geschichte des ältesten Mönchtums.* Tübingen: Mohr, 1923.

———. "Die Himmelsreise der Seele." *Archiv für Religionswissenschaft* 4 (1901): 136–69, 229–73.

Bouyer, Louis. "Mysticism: An Essay on the History of the Word." In *Understanding Mysticism,* edited by Richard Woods, O.P., 42–55. Garden City, NY: Doubleday Image Books, 1980.

———. "Die mystische Kontemplation bei den Vätern." In *Weisheit Gottes—Weisheit der Welt: Festschrift für Joseph Kardinal Ratzinger zum 60. Geburtstag,* edited by W. Baier et al., 1:637–49. 2 vols. St. Ottilien: EOS Verlag, 1987.

———. *The Spirituality of the New Testament and the Fathers.* Vol. 1 of *A History of Christian Spirituality.* 3 vols. New York: Seabury, 1982.

Bréhier, Emile. *The Philosophy of Plotinus.* Chicago: University of Chicago Press, 1958.

Bremond, Henri. *Histoire littéraire du sentiment religieux en France depuis la fin des guerres de religion jusqu'à nos jours.* 11 vols. Paris: Bloud & Gay, 1916–33. The first three volumes translated as *A Literary History of Religious Thought in France from the Wars of Religion Down to Our Own Times.* London: SPCK, 1928–36.

Brons, Bernard. *Gott und die Seienden: Untersuchungen zum Verhältnis von neuplatonischer Metaphysik und christlichen Tradition bei Dionysius Areopagita.* Göttingen: Vandenhoeck & Ruprecht, 1976.

Brown, Peter. *Augustine of Hippo: A Biography.* Berkeley: University of California Press, 1967.

——. *The Body and Society: Men, Women, and Sexual Renunciation in Early Christianity.* New York: Columbia University Press, 1988.

——. *The Cult of the Saints: Its Rise and Function in Latin Christianity.* Chicago: University of Chicago Press, 1981.

——. *The Making of Late Antiquity.* Cambridge, MA: Harvard University Press, 1978.

——. "The Notion of Virginity in the Early Church." In *Christian Spirituality: Origins to the Twelfth Century,* edited by Bernard McGinn and John Meyendorff, 427–43. WS 16. New York: Crossroad, 1986.

——. *Religion and Society in the Age of Saint Augustine.* New York: Harper & Row, 1972.

——. "The Rise and Function of the Holy Man in Late Antiquity." *Journal of Roman Studies* 61 (1971): 80–101.

——. *Society and the Holy in Late Antiquity.* Berkeley: University of California Press, 1982.

Brown, Raymond E. *The Community of the Beloved Disciple.* New York: Paulist, 1979.

——. *The Epistles of John.* Anchor Bible 30. Garden City, NY: Doubleday, 1982.

——. *The Gospel according to John.* Anchor Bible 29, 29A. Garden City, NY: Doubleday, 1966, 1970.

Browning, Don. "William James's Philosophy of Mysticism." *Journal of Religion* 59 (1979): 56–70.

Brunner, August. *Der Schritt über die Grenzen: Wesen und Sinn der Mystik.* Würzburg: Echter Verlag, 1972.

Brunner, Emil. *Die Mystik und das Wort.* Tübingen: Mohr, 1928.

Bultmann, Rudolf. "Die eschatologie des Johannes-Evangeliums." In *Glauben und Verstehen: Gesammelte Aufsätze,* 1:134–52. Tübingen: Mohr, 1933.

——. *The Gospel of John: A Commentary.* Philadelphia: Fortress, 1971.

Bunge, Gabriel. "Évagre le Pontique et les deux Macaire." *Irenikon* 56 (1983): 215–27, 323–60.

——. *Geistliche Vaterschaft: Christliche Gnosis bei Evagrios Pontikos.* Regensburg: Pustet, 1988.

——. "Origenismus—Gnostizismus: Zum geistesgeschichtliche Standort des Evagrios Pontikos." *Vigiliae Christianae* 40 (1986): 24–54.

——. "The 'Spiritual Prayer': On the Trinitarian Mysticism of Evagrius of Pontus." *Monastic Studies* 17 (1986): 191–208.

Burke, Vernon J. "Augustine of Hippo: The Approach of the Soul to God." In *The Spirituality of Western Christendom,* edited by E. Rozanne Elder, 1–12. Kalamazoo, MI: Cistercian Publications, 1976.

Burkert, Walter. *Ancient Mystery Cults.* Cambridge, MA: Harvard University Press, 1987.

Burnaby, John. *Amor Dei: A Study of the Religion of St. Augustine.* London: Houghton & Stoddard, 1938.

Burr, Ronald. "Wittgenstein's Later Language Philosophy and Some Issues in the Philosophy of Mysticism." *International Journal for Philosophy of Religion* 7 (1976): 261-87.

Butler, Cuthbert. *Western Mysticism: The Teaching of Saints Augustine, Gregory and Bernard on Contemplation and the Contemplative Life.* New York: Dutton, 1923.

Butterworth, G. W. "The Deification of Man in Clement of Alexandria." *Journal of Theological Studies* 17 (1916): 157-69.

Calati, Abbot Benedetto. "Western Mysticism." *Downside Review* 98 (1980): 201-13.

Camelot, Pierre-Thomas. *Foi et gnose: Introduction à l'étude de la connaissance mystique chez Clement d'Alexandrie.* Paris: Vrin, 1945.

——. "Gnose chrétienne." *DS* 6:509-23.

——. "Hellenisme (et spiritualité patristique)." *DS* 7:145-64.

Canévet, Mariette. "Pseudo-Macaire (Syméon). II. Doctrine." *DS* 10:27-38.

Capanaga, Victorino. "La deificacion en la soteriologia agustiniana." In *Augustinus Magister,* 2:745-54. 3 vols. Paris: L'Année théologique augustinienne, 1954.

Capelle, B. "Le progrès de la connaissance religieuse d'après s. Augustin." *Recherches de théologie ancienne et médiévale* 2 (1930): 410-19.

——. Review of *Giovanni Cassiano ed Evagrio Pontico: Dottrina sulla caritá e contemplazione,* by Salvatore Marsili, Studia Anselmiana 5. Rome: Herder, 1936. *Revue d'histoire ecclesiastique* 35 (1939): 554.

Caputo, John D. *The Mystical Element in Heidegger's Thought.* Athens, OH: Ohio University Press, 1978.

Carr, Anne E. *A Search for Wisdom and Spirit: Thomas Merton's Theology of the Self.* Notre Dame: University of Notre Dame Press, 1988.

Cavallera, F. "Saint Jerome et la vie parfaite." *Revue d'ascétique et de la mystique* 2 (1921): 101-27.

Cayré, F. *La contemplation augustinienne: Principes de spiritualité et de théologie.* 2nd ed. Paris: Desclée, 1954.

Chadwick, Henry. *Alexandrian Christianity.* Philadelphia: Westminster, 1954.

——. *Augustine.* Oxford: Oxford University Press, 1986.

——. "Christian Platonism in Origen and Augustine." *Origeniana Tertia,* 217-30. Rome: Edizioni dell'Ateneo, 1985.

——. *Early Christian Thought and the Classical Tradition: Studies in Justin, Clement, and Origen.* New York: Oxford University Press, 1966.

——. "Enkrateia." In *Reallexikon für Antike und Christentum,* 5:343-65.

Chadwick, Owen. *John Cassian: A Study in Primitive Monasticism.* Cambridge: Cambridge University Press, 1950.

——. *Western Asceticism.* Philadelphia: Westminster, 1958.

Chapman, John. "Mysticism (Christian, Roman Catholic)." *Encyclopedia of Religion and Ethics,* edited by J. Hastings, 9:90-101. New York: Scribner, 1917.

Chenu, M.-D. "La deification dans la tradition spirituelle de l'Orient." *La vie spirituelle* 43 (1935): 91-107.

——. "Une théologie de la vie mystique." *La vie spirituelle* 50 (1937): 46-50.

Clark, Henry. *The Ethical Mysticism of Albert Schweitzer.* Boston: Beacon, 1962.

Clark, Mary T. "A Neoplatonic Commentary on the Christian Trinity: Marius

Victorinus." In *Neoplatonism and Christian Thought,* edited by Dominic J. O'Meara, 24–33. Albany: State University of New York Press, 1982.

———. "The Neoplatonism of Marius Victorinus the Christian." In *Neoplatonism and Early Christian Thought: Essays in Honour of A. H. Armstrong,* edited by H. J. Blumenthal and R. A. Markus, 153–59. London: Variorum, 1981.

Clement, Olivier. *Sources: Les mystiques chrétiens des origines: Textes et commentaires.* Paris: Stock, 1982.

Cochrane, C. N. *Christianity and Classical Culture: A Study of Thought and Action from Augustus to Augustine.* New York: Oxford University Press, 1967.

Cohen, Martin Samuel. *The Shi'ur Qomah: Liturgy and Theurgy in Pre-Kabbalistic Jewish Mysticism.* Lanham, MD: University Press of America, 1983.

Colette, Jacques. "Mystique et philosophie." *Revue des sciences philosophiques et théologiques* 70 (1986): 329–48.

Collins, John J. "Apocalyptic Eschatology as the Transcendence of Death." *Catholic Biblical Quarterly* 36 (1974): 21–43.

———. *The Apocalyptic Imagination: An Introduction to the Jewish Matrix of Christianity.* New York: Crossroad, 1984.

———. *Between Athens and Jerusalem: Jewish Identity in the Hellenistic Diaspora.* New York: Crossroad, 1983.

———. "Cosmos and Salvation: Jewish Wisdom and Apocalyptic in the Hellenistic World." *History of Religions* 17 (1977): 121–42.

———, ed. *Apocalypse: Morphology of a Genre. Semeia* 14. Missoula, MT: Scholars Press, 1979.

Combés, Gustave. *La charité d'après Saint Augustin.* Paris: Desclée, 1934.

Comeau, M. "Le Christ, chemin et terme de l'ascension spirituelle, d'après saint Augustin." *Recherches de science religieuse* 40 (1952): 80–89.

Consolino, Franca Ela. "*VENI HUC A LIBANO:* La *SPONSA* del Cantico dei Cantici come modello per le vergini negli scritti esortatori di Ambrogio." *Athenaeum* n.s. 62 (1984): 399–415.

Conzelmann, Hans. *1 Corinthians.* Hermeneia. Philadelphia: Fortress, 1975.

Copleston, Frederick, S.J. *A History of Philosophy.* 9 vols. Garden City, NY: Doubleday, 1977.

Corbin, Michel. "Négation et transcendance dans l'oeuvre de Denys." *Revue des sciences philosophiques et théologiques* 69 (1985): 41–76.

Cornford, F. M. *Plato and Parmenides.* Indianapolis: Bobbs-Merrill, n.d.

Corsini, E. *Il trattato 'De Divinis Nominibus' dello Pseudo-Dionigi e i commenti neoplatonici al Parmenide.* Turin: G. Giappichelli, 1962.

Corwin, V. *St. Ignatius and Christianity at Antioch.* Yale Publications in Religion 1. New Haven: Yale University Press, 1960.

Cothenet, Edouard, et al. "Imitation du Christ." *DS* 7:1536–1601.

Couilleau, Guerric. "Perfection chrétienne. II. Pères et premiers moines." *DS* 12:1081–1118.

Countryman, L. William. *The Mystical Way in the Fourth Gospel: Crossing over into God.* Philadelphia: Fortress, 1987.

Courcelle, Pierre. "L'âme en cage." In *Parusia: Studien zur Philosophie Platons und zur Problemgeschichte des Platonismus. Festgabe für Johannes Hirschberger,* edited by Kurt Flasch, 103–16. Frankfurt: Minerva, 1965.

———. "Le corps-tombeau (Platon, Gorgias 493A; Cratyle 400C; Phédre 250C)." *Revue des études anciennes* 68 (1966): 101–22.

———. "Grab der Seele." *Reallexikon für Antike und Christentum*, 12:455–67.

———. *Late Latin Writers and their Greek Sources.* Cambridge, MA: Harvard University Press, 1969.

———. "Nouveaux aspects du Platonisme chez saint Ambroise." *Revue des études latines* 34 (1956): 220–39.

———. "Plotin et saint Ambroise." *Revue de philologie* 76 (1950): 31–45.

———. *Recherches sur les Confessions de Saint Augustin.* Paris: Boccard, 1950.

———. "Saint Ambroise devant le précepte delphique." In *Forma Futuri: Studi in Onore del Cardinale Michele Pellegrino*, 179–88. Turin: Bottega d'Erasmo, 1975.

———. "Tradition platonicienne et traditions chrétiennes du corps-prison (Phédon 62B; Cratyle 400C)." *Revue des études latines* 43 (1963): 6–43.

Cousins, Ewert. *Bonaventure and the Coincidence of Opposites.* Chicago: Franciscan Herald Press, 1978.

———. *Global Spirituality: Toward the Meeting of Mystical Paths.* Madras: University of Madras, Radhakrishnan Institute for Advanced Study in Philosophy, 1985.

Cox, Patricia. "'In My Father's House Are Many Dwelling Places': *Ktisma* in Origen's *De principiis*." *Anglican Theological Review* 62 (1980): 322–37.

———. "'Pleasure of the Text, Text of Pleasure': Origen's *Commentary on the Song of Songs*." *Journal of the American Academy of Religion* 54 (1986): 241–53.

Crouzel, Henry, "Grégoire de Nysse est-il le fondateur de la théologie mystique?" *Revue d'ascétique et de la mystique* 33 (1957): 189–202.

———. *Origen: The Life and Thought of the First Great Theologian.* San Francisco: Harper & Row, 1989.

———. "Origène." *DS* 11:933–61.

———. "Origène, précurseur du monachisme." In *Théologie de la vie monastique*, 15–38. Paris: Aubier, 1961.

———. *Origène et la "connaissance mystique".* Bruges-Paris: Desclée, 1961.

———. "Origines patristiques d'un thème mystique: Le trait et la blessure d'amour chez Origène." In *Kyriakon: Festschrift Johannes Quasten*, edited by P. Granfield and J. Jungmann, 1:311–19. Münster: Aschendorff, 1970.

———. "Spiritual Exegesis." In *Encyclopedia of Theology: The Concise Sacramentum Mundi*, edited by Karl Rahner, 126–33. New York: Seabury, 1975.

———. *Théologie de l'image de Dieu chez Origène.* Paris: Aubier, 1957.

Csányi, Daniel A. "OPTIMA PARS: Die Auslegungsgeschichte von Lk. 10,38–42 bei den Kirchenvätern der ersten vier Jahrhunderte." *Studia Monastica* 2 (1960): 5–78.

Culianu, Ioan Petru. *Expériences de l'Extase: Extase, Ascension et Récit visionnaire de l'Hellenisme au Moyen Âge.* Paris: Payot, 1984.

———. *I Miti dei Dualismi Occidentali: Dai sistemi gnostici al mondo moderno.* Milan: Jaca, 1989.

———. *Psychanodia I: A Survey of the Evidence concerning the Ascension of the Soul and its Relevance.* Leiden: Brill, 1983.

Cumont, Franz. *Astrology and Religion among the Greeks and Romans.* 1912. Reprint. New York: Dover, 1960.

———. "Le mysticisme astral dans l'antiquité." *Bulletin de l'Académie Royale de Belgique. Classe des Lettres* 5 (1909): 256–86.

d'Alès, Adhémer. "Les ailes de l'âme." *Ephemerides theologicae lovanienses* 10 (1933): 63–72.

———. "Le mysticisme de Saint Cyprien." *Revue d'ascétique et de la mystique* 2 (1921): 256–67.

Dan, Joseph. "The Religious Experience of the 'Merkavah.'" In *Jewish Spirituality: From the Bible through the Middle Ages,* edited by Arthur Green, 289–307. WS 13. New York: Crossroad, 1986.

———. *Three Types of Ancient Jewish Mysticism.* The Seventh Annual Louis Feinberg Memorial Lecture in Judaic Studies. Cincinnati: University of Cincinnati Press, 1984.

Daniélou, Jean. *A History of Early Christian Doctrine before the Council of Nicea.* Translated by David Smith and John Austin Baker. 3 vols. London: Darton, Longman & Todd; Philadelphia: Westminster, 1964–1977.

———. *Origen.* New York: Sheed & Ward, 1955.

———. *Platonisme et théologie mystique: Doctrine spirituelle de Saint Grégoire de Nysse.* Paris: Aubier, 1944.

———. "Les sources bibliques de la mystique d'Origène." *Revue d'ascétique et de la mystique* 23 (1947): 126–41.

———. "La typologie d'Isaac dans le christianisme primitif." *Biblica* 28 (1947): 363–93.

Dassmann, Ernst. *Die Frömmigkeit des Kirchenvaters Ambrosius von Mailand.* Münster: Aschendorff, 1965.

de Certeau, Michel. "L'Enonciation mystique." *Revue de science religieuse* 64 (1976): 183–215. "Mystic Speech," in *Heterologies: Discourse on the Other,* translated by Brian Massumi, 80–100. Minneapolis: University of Minnesota Press, 1986.

———. *La Fable Mystique XVIe–XVIIe Siècle.* Paris: Gallimard, 1982.

———. "Histoire et mystique." *Revue d'histoire de spiritualité* 48 (1972): 69–82.

———. "Historicités mystiques." *Revue de science religieuse* 73 (1985): 325–54.

———. "Mystique." In *Encyclopaedia universalis,* 11:521–26. Paris: Encyclopaedia universalis de France, 1968.

———. "'Mystique' au XVIIe siècle: Le problème du langage 'mystique.'" In *L'Homme devant Dieu: Mélanges offerts au Pere Henri de Lubac,* 2:267–91. 3 vols. Paris: Aubier, 1964.

Dechow, Jon F. *Dogma and Mysticism in Early Christianity: Epiphanius of Cyprus and the Legacy of Origen.* North American Patristic Society Patristic Monograph Series 13. Macon, GA: Mercer University Press, 1988.

de Grandmaison, Léonce. "L'élément mystique dans la religion." *Recherches de science religieuse* 1 (1910): 180–208.

de Guibert, Joseph, S.J. *Études de théologie mystique.* Toulouse: L'Apostolat de la prière, 1930.

———, et al. "Ascése, Ascétisme." *DS* 1:936–1010.

Deikman, Arthur J. "Deautomization and the Mystic Experience." *Psychiatry* 29 (1966): 324–38. Reprinted in *Understanding Mysticism,* edited by Richard Woods, O.P., 240–60. Garden City, NY: Image Books, 1980.

———. "Experimental Meditation." *Journal of Nervous and Mental Diseases* 136 (1963): 329–43.

———. "Implications of Experimentally Induced Contemplative Meditation." *Journal of Nervous and Mental Diseases* 142 (1966): 101–16.

——. *The Observing Self: Mysticism and Psychotherapy.* Boston: Beacon, 1982.

Deissmann, G. Adolf. *Die Neutestamentliche Formel "in Christo Jesu".* Marburg, 1893.

——. *Paul: A Study in Social and Religious History.* New York: Harper & Row, 1926.

Dekkers, E., and E. Gaar, eds. *Clavis Patrum Latinorum: Editio altera.* The Hague: Nijhoff, 1961.

Delacroix, Henri. *Essai sur la mysticisme speculatif en Allemagne au XIVe siècle.* Paris: Alcan, 1900.

——. *Études d'histoire et de psychologie du mysticisme: Les grands mystiques chrétiens.* Paris: Alcan, 1908.

de Lange, Nicholas. *Origen and the Jews.* Cambridge: Cambridge University Press, 1976.

de la Taille, Maurice, S.J. "L'oraison contemplative." *Recherches de science religieuse* 9 (1919): 273–92.

Deleani, S. *Christum sequi: Étude d'un théme dans l'oeuvre de Saint Cyprien.* Paris: Études Augustiniennes, 1979.

de Lubac, Henri. *Histoire et Espirt: L'Intelligence de l'Ecriture d'après Origène.* Paris: Aubier, 1950.

——. "Preface." In *La mystique et les mystiques,* edited by A. Ravier, S.J., 7–39. Paris: Desclée, 1965.

des Places, Édouard. "Platon et la langue des mystères." In *Études platoniciennes 1929–1979,* 83–98. Leiden: Brill, 1981.

——, et al. "Divinisation." *DS* 3:1370–1459.

Despland, Michel. *La religion en occident: Evolution des idées et du vecu.* Montreal: Fides, 1979.

Desprez, Vincent. "Pseudo-Macaire (Syméon). I. L'Oeuvre, l'auteur et son mileau." *DS* 10:20–27.

——. "Pseudo-Macaire (Syméon). III. Influence." *DS* 10:39–43.

de Vogel, C. J. "On the Platonic Character of Neoplatonism and the Neoplatonic Character of Platonism." *Mind* 62 (1953): 43–64.

de Vogüe, Adalbert. "De Jean Cassien à John Main: Reflexions sur la meditation chrétienne." *Collectanea Cisterciensia* 47 (1985): 179–81.

——. "Monachisme et Eglise dans la pensée de Cassien." In *Théologie de la vie monastique,* 213–40. Paris: Aubier, 1961.

——. "Pour comprendre Cassien: Un survol des Conferences." *Collectanea Cisterciensia* 39 (1977): 250–72.

di Berardino, Angelo, ed. *Patrology,* Vol. 4, *The Golden Age of Latin Patristic Literature from the Council of Nicea to the Council of Chalcedon.* Introduction by Johannes Quasten. Westminster: Christian Classics, 1986.

Dideberg, D. "Amor." In *Augustinus-Lexikon,* edited by Cornelius Mayer et al., 1:294–300. Basel: Schwabe, 1986–.

Dieterich, Albrecht. *Eine Mithrasliturgie.* 3rd ed. Leipzig: Teubner, 1923.

Dillon, John. *The Middle Platonists: 80 B.C. to A.D. 200.* Ithaca, NY: Cornell University Press, 1977.

——. "The Transcendence of God in Philo: Some Possible Sources." In *The Center for Hermeneutical Studies in Hellenistic and Modern Culture: Protocol of the Sixteenth Colloquy: 20 April 1975.* Berkeley, 1975.

Dodd, C. H. *The Interpretation of the Fourth Gospel.* Cambridge: Cambridge University Press, 1960.

Dodds, E. R. *The Greeks and the Irrational.* Berkeley: University of California Press, 1963.

——. *Pagan and Christian in an Age of Anxiety.* Cambridge: Cambridge University Press, 1965.

——. "The *Parmenides* of Plato and the Origin of the Neoplatonic 'One.'" *Classical Quarterly* 22 (1928): 129–42.

Dörrie, Heinrich. "Bibliographischer Bericht über den Stand der Forschung zum Mittleren und Neueren Platonismus." In *Platonica Minora,* 524–48. Munich: Fink, 1976.

——. "Das fünffach gestufte Mysterium." In *Platonica Minora,* 474–90.

Dörries, Hermann. *Symeon von Mesopotamien: Die Überlieferung der Messalianischen Makarios-Schriften.* Texte und Untersuchungen 95.1. Leipzig, 1948.

Drewery, Ben. "Deification." In *Christian Spirituality: Essays in Honor of Gordon Rupp,* edited by Peter Brooks, 35–62. London: SCM, 1975.

Drey, Johann Sebastian. "Über das Verhältnis des Mysticismus zum Katholicismus." *Theologische Quartalschrift* (1831): 25–54.

Droge, Arthur. "The Status of Peter in the Fourth Gospel: A Note on John 18:10–11." *Journal of Biblical Literature* 109 (1990): 307–11.

Dudden, F. Homes. *The Life and Times of St. Ambrose.* 2 vols. Oxford: Clarendon, 1935.

Dunne, Tad, S.J. *Lonergan and Spirituality: Towards a Spiritual Integration.* Chicago: Loyola University Press, 1985.

Dupont, Jacques. "Le chrétien, miroir de la gloire divine d'après II Cor., iii,18." *Revue biblique* 56 (1949): 392–411.

Dupré, Louis. *The Common Life: The Origins of Trinitarian Mysticism and Its Development by Jan Ruusbroec.* New York: Crossroad, 1984.

——. *The Deeper Self: An Introduction to Christian Mysticism.* New York: Crossroad, 1981.

——. "Mysticism." In *The Encyclopedia of Religion,* edited by Mircea Eliade, 10:245–61. New York: Macmillan, 1987.

——. *The Other Dimension: A Search for the Meaning of Religious Attitudes.* Garden City, NY: Doubleday, 1972.

——. "Spiritual Life in a Secular Age." *Daedalus* 111 (1982): 21–31.

——. *Transcendent Selfhood: The Loss and Recovery of the Inner Life.* New York: Seabury, 1976.

——. "*Unio mystica:* The State and the Experience." In *Mystical Union and Monotheistic Faith: An Ecumenical Dialogue,* edited by Moshe Idel and Bernard McGinn, 3–23. New York: Macmillan, 1989.

——, and James A. Wiseman, O.S.B. *Light from Light: An Anthology of Christian Mysticism.* New York: Paulist, 1988.

Dvornik, Francis. *Byzantium and the Roman Primacy.* New York: Fordham University Press, 1966.

Egan, Harvey D., S.J. *What Are They Saying about Mysticism?* New York: Paulist, 1982.

Eiten, Robert B., S.J. "Recent Theological Opinion on Infused Contemplation." *Theological Studies* 2 (1941): 89–100.

Eliade, Mircea. "Experiences of the Mystic Light." In *The Two and the One,* 19–77. New York: Harper, 1965.

————. *A History of Religious Ideas,* vol. 3. Translated by Willard R. Trask. Chicago: University of Chicago Press, 1985.

————. *Patterns of Comparative Religion.* Translated by Rosemary Sheed. Cleveland: World, 1966.

————. "Sense Experience and Mystical Experience among Primitives." In *Myths, Dreams and Mysteries,* translated by Philip Mairet, 73–98. London: Harvill, 1960.

————. *Shamanism: Archaic Techniques of Ecstasy.* Translated by Willard R. Trask. London: Routledge & Kegan Paul, 1964.

————. *Yoga: Immortality and Freedom.* Translated by Willard R. Trask. London: Routledge & Kegan Paul, 1958.

Elliot, Alison Goddard. *Roads to Paradise: Reading the Lives of the Early Saints.* Hanover: University Press of New England, 1987.

Ellwood, Robert J. *Mysticism and Religion.* Englewood Cliffs, NJ: Prentice-Hall, 1980.

Faivre, Antoine. "Hermetism." In *The Encyclopedia of Religion,* edited by Mircea Eliade, 6:283–302. New York: Macmillan, 1987.

Fallon, Francis. "The Gnostic Apocalypses." In *Apocalypse: Morphology of a Genre. Semeia* 14, edited by John J. Collins, 123–58. Missoula, MT: Scholars Press, 1979.

Farges, Albert. *Mystical Phenomena Compared with Their Human and Diabolical Counterfeits.* London: Burnes, Oates & Washbourne, 1926.

Ferwerda, R. "The Meaning of the Word *Sōma* (Body) in the Axial Age: An Interpretation of Plato's Cratylus 400C." In *The Origins and Diversity of Axial Age Civilizations,* edited by S. N. Eisenstadt, 111–24. Albany: State University of New York Press, 1986.

Festugière, André Jean. *Contemplation et vie contemplative selon Platon.* Paris: Vrin, 1936.

————. *L'Enfant d'Agrigente.* Paris: Plon, 1950.

————. *Hermétisme et mystique païenne.* Paris: Aubier-Montaigne, 1967.

————. *L'Ideal religieux des grecs et l'Évangile.* Paris: Gabalda, 1932.

————. *La révélation d'Hermes Trismégiste.* 4 vols. Paris: Gabalda, 1950–54.

————. *Personal Religion among the Greeks.* Berkeley and Los Angeles: University of California Press, 1954.

Feuillet, André. *Johannine Studies.* Staten Island: Alba House, 1964.

Finan, Thomas, "A Mystic in Milan. *Reverberasti Revisited."* In *From Augustine to Eriugena: Studies on Neoplatonism and Christianity in Honor of John O'Meara,* edited by F. X. Martin and J. A. Richmond, 77–91. Washington, DC: Catholic University Press, 1991.

Findlay, J. N. "The Logic of Mysticism." In *Ascent to the Absolute: Metaphysical Papers and Letters,* 162–83. London: Allen & Unwin, 1970.

Fischer, Klaus P. *Der Mensch als Geheimnis: Die Anthropologie Karl Rahners.* Freiburg: Herder, 1974.

Fishbane, Michael. *Biblical Interpretation in Ancient Israel.* Oxford: Clarendon, 1985.

Flew, R. Newton. *The Idea of Perfection in Christian Theology.* London: Oxford University Press, 1934.

Fontaine, Jacques. "The Practice of Christian Life: The Birth of the Laity." In

Christian Spirituality: Origins to the Twelfth Century, edited by Bernard McGinn and John Meyendorff, 453–91. WS 16. New York: Crossroad, 1986.

——. "Prose et poésie: L'interférence des genres et des styles dans la création littéraire d'Ambroise de Milan." In *Ambrosius Episcopus,* edited by Giuseppe Lazzati, 1:124–70. 2 vols. Milan: Universitá Cattolica del Sacro Cuore, 1976.

Fowden, Garth. *The Egyptian Hermes: A historical approach to the late pagan mind.* Cambridge: Cambridge University Press, 1987.

Frazer, Ruth F. "The Morphology of Desert Wisdom in the 'Apophthegmata Patrum.'" Dissertation, University of Chicago, 1977.

Frend, W. H. C. *Martyrdom and Persecution: A Study of a Conflict from the Maccabees to Donatus.* New York: New York University Press, 1967.

——. *The Rise of Christianity.* Philadelphia: Fortress, 1984.

Friedlander, Paul. *Plato: An Introduction.* New York: Harper, 1958.

Freud, Ernst, ed. *The Letters of Sigmund Freud.* New York: Basic Books, 1960.

Freud, Sigmund. *Civilization and its Discontents.* Translated by James Strachey. New York: Norton, 1961.

——. *The Future of an Illusion.* Translated by W. D. Robson-Scott. New York: H. Liveright, 1927.

Furse, Margaret. "Mysticism: Classic Modern Interpreters and their Premise of Continuity." *Anglican Theological Review* 60 (1978): 180–93.

Gabriele di Santa Maria Maddalena. *La contemplation acquise.* Paris, 1949.

Gadamer, H.-G. "Plato's Parmenides and its Influence." *Dionysius* 7 (1983): 3–16.

Gafni, Isaiah. "The Historical Background." In *Jewish Writings of the Second Temple Period,* edited by Michael E. Stone, 1–31. Compendia Rerum Iudaicarum ad Novum Testamentum, section 2. Philadelphia: Fortress, 1984.

Gale, Richard M. "Mysticism and Philosophy." *Journal of Philosophy* 57 (1960): 471–81.

Gardet, Louis. "Expérience du soi, expérience des profundeurs de Dieu." *Revue Thomiste* 78 (1978): 357–84.

——. *La mystique.* Paris: Presses universitaires de France, 1970.

——. "Théologie de la mystique." *Revue Thomiste* 71 (1971): 571–88.

——, and Olivier Lacombe. *L'expérience du soi: Étude de mystique comparée.* Paris: Desclée, 1981.

Gardiel, Ambroise. "L'expérience mystique dans le cadre des missions divins." *La vie spirituelle,* Supplement (1932): June, 129–46; July, 1–21; September, 65–76; October, 1–28.

——. *La structure de l'âme et l'expérience mystique.* 2 vols. Paris: Gabalda, 1927.

Garrigou-Lagrange, Reginald, O.P. *Christian Perfection and Contemplation according to St. Thomas Aquinas and St. John of the Cross.* St. Louis: Herder, 1951.

——. "La contemplation dans l'école dominicain." *DS* 2:2067–80.

——. *The Love of God and the Cross of Jesus.* 2 vols. St. Louis: Herder, 1947–51.

——. *The Three Ages of the Interior Life.* 2 vols. Translated by M. Timothea Doyle. St. Louis and London: Herder, 1947–48.

Garside, Bruce. "Language and the Interpretation of Mystical Experience." *International Journal for the Philosophy of Religion* 3 (1972): 93–102.

Gersh, Stephen. *From Iamblichus to Eriugena: An Investigation of the Prehistory and Evolution of the Pseudo-Dionysian Tradition.* Leiden: Brill, 1978.

———. "Ideas and Energies in Pseudo-Dionysius the Areopagite." *Studia Patristica* 15, edited by E. A. Livingstone, 297–300. Berlin: Akademie Verlag, 1984.

———. *Middle Platonism and Neoplatonism: The Latin Tradition.* 2 vols. Notre Dame: University of Notre Dame Press, 1986.

Gilson, Etienne. *The Christian Philosophy of St. Augustine.* New York: Random House, 1960.

Gimello, Robert. "Mysticism and Meditation." In *Mysticism and Philosophical Analysis,* edited by Steven T. Katz, 170–99. New York: Oxford University Press, 1978.

Goetz, Joseph, et al. "Extase." *DS* 4:2087–2109.

Goodenough, Erwin. *By Light, Light: The Mystic Gospel of Hellenistic Judaism.* New Haven: Yale University Press, 1935.

Grabowski, S. "Saint Augustine and the Doctrine of the Mystical Body of Christ." *Theological Studies* 7 (1946): 72–125.

———. "St. Augustine and the Presence of God." *Theological Studies* 13 (1952): 336–58.

Grant, Robert M. *The Early Christian Doctrine of God.* Charlottesville: University Press of Virginia, 1966.

———. *From Augustus to Constantine.* New York: Harper & Row, 1970.

———. *Gnosticism.* New York: Harper & Row, 1961.

———. *Gnosticism and Early Christianity.* New York: Harper & Row, 1959.

———. "Gnostic Spirituality." In *Christian Spirituality: Origins to the Twelfth Century,* edited by Bernard McGinn and John Meyendorff, 44–60. WS 16. New York: Crossroad, 1986.

———. *Greek Apologists of the Second Century.* Philadelphia: Westminster, 1988.

———. *The Letter and the Spirit.* New York: Macmillan, 1957.

Greenberg, Moshe. *Ezechiel 1–20.* Anchor Bible 22. Garden City, NY: Doubleday, 1983.

Gregson, Vernon J., Jr. *Lonergan: Spirituality and the Meeting of Religions.* Lanham, MD: University Press of America, 1985.

Grendle, Nicholas, O.P. "St. Irenaeus as a Mystical Theologian." *The Thomist* 39 (1975): 185–97.

Gribomont, Jean. "The Translations of Jerome and Rufinus." In *Patrology.* Vol. 4, *The Golden Age of Latin Patristic Literature From the Council of Nicea to the Council of Chalcedon,* edited by Angelo di Berardino, introduction by Johannes Quasten, 195–254. Westminster: Christian Classics, 1986.

Grof, Stanislov. "East and West: Ancient Wisdom and Modern Science." In *Ancient Wisdom and Modern Science,* edited by Stanislov Grof and Marjorie Livingston Valier, 2–23. Albany: State University of New York Press, 1984.

———, and C. Grof. *Beyond Death.* London: Thames & Hudson, 1980.

Gross, Jules. *La divinisation du chrétien d'après les pères grecs.* Paris: Gabalda, 1938.

Grossi, Vittorino. "La spiritualitá agostiniana." In *Le grandi scuole della spiritualitá cristiana,* 159–206. Rome: Teresianum, 1984.

Groves, Nicholas. "*Mundicia cordis:* A Study of the Theme of Purity of Heart in Hugh of Pontigny and the Fathers of the Undivided Church." In *One Yet Two: Monastic Traditions East and West,* edited by M. Basil Pennington, 304–31. Kalamazoo, MI: Cistercian Publications, 1976.

Gruenwald, Ithamar. *Apocalyptic and Merkavah Mysticism.* Leiden: Brill, 1980.

―――. "Jewish Apocalypticism to the Rabbinic Period." in *The Encyclopedia of Religion*, edited by Mircea Eliade, 1:336–42. New York: Macmillan, 1987.

Guerard, Christian. "La théologie négative dans l'apophatisme grec." *Revue des sciences philosophiques et théologiques* 68 (1984): 183–200.

―――. "Le théorie des Henades et la mystique de Proclus." *Dionysius* 6 (1982): 73–82.

Guillaumont, Antoine. "Étienne bar Soudaili." *DS* 4:1481–88.

―――. *Les "Kephalaia Gnostica" d'Évagre le Pontique et l'histoire d'origenisme chez les Grecs et chez les Syriens.* Paris: Seuil, 1962.

―――. "Messaliens." *DS* 10:1074–83.

―――. "Un philosophe au desert: Evagre le Pontique." *Revue de l'histoire des religions* 181 (1972): 29–56.

―――, and Claire Guillaumont. "Evagre le Pontique." *DS* 4:1731–44.

Guy, Jean-Claude. *Recherches sur la tradition grecque des "Apophthegmata Patrum."* Brussels: Société des Bollandistes, 1962.

Haas, Alois M. "Was ist Mystik?" In *Abendländische Mystik im Mittelalter: Symposion Kloster Engelberg 1984*, edited by Kurt Ruh, 319–42. Stuttgart: Metzler, 1986.

Hadot, Pierre. "Dieu comme acte d'être dans le néoplatonisme." In *Dieu et l'être: Exégèses d'Éxode 3,14 et de Coran 20,11–24*, 58–63. Paris: Études Augustiniennes, 1978.

―――. "Les divisions des parties de la philosophie dans l'Antiquité." *Museum Helveticum* 36 (1979): 218–31.

―――. "L'être et l'étant dans la Néoplatonisme." In *Études Néoplatoniciennes*, 27–41. Neuchâtel: A La Baconnière, 1973.

―――. "Forms of Life and Forms of Discourse in Ancient Philosophy." *Critical Inquiry* 16 (1990): 483–505.

―――. *Marius Victorinus: Recherches sur sa vie et ses sources.* Paris: Études Augustiniennes, 1971.

―――. "Neoplatonist Spirituality. I. Plotinus and Porphyry." In *Classical Mediterranean Spirituality: Egyptian, Greek, Roman*, edited by A. H. Armstrong, 230–49. WS 15. New York: Crossroad, 1986.

―――. "Les niveaux de conscience dans les états mystiques selon Plotin." *Journal de psychologie normale et pathologique* 77 (1980): 243–65.

―――. "Platon et Plotin dans trois sermons de saint Ambroise." *Revue des études latines* 34 (1956): 202–20.

―――. *Plotin ou la simplicité du regard.* Paris: Études Augustiniennes, 1973.

―――. *Porphyre et Victorinus.* 2 vols. Paris: Études Augustiniennes, 1968.

―――. "Théologie, exégèse, révélation, écriture, dans la philosophie grecque." In *Centre d'études des religions du livre: Les régles de l'intérpretation*, edited by Michel Tardieu, 13–34. Paris: Cerf, 1987.

―――. "L'Union de l'âme avec l'intellect divin dans l'expérience mystique plotinienne." In *Proclus et son influence: Actes du Colloque de Neuchâtel, Juin, 1985*, edited by G. Boss and G. Seel, 3–27. Neuchâtel: Editions du Grand Mich, 1986.

―――. "XXIX. Patristique Latine." In *École pratique des hauts études: Ve Section, Sciences religieuses, Annuaire 1965–66*, 151–52. Paris: Sorbonne, 1965.

Halperin, David L. "Ascension or Invasion: Implications of the Heavenly Journey in Ancient Judaism." *Religion* 18 (1988): 47–67.

————. "Heavenly Ascension in Ancient Judaism: The Nature of the Experience." In *Society of Biblical Literature 1987 Seminar Papers,* edited by K. H. Richards, 218–32. Atlanta: Scholars Press, 1987.

Halperin, David M. "Why is Diotima a Woman? Platonic *Eros* and the Figuration of Gender." In *Before Sexuality: The Construction of Erotic Experience in the Ancient Greek World,* edited by David M. Halperin, John J. Winkler, and Froma I. Zeitlin, 257–308. Princeton, NJ: Princeton University Press, 1990.

Hamman, Adalbert. "The Turnabout of the Fourth Century." In *Patrology,* vol. 4, *The Golden Age of Latin Patristic Literature From the Council of Nicea to the Council of Chalcedon,* edited by Angelo di Berardino, introduction by Johannes Quasten, 1–32. Westminster: Christian Classics, 1986.

Hanson, John S. "Dreams and Visions in the Graeco-Roman World and Early Christianity." In *Aufstieg und Niedergang der römischen Welt. II. Prinzipat,* 23.2. Berlin and New York: de Gruyter, 1980.

Happold, F. D. *Mysticism: A Study and an Anthology.* Harmondsworth: Penguin, 1963.

Harl, Marguerite. "La 'bouche' et le 'coeur' de l'apôtre: deux images bibliques du 'sens divin' de l'homme ('Proverbes' 2,5) chez Origène." In *Forma Futuri: Studi in Onore del Cardinale Michele Pellegrino,* 17–42. Turin: Bottega d'Erasmo, 1975.

————. "Le langage de l'expérience religieuse chez les pères grecs." *Rivista di storia e letteratura religiosa* 15 (1977): 5–34.

————. "Recherches sur l'origenisme d'Origène: La 'satieté' (*koros*) de la contemplation comme motif de la chute des âmes." *Studia Patristica* 8 (1966): 373–405.

Harnack, Adolph. *History of Dogma.* An unabridged republication of the 1900 translation of the 3rd German ed. 7 vols. bound as 4. New York: Dover, 1961.

Hartman, Lars. "Survey of the Problem of Apocalyptic Genre." In *Apocalypticism in the Mediterranean World and the Near East,* edited by David Hellholm, 329–43. Tübingen: Mohr, 1983.

Hathaway, Ronald F. *Hierarchy and the Definition of Order in the Letters of Pseudo-Dionysius.* The Hague: Nijhoff, 1969.

Hausherr, Irenée. "Les grands courants de la spiritualité orientale." *Orientalia Christiana Periodica* 1 (1935): 114–38.

————. "Ignorance infinie." *Orientalia Christiana Periodica* 2 (1936): 351–62.

————. "L'influence du 'Livre de Saint Hierothée.'" In *Études de spiritualité orientale,* 23–58. Orientalia Christiana Analecta 183. Rome: Pontificium Institutum Studiorum Orientalium, 1969.

————. *The Name of Jesus.* Kalamazoo, MI: Cistercian Publications, 1978.

————. "Le spiritualité des premières generations chrétiennes." In *La mystique et les mystiques,* edited by A. Rivier, 409–61. Paris: Desclée, 1965.

————. "Le Traité de l'Oraison d'Évagre le Pontique (Pseudo Nil)." *Revue d'ascétique et de la mystique* 15 (1934): 113–70.

Haussleiter, J. "Fruitio Dei." In *Reallexikon für Antike und Christentum,* 8:538–55.

Heidegger, Martin. *Der Satz vom Grund.* Pfullingen: G. Neske, 1957.

Heijke, J. "St. Augustine's Comments on 'Imago Dei.' (An Anthology from all his works exclusive of the *De Trinitate*)." *Classical Folia,* Supplement III. April 1960.

Heiler, Friedrich. *Die Bedeutung der Mystik für die Weltreligionen.* Munich: E. Reinhardt, 1919.

———. "Contemplation in Christian Mysticism." In *Spiritual Disciplines: Papers from the Eranos Yearbooks*, 186–238. New York: Pantheon, 1960.

———. *Prayer: A Study in the History and Psychology of Religion*. London: Oxford University Press, 1932.

Heim, M. *Der Enthusiasmus in den Konfessionen des hl. Augustins*. Würzburg: Augustinus Verlag, 1941.

Heine, Ronald E. *Perfection in the Virtuous Life: A Study in the Relationship Between Edification and Polemical Theology in Gregory of Nyssa's De Vita Moysis*. Philadelphia: Philadelphia Patristic Foundation, 1975.

Hendrikx, Ephraem. *Augustins Verhältnis zur Mystik*. Würzburg: Augustinus Verlag, 1936.

———. "Augustins Verhältnis zur Mystik: Ein Rückblick." In *Scientia Augustiniana: Festschrift Adolar Zumkeller*, 107–11. Würzburg: Augustinus Verlag, 1975.

Hengel, Martin. *Judaism and Hellenism*. 2 vols. Philadelphia: Fortress, 1974.

Henle, Paul. "Mysticism and Semantics." *Philosophy and Phenomenological Research* 9 (1949): 116–22.

Henry, Paul, S.J. *Plotin et l'Occident*. Louvain: Spicilegium Sacrum Lovaniense, 1934.

———. *La vision d'Ostie: Sa place dans la vie et l'oeuvre de Saint Augustin*. Paris: Vrin, 1938. Eng. trans. *The Path to Transcendence: From Philosophy to Mysticism in Saint Augustine*, translated by Francis F. Burch. Philadelphia: Pickwick Press, 1981.

Heussi, Karl. *Der Ursprung des Mönchtums*. Tübingen: Mohr, 1936.

Hick, John. "Mystical Experience as Cognition." In *Mystics and Scholars: The Calgary Conference on Mysticism 1976*, edited by Harold Coward and Terence Penelhum. *Sciences Religieuses* Supplements 13, 41–56.

Himmelfarb, Martha. "From Prophecy to Apocalypse: The *Book of Watchers* and Tours of Heaven." In *Jewish Spirituality: From the Bible through the Middle Ages*, edited by Arthur Green, 145–65. WS 13. New York: Crossroad, 1986.

Hocking, William Ernest. *The Meaning of God in Human Experience: A Philosophical Study of Religion*. New Haven: Yale University Press, 1912.

Hoffmann, Ernst. *Platonismus und Mystik im Altertum: Sitzungsberichte der Heidelberge Akademie der Wissenschaften, Philosophisch-historische Klasse, 1934–35*. 2 Abhandlung. Heidelberg: Carl Winter, 1935.

Holm, Nils G. *Religious Ecstasy*. Stockholm: Almqvist & Wiksell, 1981.

Horn, Gabriel. "Amour et extase d'après Denys l'Aréopagite." *Revue d'ascétique et de la mystique* 6 (1925): 278–89.

Horne, James R. "Tillich's Rejection of Absolute Mysticism." *Journal of Religion* 58 (1978): 130–39.

Huby, Joseph. *Mystiques paulinienne et johannique*. Paris: Desclée, 1946.

Hunter, David G. "Resistance to the Virginal Ideal in Late Fourth-Century Rome: The Case of Jovinian." *Theological Studies* 48 (1987): 45–64.

Huxley, Aldous. *The Doors of Perception* New York: Harper, 1954.

———. *The Perennial Philosophy*. New York: Harper, 1945.

Idel, Moshe. "Abraham Abulafia and *Unio Mystica*." In *Studies in Ecstatic Kabbalah*, 1–31. Albany: State University of New York Press, 1988.

———. *Kabbalah: New Perspectives*. New Haven: Yale University Press, 1988.

———. "Universalization and Integration: Two Conceptions of Mystical Union in

Jewish Mysticism." In *Mystical Union and Monotheistic Faith,* edited by Moshe Idel and Bernard McGinn, 27–55. New York: Macmillan, 1989.

———, and Bernard McGinn, eds. *Mystical Union and Monotheistic Faith: An Ecumenical Dialogue.* New York: Macmillan, 1989.

Inge, William Ralph. *Christian Mysticism.* London: Methuen, 1899.

Izutsu, Toshihiko. *Sufism and Taoism: A Comparative Study of Key Philosophical Concepts.* Berkeley: University of California Press, 1983.

Jacobs, Louis. *Jewish Mystical Traditions.* New York: Schocken, 1978.

Jaeger, Werner. *Aristotle.* Oxford: Clarendon, 1948.

James, William. "A Pluralistic Mystic." *Hibbert Journal* 8 (1910): 739–59.

———. "A Suggestion about Mysticism." In *Understanding Mysticism,* edited by Richard T. Woods, O.P., 215–22. Garden City, NY: Doubleday, 1980.

———. *The Varieties of Religious Experience: A Study in Human Nature.* New York: Collier-Macmillan, 1961.

John, Helen James. *The Thomist Spectrum.* New York: Fordham University Press, 1966.

Johnston, William, S.J. *The Inner Eye of Love: Mysticism and Religion.* New York: Harper & Row, 1978.

———. *The Still Point: Reflections on Zen and Christian Mysticism.* New York: Harper & Row, 1971.

Jonas, Hans. *Gnosis und spätantike Geist: Von der Mythologie zur mystischen Philosophie.* Göttingen: Vandenhoeck & Ruprecht, 1954.

———. "Gnosticism, Existentialism, Nihilism." Epilogue in *The Gnostic Religion,* 320–40. 2nd ed. Boston: Beacon, 1963.

———. *The Gnostic Religion: The Message of the Alien God and the Beginnings of Christianity.* Boston: Beacon, 1958.

———. "Myth and Mysticism: A Study of Objectification and Interiorization in Religious Thought." *Journal of Religion* 49 (1969): 315–29.

———. "Die origenistische Spekulation und die Mystik." *Theologische Zeitschrift* 5 (1949): 24–45.

Jones, A. H. M. *The Later Roman Empire 284–602: A Social, Economic, and Administrative Survey.* 2 vols. Norman: University of Oklahoma Press, 1964.

Jones, Rufus M. *Studies in Mystical Religion.* New York: Macmillan, 1909.

Joret, Donatien, O.P. *La contemplation mystique d'après S. Thomas d'Aquin.* Paris: Desclée, 1923.

Judge, E. A. "The Earliest Use of Monachos for Monk (P. Coll. Youtie 77) and the Origins of Monasticism." *Jahrbuch für Antike und Christentum* 20 (1977): 72–89.

Jüngel, Eberhard. *God as the Mystery of the World.* Translated by Darrell L. Guder. Grand Rapids: Eerdmans, 1983.

Kakar, Sudhir. *The Inner World.* Delhi: Oxford University Press, 1980.

Kannengiesser, Charles. "Enarratio in psalmum CXVIII: Science de la révélation et progrès spirituel." *Recherches augustiniennes* 2 (1963): 359–81.

———. "The Spiritual Message of the Great Fathers." In *Christian Spirituality: Origins to the Twelfth Century,* edited by Bernard McGinn and John Meyendorff, 61–88. WS 16. New York: Crossroad, 1986.

———, and W. Petersen, eds. *Origen of Alexandria: His World and His Legacy.* Notre Dame: University of Notre Dame Press, 1988.

Katz, Steven T. "Language, Epistemology, and Mysticism." In *Mysticism and Philosophical Analysis,* edited by Steven T. Katz, 22–74. New York: Oxford University Press, 1978.

———. "Review Article: Recent Work on Mysticism." *History of Religions* 25 (1985–86): 76–86.

———, ed. *Mysticism and Philosophical Analysis.* New York: Oxford University Press, 1978.

———, ed. *Mysticism and Religious Traditions.* New York: Oxford University Press, 1983.

Kelley, J. N. D. *Jerome: His Life, Writings and Controversies.* New York: Harper & Row, 1975.

Kelly, Anthony J. "Is Lonergan's *Method* Adequate to Christian Mystery?" *The Thomist* 39 (1975): 437–70.

Kemmer, A. "Die Mystik in Karl Barth's *Kirchliche Dogmatik.*" *Freiburger Zeitschrift für Philosophie und Theologie* 7 (1960): 3–25.

Kenney, John Peter. *Mystical Monotheism.* Hanover, NH: Brown University Press, 1991.

Kirk, Kenneth E. *The Vision of God: The Christian Doctrine of the "Summum Bonum."* London: Longmans, Green, 1932. Reprint. Cambridge: James Clarke, 1977.

Kirschner, Robert. "The Vocation of Holiness in Late Antiquity." *Vigiliae Christianae* 38 (1984): 105–24.

Kitzinger, Ernst. *Early Medieval Art.* Bloomington: Indiana University Press, 1966.

Klostermann, E. "Formen der exegetischen Arbeiten des Origenes." *Theologische Literaturzeitung* 72 (1947): 203–8.

Knowles, David. "Edward Cuthbert Butler, 1858–1934." In *The Historian and Character,* 263–362. Cambridge: University Press, 1963.

———. *The English Mystical Tradition.* New York: Harper, 1961.

———. *The Nature of Mysticism.* New York: Hawthorne Books, 1966.

Koch, Hal. *Pronoia und Paideusis: Studien über Origenes und sein Verhältnis zum Platonismus.* Berlin: de Gruyter, 1932.

Koester, Helmut. *Introduction to the New Testament.* 2 vols. Philadelphia: Fortress, 1982.

Kolakowski, Leszek. *Bergson.* Oxford and New York: Oxford University Press, 1985.

Krautheimer, Richard. *Three Christian Capitals: Topography and Politics.* Berkeley: University of California Press, 1983.

Kristeva, Julia. *Tales of Love.* New York: Columbia University Press, 1987.

Kristo, Jure. "Human Cognition and Mystical Knowledge: Joseph Maréchal's Analysis of Mystical Experience." *Mélanges de science religieuse* 37 (1980): 53–73.

———. "The Interpretation of Religious Experience: What Do Mystics Intend When They Talk about Their Experiences?" *Journal of Religion* 62 (1982): 21–38.

Kugel, James L., and Rowan A. Greer. *Early Biblical Interpretation.* Philadelphia: Westminster, 1986.

La Bonnardière, Anne-Marie. "Le Cantique des Cantiques dans l'oeuvre de saint Augustin." *Revue des études augustiniennes* 1 (1955): 225–37.

———. *Recherches de chronologie augustinienne.* Paris: Études Augustiniennes, 1965.

Ladner, Gerhard B. *The Idea of Reform: Its Impact on Christian Thought and Action in the Age of the Fathers.* Cambridge, MA: Harvard University Press, 1959.

Laeuchli, Samuel. *Power and Sexuality: The Emergence of Canon Law at the Synod of Elvira.* Philadelphia: Temple University Press, 1972.

Lamballe, Emile. *Mystical Contemplation: or, The Principles of Mystical Theology.* London: R. & T. Washbourne, 1913.

Landsberg, P.-L. "Les sens spirituels chez saint Augustin." *Dieu vivant* 11 (1948): 83–105.

Laski, Marghanita. *Ecstasy: A Study of Some Secular and Religious Experiences.* Bloomington: University of Indiana Press, 1962.

Lawless, George. *Augustine of Hippo and His Monastic Rule.* Oxford: Clarendon, 1987.

Layton, Bentley, ed. *The Rediscovery of Gnosticism.* 2 vols. Leiden: Brill, 1981.

Lebreton, Jules, et al. "Contemplation." *DS* 2:1643–2193.

Leclercq, Jean. "Monachesimo. I. Fenomenologia del monachesimo." In *Dizionario degli Istituti di Perfezione,* edited by Guerrino Pelliccia and Giancarlo Rocca, 5:1673–84. Rome: Edizioni Paoline, 1974–.

Lee, Philip R., et al. *Symposium on Consciousness.* New York: Viking Press, 1976.

Le Fevre, André, et al. "Écriture sainte et vie spirituelle." *DS* 4:128–278.

Legasse, Simon, et al. "Perfection chrétienne." *DS* 12:1074–1156.

Legrand, Lucien. *The Biblical Doctrine of Virginity.* New York: Sheed & Ward, 1963.

Lehmann, Edvard. *Mystik i Hedensgab og Kristendom.* 1904. Eng. trans. *Mysticism in Heathendom and Christendom.* London: Luzac, 1910.

Léonard, Augustin. "Recherches phenomenologiques autour de l'expérience mystique." *La vie spirituelle* Supplement 23 (November 1952): 430–94.

Leuba, James H. *The Psychology of Religious Mysticism.* 1929. Reprint. London: Routledge & Kegan Paul, 1972.

Levasti, Arrigo. "Clemente Alessandrino, iniziatore della Mistica cristiana." *Rivista di Ascetica e Mistica* 12 (1967): 127–47.

———. "La dottrina dello Pseudo Macario nelle sue cinquanta Omelie spirituali." *Rivista di Ascetica e Mistica* 14 (1969): 141–59.

———. "La dottrina mistica di S. Gregorio di Nissa." *Rivista di Ascetica e Mistica* 12 (1967): 548–62; 13 (1968): 44–61.

———. "Origene e le linee fondamentali della sua dottrina spirituale." *Rivista di Ascetica e Mistica* 12 (1967): 358–83.

———. "Il piu grande mistico del deserto: Evagrio il Pontico." *Rivista di Ascetica e Mistica* 13 (1968): 242–64.

Levenson, Jon D. "The Jerusalem Temple in Devotional and Visionary Experience." In *Jewish Spirituality: From the Bible through the Middle Ages,* edited by Arthur Green, 32–61. WS 13. New York: Crossroad, 1986.

———. *Sinai and Zion.* Minneapolis: Winston-Seabury, 1985.

Lewy, Hans. *Chaldean Oracles and Theurgy: Mysticism, Magic and Platonism in the Later Roman Empire.* Cairo: Institut français d'archéologie orientale, 1956. A revised edition by M. Tardieu, Paris, 1978.

———. *SOBRIA EBRIETAS: Untersuchungen zur Geschichte der antiken Mystik.* Beihefte zur *Zeitschrift für die neutestamentliche Wissenschaft* 9. Giessen: Töpelmann, 1929.

Lienhard, Joseph T. "On 'Discernment of Spirits' in the Early Church." *Theological Studies* 41 (1980): 505–29.

———. *Paulinus of Nola and Early Western Monasticism.* Cologne and Bonn: Peter Hanstein, 1977.

Lieske, A. *Die Theologie des Logosmystik bei Origenes.* Münster: Aschendorff, 1938.

Lion, Antoine. "Le discours blessé: Sur le langage mystique selon Michel de Certeau." *Revue des sciences philosophiques et religieuses* 71 (1987): 405–19.

Liverziani, Filippo. *Dinamismo intelletuale ed esperienza mistica nel pensiero di Joseph Maréchal.* Rome: Liber, 1974.

Lobkowicz, Nicholas. *Theory and Practice: History of a Concept from Aristotle to Marx.* Notre Dame: University of Notre Dame Press, 1967.

Loisy, Alfred. *Y a-t-il deux sources de la religion et de la morale?* Paris: E. Nourrey, 1934.

Lonergan, Bernard J. F., S.J. *Collection.* Edited by F. E. Crowe, S.J. New York: Herder & Herder, 1967.

———. *Insight: A Study of Human Understanding.* London and New York: Longmans, 1957.

———. *Method in Theology.* New York: Herder & Herder, 1972.

———. *Second Collection.* Edited by William J. Ryan, S.J., and Bernard J. Tyrrell, S.J. Philadelphia: Westminster, 1974.

———. *Third Collection.* Edited by F. E. Crowe, S.J. New York: Paulist, 1985.

———. *Verbum: Word and Idea in Aquinas.* Notre Dame: University of Notre Dame, Press, 1967.

Lorenz, Rudolf. "Die Anfänge des abendländischen Mönchtums in 4. Jahrhundert." *Zeitschrift für Kirchengeschichte* 77 (1966): 1–66.

———. "Fruitio Dei bei Augustin." *Zeitschrift für Kirchengeschichte* 63 (1950–51): 75–132.

Lossky, Vladimir. "Les éléments de 'Théologie négative' dans la pensée de saint Augustin." In *Augustinus Magister,* 1:575–81. 3 vols. Paris: L'Année théologique augustinienne, 1954.

———. *The Mystical Theology of the Eastern Church.* London: J. Clarke, 1957.

———. "La notion des 'analogies' chez Denys le Pseudo-Aréopagite." *Archives d'histoire doctrinal et littéraire du moyen âge* 5 (1930): 279–309.

———. "La théologie négative dans la doctrine de Denys l'Aréopagite." *Revue des sciences philosophiques et théologiques* 28 (1939): 204–21.

———. *The Vision of God.* London: Faith Press, 1963.

Lot-Borodine, M. *La déification de l'homme d'après les pères grecs.* Paris: Cerf, 1970.

Louth, Andrew. *The Origins of the Christian Mystical Tradition: From Plato to Denys.* Oxford: Clarendon, 1981.

Ludwig, Theodore M. "Rudolph Otto." In *The Encyclopedia of Religion,* 11:139–41.

Maas, Fritz-Dieter. *Mystik im Gespräch: Materialien zur Mystik-Diskussion in der katholischen und evangelischen Theologie Deutschlands nach dem ersten Weltkrieg.* Würzburg: Echter, 1972.

McCool, Gerald A., S.J. "Twentieth-Century Scholasticism." In *Celebrating the Medieval Heritage: A Colloquy on the Thought of Aquinas and Bonaventure.* Edited by David Tracy. *The Journal of Religion* Supplement 58 (1978): S198–S221.

McDonell, Kilian. "Prayer in the Ancient Western Tradition." *Worship* 55 (1981): 34–61.

McGinn, Bernard. "The Apocalypse and Apocalyptic Literature." In *The Apocalypse in the Middle Ages,* edited by Richard K. Emmerson and Bernard McGinn. Ithaca, NY: Cornell University Press, 1992 (to appear).

——. "Christian Monasticism." In *The Encyclopedia of Religion,* 10:44–50.

——. "Early Apocalypticism: The ongoing debate." In *The Apocalypse in English Renaissance thought and literature,* edited by C. A. Patrides and Joseph Wittreich, 2–39. Ithaca, NY: Cornell University Press, 1984.

——. "God as Eros: Reflections on Cosmic Love in the Christian Tradition." Unpublished.

——. *The Golden Chain.* Washington: Cistercian Publications, 1972.

——. "The Human Person as Image of God. II. Western Christianity." In *Christian Spirituality: Origins to the Twelfth Century,* edited by Bernard McGinn and John Meyendorff, 312–30. WS 16. New York: Crossroad, 1986.

——. "The Language of Love in Jewish and Christian Mysticism." In *Mysticism and Language,* edited by Steven Katz. New York: Oxford University Press, 1991 (to appear).

——. "Love, Knowledge and *Unio Mystica* in the Western Christian Tradition." In *Mystical Union and Monotheistic Faith: An Ecumenical Dialogue,* edited by Moshe Idel and Bernard McGinn, 59–86. New York: Macmillan, 1989.

——. "The Negative Element in the Anthropology of John the Scot." *Jean Scot Érigène et l'histoire de la philosophie,* 315–25. Paris: CNRS, 1977.

——. "Platonic and Christian: The Case of the Divine Ideas." In *Of Scholars, Savants and their Texts: Studies in Philosophy and Religious Thought: Essays in Honor of Arthur Hyman,* edited by Ruth Link-Salinger, 163–73. New York: Peter Lang, 1989.

——. "Remarks." In *Mystical Union and Monotheistic Faith,* edited by Moshe Idel and Bernard McGinn, 185–93. New York: Macmillan, 1989.

——, and John Meyendorff, eds. *Christian Spirituality: Origins to the Twelfth Century.* WS 16. New York: Crossroad, 1986.

Macleod, C. W. "Allegory and Mysticism in Origen and Gregory of Nyssa." *Journal of Theological Studies* n.s. 22 (1972) 362–79.

MacRae, George. "Apocalyptic Eschatology in Gnosticism." In *Apocalyptism in the Mediterranean World and the Near East,* edited by David Hellholm, 317–25. Tübingen: Mohr, 1983.

Madec, Goulven. "Christus, scientia et sapientia nostra: Le principe de cohérence de la doctrine augustinienne." *Recherches augustiniennes* 10 (1975): 77–85.

——. "L'homme interieur selon saint Ambroise." In *Ambroise de Milan: XVIe centenaire de son election épiscopale,* edited by Yves-Marie Duval, 283–308. Paris: Études Augustiniennes, 1974.

——. *Saint Ambroise et la philosophie.* Paris: Études Augustiniennes, 1974.

Mager, Alois. *Mystik als Lehre und Leben.* Innsbruck: Tyroliaverlag, 1934.

Mahé, Jean-Pierre. "Hermes Trismegistos." In *The Encyclopedia of Religion,* 6:287–93.

Malévez, Leopold, S.J. "Connaissance discursive et connaissance mystique des mystères du salute." In *L'homme devant dieu: Mélanges offerts à Père Henri de Lubac,* 3:167–83. 3 vols. Paris: Cerf, 1964.

——. "Théologie contemplative et théologie discursive." *Nouvelle revue théologique* 88 (1964): 225–49.

Malone, Edward E. *The Monk and the Martyr.* Washington: Catholic University Press, 1950.

Manchester, Peter. "The Religious Experience of Time and Eternity." In *Classical Mediterranean Spirituality: Egyptian, Greek, Roman,* edited by A. H. Armstrong, 384–407. WS 15. New York: Crossroad, 1986.

Mandouze, André. "L'ecstase d'Ostie." In *Augustinus Magister,* 1:67–84. 3 vols. Paris: L'Année théologique augustinienne, 1954.

———. "Où en est la question de la mystique augustinienne?" In *Augustinus Magister,* 3:103–68. 3 vols. Paris: L'Année théologique augustinienne, 1954.

———. *Saint Augustin: L'aventure de la raison et de la grace.* Paris: Études Augustiniennes, 1968.

Maréchal, Joseph. *Études sur la psychologie des mystiques.* 2 vols. Bruges: C. Beyaert, 1926, 1937. Translated in part in *Studies in the Psychology of the Mystics.* Translated by Algar Thorold. Albany: Magi Books, 1964.

———. "Les lignes essentielles du Freudisme." *Nouvelle revue théologique* 52 (1925): 537–51, 577–605; 53 (1926): 13–50.

———. *Mélanges Joseph Maréchal.* Paris and Brussels: Desclée, 1950.

———. "Note d'enseignement théologique: La notion d'extase, d'après l'enseignement traditionnel des mystiques et des théologiens." *Nouvelle revue théologique* 64 (1937): 986–98.

———. *Le point de départ de la metaphysique.* 5 vols. Bruges: C. Beyaert, 1922–1949. Translated in part in *A Maréchal Reader,* edited and translated by Joseph Donceel, S.J. New York: Herder & Herder, 1970.

———. "Sur les cimes de l'oraison: Quelques opinions récentes de théologiens." *Nouvelle revue théologique* 56 (1929): 107–27, 177–206.

———. "La vision de Dieu au sommet de la contemplation d'après saint Augustin." *Nouvelle revue théologique* 57 (1930): 89–109, 191–214.

———. "Vraie et fausse mystique." *Nouvelle revue de théologie* 67 (1945): 275–95.

Marion, J.-L. *L'idole et la distance.* Paris: Grasset, 1977.

Maritain, Jacques. "Action and Contemplation." In *Scholasticism and Politics,* 170–93. New York: Macmillan, 1940.

———. *Distinguer pour unir, ou les degrés du savoir.* 1932. Eng. trans. *Distinguish to Unite, or The Degrees of Knowledge.* Translated by Gerald B. Phelan. 4th ed. New York: Scribner, 1959.

———. "L'intelligence d'après M. Maurice Blondel." *Revue de philosophie* 30 (1923): 333–64, 484–511.

———. "On Knowledge through Connaturality." In *Jacques et Raissa Maritain. Oeuvres completes.* Paris: Editions Saint-Paul. Vol. 9 (1990): 980–1001.

———. *La philosophie bergsonienne.* 1913. *Bergsonian philosophy and Thomism.* Translated by Mabelle L. Andison. New York: Greenwood Press, 1955.

———. *Redeeming the Time.* London: G. Bles, 1944.

———, and Raissa Maritain. *De la vie d'oraison.* 1922. Eng. trans. *Prayer and Intelligence.* Translated by Algar Thorold. New York: Sheed & Ward, 1934.

———, and Raissa Maritain. *Liturgie et contemplation.* 1959. Eng. trans. *Liturgy and Contemplation.* Translated by Joseph W. Evans. New York: P. J. Kenedy, 1960.

Markus, R. A. "The Dialectic of Eros in Plato's Symposium." *Downside Review* 73 (1955): 219–30.

Marrou, H. I. "L'idée de Dieu et la divinité du Roi." *La regalità sacra,* 478–80. Leiden: Brill, 1959.

Marsili, Salvatore. *Giovanni Cassiano ed Evagrio Pontico: Dottrina sulla caritá e contemplazione.* Studia Anselmiana 5. Rome: Herder, 1936.

Massignon, Louis. *La passion de Husayn Ibn Mansūr Hāllāj, martyr mystique de l'Islam.* 1922. Eng. trans. *The Passion of al-Halaj: Mystic and Martyr of Islam.* Translated by Herbert Mason. 4 vols. Princeton, NJ: Princeton University Press, 1982.

Masson, J. Moussaieff. *The Oceanic Feeling: The Origins of Religion in Ancient India.* Dordrecht, Boston, and London: Reidel, 1980.

Matter, E. Ann. *The Voice of My Beloved: The Song of Songs in Western Medieval Christianity.* Philadelphia: University of Pennsylvania, 1990.

Mayer, Cornelius, et al., eds. *Augustinus-Lexikon.* Basel: Schwabe, 1986–.

Mealand, David L. "The Language of Mystical Union in the Johannine Writings." *Downside Review* 19 (1977): 19–34.

Meeks, Wayne A. "Moses as God and King." In *Religions in Antiquity,* edited by Jacob Neusner, 354–71. Leiden: Brill, 1968.

Mehat, André, and Aimé Solignac. "Prière. III. Dans la tradition chrétienne." *DS* 12: 2247–71.

Menard, Jacques. "Normative Self-Definition in Gnosticism." In *Jewish and Christian Self-Definition,* edited by E. P. Sanders et al., 1:134–50. 3 vols. Philadelphia: Fortress, 1980–83.

Merki, Hubert. *HOMOIOSIS THEOU: Von der platonischen Angleichung an Gott zur Gottähnlichkeit bei Gregor von Nyssa.* Freiburg: Paulusverlag, 1952.

Merkur, Daniel. "Unitive Experiences and the State of Trance." In *Mystical Union and Monotheistic Faith: An Ecumenical Dialogue,* edited by Moshe Idel and Bernard McGinn, 125–53. New York: Macmillan, 1989.

Merlan, Philip. *From Plato to Neoplatonism.* 3rd ed. The Hague: Nijhoff, 1968.

——. "Greek Philosophy from Plato to Plotinus." In *The Cambridge History of Later Greek and Early Medieval Philosophy,* edited by A. H. Armstrong, 14–132. Cambridge: Cambridge University Press, 1967.

——. *Monopsychism, Mysticism, Metaconscious.* The Hague: Nijhoff, 1963.

Mersch, Emile. *The Whole Christ.* Milwaukee: Bruce, 1938.

Merton, Thomas. *The Ascent to Truth.* New York: Harcourt, Brace, 1951.

——. *Bread in the Wilderness.* New York: New Directions, 1960.

——. *The Climate of Monastic Prayer.* Washington: Cistercian Publications, 1969. Also published under the title *Contemplative Prayer.* New York: Herder & Herder, 1969.

——. *Contemplation in a World of Action.* New York: Doubleday, 1973.

——. "The Inner Experience: Notes on Contemplation (I)–(VIII)." *Cistercian Studies* 18 (1983): 3–15, 121–34, 201–16, 288–300; 19 (1984): 62–76, 139–50, 267–82, 336–43.

——. *Mystics and Zen Masters.* New York: Farrar, Straus, Giroux, 1967.

——. *New Seeds of Contemplation.* New York: New Directions, 1972.

——. *No Man Is an Island.* New York: Harcourt, Brace, 1955.

——. *The Sign of Jonas.* New York: Harcourt, Brace, 1953.

——. "The Transforming Union in St. Bernard and St. John of the Cross." *Collectanea Ordinis Cisterciensium Reformatorum* 10 (1948): 107–17; 11 (1949): 41–52, 352–61; 12 (1950): 25–38.

Meyer, Hans. "War Augustin Intellektualist oder Mystiker?" In *Augustinus Magister,* 3:429–37. 3 vols. Paris: L'Année théologique augustinienne, 1954.

Meyendorff, John. "Messalianism or Anti-Messalianism? A Fresh Look at the 'Macarian' Problem." In *Kyriakon: Festschrift Johannes Quasten,* edited by P. Granfield and J. Jungmann, 2:585–90. 2 vols. Münster: Aschendorff, 1970.

Mieth, Dietmar. "Gotteschau und Gottesgeburt: Zwei Typen Christlicher Gotteserfahrung in der Tradition." *Freiburger Zeitschrift für Philosophie und Theologie* 27 (1980): 204–23.

Miles, Margaret. "Vision: The Eye of the Body and the Eye of the Mind in Saint Augustine's *De Trinitate* and *Confessions.*" *Journal of Religion* 63 (1983): 125–42.

Miller, Clyde Lee. "Union with the One: Ennead 6, 9, 8–11." *The New Scholasticism* 51 (1977): 182–95.

Miller, James. *Measures of Wisdom: The Cosmic Dance in Classical and Christian Antiquity.* Toronto: University of Toronto Press, 1986.

Moltmann, Jürgen. "The Theology of Mystical Experience." In *Experiences of God,* 55–80. Philadelphia: Fortress, 1980.

Momigliano, Arnaldo. *Alien Wisdom: The Limits of Hellenization.* Cambridge: Cambridge University Press, 1975.

Moore, Peter. "Mystical Experience, Mystical Doctrine, Mystical Technique." In *Mysticism and Philosophical Analysis,* edited by Steven T. Katz, 101–31. New York: Oxford University Press, 1978.

———. "Notes and Comments: A Recent Study of Mysticism." *Heythrop Journal* 25 (1984): 178–83.

———. "Recent Studies on Mysticism: A Critical Survey." *Religion* 3 (1973): 146–56.

Morris, Charles. "Mysticism and its Language." In *Writings on the General Theory of Signs,* 456–63. Paris: Mouton, 1971.

Mühlenberg, Ekkehard. *Die Unendlichkeit Gottes bei Gregor von Nyssa: Gregors Kritik am Gottesbegriff der klassischen Metaphysik.* Göttingen: Vandenhoeck & Ruprecht, 1965.

Munz, Peter. "John Cassian." *Journal of Ecclesiastical History* 11 (1960): 1–22.

Naranjo, Claudio, and Robert E. Ornstein. *On the Psychology of Mysticism.* New York: Viking, 1971.

Nasr, Seyyed Hossein. *Knowledge and the Sacred.* New York: Crossroad, 1981.

Nauroy, Gerard. "La structure du *De Isaac vel Anima* et la cohérence de l'allegorese d'Ambroise de Milan." *Revue des études latines* 63 (1985): 210–36.

Nautin, P. *Origène: Sa vie et son oeuvre.* Paris: Beauchesne, 1977.

Nedoncelle, M. "L'intersubjectivité humaine est-elle pour saint Augustine une image de la Trinité?" In *Augustinus Magister,* 1:595–602. 3 vols. Paris: L'Année théologique augustinienne, 1954.

Neumann, Erich. "Mystical Man." In *The Mystic Vision: Papers from the Eranos Yearbooks,* 375–415. Princeton, NJ: Princeton University Press, 1968.

Neusner, Jacob. "Varieties of Judaism in the Formative Age." In *Jewish Spirituality: From the Bible through the Middle Ages,* edited by Arthur Green, 171–97. WS 13. New York: Crossroad, 1986.

Niditch, Susan. "The Visionary." In *Ideal Figures in Ancient Judaism,* edited by George W. E. Nickelsburg and John J. Collins, 153–79. Chico, CA: Scholars Press, 1980.

Nikiprowetzky, V. "Philon d'Alexandrie. I. La personne et l'oeuvre." *DS* 12:1352–66.

Nock, A. D. "The Exegesis of Timaeus 28C." *Vigiliae Christianae* 16 (1982): 79–86.

———. "The Question of Jewish Mysteries." *Gnomon* 13 (1937): 156–65.

Norden, Eduard. *Die Geburt des Kindes.* Leipzig: Teubner, 1924.

Normann, Friedrich. *Teilhabe — ein Schlüsselwort der Vätertheologie.* Münster: Aschendorff, 1978.

Norrman, Christer. *Mystical Experiences and Scientific Method.* Stockholm: Almqvist & Wiksell, 1986.

Noye, Irenée, et al. "Humanité du Christ (devotion et contemplation)." *DS* 7:1033–1108.

Nussbaum, Martha C. *The Fragility of goodness: Luck and Ethics in Greek tragedy and philosophy.* Cambridge: Cambridge University Press, 1986.

Nygren, Anders. *Agape and Eros.* Philadelphia: Westminster, 1953.

O'Brien, Elmer, S.J. *The Essential Plotinus.* New York: Mentor Books, 1964.

———. *Varieties of Mystic Experience.* New York: Mentor, 1964.

O'Connell, Robert J., S.J. *The Origin of the Soul in Augustine's Later Works.* New York: Fordham University, 1987.

———. *St. Augustine's Confessions: The Odyssey of a Soul.* Cambridge, MA: Belknap Press, 1969.

———. *St. Augustine's Early Theory of Man: A.D. 386–391.* Cambridge, MA: Belknap Press, 1968.

O'Daly, Gerard J. P. "The Presence of the One in Plotinus." In *Plotino e il Neoplatonismo in Oriente e in Occidente,* 159–69. Rome: Accademia Nazionale dei Lincei, Quaderno 198, 1974.

———, and L. Verheijen. "Actio-contemplatio." In *Augustinus-Lexikon,* edited by Cornelius Mayer et al., 1:58–63. Basel: Schwabe, 1986–.

O'Donovan, Oliver. *The Problem of Self-Love in St. Augustine.* New Haven: Yale University Press, 1980.

Ohly, Friedrich. *Hohelied-Studien: Grundzüge einer Geschichte der Hoheliedauslegung des Abendlandes bis um 1200.* Wiesbaden: F. Steiner, 1958.

O'Laughlin, Michael Wallace. "Origenism in the Desert: Anthropology and Integration in Evagrius Ponticus." Dissertation, Harvard University, 1987.

Olphe-Galliard, Michel. "Cassien (Jean)." *DS* 2:214–76.

Olson, Alan M. "Jasper's Critique of Mysticism." *Journal of the American Academy of Religion* 51 (1983): 251–66.

O'Meara, Dominic. "À propos d'un témoignage sur l'expérience mystique de Plotin (*Enn.* IV 8 [6], 1, 1–11)." *Mnemosyne* 27 (1974): 238–44.

O'Meara, John J. "Augustine and Neoplatonism." *Recherches augustiniennes* 1 (1958): 91–111.

Orme-Johnson, David, and John Farrow, eds. *Scientific Research on the Transcendental Meditation Program: Collected Papers,* vol. 1. Seelisburg, Switzerland: Maharishi European Research University Press, 1977.

Otten, R. T. "Caritas and the Ascent Motif in the Exegetical Works of St. Ambrose." In *Studia Patristica,* vol. 8, edited by F. L. Cross, 442–48. Texte und Untersuchungen 93. Berlin: Akademie Verlag, 1966.

Otto, Rudolf. *Das Heilige.* 1917. *The Idea of the Holy.* London: Penguin, 1959.

———. *Mysticism East and West.* New York: Macmillan, 1970.

Ousley, David Alan. "Evagrius' Theology of Prayer and the Spiritual Life." Dissertation, University of Chicago, 1979.

Pagels, Elaine H. "Gnostic and Orthodox Views of Christ's Passion: Paradigms for Christians' Response to Persecution?" In *The Rediscovery of Gnosticism*, edited by Bentley Layton, 1:262–88. Leiden: Brill, 1981.

———. *The Gnostic Gospels*. New York: Vintage Books, 1981.

———. *The Gnostic Paul: Gnostic Exegesis of the Pauline Letters*. Philadelphia: Westminster, 1975.

———. *The Johannine Gospel in Gnostic Exegesis*. Nashville: Abingdon, 1973.

———. "Visions, Appearances, and Apostolic Authority: Gnostic and Orthodox Traditions." In *Gnosis: Festschrift für Hans Jonas*, edited by B. Aland, 415–30. Göttingen: Vandenhoeck & Ruprecht, 1978.

Palla, Roberto. "Temi del *Commento* Origeniano *al Cantico dei Cantici* nel *De Isaac* di Ambrogio." *Annali della Scuola Normale Superiore di Pisa* 9 (1979): 563–72.

Parrinder, Geofrey. *Mysticism in the World's Religions*. New York: Oxford, 1976.

Parsons, William. "Psychoanalysis and Mysticism: The Freud–Romain Rolland Correspondence." Unpublished paper.

Pellegrino, Michele. "L'imitation du Christ dans les actes des martyrs." *La vie spirituelle* 98 (1958): 38–54.

Penelhum, Terence. "Unity and Diversity in the Interpretation of Mysticism." In *Mystics and Scholars: The Calgary Conference on Mysticism 1976*, edited by Harold Coward and Terence Penelhum. *Sciences Religieuses* Supplements 13, 71–81.

Pépin, Jean. "Cosmic Piety." In *Classical Mediterranean Spirituality: Egyptian, Greek, Roman*, edited by A. H. Armstrong, 408–35. WS 15. New York: Crossroad, 1986.

———. *Mythe et allégorie: Les origines grecques et les contestations judéo-chrétiennes*. Paris: Aubier, Editions Montaigne, 1958. 2nd ed. Paris: Études Augustiniennes, 1976.

———. "Univers dionysien et univers augustinien." In *Aspects de la dialectique: Recherches de philosophie II*. Paris: Desclée, 1956.

Perella, Nicholas. *The Kiss Sacred and Profane*. Berkeley: University of California Press, 1969.

Perkins, Pheme. *The Gnostic Dialogue: The Early Church and the Crisis of Gnosticism*. New York: Paulist, 1980.

Perovich, Anthony N. "Mysticism and the Philosophy of Science." *Journal of Religion* 65 (1985): 63–82.

Perrin, Norman. *The New Testament: An Introduction*. New York: Harcourt, Brace, Jovanovich, 1974.

Petitdemange, Guy. "L'invention du commencement: *La Fable Mystique*, de Michel de Certeau. Première lecture." *Revue de science religieuse* 71 (1983): 497–520.

Philips, G. "L'influence du Christ-Chef sur son corps mystique suivant saint Augustin." In *Augustinus Magister*, 2:805–16. 3 vols. Paris: L'Année théologique augustinienne, 1954.

Piolanti, Antonio. "Il mistero del 'Cristo totale' in s. Agostino." In *Augustinus Magister*, 3:453–69.

Pizzolato, L. F. *La dottrina esegetica di San Ambrogio*. Milan: Università Cattolica del Sacro Cuore, 1978.

Pletcher, Galen K. "Mysticism, Contradiction, and Ineffability." *American Philosophical Quarterly* 10 (1973): 201–11.

Pope, Marvin H. *Song of Songs: A New Translation with Introduction and Commentary.* Anchor Bible 7C. Garden City, NY: Doubleday, 1977.

Poque, Suzanne, "L'expression de l'anabase plotinienne dans la prédication de saint Augustin et ses sources." *Recherches augustiniennes* 10 (1975): 187–215.

Poulain, Augustin-François, S.J. *The Graces of Interior Prayer: A Treatise on Mystical Theology.* Reprint. Westminster, VT: Celtic Cross Books, 1978.

Poulat, Emile. *Critique et mystique: Autour de Loisy ou la conscience catholique et l'esprit moderne.* Paris: Le Centurion, 1984.

Preiss, T. "La mystique de l'imitation du Christ et de l'unité chez Ignace d'Antioche." *Revue d'histoire et de philosophie religieuses* 18 (1938): 197–241.

Price, A. W. *Love and Friendship in Plato and Aristotle.* Oxford: Clarendon, 1990.

Price, James Robertson, III. "Lonergan and the Foundations of a Contemporary Mystical Theology." Unpublished paper.

———. "The Objectivity of Mystical Truth Claims." *The Thomist* 49 (1985): 81–98.

———. "Typologies and Cross-Cultural Analysis of Mysticism: A Critique." In *Religion and Culture: Essays in Honor of Bernard Lonergan,* edited by T. Fallon and B. Riley, 181–89. Albany: SUNY Press, 1987.

Principe, Walter "Mysticism: Its Meaning and Varieties." In *Mystics and Scholars: The Calgary Conference on Mysticism 1976,* edited by Harold Coward and Terence Penelhum. *Sciences Religieuses* Supplements 13:1–15.

Proudfoot, Wayne. *Religious Experience.* Berkeley: University of California Press, 1985.

Puech, Henri-Charles. "Un livre récent sur la mystique d'Origène." *Revue d'histoire et de philosophie religieuse* 13 (1933): 508–36.

———. "La Ténèbre mystique chez le Pseudo-Denys l'Aréopagite." In *En quête de la Gnose,* 1:119–41. 2 vols. Paris: Gallimard, 1978.

Quasten, Johannes. *Patrology.* 3 vols. Reprint. Westminster: Christian Classics, 1983.

Quell, Gottfried, and Ethelbert Stauffer. *Love: Bible Key Words from Gerhard Kittel's Theologisches Wörterbuch zum Neuen Testament,* edited by Gerhard Kittel, 1:21–55. London: A. & C. Black, 1949.

Quispel, Gilles. "Gnosis and Psychology." In *The Rediscovery of Gnosticism,* vol. 1, *The School of Valentinus,* edited by Bentley Layton, 17–31. Leiden: Brill, 1980.

———. *Makarius, das Thomasevangelium und das Lied von der Perle.* Leiden: Brill, 1967.

———. "Sein und Gestalt." In *Studies in Mysticism and Religion presented to Gershom G. Scholem,* 191–95. Jerusalem: Magnes Press, 1967.

———. "Valentinian Gnosis and the 'Apocryphon of John.'" In *The Rediscovery of Gnosticism,* edited by Bentley Layton, 1:118–32. 2 vols. Leiden: Brill, 1981.

Raasch, J. "The Monastic Conception of Purity of Heart and its Sources." *Studia Monastica* 8 (1966): 7–33, 183–213; 10 (1968): 7–55; 11 (1969): 269–314; 12 (1970): 7–41.

Rahner, Hugo. "Die Gottesgeburt: Die Lehre der Kirchenväter von der Geburt Christi aus dem Herzen der Kirche und der Gläubigen." In *Symbole der Kirche: Die Ekklesiologie der Väter,* 11–87. Salzburg: Müller, 1964.

Rahner, Karl. "'Coeur de Jesus' chez Origène?" *Revue d'ascétique et de la mystique* 15 (1934): 171–74.

———. "Die geistliche Lehre des Evagrius Ponticus." *Zeitschrift für Aszese und Mystik* 8 (1933): 31–47.

————. *Grundkurs des Glaubens: Einführung in den Begriff des Christentums.* 1976. Eng. trans. *Foundations of Christian Faith: An Introduction to the Idea of Christianity.* New York: Crossroad, 1978.

————. *I Remember: An Autobiographical Interview with Meinhold Krauss.* New York: Crossroad, 1985.

————. *Praxis des Glaubens: Geistliches Lesebuch.* 1982. Eng. trans. *The Practice of Faith: A Handbook of Contemporary Spirituality.* New York: Crossroad, 1983.

————. "The 'Spiritual Senses' according to Origen." In *Theological Investigations* 16:92–100. New York: Seabury, 1979.

————. *Theological Investigations.* 21 vols. London: Darton, Longman & Todd, et al., 1961–.

————. *Visions and Prophecies.* London: Burns & Oates, 1963.

Refoulé, François, O.P. "La Christologie d'Évagre et l'origenisme." *Orientalia Christiana Periodica* 27 (1961): 221–66.

————. "La doctrine spirituelle des Pères de l'église." *La vie spirituelle* 102 (1960): 310–26.

Rich, Audrey. "The Platonic Ideas as the Thoughts of God." *Mnemosyne,* Series IV.7 (1954): 123–33.

Ricoeur, Paul. "Response to Rahner." In *Celebrating the Medieval Heritage: A Colloquy on the Thought of Aquinas and Bonaventure,* edited by David Tracy. Chicago: University of Chicago, 1978. *The Journal of Religion* Supplement 58 (1978): S126–S131.

————. *The Symbolism of Evil.* New York: Harper & Row, 1967.

Rist, John M. *Eros and Psyche: Studies in Plato, Plotinus and Origen.* Toronto: University of Toronto Press, 1975.

————. "Mysticism and Transcendence in Later Neoplatonism." *Hermes* 92 (1964): 213–24.

————. "A Note on Eros and Agape in Pseudo-Dionysius." *Vigiliae Christianae* 20 (1966): 235–43.

————. *Plotinus: The Road to Reality.* Cambridge: Cambridge University Press, 1967.

Ritschl, Albrecht. *Geschichte der Pietismus.* 3 vols. Bonn: Marcus, 1880–86.

————. *Theologie und Metaphysik.* 2nd ed. Bonn: Marcus, 1887.

Robinson, T. M. *Plato's Psychology.* Toronto: University of Toronto Press, 1970.

Rondeau, M. J. "Le commentaire sur les Psaumes d'Évagre le Pontique." *Orientalia Christiana Periodica* 26 (1960): 307–48.

Rordorf, Willy. "Martyre. II. Théologie et spiritualité du martyre." *DS* 10:726–32.

Rorem, Paul E. *Biblical and Liturgical Symbols within the Pseudo-Dionysian Synthesis.* Toronto: Pontifical Institute of Mediaeval Studies, 1984.

————. "Iamblichus and the Anagogical Method in Pseudo-Dionysian Liturgical Theology." In *Studia Patristica* 18, edited by E. A. Livingstone, 453–60. Oxford and New York: Pergamon, 1982.

————. "The Place of *The Mystical Theology* in the Pseudo-Dionysian Corpus." *Dionysius* 4 (1980): 87–98.

————. "The Uplifting Spirituality of Pseudo-Dionysius." In *Christian Spirituality: Origins to the Twelfth Century,* edited by Bernard McGinn and John Meyendorff, 132–51. WS 16. New York: Crossroad, 1986.

Roques, René. "Contemplation chez les orientaux chrétiens. E. Le Pseudo-Denys l'Aréopagite." *DS* 2:1785–87.

———. "Contemplation, extase et ténèbre mystique chez le Pseudo-Denys." *DS* 2:1885–1911.

———. *Structures théologiques de la Gnose à Richard de Saint-Victor.* Paris: Presses universitaires de France, 1962.

———. *L'univers dionysien: Structure hierarchique du monde selon le Pseudo-Denys.* 2nd ed. Paris: Cerf, 1983.

———, et al. "Denys l'Aréopagite." *DS* 3:244–429.

Rosenberg, Joel. "Biblical Tradition: Literature and Spirit in Ancient Israel." In *Jewish Spirituality: From the Bible through the Middle Ages,* edited by Arthur Green, 82–112. WS 13. New York: Crossroad, 1986.

Rousseau, Philip. *Ascetics, Authority and the Church in the Age of Jerome and Cassian.* Oxford: Oxford University Press, 1978.

———. "Cassian, Contemplation and the Coenobitic Life." *Journal of Ecclesiastical History* 26 (1975): 113–26.

Rousselot, Pierre. *L'Intellectualism de S. Thomas d'Aquin.* Paris: Beauchesne, 1908.

Rowland, Christopher. *The Open Heaven: A Study of Apocalyptic in Judaism and Early Christianity.* New York: Crossroad, 1982.

Rudolph, Kurt. *Gnosis.* Translated by Robert McLachlan Wilson. San Francisco: Harper & Row, 1983.

———. "Mystery Religions." In *The Encyclopedia of Religion,* 10:230–39.

Runciman, G. "Plato's *Parmenides.*" 1959. Reprinted in *Studies in Plato's Metaphysics,* edited by R. E. Allen, 149–84. London: Routledge & Kegan Paul, 1967.

Runia, D. T. "God and Man in Philo of Alexandria." *Journal of Theological Studies* n.s. 39 (1988): 48–75.

Rusch, W. G. *The Trinitarian Controversy.* Philadelphia: Fortress, 1980.

Russell, Bertrand. *Mysticism and Logic and Other Essays.* London: Allen & Unwin, 1956.

Sabbatucci, Dario. *Saggio sul misticismo greco.* Rome: Edizioni dell'Atenco & Bizzarri, 1979.

Saffrey, H.-D. "Les Néoplatoniciens et les Oracles Chaldaiques." *Revue des études augustiniennes* 27 (1981): 209–25.

———. "Neoplatonist Spirituality. II. From Iamblichus to Proclus and Damascius." In *Classical Mediterranean Spirituality: Egyptian, Greek, Roman,* edited by A. H. Armstrong, 250–65. WS 15. New York: Crossroad, 1986.

———. "New Objective Links between the Pseudo-Dionysius and Proclus." In *Neoplatonism and Christian Thought,* edited by Dominic J. O'Meara, 64–74. Albany: State University of New York Press, 1982.

Sagot, Solange. "Le 'Cantique des cantiques' dans le 'De Isaac' d'Ambroise de Milan." *Recherches augustiniennes* 16 (1981): 3–57.

———. "La triple sagesse dans le *De Isaac vel anima:* Essai sur les procédes de composition de saint Ambroise." In *Ambroise de Milan: XVIe centenaire de son élection épiscopale,* edited by Yves-Marie Duval, 67–114. Paris: Études Augustiniennes, 1974.

Sanders, E. P. "The Genre of Palestinian Jewish Apocalypses." In *Apocalypticism in the Mediterranean World and the Near East,* edited by David Hellholm, 447–59. Tübingen: Mohr, 1983.

———, et al., eds. *Jewish and Christian Self-Definition.* 3 vols. Philadelphia: Fortress, 1980–83.

Saudreau, August. *The Degrees of the Spiritual Life.* 2 vols. London: Burns, Oates & Washbourne, 1907.

——. *The Life of Union with God, and the means of attaining it, according to the great masters of spirituality.* Translated by E. J. Strickland. London: Burnes, Oates & Washbourne, 1927.

——. *The Mystical State.* London: Burnes, Oates & Washbourne, 1924.

Savon, H. *Saint Ambroise devant l'exégèse de Philon le Juif.* 2 vols. Paris: Études Augustiniennes, 1977.

Schaefer, Peter. "New Testament and Hekhalot Literature: The Journey into Heaven in Paul and in Merkavah Mysticism." *Journal of Jewish Studies* 35 (1984): 19–35.

Scharfstein, Ben-Ami. *Mystical Experience.* Indianapolis and New York: Bobbs Merrill, 1973.

Schilling, Frederick Augustus. *The Mysticism of Ignatius of Antioch.* Philadelphia: University of Pennsylvania, 1932.

Schimmel, Annemarie. *As through a Veil: Mystical Poetry in Islam.* New York: Columbia University Press, 1982.

——. *Mystical Dimensions of Islam.* Chapel Hill: University of North Carolina Press, 1975.

Schleiermacher, Friedrich. *On Religion: Speeches to its Cultured Despisers.* Introduction, translation, and notes by Richard Crouty. Cambridge and New York: Cambridge University Press, 1988.

Schmithals, Walter. *The Apocalyptic Movement: Introduction and Interpretation.* Nashville: Abingdon, 1975.

Schneiders, Sandra M. "Scripture and Spirituality." In *Christian Spirituality: Origins to the Twelfth Century,* edited by Bernard McGinn and John Meyendorff, 1–20. WS 16. New York: Crossroad, 1986.

Schoedel, W. R. "Gnostic Monism and the Gospel of Truth." In *The Rediscovery of Gnosticism,* edited by Bentley Layton, 1:379–90. Leiden: Brill, 1981.

Scholem, Gershom. *Jewish Gnosticism, Merkabah Mysticism, and Talmudic Tradition.* New York: Jewish Theological Seminary of America, 1965.

——. *Major Trends in Jewish Mysticism.* New York: Schocken, 1961.

——. "Mysticism and Society." *Diogenes* 58 (1967): 1–24.

——. *Origins of the Kabbalah.* Translated by Allan Arkush. Princeton, NJ: Princeton University Press, 1987.

——. "Religious Authority and Mysticism." In *On the Kabbalah and its Symbolism.* New York: Schocken, 1965.

——. *Sabbatai Sevi: The Mystical Messiah.* Translated by R. J. Zwi Werblowsky. Princeton, NJ: Princeton University Press, 1973.

Schuon, Frithjof. *The Transcendent Unity of Religions.* Wheaton, IL: Theosophical Publishing House, 1984.

Schweitzer, Albert. *The Mysticism of Paul the Apostle.* London: A. & C. Black, 1931.

——. *The Philosophy of Civilization.* New York: Macmillan, 1950.

Segal, Alan F. "Heavenly Ascent in Hellenistic Judaism, Early Christianity and their Environment." In *Aufstieg und Niedergang der römischen Welt. II. Prinzipat,* 23.2, 1333–93. Berlin and New York: de Gruyter, 1980.

Seibel, Wolfgang. *Fleisch und Geist beim heiligen Ambrosius.* Munich: Karl Zink, 1958.

Sells, Michael. "Apophasis in Plotinus: A Critical Approach." *Harvard Theological Review* 78 (1985): 47–65.

Semmelroth, O. "Gottes geeinte Vielheit: Zur Gotteslehre des Ps.-Dionysius Areopagita." *Scholastik* 25 (1950): 389–403.

Shannon, William H. *Thomas Merton's Dark Path: The Inner Experience of a Contemplative.* New York: Farrar, Straus, Giroux, 1981.

Sheldon-Williams, I. P. "The pseudo-Dionysius." In *The Cambridge History of Later Greek and Early Medieval Philosophy,* edited by A. H. Armstrong, 457–72. Cambridge: Cambridge University Press, 1967.

Sieben, Hermann Josef, and Aimé Solignac. "Ivresse spirituelle." *DS* 7:2312–37.

Singer, Irving. *The Nature of Love: 1, From Plato to Luther.* 2nd ed. Chicago: University of Chicago Press, 1984.

Sinnige, T. G. "Metaphysical and Personal Religion in Plotinus." In *Kephalaion,* edited by J. Mansfeld and L. M. de Rijk, 147–54. Assen: Van Gorcum, 1975.

Smart, Ninian. "The Exploration of Mysticism." In *Mystics and Scholars: The Calgary Conference on Mysticism 1976,* edited by Harold Coward and Terence Penelhum. *Sciences Religieuses* Supplements 13:63–69.

——. "Interpretation and Mystical Experience." *Religious Studies* 1 (1965): 75–87.

——. "Mystical Experience." *Sophia* 1 (1962): 19–26.

——. "Mysticism, History of." In *The Encyclopedia of Philosophy,* edited by Paul Edwards, 5:419–29. New York: Macmillan, 1972.

——. "The Purification of Consciousness and the Negative Path." In *Mysticism and Religious Traditions,* edited by Steven T. Katz, 117–29. New York: Oxford University Press, 1983.

——. *Reasons and Faiths.* London: Routledge & Kegan Paul, 1958.

——. "Understanding Religious Experience." In *Mysticism and Philosophical Analysis,* edited by Steven T. Katz, 10–21. New York: Oxford University Press, 1978.

Smith, Huston. *Forgotten Truth: The Primordial Tradition.* New York: Harper, 1976.

Smith, John E. "William James's Account of Mysticism: A Critical Appraisal." In *Mysticism and Religious Traditions,* edited by Steven T. Katz, 247–79. New York: Oxford University Press, 1983.

Smith, Jonathan Z. "Birth Upside Down or Right Side Up?" *History of Religions* 9 (1970): 281–303.

Smith, Morton. "Ascent to the Heavens and the Beginning of Christianity." *Eranos Yearbook* 50 (1981): 403–30.

——. "The History of the Term Gnostikos." In *The Rediscovery of Gnosticism,* vol. 2, *Sethian Gnosticism,* edited by Bentley Layton, 796–807. Leiden: Brill, 1981.

Söderblom, Nathan. "Communion with Deity (Introductory)." In *Encyclopaedia of Religion and Ethics,* edited by James Hastings, 3:736–40. New York: Scribner, 1911.

——. *The Living God.* Oxford: Oxford University Press, 1933.

——. *The Nature of Revelation.* Philadelphia: Fortress, 1966.

Solignac, Aimé. "Jubilation." *DS* 8:1471–78.

——. "Naissance divine (mystique de la)." *DS* 11:24–28.

——. "Péchés capitaux." *DS* 12:853–62.

——. "Philon d'Alexandrie. II. Influence sur les pères de l'église." *DS* 12:1366–74.

——, and Charles Pietri. "Latine (Église)." *DS* 9:330-82.

——, et al. "Monachisme." *DS* 10:1524-1617.

Sorabji, Richard. "Myths about non-propositional thought." In *Language and Logos: Studies in ancient Greek philosophy presented to G. E. L. Owens,* edited by Malcolm Schofield and Martha Nussbaum, 295-314. Cambridge: Cambridge University Press, 1982.

Souilhé, J. "Le silence mystique." *Revue d'ascétique et de la mystique* 4 (1923): 128-40.

Spearrit, Dom Placid. "The Soul's Participation in God according to Pseudo-Dionysius." *Downside Review* 88 (1970): 378-92.

Spencer, Sidney. *Mysticism in World Religion.* Baltimore: Penguin, 1963.

Spicq, Ceslaus. *Agape in the New Testament.* 3 vols. St. Louis: Herder, 1962-66.

Staal, Frits. *Exploring Mysticism.* Berkeley: University of California Press, 1975.

Stace, W. T. *Mysticism and Philosophy.* New York and London: Macmillan, 1960.

——. *The Teaching of the Mystics.* New York: New American Library, 1960.

Steidle, B., ed. *Antonius Magnus Eremita 356-1956.* Studia Anselmiana 38. Rome, 1956.

Stewart, Columba. "John Cassian on Unceasing Prayer." *Monastic Studies* 15 (1984): 159-76.

Stolz, Anselm. *Theologie der Mystik.* Regensburg: Pustet, 1936.

Stone, Michael E. "Apocalyptic Literature." In *Jewish Writings of the Second Temple Period,* edited by Michael E. Stone, 383-440. Compendia Rerum Iudaicarum ad Novum Testamentum, section 2. Philadelphia: Fortress, 1984.

——. "Apocalyptic—Vision or Hallucination?" *Milla wa-Milla* 13 (1973): 47-56.

——. "Eschatology, Remythologization and Cosmic Aporia." In *The Origins and Diversity of Axial Age Civilizations,* edited by S. M. Einstadt, 241-51. Albany: State University of New York Press, 1986.

——. "Lists of Revealed Things in Apocalyptic Literature." In *Magnalia Dei: The Mighty Acts of God,* edited by F. M. Cross et al., 414-52. Garden City, NY: Doubleday, 1976.

——. *Scriptures, Sects and Visions: A Profile of Judaism from Ezra to the Jewish Revolts.* Philadelphia: Fortress, 1980.

——, ed. *Jewish Writings of the Second Temple Period.* Compendia Rerum Iudaicarum ad Novum Testamentum, section 2. Philadelphia: Fortress, 1984.

Streng, Frederick. "Language and Mystical Awareness." In *Mysticism and Philosophical Analysis,* edited by Steven T. Katz, 141-69. New York: Oxford University Press, 1978.

Stroumsa, G. *Another Seed: Studies in Gnostic Mythology.* Leiden: Brill, 1984.

——. "Ascèse et gnose: Aux origines de la spiritualité monastique." *Revue Thomiste* 81 (1981): 557-73.

——. "*Caro salutis cardo:* Shaping the Person in Early Christian Thought." *History of Religions* 30 (1990): 25-50.

Studer, Basil. *Zur Theophanie-Exegese Augustins.* Rome: Herder, 1971.

Sullivan, John Edward. *The Image of God: The Doctrine of St. Augustine and its Influence.* Dubuque, IA: Priory Press, 1963.

Swartley, Willard M. "The Imitatio Christi in the Ignatian Letters." *Vigiliae Christianae* 27 (1973): 81-103.

Tabor, James. *Things Unutterable: Paul's Ascent to Paradise in its Greco-Roman, Judaic and Early Christian Contexts.* Lanham, MD: University Press of America, 1986.

Tajo, Maria. "Un confronto tra S. Ambrogio e S. Agostino a proposito dell'esegesi del Cantico dei Cantici." *Revue des études augustiniennes* 7 (1961): 144–51.

Tanquerey, Adolphe. *Preçis de théologie ascetique et mystique.* Paris: Desclée, 1923–24. Eng. trans. *The Spiritual Life: A Treatise on Ascetical and Mystical Theology.* Belgium: Tournai Society of St. John the Evangelist, 1930.

Tart, Charles E. *Altered States of Consciousness.* New York: Wiley, 1969.

Tcherikover, Victor. *Hellenistic Civilization and the Jews.* New York: Atheneum, 1970.

Teselle, Eugene, "Augustine." In *An Introduction to the Medieval Mystics of Europe,* edited by Paul Szarmach, 19–35. Albany: State University of New York Press, 1984.

———. *Augustine the Theologian.* New York: Herder & Herder, 1970.

Theresia Benedicta a Cruce [Edith Stein]. "Ways to Know God: The 'Symbolic Theology' of Dionysius the Areopagite and its Factual Presuppositions." *The Thomist* 9 (1946): 379–420.

Thesaurus Augustinianus. Turnhout: CEDOC (Brepols), 1988.

Thunberg, Lars. "The Human Person as Image of God. I. Eastern Christianity." In *Christian Spirituality: Origins to the Twelfth Century,* edited by Bernard McGinn and John Meyendorff, 291–311. WS 16. New York: Crossroad, 1986.

Tillich, Paul. *Systematic Theology.* 3 vols. Chicago: University of Chicago Press, 1967.

Tomasic, Thomas Michael. "The Logical Function of Metaphor and Oppositional Coincidence in the Pseudo-Dionysius and Johannes Scottus Eriugena." *Journal of Religion* 68 (1988): 361–78.

Torjesen, Karen Jo. *Hermeneutical Procedure and Theological Method in Origen's Exegesis.* Berlin: de Gruyter, 1986.

Trapé, Agostino. "VI. Saint Augustine." In *Patrology,* vol. 4, *The Golden Age of Latin Patristic Literature From the Council of Nicea to the Council of Chalcedon,* edited by Angelo di Berardino, introduction by Johannes Quasten, 342–462. Westminster: Christian Classics, 1986.

Tremblay, Real. *La manifestation et la vision de Dieu selon saint Irenée de Lyon.* Münster: Aschendorff, 1978.

Trigg, Joseph Wilson. *Origen: The Bible and Philosophy in the Third-Century Church.* Atlanta: John Knox, 1983.

Troeltsch, Ernst. "Main Problems of the Philosophy of Religion: Psychology and Theory of Knowledge in the Science of Religion." In *Congress of Arts and Science: Universal Exposition, St. Louis, 1904,* edited by Howard J. Rogers, 1:275–88. 2 vols. Boston and New York: Houghton, Mifflin, 1908.

———. *The Social Teaching of the Christian Churches.* 2 vols. New York: Harper & Row, 1960.

Trouillard, Jean. *La mystagogie de Proclos.* Paris: Belles Lettres, 1982.

———. "Le 'Parménide' de Platon et son interprétation néoplatonicienne." In *Études Néoplatoniciennes,* 9–26. Neuchâtel: A La Baconnière, 1973.

———. "La présence de Dieu selon Plotin." *Revue de metaphysique et de morale* 59 (1954): 38–45.

———. *La procession plotinienne.* Paris: Presses universitaires de France, 1955.

———. *La purification plotinienne.* Paris: Presses universitaires de France, 1955.

———. "Raison et mystique chez Plotin." *Revue des études augustiniennes* 20 (1974): 3–14.

——. "Théologie négative et psychogonie chez Proclus." In *Plotino e il Neoplatonismo in Oriente e il Occidente,* 253–64. Accademia Normali dei Lincei. Quaderno 198. Rome, 1974.

——. *L'un et l'âme selon Proclos.* Paris: Belles Lettres, 1972.

Underhill, Evelyn. *The Essentials of Mysticism and other Essays.* New York: E. P. Dutton, 1920.

——. *Mysticism: A Study in the Nature and Development of Man's Spiritual Consciousness.* 12th ed. Cleveland and New York: World, 1965.

——. *The Mystics of the Church.* London: James Clarke, 1925.

——. *The Mystic Way: A Psychological Study in Christian Origins.* London: J. M. Dent & Sons; New York: E. P. Dutton, 1913.

——. *Practical Mysticism: A Little Book for Normal People.* New York: E. P. Dutton, 1915.

Urbach, Ephraim E. "The Homiletic Interpretations of the Sages and the Expositions of Origen on Canticles and the Jewish-Christian Disputation." *Scripta Hierosolymitana* 22 (1971): 247–75.

van Bavel, T., and F. van der Zande. *Répertoire bibliographique de Saint Augustin, 1950–60.* The Hague: Nijhoff, 1963.

van den Broek, R. "The Present State of Gnostic Studies." *Vigiliae Christianae* 37 (1983): 41–71.

Vandenbroucke, François. "Die Ursprunglichkeit der biblischen Mystik." In *Gott in Welt: Festgabe für Karl Rahner,* edited by Johannes Baptist Metz et al., 1:463–91. 2 vols. Freiburg: Herder, 1964.

van der Leeuw. *Phänomenologie der Religion.* 1933. Eng. trans. *Religion in Essence and Manifestation.* New York: Harper, 1963.

Vanneste, Jan. "Is the Mysticism of the Pseudo-Dionysius Genuine?" *International Philosophical Quarterly* 3 (1963): 286–306.

——. *Le mystère de Dieu: Essai sur la structure rationelle de la doctrine mystique du Pseudo-Dionysius l'Aréopagite.* Brussels: Desclée, 1959.

Villecourt, L. "La date et l'origine des homilies spirituelles attribuées à Macaire." *Comptes-rendus de l'académie des inscriptions et belles-lettres* (1920): 250–58.

Viller, Marcel, and Karl Rahner. *Aszese und Mystik in der Väterzeit: Ein Abriss.* Freiburg: Herder, 1939.

Völker, Walther. *Fortschrift und Vollendung bei Philo von Alexandrien.* Leipzig: Hinrichs, 1938.

——. *Gregor von Nyssa als Mystiker.* Wiesbaden: F. Steiner, 1955.

——. *Kontemplation und Ekstase bei Pseudo-Dionysius Areopagita* Wiesbaden: F. Steiner, 1958.

——. *Maximus Konfessor als Meister des geistlichen Lebens.* Wiesbaden: F. Steiner, 1965.

——. *Praxis und Theoria bei Symeon dem Neuen Theologen.* Wiesbaden: F. Steiner, 1974.

——. *Scala Paradisi: Eine Studie zu Johannes Climacus und zugleich eine Vorstudie zu Symeon dem Neuen Theologen.* Wiesbaden: F. Steiner, 1968.

——. *Das Vollkommenheitsideal des Origenes.* Tübingen: Mohr, 1931.

——. *Die wahre Gnostiker nach Clemens Alexandrinus.* Berlin: Akademie-Verlag, 1952.

von Balthasar, Hans Urs. *Herrlichkeit: Eine Theologische Ästhetik.* 3 vols. Various parts are available in English translation in *The Glory of the Lord: A Theological Aesthetics.* New York: Crossroad; San Francisco: Ignatius Press, 1982, 1984, 1986.

———. *Kosmische Liturgie: Maximus der Bekenner.* Freiburg-im-Breisgau: Herder, 1941.

———. "Metaphysik und Mystik des Evagrius Pontikos." *Zeitschrift für Aszese und Mystik* 14 (1939): 31–47. Eng. trans. "The Metaphysics and Mystical Theology of Evagrius." *Monastic Studies* 3 (1965): 183–95.

———. *Origenes: Geist und Feuer: Ein Aufbau aus seiner Schriften.* Salzburg: Otto Müller, 1938. Eng. trans. *Origen, Spirit and Fire: A Thematic Anthology of His Writings.* Translated by Robert J. Daly. Washington: Catholic University of America Press, 1984.

———. *Parole et mystère chez Origène.* Paris: Cerf, 1957.

———. *Présence et pensée: Étude sur la philosophie religieuse de Grégoire de Nysse.* Paris: Beauchesne, 1942.

———. *Schwestern im Geist: Thérese von Lisieux und Elisabeth von Dijon.* 2nd ed. Einsiedeln: Johannes-Verlag, 1970.

———. "Zur Ortsbestimmung christlicher Mystik." In *Grundfragen der Mystik,* 37–71. Einsiedeln: Johannes-Verlag, 1974.

von Campenhausen, Hans. *Die Idee des Martyriums in der alten Kirche.* 2nd ed. Göttingen: Vandenhoeck & Ruprecht, 1964.

von Görres, Johann Joseph. *Christliche Mystik.* 4 vols. Regensburg: G. Manz, 1836–42.

von Hügel, Baron Friedrich. "Experience and Transcendence." *Dublin Review* 29 (1906): 357–79.

———. *The Mystical Element of Religion as Studied in Saint Catherine of Genoa and her Friends.* 2 vols. Reprint. London: James Clarke & J. M. Dent, 1961.

von Ivánka, Endre. *Plato Christianus: Übernahme und Umgestaltung des Platonismus durch die Väter.* Einsiedeln: Johannes-Verlag, 1964.

———. "La signification historique du 'Corpus Areopageticum.'" *Recherches des sciences religieuses* 36 (1949): 15–19.

von Simson, Otto. *The Gothic Cathedral.* New York: Harper & Row, 1964.

Wach, Joachim. *The Sociology of Religion.* Chicago: University of Chicago Press, 1944.

———. *Types of Religious Experience: Christian and Non-Christian.* Chicago: University of Chicago Press, 1951.

Wainwright, William J. *Mysticism: A Study of its Nature, Cognitive Value and Moral Implications.* Madison: University of Wisconsin Press, 1981.

Wallis, R. T. *Neoplatonism.* New York: Scribner, 1972.

———. "NOUS as Experience." In *The Significance of Neoplatonism,* edited by R. Baine Harris, 121–53. Norfolk, VA: Old Dominion University Press, 1976.

———. "The Spiritual Importance of Not Knowing." In *Classical Mediterranean Spirituality: Egyptian, Greek, Roman,* edited by A. H. Armstrong, 460–80. WS 15. New York: Crossroad, 1986.

Watkin, E. I. "Mysticism and the Supernatural." *The Month* 18 (1957): 274–81.

———. "The Mysticism of St. Augustine." In *St Augustine: His Age, Life and Thought,* 105–19. Cleveland and New York: Meridian, 1957.

————. *The Philosophy of Mysticism.* London: Grant Richards, 1920.

————. *Poets and Mystics.* London: Sheed & Ward, 1953.

Weil, Simone. *The Notebooks of Simone Weil.* Translated by Arthur Wills. 2 vols. London: Routledge & Kegan Paul, 1976.

Westra, Laura. "Proclus' Ascent of the Soul towards the One in the *Elements of Theology:* Is it Plotinian?" In *Proclus et son influence: Actes du Colloque de Neuchâtel, Juin, 1985,* edited by G. Boss and G. Seel, 129–43. Neuchâtel: Editions du Grand Mich, 1986.

Whittaker, John. *Studies in Platonism and Patristic Thought.* London: Variorum, 1984.

Wikenhauser, Alfred. *Pauline Mysticism.* New York: Herder, 1955.

Wilbrand, W. "Ambrosius und Platon." *Römische Quartalschrift für christliche Altertumskunde und für Kirchengeschichte* 25 (1911): 42–49.

Wiles, M. F. *The Divine Apostle.* Cambridge: Cambridge University Press, 1967.

————. *The Spiritual Gospel: The Interpretation of the Fourth Gospel in the Early Church.* Cambridge: Cambridge University Press, 1960.

Wilken, Robert L. "Diversity and Unity in Early Christianity." *The Second Century* 1 (1981): 101–11.

Williams, Rowan. "Butler's *Western Mysticism:* Towards an Assessment." *Downside Review* 102 (1984): 197–215.

————. *Christian Spirituality.* Atlanta: John Knox, 1979.

————. "The Prophetic and the Mystical: Heiler Revisited." *New Blackfriars* 64 (1983): 330–44.

Winston, David. *Logos and Mystical Theology in Philo of Alexandria.* Cincinnati: Hebrew Union College Press, 1985.

————. "Philo and the Contemplative Life." In *Jewish Spirituality: From the Bible through the Middle Ages,* edited by Arthur Green, 198–231. WS 13. New York: Crossroad, 1986.

————. "Was Philo a Mystic?" In *Studies in Jewish Mysticism,* edited by Joseph Dan and Frank Talmadge, 15–41. Cambridge, MA: Harvard University Press, 1982.

Wolfson, H. A. "Extradeical and Intradeical Interpretations of the Platonic Ideas." In *Religious Philosophy: A Group of Essays,* 27–68. Cambridge, MA: Belknap Press, 1961.

————. *Philo.* 2 vols. Cambridge, MA: Harvard University Press, 1947.

Woods, Richard. "Mysticism, Protestantism and Ecumenism: The Spiritual Theology of W. E. Hocking." In *Western Spirituality: Historical Roots, Ecumenical Roots,* edited by Matthew Fox, 414–35. Santa Fe: Bear, 1981.

————, ed. *Understanding Mysticism.* Garden City, NY: Doubleday, 1980.

Worgul, George S., Jr. "M. Blondel and the Problem of Mysticism." *Ephemerides theologiae lovanienses* 71 (1985): 100–122.

Yates, Frances. *Giordano Bruno and the Hermetic Tradition.* Chicago: University of Chicago Press, 1964.

Zaehner, Robert Charles. *Concordant Discord.* Oxford: Clarendon, 1970.

————. *Drugs, Mysticism and Make-believe.* London: Collins, 1972.

————. *Mysticism Sacred and Profane: An Inquiry into some Varieties of Praeternatural Experience.* New York: Oxford, 1961.

———. "Mysticism without Love." *Religious Studies* 10 (1974): 257–64.

Zahn, Joseph. *Einführung in die christliche Mystik.* Paderborn: F. Schöningh, 1918.

Zemach, E. "Wittgenstein's Philosophy of the Mystical." *Review of Metaphysics* 18 (1964): 38–57.

Zumkeller, Adolar. *Augustine's Ideal of the Religious Life.* New York: Fordham University Press, 1986.

Index

Names

Biblical Passages

Subjects

Apophatic language and theology (*cont.*), 306-7, 324. *See also* Absence, Cataphatic, Nothingness
Arianism, 139-40, 144, 150, 152, 156, 194, 197, 199, 202-3
Aristotelianism, 34, 35, 46
Ascent (to heaven, to God), 6, 11, 13-20, 22, 26-29, 30, 39, 42-43, 47, 62, 70, 74, 92-94, 112, 114, 115-18, 120, 129, 149-50, 156, 159, 166, 171, 181, 199-200, 203, 205-8, 221, 233-37, 239, 241-42, 245-46, 248, 258, 261, 281, 337. *See also* Itinerary
Asceticism, 3, 24, 25, 29, 30, 39, 47, 83, 92, 95, 99, 109-10, 117, 126, 132, 133-35, 137, 139, 142, 144-46, 148-49, 151, 155, 157, 164-65, 172-73, 194-95, 205, 209-11, 216, 218, 221, 226, 231, 249, 261, 280, 295, 319, 337
Autobiography (as mystical genre), xiv-xv, 3-4, 45, 57, 70, 130, 170, 206, 236

Baptism, 6, 63, 73, 79, 142-43, 165, 181, 194, 204, 211-12, 228, 249, 252, 289, 304, 308
Beatitude, 25-27, 28, 30, 34, 39, 53, 68, 119, 128, 151, 232, 235, 238, 245, 255, 257, .262, 275, 286, 303, 308
Beauty (and the Beautiful), 25, 26-28, 30, 32, 33, 47-48, 59, 109, 126, 158, 160-61, 164-67, 174, 206-7, 233, 235, 260
Being, 27-28, 29, 31-33, 37, 39, 47, 49, 50-51, 56-57, 58, 60, 112, 144, 152, 160-62, 168-69, 173, 176-77, 199, 269, 272, 276, 295, 299, 301, 302, 306, 308, 319, 328, 336. *See also* Existence
Benedictinism. See Monasticism
Bible (exegesis of), 3-4, 6, 11-12, 17, 21-22, 36-39, 64, 66, 68-69, 83, 85-86, 89, 98-99, 102, 104, 110-12, 116-17, 124, 158, 161-62, 171, 173-74, 179, 184, 197-98, 199, 204-5, 209-10, 212, 220-21, 223-24, 232, 242, 252, 281, 312. *See also* Allegory, Canon, Hermeneutics, Song of Songs, Typology
Birth of the Word, xvii, 74, 78-80, 85, 125, 208, 268. *See also* Sonship with Christ
Body, 15, 26-28, 30, 36, 45, 47, 52, 54, 59, 74, 79, 102, 105, 111, 113-15, 117, 120-21, 127, 135, 143, 148, 153, 156, 202, 205-8, 212, 214-15, 216-17, 221-22, 225, 240-41, 254, 258, 260, 312. *See also* Asceticism, Soul

Canon (of Scripture), 6, 11-12, 20, 22, 64, 68, 79, 87, 89
caritas. See Agape
Cataphatic (i.e., positive) language and theology, xviii, 118, 159, 161-65, 169, 171, 173-74, 179, 181. *See also* Apophatic
Chaldean Oracles, 35, 42, 43, 57, 60
Christ, xiii, 4, 6, 16, 17, 21, 29, 34, 55, 63-64, 65, 67, 71, 73-81 passim, 84-85, 89, 91-92, 94, 101-2, 104-8, 113, 115-18, 122-24, 126-28, 134-35, 143, 147-50, 165, 180-81, 185, 191, 198, 199-200, 206-7, 209-13, 214-15, 217, 223, 225, 228, 231-32, 233-34, 236, 238, 242, 243, 248-51, 252, 255, 260, 262, 268, 272, 281, 287-88, 289-90, 295, 315, 322
Christianity, xv-xvii, 3, 7, 15, 20, 35, 62, 64-66, 70, 72, 76, 83, 84-90, 92, 96, 98,

99-100, 101, 103, 108, 133, 138-40, 144, 148, 157, 182, 183, 201, 230-31, 252, 267-69, 270, 272-73, 275, 285, 286-87, 290, 294-95, 300, 302, 305, 307, 311-12, 327, 330; Catholic (Roman), 7, 42, 65, 158, 230, 268, 269, 270, 273, 275, 276-91, 304-5, 320, 330, 338-39; Eastern Orthodox, 7, 65, 68, 76, 100, 107, 142-44, 147, 193, 268, 270, 275, 281; Latin, 189-96, 197, 202, 230, 252; Protestant, 7, 24, 65, 230, 267-72, 275, 277, 282, 288, 290, 327, 330, 333
Church, xv, 21, 55, 63, 64, 66, 80, 83, 86-87, 89, 99, 101, 103, 109-11, 113, 122-24, 127, 132-33, 138-39, 143, 159, 160-61, 170, 172-73, 182, 183-85, 189-90, 192-94, 196, 197, 201, 203, 209-10, 212, 213, 216, 218, 231-32, 233-43 passim, 244, 248-51, 252, 259-62, 267, 270, 272, 279, 281-82, 285, 287-88, 311-12, 336
circle. See Symbol
Connaturality, 221, 280-81, 302-3, 306-9. *See also* Consciousness, Knowledge
Consciousness (mystical), xiii, xv, xvii-xx, 41, 45-46, 64-65, 67, 182, 224, 226, 230, 235, 237-38, 241, 253, 256, 259, 262, 284, 291-93, 298, 300, 311-12, 318-19, 323, 324, 325, 326, 331, 332-33, 335, 340-42. *See also* Presence
Contemplation, xvii, 6-7, 24, 25-30, 31, 34, 36, 39, 40-41, 42, 45, 52-55, 59, 61, 65, 69, 71-72, 83, 85, 92, 100, 104-5, 111, 113-15, 117-18, 125-26, 128-30, 141, 146-49, 152-56, 170, 172, 179, 184, 205, 219-26 passim, 231, 232, 234, 236, 238-39, 243, 245, 275, 276-79, 283, 307-9, 318, 330, 338, 340, 343; acquired and infused, 230, 278-80; contemplation and action, 29, 69, 78, 83, 106-7, 126-28, 142, 148-49, 151, 185, 215, 225-26, 256-57, 274, 275, 276, 305, 341. *See also* Theoria, Vision
Conversion, 70, 75, 88, 100, 117, 134, 191-92, 195, 198, 200, 228, 283-84
Cosmos, 11, 19, 20, 26, 43, 47, 55, 59, 61, 95-96, 110-12, 130, 161, 166-68, 261, 342
Creation, 37-38, 39, 54, 58, 76, 91-92, 96, 112-14, 115, 119-20, 126, 140-41, 147-48, 152, 154-55, 157-58, 161, 163-65, 167, 168-70, 178-79, 181, 184, 200, 207, 232, 240, 242, 247, 295, 304-5, 308, 327

deification. See Divinization
Demons, 69, 114-15, 118, 127, 134-37, 142, 147-48, 151, 215, 276, 279, 281
Dialectic, xviii, 32-33, 47, 49-52, 54, 56, 61, 76, 93, 108, 158, 162, 167, 169, 170, 173-74, 176, 178-80, 211, 275, 294, 296, 319, 325, 329, 335-36, 339
Discernment (of spirits), 118, 135, 137, 149
Divinization, xvii, 33, 39-40, 42-43, 47, 52-53, 74, 78-79, 85, 92-93, 96, 101-3, 105, 107-8, 128-29, 137, 142, 149-50, 152, 162, 164-65, 177-78, 179, 182, 184, 251, 268, 273, 274. *See also* Soul
Dualism and Duality, 30, 53, 90-92, 93, 95, 98, 154, 300

Ecstasy, 18, 39-41, 44, 52-53, 61, 67, 79, 85,